Lecture Notes in Computer Science 16627

The series Lecture Notes in Computer Science (LNCS), including its subseries Lecture Notes in Artificial Intelligence (LNAI) and Lecture Notes in Bioinformatics (LNBI), has established itself as a medium for the publication of new developments in computer science and information technology research, teaching, and education.

LNCS enjoys close cooperation with the computer science R & D community, the series counts many renowned academics among its volume editors and paper authors, and collaborates with prestigious societies. Its mission is to serve this international community by providing an invaluable service, mainly focused on the publication of conference and workshop proceedings and postproceedings. LNCS commenced publication in 1973.

Jiří Novotný · Jan Mazal · Petr Vašík ·
Marco Gotelli · Petr Stodola · Pavel Loučka ·
Stefan Pickl · Adriano Fagiolini ·
Vlastimil Neumann
Editors

Modelling and Simulation for Autonomous Systems

12th International Conference, MESAS 2025
Istanbul, Turkey, October 21–23, 2025
Revised Selected Papers

Springer

Editors
Jiří Novotný
University of Defence
Brno, Czech Republic

Jan Mazal
University of Defence
Brno, Czech Republic

Petr Vašík
Brno University of Technology
Brno, Czech Republic

Marco Gotelli
University of Genoa
Genoa, Italy

Petr Stodola
University of Defence
Brno, Czech Republic

Pavel Loučka
Brno University of Technology
Brno, Czech Republic

Stefan Pickl
Universität der Bundeswehr München
Neubiberg, Germany

Adriano Fagiolini
University of Palermo
Palermo, Italy

Vlastimil Neumann
University of Defence
Brno, Czech Republic

ISSN 0302-9743 ISSN 1611-3349 (electronic)
Lecture Notes in Computer Science
ISBN 978-3-032-33181-6 ISBN 978-3-032-33182-3 (eBook)
https://doi.org/10.1007/978-3-032-33182-3

This Springer imprint is published by the registered company Springer Nature Switzerland AG
The registered company address is: Gewerbestrasse 11, 6330 Cham, Switzerland

Preface

This volume contains selected papers presented at the Modelling and Simulation for Autonomous Systems (MESAS) Conference, held from October 21–23, 2025, at the Multinational Joint Warfare Centre (MJWC) in Istanbul, Turkey.

The MESAS initiative, launched by the NATO Modelling and Simulation Centre of Excellence (MSCOE) in 2013, aims to bring together the Modelling and Simulation and the Autonomous Systems and Robotics communities. Its objective is to provide a platform for the exchange of innovative ideas, concept development, and the advancement of technologies relevant to autonomous systems.

Over the years, MESAS has attracted experts from military, academic, and industrial domains, fostering a multidisciplinary environment that supports collaboration and knowledge sharing across communities of interest.

For the 2025 edition of MESAS, a total of 32 papers were submitted. All submissions underwent a rigorous double-blind peer-review process, with each contribution evaluated by at least three members of the Technical Committee or independent reviewers. As a result of this evaluation process, 21 high-quality papers were selected for inclusion in these proceedings.

The editors would like to thank all authors for their valuable contributions, as well as the reviewers for their careful and constructive evaluations, which ensured the scientific quality of this volume.

We would also like to honor the memory of Agostino G. Bruzzone, who sadly passed away in 2025. Bruzzone made a significant contribution to the MESAS community and to the broader field of modelling and simulation. His work and legacy will continue to inspire future research and collaboration.

MESAS25

MODELLING & SIMULATION FOR AUTONOMOUS SYSTEMS CONFERENCE

December 2025

Jiří Novotný
Jan Mazal
Petr Vašík
Marco Gotelli
Petr Stodola
Pavel Loučka
Stefan Pickl
Adriano Fagiolini
Vlastimil Neumann

Organization

Program Committee Chairs

Agostino Bruzzone	University of Genoa, Italy
Pavel Loučka	Brno University of Technology, Czech Republic
Jan Mazal	University of Defence, Czech Republic
Jiří Novotný	University of Defence, Czech Republic
Petr Stodola	University of Defence, Czech Republic
Petr Vašík	Brno University of Technology, Czech Republic
Adriano Fagiolini	Università degli Studi di Palermo, Italy
Stefan Pickl	Universität der Bundeswehr München, Germany
Vlastimil Neumann	University of Defence, Czech Republic

Program Committee

Adrian Albert	Universität der Bundeswehr München, Germany
Erkin Çilden	STM Defense Technologies Engineering and Trade Inc., Türkiye
Jaroslav Kompan	Armed Forces Academy of General Milan Rastislav Štefánik, Slovak Republic
Jan Nohel	University of Defence, Czech Republic
Peter Stütz	Universität der Bundeswehr München, Germany
David Žůrek	NATO M&S COE, Italy

Reviewers

Adrian Albert	Universität der Bundeswehr München, Germany
Martin Blaha	University of Defence, Czech Republic
Tomáš Brázda	Brno University of Technology, Czech Republic
Johanka Brdečková	Brno University of Technology, Czech Republic
Jindřiška Deckerová	Czech Technical University in Prague, Czech Republic
Jan Drábek	University of Defence, Czech Republic
Hana Druckmüllerová	Brno University of Technology, Czech Republic
Branislav Dubec	University of Defence, Czech Republic
Adéla Felcmanová	Brno University of Technology, Czech Republic

Natálie Gottvaldová	University of Defence, Czech Republic
Natálie Hanáková	University of Defence, Czech Republic
Kamila Hasilová	University of Defence, Czech Republic
Tomáš Havlík	University of Defence, Czech Republic
Danisa Jokanovich	Universidad Abierta Interamericana, Argentina
Josef Kříž	University of Defence, Czech Republic
Rayen Laabidi	Sorbonne Université, France
Pavel Loučka	Brno University of Technology, Czech Republic
Jan Mazal	University of Defence, Czech Republic
Pavel Mikuláček	Brno University of Technology, Czech Republic
Jan Nohel	University of Defence, Czech Republic
Jiří Novotný	University of Defence, Czech Republic
Marek Nowakowski	Military Institute of Armoured and Automotive Technology, Poland
Tibor Palasiewicz	University of Defence, Czech Republic
Ondřej Pekař	University of Defence, Czech Republic
Dalibor Procházka	University of Defence, Czech Republic
Jana Procházková	Brno University of Technology, Czech Republic
Jan Prokop	Brno University of Technology, Czech Republic
Fabian Rainisch	Universität der Bundeswehr München, Germany
Luděk Rak	University of Defence, Czech Republic
Tyler Sadler	Defence Research and Development, Canada
Jakub Sláma	Czech Technical University in Prague, Czech Republic
Martin Sedláček	University of Defence, Czech Republic
Sofia Schön	Blekinge Institute of Technology, Sweden
Filip Šalamon	Brno University of Technology, Czech Republic
Vlastimil Šlouf	University of Defence, Czech Republic
Levent Hakki Şenyürek	STM Defense Technologies Engineering and Trade Inc., Türkiye
Stefan Pickl	Universität der Bundeswehr München, Germany
Peter Stütz	Universität der Bundeswehr München, Germany
Esra Hicret Uzer	Czech Technical University in Prague, Czech Republic
Petr Vašík	Brno University of Technology, Czech Republic
David Žůrek	NATO M&S COE, Italy

Contents

AxS/AI in Context of Future Warfare and Security Environment (Concepts, Applications, Standards, etc.)

Artificial Intelligence in the Space Domain: Trends, Opportunities and Challenges

Walter David(✉)

Climate & Security Consulting LLC, Virginia Beach, VA 23452, USA
walterdavid.xyz@gmail.com

Abstract. The integration of Artificial Intelligence (AI) in space-based systems is transforming strategic and operational paradigms across civil, commercial, and military sectors. This paper presents a comprehensive literature review of current trends, applications, opportunities and challenges of AI-enabled space operations, drawing on peer-reviewed articles, international agencies technical reports and policy documents. AI capabilities, such as onboard data processing, machine learning for anomaly detection, reinforcement learning for navigation, and predictive analytics for early warning, are increasingly embedded in satellite constellations management, control, and decision-support. Special attention is given to applications in Earth observation, intelligence, surveillance, and reconnaissance, space situational awareness, autonomous navigation. The convergence of civil/commercial and military space actors is also highlighted. The paper explores the implications of this transformation. Emerging governance challenges, such as algorithm transparency, dual-use technology, lack of updated international norms, are discussed with relevance to NATO, EU policy and the Outer Space Treaty. Key findings emphasize the role of hybrid AI architectures, cross-domain interoperability, and the role of simulation-based validation. The paper concludes by identifying gaps in empirical validation and policy integration, recommending a way forward focused on standardization, explainability, and cross-sector collaboration. This synthesis aims to support decision makers, planners, and researchers in responsibly accelerating AI adoption for secure and sustainable space operations.

Keywords: Artificial Intelligence · Space Operations · Satellite Autonomy · Space Situational Awareness · Constellation Management

1 Introduction

1.1 Background

The integration of artificial intelligence (AI) into the space domain represents a transformative shift in the space domain [1], enabling new capabilities in satellite operations, mission design, data processing, and autonomous systems.

In 2019, Allies recognized space as an operational domain and adopted NATO's Overarching Space Policy (OSP) [2]. Meanwhile, over the past decade, the commercial

J. Novotný et al. (Eds.): MESAS 2025, LNCS 16627, pp. 3–16, 2027.
https://doi.org/10.1007/978-3-032-33182-3_1

space sector has experienced unprecedented growth and innovation [3]. As NATO continues to operationalize the Multi-Domain Operations (MDO) concept [4], integrating land, maritime, air, cyber, and space domains demands an evolution from the traditional Command and Control (C2) approach. The Cross-Domain Command (CDC) concept aims to achieve decision advantage by orchestrating and synchronizing activities across multiple domains with the crucial role of non-military instruments of power; aspect particularly relevant for space as NATO does not own satellites [5, 6].

Private companies are leading the space revolution and offer services that in the past only governmental or international agencies could deliver [3]. NATO's Commercial Space Strategy [7] aims to strengthen the relationships with commercial partners and leverage their services. With the deployment of large constellations in low Earth orbits (LEO), and the growing reliance on space services, AI has emerged as a dual-use enabler of space technologies for the civil, commercial, and military sectors.

1.2 Methodology

The study was conducted using a structured literature review of recent relevant scientific publications and institutional and operational reports addressing the intersection of artificial intelligence and space technology.

The selection process included search of academic databases Scopus, Web of Science, IEEE Xplore, SpringerLink, and Google Scholar for years 2004–2025. The author has tested the Open AI large language model (LLM) ChatGPT-5; it proved more accurate than its previous versions and Gemini 2.5 pro, but it still experienced hallucinates in quoting and citing sources and produced links to non-existent papers and links to papers on different topics. Consensus app has also been tested; it does not use a general AI model's internal memory to "guess" an answer. Apparently, it does not fabricate sources and provides links to real, peer-reviewed papers. However, for precautionary reasons, the author has chosen a traditional sources search approach; by selecting sources for their technical depth, policy relevance, or value as best practices.

References Include Institutional Policy, Programmatic and Technical Reports Retrieved from the United Nations Office for Outer Space Affairs (UNOOSA), European Union, European Space Agency (ESA), European Defence Agency (EDA), and NASA.

The author has been involved in NATO space policy and doctrine development; public release versions of policy documents have been considered. Where civil/commercial and military sectors use the same capabilities and address similar challenges, the convergence points have been highlighted.

2 Major Trends and Opportunities in Space – AI Integration

This section synthesizes the most relevant trends in the adoption of AI [8, 9] and a significant shift to the privatization of space access. Opportunities are growing areas like satellite communications (SATCOM), intelligence, surveillance and reconnaissance (ISR), land use, off-Earth missions [10], positioning, navigation and timing (PNT), meteorology and oceanography (METOC), space situational awareness (SSA), early warning. UN agencies explore the use of AI in anticipatory action in humanitarian crises through predictive analytics [11].

2.1 Onboard Data Processing and Edge AI

Earth observation (EO) initial paradigm included transferring raw data to ground stations for processing, with significant issues in terms of latency, and bandwidth.

Case Study. ESA Φ-Sat-1. Convolutional Neural Networks (CNN) are designed to process data in multiple arrays and are mainly used to analyse visual images [12]. The Φ -sat-1 nano satellite, first of two 6 U CubeSats developed by the ESA, in a first in-orbit demonstration of Deep Neural Network (DNN) processing data on the edge successfully detected and discarded cloud-covered images [13].

As noted in [14], satellite edge AI is a reliable tool for EO and remote sensing [10] and represents a paradigm shift from ground-based to on-board space data processing, enabling the transmission to the ground segment of only the meaningful data, with reduction of data bandwidth and latency [15].

Temporal models such as DeepSat V2 and TempCNN, demonstrate high accuracy in annotating satellite imagery (e.g.: Sentinel-2) [9, 16, 17]. METOC and EO are increasingly automated with Machine Learning (ML) applied to multispectral and synthetic aperture radar (SAR) satellite data for environmental monitoring, agriculture, crop classification, land use analysis, rapid wildfire detection, flood forecasting, predictive drought mapping, and near-real-time disaster response [18].

2.2 Guidance, Navigation, and Control

One of the most critical stages of a mission are the entry, descent and landing (EDL); implementing pre-planned sequences might not be sufficient [19]. Autonomous Guidance, Navigation and Control (GNC) became essential for exploration, rendezvous, and swarm coordination.

Case Study. NASA Mars 2020 Perseverance Rover. This mission incorporates Deep Reinforcement Learning (DRL) to optimize operations, autonomous positioning of instruments, adjusting of drives, data collection, and reactive decision making in an unpredictable environment [9]. By utilizing Deep Neural Networks (DNN) as function approximators, DRL empowers agents to learn directly from raw sensory input [19]. The rover navigates rough Martian terrain without need of constant command from Earth; basically:

- The AI agent (DRL software) is trained in a virtual environment that simulates Mars' environment.
- Control theory for controlling systems is still used but alongside the DRL because it helps reduce the learning burden and facilitates the transfer of the learned behavior from simulation to reality [20, 21].
- The agent learns the behaviors leading to success versus those leading to failure by receiving "rewards" and "punishments".
- The agent develops an optimal policy for movement and navigation, and autonomously make safe, efficient decisions on Mars.

This technology is a key component of the autonomous navigation that allows the rover to land and drive on Mars terrain. DRL harnesses the DNN capabilities to tackle problems that traditional RL struggled to handle, enabling spacecraft to learn optimal EDL and navigation trajectories in simulation and transfer them to reality [19, 21]. In effect, Perseverance represents an outstanding achievement in space exploration. Moreover, with emerging developments of connectivity and computing technologies [22], the convergence between AI and Blockchain will bring significant benefits to the Internet of Space Things, SATCOM, and Spacecraft Data Security [23].

2.3 Anomaly Detection

It is essential to track in real-time the status and health of the spacecraft, quickly identify unexpected or abnormal behaviour and take appropriate corrective action [24]. This requires predictive maintenance and rapid anomaly identification.

Case Study. OPS-SAT ESA Mission. OPS-SAT (Operations nanosatellite) is the world's first mission dedicated to testing satellite control technology in orbit, designed to drive innovation and experimentation. In effect, telemetry data plays a crucial role in ensuring the safeguard and the integrity of space systems. [25].

Recurrent Neural Networks (RNNs) interpret sequential and temporal information, analyse time series, audio, text, and speech [12]. Long Short-Term Memory (LSTM) models learn temporal dependencies in data to distinguish nominal behaviour from emerging threats and identify anomalies before critical failures occur in satellite subsystems [24, 26], shifting maintenance strategies from reactive to proactive, extending spacecraft lifespan.

2.4 Satellite Communication Constellations Management

Mega constellation networks (MCN) (e.g. Starlink and OneWeb) satellites in LEO represent a promising solution to global internet access but present significant management challenges, requiring innovative approaches for efficient, scalable, and resilient operations. Stock et al. [27] investigated the optimization of MCN operations, drawing from the ESA ConstellAI initiative to develop AI algorithms for managing satellite mega-constellations. AI proved effective over traditional data routing methods, in a critical shift toward decentralized control, with benefits for load balancing, link optimization, and routing decisions [28].

In fact, the growing demand for space services requires establishing simultaneous multiple paths for transmission of flows in parallel. DRL-based Multipath Routing (DMR) enabled by a Graph Neural Network (GNN) is proposed [28–30] for enhancing the transmission performance of MCNs in low orbits.

Hybrid models where GNNs capture the complex relationships between satellites, while the DRL-based routing improves latency and resource allocation, and optimizes dynamic routing [27] demonstrate superior performance in reducing latency and improving link utilization compared to traditional approaches [31].

2.5 Space Situational Awareness

The number of satellites in LEO has increased dramatically. Currently around 1 million resident space objects (RSO) larger than 1 cm are orbiting the Earth but only thirty thousand that are larger than 10 cm are tracked. Space Situational Awareness (SSA) becomes crucial to accurately track and predict debris and orbits of satellites to avoid a Kessler Syndrome's chain reaction of collisions [32].

DL methods for object detection and classification leverage CNNs to identify and track RSOs (satellites and debris), improving the fidelity of orbital catalogs and maneuvers, thus avoiding collisions [8, 33]. RL has been successfully applied to optimize sensor scheduling across dense RSO fields. A DRL agent tasks a space-based narrow field of view sensor in LEO using the proximal policy optimization algorithm [34]. Fig. 1 illustrates the end-to-end data processing architecture for an SSA system where the AI-enabled workflow is structured into three functional blocks.

Sensors (data sources). Heterogeneous sources collect raw observational data.

- *Ground-Based Sensors.* Ground-based radars and space-based optical telescopes, and laser ranging systems that monitor objects from Earth.
- *Space-Based Sensors.* Satellites with onboard cameras, infrared sensors, and radar instruments that observe other space objects.
- *External Data.* Feeds from partners, commercial providers, or historical datasets.

AI Processing. This includes:

- *Object Detection & Tracking.* CNNs are used to detect objects in orbital imagery or radar data. Kalman filters or neural net regressors track motion and update positional predictions.
- *Threat Classification.* Using pattern recognition, anomaly detection, and RL, the system assesses whether an object poses a threat (e.g., potential collision, anti-satellite behavior, uncontrolled debris).

Outputs include:

- *Object Catalog.* A continuously updated database of RSOs, including their trajectories and behavioral patterns.
- *Threat Alerts.* Automated warnings about potential collisions, close approaches, or hostile actions are issued to mission operators.

This pipeline enables rapid interpretation of raw sensor data turning them into actionable situational awareness for space traffic management and defense operation.

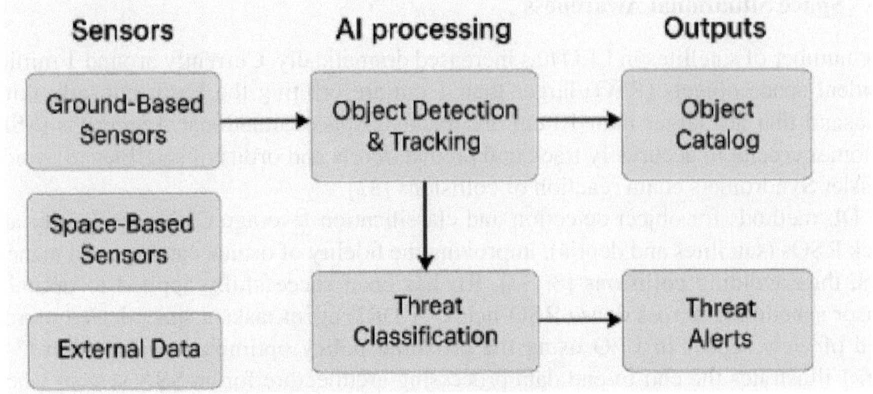

Fig. 1. Conceptual framework of an AI-enabled SSA workflow

3 Key Challenges in AI–Space Integration

Despite rapid advances, the integration of AI in the space domain faces critical challenges that can be grouped into short-term (0–5 years), concerning data reliability, availability and vulnerabilities affecting near-term missions, and long-term (5–15 years), which concern sustainability, governance, and legal frameworks (see Table 1).

Table 1. Short-term vs. long-term challenges in AI–Space integration

Horizon	Challenges
Short-Term	Operational Safety and Reliability; Explainability and Trust; Data Integrity and Availability; Cyber vulnerability
Long-Term	Legal and Ethical Implications; International Norms and Regulation; Standardization and Interoperability; Bias risks

3.1 Short-Term Challenges

Operational Safety and Reliability. During autonomous guidance or anomaly response, it is vital to ensure fail-safe behavior and appropriate human-in-the-loop (HITL) design, to avoid errors escalating into critical failures [35].

Explainability and Trust. Complex black-box models, e.g. DNN and RL agents, often lack interpretability, making real-time decision justification difficult [36], undermining human confidence and acceptance.

The principles of explainable AI (XAI) are particularly relevant where failures could have catastrophic consequences, providing transparency into the decision-making processes of AI models, essential for ensuring the safety, trustworthiness, and effectiveness of space missions. ESA policy drafts emphasize the need to integrate XAI into space operations [37] while the EDA white paper 'Trustworthiness for AI in Defence' (TAID) recognizes this topic as crucial for the military [38]. NASA applies XAI key principles to its mission-critical systems, established a Framework for the Ethical Use of Artificial Intelligence (AI), and developed NASA's Responsible AI Plan in 2022 [39]. Graham et al. [40] introduced the concept of Responsible AI and its applicability in the space industry.

Data Integrity and Availability. Training DL models demand a large amount of data to achieve exceptional performance, but high-quality, labelled datasets remain scarce for specific contexts such as orbital dynamics, deep-space telemetry, and mission anomaly logs [35, 41].

Cyber vulnerability. AI-enabled space architectures present novel vulnerabilities. Potential threats include spoofing of space links, and adversarial ML attacks (e.g. image perturbation or data poisoning) [42]. Frameworks should incorporate resilience to adversarial learning, zero-day threats, and spoofing attacks.

The EU Agency for Cybersecurity (ENISA) report [43] examines how standardization can support the implementation of the cybersecurity aspects. The U.S. National Institute of Standards and Technology (NIST) is working toward cross-domain cybersecurity benchmarks (see NIST Internal Report (NIST IR) 8403, Blockchain for Access Control Systems) [44].

3.2 Long-Term Challenges

Legal and Ethical Implications. AI-enabled space capabilities bring up complex considerations involving the Law of Armed Conflict, codes of conduct [3] and the Treaty on Principles Governing the Activities of States in the Exploration and Use of Outer Space, including the Moon and Other Celestial Bodies, 1967, known as the Outer Space Treaty (OST) that, together with four other key treaties, provide a legal foundation.

However, the OST does not adequately cover autonomous decision making in space. There is a need for nations to update legal frameworks to account for autonomous systems while upholding the OST core principles of international cooperation and mutual benefit in space activities [45] but also to adapt to the new reality of AI [46]; the status quo risks rendering the OST Article IX on harmful interference meaningless.

4 Findings and Discussion

AI is moving toward systemic integration in the space domain. The analysis reveals four main patterns: (1) AI permeates all phases of the space system lifecycle; (2) a shift toward distributed and autonomous systems; (3) convergence across civilian, commercial, and uses; (4) reliance on simulation-based validation as a bridge between experimentation and operations.

International Norms and Regulation. AI operationalization in space requires an evolution of international norms. The EU AI Act (Regulation 2024/1689), originally proposed as COM (2021) 206, is the world's first comprehensive regulation on AI, establishing harmonized rules for development, deployment, and use of AI within the EU [37, 38] but does not address outer space applications.

Standardization and Interoperability. Without common technical benchmarks, interoperability across civil, commercial and military actors will remain fragmented. The lack of shared datasets and testing environments slows validation and adoption.

Bias and Ethical Risks. AI models may reproduce bias in ISR data, with geopolitical implications. Long-term governance must ensure that AI-enabled decisions do not inadvertently escalate tensions or discriminate in humanitarian contexts.

4.1 AI Applications across Satellite Lifecycle

Mission Lifecycle Optimization. Experiments conducted on the OPS-SAT satellite successfully verified onboard learning models that can autonomously adapt mission parameters in real-time [47]. Fig. 2 proposes a visualization of how AI technologies can be mapped across five key satellite lifecycle phases. Lifecycle Phases include:

- *Mission Planning.* Concept development, trajectory design, and risk modeling.
- *Assembly and Testing.* Hardware integration, system diagnostics, and simulation tests.
- *Orbit Operations.* Satellite control, maneuvering, and payload operation.
- *Anomaly Detection.* Monitoring for faults, degradation, or cyber anomalies.
- *Deorbiting and Disposal.* End-of-life planning, collision-avoidance during reentry.

AI Applications. These include:

- *Path Optimization.* AI plans efficient orbital trajectories, especially for interplanetary missions or satellite constellations (applied in mission planning).
- *System Design.* AI assists in optimizing component layout, mass distribution, and thermal control (applied in satellite assembly).
- *Fault Diagnosis.* Predictive maintenance and error classification using ML (from assembly to orbit).
- *Autonomous Navigation.* RL enables self-guided repositioning and docking maneuvers (orbit operations).
- *Image Analysis.* CNNs and other classifiers interpret Earth observation or surveillance imagery (from orbit to anomaly detection).
- *Collision Avoidance.* AI predicts conjunctions and proposes evasive maneuvers (from anomaly detection to deorbiting).

The diagram illustrates how different AI methods (on the vertical axis) are applied across five key phases of a satellite's lifecycle (on the horizontal axis):

- *Path Optimization.* (blue line, top): Applied only at the Mission Planning stage (design of optimal trajectories).
- *System Design.* (orange line): Relevant during Assembly & Testing for component layout and diagnostics.
- *Autonomous Navigation.* (green line): Becomes critical in Orbit Operations (self-guided docking, manoeuvring).

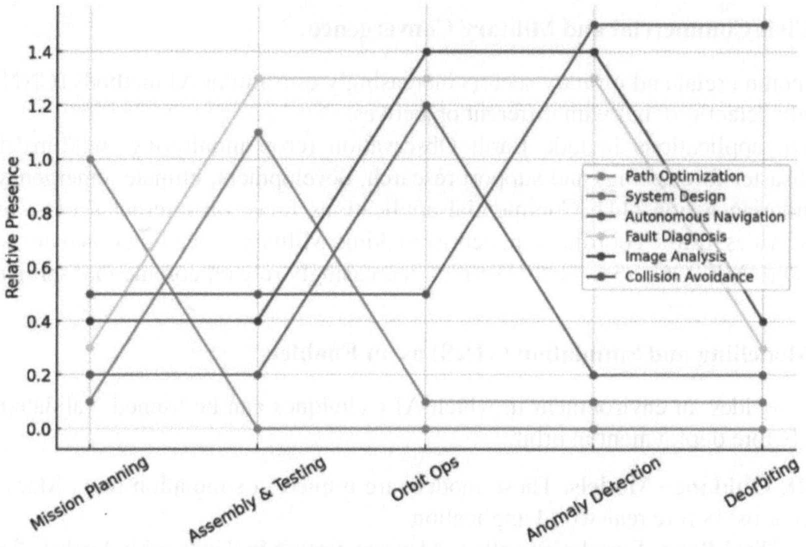

Fig. 2 AI applications applied across satellite lifecycle

- *Fault Diagnosis.* (red line): Spans Assembly, Orbit, and Anomaly Detection, reflecting predictive maintenance across multiple stages.
- *Image Analysis.* (purple line): Applied in Orbit Operations and Anomaly Detection, e.g., EO interpretation or identifying system failures.
- *Collision Avoidance.* (brown line): Used in Anomaly Detection and Deorbiting, for safe end-of-life disposal and manoeuvring.

The figure highlights how AI permeates all lifecycle phases, with different emphases. Early phases (Mission Planning, Assembly) rely on optimization and diagnostics. Mid-phases (Orbit Operations, Anomaly Detection) are AI-intensive, combining navigation, analysis, and predictive monitoring. End-of-life (Deorbiting) rely on safety and collision avoidance.

4.2 Shift toward Distributed and Autonomous Systems

Traditional monolithic space systems are being replaced by distributed constellations [47, 48]. RL agents learn optimal policies for trajectory control in rapidly changing environments, supporting planetary EDL, where reactivity is critical. AI enables:

- Dynamic routing data, optimize link connectivity, and adapt to network congestion.
- Onboard decision-making in exploratory missions.
- Real-time anomaly detection using OPS-SAT benchmarks.
- Edge AI reducing latency and bandwidth.

4.3 Civil/Commercial and Military Convergence

Civil, commercial and military sectors increasingly use similar AI methods (CNN, RL, anomaly detection), but with different objectives.

Civil applications include Earth Observation (crop monitoring, wildfire detection, disaster forecasting) and support research, development, climate, emergency and humanitarian action [11]. Commercial applications focus on internet access, broadband services, traffic coordination, debris tracking. Military space functional areas ISR, SATCOM, METOC, SSA, Early Warning increasingly rely on commercial services.

4.4 Modelling and Simulation (M&S) as an Enabler

M&S provides an environment in which AI techniques can be trained, validated, and tested before deployment in orbit.

- **DRL Guidance Models.** These models are trained in simulation (e.g., Mars EDL scenarios) before real-world application.
- **SSA Workflows.** Simulations allow AI stress-testing in dense orbital debris fields.
- **Constellation Routing.** GNN–DRL models are tested in virtual environments to optimize link connectivity.

This paper contributes to scientific and policy debates by offering a structured synthesis of AI-enabled space applications, highlighting case studies, and identifying research gaps relevant to space domain civil/commercial, and military stakeholders.

5 Conclusions and Way Ahead

Major Trends and Applications. AI is essential for preventing collisions and extending spacecraft lifespan but also for addressing sustainability challenges in orbital regimes, vulnerable to congestion and threatened by debris. Distributed AI architectures reduce single points of failure and support enhanced resilience.

AI is driving advances in autonomous navigation, health monitoring, and operational management of orbital assets, including distributed satellite systems and trusted autonomous orbital operations [12, 48]. Powerful AI-driven onboard data processing is enabled using commercial off-the-shelf system-on-chip technologies deployed directly on spacecraft, thus reducing bandwidth needs and enabling real-time decision making [48]. Efficiency of SSA capabilities is improved by AI enhanced orbit determination and prediction of space debris. Imaging from space is improved by AI, though challenges remain in data processing and algorithm optimization [49].

Key Opportunities. AI-driven geospatial analytics enable novel insights from large-scale spatial data, supporting Earth observation and exploration [50]. The convergence of AI with Internet of Things (IoT) and blockchain technologies opens new avenues for efficient space communications and data management [22]. ML, DL, and evolutionary algorithms are evolving mission planning, spacecraft guidance, and control [48].

Challenges. Technical hurdles such as scarce availability of data and limited onboard computing power, radiation tolerance, and the need for efficient, robust algorithms remain significant obstacles. Legal and ethical questions concern autonomous systems questions of accountability, liability, acceptance, regulation for AI-driven decision making in outer space [51] because adoption of AI without governance poses new imperatives for governance to avoid undermining international space law. Ensuring data integrity, cybersecurity, and privacy in interconnected space systems is also a growing concern [22, 50]. Gaps in standardization, lack of shared datasets and benchmarks create barriers to interoperability across different sectors and nations.

Way ahead. AI holds transformative potential, enabling unprecedented levels of autonomy, optimizing performance, responsiveness, and mission complexity but its responsible adoption hinges on addressing foundational challenges in transparency, security, and regulation.

As the space domain evolves, the integration of AI becomes a strategic imperative. AI is being embedded in the architecture design [51–54]. The ability to anticipate threats, adapt to uncertain conditions, and coordinate across distributed assets marks a transformation in space planning and execution. Successful deployment depends on integrating insights from space engineering, computer science, ethics, international law, and policy. Challenges in bias mitigation, accountability, and algorithm auditing require broader international collaboration and adaptive policies. Governance mechanisms, including AI auditing protocols, international norms for human oversight, and transparent algorithm certification, will be essential.

The integration of AI in space must proceed with strategic foresight. While this paper presents a conceptual synthesis, empirical validation is needed. Real-world experimentation, simulation-based validation, and performance benchmarking across AI models in orbital conditions should be prioritized. Research should focus on standardizing performance benchmarks for AI in space, integrating explainable AI approaches.

Disclosure of Interests. The author declares that there are no competing interests, financial or non-financial, related to this work.

References

1. Ben-Itzhak, S.: The use of artificial Intelligence in outer space capabilities. SAIS Rev. Int. Aff. **44**(2), 5–30 (2024). https://doi.org/10.1353/sais.2024.a950954
2. NATO., https://www.nato.int/cps/en/natohq/official_texts_190862.htm
3. NATO Standard AJP-3.3 https://assets.publishing.service.gov.uk/media/5a82d7bc40f0b62305b94a32/doctrine_nato_air_space_ops_ajp_3_3.pdf
4. Takabatake, F.: NATO's approach to multi-domain operations: from the perspective of the economics of alliances. Defence and Peace Economics. **35**(3), 281–294 (2023). https://doi.org/10.1080/10242694.2023.2235502
5. NATO ACT., https://www.act.nato.int/article/next-generation-c2/, Last Accessed 17 Sep 2025
6. NATO C2 Centre of Excellence., https://c2coe.org/cross-domain-command-concept-workshop-5-orchestration-is-needed-but-what-is-it/#:~:text=The%20fifth%20Cross%2DDomain%20Command,Course%20at%20NATO%20School%20Oberammergau, last accessed 2025/09/17

7. NATO Commercial Space Strategy, https://www.nato.int/cps/en/natohq/official_texts_236520.htm , Last Accessed 17 Sep 2025
8. Thangavel, K., et al.: Artificial Intelligence for Trusted Autonomous Satellite Operations. Progress in Aerospace Sciences. **144**, 100960, ISSN 0376-0421 (2024). https://doi.org/10.1016/j.paerosci.2023.100960
9. Liu, Q., et al.: DeepSat V2: feature augmented convolutional neural nets for satellite image classification. Remote sensing letters. **11**(2), 156–165 (2019). https://doi.org/10.1080/2150704X.2019.1693071
10. Denis, G., Alary, D., Pasco, X., Pisot, N., Texier, D., Toulza, S.: From new space to big space: How commercial space dream is becoming a reality. Acta Astronautica. **166**, 431–443, ISSN 0094-5765 (2020). https://doi.org/10.1016/j.actaastro.2019.08.031
11. David, W., King-Okoye, M., Garmendia-Doval, B.: Artificial Intelligence support to the paradigm shift from reactive to anticipatory action in humanitarian responses. In: Mazal, J., et al. (eds.) Modelling and Simulation for Autonomous Systems: MESAS 2022, pp. 145–162. Springer (2023). https://doi.org/10.1007/978-3-031-31268-7_9
12. Russo, A., Lax, G.: Using artificial Intelligence for space challenges: a survey. Appl. Sci. **12**(10), 5106 (2022). https://doi.org/10.3390/app12105106
13. Fonseca, R.M., María-Paz Zorzano, M.P., Martín-Torres, J.: MARSWRF Prediction of Entry Descent Landing Profiles: Applications to Mars Exploration. Earth and Space Science. **6**(8), 1319–1577 (2019). https://doi.org/10.1029/2019EA000575
14. Giuffrida, G., et al.: The Φ-Sat-1 Mission: The First On-Board Deep Neural Network Demonstrator for Satellite Earth Observation. IEEE Transactions on Geoscience and Remote Sensing. **60**, 1–14 (2022, Art no. 5517414). https://doi.org/10.1109/TGRS.2021.3125567
15. Shi, Y., Zhu, J., Jiang, C., Kuang, L., Letaief, K.B.: Satellite edge artificial intelligence with large models: Architectures and technologies. https://arxiv.org/html/2504.01676v1
16. Pelletier, C., et al.: Temporal convolutional neural networks for satellite time series. Remote sensing letters. **9**(11), 1049–1058 (2018). https://doi.org/10.1080/2150704X.2018.1478926
17. Cheng, X., Sun, Y., Zhang, W., Wang, Y., Cao, X., Wang, Y.. Application of deep learning in multitemporal remote sensing image classification. Remote Sens., 15(15), 3859. (2023). doi:https://doi.org/10.3390/rs15153859
18. Feng, F., Maofang Gao, M., Liu, R., Yao, S., Yang, G.: A deep learning framework for crop mapping with reconstructed Sentinel-2 time series images. Computers and Electronics in Agriculture. **213**, 108227, ISSN 0168-1699, (https://www.sciencedirect.com/science/article/pii/S0168169923006154) (2023). https://doi.org/10.1016/j.compag.2023.108227
19. Alma Better, https://www.almabetter.com/bytes/articles/deep-reinforcement-learning.
20. Ayık, F. (2023) Utilizing deep reinforcement learning in control: release the power of intelligent systems (2023). https://github.com/frknayk/Reinforcement-Learning-In-Control
21. Hovell, K., Steve Ulrich, S.: Deep Reinforcement Learning for Spacecraft Proximity Operations Guidance. JSR. **58**(2), 254 (2021). https://doi.org/10.2514/1.A34838
22. Kua, J., Arora, C., Loke, S., Fernando, N., Ranaweera, C.: Internet of things in space: a review of opportunities and challenges from satellite-aided computing to digitally-enhanced space living. Sensors (Basel, Switzerland). **21**, 8117 (2021). https://doi.org/10.3390/s21238117
23. Oche, P., Ewa, G., Ibekwe, N.: Applications and challenges of artificial Intelligence in space missions. IEEE Access. **12**, 1–1 (2021). https://doi.org/10.1109/ACCESS.2021.3132500
24. Cuéllar, S., Santos, M., Alonso, F., Fabregas, E., Farias, G.: Explainable anomaly detection in spacecraft telemetry. engineering applications of artificial Intelligence. **133**, 108083, ISSN 0952-1976 (2024). https://doi.org/10.1016/j.engappai.2024.108083
25. Fejjari, A., Delavault, A., Camilleri, R., Valentino, G.: A review of anomaly detection in spacecraft telemetry data. Appl. Sci. **15**(10), 5653 (2025). https://doi.org/10.3390/app15105653

26. Lindemann, B., Müller, T., Vietz, H., Nasser Jazdi, N., Weyrich, M.: A survey on long short-term memory networks for time series prediction. Procedia CIRP. **99**, 650–655, ISSN 2212-8271 (2021). https://doi.org/10.1016/j.procir.2021.03.088
27. Stock, G.F. et al, (2025). On the Role of AI in Managing Satellite Constellations: Insights from the ConstellAI Project, https://arxiv.org/abs/2507.15574
28. Han, C., Xiong, W., Yu, R.: Deep reinforcement learning-based multipath Routing for LEO Megaconstellation networks. Electronics. **13**(15), 3054 (2024). https://doi.org/10.3390/electronics13153054
29. Chen, Y., et al.: Deep reinforcement learning-based Routing method for low earth orbit mega-constellation satellite networks with service function constraints. Sensors. **25**(4), 1232 (2025). https://doi.org/10.3390/s25041232
30. Xu, P., Feng, M., Zhou, J., Xiao, L., Xiao, P., Jiang, T.: Inter-satellite routing for LEO satellite networks: A GNN and DRL integrated approach. In: 2024 IEEE/CIC International Conference on Communications in China, ICCC, pp. 1346–1351 (2024). https://doi.org/10.1109/ICCC62479.2024.10681995
31. Toka, L., Illes, Z., Papp, E.A., Hevizi, L., Godor, I.: Routing LEO satellite traffic in adverse weather. Computer Networks. **270**, 111559, ISSN 1389-1286 (2025). https://doi.org/10.1016/j.comnet.2025.111559
32. Caldas, F., Cláudia Soares, C.: Machine learning in orbit estimation: A survey. Acta Astronautica. **220**, 97–107, ISSN 0094-5765, .(https://www.sciencedirect.com/science/article/pii/S0094576524001917) (2024). https://doi.org/10.1016/j.actaastro.2024.03.072
33. Massimi, F., Ferrara, P., Petrucci, R., Benedetto, F.: Deep learning-based space debris detection for spacesituational awareness: a feasibility study applied to the radar processing. IET Radar Sonar Navig. **18**(4), 635–648 (2024). https://doi.org/10.1049/rsn2.12547
34. Siew, P.M., Jang, D., Roberts, T.G., et al.: Space-based sensor tasking using deep reinforcement learning. J. Astronaut. Sci. **69**, 1855–1892 (2022). https://doi.org/10.1007/s40295-022-00354-8
35. Nesnas, I.A., Fesq, L.M. Volpe, R.A. Autonomy for space robots: past, present, and future. Curr. Robot. Rep. 2, 251–263 (2021). doi:https://doi.org/10.1007/s43154-021-00057-2
36. Zuiderwijk, A., Chen, Y.C., Salem, F.: Implications of the use of artificial intelligence in public governance: a systematic literature review and a research agenda. Gov. Inf. Q. **38**(3), 101577, ISSN 0740-624X (2021). https://doi.org/10.1016/j.giq.2021.101577
37. European Space Agency.: https://esastar-publication-ext.sso.esa.int/ESATenderActions/details/143599;
38. European Defence Agency.: https://eda.europa.eu/docs/default-source/brochures/taid-white-paper-final-09052025.pdf
39. NASA., https://oig.nasa.gov/wp-content/uploads/2023/12/ig-23-012.pdf
40. Graham, T., Thangavel, K.: Artificial Intelligence in space: an analysis of responsible AI principles for the space domain. In: October 2023 Conference: 74th International Astronautical Congress (IAC) at, Baku, Azerbaijan (2023)
41. Alzubaidi, L., Bai, J., Al-Sabaawi, A., et al.: A survey on deep learning tools dealing with data scarcity: definitions, challenges, solutions, tips, and applications. J. Big Data. **10**, 46 (2023). https://doi.org/10.1186/s40537-023-00727-2
42. Vassilev A, Oprea A, Fordyce A, Anderson H, Davies X, Hamin M (2025) Adversarial Machine Learning: a Taxonomy and Terminology of Attacks and Mitigations. (National Institute of Standards and Technology, Gaithersburg, MD) NIST Trustworthy and Responsible AI, NIST AI 100-2e2025. https://doi.org/10.6028/NIST.AI.100-2e202
43. European Union Agency for Cybersecurity. (ENISA), Cybersecurity for Artificial Intelligence.. https://www.enisa.europa.eu/publications/cybersecurity-for-ai

44. National Institute of Standards and Technology (NIST).: https://csrc.nist.gov/News/2022/blockchain-for-access-control-systems-nist-ir-8403#:~:text=Updates%202022-,Blockchain%20for%20Access%20Control%20Systems%3A%20NIST%20IR,May%2026%2C%202022&text=NIST%20has%20published%20NIST%20Internal,of%20an%20access%20control%20system. Accessed 23 Sep 2025
45. United Nations Office for Outer Space Affairs (UNOSA).: https://www.unoosa.org/oosa/en/ourwork/spacelaw/treaties/outerspacetreaty.html.
46. War on the Rocks, https://warontherocks.com/2025/03/autonomy-has-outpaced-international-space-law/, last accessed 2025/09/23
47. Ruszczak, B., Kotowski, K., Evans, D., et al.: The OPS-SAT benchmark for detecting anomalies in satellite telemetry. Sci. Data. **12**, 710 (2025). https://doi.org/10.1038/s41597-025-05035-3
48. Izzo, D., Märtens, M., Pan, B.: A survey on artificial intelligence trends in spacecraft guidance dynamics and control. Astrodynamics. **3**, 287–299 (2018). https://doi.org/10.1007/s42064-018-0053-6
49. Jia, Q., Xiao, J., Bai, L., Zhang, Y., Zhang, R., Feroskhan, M.: Space situational awareness systems: bridging traditional methods and artificial intelligence. Acta Astronaut. **228**, 321 (2024). https://doi.org/10.1016/j.actaastro.2024.11.025
50. Chen, M., et al.: Artificial intelligence and visual analytics in geographical space and cyberspace: research opportunities and challenges. Earth Sci. Rev. **241**, 104438 (2023). https://doi.org/10.1016/j.earscirev.2023.104438
51. Martin, A., Freeland, S.: The advent of artificial Intelligence in space activities: new legal challenges. Space Policy. **55**, 101408 (2021). https://doi.org/10.1016/j.spacepol.2020.101408
52. Jeong, Y., Suthakar, V., Qashoa, R., Sohn, G., Lee, R.S.: Orbit track: advanced RSO detection and tracking from wide field-of-view on-orbit images. Adv. Space Res., ISSN 0273-1177. (2025). https://doi.org/10.1016/j.asr.2025.08.006
53. Kyuroson, A., Banerjee, A., Tafanidis, N.A., Satpute, S., Nikolakopoulos, G.: Towards fully autonomous orbit management for low-earth orbit satellites based on neuro-evolutionary algorithms and deep reinforcement learning. European Journal of Control. **80**, 101052, ISSN 0947-3580 (2024). https://doi.org/10.1016/j.ejcon.2024.101052
54. Botezatu, U.E., Ciuperca, E.M.: AI-Driven space security: Future trends and strategic imperatives for critical infrastructures. Romanian Journal of Information Technology and Automatic ControlISSN 1220–1758. **35**(1), 7–22 (2025). https://doi.org/10.33436/v35i1y202501

The Impact of Contemporary Armed Conflicts on the Acquisition and Modernization of UAVs in the Armed Forces of Central Europe

Jaroslav Galba(✉), Markéta Licková, Michaela Pavlisová, and Vladimír Vyklický

University of Defence, Kounicova 65, Brno, 662 10 Brno, Czech Republic
jaroslav.galba@unob.cz

Abstract. This study examines the influence of selected contemporary armed conflicts, namely the Second Nagorno-Karabakh War (2020), the Russian aggression against Ukraine (2022 to present), and the Israeli-Palestinian conflict (2023 to present), on the planned acquisition of unmanned aerial vehicles (UAVs) within the armed forces of Central European states. Employing a comparative case study methodology, the research analyses acquisition processes in six countries: Poland, the Czech Republic, Slovakia, Hungary, Austria, and Germany. The study identifies key operational characteristics of UAVs deployment in these conflicts and surveys the specific acquisition decisions made by the selected states since 2015.

Keywords: Acquisition · Central Europe · Unmanned Aerial Vehicles

1 Introduction

The role of unmanned aerial vehicles (UAVs) in contemporary armed conflicts has undergone a profound transformation over the past two decades. Initially employed primarily for reconnaissance, surveillance, and target acquisition, UAVs have evolved into versatile assets capable of performing both kinetic and non-kinetic functions across the full spectrum of military operations. The shift from specialized intelligence platforms to multi-role systems and loitering munitions (LMs) reflects broader changes in the conduct of warfare, where speed, adaptability, and the ability to operate in contested environments have become increasingly decisive factors.

Simultaneously, the mass proliferation of commercially available drones has blurred the line between state and non-state actors, introducing elements of asymmetry and improvisation that challenge traditional military doctrines.

Recent conflicts have provided empirical evidence of these developments. The Second Nagorno-Karabakh War (2020) marked a turning point, demonstrating the decisive role of UAVs in suppressing enemy air defences and enabling precision strikes during a short, high-intensity campaign. In contrast, the ongoing Russian aggression against Ukraine highlights both the opportunities and limitations of UAVs in a protracted, large-scale conventional war, where advanced electronic warfare and layered air defence systems impose significant attrition on aerial platforms. Meanwhile, the escalation of the

J. Novotný et al. (Eds.): MESAS 2025, LNCS 16627, pp. 17–43, 2027.
https://doi.org/10.1007/978-3-032-33182-3_2

Israeli-Palestinian conflict since 2023 illustrates how both state and non-state actors integrate UAVs - from sophisticated MALE systems to improvised commercial drones - into complex urban and hybrid operations. Collectively, these cases underscore the extent to which UAVs have become integral to modern combat, while also revealing the highly context-dependent nature of their effectiveness.

For the armed forces of Central European states, these experiences are particularly relevant. Situated in geographic proximity to the war in Ukraine and embedded within Euro-Atlantic security structures, countries such as Poland, the Czech Republic, Slovakia, Hungary, Austria, and Germany face the dual imperative of adapting to rapidly evolving operational realities while balancing political, economic, and industrial constraints. The acquisition and modernization of UAVs thus represent not merely a technological choice, but a strategic response to the shifting security environment. These decisions are shaped by lessons drawn from contemporary conflicts, national defence doctrines, and the broader dynamics of European defence cooperation.

The purpose of this study is to examine how selected Central European states have responded to these challenges between 2015 and 2025. Employing a comparative case study design, the research aims to identify both common patterns and national divergences, contributing to a deeper understanding of how technological innovation, operational experience, and strategic necessity interact in military modernization. More broadly, the analysis engages with the ongoing debate over whether UAVs constitute a revolutionary transformation of warfare or an evolutionary adaptation that reinforces existing paradigms while expanding the range of available operational options.

2 Reflection of Previous Research

UAVs are aerial platforms operated without an onboard pilot, either remotely from a Ground Control Station (GCS) or autonomously according to pre-programmed tasks [1, 2]. UAVs are most commonly employed for ISR/ISTAR (Intelligence, Surveillance, Target Acquisition, and Reconnaissance). A subcategory is Unmanned Combat Aerial Vehicles (UCAVs), which are designed to conduct offensive operations and typically carry integrated or payload-mounted weapon systems [3]. Another subcategory consists of LMs, which are expendable, one-way platforms capable of combining ISR/ISTAR tasks with direct target engagement [4]. It is also important to distinguish UAVs from Unmanned Aerial Systems (UAS), a broader term that refers to the entire operational architecture, including the UAV itself, the GCS, communications links, and supporting infrastructure [3].

Research on military UAVs has undergone significant changes over the past decade, reflecting shifts in their operational use on the battlefield. Early studies, such as Sullivan [5], primarily viewed UAVs as a symbol of technological advancement, particularly in connection with MALE and HALE platforms used in counterterrorism operations. After 2014, however, the focus of research shifted. Yevtodyeva [6] shows that this period marked a change in acquisition trends, with states increasingly favouring smaller and more cost-effective platforms, including LMs and tactical ISR–strike systems capable of operating even in areas fully covered by air defence. This shift is linked to contemporary conflicts, especially the conflict in Ukraine, where UAVs have become an integral part of all phases of operations, while also serving as a symbol of improvisation and rapid technological adaptation.

Several studies examine the doctrinal and strategic implications of these developments. Tolstonosov et al. [7] highlight how innovative applications of small drones in Ukraine reshaped both tactical manoeuvre and broader operational concepts. Similarly, Minculete and Păstae [8] emphasize that the combination of low cost, ease of operation, and operational flexibility grants a significant advantage to armed forces, particularly in resource-constrained contexts. These studies underscore how UAVs enable persistent surveillance, accelerate the sensor-to-shooter cycle, and allow for continuous battlefield presence at relatively low financial cost.

A major point of debate is whether UAVs represent a revolutionary transformation of warfare. Rogers [9] argues that armed drones redefine military power by lowering the threshold for precision strikes, allowing smaller states and non-state actors to project force previously reserved for major powers. Plichta and Rossiter [10] similarly suggest that inexpensive, scalable one-way attack drones democratize precision warfare and reshape the economics of combat. Yet other scholars take a more cautious perspective. Calcara et al. [11] note that, despite tactical innovations, the fundamental dynamics of war remain largely unchanged. Kunertova [12], drawing on evidence from Ukraine, emphasizes that the impact of UAVs is context-dependent: they can be decisive when enhancing specific capabilities but often act as supplementary assets in other scenarios. This debate represents one of the most contested issues in the literature, highlighting the tension between those who regard UAVs as a disruptive technology and those who see them as an incremental, yet still significant, evolution.

An important area of research concerns the techno-industrial dimension. Nefodova et al. [13] analyse how the Ukrainian experience has influenced the global arms market and led to changes in acquisition processes, emphasizing flexibility and the use of civilian supply chains. Yevtodyeva [6] further confirms that, after 2014, the focus of acquisitions shifted toward smaller and modular systems, and she shows that research and development increasingly targeted platforms more resilient to air defence and electronic warfare.

Researchers agree that armed forces must anticipate high attrition rates of small UAVs and establish logistics capable of rapid replacement [6, 13]. Counter-drone measures need to be institutionalized at the brigade and battalion levels and integrated with electronic warfare and M-SHORAD systems [8, 14]. Finally, acquisition strategies must consider the dual-use reality, involving the civilian sector in both development and production [6, 13].

2.1 Evolutions of UAVs and Analysis of Contemporary Conflicts

The history of UAVs dates back to the first half of the 20th century, when these platforms were primarily used as training or decoy targets for manned aircraft. In this early phase, they were relatively simple technological systems, whose main function was to support pilot training and preparation [15]. Systematic military use began in the 1950s, driven by Cold War tensions and the Vietnam conflict, which necessitated more sophisticated reconnaissance tools. Early significant UAVs included the SD-1 Observer and

Ryan Aeronautical designs, valued for battlefield monitoring rather than direct combat engagement [15, 16].

During the 1960s and early 1970s, UAV deployment expanded notably in Israel, particularly during the Yom Kippur War. Platforms such as the American Firebee and domestic UAVs like the Chukar, with experimental kamikaze capabilities, were employed. A key milestone came in 1973 with Tadiran's Mastiff, the first modern UAV capable of transmitting high-resolution imagery, advancing real-time Reconnaissance [17, 18]. Shortly thereafter, Israel Aerospace Industries (IAI) introduced the Scout UAV, which significantly improved artillery accuracy during the First Lebanon War [18, 19]. These developments influenced U.S. programs, leading to collaboration with IAI on the RQ-2 Pioneer and the independent development of the GNAT 750, later modified into the RQ-1 Predator, the first systematically deployed MALE UAV for ISTAR missions in the 1990s [19]. Concurrently, the HALE RQ-4 Global Hawk was introduced, providing long-endurance surveillance under all weather conditions and accumulating extensive operational hours in Iraq and Afghanistan [18].

Israel continued advancing MALE UAVs with the Heron, an unarmed ISTAR platform featuring modular sensor capabilities. Modern variants, including the Heron TP, Hermes 450 and 900, and the smaller Skylark UAV, demonstrate the operational benefits of flexible, modular designs integrating various sensors and real-time data links [19–21].

In the 1990s, UAV technology began to be employed not only as a reconnaissance tool but also as a means to shorten the decision-making cycle. Lambeth [22] notes that during Operation Allied Force in Kosovo (1999), the Predator reduced the "sensor-to-shooter" time, providing continuous full-motion video and enabling identification of mobile targets, as well as direct guidance of A-10 and F-16 aircraft for strikes.

Following the September 11, 2001 attacks, UAVs transitioned decisively from reconnaissance to armed systems. The RQ-1 Predator evolved into the armed MQ-1, deployed in Operation Enduring Freedom, and later replaced by the MQ-1C Grey Eagle and MQ-9 Reaper [20]. The second decade of the 21st century saw further shift due to global UCAV market expansion, notably with China's entry, enabling previously excluded states to acquire both armed and reconnaissance platforms. UCAV acquisition often reflects defensive, prestige, and strategic considerations [23, 24].

The proliferation of UCAVs has also influenced non-state actors, who adapted commercial drones, such as quadcopters and FPV platforms, for both reconnaissance and offensive operations. This iterative dynamic, in which state and non-state actors observe and adapt to each other's tactics, has shaped contemporary UAV employment [25].

However, the most significant milestone in UAV development has been their deployment in recent conflicts, where their use has reached unprecedented levels.

2.2 Analysis of UAV Utilization in the Second Nagorno-Karabakh War

The intensity of UAVs use was partly a consequence of the limited number of manned aircraft available to both sides. The conflict thus provided an opportunity to demonstrate new capabilities of UAVs and LMs under real combat conditions. Various types of UAVs were deployed, including domestic platforms as well as Israeli, Turkish, and Russian systems, with integration of both multi-role UAVs and small tactical drones and LMs [26, 27].

Armenia did not achieve a comparable development of UAVs capabilities to Azerbaijan, and its deployment was largely limited to smaller, primarily domestic tactical platforms intended for ISR missions, along with a low number of LMs [26, 27]. In contrast, Azerbaijani forces possessed a modern and diverse UAVs arsenal, including Turkish Bayraktar TB2s and Israeli systems, capable of conducting complex ISTAR operations, providing support to artillery units, and executing direct strikes on strategic targets. This level of deployment enabled Azerbaijan to achieve near-complete air superiority over the contested territory [26, 28, 29].

In the initial offensive phase, multi-role TB2 UAVs were extensively employed [27, 28]. These platforms were deployed to locate and neutralize Armenian air defence systems while simultaneously providing ISTAR support for the subsequent employment of LMs The success of the TB2 was associated with the prompt neutralization of a significant portion of Armenian air defence and electronic warfare assets, thereby creating opportunities for further air operations [27, 30]. Detailed analyses indicate that Azerbaijan deployed UAVs as part of coordinated SEAD/DEAD operations: Harop/Harpy LMs targeted radars and SAMs, while TB2 UAVs conducted ISR, target acquisition, and precision strikes where air defences permitted. Small UAS and commercial platforms were also employed to provide battle damage assessment and fire correction [31].

The TB2 was subsequently extensively employed by Azerbaijan in the more advanced phases of the conflict to provide ISTAR information to reconnaissance and artillery units. Due to its ability to integrate weapon systems, it could also independently acquire and strike enemy targets, including both heavy and light armoured vehicles, command centres, and other assets. The effectiveness of these operations was significant, with estimates of damage inflicted on the Armenian armed forces by TB2 strikes reaching at least one billion USD [32]. Armenian forces responded by implementing countermeasures, including EMCON, the use of decoys, and increased mobility and dispersion of equipment, which gradually limited the direct effectiveness of the TB2. Nevertheless, these UAVs continued to contribute significantly to ISR and coordination functions [31, 33]. TB2s were also employed in psychological operations, for instance through the publication of successful strike footage on social media and numerous billboards in the capital, Baku [26]

During the conflict, Azerbaijan also employed other multi-role UAVs of the same category, specifically the Heron 1 and armed variants of the Hermes 450 and 900 [28, 30]. According to available sources, there is no evidence that the Armenian armed forces deployed any MALE UAVs or UCAVs during the conflict; however, they did operate several types of small domestic tactical UAVs, namely the Krunk and X-55 (Kh-55), a counterpart to the Russian Ptero UAV [28]. None of these Armenian UAVs possessed weapon integration capabilities and were therefore primarily intended for ISR missions. In later operations, Armenian forces also deployed Russian Orlan-10 UAVs, again mainly for reconnaissance purposes. The extent to which, if at all, Armenian UAVs were operated in coordination to support artillery fire remains unknown [26]. Azerbaijan additionally employed small UAVs, specifically imported Israeli platforms such as the Orbiter 3, IAI Searcher, and Aerostar, tasked with ISTAR missions, enabling effective detection of Armenian positions and indirect fire targeting even in mountainous and forested terrain [29].

LMs were also employed by both sides during the Nagorno-Karabakh conflict, particularly affecting the initial phase of the fighting, where IAI Harop munitions were effectively combined with TB2 UAVs to target Armenian air defence systems. LMs were also used in later stages during extensive mountain operations, with the Turkish-made STM KARGU proving particularly effective [30]. In addition to the aforementioned systems, Azerbaijani forces deployed the Israeli LM Aeronautics Orbiter 1 K and Elbit Skystriker. Armenian forces also employed LMs, specifically the domestic HREESH system [26].

2.3 Analysis of UAV Utilization in the Ukraine Conflict

By the outbreak of Russian aggression against Ukraine in 2022, unmanned aerial systems became one of the key elements of the modern battlefield. While the Russian Federation entered the conflict with significantly more limited UAVs capabilities, Ukraine had been systematically developing its own UAV capabilities in terms of design and production since 2014, following the first invasion of Crimea. This process has been further strengthened by extensive deliveries of foreign UAVs during the war, substantially enhancing Ukraine's position [34]. The conflict involves the use of both military and commercial UAVs. The types of UAVs deployed have continuously evolved throughout the conflict, resulting in a wide variety of systems in operation [12].

On the Russian side, UAVs, including the ENIKS E95M, were deployed as aerial targets to simulate airborne decoys for air defence systems [35]. At the same time, multi-role MALE systems, such as the Orion UAV, were introduced. However, their operational employment was limited due to insufficient production capacities, which were affected by international sanctions [34]. In addition to the Orion, Russian forces also employed domestically produced multi-role aircraft such as the Luch Korsar, the Iranian Mohajer-6, and the Russian Forpost-R [12, 36].

On the Ukrainian side, multi-role TB2 UAVs were extensively employed. These UAVs played a key role, particularly during the first weeks of the conflict, conducting several dozens of successful strikes. It is important to note, however, that significant losses of these aircraft occurred later due to the full activation of Russian air defence and electronic warfare systems. The combination of high attrition rates, limited availability, and the high cost of these platforms resulted in TB2s being deployed primarily in lower-risk operational environments [35].

In contrast to the multi-role UAVs employed during the initial phase of the conflict, smaller UAVs were continuously deployed by ground forces on both sides. Russian armed forces primarily utilized domestically produced systems, such as the ZALA 421, Eleron-3, Orlan-10, and Orlan-30, and to a limited extent, modified commercial drones [36, 37]. Ukraine deployed a combination of foreign systems, including the ScanEagle, RQ-20B Puma 3 AE/LE, and Raven RQ-11, as well as indigenous designs such as the A1-CM Furia, PD-1, and Leleka-100, alongside modified commercial UAVs [38, 39].

Since 2022, the importance of LMs has increased significantly. Russian forces most frequently employed systems such as the ZALA KUB-BLA (KYB-UAV), ZALA Lancet-3, and Iranian Shahed-136 (Geran-2). While the KYB-UAV demonstrated low reliability and accuracy, the Lancet-3 gradually established itself as an effective tool for striking selected targets [40]. The Lancet was typically used in combination with reconnaissance platforms such as the SuperCam S350, enabling the creation of a loitering kill chain, i.e., the integration of ISR and immediate strike capability [39]. The Ukrainian armed forces, supported by international partners, have access to LMs including the Switchblade 300, Switchblade 600, Phoenix Ghost, and the Polish LM Warmate [12, 41], while also deploying domestically produced LMs, specifically kamikaze UCAVs such as the Bober, Morok, RMA II, and ST-35 Silent Thunder, among others [42]. On both sides, the use of improvised FPV kamikaze drones has also expanded; due to their low cost and accessibility, they provide a cost-effective alternative to traditional LMs [37].

The most significant transformation was the aforementioned proliferation of FPV drones. Originally an improvised solution, these UAVs gradually evolved into a central tool of combat operations. In 2022, smaller fixed-wing drones (e.g., Raven, Puma, ScanEagle) still dominated [42] primarily serving reconnaissance and fire-correction roles, while strike operations remained largely improvised. Over time, however, the adaptability of inexpensive FPV platforms became increasingly prominent, allowing them to operate effectively even in environments with strong C-UAS and electronic warfare measures [43].

A decisive change occurred in 2023, when the Ukrainian Ministry of Defence approved twenty standardized models of multirotor FPV drones, thereby establishing a production and logistical framework for their widespread deployment. These systems began performing tasks in ISR, fire guidance, battle damage assessment, electronic warfare, and direct strike operations [43, 44].

The following year, 2024, proved to be a turning point in terms of the scale and complexity of UAVs deployment. FPV drones evolved from improvised tools into mass-produced consumables. Both sides implemented new tactics, including the carousel (repeatedly deploying FPVs against the same target), swarming attacks, and drone-on-drone missions, in which FPVs neutralized enemy reconnaissance assets [45]. In parallel, the Ukrainian arsenal incorporated FO-FPV (fiber-optic) technology, enabling man-in-the-loop control of drones in environments with strong electronic interference. This system supported coordinated multi-wave attacks [46].

2.4 Evaluation of UAV Employment and Implications

An analysis of UAV deployment in conflicts such as Ukraine, Nagorno-Karabakh, and the Gaza Strip indicates that the effectiveness of UAVs is strongly determined by the adversary's capabilities in air defence and electronic warfare. In environments with advanced air defence systems and active electronic countermeasures, the extensive use of MALE or HALE UAVs becomes risky and often ineffective. In such contexts, the employment of small and mini-UAS, complemented by LMs, has proven effective. Their low cost and operational flexibility enable rapid strikes, overcome enemy defensive systems, and support tactical operations.

In asymmetric conflicts, where the adversary lacks permanently established air defence systems or electronic warfare capabilities, larger platforms such as MALE/HALE UAVs can be employed for reconnaissance, target acquisition, and stand-off operations. Even in such contexts, however, a layered operational concept proves effective, whereby large platforms provide strategic situational awareness and coordination, while smaller drones and LMs carry out the primary strike role and enable rapid kill-chain operations. This approach maximizes the efficiency of reconnaissance, targeting, and integration with ground forces or artillery, thereby reducing the time from target detection to engagement (sensor-to-shooter).

Overall, available evidence indicates that small UAVs and LMs constitute a critical component of the modern battlefield. Their effectiveness is best realized within a layered and networked deployment, enabling adaptive and efficient operations across diverse operational environments.

3 Methods

The objective of this study is to analyse the deployment of UAVs in selected contemporary armed conflicts and to examine how these deployments are reflected in publicly available acquisition decisions made by the armed forces of selected Central European states between 2015 and 2025.

The primary focus is to assess how experiences from selected contemporary armed conflicts have influenced UAVs acquisition strategies in Central European militaries. To guide this analysis, the study addresses the following research questions:

- What are the key characteristics and deployment patterns of UAVs in the selected conflicts, specifically in Ukraine, Nagorno-Karabakh, and the Gaza Strip?
- Which acquisition decisions (including system types, quantities, and suppliers) were made by selected Central European states after September 2020, and how do these decisions differ from prior plans?
- What are the main similarities and differences in how individual Central European states have responded to lessons learned from the selected conflicts?

The analysis was conducted using a structured comparative approach. As a first step, operational lessons from recent conflicts – most notably the wars in Ukraine, Nagorno-Karabakh, and the Gaza Strip – were examined to define key capability areas relevant for UAV employment (ISR, precision strike, layered force integration). These findings served as the analytical framework for the subsequent national case studies.

The time window of the analysis was set from 2015 to 2025 to capture a sufficiently long period both before and after the outbreak of the war in Ukraine. This allows for the identification of structural trends as well as conflict-driven accelerations in UAV procurement.

The sample includes six Central European states – Germany, Austria, Slovakia, Hungary, the Czech Republic, and Poland – selected based on geographic proximity, broadly comparable security environments, and, for five of them, membership in NATO and the EU. Austria, although neutral, was included due to its shared regional context and exposure to similar security dynamics. Importantly, all six countries are located in the immediate or near vicinity of Ukraine, ensuring that the war has had strong impact on their defence planning.

The research process consisted of several steps. First, data on UAV procurement within the selected time frame were collected from official defence documents, acquisition announcements, parliamentary records, and verified secondary sources. Second, the structure of the dataset was designed to define the main variables to be traced. Third, a codebook was developed to ensure consistency in coding across countries, specifying rules for classification, coding procedures, and the treatment of incomplete or ambiguous entries. All data were then coded accordingly and stored in tabular form.

The initial aim was to include a wide range of variables, such as contractual details (e.g., contract values, suppliers, delivery schedules, quantities) and acquisition contexts (e.g., political debates, industrial involvement, operational allocation). However, the availability of such information proved highly uneven across countries, resulting in gaps in the dataset. Consequently, the final dataset was streamlined to include consistently traceable variables, while retaining qualitative notes to preserve contextual depth.

To complement the quantitative dataset and partially compensate for missing detail, qualitative content analysis of the collected sources was also applied. This approach provided context for each national case study and enabled a more robust comparative synthesis. All coded data were used in the analysis, with variables suitable for chronological comparison visualized as timelines to illustrate procurement dynamics, continuities, and turning points. Each national trajectory was first analysed individually, and the results were subsequently synthesized into a cross-country comparison.

This integration of conflict analysis, structured dataset design, codebook-supported coding, qualitative content analysis, and timeline visualization forms the empirical foundation for the comparative outcomes presented in this paper.

4 National Case Studies: UAV Development in Central Europe

4.1 Germany

While the Bundeswehr's tradition of having drones in its arsenal can be traced several decades back, Germany is rarely labeled as an "inventor" when it comes to discussions about attacking unmanned aerial vehicles. Although, the country has deployed Heron 1 MALE UAVs and other smaller systems since 2010 in Afghanistan and since 2016 in Mali as part of its Air force missions [51] it is important to note that these drones do not possess weapon-carrying capabilities [52].

Multiple defense ministers tried to advance the issue of procuring more capable UAVs in recent years, consistently sparking public debate over whether in the country whether Bundeswehr should modernize its drone fleet or not. The issue of the debate was less about acquiring the drones themselves and more about the intention to arm them. After intense discussions, the German Parliament approved the acquisition of modern non-weaponized in 2018, supported by the then government coalition [53]. However, the procurement was limited to just five units of the Israeli made Heron TP MALE UAV [54]. It was declared that at least some of Heron TPs were initially leased by Germany and, as of 2024, were remained stationed in Israel [55].

This reflects a broader among Western powers when it comes to purchasing modern military hardware – often acquired in very limited quantities. It could be assumed that footages of drone deployments in various conflict zones around the world has made the topic less appealing to Germany's traditionally war-sensitive public [52]. In addition, the Bundeswehr Conception from 2018 (an umbrella document issued by the German Ministry of Defense aimed on providing long term development plans for the German armed forces) mentions UAVs only briefly, stating an intent to use them as a supporting element [56]. On the other hand, the Germany serves as the coordinator of the PESCO project aimed at developing a MALE remotely piloted aircraft system.

Unfortunately, the 2018 version of the Bundeswehr Conception remains the most recent publication to date, making it impossible to deduce any potential shifts in German operational thinking through the comparison with newer documents of the same type. The most up-to-date German defense document – Defence Policy Guidelines from 2023, operates at strategic level and provides only general guidance regarding importance of robotics and autonomy [57].

In 2022, the paradigm shifted when Germany decided to procure armaments for its drones, specifically 140 Israeli-made missiles. The procurement was officially authorized by Parliament in 2022 [52], signaling a clear intent to use unmanned autonomous vehicles in potential combat operations. The following year, another contract was awarded – this time to domestic producer Rheinmetall for 13 LUNA NG tactical UAVs [58]. Again, this was a small-scale purchase, but the Bundeswehr focused on acquiring a smaller type of drones.

However, this acquisition should not be interpreted as a broader trend toward smaller UAVs in the German armed forces in the context of war in Ukraine as it was intended at least few years before finalizing the deal and new assets should replace older German KZO drones [59].

On the other hand, there is no doubt that Germany analyzes contemporary conflicts and reaches similar conclusions as many other member states. Members of the Bundeswehr have expressed their views on the tactical and operational advantages of using UAVs on the battlefield, as well as the associated risks – such as the vulnerability of forces to rapid ISR and the detection capabilities of enemy drones [60].

The final and most significant development on the German side came in April 2025, when two contracts for LMs were awarded. Germany described this as "the highest priority for both the Ministry of Defense and the Armed forces." The systems - Helsing HX-2 and Stark Virtus – are designed with an estimated range of up to 100 km and a payload till 5 kg.

In this case, we are talking about moderate LMs assets, not suitable for long-range strategic strikes, but also not man-handled compact weapons to support small tactical units in the way mortars do.

The final decision followed a long and widespread public debate in Germany about whether the country should procure such assets. Germany is now ordering a "large number" of these systems to begin testing as soon as possible, in order to determine whether to procure more for its units or shift focus toward alternative solutions. The General Inspector of the Bundeswehr, General Breuer, described LMs as a "game changer in modern warfare." [61]. Thus, this capability is undoubtedly considered crucial by the German Armed Forces for both current and future conflicts.

As outlined above and illustrated in Fig. 1, Germany's UAV/UAS trajectory reflects a post-2022 shift from an ISR-first approach to a consolidated, multi-layered ecosystem combining reconnaissance and strike capabilities across MALE, tactical, and loitering systems.

From a terminological point of view, it is interesting that the German military does not consider LMs to be drones, but rather views them as a specific type of ammunition

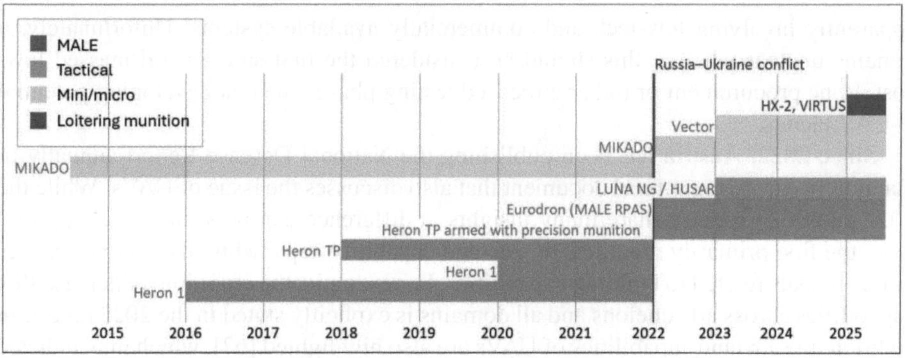

Fig. 1. Germany's UAV/UAS procurement trajectory, 2015–2025

[62]. Geiger argues that this distinction is tied to legal and ethical considerations, and that if such systems were classified as drones, their procurement would be significantly more difficult and complex [63].

This is in line with the Federal Republic of Germany's stance in international forums, such as the Report of the Secretary-General of United Nations on the Lethal autonomous weapons systems. In expressing its views, Germany considers LAWS "incompatible with international law" [64], although the understanding of which systems fall under the "label LAWS" typically varies from state to state.

To summarize, the authors observe a significant shift in Germany's attitude toward UAVs in recent years and view its ambition to equip the German Armed Forces with various types of modern drones and LMs as part of a broader trend.

4.2 Austria

Despite its politics of neutrality, defense spending reaching only 1% of GDP, and being the only state analyzed in this paper that is not a NATO member, it is worth noting that Austria is also the only one among the analyzed states with active conscription [65]. Additionally, Austria's absolute defense budget is higher than that of Slovakia and is approximately on par with Hungary's investment.

As discussed above, UAVs are a relatively cost-effective way to enhance military capability, so it is theoretically possible that Austria could afford to procure such systems.

On the other hand, there is very little to say about UAVs in Austria before 2013. The army had few conceptual ideas and was testing potential armaments, but the first significant contract was awarded that year for six Tracker UAV systems. These assets could be classified as "mini" according to NATO drone classification, meaning they are characterized by very limited payload and a range of approximately 25 km.

The intent – besides establishing a drone training component – was to distribute the assets among reconnaissance and artillery units to provide support and intelligence [66]. This mirrors a common pattern among many armed forces and could be considered a typical (and least transformative in terms of impact) first step toward integration of UAVs into military. In 2015, a small procurement was also made for testing purposes, apparently involving low-tech and commercially available systems. Unfortunately, it remains unclear whether this should be considered the first step toward massed low-cost drone procurement or rather a focused testing phase aimed at developing potential C-UAV tactics.

Since 2022, Austria has been publishing the National Defense Report annually or biannually – a strategic-level document that also discusses the issue of UAVs. While the 2022 and 2023 reports share many insights, a difference can be seen in their general tone: the first primarily identifies threats and capability gaps, while the second focuses more on goals related to building capabilities. For example, the ambition to increase ISR capabilities across all echelons and all domains is explicitly stated in the 2023 report. In addition, the air-land capabilities of UAVs are also highlighted [67], which may indicate an intent to broaden their utilization by the Armed Forces.

At the same time, the Bundesheer announced its intent to procure a larger number of small UAVs, and the contract with Elbit Systems for 315 units of the Magni-X quadcopter was officially concluded in July 2025 [68]. Training of operators began even earlier, with some reaching FOC as early as January 2025. With this acquisition, the Austrian Armed Forces remain at the lower end in terms of UAV size and long-range capabilities, but there has been a rapid increase in quantity – particularly in the field of reconnaissance at the company and platoon levels.

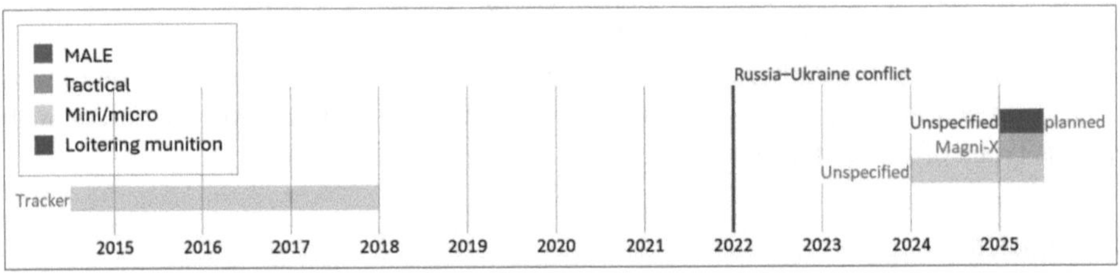

Fig. 2. Austria's UAV/UAS procurement trajectory, 2015–2025

At the same time, Bundesheer declared its interest in LMs and took specific steps in this direction – including participating in a demonstration of LMs in Slovenia as well as "working on the introduction of such systems" [70]. While no further information has been provided so far, this marks another significant step in the development of Austria's UAV capabilities, now extending into the direct strike and kinetic domain. Because National Defense Reports were not published prior to the start of the war in Ukraine, a comparison at this level cannot be made.

As mentioned above and illustrated in Fig. 2, Austria's UAV/UAS development transitioned from limited early activity to a rapid post-2022 expansion in scale and capability—driven by new procurements and likely influenced by the war in Ukraine.

To summarize, the authors are convinced that these substantial procurements are closely linked to the current operational environment.

4.3 Slovakia

The Slovak Armed Forces are the smallest among the six militaries analyzed, yet they share border with Ukraine, which makes the war resonate strongly within the country. Regarding the introduction of UAVs into service, Slovakia could be considered cautious. According to available reports, the Slovak Armed Forces acquired only a few small drone systems in the micro/mini categories before 2015. A notable purchase was the Israeli Skylark I-LE, with an extended range of 40 km, which replaced older systems [71]. Although the exact number of these systems was not reveled, it is understood that they are designated for special forces, and thus their impact on conventional military operations would likely be limited. Some secondary sources suggest the possible presence of the RQ-11 Raven in the Slovak Armed Forces; however, without official confirmation or procurement records this remains unverified.

In 2018, Slovakia attempted to procure fixed-wing UAVs – likely larger and more capable tactical assets – but the process was halted, and the public tender was canceled without a contract being concluded [72]. Regarding developments since 2022, the Slovak cabinet approved the Long-Term Defense Development Plan with Outlook to 2035, drafted by the Ministry of Defense shortly after the outbreak of the war in Ukraine [73]. The plan includes the acquisition project titled "Unmanned aerial systems" which is scheduled to run from 2024 until at least 2035 [74].

In 2022, media also reported ongoing discussions about the need to procure combat drones, with the Bayraktar TB2 system specifically considered, alongside negotiations with several potential producers. However, systematic analysis of available evidence has not revealed any indications that these discussions resulted in contractual follow-up or concrete procurement steps.

In public discourse, UAVs have primarily been discussed in the context of threats, with an increased emphasis in recent years on the need for more capable and layered air defense. On the other hand, the idea of further UAV procurement is frequently mentioned by army and ministry officials [75], including in the context of small FPV drones [76]. By September 2025, however, a systematic review of available data has not revealed any evidence of awarded contracts.

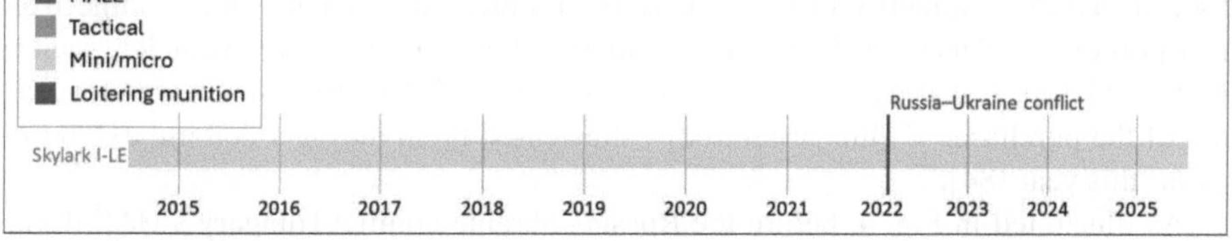

Fig. 3. Slovakia's UAV/UAS procurement trajectory, 2015–2025

As illustrated in Fig. 3, Slovakia's UAV procurement trajectory is characterized by long-term stagnation with only minimal capability development and an absence of diversification across categories. The graph highlights the dominance of a single small-scale system over the entire observed period and the lack of new acquisitions even after 2022, when other analyzed countries accelerated their efforts.

It can be concluded that Slovakia remains the least active actor among those observed. However, there is a clear understanding of the importance of unmanned systems in contemporary conflicts, and it is highly likely that the Slovak Armed Forces will acquire drones in the near to mid-term future.

4.4 Hungary

The development of UAVs in the Hungarian Armed Forces appears similar to that of other Central European countries. Prior to 2022, Hungary primarily acquired mini/micro drones of Israeli origin for its reconnaissance units, such as the Skylark I-E manufactured by Elbit.

In 2017, the country launched a large-scale, long-term modernization program for its Armed Forces (Zrínyi 2026). While the exact contents of the program were not published, UAVs are generally not considered a central focus of Hungary's efforts. Nevertheless, the program acknowledges their utility and value in supporting commanders with valid, real-time decision-making [77].

In 2018, a UAV reconnaissance squadron was established within the 24th Regiment and equipped with more modern mini Skylark I-LEX ISR drones, enhancing Hungary's capabilities in this domain [78]. These capabilities were later further strengthened with the addition of the Skylark 3, also a mini UAV, specifically designed for ISTAR missions [79, 80].

Parallel to these developments, Hungary has fostered a domestic UAV industry, with companies such as ProTAR [81]. Public statements in 2022 indicated interest in Turkish MALE UAVs (Bayraktar TB2, Karayel) [82], likely influenced by their strong performance in the early months of the war in Ukraine. However, no contract has been confirmed to date.

Hungary has also made significant progress in developing LM capability – doing so earlier than most of the countries analyzed here. Shortly after the outbreak of the war in Ukraine, Hungary reached a deal with Rheinmetall and UVision in 2023, aiming for full delivery of Hero LMs by the end of 2025 [83]. While the official sources didn't disclose the exact quantity or types of LMs procured, the systems likely range from man-portable models to tactical variants capable of engaging armored vehicles, such as the HERO 120. It can be confirmed that short-range HERO 30 systems were at least part of the purchase, as Hungarian troops showcased them during a defense exhibition earlier this year [84].

As illustrated in Fig. 4, before the Russia–Ukraine conflict Hungary's UAS development concentrated primarily on ISR capabilities at the mini/micro and tactical levels. In the initial phase the portfolio was dominated by Skylark I-LE, followed by Skylark I-LEX, and over time Skylark 3 emerged as the backbone of tactical reconnaissance due to its extended range and endurance. The acquisition path was incremental—broadening sensor suites and operational maturity—without a deliberate move into MALE or offensive classes. After the 2022 inflection point the Skylark 3 and the mini/micro fleet

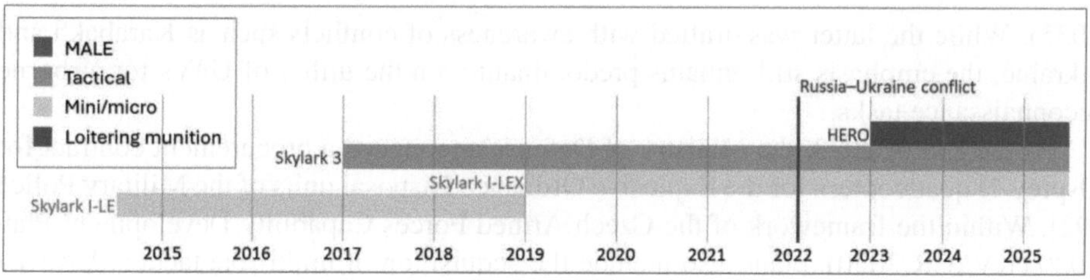

Fig. 4. Hungary's UAV/UAS procurement trajectory, 2015–2025

remained central, but from 2023 the portfolio exhibits a qualitative change: the introduction of HERO-series LMs supplements the primarily reconnaissance profile with precision kinetic effects at tactical depth. Overall, Hungary's posture therefore appears to be shifting from an ISR-first model toward an ISR–strike orientation focused on rapid operationalization of strike capability, while MALE systems remain outside the scope of the analyzed period.

Finally, it can be concluded that the synergy between LMs and ground forces is well understood by Hungarian authorities, as there is intent to arm the new Lynx IFVs with these weapons [85]. This reflects a broader trend currently pursued by some of the most advanced militaries, such as the U.S. Marine Corps [86].

4.5 Czech Republic

The moderately sized Czech Armed Forces have a long tradition of employing UAVs, including domestic systems such as the Sojka. In the 2000s, modern mini UAVs were introduced into the inventory, most notably the RQ-11B Raven from AeroVironment (operated by the 102nd Reconnaissance Battalion), the Skylark I-LE from Elbit Systems, and the miniature Black Hornet 3 used by the 601st Special Forces Battalion [87]. As in other countries in the region, special forces and ISR-designated units were among the first to integrate UAVs into their arsenals.

In 2015, capabilities were expanded with the ScanEagle (a small system with payload capacity up to 25 kg, operationally deployed in Afghanistan), complemented by additional micro and mini platforms, including the RQ-12A Wasp AE, later the Puma 3 LE, and the domestically developed quadcopter Vážka A, which was also designed for tasks such as fire monitoring [88, 89]. Although the Czech industry retains the ability to develop domestic drones, the Ministry of Defense has generally preferred to procure proven Western or Israeli systems, reflecting broader patterns across the analyzed countries.

Most of these UAVs (with the exception of Skylark I-LE, Black Hornet 3, and RQ-12A Wasp) are operated by the 533rd Reconnaissance Battalion, established in 2020 by expanding the former UAV company. Full operational capability of this battalion is expected by 2025 [90, 91]. This reflects an initial principle of concentrating UAV assets. However, the ongoing war in Ukraine has underscored the need to distribute such systems more widely, a lesson the Czech Armed Forces have begun to absorb.

UAVs are briefly referenced in both recent Czech Armed Forces Development Concepts (the 2019 version with outlook to 2030 and the 2024 version with outlook to

2035). While the latter was drafted with awareness of conflicts such as Karabakh and Ukraine, the emphasis still remains predominantly on the utility of UAVs for airborne reconnaissance tasks.

At the end of 2023, the Ministry of Defense announced a procurement contract for Osprey-H quadcopters for the Explosive Ordnance Disposal units of the Military Police [92]. Within the framework of the Czech Armed Forces Capability Development Plan 2030 (KVAČR 2030), plans also include the acquisition of multi-role tactical UAS III [93]. Negotiations with the Israeli company IAI for Heron 1 were postponed in May 2023 [94–96]. In parallel, an initiative was launched to procure 200 small UAVs (ranging from quadcopters to platforms with an MTOW of approximately 20 kg and longer endurance), intended primarily for the 4th Rapid Deployment Brigade, the 7th Mechanized Brigade, and the 43rd Airborne Regiment [96]. This indicates a re-prioritization of acquisitions in 2023: the originally considered three MALE systems were postponed in favor of smaller UAVs, with the declared intent of rapidly equipping tactical units while maintaining continuity with the existing portfolio (Wasp, Raven, Puma, Vážka A).

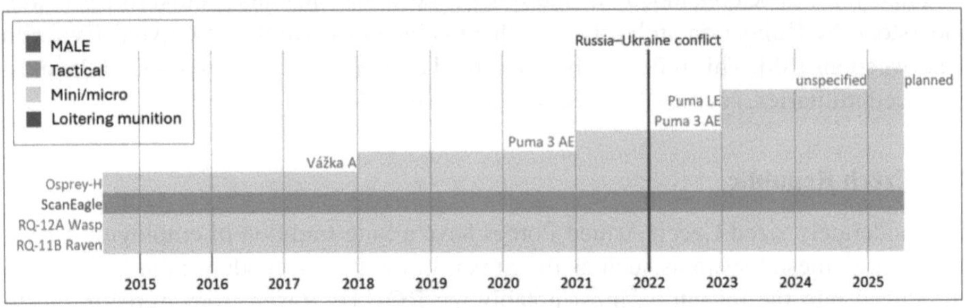

Fig. 5. Czech Republic's UAV/UAS procurement trajectory, 2015–2025

As illustrated in Fig. 5, the Czech Republic's UAV/UAS procurement trajectory reveals continuity in small (mini/micro) and tactical ISR capabilities throughout the observed period. Long-standing systems include the RQ-11B Raven, RQ-12A Wasp, and the ScanEagle, complemented by Osprey-H. A modernization wave is identifiable in 2021 with the Puma 3 AE and in 2023 with the Puma LE. The timeline highlights a turning point in 2022, followed by accelerated acquisition activity and diversification of tactical and mini/micro assets. Notably, the contracting record confirms that no transition toward MALE or loitering munition occurred during the observed period. However, the Czech Ministry of Defense has announced negotiations for LMs - a capability that, based on the statements from senior commanders, could realistically be integrated into maneuver units to enhance their firepower [97].

It can be concluded, the Czech Armed Forces are adapting their UAV strategy by prioritizing smaller, tactical systems over large MALE platforms, aiming for rapid deployment across frontline units while maintaining continuity with their existing drone portfolio.

4.6 Poland

With its geopolitical position, strong will to resist foreign aggression, and a military budget targeting 4.5% GDP - focused on both quantity and quality - Poland stands out as the most advanced among the countries analyzed in terms of progress over the past decade and current UAV capabilities.

Over the last ten years, the Polish military has achieved contracts for a wide range of UAVs, including the mini Wizjer, tactical Orlik and the Warmate loitering munition. Unlike other countries analyzed, Poland's acceleration in UAV procurement began not after 2022, but in response to the 2014 Russian occupation of Crimea, reflecting a distinct perception of national security. For example, Poland contracted 24 Turkish Bayraktar TB2 UAVs in 2021, prior to Russia's full-scale invasion [98].

In recent years, Poland has increasingly focused on developing and acquiring domestic systems, such as the Warmate loitering munition (approximately 5 kg payload, comparable to the Russian Lancet), with a framework agreement signed by Polish Armament Agency to procure 10 000 units [99].

As illustrated in Fig. 6, Poland's UAV/UAS procurement trajectory demonstrates a bottom-up build-up of capabilities before 2022, followed by a rapid transition toward a layered ISR–strike ecosystem. Pre-2022 period, the tactical ORLIK/PGZ-19R programme formed the backbone, while Poland was also among the first regional militaries to integrate loitering munition (the Warmate). The 2021 contract for Bayraktar TB2 marked an early entry into the MALE category. After 2022, the portfolio expanded both qualitatively and quantitatively: major contracts were concluded for GLADIUS (May 2022) and its successor GLADIUS-2 (September 2022), MQ-9A Reaper was leased and MQ-9B SkyGuardian ordered in 2024, while large-scale procurement of FlyEye (~400 sets, with follow-on contracts in 2024–2025) and NeoX-2 (Wizjer) further strengthened organic reconnaissance assets. The trajectory culminates with a framework agreement for nearly 10,000 Warmate units in 2025.

Taken together, the timeline visualised in the graph illustrates Poland's shift from an ISR-first model with early LM integration to a fully multi-layered ecosystem across mini/micro, tactical, and MALE tiers, in which reconnaissance, targeting, and precision strike are integrated across command levels.

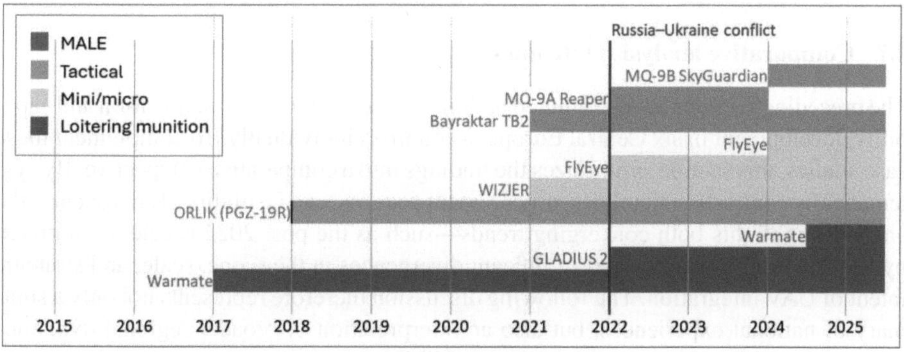

Fig. 6. Poland's UAV/UAS procurement trajectory, 2015–2025

The scale of Poland's current UAV purchases and plans is massive, far surpassing the ambition of other countries analyzed. While the types of assets being procured have not changed dramatically, the shift since 2022 is evident at the organizational level and in overall scale. The Polish military has taken lessons from the war in Ukraine seriously, with senior leadership stating that "every soldier" needs to have contact with drones across all physical domains [100]. According to the Polish Ministry of National Defense, the aim is to have hundreds of thousands of UAVs at the army's disposal within a few years [101]. The pace and scope of these developments are described by the Ministry itself as a "drone revolution," emphasizing that the character of war in Ukraine is an absolute game-changer for technological innovation and modern warfare [102].

This strong focus on drones reflects both the global trend of rising UAV importance and Poland's asymmetric strategy to counterbalance Russia's numerical superiority. In 2025, Poland established the Inspectorate for Unmanned Aerial Systems Forces within the structure of the General Command, signaling an effort to create a dedicated branch for UAV operations within current polish defense system [103]. This highlights the strategic value the Polish military places on unmanned systems. Many Polish UAVs, including the FlyEye and Warmate, have been delivered to Ukraine and are actively operated there. This provides Poland with valuable performance feedback for further development.

The "drone revolution" in Poland extends beyond the armed forces to industry and legislation. Poland's rearmament and capability-building efforts are increasingly seen as a whole-of-government and societal endeavor [102]. One example is the "Drone Space Valley" initiative - a cluster-like cooperation among Polish companies aimed at accelerating UAS research and services – which has gained public attention for its scale and ambition [104, 105]. Additionally, the Special Defense Investment Act, which came into force in September 2025, represents a legal and bureaucratic effort to streamline armament procedures. Under this act, drones now benefit from a simplified regulatory framework, enabling faster and more flexible acquisition [106].

To summarize, the authors are convinced that Poland has emerged as a regional leader in UAV development, transitioning from early ISR-focused systems to a comprehensive, multi-layered drone ecosystem. Since 2014, and especially after 2022, it has rapidly expanded procurement across mini, tactical, loitering munition, and MALE categories—emphasizing domestic production (e.g. Warmate, FlyEye) and integrating UAVs across all military levels.

4.7 Comparative analysis Outcomes

The preceding sections have examined national trajectories of UAV acquisition and capability development in six Central European countries individually. To complement these case studies, this section synthesizes the findings into a comparative perspective. By systematically contrasting timelines, procurement patterns, and institutional approaches, the analysis highlights both converging trends—such as the post-2022 acceleration driven by lessons from Ukraine—and significant divergences in the scope, scale, and strategic intent of UAV integration. The following discussion therefore represents not only a summary of national experiences, but also an interpretation of broader regional dynamics shaping the future of unmanned aerial capabilities.

When comparing the six Central European countries analysed—Germany, Austria, Slovakia, Hungary, the Czech Republic, and Poland—significant differences emerge in both the pace and direction of UAV acquisition and development. While all of them were influenced by lessons learned from contemporary conflicts such as Nagorno-Karabakh and Ukraine, the degree of responsiveness, strategic prioritization, and institutionalization varies substantially.

Germany represents a case of gradual adaptation shaped by strong political and ethical sensitivities. Despite early deployments of the Heron 1 in Afghanistan and Mali, acquisitions remained limited in quantity and constrained by domestic debates over armed drones. Only in 2022 did Berlin authorize the arming of UAVs, marking a paradigm shift toward integrating precision-strike capabilities. Subsequent contracts for LUNA NG and LMs further underline a cautious but layered ISR–strike trajectory. However, Germany's approach continues to be influenced by normative and ethical considerations, which slow procurement compared to regional peers.

Austria demonstrates a late but accelerating trajectory in UAV development. Prior to 2013, UAV presence was negligible, with the Tracker system representing a modest initial step. Real momentum emerged only after 2022, following the publication of National Defence Reports and subsequent acquisitions, most notably the large 2025 contract for 315 Magni-X quadcopters. Although Austria's UAV portfolio remains concentrated in the mini/micro segment, its declared interest in LMs signals an intention to expand capabilities into the kinetic domain. Historically, Austria's neutrality and modest defence budgets delayed UAV integration, but the war in Ukraine has clearly acted as a catalyst.

Slovakia, in contrast, stands out as the least active actor. Apart from limited acquisitions of Skylark I-LE and possibly small numbers of Ravens, capability development has stagnated. Efforts to procure more advanced UAVs failed in 2018, and although strategic documents published after 2022 mention UAV-related projects, no concrete contracts had materialized by 2025. Discussions about acquiring combat drones such as Bayraktar TB2 remained inconclusive. The Slovak case thus illustrates a persistent gap between strategic recognition of UAV importance and the absence of tangible outcomes, highlighting institutional and budgetary constraints.

Hungary has followed an incremental, ISR-first pathway, relying heavily on Israeli Skylark systems. Gradual modernization has produced a layered reconnaissance portfolio, culminating in the Skylark 3 as the tactical backbone. After 2022, Hungary became one of the earliest adopters of LMs, contracting Hero systems from Rheinmetall/UVision in 2023. This marked a qualitative shift from pure ISR to ISR–strike, although MALE platforms remain absent. Hungary's approach is characterized by combination of foreign acquisitions and a nascent domestic industry, aiming to build both operational capability and industrial know-how.

The Czech Republic's UAV trajectory reflects continuity and pragmatism. UAVs have been present for decades, with systems like Ravens, Wasp, and ScanEagle forming a long-standing reconnaissance layer. Modernization has been gradual, with Puma systems added after 2021. A turning point came in 2023, when plans for MALE acquisitions were postponed in favour of a large-scale procurement of 200 small UAVs for tactical units. This decision highlights the intent to rapidly equip brigades and airborne forces with organic ISR assets, while ongoing negotiations for LMs suggest a potential expansion into strike capabilities. The Czech model demonstrates a clear prioritization of tactical flexibility over strategic platforms.

Poland stands in sharp contrast as the regional frontrunner. Unlike most neighbours, Poland's acceleration began as early as 2014, reflecting a heightened threat perception following the annexation of Crimea. By 2021, Poland had contracted Bayraktar TB2 systems, entering the MALE category head of others, while simultaneously expanding loitering munition capabilities through large Warmate contracts. After 2022, the scale of acquisitions surged, including the Gladius and Gladius-2 programs, MQ-9A Reaper leasing, MQ-9B SkyGuardian procurement, and extensive orders for FlyEye and NeoX-2. By 2025, Poland envisions a "drone revolution," institutionalizing UAVs across command levels and aiming to deploy hundreds of thousands of units. Its trajectory is unique in both scale and institutional integration, exemplified by the creation of a dedicated Inspectorate for UAS.

Taken together, the comparison reveals three distinct models of UAV development in Central Europe. First, the frontrunner model, represented by Poland, is marked by early adoption, large-scale procurement, and integration of both ISR and strike capabilities. Second, the incremental adapters - Germany, Hungary, and the Czech Republic - demonstrate continuity in ISR operations with gradual post-2022 expansion into LMs and armed platforms, shaped by varying political and industrial contexts. Third, the late or minimal adopters (Austria, Slovakia), show either delayed engagement (Austria) or continued stagnation (Slovakia). The divergence underscores how national threat perceptions, political culture, and budgetary priorities shape the pace a depth of UAV integration across the region.

5 Conclusion

This study set out to analyse and compare the trajectories of UAV acquisition and capability development across six Central European states—Germany, Austria, Slovakia, Hungary, the Czech Republic, and Poland—over the period 2015–2025. By combining detailed national case studies with a comparative synthesis, the analysis has provided insights into both converging patterns and marked divergences in how UAVs are integrated into national defence portfolios.

The findings demonstrate that all six states recognize the growing importance of unmanned aerial systems, yet their approaches differ significantly in timing, scale, and strategic framing. Poland stands out as the regional frontrunner, pursuing what has been labelled a "drone revolution," characterized by early adoption, large-scale procurement, and institutional embedding across all command levels. At the opposite end of the spectrum, Slovakia and Austria remain late or hesitant adopters, with Slovakia showing minimal progress in material acquisitions and Austria beginning to accelerate only after 2022. Germany, Hungary, and the Czech Republic occupy intermediate positions: they illustrate gradual adaptation, with continuity in ISR-first portfolios and incremental post-2022 expansion into armed and loitering systems.

These variations are shaped by broader context. Poland's early acceleration is closely tied to the 2014 annexation of Crimea, highlighting acute threat perceptions and the drive for asymmetric balancing against Russia. Germany's trajectory is slowed by domestic political and ethical debates about armed drones, while Austria's neutrality and budgetary constraints delayed early adoption. The Czech Republic's prioritization of tactical flexibility over MALE systems demonstrates pragmatism under resource limits, and Hungary's integration of LMs reflects both operational and industrial objectives. Despite these differences, the war in Ukraine emerges as a decisive catalyst, accelerating procurement and pushing even late adopters to reconsider their approaches.

The comparative evidence also points to a gradual convergence. Across the region, ISR platforms remain central, but a shift toward ISR–strike ecosystems is visible, with LMs emerging as a common vector of capability growth. This suggests that, although national contexts produce different speeds and scales of adoption, Central Europe as a whole is moving toward layered ISR–strike ecosystems in a gradual process significantly constrained by economic resources, institutional limitations and broader societal factors.

Disclosure of Interests. The authors declare no competing interests.

References

1. Udeanu, G., Dobrescu, A., Oltean, M.: Unmanned aerial vehicle in military operations. Sci. Res. Educ. Air Force. **18**, 199–206 (2016). https://doi.org/10.19062/2247-3173.2016.18.1.26
2. Scharre, P.: Army of None: Autonomous Weapons and the Future of War. W.W. Norton, New York (2018)
3. Joint Doctrine Note 3/10: Unmanned Aircraft Systems: Terminology, Definitions and Classification (2010)
4. Gilli, A., Gilli, M.: The diffusion of drone warfare? Industrial, organizational, and infrastructural constraints. Secur. Stud. **25**, 50–84 (2016). https://doi.org/10.1080/09636412.2016.1134189
5. Sullivan, J.M.: Revolution or evolution? The rise of the UAVs. In: Proceedings of the 2005 International Symposium on Technology and Society, pp. 95–102. IEEE Press, New York (2005). https://doi.org/10.1109/ISTAS.2005.1452718
6. Yevtodyeva, M.G.: New trends in the procurement and use of unmanned aerial vehicles. Obŝestvennye Nauki i Sovremennost′, 97–109 (2024). https://doi.org/10.31857/s0869049924030073
7. Tolstonosov, Y., Tolstonosov, D., Bondarenko, O.: Formation and development of the concept of using unmanned aerial vehicles and their innovative application in modern wars and military conflicts. State Secur. **2**, 98–105 (2024). https://doi.org/10.33405/2786-8613/2024/2/4/323394
8. Minculete, G., Păstae, V.: Essential approaches to combat the use of drones: specific elements of the armed conflict in Ukraine. Bull. "Carol I" Natl. Defence Univ. **12**, 208–224 (2024). https://doi.org/10.53477/2284-9378-23-58
9. Rogers, J.: The second drone age: defining war in the 2020s. Defense Secur. Anal. **39**, 256–259 (2023). https://doi.org/10.1080/14751798.2023.2178519
10. Plichta, M., Rossiter, A.: A one-way attack drone revolution? Affordable mass precision in modern conflict. J. Strateg. Stud. **47**, 1001–1031 (2024). https://doi.org/10.1080/01402390.2024.2385843
11. Calcara, A., Zaccagnini, I., Gilli, M., Gilli, A.: Military drones, air defence, and the hider-finder competition in air warfare. Defense Secur. Anal. **39**, 260–262 (2023). https://doi.org/10.1080/14751798.2023.2178541

12. Kunertova, D.: The war in Ukraine shows the game-changing effect of drones depends on the game. Bull. At. Sci. **79**, 95–102 (2023). https://doi.org/10.1080/00963402.2023.2178180
13. Nefodova, L., Kushch, V., Cherneha, T.: Global arms market transformation and the rise of drone warfare: strategic lessons from Ukraine's experience. Polit. Sci. Secur. Stud. J. **5**, 62–67 (2024). https://doi.org/10.33445/psssj.2024.5.3.6
14. Panait, C.: The evolution of aerial threats and their implications on Army operations. Land Forces Acad. Rev. **29**, 481–488 (2024). https://doi.org/10.2478/raft-2024-0050
15. Blom, J.D.: Unmanned Aerial Systems: A Historical Perspective. Combat Studies Institute Press, Fort Leavenworth, KS (2010)
16. Hall, A.R., Coyne, C.J.: The political economy of drones. SSRN Electron. J. (2013). https://doi.org/10.2139/ssrn.2285820
17. Merrin, W.: Digital War: A Critical Introduction. Routledge, New York (2019)
18. Frantzman, S.J.: Drone Wars: Pioneers, Killing Machines, Artificial Intelligence, and the Battle for the Future. Bombardier Books, New York (2021)
19. Katz, Y., Bohbot, A.: The Weapon Wizards: How Israel Became a High-Tech Military Superpower. St. Martin's Press, New York (2017)
20. Rýznar, B., Zezula, J., Rak, L.: Přehled bezpilotních systémů vyspělých armád. Univerzita obrany, Brno (2022)
21. Królikowski, H.: The use of unmanned aerial vehicles in contemporary armed conflicts – selected issues. Politeja. **19**, 17–34 (2022). https://doi.org/10.12797/Politeja.19.2022.79.02
22. Lambeth, B.S.: NATO's Air War for Kosovo: A Strategic and Operational Assessment. RAND, Santa Monica, CA (2001)
23. Tabrizi, A.B., Bronk, J.: Armed Drones in the Middle East: Proliferation and Norms in the Region. Royal United Services Institute for Defence and Security Studies, London (2018)
24. Horowitz, M., Schwartz, J.A., Fuhrmann, M.: Who's prone to drone? A global time-series analysis of armed uninhabited aerial vehicle proliferation. Confl. Manag. Peace Sci. **39**, 119–142 (2020). https://doi.org/10.1177/0738894220966572
25. Haugstvedt, H.: A flying reign of terror? The who, where, when, what, and how of non-state actors and armed drones. J. Hum. Secur. **19**, 1–17 (2023). https://doi.org/10.12924/johs2023.19010001
26. Shaikh, S., Rumbaugh, W.: The Air and Missile War in Nagorno-Karabakh: Lessons for the Future of Strike and Defense. CSIS, Washington, DC (2020)
27. Gady, F.-S., Stronell, A.: What the Nagorno-Karabakh Conflict Revealed About Future Warfighting. https://www.worldpoliticsreview.com/what-the-nagorno-karabakh-conflict-revealed-about-future-warfighting, last Accessed 23 Sep 2025
28. Postma, J.: Drones over Nagorno-Karabakh: a glimpse at the future of war? Atlantisch Perspectief. **45**, 15–20 (2021)
29. Andrews, P.: Lessons from the Nagorno-Karabakh 2020 Conflict. https://api.army.mil/e2/c/downloads/2023/01/31/693ac148/21-655-nagorno-karabakh-2020-conflict-catalog-aug-21-public.pdf, last Accessed 23 Sep 2025
30. Jones, S.G., Harrington, J., Reid, C.K., Strohmeyer, M.: Combined Arms Warfare and Unmanned Aircraft Systems: A New Era of Strategic Competition. CSIS, Lanham (2022)
31. Terzić, M.: Critical review of the protection of aircraft Defense forces during the conflict in Nagorno-Karabakh in 2020. Small Wars Insurgencies. **33**, 1017–1031 (2022). https://doi.org/10.1080/09592318.2021.2025286
32. Kınık, H., Çelik, S.: The role of Turkish drones in Azerbaijan's increasing military effectiveness: an assessment of the second Nagorno-Karabakh war. Insight Turkey. **23**, 169–191 (2021). https://doi.org/10.25253/99.2021234.10

33. Cherednychenko, O., Protsiuk, Y., Shemendiuk, O., Lebed, E.: Analysis of the experience of the combat use of unmanned aerial vehicles against anti-aircraft missile Systems in the Military Conflict in Nagorno-Karabakh. Commun. Informatization Cybersecurity Syst. Technol. **2** (2022). https://doi.org/10.58254/viti.2.2022.10.70
34. Sanders, G., Butchart, R., Price, A., Steinberg, D., Holderness, A.: Rising Demand and Proliferating Supply of Military UAS. CSIS, Washington, DC (2023)
35. Zabrodskyi, M., Watling, J., Danylyuk, O.V., Reynolds, N.: Preliminary Lessons in Conventional Warfighting from Russia's Invasion of Ukraine: February–July 2022. Royal United Services Institute for Defence and Security Studies, London (2022)
36. Poulsen, N.B., Staun, J.: Russia at War: Intention and Military Capability After Ukraine. Djøf Forlag, Copenhagen (2025)
37. Edmonds, J., Bendett, S.: Russia's use of Uncrewed systems in Ukraine. CNA, 1–58 (2023)
38. Roblin, S.: Drone War Accelerates Over Ukraine. Inside Unmanned Systems (2022)
39. Samus, M.: Lessons Learned from the War in Ukraine: The Impact of Drones. New Strategy Center, Bucharest (2024)
40. Janovsky, J.: Hit or Miss: The Russian Loitering Munition Kill List. https://www.oryxspioenkop.com/2022/11/hit-or-miss-russian-loitering-munition.html, last Accessed 23 Sep 2025
41. Edmonds, J., Bendett, S.: Russian Military Autonomy in Ukraine: Four Months In. CNA, pp. 1–12 (2022)
42. Sotoudehfar, S., Sarkin, J.J.: Drones on the frontline: charting the use of drones in the Russo-Ukrainian conflict and how their use may be violating international humanitarian law. Int. Comp. Law Rev. **23**, 129–169 (2023). https://doi.org/10.2478/iclr-2023-0018
43. Oleksenko, O., Misiuk, H., Ikaiev, D., Korshok, V., Palka, V.: Main trends in the use of unmanned Aircraft in the Russian-Ukrainian war. Наукові праці Державного науково-дослідного інституту випробувань і сертифікації озброєння та військової техніки. **20**, 99–105 (2024). https://doi.org/10.37701/dndivsovt.21.2024.12
44. Oleksenko, O., Huk, O., Snitsarenko, V., Ikaiev, D., Rahulin, V.: Regarding the features of the combat application of FPV drones in the war between Russia and Ukraine. Наукові праці Державного науково-дослідного інституту випробувань і сертифікації озброєння та військової техніки. **22**, 99–105 (2024). https://doi.org/10.37701/dndivsovt.22.2024.12
45. Bojor, L., Grigore, L.: Tactical network-centric warfare in practice: FPV drones and the architecture of a new RMA. In: International Conference Knowledge-Based Organization, vol. 31, pp. 30–45 (2025). https://doi.org/10.2478/kbo-2025-0004
46. Oleksenko, O., Huk, O., Snitsarenko, V., Ikaiev, D., Snitsarenko, O.: Key features of the combat use of unmanned aerial vehicles by the armed forces of the Russian Federation against Ukraine in 2024. Випробування та сертифікація, 57–63 (2025). https://doi.org/10.37701/ts.08.2025.06
47. Page, J.M.: Drones and the Hamas-led attack of 7 October 2023: innovation and implications. Perspect. Terrorism. **19**, 1–33 (2025). https://doi.org/10.19165/2025.8488
48. Borg, S.: Assembling Israeli drone warfare: loitering surveillance and operational sustainability. Secur. Dialogue. **52**, 401–417 (2020). https://doi.org/10.1177/0967010620956796
49. Özdemir, G.S.: Remote warfare: evaluating the combat effectiveness of drones in the context of the war on Gaza. In: October 7 One Year On: Strategic Analyses, pp. 1–11. Arab Center for Research and Policy Studies, Qatar (2024)
50. Selján, P.: The 7 October Hamas attack: a preliminary assessment of the Israeli intelligence, military and policy failures. Acad. Appl. Res. Mil. Public Manage. Sci. **23**, 81–98 (2024). https://doi.org/10.32565/aarms.2024.1.5
51. Airbus: Germany Extends the Contracts for the Operation of the Heron 1 Drones in Afghanistan and Mali. https://www.airbus.com/en/newsroom/press-releases/2018-12-germany-extends-the-contracts-for-the-operation-of-the-heron-1, last Accessed 25 Sep 2025

52. Wachs, L.: The Latecomer: Germany's Debate on Armed Drones. https://www.rusi.org/explore-our-research/publications/commentary/latecomer-germanys-debate-armed-drones, last Accessed 25 Sep 2025
53. The Defense Post: Germany to Get Weaponized Drones for the First Time. https://thedefensepost.com/2022/04/06/germany-weaponized-drones, last Accessed 25 Sep 2025
54. Bundesministerium der Verteidigung: Unterzeichnet: Vertrag über Nutzung der Drohne Heron TP. https://www.bmvg.de/de/themen/unterzeichnet-vertrag-nutzung-drohne-heron-tp-25572, last Accessed 25 Sep 2025
55. Knight, B.: Israel May Be Using German-Leased Heron War Drones. https://www.dw.com/en/israel-may-be-using-german-leased-heron-war-drones/a-70407675, last Accessed 25 Sep 2025
56. Bundesministerium der Verteidigung: Konzeption der Bundeswehr. Bundesministerium der Verteidigung, Berlin (2018)
57. Bundesministerium der Verteidigung: Defence Policy Guidelines 2023. Bundesministerium der Verteidigung, Berlin (2023)
58. Bundesministerium der Verteidigung: Aufklärungsdrohne: Bundestag genehmigt 13 neue LUNA-Systeme. https://www.bmvg.de/de/aktuelles/aenderungsvertrag-projektfortfuehrung-neuer-auftragnehmer-5680352, last Accessed 25 Sep 2025
59. Fiorenza, N.: Germany funds LUNA NG UAS to replace KZO. https://www.janes.com/osint-insights/defence-news/air/germany-funds-luna-ng-uas-to-replace-kzo, last Accessed 25 Sep 2025
60. Kather, T.: "Wir sehen einen permanenten Wechsel von Lernen und Anpassung", https://www.bundeswehr.de/de/meldungen/nachgefragt-taktik-lehren-krieg-ukraine-5758614?, Last Accessed 25 Sep 2025
61. Fiorenza, N.: Bundeswehr procures loitering munition, and together with Latvia and Norway, anti-tank mines, https://www.janes.com/osint-insights/defence-news/air/bundeswehr-procures-loitering-munition-and-together-with-latvia-and-norway-anti-tank-mines, Last Accessed 25 Sep 2025
62. Kather, T., Henckel, O.: Bundeswehr beschafft Loitering Munition, https://www.bundeswehr.de/de/meldungen/bundeswehr-beschafft-loitering-munition, Last Accessed 25 Sep 2025
63. Geiger, W.: Bundesregierung definiert Loitering Munition als Munition und nicht als Drohne, https://www.hartpunkt.de/bundesregierung-definiert-loitering-munition-als-munition-und-nicht-als-drohne/?utm_source=chatgpt.com, Last Accessed 25 Sep 2025
64. UN General Assembly: Lethal autonomous weapons systems. UN General Assembly (2024)
65. Oesterreich GV: Military service and civilian service, https://www.oesterreich.gv.at/en/themen/gesetze_und_recht/wehrpflicht-und-zivildienst, Last Accessed 25 Sep 2025
66. Rechnungshof Österreich: Beschaffung und Einsatz von Drohnen im Bundesheer. Rechnungshof Österreich (2020)
67. Bundesministerium für Landesverteidigung: Landesverteidigungsbericht 2023: gemäß Landesverteidigungs-Finanzierungsgesetz (LV-FinG). Bundesministerium für Landesverteidigung (2023)
68. Wall, R.: Austria Buys Elbit's Magni-X Quadcopter For Army, https://aviationweek.com/defense/sensors-electronic-warfare/austria-buys-elbits-magni-x-quadcopter-army, Last Accessed 25 Sep 2025
69. Tesch, S.: The flying binoculars of the Austrian Armed Forces, https://militaeraktuell.at/en/the-flying-binoculars-of-the-austrian-armed-forces/, Last Accessed 25 Sep 2025.
70. Militär Aktuell: Austrian Armed Forces want to procure loitering ammunition, https://militaeraktuell.at/en/austrian-armed-forces-want-to-procure-loitering-ammunition/?utm_source=chatgpt.com, Last Accessed 25 Sep 2025

71. UVision: Slovak Special Forces Deploy Skylark I-LEX, https://www.uasvision.com/2017/02/21/slovak-special-forces-deploy-skylark-i-lex/, Last Accessed 25 Sep 2025
72. UVO: Oznámenie 2173 - ZUT, https://www.uvo.gov.sk/vestnik-a-registre/vestnik/oznamenie/detail/375648?cHash=399e16520a57833e451f2fe15feebf6c, Last Accessed 25 Sep 2025
73. SKV MOD: Cabinet approves Ministry of Defence's Long-Term Defence Development Plan with Outlook to 2035, https://www.mosr.sk/51591-en/vlada-odsuhlasila-dlhodoby-plan-rozvoja-rezortu-ministerstva-obrany-s-vyhladom-do-roku-2035/?utm_source=chatgpt.com, Last Accessed 25 Sep 2025
74. Dlhodobý plán rozvoja rezortu Ministerstva obrany s výhľadom do roku 2035. (2022)
75. Dóka, O..: Ministerstvo obrany SR hovoří o dalších modernizačních projektech, https://www.czdefence.cz/clanek/ministerstvo-obrany-sr-mluvi-o-dalsich-modernizacnich-projektech, last accessed 2025/09/25
76. Poloha, N.L.: Armáda chystá dronovú divíziu, chce mať operátora v každej čate. Strojov však nemáme dosť, upozorňuje expert, https://spravy.pravda.sk/domace/clanok/742343-moderna-armada-bez-dronov-neexistuje-slovensko-zaspalo-dobu-a-musi-to-napravit-co-najskor-varuje-odbornik/, Last Accessed 25 Sep 2025
77. Balogh, O.: The Hungarian governmental defence and military development program, "Zrínyi 2026" as a response to the new threats in the region. Natl. Secur. Stud. **15**, 245–260 (2018). https://doi.org/10.37055/sbn/132160
78. Sándor, O.: Elbit Skylark I-LEX pilóta nélküli felderítő repülőgép rendszeresítése a Magyar Honvédségben. Haditechnika. **57**, 57–60 (2023). https://doi.org/10.23713/ht.57.6.12
79. Honvédelem: Végéhez ért az ötéves Skylark beszerzési projekt, a KFOR-ban is bizonyít az új típus, https://honvedelem.hu/hirek/vegehez-ert-az-oteves-skylark-beszerzesi-projekt-a-kfor-ban-is-bizonyit-az-uj-tipus.html?utm_source=openai, Last Accessed 25 Sep 2025
80. Sándor, O.: ELBIT Skylark 3 pilóta nélküli felderítő repülőgép rendszeresítése a Magyar Honvédségben. Haditechnika. **58**, 50–55 (2024). https://doi.org/10.23713/ht.58.5.10
81. Gallai, S., Gyuriss, D.: Maverick or front-runner? Army modernization in Hungary in the light of the other Visegrad countries. UNISCI J. **22**, 129–155 (2024). https://doi.org/10.31439/unisci-214
82. Woods, J.: Hungary to strengthen its army with Turkish Bayraktar drones, https://dailynewshungary.com/hungary-to-strengthen-its-army-with-turkish-bayraktar-drones/, Last Accessed 25 Sep 2025
83. Rheinmettal: Hungary awards Rheinmetall and UVision a major contract for the Hero loitering munitions – order volume in the three-digit million-euro range, https://www.rheinmetall.com/en/media/news-watch/news/2023/7/2023-07-20-hungary-awards-rheinmetall-and-uvision-a-major-contract-for-the-hero-loitering-munitions?utm_source=chatgpt.com, Last Accessed 25 Sep 2025
84. Defense News Army: Hungary Deploys HERO 30 to Enhance Tactical Precision Strike Capabilities on the Battlefield, https://armyrecognition.com/news/army-news/2025/hungary-deploys-hero-30-to-enhance-tactical-precision-strike-capabilities-on-the-battlefield, Last Accessed 25 Sep 2025
85. Fiorenza, N.: IAV 2024: Hungary arms its Lynx IFVs with Hero loitering munitions, https://www.janes.com/osint-insights/defence-news/land/iav-2024-hungary-arms-its-lynx-ifvs-with-hero-loitering-munitions?utm_source=chatgpt.com, Last Accessed 25 Sep 2025
86. Trevithick, J.: This Is Our First Look At The Marines' Loitering Munition-Armed Light Armored Vehicle, https://www.twz.com/42707/this-is-our-first-look-at-the-marines-loitering-munition-armed-light-armored-vehicle, Last Accessed 25 Sep 2025
87. Štrbík, J.: Vznik 533. praporu bezpilotních systémů. A report. 2019, pp. 10–13 (2019)

88. Starfos: MINI VTOL UAS - průzkumný bezpilotní prostředek kategorie VTOL, https://starfos.tacr.cz/projekty/OWVTUP2018006#project-main, Last Accessed 26 Sep 2025
89. Cyprisová, V.: Armáda vyšle do Hřenska drony, které budou monitorovat ohniska požáru, https://acr.mo.gov.cz/informacni-servis/zpravodajstvi/armada-vysle-do-hrenskadrony%2D%2Dktere-budou-monitorovat-ohniska-pozaru-237877/, Last Accessed 25 Sep 2025
90. Želinský, L., Herber, D.: V české armádě od ledna vznikl nový prapor bezpilotních systémů, https://acr.mo.gov.cz/informacni-servis/zpravodajstvi/v-ceske-armade-od-lednavznikl-novy-prapor-bezpilotnich-systemu-218687/, Last Accessed 25 Sep 2025
91. 533. prapor bezpilotních systémů, https://53pluk.cz/533-prapor/, Last Accessed 25 Sep 2025
92. MO ČR: Bezpilotní prostředek odstupného sledování pro potřeby pyrotechnické služby VP - nákup, https://nen.nipez.cz/en/verejne-zakazky/p:vestnik:page=15652;vz:query=bezpilotn%C3%AD%20prost%C5%99edek%20odstupn%C3%A9ho;dns:page=4/detail-zakazky/N006-23-V00035748, Last Accessed 25 Sep 2025
93. MO ČR: Koncepce výstavby armády České republiky 2035. Ministerstvo obrany České republiky - VHÚ Praha, Praha (2024)
94. Havrdová, H.: Armáda v příštích letech plánuje pořídit víceúčelové bezpilotní prostředky, https://mocr.mo.gov.cz/informacni-servis/zpravodajstvi/armada-v-pristich-letech-planuje-poridit-viceucelove-bezpilotni-prostredky-204103/, Last Accessed 25 Sep 2025
95. Táborský, J.: Ministerstvo obrany zahájí jednání s izraelskou vládou o pořízení tří bezpilotních letounů, https://mocr.mo.gov.cz/informacni-servis/zpravodajstvi/ministerstvo-obrany-zahajijednani-s-izraelskou-vladou-o-porizeni-tri-bezpilotnich-letounu-237834/, Last Accessed 25 Sep 2025
96. OdKV GŠ: Armáda upřednostní potřeby taktických jednotek: Nejdříve nakoupí 200 menších dronů, až pak střední, https://acr.mo.gov.cz/informacni-servis/zpravodajstvi/armada-uprednostni-potreby-taktickych-jednotek:-nejdrive-nakoupi-200-mensich-dronu%2D%2Daz-pakstredni%2D%2D244103/, Last Accessed 25 Sep 2025
97. MO ČR: Ministerstvo obrany vypracovalo rámec pro nákup vojenské munice, https://mocr.mo.gov.cz/informacni-servis/zpravodajstvi/ministerstvo-obrany-vypracovalo-ramec-pro-nakup-vojenske-munice-259749/, Last Accessed 25 Sep 2025
98. Dönmez, B.B.: Polish defense minister calls Turkish drones 'proven, effective' weapons, https://www.aa.com.tr/en/europe/polish-defense-minister-calls-turkish-drones-proven-effective-weapons/2253983, Last Accessed 25 Sep 2025
99. WB Group: 10,000 Warmates for the Poland, https://www.wbgroup.pl/en/aktualnosci/10000-warmates-for-the-poland/, Last Accessed 25 Sep 2025
100. Ministerstwo Obrony Narodowej: Nie będzie bezpiecznej Polski bez armii dronów, https://www.gov.pl/web/obrona-narodowa/nie-bedzie-bezpiecznej-polski-bez-armii-dronow?utm_source=chatgpt.com, Last Accessed 25 Sep 2025
101. Wilewski, K.: Drones on the Offensive, https://www.polska-zbrojna.pl/home/articleshow/44591?t=Drones-on-the-Offensive, Last Accessed 25 Sep 2025
102. Ministerstwo Obrony Narodowej: Rewolucja dronowa w Siłach Zbrojnych RP, https://www.gov.pl/web/obrona-narodowa/rewolucja-dronowa-w-silach-zbrojnych-rp, Last Accessed 25 Sep 2025
103. International Trade Administration: Poland Aerospace and Defense Military Drone Force Established. https://www.trade.gov/market-intelligence/poland-aerospace-defense-military-drone-force-established, Last Accessed 25 Sep 2025
104. Drone Space Valley, https://www.dronespacevalley.com/, Last Accessed 25 Sep 2025

105. Rubryka: Poland plans to create Valley of Drones, https://rubryka.com/en/2022/07/27/u-polshhi-planuyut-stvoryty-dolynu-bespilotnykiv/?utm_source=chatgpt.com, Last Accessed 25 Sep 2025
106. Dentons: Polish special act to accelerate defense investments, https://www.dentons.com/en/insights/guides-reports-and-whitepapers/2025/september/9/polish-special-act-to-accelerate-defense-investments, Last Accessed 25 Sep 2025

Unmanned Systems: A Way to Enhance Environmental Assessment Process

Natálie Hanáková[1](✉), Adam Jančařík[2], and Tibor Palasiewicz[1]

[1] University of Defence, Kounicova 65, 662 10 Brno, Czech Republic
{natalie.hanakova,tibor.palasiewicz}@unob.cz
[2] 602 00 Brno, Czech Republic
admjan@pm.me

Abstract. Climate change and the growing emphasis on environmental protection present significant challenges to environmental security and operational safety in NATO missions. This paper presents a conceptual framework for the deployment of autonomous unmanned systems to support key environmental assessment processes. The research builds on a qualitative design combining analysis, synthesis, comparison, and analogical reasoning. The approach integrates UAV capabilities across the entire lifecycle of NATO-relevant procedures, including Environmental Baseline Studies (EBS), Environmental Impact Assessments (EIA), and Environmental Close-out Studies (ECS). Focus is placed on the fusion of advanced airborne sensing technologies with onboard data processing and analytics. Key use cases include pre-deployment baseline mapping, real-time hazard surveillance during operations, and post-mission environmental verification—each contributing to enhanced force protection, faster decision-making, and strategic environmental accountability. The discussion also addresses the emerging legal concept of ecocide and its implications for NATO's environmental responsibilities. Finally, the paper outlines future directions in autonomous environmental response, including the potential deployment of UAVs for in situ mitigation via the targeted release of decontaminating or bioremediating agents. The study concludes by emphasizing both the benefits and the current limitations of UAV-based environmental monitoring while highlighting the need for standardized validation procedures within NATO- and UN-led operations.

Keywords: Environmental Impact Assessment · Environmental Protection · NATO Operations · Post-Conflict Recovery · UAV · UGV

1 Introduction

Accelerating climate change, the imperative of economy-wide carbon neutrality, and the concomitant shift toward renewable and low-carbon energy sources now define the strategic context in which both civil- and defense-sector environmental policies are formulated. International commitments—anchored in the European Green Deal and echoed

a. Adam Jančařík—Independent Researcher

J. Novotný et al. (Eds.): MESAS 2025, LNCS 16627, pp. 44–60, 2027.
https://doi.org/10.1007/978-3-032-33182-3_3

across NATO's climate-security agenda—serve as key reference points, yet their real-world implementation is mediated by the legal, political, and operational specificities of individual member states.

In recent years, environmental protection has garnered increasing attention at the NATO level. According to NATO terminology, environmental protection refers to "the prevention or mitigation of adverse environmental impacts" [1]. This definition emphasizes the prevention of military-induced environmental damage, rather than the protection of armed forces from the environment. Nevertheless, this may appear to be a conceptual distinction; however, it is precisely the latter perspective—the impact of environmental conditions on military operations—that has significantly contributed to the growing prominence of environmental considerations within NATO. The threat posed by climate change, which compels armed forces to operate under increasingly extreme temperature fluctuations and weather anomalies, exemplifies this second dimension. The establishment of the Climate Change and Security Centre of Excellence (CCAS CoE) in Canada in late 2023 [2] further confirmed the urgency of addressing this issue.

The outbreak of high-intensity warfare in Ukraine has added a further layer of complexity. The conflict has produced environmental devastation on a scale unseen since the era of symmetric warfare in the twentieth century [3, 4], thereby exposing critical gaps in existing environmental impact assessment (EIA) frameworks, which were largely designed for industrial projects or low-intensity conflicts. Heavy metal and organic contamination, ecosystem destruction and large-scale emissions from military operations underscore the need to rethink how EIAs account for the full life cycle impacts of extensive armed engagements—both during hostilities and throughout the subsequent remediation phase.

Although environmental impacts caused by military operations will primarily be addressed after the cessation of hostilities, expert discussions are already underway regarding methodologies for quantifying these impacts with the aim of determining the scale of war reparations in the context of the emerging concept of ecocide [5, 6]. In this regard, the deployment of technologies based on unmanned systems—particularly unmanned aerial vehicles (UAVs) and unmanned ground vehicles (UGVs)—appears critical. These systems enable real-time environmental monitoring without the need for direct human involvement in hazardous or inaccessible areas, thereby significantly enhancing the safety, efficiency, and scope of data acquisition [7–11]. By integrating advanced sensor systems (e.g., optical, chemical, hyperspectral) with onboard data processing capabilities, UAVs and UGVs can provide highly accurate information on heavy metal contamination, the presence of organic pollutants, and ecosystem destruction [7, 8]. Such data can be used not only for conducting EIA in post-conflict settings, but also to support decision-making in remediation planning and to provide objective evidence for the determination of damage and reparations.

Despite growing attention to environmental protection within NATO, no standardized operational framework currently exists for incorporating unmanned systems into EIA or EBS/ECS procedures. This paper seeks to bridge this gap systematically outlining the potential applications of unmanned systems in post-conflict EIA and demonstrating how data collected through these technologies can enhance the quality and credibility of assessment outputs, while supporting post-conflict recovery and environmental justice.

2 Literature Review

2.1 Ecocide, Ecotone and Badland: Impact of War on the Environment

The concept of ecocide constitutes an emerging legal construct, most widely defined as "unlawful or wanton acts committed with knowledge that there is a substantial likelihood of severe and either widespread or long-term damage to the environment being caused by those acts" [12]. Although the term was first introduced in 1970 by the American biologist Arthur W. Galston, who proposed an international treaty for its prevention at the Conference on War and National Responsibility [13], the notion has only recently attracted significant attention within the realm of international criminal law [5]. This discourse has progressed from general debate to an active consideration of its potential incorporation into the existing legal framework. At the heart of the discussion lies the question of whether ecocide can be subsumed under the existing crimes defined in the Rome Statute, or whether it warrants recognition as a distinct, fifth core international crime [5].

The current legal framework penalizes environmental damage primarily when it is associated with other criminal offenses; environmental protection has not yet been fully recognized as an autonomous object of criminal law [14]. As a result, both scientific and legal-political discourse is increasingly shifting from merely naming ecocide to the implementation of concrete tools for prevention, accountability, and legal classification of environmental destruction. Some countries have already adopted their own legal frameworks defining ecocide as a distinct criminal offense—for example, France's Climate and Resilience Act (2021) [15]. At the international level, there are ongoing discussions about amending the Rome Statute of the International Criminal Court (ICC) to include ecocide as a fifth core international crime, alongside genocide, crimes against humanity, war crimes, and the crime of aggression.

Empirical data on the long-term environmental consequences of armed conflicts—such as those in Vietnam, the Persian Gulf, or the Balkans [16]—have repeatedly confirmed that environmental devastation can amount to a structural assault on the fundamental conditions of life, including large-scale biodiversity loss, soil and water contamination, and accelerated greenhouse gas emissions. In the context of the war in Ukraine, there is an increasing recognition of the need to develop a new ecological paradigm of warfare that accounts for both the direct and cumulative impacts of military activities. Within this framework, emerging concepts such as military ecotone and military badland offer valuable analytical tools for understanding these phenomena [17].

The military ecotone can be defined as a transitional landscape zone formed as a result of intensive military activity with the intent to destabilize and destroy the local ecological and cultural systems. Unlike natural ecotones, which evolve gradually through long-term ecological processes, military ecotones arise abruptly, are characterized by high levels of environmental disruption, and often result in long-term contamination of the environment, posing risks to public health and human well-being for generations [18]. The military badland represents an advanced stage of territorial degradation where uninhabitability itself becomes the intended outcome. Unlike the military ecotone, which can be understood as a processual and potentially reversible phenomenon, the badland denotes a morphologically fixed and environmentally irreversible transformation of the territory into a permanently hostile and toxic environment. These areas are marked by extreme levels of pollution, newly established ecological gradients, and substantial impacts on biota, while being deliberately constructed as zones unsuitable for human habitation—as exemplified by conditions in eastern Ukraine [6, 18].

In the context of NATO allied operations, these findings underscore the urgent need to integrate EIA into the early planning phases of missions, to strengthen continuous ecological monitoring, and to codify the obligation to prevent acts that could meet the legal definition of ecocide. The concepts of military ecotone and badland thus provide a crucial framework for assessing the environmental consequences of armed conflict and for designing appropriate mechanisms for ecological restoration and post-conflict territorial rehabilitation [18].

2.2 Approaches to Environmental Impact Assessment

Environmental Impacts of Armed Conflicts. Armed conflicts typically generate both immediate and long-term, multifaceted environmental consequences, which affect all components of the natural environment in complex and interrelated ways [19]. These impacts include mechanical disturbances (e.g., soil compaction or crater formation), physico-chemical contamination (e.g., the presence of heavy metals, petroleum products, explosives, toxic and particulate gases, and combustion by-products), as well as biological degradation such as biodiversity loss and disruption of ecosystem functions [3]. These processes are often cumulative and may persist even for decades after hostilities cease.

The war in Ukraine has, in terms of both scale and intensity, surpassed the environmental impacts of all other armed conflicts studied over the past eight decades [3]. As of August 2024, the estimated environmental damage exceeded USD 60 billion [3, 4]. The destruction of the Kakhovka Dam is considered the most significant ecological disaster since the Chernobyl nuclear accident [20]. This event resulted in direct losses to infrastructure and property amounting to USD 2.79 billion, and total damages exceeding USD 11 billion, with environmental losses alone accounting for more than USD 6.4 billion—approximately 58% of the total [21]. Furthermore, approximately one-third of Ukraine's territory (around 174,000 km^2) is contaminated by landmines and explosive remnants of war, representing a prolonged ecological and security threat [4, 20].

Environmental Protection in NATO. In recent years, environmental protection has garnered increasing attention at the NATO level. According to NATO terminology, environmental protection refers to "the prevention or mitigation of adverse environmental impacts." This definition emphasizes the prevention of military-induced environmental damage, rather than the protection of armed forces from the environment.

In June 2021, the NATO Summit in Brussels culminated in the approval of the Climate Change and Security Action Plan (CCSAP), mandating the Alliance to: (i) conduct annual assessments of climate-security threats, (ii) reduce NATO's own greenhouse gas emissions, and (iii) systematically integrate climate adaptation into capability development and military operations [22]. The plan (issued in 2023) also endorsed the establishment of the CCAS CoE, subsequently hosted by Canada. In October of the same year, MC 469/1 was revised. In June 2022, the Madrid Strategic Concept was adopted, marking the first time that climate change was identified as a "decisive challenge" and directing Allied Commanders to incorporate climate-related scenarios into NATO's defense planning process [23]. That same year also saw updates to doctrinal documents MC 560/2 and AJEPP-2 [24].

In February 2023, NATO carried out its inaugural Climate Change and Security Impact Assessment, mapping climate-related risks across 19 mission-critical domains—ranging from Arctic mobility to munitions safety [25]. Concurrently, AJEPP-3 was updated [26], and AJEPP-6.1 Manual for Environmental Sampling Protocols was issued as a Standard Related Document (SRD) [27]. It is also essential to note that version B of ATP-3.12.1 was promulgated in June 2023 [28]. This new tactical doctrine introduced partial changes in the approach to EP. Unlike the previous ATP-3.12.1 Version A, it classifies support to environmental protection under general engineer support as an engineering activity, alongside horizontal and vertical works, support to logistics, and railway construction/repair. In 2024, the third edition of Climate Change and Security Impact Assessment report was released. It highlighted successful pilot initiatives involving hybrid micro-grid systems (e.g., within KFOR) and recommended the mandatory application of life-cycle cost analysis in equipment procurement beginning in 2026 [29]. For clarity, Table 1 provides a comprehensive list of current NATO documents addressing EP.

Table 1. List of current NATO's EP-related documents (as of 30 July 2025)

Code	Title
MC 469/1	NATO Military Principles and Policies for Environmental Protection
MC 560/2	Military Committee Policy for Military Engineering
AJEPP-2	Environmental Protection Best Practices and Standards for Military Camps in NATO Operations
AJEPP-3	Environmental Management System in NATO Military Activities
AJEPP-4	Joint NATO Doctrine for Environmental Protection During NATO-Led Military Activities
AJEPP-6	NATO Environmental File During NATO-led Activities
AJEPP-6.1	Manual for Sampling Protocols
AJEPP-7	Best Environmental Protection Practices for Sustainability of Military Training Areas
AMEPP-1	NATO Navies Pollution Abatement Policies
AMEPP-2	National Navy Regulations for the Disposal of Waste
AMEPP-3	Shipboard pollution Abatement Equipment Catalogue
AMEPP-4	Guidance for the integration of Maritime Environmental Protection (MEP) functional requirements in to ship design
AMEPP-9	Health care waste management procedures aboard Navy vessels
AMedP-4.9	Water / wastewater management

The Allied Joint Environmental Protection Publication AJEPP-2 [1] identifies key environmental aspects that must be considered during the planning, execution, and termination phases of military operations. These aspects include:

- Infrastructure Planning
- Energy Management
- Potable / Non-Potable Water
- Waste Water – Black
- Waste Water – Grey
- Storm Water
- Solid Waste
- Hazardous Waste
- Health Care Waste
- Petroleum, Oils and Lubricants (POL)
- HAZMAT
- Air Quality
- Natural Resources Protection
- Cultural Property Protection.

These domains represent the primary environmental concerns that must be systematically addressed throughout the operational lifecycle. According to MC 560/2, responsibility for implementing environmental protection measures during operations lies primarily with military engineering units [30].

Until 2023, the valid Tactical Doctrine for Military Engineering was ATP-3.12.1 Version A [31], which defined the so-called 17 areas of environmental concern—a comprehensive set of categories in which military activities may pose risks to the environment. This framework served as a detailed guideline for identifying and mitigating environmental hazards. However, as of June 2023, a new version of the doctrine (Version B) has come into force, which no longer includes this list [28].

Challenges in Environmental Impact Assessment. EIA is closely linked to the concept of ecocide, military ecotone and badland, as it constitutes a fundamental tool for identifying, quantifying, and potentially classifying environmental damage resulting from armed conflict. To enable a meaningful evaluation of such impacts, it is essential to establish a unified, up-to-date, and operational assessment framework. As shown in Table 1, the NATO currently lacks a dedicated document that explicitly regulates EIA procedures in NATO-led operations. Each member state applies its own national methodology; therefore, for joint exercises and deployments, a context-specific Standard Operating Procedure (SOP) is developed to guide EIA practices in the given operational setting.

National standards are typically based on broader international and European frameworks, particularly when a NATO member state is also a member of the European Union. Nevertheless, at the international level, a unified methodology for assessing environmental damage caused by military operations is still lacking. This absence significantly hinders the legal attribution of such damage, particularly in proceedings before international judicial bodies [21].

2.3 Unmanned Systems and AI Technologies in Environmental Monitoring

Unmanned systems are becoming indispensable tools in the field of environmental monitoring [8]. Despite ongoing challenges related to the standardization and regulatory framework of environmental assessment, these technologies offer promising solutions for improving both the efficiency and accuracy of environmental data acquisition. Their potential is particularly relevant in complex or inaccessible areas, where conventional methods are limited.

High-Resolution and Multi-parameter Data Collection. A key advantage of unmanned systems lies in their ability to perform high-resolution and multi-parameter data collection. UAVs can be equipped with advanced sensor payloads—including multispectral, hyperspectral, thermal, and LiDAR systems [7, 32–34]—capable of capturing data on wind speed and direction, temperature, relative humidity, atmospheric pressure, and fine particulate matter [33]. The integration of these sensors with onboard data processing units enables real-time analysis and delivery of actionable information (e.g., damage maps or pollution hotspots), thereby reducing the need for manual intervention.

Real-Time Monitoring. Unmanned systems allow real-time environmental monitoring, which is critical for rapid disaster response and impact assessment [7, 33]. In the context of pollution detection, UAVs using image recognition models (e.g., YOLOv8n-BWG) have demonstrated high precision in locating and characterizing industrial smoke emissions, significantly accelerating the identification of environmental threats [35].

Autonomy. The increasing level of autonomy in drone platforms—driven by onboard sensors, AI algorithms, and GPS-based navigation—enables them to execute missions independently, even in hazardous or remote areas [3, 36, 37]. This makes them particularly suitable for deployment in disaster zones and post-conflict settings.

Swarm Robotics. The development of swarm robotics allows multiple UAVs to cooperate on complex tasks, share data in real time, and collectively cover larger geographic areas while optimizing spatial data acquisition and analysis [7, 36].

Post-Conflict Recovery. In the context of post-conflict recovery and environmental remediation, UAVs can be used to track long-term air quality trends, visualize habitat degradation, and monitor vegetation dynamics before, during, and after armed conflicts [6, 38]. Furthermore, unmanned platforms may be deployed for the targeted application of neutralizing or bioremediating agents, offering a remote and scalable solution for decontamination in polluted or otherwise hazardous environments [39, 40].

3 Methods

This study is based on a qualitative and conceptual research design utilizing analysis, synthesis, comparison, and analogical reasoning. The primary objective was to formulate a framework for the integration of unmanned systems into environmental assessment processes—particularly within the framework of NATO-led missions. The methodological approach was designed to bridge the gap between civil-sector technological advances and military environmental doctrines.

3.1 Research Design and Analytical Framework

The methodological workflow consisted of four sequential stages.

1. **Literature Synthesis.** An analytical review of current literature was conducted, focusing on civil-sector applications of unmanned systems (UAVs, UGVs, USVs) in environmental monitoring. These sources provided insights into the technological capabilities in areas such as soil and water analysis, pollution detection, habitat mapping, and chemical application.
2. **Doctrinal Mapping.** NATO environmental doctrines (AJEPP-2, 3, 4, 6, 6.1, 7 and MC 469/1) and ATP-3.12.1 Version A and B were analyzed to identify existing environmental protection domains and procedural gaps.
3. **Analogical Reasoning.** Given that most UAV/UGV applications originate from civilian contexts, analogical reasoning was applied to infer their transferability to defense operations. Each civil application was compared with its functional equivalent in military context (e.g., chemical spraying into application of decontaminants; crop monitoring into post-conflict biodiversity recovery). This analogical reasoning formed the basis for identifying the potential of unmanned systems in environmental management within military domain.
4. **Comparison and Framework Formulation.** The identified technical capabilities were compared with the environmental domains defined in *Allied Joint Environmental Protection Publication* AJEPP-2 and the earlier version of tactical doctrine ATP-3.12.1 (Version A), which contained a comprehensive list of environmental concern areas relevant to military activities. While AJEPP-2 remains the core reference for environmental protection in NATO operations, ATP-3.12.1 Version A offered a broader operational context and therefore served as a valuable complementary source. For each domain, suitable unmanned system types (UAV, UGV, USV) and corresponding sensors or payloads were assigned.

3.2 Evaluation Criteria

To assess the practical feasibility of each proposed application, two evaluation criteria were used: (i) operational feasibility – the capability to deploy the system in NATO/UN operational environments considering climate, logistics, and interoperability constraints, and (ii) environmental relevance – the extent to which the system directly contributes to EIA/EBS/ECS objectives or risk mitigation. These criteria were applied qualitatively, following expert judgment and comparison with existing NATO practices.

3.3 Limitations

As this research is conceptual in nature, no field experiments or simulations were conducted. Nevertheless, the proposed framework is deliberately structured to enable subsequent empirical testing through pilot studies or simulation modelling. The qualitative character of the study limits the generalizability, as analogical reasoning relies on the assumption that civilian use cases can be transferred to military contexts—an assumption that may not always hold true due to operational and security constraints. Consequently, empirical validation lies beyond the scope of this study but remains an essential next step to verify the applicability and robustness of the proposed framework.

4 Results and Discussion

Although the successful completion of a mission remains the primary objective during armed conflict, NATO forces and United Nations (UN) military units bear an environmental responsibility that obliges them to prevent unnecessary damage to the environment. This obligation stems from international legal commitments as well as from NATO doctrinal and operational planning standards. In practice, however, environmental measures are primarily concentrated in phases of deployment or in non-combat conditions—such as garrison conditions and international military exercises—while their application during active combat operations remains limited.

As previously noted, the AJEPP-2 outlines several domains of environmental management that should be addressed during missions. However, for the purpose of systematically integrating unmanned systems into environmental protection efforts within NATO- and UN-led operations, the list provided in AJEPP-2 is not entirely sufficient. It has therefore been extended to include additional areas formerly covered by the tactical doctrine ATP-3.12.1 Version A, which primarily applied to peace support operations. These additional domains include the preparation of Environmental Baseline Studies (EBS) and Environmental Closeout Studies (ECS), EIA, environmental risk management, sustainability, and noise pollution. A proposal for the integration of unmanned systems into these relevant environmental protection areas in NATO operations is presented in Table 2 a graphically displayed in Fig. 1.

Air. Military activities are frequently associated with deteriorated air quality, resulting both from increased concentrations of combat vehicles and direct combat operations, as well as from operations conducted in contaminated environments. In this context, unmanned systems offer an effective tool for real-time air quality monitoring and decision-making support. Drones equipped with specialized sensors (e.g., Sniffer4D) can collect time-series data on concentrations of suspended particulate matter ($PM_{2.5}$, PM_{10}), greenhouse gases, and other airborne pollutants [8, 41]. Thanks to their ability to simultaneously measure meteorological parameters such as wind speed and direction, humidity, and temperature, unmanned aerial platforms can provide a comprehensive overview of the current microclimatic conditions within the operational environment [41]. These data are applicable not only for environmental monitoring but also for use by chemical defense units in assessing and tracking chemical threats in the field. Furthermore, the integration of advanced machine learning algorithms—such as YOLOv8n-BWG—enables accurate detection and localization of emission sources, thereby enhancing the efficiency of environmental surveillance operations [35]. This capability is particularly valuable in areas with restricted access, where personnel presence is hazardous or infeasible. Nevertheless, meteorological conditions remain a limiting factor, especially strong winds and precipitation, which significantly reduce the number of viable flight days and thus impact the overall operational effectiveness of UAS deployments during military missions [42].

EBS/ECS. UAS play a significant role in enhancing the efficiency of environmental studies by enabling rapid, real-time data acquisition at high spatial and temporal resolution [42]. They allow for the collection of high-quality data from remote and otherwise inaccessible areas within a fraction of the time required by conventional methods [8].

Table 2. Proposal of unmanned systems use for areas of environmental concern

Area	Type of US	Use of US
Air	UAVs	Detection of $PM_{2.5}$ and PM_{10}; wind, humidity and temperature measurements; input for chemical threat assessment.
EBS/ECS	UAVs, LiDAR, USVs	High-resolution data collection; mapping of sensitive zones, planning of sampling points, infrastructure siting risk analysis.
Ecosystem	UAVs (IR, LiDAR), UGVs	2D/3D habitat mapping, biodiversity assessment, species distribution and migration modelling; detection of erosion and invasive species.
EIA	UAVs, LiDAR	Environmental data collection (even from hardly accessible environments).
Energy Management	UAVs	Reduced fuel consumption via targeted applications.
Hazardous Materiel Management + POL	UAVs	Precise application for decontamination; detection of gas leaks and hazardous material spills.
Noise Pollution	UAVs	Measurement of noise levels; 3D noise propagation modelling.
Risk Management	UAVs, UGVs, USVs	Detection of air, water and soil contamination; monitoring of gas leaks and fires; damage assessment; emergency coordination.
Soil	UAVs, UGVs	Detection of soil degradation, compaction, pH, moisture and temperature monitoring; support post-conflict land restoration.

(continued)

UAS can be employed to monitor water bodies, gathering information on water quality, pollution levels, and aquatic ecosystems [8]. The ability to obtain timely and accurate

Table 2. (*continued*)

Area	Type of US	Use of US
Sustainability	UAVs	Monitoring of ecological footprint; identification of zones for remediation.
Waste Management	UAVs	Surveillance of waste accumulation, illegal dumping and open burning; mapping of waste streams.
Water and Wastewater	UAVs, USVs, underwater drones, LiDAR	Monitoring of water quality, pollutant concentration; GIS-based 2D/3D visualizations of changes in water systems and groundwater

environmental data greatly improves the planning process, particularly in identifying and prioritizing areas for targeted ground sampling. This is especially relevant when assessing future sites intended for infrastructure development that may pose environmental risks—such as vehicle wash points, fuel and lubricant storage facilities, or waste accumulation zones.

Ecosystem. Impacts on fauna and flora represent a critical component of environmental assessment during military activities. Digital habitat surveys conducted using unmanned aerial systems (UAS) and stationary LiDAR platforms are designed to collect high-resolution 2D and 3D data on biodiversity, species distribution, habitat structure, and ecological connectivity [41]. UAS can also support the identification of alternative compensatory habitats for protected species, which is essential in cases where military activities disrupt ecologically sensitive zones. Infrared-equipped drones further enhance predictive modeling of habitat suitability and species migration patterns, enabling proactive environmental risk management during deployment [41]. The integration of such data into operational planning supports mitigation strategies aimed at minimizing long-term ecological damage during military operations.

EIA. A recent study [38] proposed and tested a digital framework for conducting EIA using drones and LiDAR to collect quantitative environmental data. The study, conducted in the context of railway infrastructure projects in South Korea, demonstrated that the digitalization of EIA enables rapid prediction and evaluation of potential impacts [41]. In military operations, where time constraints and access limitations are common, the use of UAS offers a significant advantage. Drones can compensate for gaps in existing environmental datasets by providing real-time data collection, even in remote or hazardous areas that are otherwise difficult to access [41].

Energy Management. According to a study by [39], conventional spraying methods—currently applied in agriculture but transferable to military remediation contexts—consume approximately 2.43 times more energy than drone-assisted spraying (365.26 MJ/ha compared to 146.84 MJ/ha). This substantial difference highlights the energy efficiency potential of UAS in operational environments where resource optimization is critical. Drones further reduce fuel consumption and related emissions by providing highly targeted and spatially precise data, thereby minimizing the need for large-scale deployment of heavy machinery [43]. This capability is particularly valuable in military field operations, where reducing logistical burdens and fulfillment of the Zero Footprint Basis commitment play significant role. However, the environmental burden associated with drone operations lies primarily in the production and charging of batteries. This impact can be significantly mitigated through the integration of renewable energy sources—such as portable solar panels—which offer a promising solution for maintaining drone functionality with minimal ecological cost [39].

Hazardous Materiel Management and POL. Drone-based spraying systems enable highly localized application of chemical agents, thereby minimizing the volume of hazardous substances introduced into ecosystems and reducing adverse effects on non-target organisms [43]. This targeted precision not only decreases overall chemical usage but also significantly mitigates collateral ecological damage, which is particularly relevant during military decontamination or remediation operations. Moreover, drones can be equipped with sensors to detect gas leaks and other hazardous material releases, providing critical real-time data for risk assessment and incident response [8].

Noise Pollution. Noise and vibration are critical environmental impact indicators, particularly in military contexts where training activities have been associated with wildlife mortality. UAS can be employed to measure noise levels using onboard sound level meters; however, it is essential to apply correction factors to account for the drone's own acoustic emissions [41]. Drones also support 3D noise prediction modeling by integrating data on topography and the spatial distribution of built structures. This capability enhances the assessment of noise propagation in complex operational environments and supports the development of mitigation strategies to reduce acoustic disturbances during military exercises and deployments [41].

Risk Management. Unmanned systems are highly effective tools for environmental risk assessment, particularly in detecting air (UAVs), water (UWVs) and soil contamination (UGVs). Such early detection capabilities support the implementation of preventive measures during military operations [43]. An illustrative example might be the identification of parasitic outbreaks affecting salmonid populations during international military exercises in Norway, which led to the establishment of mandatory decontamination points for military vehicles exiting aquatic environments. Drones are also valuable for damage assessment, search and rescue operations, and the coordination of emergency responses [8]. Furthermore, they play a key role in the continuous monitoring of environmental hazards, including gas leaks, landslides, and wildfires [8]. Their deployment enhances situational awareness, reduces response times, and facilitates more effective risk mitigation strategies in military operations.

Soil. UAVs can detect early indicators of soil degradation, enabling proactive environmental management in military operational areas [43]. In agricultural contexts, drones have been shown to reduce fuel consumption and associated emissions through targeted applications—a principle that can be adapted for use in remediation and decontamination scenarios within military settings. UGVs are particularly suitable for monitoring soil quality. Equipped with soil sensors, these platforms can measure parameters such as moisture content, temperature, and pH levels [8]. Additionally, UGVs can be employed to assess soil compaction and the decline of organic matter—both of which are critical indicators of anthropogenic disturbance resulting from intensive vehicle movement, construction, POL leakages or other post-conflict land degradation [43].

Sustainability. Through high-resolution spatial data, drones facilitate the targeted and efficient application of inputs, thereby reducing waste and minimizing ecological footprints [43]. While this approach has been widely applied in the agricultural sector (e.g. fertilizer application), its principles are directly transferable to the remediation of areas affected by military activity. Especially, in post-conflict or contaminated zones, drones can support sustainable land restoration efforts by identifying zones requiring decontamination. In addition, drones can assist in identifying areas vulnerable to soil erosion, nutrient depletion, or the spread of invasive species, thereby supporting early intervention and habitat conservation strategies [43].

Waste Management. UAS can support waste monitoring by providing real-time surveillance of waste accumulation sites, unauthorized dumping, and spatial distribution of waste streams [8, 34]. This capability is particularly useful during the planning and sustainment phases of operations, where logistical constraints often complicate waste segregation, transport, and disposal [6]. Drones equipped with optical and thermal sensors can detect open burning. This enhances situational awareness, reduces environmental and health risks, and supports compliance with AJEPP-2 guidelines, contributing to a more sustainable and operationally resilient mission footprint.

Water and Wastewater. UAVs can be deployed to collect data on water quality, pollutant concentrations, and the status of aquatic ecosystems, supporting early detection of contamination and informing mitigation strategies. For more detailed analyses, unmanned surface vessels (USVs) are proposed for direct water sampling, while underwater drones may be utilized to gather multiphase time-series data [41]. In addition, drone and LiDAR technologies enable the evaluation of thermal impacts from surrounding land use on surface water systems and groundwater reserves. Water quality changes can be visualized using 2D and 3D GIS-based mapping tools, enhancing situational awareness and supporting transparent documentation [41].

Although the proposed framework shows strong potential to improve environmental assessment process within NATO-led operations, several operational constraints remain. UAV, UGV and USV performance is affected by weather conditions [8, 42, 43], battery endurance [34, 42], and communication range [7, 42]. The current absence of standardized data formats and procedures [34] also complicates integration into existing environmental systems of NATO. These limitations underline the need for a unified NATO guideline defining technical standards and interoperability protocols for unmanned environmental monitoring.

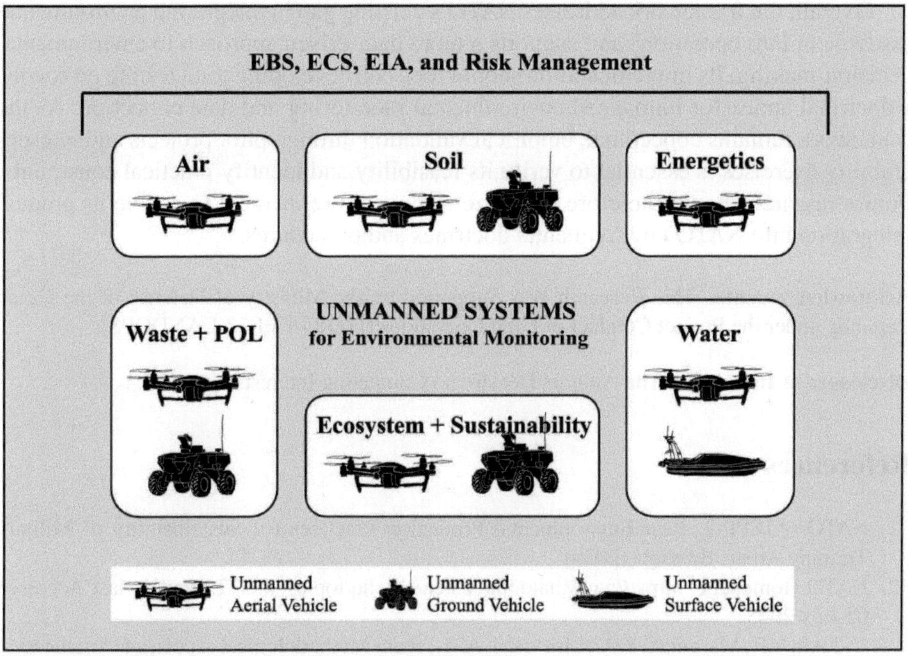

Fig. 1. Proposal for the use of unmanned systems in the environmental assessment process

5 Conclusion

The active deployment of unmanned systems has become an integral part of the modern battlespace. Although these technologies are primarily used for reconnaissance and combat purposes, their potential can also be effectively harnessed in the domain of environmental protection. While environmental considerations are not typically prioritized during armed operations, NATO member states are bound by international commitments to prevent and mitigate adverse environmental impacts caused by military activities. Integrating unmanned systems into EIA processes in NATO- and UN-led operations thus represents a significant opportunity to enhance both the scope and quality of environmental monitoring in complex, hazardous, or otherwise inaccessible operational environments. In this context, lessons learned from the civilian sector—particularly from applications in agriculture—can be leveraged to improve situational awareness, accelerate decision-making, and reduce the ecological footprint across all operational phases.

This paper proposes a conceptual framework for the deployment of UAVs, UGVs, and USVs in support of EBS, ECS, and EIA. By aligning key environmental domains identified in NATO doctrinal documents with the technological capabilities of unmanned systems, the study outlines specific use cases in the areas of air, soil, and water monitoring, ecosystem assessment, and hazardous material management. The proposed approach contributes to NATO's broader climate-security agenda and enhances the environmental dimension of operational resilience, while also engaging with ongoing legal and strategic debates on ecocide and post-conflict environmental justice.

Overall, the framework addresses NATO's existing gap in integrating environmental assessment into operations and supports a more data-driven approach to environmental decision-making. Its implementation should focus on developing joint testing protocols, a doctrinal annex for unmanned environmental monitoring and data collection. As the framework remains conceptual, empirical validation through pilot projects and interoperability exercises is essential to verify its feasibility and identify practical constraints. Future research should therefore prioritize testing and refinement to enable its gradual integration into NATO environmental doctrines and procedures.

Acknowledgements. This Research Was Supported by the Ministry of Defence of the Czech Republic under the Project Conduct of Land Operations (DZRO-FVL22-LANDOPS).

Disclosure of Interests. The Authors Declare no Competing Interests.

References

1. NATO: AJEPP-2. Best Environmental Protection Practices for Sustainability of Military Training Areas. Brussels (2020)
2. NATO Homepage, https://www.nato.int/cps/en/natohq/topics_68372.htm#29, last Accessed 05 July 2025
3. Didukh, Y.P., Maruniak, S.A., Lisovskyi, A.A., et al.: Methodological aspects of classification of environmental impact caused by Russian aggression in Ukraine. Ukrainian Geographical Journal. **2**, 3–12 (2024)
4. Maslak, O., Yakovenko, Y., Maslak, M., et al.: Methods of environmental monitoring, analysis and assessment of the consequences of military actions. In: 18th International Conference Monitoring of Geological Processes and Ecological Condition of the Environment, pp. 1–5. European Association of Geoscientists and Engineers (2025)
5. Pazvantoglu, C.A.: Ecocide as a separate crime under the Rome statute: a legal analysis of the discourse. Environmental Policy and Law. **55**, 1–11 (2025)
6. Wirtu, Y.D., Abdela, U.: Impact of war on the environment: ecocide. Front. Environ. Sci. **13**, 1539520 (2025)
7. Nasiri, N., Al-Maashri, A., Bourdoucen, H., et al.: Environmental Monitoring in the Oil and Gas Industry Using Machine Vision Associated with Robotics and AI. In: Advances in Unmanned Aerial Vehicles – Technology and Applications – Big Issues Solved with Drone Technology. IntechOpen (2025)
8. Manjunath, T., Prabhu, P.: The future of autonomous drones in environmental monitoring and disaster management. International Journal of Scientific Research and Engineering Trends. **11**(2) (2025)
9. Sedlacek, M., Dohnal, F., Rolenec, O.: Proposal of an algorithm for evaluation of wet gap crossing using geoprocessing tool. In: Transbaltica XII: Transportation Science and Technology Lecture Notes in Intelligent Transportation and Infrastructure, pp. 542–551 (2022)
10. Rolenec, O., Bilina, M., Pekar, O., et al.: Unmanned Aerial Vehicle LiDAR Scanning for Railway Security: Pre- and Post-Explosion Analysis. In: 10th International Conference on Military Technologies (ICMT) (2025)
11. Havlik, T., Sustr, M., Ivan, J.: Evaluation of the effectiveness of a firing battery in self-defense and protection in the area of firing postitions using constructive simulation. Journal of Defense Modeling and Simulation. **23**, 335 (2024)

12. Stop Ecocide International., https://www.stopecocide.earth/legal-definition, last Accessed 2025 July 08
13. Ecocide Law, https://ecocidelaw.com/history/, last Accessed 2025 July 08
14. Winter, E.: Stop ecocide International's blueprint for ecocide is compromised by anthropocentrism: a new architect must be found. Isr Law Rev. **57**, 175–209 (2024)
15. European Commission., https://commission.europa.eu/projects/climate-and-resilience-law_en, last accessed 2025/07/15.
16. Melas, D., Zerefos, S., Rapsomanikis, N., et al.: The war in Kosovo: evidence of pollution transport in the Balkans during operation 'allied force. Environ. Sci. Pollut. Res. **7**(2), 97–104 (2000)
17. Nikolaenko, D.: The Military Ecotone and Military Badland of Ukraine Are Subjects of Geographical and Environmental Research (2024)
18. Nikolaenko, D.: Ecological Successions of the Cultural Landscape and Targeted Depopulation of the Territory: Patterns on the Environmental Consequences of the Military Aggression of the Russian Federation against Ukraine (2024)
19. Honcharov, G., Novitskyi, R., Hapich, H.: Preliminary assessment of losses for fish farming of the Kharkiv region due to military actions. Ribogospodars′ka nauka Ukraïni. **1**(67), 4–25 (2024)
20. Golovko, L.: International legal aspects of the assessment of environmental damage caused by military actions. Bratislava Law Review. **8**(1), 99–110 (2024)
21. Golovko, L., Ladychenko, V., Yara, O.: Protection of the environment during armed conflicts: economic and international legal aspects. Baltic Journal of Economic Studies. **11**(2), 346–351 (2025)
22. NATO: NATO Climate Change and Security Action Plan. Brussels (2023)
23. NATO: NATO 2022 Strategic Concept. Brussels (2022)
24. NATO: Environmental Protection for Military Camps in NATO Operations. Brussels (2022)
25. NATO: NATO Climate Change and Security Impact Assessment. Brussels (2023)
26. NATO: Environmental Management System in NATO Military Activities. Brussels (2023)
27. NATO: Manual for Environmental Sampling Protocols. Brussels (2022)
28. NATO: Allied Tactical Doctrine for Military Engineering. Brussels (2023)
29. NATO: NATO Climate Change and Security Impact Assessment. Brussels (2024)
30. NATO: Policy for Military Engineering. Brussels (2016)
31. NATO: Allied Tactical Doctrine for Military Engineering. Brussels (2016)
32. Marsella, E., Giordano, L., Evangelista, A., et al.: An innovative unmanned system for advanced environmental monitoring: design and development. In: EGU General Assembly, Vienna (2015)
33. Jung, S., Kim, W.: Development of an Unmanned Aerial System for Maritime Environmental Observation. In: IEEE, pp. 132746–132765 (2021)
34. Manfreda, S., McCabe, M.F., Miller, P.E., et al.: On the use of unmanned aerial Systems for Environmental Monitoring. Remote Sens. **10**(4), 641 (2018)
35. Zhang, Y., Wu, G.: YOLOv8n-BWG-enhanced drone smoke detection: advancing environmental monitoring efficiency. PLoS One. **20**(5) (2025)
36. Douabul, A.: The Vengeance of Iraq's Environment Analyzing the Impact of War on Natural Resources. (2014)
37. Ferreira, C., Freire, F., Ribeiro, J.: Environmental Assessment of Military Systems with the Life-Cycle Assessment Methodology. In: Energetic Materials and Munitions: Life Cycle Management, Environmental Impact, and Demilitarization, 1st edn, pp. 169–197. Wiley (2019)
38. Mohamadi, B., Abu Ghazala, M.O., Al.Sabbagh, T.A., et al.: Integrating InSAR coherence and air pollution detection satellites to study the impact of war on air quality. Int. J. Appl. Earth Obs. Geoinf. **142**, 104687 (2025)

39. Safaenejad, M., Ghasemi-Nejad-Raeni, M., Taki, M.: Reducing energy and environmental footprint in agriculture: a study on drone spraying vs. conventional methods. PLoS One. **20**(6), e0323779 (2025)
40. Maranda, A., Wachowski, L., Kukfisz, B.: Valorization of energetic materials from obsolete military ammunition through life cycle assessment (LCA): a circular economy approach to environmental impact reduction. Sustainability. **17**(1), 346 (2025)
41. Kim, M., Park, D., Hwang, D., et al.: Digitalization for the Environmental Impact Assessment of Railway Projects Using Drones and Lidar. (2024).
42. Komarek, J.: When the wind blows: exposing the constraints of drone-based environmental mapping. Nat. Sci. **5**(1–2), e70003 (2025)
43. Takhumova, O., Pustuev, A., Eiryan, A., et al.: Integrating drone technology in sustainable agriculture: Precision environmental monitoring and resource management. In: E3S Web of Conferences, vol. 633, (2025)

Modelling of UGV's Manoeuvre in the Light of Tactical Variables

Pavel Zahradníček(✉), Jan Hrdinka, and Jan Nohel

University of Defence, Brno, Czech Republic
{pavel.zahradnicek,jan.hrdinka,jan.nohel}@unob.cz

Abstract. The unmanned ground vehicles are and will be in the close future an essential part of the formation of maneuvering units. The mission of these hybrid teams has to respect tactical variables. The variable terrain is extremely significant for this kind of device; despite this, it is necessary to find relations and limitations and how to calculate with the utilization of unmanned ground vehicles. The article presents relations between tactical variables for the main element—the unmanned ground vehicle. The approach is holistic. For exact interpretation and possible operational calculation, the relations are mathematically expressed. For validation, the Maneuver Control System CZ for Wargaming Modelling and Simulation has been chosen. The article combines principles of warfighting at the tactical level and exact scientific methods. The results can be used as a part of the military decision-making process, esp. Order of battle creation.

Keywords: Tactical variables · Terrain · Unmanned Ground Vehicle

1 Introduction

Tactical problems are resolved by using a combination of tactics, techniques, and procedures (TTPs) as well as by using combat power. Choosing appropriate combinations of TTPs is related to understanding the situation according to tactical variables (Mission, Enemy, Terrain and Weather, Troops available, Time available, Civil considerations—METT-TC) [1]. Tactical (also mission) variables are used by decision-makers after a specific mission is assigned, and they are used to understand matters that have an impact on mission execution.

The above-mentioned sentence is valid for all tools and elements making some kind of decision, including sub-systems of unmanned ground vehicles (UGVs). Autonomous systems are specific and still have significant limitations, technical and algorithmic also. The relations between tactical variables are crucial for correct decision-making of commanders, operators, or the autonomous system itself. The goal is to make the unmanned system as autonomous as possible and save the human power for decision-making or key operations.

The UGV, reflecting as many variables as possible, can be more autonomous in specific operations. Therefore, the general approach is inspired by the Maneuver Control System CZ (MCS CZ) [2], developed at the University of Defense, whose calculations

J. Novotný et al. (Eds.): MESAS 2025, LNCS 16627, pp. 61–75, 2027.
https://doi.org/10.1007/978-3-032-33182-3_4

come from the Tactical Decision Support System (TDSS) [3], developed at the University of Defense in 2006.

The aim of the article is to describe and find out the relations of tactical variables, which are necessary to implement into the decision-making process, because they can influence the maneuver.

The article is focused on combat UGVs equipped with weapon stations and supporting the warfighting function "maneuver."

2 Literature Review

A number of publications deal with the issue of automation and robotization of unmanned systems, motion modeling, and obstacle avoidance. The characteristics of different types of UGVs in the world can be observed in [4–6]. These characteristics are significant for types of operations and actions. Platforms can move heavy weapons; what determines the kinetic effect. Also, other capabilities are influenced: mobility, protection, endurance, etc. The use of robotic and autonomous systems, artificial intelligence, and their implementation on the battlefield are described in [7–9]. The Ukrainian conflict catalyzed this field. Some sub-operations of unmanned systems are done automatically; nevertheless, a human dominates decision-making and key operations. The operational utilization of robotic autonomous systems is explained in [10–16]. The authors are approaching this field with respect to technical limitations but are finding the opportunities and how to reasonably support the combat as a key topic. The outcome is that tactical tasks are significantly limited. UGV in the close future will be "only" a supportive tool. The manned-unmanned teaming (MUM-T) will be a reality. The man will "authorize" kinetic effects, and autonomous fire missions are not real in the close future. In relation to this, the definition of tactics and effectiveness of the use of small units in ground unit operations and the aspect description of the decision-making process of commanders in military operations for the effective use of UGVs can be found in [17, 18]. The tactical variables are explained in [1, 19, 20].

3 Tactical Variables

The analysis and evaluation of individual tactical variables, but in relations and context, enables commanders at a tactical level to understand and visualize their role in specific tactical operations. The commanders constantly face adapting enemies, varying views of the public, and contradictory priorities of various non-military organizations in AOO [21]. Understanding the situation in the planning phase is essential, but still, the situation awareness has to be updated repeatedly and constantly during the execution phase. Every tool (unit, element, device) is a sensor, and part of them are the effectors, which can change or influence the situation.

3.1 Mission

Mission represents "a clear, concise statement of the task of the command and its purpose" [22]. The mission thus defines the tactical tasks for subordinate units and at the same time specifies the purpose of these tasks. The "5 W" rule applies when formulating the mission by specifying Who, What, When, Where and Why the unit should perform. The tactical task determines the activity to be performed and the effect to be achieved by this activity. In their expression, meaningful verbs are used, e.g., attack, destroy, divert, disrupt, seize, block, retain, clear, secure, and others [1]. In the language of algorithms, it is extremely heavy to define what the device is allowed to do and what not. The simplicity can be a solution, and it is important to orient basic or selected tasks. The MCS CZ offers an optimal maneuver route, which is not a "mission," represented by a specific task and purpose. The algorithmizing of tactical tasks is crucial for the automatization of UGVs and is not developed at an appropriate level.

3.2 Enemy

An analysis of the enemy must be aimed at identifying the basic information about their composition, activity, deployment, disposition (strengths and weaknesses), and other factors that are covered by the SALUTE acronym (Size, Activity, Location, Unit, Time, Equipment) [23] or ENVAOH (type of Enemy, Nature, Volume, Amplitude, Objects of interest, Hours-reaction times). In the light of basic information, according to SALUTE, the "mission" can be optimized, meaning routes for approaching, defining fire lines, etc. The operator has to approve the type of maneuver. The MCS CZ defines the horizontal factor of "enemy influence" as the general position of the enemy and its ability to hit its own forces. Similarly as in 3.1, for automatization, this variable has to be more developed.

3.3 Terrain and Weather

The terrain includes the natural terrain features, such as rivers, mountains, meadows, as well as artificial terrain features created by human activities, such as cities, airports, bridges, and others. Weather describes AOO's climate and it is focused on temperatures, air humidity, visibility, wind, precipitation (rain, snow) and cloud at a specific location and at a specific time. Generally, the terrain and weather directly affect the deployment of military capabilities, use of weaponry and equipment and has an impact on observation and mobility [24]. The impact of the terrain and weather on the operation of his unit, as well as on the activity of the enemy. In practice, the analysis of the military aspects of the terrain is realized through an acronym OAKOC (Observation and fields of fire, Avenues of approach, Key terrain, Obstacles, Cover and Concealment). All mentioned attributes of this tactical variable are well counted in MCS CZ and specifically influence the maneuver and observation, including microrelief [25].

3.4 Troops Available

This tactical variable factor represents the combat power of a particular unit expressed by human / device power, its moral state, its level of training and experience. Additionally, it includes the species, the number and status of equipment, ammunition and supplies. The commander shall specify the strengths and weaknesses of his unit through analysis, in relation to the particular conditions of the operation, what can cause limitations during maneuvers or select specific types of actions [26, 27]. The availability of troops is meant in MCS CZ by the Horizontal Factor of Own Units, which represents the supporting effect of friendly units in a military operation on the terrain trafficability through tasked maneuvering units [16]. The combat ratio in relation to tactical variables is covered only partially. The operations in the environment with presents of non-military elements are not covered and, for purposes of purpose of maneuver, it is not crucial, despite the fact that human decision-makers must count on it (esp. in counter-insurgency operations).

3.5 Time Available

Time available is a time-spatial aspect of the preparation and implementation of a particular operation or action. The factor of time has a different role in the planning phase and in the execution phase. The frequency of the OODA (observe-orient-decide-act) cycle has [28] to be extremely quick in the execution phase, which can partially substitute for human decision-makers. The OODA process, based on time, can be for the purpose of machine decision-making "basic-hasty", which safes time, or "advanced-deliberate", which gives outputs more detailed. In real combat, hasty planning and decisions led by intuition and drills are often.

3.6 Civil Considerations

In current operations, notably in non-conventional/irregular warfare, the host nation is a vital factor because the advantage of the conflict is that of the indigenous people. As a result, the civil aspects represent the most important tactical variable factor that requires in-depth analysis and evaluation. It concerns the consideration of the impact of civilian institutions and civilian authorities, the views and reactions of the local population, as well as the ROE (Rules of engagement) restrictions that have a complex impact on the operation and its resulting impact on the overall campaign. The possibility of successfully interacting with the external surrounding environment can be fulfilled only under the conditions of sound internal management, able to manage the surrounding external issues. It includes six areas that are labeled with the acronym ASCOPE (Areas, Structures, Capabilities, Organizations, People, and Events): [1, 28]

- Areas represent specific areas (locations) in AOO (Area of operation) where individual demographic groups live (e.g. tribal, religious, economic, political, and other).
- Structures consist of important structures (bridges, road networks, power stations, churches, mosques, hospitals, cultural monuments and others) located in the AOO. Analysis of these structures involves identifying how their location, function and facilities can support a particular operation. It has to be clearly defined which of these structures is prohibited from impacting or which of them is possible to utilize for maneuver.
- Capabilities represent the capabilities of local authorities to provide local people with key services, such as public administration, security, healthcare, etc. The analysis of this area is aimed at identifying the needs of the local population, its security, and availability of health care, education, living standards and so on. This analysis also provides the basis for identifying the causes of the crisis (conflict);

- Organizations are civilian groups or institutions deployed in the AOO, which cooperate with the local population and military units. Their goal is to provide financial or logistical support. Some organizations may come from the internal environment (local tribes, ethnic, religious, patriotic or political groups, etc.), others from external areas outside AOO (transnational corporations, GOs, NGOs, and others);
- People include the civilian population located in the AOO or Area of Interest (AI), whose activities and views may affect the operation. An important aspect of this factor is the communication channels that allow the flow of information between the local populations. These include visual signals (graffiti, posters, billboards, paintings, videos, television broadcasts, etc.) or acoustic methods of information dissemination (legal and illegal broadcasting, amplification of information from minarets or squares, religious manifestations and education);
- Events include events or aspects of public or private life, routine, cyclical, planned or spontaneous activities (celebrations, national or religious holidays, harvest celebrations, elections, civil unrest, etc.) affecting the people, the organizational activity and military operations; During the Intelligence Preparation of the Battle space (IPB), the tactical commander and his staff analyze the civil aspects from three perspectives: from the perspective of the local population, the enemy and their own forces. Its purpose is to determine the impact of the civil aspects on the course of action of its own forces and of the enemy.

4 Mathematically – Empiric Explanation

4.1 Theoretical Design

The human thinking about METT-TC analysis is based on relations, which are probable in combat. According to [29], the "background" information is desirable, but the combat deployment of troops requires context. Therefore, the authors give preference to an approach "based on clear data – searching for variations and context." This approach is in a wide range as represented by [30] in Fig. 1, but for the purpose of small unit is introduced METT-TC matrix (Fig. 2).

Having answers to questions mentioned in Fig. 2, it is possible to achieve decisions, it does not matter if done by a human or a machine. The systems with a specific level of autonomy must make decisions by themselves. Minimally, immediate decisions to fulfill the ordered mission are necessary. Then, the UGV (as a single device) or swarm of UGV's can be deployed and can significantly help. A possible solution is MUM-T, where the operator only partially controls the UGV or swarm. In this case, the MCS CZ, a "reference" software, has been utilized. The structure of the MCS CZ tactical decision support system is as follows (Fig. 3):

The structure of MCS CZ is sorted according to METT-TC:

- **Mission** is a specific activity defined with effect on the enemy or the activity of our own troops, edited by the operator.
- •**Enemy** is defined by, according to SALUTE, layered enemy forces (HF5).
- •**Terrain and** weather are represented by surface, slow go / no-go areas, as (CS1) + NO GO and SLOW GO zones (CS1,2).

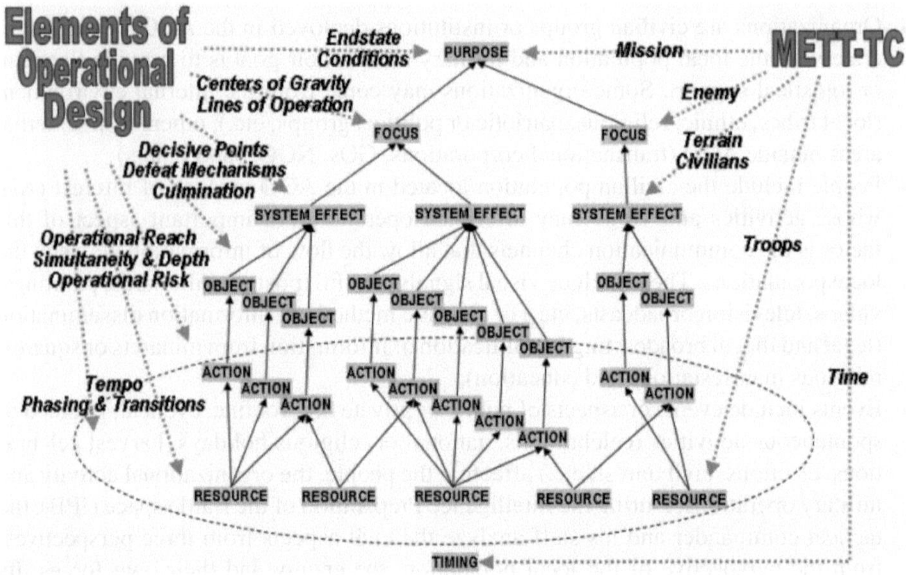

Fig. 1. Mapping of METT-TC and Elements of Operational Design onto Visualization Space [30].

Relief (VF2)
Weather (HF3)
Visibility of your own forces and visibility of the enemy according to OAKOC using geographical data from map overlay.
Cost of crossing the surface

- **Troops** are represented according to SALUTE; the player's own forces (HF4) and movements of their own forces, movements of subordinate units.
- **Time** is represented by limitation for the whole mission.
- **Civilian** consideration is represented by reduced ASCOPE, esp. buildings, infrastructure or restrictions (no-go zones).

In total, eleven types of data and overlays are counted, using the Floyd-Marshall algorithm to find an optimized route for maneuvers from the perspective of length, time and safety.

Mathematically can be the relation explained as:

$$CCS = \frac{CS_1 \cdot CS_{1.2}}{VF_2 \cdot HF_3 \cdot \min(1, HF_4 \cdot HF_5)}$$

Formula 1: Relation of METT-TC used in MCS CZ

4.2 Experiment

The methodological concept of the experiment is based on the triangular method [31], which consists of 2 parts: first is the theoretical design verified in planner MCS CZ.

	Mission	Enemy	Terrain and weather	Troops	Time	Civil consideration
Mission	x	How will be enemy impacted? What will be his reaction?	Is the terrain adequate for fulfilling the mission?	Do we have enough troops regarding to the maneuver?	Do we have enough time for planning, execution?	Regarding to civilian consideration, is the mission possible to fulfill?
Enemy	x	x	How will be the terrain utilized by enemy (according to OAKOC)	Do the combat ratio favorize own forces or enemy forces?	What are reaction times of enemy?	How influence the enemy civilian considerations?
Terrain and weather	x	x	x	How will be affected own forces by terrain and weather, according to OAKOC?	How will affect the terrain timing of actions? Will be influenced synchronization during maneuver?	How do impact terrain and weather conditions the civil sphere, according to ASCOPE? Is there impact on maneuvering units?
Troops	x	x	x	x	Do we have enough time for preparation and execution? Which steps is necessary to reduce?	How will be civil sphere impacted by activity of own forces and what are possible tactical results?
Time	x	x	x	x	x	How will tempo of operations, frequence and sequence impact civil sphere?
Civil consideration	x	x	x	x	x	x

Fig. 2 METT-TC matix (own)

The goal of the experiment is to gain the course of action of maneuver of the UGV unit, based on a specified tactical task. Then, comparing expert knowledge, discuss the advantages and disadvantages of maneuvers and recommend solutions for improvement of autonomous or semiautonomous planning.

Secondly, field tests are conducted, where the results from MCS CZ, and through this the idea of theoretical design is verified.

The results of the planned COA and field tests have been validated by an independent committee of 3 experts in the field of tactics.

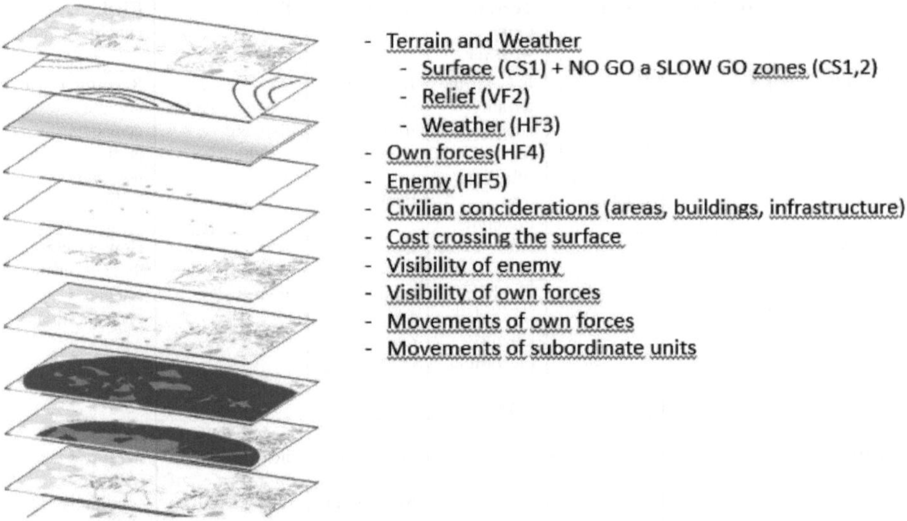

Fig. 3. Overlay structure

Basic Data-Set for Experiment, According to METT-TC Acronym Planned and Tested in MCS CZ

Mission:

Who: UGV company (9 UGVs)

What: attack to seize OBJ. 1

Where: OBJ.1 — rural agricultural complex

When: TBD (no limitations)

Why: allow an attack on OBJ. 2 (approx. 800 m north)

Enemy:

Size – infantry platoon

Activity -defending area

Location – OBJ-1, OBJ-2

Unit – 3 infantry squads

Time – not determined

Equipment – assault rifles, 3 x machine guns, 3x antitank weapons

Terrain and weather:

Slow downhill terrain, dry surface, crops 30 cm tall, no significant barriers and obstacles, 20 dgr of Celius, no rain, sunny. OBJ-1 is a rural area consisting of buildings.

Troops:

Size – UGV company (9 vehicles)

Activity -attack to seize

Location – OBJ.1, OBJ. 2

Unit – UGV squadron, 5 UGV companies

Time – not determined

Equipment – wheeled moderate type of UGV's and 12.7 mm machinegun assault rifles

Civil considerations:

No significant object or presence of civilians. Buildings in OBJ 1 and OBJ 2 (Figs. 4, 5, 6, 7).

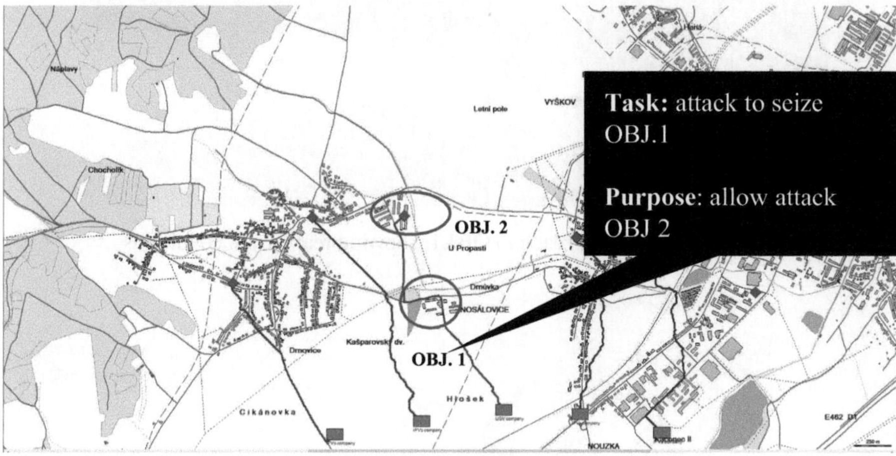

Fig. 4. Mission of UGV unit

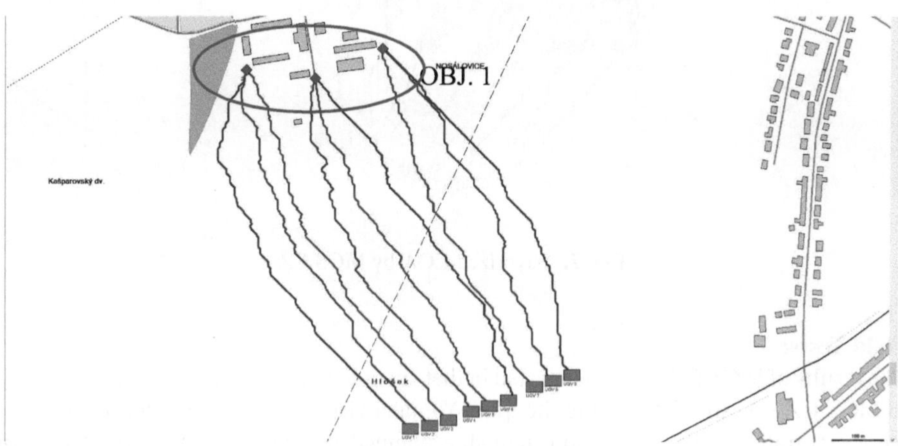

Fig. 5. Detail of mission of UGV unit

Result no.1 (of the planned COA in MCS CZ): the maneuver has been planned as a frontal attack, where the terrain enables continuous movement. The basic formation is the line. The movement lasts approx. 7 min. All the criteria have been respected. Results analyzed and decomposed fit with the basic design, according to chapter 4.1 and the doctrinal apparat (Fig. 8).

Fig. 6. Avenue of approach to OBJ.1, showing real terrain conditions

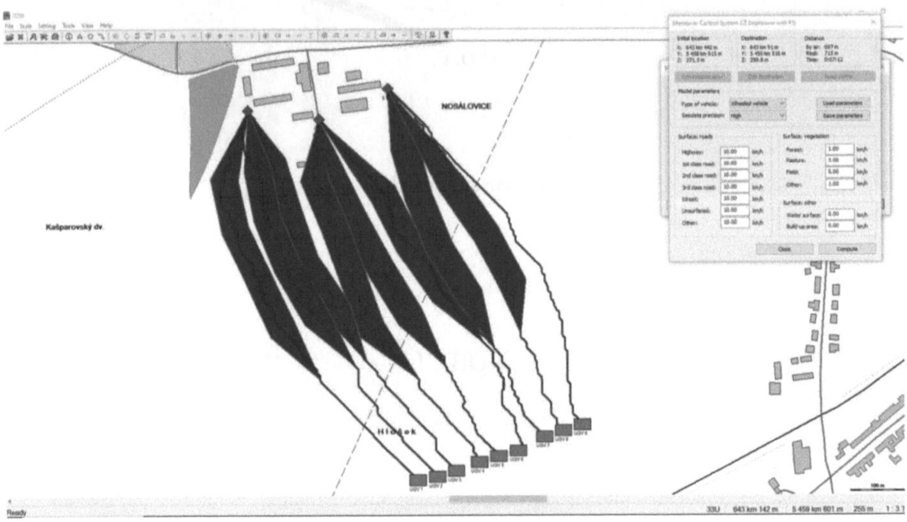

Fig. 7. Favorized COA by MCS CZ

Field Tests:
The results of MCS CZ have been tested in that specific terrain. The maneuver according to MCS CZ was simulated using the quad Yamaha Grizzly 450. The criteria compared were real trafficability, ability to establish a planned formation, keeping the tempo of maneuver, visibility of the object.

The committee consisting of authors independently checked criteria with the result of 91.6% of matches, which means that the results are acceptable and most likely probable, if the conditions according to METT-TC were optimal and enemy would not do any kind of dynamic maneuver.

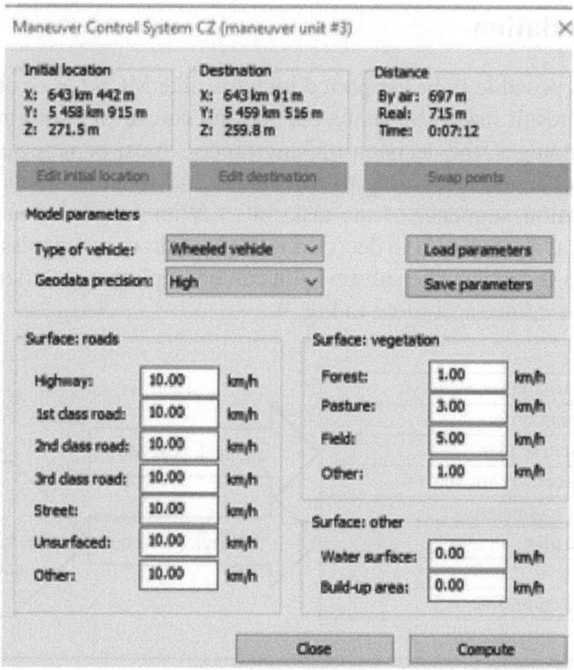

Fig. 8. Basic data about COA maneuver (in Fig. 7 right-upper corner)

4.3 Discussion

Based on personal presence in the terrain and using indicative-empiric knowledge [32], can be presented following comment:

- The mission is adequate to other tactical variables.
- The enemy will probably use movement and hiding in the object. It means, the formation of UGV must be modified (for. ex. L- shape), using flanking and not continuous movement.
- The time in reaction of enemy will be longer, can be approx. between 15–30 min, depending on results of fire.
- Some vehicles will be lost, approx. 30–50% of them.
- The consumption of ammo will be crucial. In case of reaching 30% level is necessary to decide, if continue or stop the maneuver.
- Significant role will play microrelief, esp. in agricultural surface. Every week can be different, during spring and summertime. The terrain is gamechanger for this type of operation and vehicles.
- The algorithm of reactions of enemy is not in-counted and can be only predicted.
- The civilian considerations are not in-counted, but for kinetic operation this factor is minor.
- The advantage of MCS CZ or similar systems is in short time prepared COAs, which can be accepted or slightly modified, what saves time. The intended solution can be re-counted with different inputs, when necessary.

5 Recommendation

For planning it is possible to be supported by tools, like MCS CZ or other for. ex. [33, 34] or [35]. The result has to be analyzed, and the course of action must be revised. If there are any changes, the decision-making process must be repeated and the phase of creating plan changed, according to METT-TC and specific inputs (for ex. axis of movement, formation, sequence of sub-tasks etc..). With support of autonomy, can this process last several minutes. If the decision is made without reconnaissance, the risk of changing the plan is higher. The sub-revision can be implemented after step 3 and 6 of Troop leading procedure, according to Fig. 9.

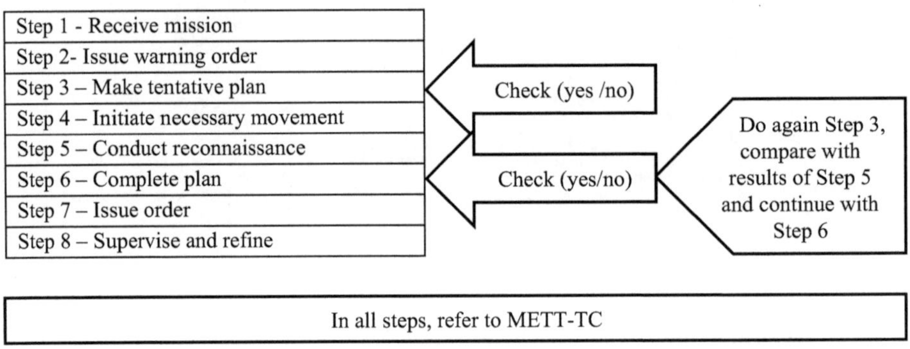

Fig. 9. Recommended revisions during TLP

From a practical point of view, contingency plans have to be prepared for the unit. The most probable complication is trafficability, esp. microrelief and identification of the enemy. It has to solve the problem of "friendly fire", where units without identifiers can be hit. It has to be possible to take over control by a human operator. Possible unpredictable situations can be solved by man more quickly, then automatically by machine.

For development, MCS CZ or a similar type of software, it is necessary to prepare a set of algorithms, following the METT-TC and the OODA loop at very quick frequency. All elements of these algorithms have to work as complex, not separately. The sensors and informational inputs are the key.

6 Conclusion

The maneuverability of a UGV unit is crucial ability to effectively use these devices, not only as combat vehicles, or also as supportive vehicles. The operations and maneuvers have to be planned at some level of latitude, having the opportunity to act according to the situation. Therefore, the set of algorithms, sensors and information systems play a crucial role.

The authors described a proven sequence of overall analyzing a mission, which has to be incorporated into modeling programs, who supports decisions or, better, makes decisions automatically. Automatic decisions have to be made at the level of a single device, which follows the mission (5 W's).

The experiment reproduced the general approach, how this software works and where is the difference is between deciding of man and a machine. As the biggest advantage is necessary to mention the quickly offered COA, respecting time, safety, length and other attributes in-counted in **Formula 1**. For the next research and development, the MCS CZ is planned to be utilized as supporting software for planning the maneuvers of combat units in experimental exercise MORAVIAN LANCE 2026. Based on this study and experiment, the recommendations have been in-traduced: making comparisons of courses of action more often and going deeply into detail, have been presented practical insights and have been introduced recommendations for development the architecture of software.

References

1. Hrnčiar, Michal. "Tactical variables – a tool for Mission analysis" International Conference Knowledge-Based Organization, vol. 25, no. 1, Sciendo, 2019, pp. 86–90. https://doi.org/10.2478/kbo-2019-0014
2. Nohel, J., Flasar, Z.: Maneuver control system CZ. In: Mazal, J., Fagiolini, A., Vasik, P. (eds.) Modeling and Simulation for Autonomous Systems. MESAS 2019. Lecture Notes in Computer Science, vol. 11995, pp. 379–388. Springer, Switzerland, Cham (2020). https://doi.org/10.1007/978-3-030-43890-6_31. ISBN 978-3-030-43889-0
3. Stodola, P., Mazal, J.: Tactical decision support system to aid commanders in their decision-making. In: Hodicky, J. (ed.) MESAS 2016. LNCS, vol. 9991, pp. 396–406. Springer, Cham (2016). https://doi.org/10.1007/978-3-319-47605-6_32. ISBN 978-3-319-47605-6
4. The Buzz. [Top 10 Unmanned Ground Combat Vehicles (UGCVs), Top Military Robots in the World (2019)] In: YouTube [online]. November 23, (2019).
5. Top 10 military robots and unmanned ground vehicles in the world. RoboticsBiz (2020). https://roboticsbiz.com/top-10-military-robots-and-unmanned-ground-vehiclesin-the-world/
6. Top 10 best military robots in the world, Auto journalism, Jim Carrey (2021). https://autojournalism.com/top-10-best-military-robots-in-the-world/
7. Feickert, A., Kapp, L., Elsea, J. K., Harris, L. A.: U.S. Ground Forces Robotics and Autonomous Systems (RAS) and Artificial Intelligence (AI): Considerations for Congress, Washington D.C. (2018), pp. 47. https://digital.library.unt.edu/ark:/67531/metadc1442984/m1/.
8. Bērziņa, I., et al.: Digital Infantry Battlefield Solution, Research and Innovation, Part III, Milrem Robotics, Tallinn, Estonia, pp. 120. (2019). ISBN 978-9934-567-37-7,
9. Andžāns, M., et al.: Digital infantry battlefield solution, introduction to ground robo
10. Braun, W.G., Nossal, K.R., Hlatky, S.: Robotics and military operations. In: Kingston Conference on International Security. U.S, p. 77. Army War College, New York (2018). https://doi.org/10.1117/12.720422. ISBN 1-58487-780-4.
11. Ivan, J., Potužák, J., Šotnar, J.: Dělostřelecká rekognoskace pro zabezpečení činnosti autonomních zbraňových systémů a základní požadavky na rekognoskační jednotky. Vojenské rozhledy. 2019, 28 (4), pp. 063–077. ISSN 1210–3292 (print), pp. 2336–2995 (on-line). Available at: www.vojenskerozhledy.cz. https://doi.org/10.3849/2336-2995.28.2019.04.063-077
12. Tilenni, G.: Unmanned Ground Vehicles for Combat Support. In: European Security & Defence, pp. 74–77. Mittler Report Verlag, Bonn (2019) ISSN 1617-7983. https://eurosd.com/2019/11/articles/15191/unmanned-ground-vehicles-for-comba
13. Hrdinka, J., Nohel, J., Zezula, J., Mazal, J.: Možnosti podpory činnosti pěších jednotek bojovými bezosádkovými prostředky za útoku. Vojenské rozhledy. **1**, 120–135. ISSN 1210-3292. (2025). https://doi.org/10.3849/2336-2995.34.2025.01.120-135

14. Zahradníček, P., Zezula, J.: Basic statement to development and implementation of unmanned systems into ground forces units. Int. Electron. Sci. Pract. J. Way Sci. **6**(2), 107–112 (2023) ISSN 2664-4819.
15. Nohel, J., SRB, D., Hrdinka, J., Hrnčiar, M. Pozemní robotické systémy jako ochrana vnějšího perimetru míst velení. Vojenské rozhledy. ISSN 1210-3292 (2025)
16. Nohel, J., Stodola, P., Flasar, Z., Křišťálová, D., Zahradníček, P., Rak, L.: Swarm Maneuver of Combat UGVs on the Future Digital Battlefield. In: Modelling and Simulation for Autonomous Systems MESAS 2022, vol. 13866, pp. 209–230. ISSN 0302-9743. ISBN 978-3-031-31267-0. Springer, Cham (2023). https://doi.org/10.1007/978-3-031-31268-7_12
17. Zahradnicek, P., Rak, L.: Combat UGV: The Challenge of Their Implementation in Combat Units. In: International Conference Knowledge-Based Organization, vol. 27, pp. 105–109 (2021). https://doi.org/10.2478/kbo-2021-009638
18. Rak, L., Zahranicek, P., Polach, M.: The effectiveness of infantry squad combat and pre-combat formations for warfighting International Conference Knowledge-Based Organization, 27, 1, 2021, pp. 106–111.https://doi.org/10.2478/kbo-2021-0017
19. Thomas M. Cook, Dennis K. Leedom, Jock O. Giynovicki, Michael G. Golden: Cognitive representations of battlespace complexity: Six fundamental variables of combat. PsycEXTRA Dataset, January (2000). https://doi.org/10.1037/e437812006-001.
20. Higuchi, Shunsaku: Operational Art and Tactics of the United States Army. 10 (2021). Https://www.nids.mod.go.jp/english/publication/briefing/pdf/2021/briefing_e202106.pdf.
21. Wesselényi, J., Kompan, J.: Miesto a úlohy medzinárodného kurzu štábnych dôstojníkov (ISOC) v rámci kariérneho a odborného vzdelávania v OS SR a NATO (in Slovak). Vojenské reflexie. ISSN 1336-9202. **13**(1/2018), 44–55 (2018)
22. STANAG 3680 AAP-6 NATO Glossary of Terms and Definitions. Edition (2017)
23. Hrnčiar, M. Možnosti zvýšenia efektívnosti operácií proti povstaniu (in Slovak). [Dissertation Thesis]. Liptovský Mikuláš, Slovak Republic (2017)
24. Hrnčiar, M.: The counterinsurgency operating environment. In: The 24th International Conference. The Knowledge-Based Organization: Conference Proceedings 1. Management and Military Sciences. ISBN 978-973-153-325-4,, pp. 87–92, Sibiu, Romania (2018)
25. Křišťálová, D., Túró, T., Nohel, J., Rybanský, M., Zezula, J., Hütter, M.: Modelling and simulation of microrelief impact on ground path extension. In: Mazal, J., et al. (eds.) Modelling and Simulation for Autonomous Systems (MESAS 2021), vol. 13207, pp. 93–112. ISSN 0302-9743. ISBN 978-3-030-98259-1. Springer International Publishing Ag, Cham (2022). https://doi.org/10.1007/978-3-030-98260-7_6
26. Varecha, J.: Možný pohľad na parameter bojového potenciálu (in Slovak). In: National and International Security 2016: Proceedings of 7 Th International Scientific Conference. ISBN 978-80-8040-534-2, pp. 569–577, Liptovský Mikuláš, Slovak Republic (2016)
27. Kress, M., Talmor, I.: A new look at the 3:1 rule of combat through Markov stochastic Lanchester models. J. Oper. Res. Soc. **50**(7), 733–744 (1999). https://doi.org/10.1057/palgrave.jors.2600758
28. Jeffrey N. Rule, and Army War College (U.S.): A Symbiotic Relationship: The OODA Loop, Intuition, and Strategic Thought (2013)
29. Ulicny, Brian, Christopher J. Matheus, Gerald Powell, Robert Dionne, Mitch Kokar: Representability of METT-TC Factors in JC3IEDM (2007)
30. Dennis K. Leedom, et al.: Cognitive Task Analysis of the Battalion Level Visualization Process. PsycEXTRA Dataset (2007). https://doi.org/10.1037/e587402011-001.
31. Noble, H., Heale, R.: Triangulation in research, with examples. Evid Based Nurs. **22**, 67–68 (2019). https://doi.org/10.1136/ebnurs-2019-103145
32. Douven, I., Verbrugge, S.: Indicatives, concessives, and evidential support. Think. Reason. **18**, 480–499 (2012). https://doi.org/10.1080/13546783.2012.716009

33. Palasiewicz, T., Rolenec, O., Lacinová, V., Bilina, M.: A simulation-based analysis for optimal placement of anti-tank obstacles in armored wearfare. The Journal of Defense Modeling and Simulation: Applications, Methodology, Technology (2025). https://doi.org/10.1177/15485129251339485
34. Nohel, J., Hradský, L., Flasar, Z., Zahradníček, P., Kristalova, D.: Utilizing the maneuver control system CZ in the course of Wargaming modelling and simulation. In: Lecture Notes in Computer Science, pp. 357–373. Springer International Publishing, Cham (2022)
35. Martin, G., Schamburg, J., Kwinn, M.J.: Acquisition-based simulation. In: Proceedings of the Winter Simulation Conference, pp. 1213–1219. IEEE (2005)

Hybrid Warfare in the Electromagnetic Domain: Modelling, Detection and Legal Assessment of State-Financed GNSS Spoofing Campaigns Targeting Autonomous Systems in Europe (2015–2025)

Danisa Jokanovich[1(✉)], Amna Adnan[2], Antonio Carlo[3], Cláudia Faria[4], Maria Paula Gomez Hernandez[5], Anh T. Truong[6], Rayen Laabidi[7], and Luca Brocca[8]

[1] Universidad Abierta Interamericana, Buenos Aires, Argentina
djokanovich@gmail.com
[2] University of Calgary, Calgary, Canada
[3] Tallinn University of Technology, Tallinn, Estonia
[4] University of Minho, Braga, Portugal
[5] Universidad Argentina de la Empresa, Buenos Aires, Argentina
[6] University of Northampton, Northampton, UK
[7] Sorbonne Université, Paris, France
[8] Katholieke Universiteit Leuven, Leuven, Belgium

Abstract. Global Navigation Satellite Systems (GNSS) are central to positioning, navigation and timing services used by civil infrastructure, autonomous systems and military platforms. This paper examines GNSS spoofing and jamming as instruments of hybrid warfare in Europe between 2015 and 2025, connecting geopolitical patterns with technical mechanisms, operational consequences and legal accountability gaps. It analyses attack modalities, impacts on autonomous systems, and layered prevention, detection, containment and mitigation strategies, including signal authentication, multi-constellation receiver design, INS/GNSS sensor fusion, Kalman innovation monitoring, physical signal analysis and spectrum-level monitoring. The paper argues that GNSS interference is not only an engineering problem but also a governance and human-rights challenge because electromagnetic manipulation can affect safety, mobility, privacy and trust in automated decision-making.

Keywords: GNSS spoofing · GNSS jamming · hybrid warfare · autonomous systems · electromagnetic warfare · Kalman filtering · international law

J. Novotný et al. (Eds.): MESAS 2025, LNCS 16627, pp. 76–99, 2027.
https://doi.org/10.1007/978-3-032-33182-3_5

Glossary

Electromagnetic Warfare (EW): Military action that exploits electromagnetic energy to provide situational awareness and create offensive and defensive effects.

Cyber Warfare: An armed conflict conducted in whole or in part by cyber means, including cyber attack, cyber defence and cyber enabling actions, conducted to deny an opposing force the effective use of cyberspace systems and weapons.

Information Warfare (IW): The battlespace use and management of information and communication technology in pursuit of a competitive advantage over an opponent.

Information-Psychological Warfare (IPW): The deliberate use of information and communication tools to influence, manipulate or undermine the perceptions, emotions and decision-making of target audiences during peace or war.

1 Introduction

Global Navigation Satellite Systems (GNSS) have become a fundamental tool for positioning, navigation, and timing (PNT) services in both civilian and military domains. From synchronising power grids to the navigation of autonomous vehicles, a vast number of critical infrastructures depend on GNSS signals such as the Global Positioning System (GPS), Galileo, Global'naya Navigatsionnaya Sputnikovaya Sistema (GLONASS), or BeiDou. This increasing reliance means that any intentional or accidental interference in these signals can have serious consequences for the safety and operation of autonomous systems and essential infrastructure.

There are two main categories of GNSS interference attacks: jamming, which suppresses the legitimate signal through noise, and spoofing, which deceives the receiver by generating counterfeit navigation data. Whereas jamming creates a denial-of-service condition by saturating the target's receiver bandwidth, spoofing manipulates the navigation solution while maintaining apparent signal continuity. Both techniques have evolved into standard tools within modern electronic warfare arsenals and are now routinely employed in hybrid satellite-interference campaigns operating below the threshold of open conflict. Particularly concerning is the rise of so-called smart or subtle spoofing, which does not induce total signal loss but instead introduces controlled errors into the position or timing solution. In such cases, the affected platform may continue to operate normally while unknowingly using false information, potentially leading to hazardous decision-making. This makes early detection and mitigation significantly more challenging, especially for autonomous systems whose situational awareness depends heavily on GNSS inputs. In recent years, the threat landscape has intensified. A substantial increase in users reporting position errors of hundreds of kilometres has been documented, especially in sensitive regions such as the

Baltic Sea, the Black Sea, and parts of the Middle East. These deliberately engineered "GNSS-denied zones" pose a serious operational hazard for autonomous platforms—unmanned aerial systems, surface drones, driverless ground vehicles, and robotic systems—which require stable and uninterrupted PNT services to function safely. Although the primary scope of this paper focuses on GNSS interference campaigns between 2015 and 2025, it is important to highlight that such incidents have continued to escalate beyond this period. A notable example occurred in early 2024, when the aircraft carrying the President of the European Commission, Ursula von der Leyen, experienced significant GNSS degradation while approaching the Baltic region. The flight crew were forced to transition to inertial and ground-based navigation as jamming in the area rendered GPS unreliable. While this episode falls outside the core timeframe of our analysis, its political relevance and proximity to European airspace demonstrate vividly how GNSS interference has evolved into a strategic signalling tool, capable of affecting even high-level governmental transport. Including this reference here underscores the urgency and contemporary relevance of the threat discussed throughout this study. This paper examines the full lifecycle of GNSS interference as a hybrid threat—from its geopolitical origins and technical operation to its operational, legal, and human consequences. It analyses the progression of interference and spoofing campaigns across Europe, assesses the mechanisms through which these actions degrade autonomous and critical systems, and evaluates viable technical and regulatory responses across three key phases: prevention, detection, and mitigation. As will be explored, malicious actors can disrupt GNSS using a broad spectrum of technologies ranging from commercial off-the-shelf devices to military-grade jamming and spoofing platforms deployed from land, sea, air, and even space. Accordingly, this paper evaluates technical strategies capable of preventing, detecting, containing, and mitigating these attacks in the context of autonomous systems. Finally, the paper investigates how GNSS interference campaigns across Europe between 2015 and

2 Align with Broader Geopolitical Developments, and How These Operations Have Produced Tangible

Implications for human rights and international norms. By analysing the legal and regulatory gaps surrounding these actions, the study aims to expose the underlying accountability challenges and propose a framework to address the strategic, technical, and ethical dimensions of hybrid electromagnetic threats.

3 Key Geopolitical Events, Legal Gaps and Human Rights

Interference (2015–2025) Between 2015 and 2025, incidents of GNSS spoofing and jamming across Europe have followed a discernible pattern aligned with geopolitical developments. Far from being isolated technical anomalies, these electromagnetic operations are integral to broader hybrid strategies. They serve to send strategic signals, undermine trust in NATO-aligned critical infrastructure, and shift the operational balance in contested areas without the need for open armed conflict. Analysis of the incidents reveals three primary geographical clusters where GNSS interference has been recurrent:

- Northeastern Europe, particularly the Baltic Sea region, Finland, and Sweden.
- The Black Sea and Eastern Mediterranean basins, including maritime choke points.
- Active conflict zones, such as Ukraine and Syria. Each cluster corresponds to specific strategic developments. In Northeastern Europe, the accession of Finland (2023) and Sweden (2024) to NATO was followed by increased electromagnetic interference, notably targeting civil aviation. This pattern indicates a deliberate attempt by offensive state actors to signal their opposition to NATO expansion and demonstrate their capacity to degrade regional stability. In the Black Sea basin, mass spoofing campaigns between 2016 and 2018 targeted civilian maritime navigation near Russian installations, disrupting shipping lanes and asserting control over strategic waters through non-kinetic means. Similarly, the 2019 spoofing incident affecting Ben Gurion Airport occurred amid heightened tensions in Syria, likely serving as a live test of electromagnetic disruption in a multiparty conflict environment. The timing of these operations is not coincidental. For instance, during NATO's Trident Juncture 2018—the largest alliance mobilisation since the Cold War—multiple GNSS jamming incidents were documented, affecting both military and civilian airspace. Likewise, during the 2022–2023 escalation in Ukraine, platforms such as Tirada-2S and Zhitel, alongside malware like AcidRain, were deployed to degrade drone navigation and disrupt dual-use satellite communications (e.g., Starlink). These campaigns exhibit not only advanced technical capabilities but also strategic intent to project power through control of the electromagnetic spectrum, directly impacting civilian infrastructure during high-profile international events. While the International Telecommunication Union (ITU) Constitution and Radio Regulations (Articles 45, 15.1, and 15.28) formally prohibit harmful interference between states, enforcement mechanisms remain weak. The ITU relies primarily on technical coordination rather than punitive measures. As a result, even severe violations—such as the GNSS disruption that affected over 1,600 commercial flights across the Baltic region—have led to no substantive legal consequences for the responsible states. This institutional weakness is compounded by the ambiguity of international law regarding electronic warfare activities. GNSS interference rarely meets the threshold of "use of force" under Article 2(4) of the UN Charter, nor does it clearly qualify as an "armed attack" under Article 51. It also remains ambiguously placed within the definition of "aggression" provided by UNGA Resolution 3314. This legal grey zone enables state actors to deny involvement or reframe operations as technical anomalies or defensive tests. Furthermore, fragmentation across legal regimes—including space

law, cyber law, telecommunications, and human rights law—has produced a disjointed governance structure. For example, while the Outer Space Treaty holds states accountable for national activities (Article VI), it does not explicitly cover the manipulation of GNSS signals with civilian consequences. This lack of doctrinal integration hampers effective legal responses. The civilian impacts of GNSS interference extend beyond technical disruption, directly infringing upon internationally recognised human rights. Spoofing and jamming campaigns have affected:

- The right to privacy, by manipulating location data in mobile applications and navigation sys- tems without consent.
- The right to life and physical security, through interference with aviation safety, medical evacuations, and humanitarian drone operations.
- The right to freedom of movement and access to services, by disrupting civilian transport networks and maritime navigation. Despite legal protections under instruments such as the ICCPR and ECHR, victims lack access to effective accountability mechanisms. Attribution remains difficult, and existing legal regimes do not adequately cover hybrid electromagnetic operations targeting civilians. The absence of dedicated enforcement mechanisms reinforces a permissive environment where the infringement of fundamental rights can occur without remedy. Collectively, these legal and institutional gaps facilitate the use of GNSS spoofing and jamming as low-cost, high-impact tools of hybrid warfare—tactically precise, politically deniable, and legally opaque.

4 Types of GNSS Attacks and Their Technical Operation

As previously described, attacks against GNSS can be classified into two main modalities: signal inhibition (jamming), where the attacker blocks or degrades satellite signals, and signal spoofing, where the receiver is deceived with false signals. Below, the technical functioning of each type is explained, with particular emphasis on spoofing as it is the main focus of this study. Known cases and employed tools are also described to understand how these attacks operate in practice.

4.1 GNSS Signal Inhibition (Jamming)

Jamming consists of transmitting radio frequency signals of sufficient power in the GNSS signal band (around 1.2–1.6 GHz) to blind or stun the receiver. Since satellite signals reach Earth at extremely low power levels (around -130 dBm), a nearby low-power terrestrial transmitter can raise the noise floor above the receiver detection threshold, blocking reception. Simply put, the attacker "shouts" louder than the satellites, preventing the receiver from acquiring valid navigation data. Real examples: Numerous GNSS jamming incidents have been documented globally. For example, during NATO military exercises in Scandinavia, Norway and Finland reported that GPS signals were blocked by electronic warfare equipment, affecting even civil aviation in 2018. It is also common for truck drivers or individuals (illegal in most countries) to use small jammers to evade GPS trackers; these devices, costing a few hundred euros, can cause micro GPS blackouts on highways. The consequences of jamming are immediate and evident: the GNSS receiver typically shows signal loss or a drastic drop in precision. If an autonomous vehicle relies solely on GNSS, it could completely lose its navigational capability. However, since the failure is relatively abrupt due to the cessation of position updates, many systems have degraded modes prepared in case of GPS failure. In summary, although jamming can be disruptive, it is easier to detect (due to total signal loss) and counter (using anti-jam antennas, filters, or contingency plans) than spoofing, as elaborated in the following sections.

4.2 GNSS Signal Spoofing

GNSS spoofing is a more insidious form of interference, in which the attacker emits false signals that mimic genuine satellite signals with the aim of deceiving the receiver into computing erroneous position, velocity, or time data. Unlike jamming, spoofing does not seek to disable the receiver but to subtly deceive it by providing plausible yet manipulated navigation data. According to the technical literature, "GNSS spoofing is the deliberate transmission of false satellite signals with the intention of inducing the receiver to compute incorrect PNT data." In other words, the attacker impersonates the satellites by "spoofing" their signals.

5 Technical Basis of Spoofing

To understand spoofing from a technical perspective, it is helpful to review how a GNSS receiver determines its position. Satellites transmit pseudo-random noise (PRN) code sequences and navigation messages that allow the receiver to measure propagation times and calculate pseudoranges. In simplified terms, the apparent distance ρi from the receiver to satellite i is given by:

ρi = c (trx - ttxi) + d + Ii + Ti + . . . (1) where c is the speed of light, ttxi is the transmission time at the satellite (contained in the GNSS message), trx is the reception time on the receiver's internal clock, d is the receiver clock bias (unknown), and Ii and Ti represent ionospheric and tropospheric delays, among other factors. Solving the equations for at least four satellites, the receiver computes its position (x, y, z) and a correction for its clock. A spoofing attacker transmits signals with PRN codes identical to those of genuine satellites, but with falsified transmission times (t'txi) or even altered navigation messages, so that the calculated pseudoranges ρ'i lead to a solution (x', y', z') desired by the attacker instead of the true position. In essence, the spoofer deceives the receiver by modifying the time terms in the received signal. For example, if it introduces a common additional delay Δt in all signals, the receiver will interpret itself as being further from all satellites than it actually is, which mainly affects the clock bias term (placing itself in nearly the same location but believing its clock is ahead). However, if it introduces unequal delays per satellite (or alters orbital data in the messages), the position calculation can result in completely different coordinates. Thus, spoofing can artificially shift the perceived position or synchronised time of the receiver. Achieving such deception requires overcoming several technical challenges. First, the spoofer must capture the receiver's attention: the fake signals must arrive with sufficient power to overpower the authentic signals at the receiver input. This often involves initially transmitting a nearly identical signal.

To the real one (same information and phase synchronisation) and then gradually deviating it (e.g., introducing a slowly increasing delay) to drag the receiver away from the genuine signal without triggering alarms. This "carry-off" technique avoids abrupt changes that would be more easily detectable. Second, the spoofer must consistently emulate multiple satellites simultaneously. If only one satellite is spoofed while the rest are real, a receiver with integrity checks will detect the inconsistency. Therefore, in a sophisticated attack, the adversary generates a virtual constellation of coherent fake satellites (often initially aligned with the real one, then diverging). This can be achieved using synchronised multi-frequency transmitters or a single transmitter rapidly alternating between simulated satellite signals. A related variant is meaconing, in which the adversary simply captures real GNSS signals and re- transmits them with delay. Meaconing is simpler (it does not require knowledge or generation of the message content, just repeating what is received), but it typically introduces the same delay to all signals. As mentioned, a common delay mainly affects the receiver's calculated time rather than position, which is why meaconing is typically used for time synchronisation attacks rather than position spoofing. In any case, the distinction is subtle: meaconing can be considered a subset of spoofing (passive spoofing), whereas sophisticated spoofing implies the active generation of fake signals ex nihilo.

5.1 Tools and Documented Cases of Spoofing Attacks

Traditionally, generating fake GNSS signals required specialised (and costly) equipment such as GPS simulators used in laboratories. However, for over a decade it has been known that it is possible to build a portable and inexpensive GPS spoofer using commercial components. In 2008, researchers demonstrated a prototype for only $2500 USD, based on software-defined radio (SDR). Today, there are open-source tools and accessible hardware that facilitate these attacks. For example, the GPS-SDR-SIM project allows the generation of pre-recorded GPS L1 signals (IQ data) from a desired trajectory and time; these signals can then be emitted using popular SDR platforms such as HackRF, bladeRF, ADALM-Pluto or USRP. In this way, an attacker with moderate knowledge can programme a spoofing scenario (e.g., setting a false location) and broadcast it with an SDR, causing nearby receivers to compute the spoofed position. Other GNSS simulation suites (e.g., Spirent GSS, Safran Skydel), legally used for receiver testing, could be repurposed for malicious intent. In summary, spoofing tools have been democratised, reducing the barrier of entry for hostile actors. Academic demonstrations: In 2012, a team from the University of Texas at Austin successfully hijacked a civilian unmanned aerial vehicle (UAV) using GPS spoofing, redirecting its path without system detection. That same year, Professor Todd Humphreys testified before the U.S. Congress about UAV vulnerabilities to such attacks. In 2013, the same group used spoofing to cause an 80-metre yacht in the Mediterranean to change course without the captain noticing, demonstrating the potential to deceive maritime navigation systems. Maritime transport incidents: In 2017, approximately 20 ships navigating the Black Sea reported erroneous GPS coordinates showing them at an inland airport—an early large-scale spoofing case un- officially attributed to Russian equipment. Since then, spoofing reports have become common in ports and coastal zones: for example, near the Kremlin in Moscow, satellite receivers often indicate false locations—a deliberate mechanism to protect sensitive areas by creating adulterated GNSS "bubbles." Civil aviation: From 2019 to 2023, commercial pilots in regions such as the Middle East reported interruptions and anomalous GPS behaviour. An IEEE Spectrum article in 2024 revealed that airliners on certain routes were being misdirected by spoofed GNSS data, increasing pilot workload and posing a safety risk. The International Civil Aviation Organization (ICAO) has acknowledged the issue; in fact, Galileo OSNMA authentication is being standardised for future aviation use as a preventive measure. Critical infrastructure: Beyond transport, time spoofing attacks have been considered against power grids (to be detailed in later sections). There is also suspicion that some financial and telecommunications systems have experienced attempts to manipulate timing via false GNSS signals. UN agency reports from 2023 warned of a global increase in GNSS interference threatening civil aviation, maritime safety, and telecommunications networks. In all these cases, a common factor is that spoofing can go unnoticed by users or systems: unlike jamming, GNSS devices typically continue to deliver data—albeit incorrect. Without countermeasures, a standard civil receiver has no way of distinguishing fake signals from legitimate ones. This underscores the need to develop robust strategies for spoofing prevention, detection, and mitigation.

6 Impact on Autonomous Systems

Autonomous systems—self-driving vehicles, drones, industrial or military robots, and similar platforms—are particularly vulnerable to GNSS attacks due to their heavy reliance on satellite navigation to situate themselves within the physical environment. By definition, an autonomous system must make decisions and update its internal state without continuous human supervision, a process that frequently depends on external sensors such as GPS for determining position and time. This heavy reliance on GNSS can be exploited by adversaries to induce unsafe behaviour or even assume control of the platform. Many autonomous systems incorporate GNSS as a core component of their navigation stack. For instance, civilian drones employ GPS to maintain stability during hovering, follow pre-programmed routes, and return to their take-off coordinates. Should an attacker spoof the GPS signal to suggest the drone is slightly offset from its true position, the flight controller may compensate for this perceived error by physically shifting the drone—an example of direct spoofing. In more extreme scenarios, the drone may veer kilometres off its intended course without detection, as demonstrated by the University of Texas at Austin, where researchers successfully manipulated a UAV's trajectory using false GPS signals. In military contexts, this technique could hypothetically be used to "capture" hostile drones by luring them to land within controlled territory, a tactic that Iran claimed to have employed in 2011 against a U.S. reconnaissance drone—although the details remain unverified. In the case of ground-based autonomous vehicles—robotic cars, automated buses, and similar—the threat posed by GNSS attacks is more nuanced but equally real. A typical autonomous vehicle fuses data from multiple sensors (e.g., LIDAR, cameras, odometry, and HD maps) in addition to GNSS. Therefore, a GPS error may not immediately result in a crash, thanks to this sensory redundancy. However, it could nonetheless impact the vehicle's global navigation subsystem, causing it to believe it is located on a different street or skewing its route-planning module. Consider, for example, an autonomous taxi whose GPS indicates a position 50 m off the road; the navigation software might recalculate an unnecessary detour or enter a state of uncertainty, thereby degrading service quality. In operational contexts where GPS is the principal navigational reference, a false signal could lead the vehicle outside its safe route. Researchers have warned that as driverless cars become more widespread, securing GPS signals is essential, noting that "hijacking the geolocation capability of an autonomous vehicle could prove extremely dangerous." In short, a successful spoofing attack could misdirect a vehicle—potentially into a trap—without the knowledge of its occupants or controllers until it is too late. Timing represents another critical dimension. Many distributed autonomous systems—robot fleets, coordinated sensor networks, etc.—require precise synchronisation, often derived from GNSS. A spoofing attack that introduces time bias could desynchronise the actions of autonomous agents. Cooperative vehicles, for example, may lose alignment in their coordinated manoeuvres. Likewise, intelligent infrastructures—traffic lights, V2X signalling—synchronised via GPS could fall out of phase, causing systemic disorder in autonomous traffic management. In summary, GNSS attacks can erode the reliability and safety of autonomous systems in multiple ways: by corrupting navigation, disrupting synchronisation, or introducing uncertainty into control algorithms. Given that autonomy removes direct human oversight, it is imperative to equip these systems with robust prevention and detection mechanisms against GNSS interference.

7 GNSS Interference Prevention Strategies

As reliance on satellite-based PNT increases across autonomous, civil, and military domains, defending against GNSS interference—particularly spoofing—has become a strategic imperative. This section outlines the four most widely implemented prevention strategies based on current deployments, regulatory frameworks, and technical evaluations.

7.1 Signal Authentication via OSNMA and Encrypted Services

One of the most direct defences against spoofing involves authenticating GNSS signals to verify their legitimacy. Military systems achieve this through encrypted signals such as GPS M-code or Galileo PRS, which are inaccessible to unauthorised receivers. However, civilian services have historically relied on open, unauthenticated signals—especially GPS L1 C/A—leaving them exposed to spoofing attacks. To address this vulnerability, the European Union launched the OSNMA (Open Service Navigation Message Authentication) protocol for Galileo. As of mid-2025, OSNMA has entered operational deployment and introduces digital signatures into the navigation message, enabling receivers to verify that the orbital and timing data originate from Galileo and have not been tampered with. This significantly reduces the feasibility of forging navigation messages or fabricating satellite ephemerides. Commercial receivers compliant with OSNMA are already being deployed—most notably within the EU's mandatory Smart Tachograph for commercial vehicles. ICAO is also in the process of standardising OSNMA for future civil aviation use. While OSNMA does not prevent replay attacks or spoofing against non-compliant receivers, it raises the bar considerably for adversaries, particularly in regions where spoofing is frequently reported.

7.2 Multi-constellation, Multi-frequency Receiver Design

Receivers that track multiple GNSS constellations (e.g., GPS, Galileo, GLONASS, BeiDou) and operate across several frequency bands inherently exhibit greater resilience to interference. By increasing the diversity of signals, the likelihood that an attacker can successfully spoof or jam all of them simultaneously is dramatically reduced. Modern dual-frequency receivers, for example those using L1/E1 and L5/E5 bands, benefit from cross-validation between signals. If one frequency is spoofed or degraded, the receiver can detect inconsistencies with the alternate band. Signals in the L5/E5 range also possess wider bandwidths and complex modulation schemes, which make them more difficult to replicate without specialised equipment. In military applications, this approach is reinforced by fusing encrypted and unencrypted signals. U.S. Department of Defense systems can concurrently process GPS M-code and Galileo PRS, creating redundancy across systems with separate key infrastructures. Civil systems increasingly follow suit, as seen in integrated multi-constellation GNSS receivers in commercial aviation and automotive safety platforms.

7.3 Sensor Fusion with Inertial Navigation Systems (INS)

A critical redundancy strategy involves integrating GNSS with inertial navigation systems (INS), which use accelerometers and gyroscopes to estimate motion independently of external signals. INS are immune to RF interference and thus offer a trustworthy cross-check against GNSS-derived data. Kalman filters or similar algorithms are typically employed to fuse the two data sources. In normal operation, the GNSS corrects the drift of the INS, while the INS can verify

GNSS consistency. In the presence of spoofing, discrepancies between inertial and GNSS predictions become detectable—allowing systems to flag anomalies, reject corrupted signals, and revert to inertial-only operation if necessary. This approach is already standard in commercial aviation and in high-end autonomous vehicles, where continuity of navigation is essential even in degraded environments. Its efficacy is further enhanced when combined with vision systems, radar, barometric altimeters, and magnetometers.

7.4 Controlled Antenna Patterns and Directional Filtering

Physical-layer defences play an increasingly vital role in modern GNSS receivers. Controlled Radiation Pattern Antennas (CRPAs), vector-tracking arrays, and polarisation-sensitive elements can all be used to reject suspicious signals based on direction-of-arrival or polarisation profile. Spoofed signals generally originate from a single emitter at fixed ground level, producing uncharacteristic angles of arrival compared to genuine GNSS sources dispersed across the sky. By shaping nulls in the antenna pattern toward these signals, or detecting abnormal polarisation, such spoofing attempts can be suppressed or flagged. Interferometric antenna systems can further discriminate spoofed constellations by assessing coherence in signal direction. These defences are already employed in military navigation platforms and maritime GNSS receivers operating in high-risk regions. Although they increase system cost and complexity, they provide a robust defence layer that is independent of the signal content itself.

7.5 Other Strategies

In addition to the four primary techniques outlined above, other prevention strategies are being developed or implemented across civil and defence sectors:

- Real-time GNSS interference monitoring networks, such as those operated by EUSPA, ESA, and NATO mobile units, provide situational awareness and early warnings for users and authorities.
- PNT backup systems, such as eLoran and secure terrestrial timing services, are being reintro- duced or trialled in Europe, the U.S., and the U.K. to mitigate the consequences of GNSS outages.
- Machine learning models embedded in GNSS chipsets can detect subtle spoofing artefacts by analysing Doppler shifts, phase consistency, and carrier-to-noise ratios.
- Legal and regulatory deterrents in the EU and U.S. criminalise GNSS interference, and moni- toring systems support enforcement by geolocating signal sources.

While none of these measures is sufficient alone, their layered application significantly improves the robustness of GNSS-dependent systems, particularly in the context of autonomous navigation and critical infrastructure protection.

8 Detection and Containment of GNSS Attacks

Having analysed how state-financed GNSS interference campaigns emerged between 2015 and 2025 and how they affect autonomous platforms, this section turns to what systems can actually do when faced with jamming and spoofing in practice. Detection focuses on recognising deviations in signal behaviour or system performance, while containment deals with immediate countermeasures to limit the impact. As spoofing and jamming campaigns become increasingly sophisticated, autonomous and critical systems must be able not only to prevent but also to detect and contain GNSS interference. Detection involves recognising deviations in signal behaviour or system performance, while containment entails immediate countermeasures to limit the impact—ranging from rejecting corrupted data to switching to fail-safe navigation modes. This section outlines four key detection and containment methods currently deployed in both civil and defence-grade systems.

8.1 Receiver Autonomous Integrity Monitoring (RAIM) and Redundancy

Checks RAIM has long served as the baseline mechanism for GNSS integrity in aviation. By exploiting redundant satellite signals, the receiver evaluates whether any measurement is inconsistent with the overall solution. If a single satellite produces an outlier, it is excluded from the position calculation. While classical RAIM may struggle with coordinated spoofing—where all signals are falsified but self-consistent—it remains a valuable first layer of defence. Modern GNSS receivers often integrate enhanced RAIM logic, capable of issuing warnings or entering degraded navigation modes. In autonomous platforms, such a trigger may prompt a shift to local navigation systems or cautious operation.

8.2 Cross-Sensor Comparison: INS/GNSS Kalman Innovation Monitoring

A practical method to detect GNSS spoofing is by comparing satellite-based positioning with inertial estimates using a Kalman filter. This filter predicts the system's next position based on motion sensors (INS), and then checks how much the GNSS reading deviates from that prediction. This deviation is called the innovation:

$$\text{Innovation} = \text{GNSS measurement} - \text{Predicted position} \tag{1}$$

Under normal conditions, this difference fluctuates randomly around zero. But if spoofed signals are introduced, the innovation will show a sudden and sustained increase beyond what is statistically expected. A simple threshold rule is often applied: if the innovation is greater than three times the expected noise (3σ), and this happens in three consecutive steps, a spoofing event is flagged. This method was tested in the simulation annex. A one-dimensional object moving at

1 m/s was subjected to spoofing after 30 s, with the fake GNSS signal gradually diverging by 20 m. The Kalman filter, using only position and velocity states, detected the spoofing once the innovations breached the threshold three times in a row. An alarm was then triggered, showing the system's ability to identify the attack even though the GNSS continued to provide plausible readings. This approach is efficient, easy to implement, and suitable for real-time detection in resource-limited autonomous systems. It does not require external verification or secure GNSS signals—only consistency between what the system senses and what it is told by satellites.

Prescriptive Measures for the Use of Kalman Filters for Spoofing Detection. As mentioned in Sect. 7.2 and described by Liu et al. [56], we can formalise the INS/GNSS navigation stack using a standard error-state model. We consider the state vector

x = [ϕT δvnT δpT ϵTb ∇Tb]T

which is a 15-dimensional vector with five groups of three components each, where $\phi = [\phi_x, \phi_y, \phi_z]^T$ are the misalignment angles, δv_n is the velocity error in the navigation frame, δp is the position error, ϵ_b is the gyro bias, and ∇_b is the accelerometer bias. Intuitively, the INS delivers the raw motion estimate, while the Kalman filter is built as an error-state filter that tracks how wrong the INS solution is. This is precisely what makes it useful for spoofing detection: under nominal conditions, the estimated errors remain statistically consistent with the expected noise; under spoofed conditions, the errors start to look statistically implausible. The measurement model can be written as the difference between INS and GNSS positions:

$$z_k = \tilde{p}_{INS,k} - \tilde{p}_{GNSS,k} = H_k x_k + v_k, \tag{2}$$

where $H_k = [0_{3\times3}, 0_{3\times3}, I_{3\times3}, 0_{3\times3}, 0_{3\times3}]$ and v_k is the measurement noise. The navigation Extended Kalman Filter (EKF) already computes the innovation

$$\gamma_k = z_k - H_k \hat{x}_{k|k-1}, \tag{3}$$

with covariance

$$P_{\gamma,k} = H_k P_{k|k-1} H_k^T + R_k, \tag{4}$$

where $P_{k|k-1}$ is the a priori state covariance and R_k is the measurement-noise covariance. Liu et al. show that, under nominal (no-spoofing) conditions, the innovation satisfies

$$\gamma_k \sim \mathcal{N}(0, P_{\gamma,k}), \tag{5}$$

which means that the quadratic form

$$q_k = \gamma_k^T P_{\gamma,k}^{-1} \gamma_k \tag{6}$$

follows a chi-square (χ^2) distribution with degrees of freedom equal to the dimension of γ_k. On this basis, a snapshot chi-square test can be used to detect large attacks by computing qk at each update and comparing it with a threshold chosen according to a desired false-alarm probability. Liu et al. also describe a sequential detection method for ramp-type, "slow-drift" spoofing attacks, where evidence is accumulated over a time window instead of looking at a single epoch.

Prescription. We recommend that UAV navigation systems implement an INS/GNSS integrated EKF with innovation- based spoofing detection following this approach. In practice, the detector should combine both a snapshot chi-square test and a sequential chi-square test, with false-alarm probabilities set according to the level of operational risk that the user is willing to accept. For a UAV equipped with an IMU and a coupled INS/GNSS EKF, the onboard logic should, at each GNSS update, compute the innovation γk, evaluate qk, and compare it with the appropriate chi-square threshold. A similar process applies for the sequential detector over a sliding time window. Once an alarm is raised by either the snapshot or the sequential detector, the system must apply predefined decision logic. For example, if spoofing is suspected, the UAV can switch to INS-only mode, restrict manoeuvres, or initiate a return-to-base procedure. In this way, the existing INS/GNSS EKF infrastructure is leveraged not only for navigation but also as a real-time spoofing detector with tunable sensitivity.

8.3 Physical Signal Feature Analysis (Doppler, Phase, Power)

Spoofing attempts often exhibit physical characteristics that deviate from expected GNSS signal profiles. For example, if all signals share an identical Doppler shift or exhibit simultaneous power fluctuations, this may suggest a single-source spoofer. Abnormalities in carrier phase or polarisation are also indicative.

Recent detection methods employ machine learning models trained on these signal attributes, the carrier-to-noise ratio, the Doppler profile, and temporal consistency, to classify suspicious transmissions. Next-generation GNSS chipsets increasingly embed these models directly into the receiver firmware, allowing real-time spoofing detection without reliance on external infrastructure. Once identified, forged signals are excluded from the PNT solution and, in some systems, logged or reported to external monitoring networks.

8.4 Spectrum Monitoring and Directional Anomaly Detection

Spectrum-level monitoring allows systems to observe RF energy in GNSS bands and detect unusual emissions. For instance, the presence of double signals for the same satellite—one authentic and one spoofed—may reveal itself as duplicate correlation peaks or abrupt phase jumps. These can trigger a freeze in the navigation solution, locking position and time to the last trusted state. Some platforms use interferometric antenna arrays or vector-tracking methods to assess signal directionality. Since genuine GNSS signals originate from different positions in the sky, while spoofed signals often arrive from a common source, any convergence in angle-of-arrival is suspect. These physical signatures offer robust evidence of an ongoing attack, prompting the system to switch to inertial fallback or dead-reckoning.

8.5 Other Techniques

Beyond the four principal approaches, several complementary detection and containment strategies are in operational or experimental use:

- Collaborative detection networks, where platforms share GNSS readings and identify discrep- ancies across nearby units to isolate spoofed devices.
- Dedicated scout platforms, such as UAVs equipped with advanced spoofing detectors, which act as sentinels and broadcast alerts to companion units.
- GNSS interference monitoring infrastructure, including mobile NATO units and national regulatory sensors, which can issue real-time alerts or geolocate the source of interference.
- Operational protocols for containment, especially in aviation and robotics, define safe-state procedures when GNSS signals are deemed unreliable—such as reducing speed, holding position, or reverting to manual control. While early detection remains the preferred outcome, containment ensures that even undetected spoofing attempts do not compromise system safety or mission continuity. These measures, particularly when combined, provide the final defensive barrier in the GNSS threat landscape.

9 Mitigation Techniques

Mitigation refers to operational responses designed to reduce the impact of GNSS interference or facilitate recovery. Several of the strategies previously discussed for detection also serve as mitigation tools. The focus here is on how each contributes to preserving system safety and operability during a confirmed attack, with an assessment of their known effectiveness in realistic scenarios.

Switching to Degraded Modes. Autonomous platforms often support degraded or contingency navigation modes triggered upon loss of GNSS. Unmanned aerial vehicles, for example, may execute a return-to-home procedure relying on the last known GPS position in combination with inertial measurements and barometric altitude. Autonomous vehicles can reduce speed, restrict manoeuvres, or rely solely on onboard sensors such as cameras and LiDAR until a safe stop is achieved. Such measures mitigate the risk of complete system failure and buy critical time during short-term outages. While effective for brief disruptions, performance deteriorates over longer durations due to inertial drift. Nonetheless, most commercial drones and vehicles are able to maintain adequate control for several minutes—sufficient to land or halt safely.

Rejection of Compromised Signals. When spoofing affects only a subset of visible satellites, robust GNSS receivers can isolate and disregard the inconsistent sources using integrity monitoring algorithms. In multi-constellation systems, if spoofed GPS signals are detected while Galileo or GLONASS remain unaffected, the receiver may compute position using only trusted data. This approach has proven effective in operational contexts. Pilots navigating in interference-prone regions have successfully switched to alternative constellations after GPS compromise. Such signal- level mitigation depends on the spoofing attack not being perfectly coordinated across all constellations—something technically challenging even for state-level actors.

Time Restoration Algorithms. GNSS time manipulation is especially disruptive to critical infrastructures, such as energy distribution and telecom networks. Mitigation methods under development aim to restore synchronisation by detecting anomalies and extrapolating a corrected time reference. Algorithms designed to estimate spoof-induced timing bias by comparing it with historical patterns offer a promising line of defence. While currently at the research stage, these techniques may allow affected systems to continue operating with internally corrected clocks during attacks. Their success depends on prior detection of the interference and the availability of clean pre-attack timing data.

Adaptive Antennas and Null Steering. Adaptive antennas such as Controlled Radiation Pattern Antennas (CRPAs) are capable of actively nulling interference by directing antenna pattern minima toward the source of jamming or spoofing. These systems are particularly effective against jammers emitting from a fixed ground-based position. In spoofing scenarios, direction-of-arrival filtering can help reject signals that do not conform to the expected spatial distribution of satellite sources. While advanced adversaries could theoretically simulate a distributed satellite geometry using multiple emitters or drones, such attacks are rarely observed in the field due to their logistical complexity. As such, directional filtering remains highly effective in real-world deployments. Procedural readiness also plays a crucial role. Operator training, clear contingency protocols, and conservative behaviour programming allow systems to respond prudently when confidence in GNSS data declines. This includes deferring lane changes, activating hazard signals, or requesting human intervention when required. Redundant PNT sources such as eLoran provide additional assurance, although real-world effectiveness is limited by current adoption. Where deployed—such as in port facilities with terrestrial beacons—these systems have prevented service disruption during jamming events.

10 From Recommendations to Practice: Concrete Examples of

Implementation The recommendations presented earlier are not merely conceptual. Over the past decade, multiple states, international organisations and industrial actors have begun deploying measures that closely resemble the resilience agenda proposed here. This section illustrates each recommendation with concrete examples so that the reader can clearly understand what "should be done" and how it is already being implemented in practice.

10.1 Shared Spectrum-Monitoring Networks and Certification

Within Europe, one of the most significant steps towards shared GNSS interference monitoring is the development of continent-wide cooperative networks funded by the European Union. A representative example of this trend can be seen in European Global Interference PROtection Network (EGIPRON)-type initiatives coordinated by companies such as Qascom and Leonardo under EUSPA. EGIPRON aims to deploy a scalable network of sensors distributed across Europe, capable of detecting and characterising GNSS jamming and spoofing in near real time, aggregating data from ground-based stations, mobile platforms and even satellites. The operational logic is straightforward: when each state operates sensors following a common standard, the resulting data can be fused into a continental GNSS interference map.

In parallel, the EU has launched Galileo's OSNMA open authentication service, which embeds cryptographic signatures in the E1 navigation message. Several manufacturers have begun offering "OSNMA- ready" receivers capable of verifying signal authenticity. For operators, the implication is clear: GNSS certification is evolving from simply checking that a receiver obtains a position fix, to ensuring that it can identify unauthenticated or suspicious signals. It is reasonable to anticipate that sectors such as aviation and critical transport will begin requiring explicit anti-spoofing and anti-jamming capabilities for certification. Commercial actors are also contributing. Spire Global, for example, has repurposed its low-Earth orbit nanosatellite constellation to act as a space-based GNSS interference sensor grid. Using simultane- ous L1/L2 observations, Spire demonstrated detection and coarse localisation of jamming sources in the Eastern Mediterranean. This shows that a truly shared monitoring architecture will likely need to combine state-operated ground sensors, critical infrastructure monitoring nodes and commercially operated SIGINT-capable satellites.

10.2 Realistic Attack Simulation as a Validation Tool

The United States offers perhaps the most mature example of routine training in GNSS-denied environments. Since 2019, the US Army has held the annual PNT Assessment Exercise (PNTAX) at the White Sands proving ground. During PNTAX, units from various divisions and selected allies operate vehicles, command systems and autonomous platforms in an environment where GPS is deliberately denied or spoofed using a broad range of realistic interference sources. The premise is simple: resilience cannot be certified solely through laboratory simulations; it must be demonstrated by soldiers operating real systems in a contested electromagnetic spectrum. In civil aviation, GNSS-denial scenarios have begun to appear in training manuals and simulator curricula. EASA has issued safety bulletins recommending that airlines train crews to react to sudden GNSS outages and revert to conventional navigation aids. In some cases, states have conducted controlled jamming campaigns in remote areas—such as the officially authorised UK trials in Wales—to observe how real receivers respond, assess NOTAM dissemination, and evaluate the robustness of avionics. At the industrial level, SDR-based laboratories and commercial GNSS simulators now enable hardware- in-the-loop spoofing and jamming experiments under legally confined conditions. Operators typically design test campaigns combining nominal conditions, broadband/narrowband jamming, and various spoofing profiles. For each scenario, they record performance degradation, lock loss, and detection latency. These practices translate the recommendation of "train and test in contested spectrum" into actionable engineering procedures.

10.3 Common Protocols for Technical Evidence After Interference Incidents

Aviation regulators provide an instructive case of harmonisation. EASA and IATA have agreed to standardise radio phraseology for GNSS interference reports as well as the NOTAM "Q-codes" used to disseminate alerts. This ensures that a pilot experiencing GNSS degradation in Riga or Athens uses identical terminology, enabling controllers to identify the situation immediately. Their joint action plan also recommends that states establish clear procedures for collecting technical evidence after incidents: time, flight phase, affected systems, approximate location, duration, and any available logs (FDR data, receiver logs, spectrum snapshots). At the European level, EASA's Safety Information Bulletin SIB 2022-02 distinguishes between events requiring mandatory reporting (such as confirmed spoofing or any interference affecting safety) and those manageable within the operator's internal safety management system. The practical result is a relatively homogeneous reporting format across jurisdictions. Beyond Europe, some states have adopted stricter measures. India's DGCA, for instance, mandated that all suspected spoofing or GPS interference events be reported within minutes after identifying recurrent incidents near borders and at Delhi Airport. This requirement produced hundreds of incident records in a year, enabling authorities to identify hot spots and adjust procedures. The lesson is clear: even without a global standard, a well-defined national evidence protocol significantly strengthens incident understanding and response.

10.4 Strengthening the Role of the ITU in Notification and Technical Assessment

The ITU has begun acknowledging the growing scale of harmful RNSS interference, although its enforcement capacity remains limited. At WRC-23, Resolution 676 urged administrations to curb the proliferation of jamming devices, improve regulator–operator coordination, and report harmful interference. However, it also affirmed states' rights to restrict RNSS access for "security or defence" purposes, leaving a grey zone that certain states may use to justify deliberate interference. In March 2025, the ITU, ICAO and IMO issued a joint statement urging states to report GNSS interference not only to aviation and maritime authorities but also to the ITU Radiocommunication Bureau. This is the first explicit attempt to establish a unified global notification channel. While the ITU still lacks investigative powers, nothing prevents states—individually or via regional alliances—from supplying consolidated evidence packages (spectral recordings, geolocation analyses, operational impacts) for deliberation in multilateral forums. The practical takeaway is twofold: states need internal procedures for compiling interference evidence for ITU submission, and regional alliances (e.g., NATO, the EU) should provide coordinated evidence dossiers in severe cases.

10.5 Towards a Joint NATO–EU Electromagnetic Operations Centre

A formal NATO–EU electromagnetic operations centre does not yet exist. However, key building blocks are emerging. In 2023, the two organisations established a joint task force on critical infrastructure resilience, which explicitly includes space-based systems. NATO leadership has publicly acknowledged that large-scale GPS jamming campaigns pose a direct threat to European security, prompting deeper NATO–EU cooperation. A hypothetical joint centre could fuse NATO's military EW sensor network with Europe's civil GNSS monitoring architecture (including Galileo's GSMC and emerging EU-wide interference-monitoring networks). Such a centre would produce a unified electromagnetic operating picture, perform technical attribution, issue tactical and civil advisories, and coordinate responses ranging from diplomatic actions to operational mitigation. Several informal mechanisms already approximate this model. During heightened interference around the Baltic and Black Sea regions, NATO and EU agencies regularly exchanged interference data, with NATO providing military SIGINT assessments and EU agencies (EASA, EUSPA, EUROCONTROL) contributing operational incident data. These practices suggest a gradual convergence towards an institutionalised shared EM domain capability.

10.6 Spatial and Digital Integrity as an Emerging Rights-Based Concept

Although no binding legal instrument currently enshrines a "right to spatial and digital integrity", recent interference campaigns have highlighted the human-rights dimensions of GNSS manipulation. Large-scale spoofing episodes over urban areas have altered the perceived location of thousands of civilians; jamming near borders has disrupted civil aviation, emergency flights and medical evacuations; and persistent GNSS interference has compromised freedom of movement and access to essential services. Legally, such conduct is often shoehorned into existing rights—life, personal security, freedom of movement, data protection—but these frameworks do not fully capture the nature of electromagnetic harm. As a result, scholars have begun calling for explicit recognition of spatial/digital integrity as a bridging right: a principle ensuring that individuals are not exposed to arbitrary manipulation of the electromagnetic environment that underpins navigation, timing and basic digital functions. While no state or international organisation has codified the right to date, discussions within UN human-rights bodies and the Council of Europe hint at an evolving understanding. The practical implication is that states should begin incorporating EM-interference considerations into human-rights policy, and support soft-law initiatives that frame deliberate large-scale GNSS manipulation against civilians as incompatible with modern rights obligations. Taken together, these examples show that many of the recommended measures are not aspirational abstractions but logical extensions of practices already emerging in different operational and regulatory settings. For states and organisations that have not yet progressed in these areas, the practical path forward involves adapting these experiences to their own conditions: investing in shared monitoring networks, institutionalising contested-spectrum training, formalising technical evidence protocols and, crucially, recognising that GNSS resilience is not solely an engineering matter but also a question of governance and societal protection.

11 Conclusions

GNSS spoofing and jamming have evolved into silent forms of intervention over the physical world, capable of altering trajectories, timing, and decisions without leaving visible traces. Unlike more overt expressions of hybrid warfare, these practices do not seek immediate system collapse. Their effect is subtler and, over time, more corrosive: they introduce uncertainty where precision was assumed, and doubt where trust once prevailed. The incidents documented across Europe between 2015 and 2025 suggest that electromagnetic interference increasingly operates as a persistent background disturbance—normalised, often unnoticed, and rarely addressed in isolation. Its impact is not always expressed through dramatic failures or total outages, but through slight deviations, unexplained anomalies, and automated decisions that slowly drift away from their intended outcomes. In systems that are progressively more autonomous, such deviations do not simply disappear; they accumulate. The episode involving an aircraft carrying the President of the European Commission, :contentReference[oaicite:0]index=0, acquires in this context a significance that goes beyond the technical details of the event itself. What matters is not only that an official flight may have been exposed to GNSS interference, but what this exposure reveals: even systems assumed to be among the most protected remain dependent on signals that can be discreetly manipulated. The implicit message is unsettling. If such interference can occur at the very centre of European political power, it can occur wherever navigation, synchronisation, and automation rely on GNSS. This study has shown that spoofing does not operate as an external disruption, but as a form of internal deception. By gradually manipulating positioning, navigation, and timing information, these attacks exploit the internal logic of the systems they target. Navigation filters continue to operate, algorithms converge, control loops remain stable—but they do so on a displaced reality. The system does not fail abruptly; it simply ceases to be where it believes it is. This characteristic lies at the core of spoofing's danger in autonomous and semi-autonomous environments. From a technical standpoint, the modelling and simulation work presented here makes this dynamic observable without waiting for its consequences to materialise in real-world operations. Innovation- based detection methods, grounded in Kalman filtering and inertial consistency, demonstrate that such deviations can be identified before they translate into catastrophic outcomes. Yet the effectiveness of these defences depends on recognising spoofing as a structural vulnerability rather than an exceptional anomaly. More troubling still is the gap between this technical reality and existing governance frameworks. GNSS interference rarely fits neatly into established categories of international law or collective security. It does not always cross the threshold of armed conflict, yet it cannot be dismissed as a purely technical malfunction. Its effects—on safety, mobility, trust in digital systems, and ultimately on fundamental rights—are often absorbed into grey zones of responsibility where accountability remains diffuse. Taken together, the findings of this study suggest that GNSS spoofing is more than an emerging threat; it is a symptom of a deeper transformation in how power is exercised within the electromagnetic domain. As societies continue to delegate critical decisions to automated and autonomous systems, the quiet manipulation of the signals that underpin them acquires strategic weight. Without a more integrated technical, legal, and political understanding of this phenomenon, the risk is not only that systems may fail, but that they may gradually cease to be trustworthy—without a clear moment at which that trust was lost.

Acknowledgements. This research was carried out by members of the Space Generation Advisory Council (SGAC), a global non-governmental organisation that represents students and young professionals in the space sector. SGAC works in support of the United Nations Programme on Space Applications and provides a platform for the next generation to engage in international discussions on space policy, security and development. The contributing members, from diverse academic and professional backgrounds, collaborated through SGAC's Space and Cyber Security Project Group to investigate the role of satellite interference in the context of hybrid warfare and electromagnetic operations.

Disclosure of Interests. The authors have no competing interests to declare that are relevant to the content of this article.

References

1. NATO Military Committee. (2009). MC 0064/10 NATO electronic warfare (EW) policy (para. 6). NATO
2. U.S. Department of Defense. Joint Terminology for Cyberspace Operations (JP 1-02) (2010). https://info.publicintelligence.net/DoD-JointCyberTerms.pdf
3. Glenn, J.C.: Global Challenge 10, State of the Future 19.1. The Millennium Project, Washington, DC (2018)

4. Daseking, F. I. S. R. M.: A systematic review of cognitive and psychological warfare. Defence Horiz. J. (2025). https://tdhj.org/blog/post/cognitive-psychological-warfare/
5. Browne, R.: Russia jammed GPS during major NATO military exercise. CNN (2018). https://www.cnn.com/2018/11/14/politics/russia-nato-jamming
6. C4ADS. Above Us Only Stars: Exposing GPS Spoofing in Russia and Syria (2019). https://c4ads.org/reports/above-us-only-stars/
7. European Court of Human Rights. Libert v. France (2018). https://hudoc.echr.coe.int/eng?i=001-181273
8. Council of Europe. Convention for the Protection of Human Rights and Fundamental Freedoms (1950). https://echr.coe.int/Documents/Convention_ENG.pdf
9. European Union. General Data Protection Regulation (EU 2016/679) (2016). https://eur-lex.europa.eu/eli/reg/2016/679/oj
10. Emanuilov, I.: From Space Big Data to Big Space Brother. KU Leuven CiTiP Blog (2019). https://www.law.kuleuven.be/citip/blog/from-space-big-data-to-big-space-brother-do-states-have-a-
11. Spirent Federal. GNSS Signal Spoofing (2023). https://spirentfederal.com/wp-content/uploads/Federal-DWP0
12. Humphreys, T.E.: Statement on GPS Spoofing before the U.S. Congress (2012). https://radionavlab.ae.utexas.edu
13. Goff, S.: Mass GPS spoofing attack in the Black Sea. Inside GNSS (2017). https://insidegnss.com/reports-of-mass-gps-spoofing-attack-in-the-black-sea-strengthen-calls-for-
14. International Telecommunication Union. Warning: Harmful Interference to RNSS (2022). https://www.itu.int/hub/2022/08/warning-harmful-interference-rnss/
15. Safran Electronics & Defense. Skydel GSG-8 Gen2 GNSS Simulator (2025). https://www.safran-group.com/products-services/skydel-gsg-8-gen2-gnss-simulator
16. Spirent Communications. GSS7765 Interference Simulation System (2025). https://www.spirent.com/products/gnss-interference-generator-gss7765
17. VectorNav Technologies. GNSS–Aided Inertial Navigation System (GNSS/INS) (n.d.). https://www.vectornav.com/resources/inertial-navigation-primer/theory-of-operation/theory-gpsins
18. Hamad, M., Steinhorst, S.: Security challenges in autonomous systems design. arXiv:2312.00018v2. https://arxiv.org/abs/2312.00018 (2023)
19. Hozint. The threat of GPS interference in aviation. Horiz. Intell. (2025). https://www.hozint.com/the-threat-of-gps-interference-in-aviation/
20. Khalil, J.: GNSS spoofing threatens airline safety, alarming pilots and aviation officials. GPS World (2024). https://www.gpsworld.com/gnss-spoofing-threatens-airline-safety/
21. Tobin, J., et al.: Domain randomization for transferring deep neural networks from sim- ulation to the real world. In: IEEE/RSJ International Conference on Intelligent Robots and Systems (IROS) (2017). https://doi.org/10.1109/IROS.2017.8202133
22. Humphreys, T.E., Bhatti, J., Shepard, D.P., Wesson, K.D.: Demonstration of a Civil GPS Spoofing Attack on a Civilian Unmanned Aerial Vehicle and an 80-Metre Yacht. University of Texas at Austin, Radionavigation Laboratory (2013). https://radionavlab.ae.utexas.edu/gps-spoofing
23. Open Access Government. Galileo launches OSNMA to combat satellite spoofing threats (2025). https://www.openaccessgovernment.org/article/galileo-launches-osnma-to-combat-satellite-spoofing-

24. Sun, H., Khanafseh, S., Joerger, M., Pervan, B.: Real-time Bayesian detection of drift- evasive GNSS spoofing. arXiv preprint. https://arxiv.org/abs/2312.10571 (2023)
25. Goff, S.: Reports of Mass GPS Spoofing Attack in the Black Sea. Inside GNSS (2017). https://insidegnss.com/reports-of-mass-gps-spoofing-attack-in-the-black-sea-strengthen-calls-for-
26. Browne, R.: Russia jammed GPS during major NATO exercise. CNN (2018). https://www.cnn.com/2018/11/14/politics/russia-nato-jamming
27. GPS World. ICAO adopts international standards for Galileo (2023). https://www.gpsworld.com/icao-adopts-international-standards-for-galileo/
28. Misra, P., Enge, P.: Global Positioning System: Signals, Measurements, and Performance. 2nd ed. Ganga-Jamuna Press (2006)
29. Kaplan, E.D., Hegarty, C.J.: Artech House. In: Understanding GPS/GNSS: Principles and Applications. 3rd ed (2017)
30. Borkar, S.: GPS and GNSS Technology in Geosciences. Springer, Heidelberg (2019)
31. Schubert, F., Wiesbeck, W.: Handbook of RF and Microwave Power Amplifiers. Cambridge University Press, Cambridge (2015)
32. United Nations. Treaty on Principles Governing the Activities of States in the Exploration and Use of Outer Space, Including the Moon and Other Celestial Bodies. General Assembly, RES 2222(XXI) (1967)
33. Metcalf, K.: A legal view on outer space and cyberspace. NATO Cooperative Cyber Defence Centre of Excellence (2018)
34. Carlo, A., Obergfaell, K.: Cyber attacks on critical infrastructure and satellite communications. Int. J. Crit. Infrastruct. Prot. (2024)
35. Nicolas, P.: Electronic Warfare Target Location Methods. 2nd ed. Artech House (2020)
36. Lyall, F., Larsen, P.B.: Space Law: A Treatise (2nd ed.). Routledge (2017)
37. Benatar, M.: International Humanitarian Law and the Changing Technology of War. Cambridge University Press, Cambridge (2021)
38. Hathaway, O.A., Shapiro, S.: The Internationalists: How a Radical Plan to Outlaw War Remade the World. Penguin Books (2019)
39. Andress, J., Winterfeld, S.: Cyber Warfare: Techniques, Tactics and Tools for Security Practitioners. (2nd ed). Elsevier (2019)
40. GPS World. GNSS interference affects aircraft carrying European Commission President in the Baltic region (2024)
41. EUROCONTROL. GNSS interference and spoofing in the Baltic Sea region: Operational impact assessment (2024)
42. Finnish Transport and Communications Agency (Traficom). Repeated GNSS interference reports affecting Eastern Finland airspace (2024)
43. Estonian Civil Aviation Administration. GNSS degradation notifications within the Gulf of Finland FIR (2024)
44. OSCE Special Monitoring Mission to Ukraine. Technical analysis of the loss of a long-range UAV in Donbas. OSCE Monitoring Report (2018)
45. Resilient Navigation and Timing Foundation. GNSS interference trends and PNT vulnerability in Europe (2020)
46. European Union Aviation Safety Agency (EASA). Safety Information Bulletin 2022-02: GNSS Interference v
47. Europol: Criminal misuse of GNSS jammers and interference devices across EU Member States (2023)
48. Humphreys, T.: Analysis of GNSS spoofing patterns in Eastern Europe and the Eastern Mediterranean. University of Texas Radionavigation Laboratory (2023)

49. UK Ministry of Defence. Electronic Warfare and PNT Resilience: Annual Threat Assessment (2021)
50. NATO StratCom COE. Electromagnetic interference campaigns near NATO borders (2024)
51. European Union and NATO. Joint Declaration on Hybrid Threats and Electromagnetic Domain Resilience (2023)
52. Finnish Transport and Communications Agency (Traficom). GNSS jamming source analysis indicating emissions from Kaliningrad oblast (2024)
53. International Civil Aviation Organization (ICAO). Guidance on detection and mitigation of GNSS spoofing and meaconing (2024)
54. International Maritime Organization (IMO). Recommendations to enhance maritime PNT resilience against GNSS interference (2023)
55. C4ADS. Global GNSS Interference Mapping Dataset (2015–2023) (2023)
56. Liu, Y., Li, S., Fu, Q., Liu, Z., Zhou, Q.: Analysis of Kalman filter innovation-based GNSS spoofing detection method for INS/GNSS integrated navigation system. IEEE Sens. J. **19**(13), 5167–5178 (2019). https://doi.org/10.1109/JSEN.2019.2902178

M&S of Intelligent Systems – R&D and Application

Notes on the Mathematical Analysis of Minefield Efficiency

Jiří Neubauer(✉) and Tibor Palasiewicz

University of Defence, Kounicova 65, 662 10 Brno, Czech Republic
jiri.neubauer@unob.cz

Abstract. The present paper employs a mathematical analysis to assess the effectiveness of a minefield composed of a single row of mines. Two types of mine distribution are considered: uniform and random. The probability of successful crossing is evaluated for two approach directions: perpendicular and at an arbitrary angle. The derived analytical expressions are verified through simulations, thereby confirming their validity and illustrating the influence of entry angle and mine distribution on the likelihood of penetration. This study makes a foundational contribution to the field of minefield performance modeling.

Keywords: Minefield efficiency · Probability · Simulation

1 Introduction

Minefields continue to serve as key tools in modern armed conflicts and have a significant impact on the conduct of military operations [1,2]. This is evidenced by their extensive deployment in conflicts such as that in Ukraine [3]. Anti-tank mines are mainly used to stop the enemy's advance and direct it into confined spaces, thereby facilitating more effective use of other weapon systems [4,5].

Given the key role of minefields, it is necessary to evaluate and optimize the doctrinal basis for their deployment. The current doctrinal basis for engineering support often fails to address specific requirements of contemporary battlefields. An analysis of the development of the doctrinal framework in the Army of the Czech Republic (ACR) shows that although alliance standards are being adopted, this process occurs without thorough systematic integration and without adaptation to specific current tactical situations. The disorganized way these standards are implemented makes them less useful, especially for obstacle operations. Modern conflicts require detailed procedures that these standards do not always provide [6].

Modern armed conflicts have shown that the free movement of military units, their ability to manoeuvre and adapt to changing battlefield conditions, is essential not only for the fulfillment of assigned tasks but also, more importantly, for the logistical support and survival of forces [7–9]. Engineer units play a key role in this regard, as they facilitate mobility support through activities such as mine

J. Novotný et al. (Eds.): MESAS 2025, LNCS 16627, pp. 103–113, 2027.
https://doi.org/10.1007/978-3-032-33182-3_6

clearance and bridge building while simultaneously limiting the mobility of the enemy. Engineers are also important in hybrid and undefined conflicts, where their ability to react quickly, carry out technical interventions, and adapt to the prevailing conditions is increasingly important [10].

A fundamental method of limiting the mobility of the enemy is the establishment of minefields, which form the basis of movement restrictions owing to their rapid deployment, high efficiency, and significant psychological impact [11,12]. Unlike nonexplosive obstacles, minefields can also cause direct losses to adversaries [13]. Effective minefield use requires integration into a defense system in coordination with firepower, terrain, and other obstacles. Strategic minefield placement and timing can fundamentally affect the outcome of an operation and inflict significant losses to the enemy [14–16].

Understanding the tactical significance of minefields paves the way for evaluating the current planning methodologies [17]. This underscores the need for advanced simulation tools and methodologies to develop more effective deployment strategies. Recognizing the limitations of traditional minefield planning methods emphasizes the importance of using advanced simulation tools, such as constructive simulations, as exemplified by MASA SWORD, which can be crucial for minefield planning [18]. These tools facilitate the evaluation of various obstacle placement options, assess their impact on the development of tactical scenarios, and optimize the deployment of engineering resources [19]. Empirical evidence suggests that integrating engineering components into defense strategies significantly increases the likelihood of mission success and unit survival.

To optimize minefield deployment, it is necessary to complement empirical experience with theoretical and computational assessments of their effectiveness. Traditional geometric models for assessing the effectiveness of minefields often suffer from simplification and do not sufficiently consider critical factors, such as edge effects in minefields composed of full-width mines [20]. A significant step in this area has been the introduction of the concept of "active length", which improves the estimation of vehicle hit probability, especially in the context of short minefields [21].

In addition to simple geometric models, advanced methodologies such as hybrid intelligent models (IHHO-MCNN) using machine learning, as well as probabilistic models using real-world vehicle movements and mine locations, are increasingly being used [22]. Therefore, accurate mine deployment planning requires more sophisticated theoretical approaches.

2 Methods

For the purpose of describing the efficiency of the minefield, we will use the tools of probability, in particular geometric probability, conditional probability and the law of total probability, see for example [23,24].

Geometric probability is a tool to deal with the problem of infinite outcomes of the random event by measuring the number of outcomes geometrically, in terms of length, area, or volume. Let the sample space Ω be continuous creating some area which is bounded, closed and has size $V(\Omega)$ (described by the length, eventually the area or the volume). Similarly if an event $A \subset \Omega$, it creates area of the size $V(A)$. Then the *geometric probability* of the event A is defined by

$$P(A) = \frac{V(A)}{V(\Omega)}. \tag{1}$$

Conditional probability is the probability that an random event will occur given that another event has already occurred. If A and B are two events, then the conditional probability of A given B is written as $P(A|B)$ (read "the probability of A given that B has already occurred") and is defined as

$$P(A|B) = \frac{P(A \cap B)}{P(B)}, \quad P(B) > 0. \tag{2}$$

Two events are said to be *independent* if the occurrence of one does not affect the probability of the occurrence of the other one, $P(A|B) = P(A)$, $P(B|A) = P(B)$. In other words, A and B are independent events if

$$P(A \cap B) = P(A)P(B).$$

This formula can be generalized to more than two events.

Assume $H_1, \ldots, H_n$ are n mutually exclusive random events ($H_i \cap H_j = \emptyset$, $i, j = 1, 2, \ldots, n$, $i \neq j$) and exhaustive sets ($\bigcup_{i=1}^{n} H_i = \Omega$) and $P(H_i) > 0$ for each $i = 1, 2, \ldots, n$, then for the probability of the event A

$$P(A) = \sum_{i=1}^{n} P(H_i)P(A|H_i). \tag{3}$$

The expression (3) is called the *law of total probability.*

3 Minefield Efficiency

First, we focus on the basic situation where mines are placed regularly in only one row, the row itself is infinite. We will use the following notation:

- a ... distance between mine centres in meters
- m ... mine width in meters
- t ... tank width in meters

We assume that $m + t \leq a$. If a tank runs perpendicularly on a row of mines, the probability of its destruction (an event Z), i.e. the probability that some part of it will run on a mine, is determined by the geometric probability

$$P(Z) = \frac{m + t}{a}. \tag{4}$$

For parameters $a = 5$, $m = 0.2$ and $t = 3.5$ we get $P(Z) = 0.74$ We will assume that the tank will run into a row of mines regularly spaced on a straight line at

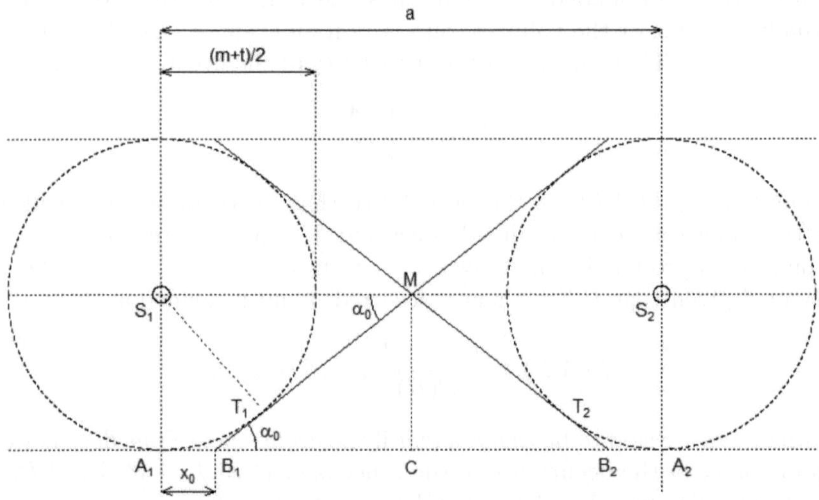

Fig. 1. Entering a minefield – the limiting angle.

an arbitrary angle $\alpha \in (0, \pi)$. We will consider the center of the tank. First, we consider the situation shown in Fig. 1.

Without loss of generality, we will focus only on the area between the two mines, namely between the centers of the mines. If a tank enters the minefield between points A_1B_1 or A_2B_2 at any angle, it will be destroyed with certainty. The limiting angle α_0 of the triangle $\triangle MS_1T_1$ is

$$\sin\alpha_0 = \frac{|S_1T_1|}{|S_1M|} = \frac{(m+t)/2}{a/2} = \frac{m+t}{a} \Rightarrow \alpha_0 = \arcsin\frac{m+t}{a}. \tag{5}$$

Denote the length of the line segment A_1B_1 by x_0. From the triangle $\triangle MCB_1$ we get

$$\tan\alpha_0 = \frac{|MC|}{|B_1C|} = \frac{(m+t)/2}{|B_1C|} \Rightarrow |B_1C| = \frac{t+m}{2\tan\alpha_0}, \tag{6}$$

then

$$x_0 = |A_1B_1| = |A_1C| - |B_1C| = \frac{a}{2} - \frac{t+m}{2\tan\alpha_0}. \tag{7}$$

The situation when the tank enters the space between the mines outside the areas A_1B_1 or A_2B_2 is shown in Fig. 2.

The tank will be destroyed if the α angle is $\alpha \leq \alpha_1$ or $\alpha \leq \alpha_2$. Obviously, the tank will not be destroyed for $\alpha_2 < \alpha < \pi - \alpha_1$, $\alpha \in (\alpha_2, \pi - \alpha_1)$. Let us denote the length of the line segment A_1T as x. From the triangle $\triangle S_1TA_1$ we get

$$\tan\frac{\alpha_1}{2} = \frac{|A_1S_1|}{|A_1T|} = \frac{(m+t)/2}{x} \Rightarrow \alpha_1 = 2\arctan\frac{m+t}{2x}. \tag{8}$$

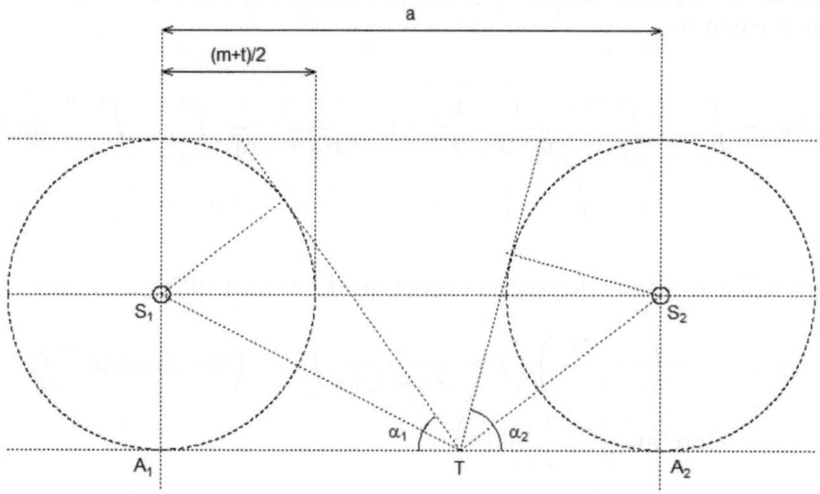

Fig. 2. Entering a minefield outside the limiting angle.

Similarly, from the triangle $\triangle S_2TA_2$ we obtain

$$\tan\frac{\alpha_2}{2} = \frac{|A_2S_2|}{|A_2T|} = \frac{(m+t)/2}{a-x} \Rightarrow \alpha_1 = 2\arctan\frac{m+t}{2(a-x)}. \tag{9}$$

Now we move on to calculating the probability of destroying the tank. Let us denote

Z: event when the tank is destroyed;

H_1: event when the tank drives between mines in the area A_1B_1 or A_2B_2;

H_2: event when the tank drives between mines outside the area A_1B_1 or A_2B_2.

We determine the probability of tank destruction using the law of total probability formula (3)

$$P(Z) = P(H_1)P(Z|H_1) + P(H_2)P(Z|H_2). \tag{10}$$

If the tank enters the minefield in area A_1B_1 or A_2B_2, it will definitely be destroyed, i.e., $P(Z|H_1) = 1$. It remains to determine the conditional probability $P(Z|H_2)$, i.e., the probability of the tank being destroyed when the entry point is outside the above-mentioned area. For the purposes of calculation, it will be easier to determine the probability of the opposite event $P(\overline{Z|H_2})$, i.e., that the tank will not be destroyed if the point of entry is outside the above-mentioned area. We will assume that the point of entry has a uniform distribution (see for example [23]) with density $\frac{1}{a-2x_0}$ on the interval $(x_0, a-x_0)$, and further assume that the angle of approach takes values from the interval $(0,\pi)$ and has a uniform distribution with density $\frac{1}{\pi}$. The entry point and angle are independent.

The values of angles α_1 and α_2 are given by formulas (8) and (9). The probability sought is equal to

$$P(\overline{Z|H_2}) = \int_{x_0}^{a-x_0}\int_{\alpha_2}^{\pi-\alpha_1} \frac{1}{a-2x_0}\frac{1}{\pi}\mathrm{d}\alpha \mathrm{d}x = \frac{1}{\pi(a-2x_0)}\int_{x_0}^{a-x_0}\int_{\alpha_2}^{\pi-\alpha_1} \mathrm{d}\alpha \mathrm{d}x =$$
$$= \frac{1}{\pi(a-2x_0)}\int_{x_0}^{a-x_0}\left(\pi - 2\arctan\frac{m+t}{2x} - 2\arctan\frac{m+t}{2(a-x)}\right)\mathrm{d}x. \tag{11}$$

The probability of tank destruction is obtained by substituting into (10)

$$P(Z) = \frac{2x_0}{a} + \left(\frac{a-2x_0}{a}\right)\left(1 - \frac{1}{\pi(a-2x_0)}\int_{x_0}^{a-x_0}\left(\pi - 2\arctan\frac{m+t}{2x} - \right.\right.$$
$$\left.\left. -2\arctan\frac{m+t}{2(a-x)}\right)\mathrm{d}x\right) =$$
$$= 1 - \frac{1}{a\pi}\int_{x_0}^{a-x_0}\left(\pi - 2\arctan\frac{m+t}{2x} - 2\arctan\frac{m+t}{2(a-x)}\right)\mathrm{d}x. \tag{12}$$

The integral can be computed numerically for specific values of parameters a, m and t. It can also be solved analytically (the calculation is longer, we will not show it here), the probability is equal to

$$P(Z) = \frac{1}{a}\left[2x_0 + \frac{1}{\pi}\left(4(a-x_0)\arctan\frac{m+t}{2(a-x_0)} - \right.\right.$$
$$\left.\left. -4x_0\arctan\frac{m+t}{2x_0} + \ln\frac{4(a-x_0)^2+(m+t)^2}{4x_0^2+(m+t)^2}\right)\right]. \tag{13}$$

From formula (13), it is clear that the probability $P(Z)$ is not a function of the parameters p and t separately, but depends on the sum $m+t$.

Table 1 contains the results of the probability of tank destruction for several parameter values, as well as the results of simulations, where 101 mines were considered for Simulation I and 1001 mines for Simulation II. The number of simulations was $N = 10^5$ for both variants. For each individual simulation, the position of the tank's center and the angle of approach were randomly simulated, and it was determined whether or not the tank was destroyed for this combination. The estimated probabilities are then the ratio of the number of cases in which the tank was destroyed to the total number of simulations N. The results show that the estimated probabilities of tank destruction are very close to the theoretical probabilities determined from formula (13). For a higher number of mines (longer minefield), the estimate is usually better.

Now, let us focus on the case where the mine placement geometry is not fixed, but rather, the mines (mine centres) are placed randomly and independently along a line of width l. Under this assumption, a situation may arise where mines overlap. We will choose a sufficiently large length l to avoid problems associated with placing mines at the edges. We will consider a uniform distribution. Suppose

Table 1. Probability and estimated probability of tank destruction

m	t	a	$P(Z)$	Simulation I	Simulation II
0.2	3.5	5	0.915	0.912	0.913
0.2	3.5	6	0.841	0.837	0.839
0.2	3.5	7	0.776	0.773	0.774
0.2	3.5	8	0.720	0.718	0.717
0.2	3.5	9	0.671	0.668	0.670
0.2	3.5	10	0.630	0.628	0.627
0.2	3.5	15	0.485	0.483	0.484
0.2	3.5	20	0.398	0.396	0.397
0.2	3.5	25	0.339	0.338	0.338
0.2	3.5	30	0.297	0.295	0.296

we have n mines. One mine will destroy a tank with probability $\frac{m+t}{l}$. To calculate the probability of a tank being destroyed by n mines we use complement event. A tank will not be destroyed by one mine with probability $1 - \frac{m+t}{l}$. Mines are deployed independently of each other, so the destruction, respectively non-destruction of the tank by individual mines are independent events. This means that n mines do not destroy a tank with probability $\left(1 - \frac{m+t}{l}\right)^n$. Thus, the probability of destroying a tank (the probability that at least one mine destroys a tank) is given by the expression

$$P(Z) = 1 - \left(1 - \frac{m+t}{l}\right)^n, \tag{14}$$

We use simulations to verify formula (14). For simulation purposes, set the parameters as follows: $m = 0.2$, $t = 3.5$, $l = 500$, $n = 101$. In a regular mine placement, where the first mine is placed at the beginning and the last mine at the end of the line, this setting corresponds to a mine distance of $a = 5$. Calculation according to formula (14) gives the probability value $P(Z) = 0.528$. The simulation results for $N = 10^5$ repetitions are shown in Fig. 3. The probability of tank destruction was determined for each simulation of random mine deployment. As can be seen in the graph, there is variability in the simulation results. However, the average of these values can be used to estimate the desired probability, which is 0.527 and is shown by the dashed line on the graph. As calculated at the beginning of this section, if mines are deployed regularly, the probability of destroying a tank is 0.74. Random deployment leads to lower probability values.

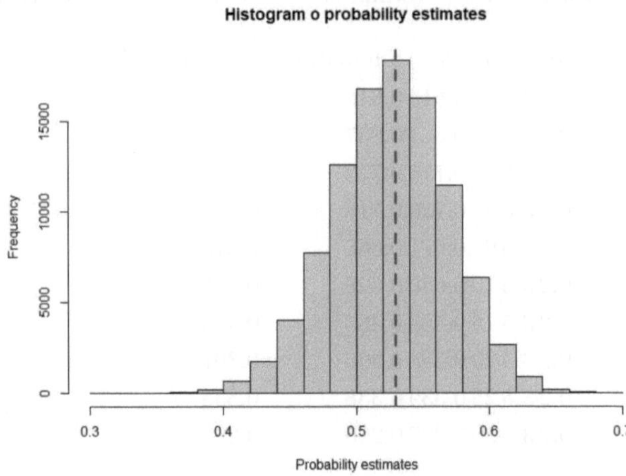

Fig. 3. Histogram of probability estimates – uniform distribution of mines, mean value – dashed line.

If we required that the mines not overlap, it would not be possible to use the formula (14). The events are no longer independent. The probability of destroying a tank is then equal to

$$P(Z) = 1 - \left(1 - \frac{(m+t)}{l}\right)\left(1 - \frac{(m+t)}{l-(m+t)}\right)\cdots\left(1 - \frac{(m+t)}{l-(n-1)(m+t)}\right) = \\ = 1 - \prod_{i=1}^{n}\left(1 - \frac{(m+t)}{l-(i-1)(m+t)}\right). \tag{15}$$

The above expression can be simplified as follows

$$P(Z) = 1 - \prod_{i=1}^{n}\left(1 - \frac{(m+t)}{l-(i-1)(m+t)}\right) = 1 - \prod_{i=1}^{n}\frac{l-i(m+t)}{l-(i-1)(m+t)} = \\ = 1 - \frac{l-(m+t)}{l}\cdot\frac{l-2(m+t)}{l-(m+t)}\cdot\frac{l-3(m+t)}{l-2(m+t)}\cdots \\ \cdots\frac{l-(n-1)(m+t)}{l-(n-2)(m+t)}\cdot\frac{l-n(m+t)}{l-(n-1)(m+t)} = \\ = 1 - \frac{l-n(m+t)}{l} = 1 - \left(1 - \frac{n(m+t)}{l}\right) = \frac{n(m+t)}{l}, \tag{16}$$

which is n times the probability of destruction by a single mine. For parameters $m = 0.2$, $t = 3.5$, $l = 500$, and $n = 101$ we obtain a probability of destruction of 0.747. This probability is surprisingly higher than for a regular array, where we obtained a value of 0.74. The explanation is related to edge effects. With regular placement, it was assumed that the center of the first mine was at the beginning of the section (at position 0) and the center of the last mine was at the end of the section (at position l). However, this reduces the probability of destruction by these mines by half, which actually corresponds to a situation where we have one less mine, i.e., only 100. After this adjustment, the probability of destruction is 0.74. The example above shows how the aforementioned edge effect can be reflected in the resulting probability. For small l, the effect is greater, while for large l and a smaller number of mines, it is negligible.

4 Conclusion

The analytical calculation of minefield effectiveness using geometric probability in cases involving a more general mine distribution (multiple rows and/or irregular placement) is a relatively complex problem, and describing the solution explicitly is difficult. However, as the results of the analyzed cases demonstrate, simulations can be used to reliably estimate the desired probabilities. Upon analysis, it is evident that the effectiveness of minefields is contingent not only on the spacing of the mines and the dimensions of the vehicles but also on the deployment strategy. The findings indicate that the likelihood of vehicle destruction is significantly influenced by both the regularity and randomness of the mine placement. Calculations utilizing geometric probability and the law of total probability yield a more precise and realistic estimation of minefield effectiveness than simple geometric methods, which fail to consider critical factors such as edge effects.

The analytical calculations provided a solid foundation for understanding the probabilities of vehicle hit in minefields. Simulation experiments were conducted to verify the theoretical results, offering a practical validation of the mathematical models. The simulations not only confirmed the analytical findings but also uncovered additional insights into mine placement strategies. Specifically, they demonstrated that randomly distributed mines are less likely to result in vehicle hits than regularly spaced mines. This discovery has significant implications for military and security operations, as it challenges general convictions regarding minefield design. The findings suggest that adopting random placement techniques could potentially enhance the effectiveness of minefields, while potentially reducing the overall number of mines required, leading to more efficient and cost-effective defensive strategies.

Future research on minefield effectiveness assessment should prioritize the integration of dynamic vehicle properties, terrain variability, and tactical situations that influence existing models. These enhancements would provide a more comprehensive and realistic representation of the complex factors affecting minefield efficiency in real-world scenarios. Incorporating probabilistic models based on empirical data can significantly improve the accuracy and reliability of the effectiveness predictions. Additionally, the development of hybrid intelligent methods that combine traditional analytical approaches with machine learning techniques could offer novel insights and enhance the adaptability of minefield assessment tools to diverse operational environments.

Acknowledgments. The paper was supported by institutional funding aimed at the development of the research organization (Long-Term Organisation Development Goals – LANDOPS at the Faculty of Military Leadership, University of Defence, Brno, Czech Republic).

Disclosure of Interests. The authors declare no competing interests.

References

1. Abdelwahab, S.: Defensive Barriers. Effectiveness in modern warfare. https://www.aljundi.ae/en/studies-and-analysis/defensive-barriers-effectiveness-in-modern-warfare/. Accessed 26 Jan 2025
2. Walker, B.C.: Landmine warfare in support of multi-domain battle: balancing discrimination and military effectiveness. In: Presented at the (2017)
3. Gady, F.-S., Kofman, M.: Making attrition work: a viable theory of victory for Ukraine. Survival (Lond). **66**, 7–24 (2024). https://doi.org/10.1080/00396338.2024.2309068
4. NSA: STANAG 2036. Land Mine Laying, Marking, Recording and Reporting Procedures (2005)
5. Palasiewicz, T., Skalický, P.: The possibilities of antitank mine-laying with mine delivered systems in conditions of ACR. Vojenské rozhledy. **26**, 109–117 (2017)
6. Zizka, P., Saibert, R.: Development of the Czech armed forces doctrinal framework. Vojenské rozhledy. **33**, 3–20 (2024). https://doi.org/10.3849/2336-2995.33.2024.01.003-020
7. Hrnčiar, M., Kompan, J., Nohel, J.: The future of the battlefield: Technology-driven predictions in the land domain. Revista Científica General José María Córdova 23 (2025). https://doi.org/10.21830/19006586.1323
8. Havlík, T., Šustr, M., Ivan, J., Pekař, O., Mušinka, M.: Evaluation of the effectiveness of a firing battery in self-defense and protection in the area of firing positions using constructive simulation. J. Defense Model. Simul. 0, 15485129241291580. https://doi.org/10.1177/15485129241291579
9. Repík, D., Hanáková, N., Kotisa, J., Foltin, P.: Present trends, emergencies and their impact on supply chain security. Vojenské rozhledy. **32**, 063–081 (2023). https://doi.org/10.3849/2336-2995.32.2023.03.063-081
10. Kompan, J., Hrnčiar, M., Brezina, D.: AI in mobility support management in hybrid warfare. In: Kabashkin, I., Yatskiv, I., Prentkovskis, O. (eds.) Reliability and Statistics in Transportation and Communication: Human Sustainability and Resilience in the Digital Age, pp. 99–109. Springer, Cham (2025)
11. Palasiewicz, T., Kyjovský, J.: Criteria determination for obstacle effectiveness evaluation. In: International Conference Knowledge-Based Organization (2017)
12. Park, B.-H., Sim, J.: The future of countermobility capability with a literature analysis from FASCAM to terrain shaping obstacle (TSO). J. Korea Academia-Ind. Cooperation Soc. **22**, 291–298 (2021)
13. Sedláček, M., Dohnal, F., Ivan, J., Šustr, M.: Possible approaches to assessing terrain mobility after the effects of artillery munition. Cogent Soc. Sci. **10** (2024). https://doi.org/10.1080/23311886.2024.2368096
14. Palasiewicz, T., Rolenec, O., Lacinová, V., Bilina, M.: A simulation-based analysis for optimal placement of anti-tank obstacles in armored warfare. J. Defense Model. Simul. 15485129251339484 (2025). https://doi.org/10.1177/15485129251339485

15. Jacobs, P.A.: A Model for the Defense of a Mine Field, Monterey (1979)
16. Lee, Y.U.: Probabilistic model and analysis of a conventional preinstalled mine field defense. J. Mil. Oper. Res. Soc. Korea. **6**, 151–184 (1980)
17. Rolenec, O., Šilinger, K., Sedláček, M.: Algorithm development of the decision-making process of an engineer specialization officer. In: Presented at the June (2022). https://doi.org/10.1007/978-3-030-98260-7_18
18. Rolenec, O., Sedláček, M., Vlkovský, M.: Constructive simulation in tactical level planning: options for optimizing engineer support. Vojenské rozhledy. **33**, 51–69 (2024). https://doi.org/10.3849/2336-2995.33.2024.04.051-069
19. Němec, P., Stodola, P., Pecina, M., Neubauer, J., Blaha, M.: Optimization of the weighted multi-facility location problem using MS Excel. Algorithms. **14**, 191 (2021). https://doi.org/10.3390/a14070191
20. Bilina, M., Hasilova, K., Palasiewicz, T.: Drone swarming and its use in minefield laying using mathematical methods. In: CNDCGS 2024, p. 125 (2024)
21. Palasiewicz, T., Baláž, T., Bilina, M., Poročák, L: Enhancing minefield row efficiency model precision through active length integration for improved accuracy. In: 2025 International Conference on Military Technologies (ICMT), pp. 1–5 (2025). https://doi.org/10.1109/ICMT65201.2025.11061333
22. Li, Z., Wu, J., Kong, X., Tang, H., Chen, W.: Research of effectiveness evaluation of anti-tank minefield based on IHHO-MCNN. Command Control Simul. **45**, 87–93 (2023). https://doi.org/10.3969/j.issn.1673-3819.2023.03.013
23. Olofsson, P., Andersson, M.: Probability, Statistics, and Stochastic Processes. Wiley, New York (2012)
24. Klain, D.A., Rota, G.-C.: Introduction to Geometric Probability. Cambridge University Press, Cambridge (1997)

Adaptive Risk Evaluation for Defence Technology Under Uncertain Operational Conditions

Jaroslav Varecha[1], Luděk Rak[2], Kateřina Jelínková[3](✉), and Natálie Gottvaldová[3]

[1] Department of Military Tactics and Operational Art, Armed Forces Academy of General M. R. Štefánik, Liptovský Mikuláš, Slovakia
[2] Department of Tactics, Faculty of Military Leadership, University of Defence, Brno, Czech Republic
[3] Department of Fire Support, Faculty of Military Leadership, University of Defence, Brno, Czech Republic
katerina.jelinkova2@unob.cz

Abstract. Risk analysis plays a key role in the defense environment, especially in operations burdened by uncertainty and the risk of technical or information failure. Such failures can significantly limit the ability to respond quickly and accurately to emerging threats. Unlike the civilian sector, where economic or operational impacts are often sufficient, military applications also require the protection of lives, continuity of command, support for decision-making under pressure, and the implementation of rational decisions concerning real-time resources.

Current approaches based on known states and predictable probabilities are often insufficient for the rational determination of risk mitigation strategies and their financial planning in conditions of uncertainty. The dynamic introduction of new technologies puts users in situations where they must deal with entirely new tactical and technical aspects of their deployment. Risk analysis must therefore be carried out even in cases where knowledge of new systems is limited, which further increases the degree of uncertainty.

The authors therefore consider it essential to examine applications of methods that can support decision-making processes, reliably identify vulnerabilities in newly introduced systems, and contribute to the design of targeted measures to increase their overall resilience and effectiveness in conditions burdened by uncertainty.

This article discusses the use of fuzzy set mathematics in the risk analysis of newly introduced command and control system technologies, whose architecture must ensure communication in a classified environment and in real time. The approach described combines risk prioritization with the financial and time resources available to the system user at a given moment.

Keywords: Asset · Command and control center · Fuzzy set · Re-source and time frame · Risk · Risk analysis · Risk management

J. Novotný et al. (Eds.): MESAS 2025, LNCS 16627, pp. 114–136, 2027.
https://doi.org/10.1007/978-3-032-33182-3_7

1 Introduction

The current international and security environment is deteriorating. In particular, the conflict between Ukraine and the Russian Federation, which began with the annexation of Crimea in 2014 and culminated in a large-scale war in 2022, has objectively increased the likelihood of armed conflict. This is leading to a growing demand for modern weapon systems, as evidenced by the increase in defence spending by NATO countries after 2014 and even more significantly after 2022. Empirical analyses show that the growth rate and structure of these expenditures vary significantly among member states, which affects their ability to respond to new threats and adapt military capabilities to current needs [1]. Companies organised in defence industry associations are responding to this situation by expanding their workforce, adjusting their product portfolios, and introducing new technologies to counter emerging threats. If current conditions persist, similar developments can be expected in the coming years.

However, this process is not without risks. These include uncertainty about future needs, types of threats, and the introduction of new, often untested technologies. The key dilemma is the choice between deploying a smaller number of advanced technologies and a larger number of older systems. In the context of a shortage of qualified technical personnel in the labour market, it is necessary to strike a balance between investment in research and development and production capacities, or a combination of the two. The state's ability to respond to these challenges is also influenced by the way risks are financed at the regional level, which can strengthen or weaken the overall resilience of the security system [2]. As a result, both the defence industry and system users operate in a highly uncertain environment in which it is difficult to predict whether, how, and to what extent an armed conflict may escalate.

This article addresses issues of effectiveness, reliability, and cybersecurity in the context of risk analysis of newly introduced command and control nodes. Given the growing importance of integrated military systems and the increasing complexity of security threats, it is essential to assess risks not only in terms of operational safety, but also with a focus on cyber and technical aspects. The research questions are:

"How can fuzzy set theory be applied in risk analysis and decision-making processes related to the application of new military technologies in tactical conditions?"

"Is there a suitable mathematical framework, and how can it be applied to assess various threats and strategies for mitigating them in conditions of uncertainty?"

Using a case study, we present a method for analysing security threats affecting a new command and control node using fuzzy set theory. Partial threat assessments are based on expert confidence levels derived from analogous scenarios and are then aggregated using a compensatory decision-making method. Unlike traditional approaches, this approach creates fuzzy boundaries between risk levels. The goal is to identify pessimistic and optimistic scenarios, giving decision-makers more flexibility in formulating context-sensitive responses.

The proposed method is beneficial in borderline cases where the assessed threats are close to the thresholds between predefined risk categories (e.g., between medium and high risk). In such situations, even a slight change can shift the risk to a different category, leading to a different response. In contrast, the fuzzy approach allows for smooth scaling of outputs, reducing sudden jumps in evaluation and increasing the stability of results.

This makes the method particularly suitable for environments with data uncertainty, where consistency and predictability of decision-making processes are essential. To implement this approach, Mamdani's fuzzy inference system is chosen, which is suitable for expert-driven decision-making in situations with vague and incomplete data. The model uses three input variables: the probability of a threat occurring, the level of system vulnerability, and the degree of possible impact. Each of the variables is divided into three fuzzy sets (i.e., low, medium, high), with fuzzy membership functions determined based on expert assessment by specialists in operational-tactical, system, and technical architecture.

The output of the model is an aggregated risk value expressed by a linguistic variable with fuzzy sets of "low," "medium," and "high" risk. IF–THEN fuzzy rules are created by experts in the field of defence research to reflect decision-making scenarios in a military environment. This specific fuzzy apparatus not only ensures more flexible responses to borderline situations but also increases the transparency of the assessment and enables the traceability of decision-making steps. Risk analysis is an essential discipline for the armed forces. In an environment characterised by a high degree of uncertainty, insecurity, and risk, dynamic operations, and changing potential threats, the ability to effectively identify, analyse, and manage risks is key to achieving strategic goals, completing operational and tactical tasks, protecting personnel, and ensuring the required technical condition of deployed systems. The fuzzy model must be constructed in such a way that it accurately reflects the real decision-making priorities of the military environment, including multi-criteria evaluation, working with uncertain inputs, and expert weighting. A model based on second-order fuzzy sets was applied to select the optimal solution for the tactical deployment of engineering units. It has been proven that without a carefully defined structure of fuzzy rules and membership functions, the system loses its informative value and may provide unrepresentative results [3].

However, the military context differs in many ways from the civilian context and requires a specific understanding and application of risk analysis principles. In the armed forces, risk analysis is not limited to the protection of information systems or property, but also includes the lives of soldiers, the success of missions, the defence capability of the state, and international security commitments. The consequences of misjudging or underestimating risks can be fatal and far-reaching in a military environment. Therefore, thorough and systematic risk analysis is an integral part of planning, operational and tactical command, logistics, training, acquisitions, and all other key military processes. The importance of the human factor in this process is also demonstrated by a comparison of the Czech and Slovak approaches to the training of artillery officers for Joint Fires coordination, which shows that unified standards and training methodologies increase interoperability and improve the quality of decision-making in complex combat conditions [4].

In this context, MKPP[1] plays a vital role as a means of effective coordination and control of artillery fire, missile systems, air defence systems (hereinafter referred to as PVO), and air support. Its main contribution is the coordination and increased accuracy of fire, the minimisation of collateral damage, and rapid response to changing battlefield conditions. Thanks to advanced processing of sensor data and combat situation

[1] A command-and-control vehicle

information, this enables the correct assessment of risks in real time. To maintain these capabilities in demanding conditions, it is necessary to build a resilient and secure communications infrastructure that ensures reliable data transmission, for example, in the event of electronic interference [5].

Given the importance of the topic, the motivation for presenting the partial results of the research is to compare different methods of risk analysis. Two methods are compared: one that complies with the order of the Minister of Defence [6] and an alternative technique that uses fuzzy set mathematics to determine the criticality of assets, the degree of criticality of threats, and the degree of criticality of risks. The scope of threats is selected using the results of a questionnaire survey among experts from the artillery community and students of the "Artillery Unit Commander" program, which is organised as part of the research activities of the Department of Fire Support.

Although the case study is grounded in the specific organisational, doctrinal, and technical context of the Czech Armed Forces, the underlying structure of the proposed method is not limited to a single national environment. The framework can be adapted to other armed forces and security organisations by redefining the set of assets and threats, recalibrating the fuzzy scales, and involving domain experts familiar with the respective command-and-control architecture. This makes the approach applicable to a wide range of multinational and allied settings, provided that the necessary expert knowledge and contextual data are available.

2 Literature Review

Current technological innovations are taking place in an environment that is highly dynamic, full of uncertainty, and incomplete data. High costs and time-consuming development must be balanced with the need to make quick and informed decisions while making the best use of limited resources. Therefore, accurate and flexible risk analysis methods are indispensable for planning during development and subsequent operational support of already established systems. Over the past decade, risk analysis has shifted from fixed, precisely defined models to hybrid approaches that combine statistical models, Bayesian learning, fuzzy logic, and system dynamics with algorithms based on real data. However, analytical processes set up in this way are very diverse, and their advantages are not always apparent without deeper comparison.

An analysis of environmental risks [7] shows that even large and complex data sets can be effectively simplified and converted into comprehensible output using a screening method that employs traffic light classification. This method combines multi-year monitoring of dozens of data sets and works with predefined extreme values, i.e., the worst and best scenarios. The result is a single synthetic indicator, also called an environmental risk score, which is classified into a colour band (green, yellow, red) that visually indicates the level of threat. This traffic light scale ensures immediate interpretability even for users without specialist training. The importance of environmental factors for the security environment is also confirmed by a study focusing on anthropogenic sources of mercury in the Baltic Sea, which emphasizes the need for systematic identification and mitigation of these threats to maintain the stability and operational capabilities of the armed forces [8]. From a methodological point of view and in terms of the issue under investigation, this approach is particularly valuable in that it transforms diverse and often incomplete data into a unified framework that allows for comparison.

The use of military technologies, in particular artillery systems and special ammunition, to mitigate the risk of forest fires starting and spreading in difficult-to-access terrain, where conventional suppression methods are ineffective, is analyzed based on numerical simulations. These simulations show that a single salvo (eight shots) is capable of applying fire extinguishing agent to an area of up to 650 m^2. This concept represents an alternative approach, but its implementation requires a comprehensive assessment of safety aspects, logistical demands, and environmental impacts. Further research focused on the synergistic integration of military and civilian technologies is recommended to enhance disaster response effectiveness [9, 10].

The same emphasis on the interpretability of results is also evident in a study based on an extensive statistical analysis of more than a thousand cases of occupational accidents. The analysis shows that even relatively small changes in the weights of individual risk factors, such as the absence of personal protective equipment or insufficient supervision of the workplace, can lead to significant shifts in the prioritization of preventive measures. Using multidimensional contingency tables and logistic regression, it is demonstrated that the weights assigned to these factors are not stable and that their modification affects the resulting risk level. The results confirm that fixed parameters may not always reflect actual conditions and that it is necessary to verify how the overall assessment changes when the input data is modified. This approach is potentially applicable in other specific areas, such as military logistics, where, as in construction, the human factor, standards, and regulations play a key role. The model can be adapted to a specific environment by adjusting the weights or adding particular variables, while the statistical basis of the model remains unchanged [11].

An alternative approach is based on a method that combines rough set theory and information entropy intending to eliminate redundant values while objectively determining the weights of individual criteria. In the first phase, the original set of variables is reduced using rough set analysis, retaining only those that exhibit decision-making ability without loss of information content. Subsequently, an entropic weighting procedure is applied to the reduced set, which assigns greater importance to variables with the most significant variability of values in the cases under consideration, i.e., those that carry the most tremendous amount of information. The result is a model that is both economical and information-rich, providing a so-called "data-clean" starting framework that can be directly used in quantitative decision-making [12].

An analysis of the development of weapon systems shows that the time dimension of risk is of fundamental importance, particularly in dynamic risk analysis models. In particular, it has been identified that delayed resource allocation triggers a chain reaction leading to increased costs, extended timelines, and reduced production quality. The system-dynamic model describes these causal relationships and defines key variables with precisely defined minimum and maximum impact values. It allows the simulation of scenarios in which even relatively small delays can lead to significant financial and qualitative consequences, while also providing a basis for timely intervention and the allocation of reserve resources [13]. This approach is in line with the risk management methodology in transport infrastructure, which links the phases of identification, analysis, evaluation, design of measures, and monitoring into a closed feedback loop. This framework allows for continuous updating of input data depending on the current traffic load. An innovative feature is the ability to recalculate variable weights through machine learning automatically [14].

Both approaches point out that in an environment with a high degree of uncertainty, risk must be perceived as a highly variable quantity. At the same time, they provide tools that estimate the future impacts of current decisions and continuously adjust the weights of input data. It is this flexibility that makes dynamic models suitable for use in specific environments, such as the military sector, where there is a lack of time, limited resources, and a need to respond to unpredictable situations. To complement these analytical methods, constructive simulation can be used to evaluate the operational effectiveness of planned measures in realistic scenarios and minimize the risks associated with their implementation [15].

The use of discrete event simulation (DES) in professional training focused on analysis, planning, and decision support during highly complex and dynamic military operations is primarily focused on the RSOM[2] process, which requires finding the optimal balance between time, cost, and quality. The study shows that this type of simulation can effectively support logistics planning and preparation for future scenarios, including the integration of autonomous systems. The approach also makes it possible to identify and minimize risks associated with supply chain disruptions, time delays, and critical resource failures [16].

The development of an advanced simulation system based on VR[3]/AR[4] technologies for teaching the principles of fire support, particularly within artillery units, involves the use of realistic models of military equipment and the integration of data from UAV[5]s and laser scanning to increase the credibility of the simulation. The main benefit is the possibility of conducting training in an environment without the risks associated with live firing, while reducing financial and logistical demands. The solution represents a significant step towards reducing safety risks and more effective risk management in military training [17]. The impact of risks on the expected capabilities of an army unit is examined through an experiment using simulations to identify potential threats to the unit's area of operation. The experiment is conducted under conditions characterized by a high degree of uncertainty, and its goal is to determine the unit's survivability and the need to allocate resources to eliminate the identified risks [18]. The risks associated with the specific deployment of artillery and engineering units are analyzed in this case primarily from the perspective of operational factors, without direct consideration of economic aspects. A scenario is described in which the protection of human resources is prioritized over the costs of risk elimination, in an environment with a high degree of uncertainty and a significant potential for loss of life. Non-standard procedures for the use of artillery units are proposed to reduce these risks [19].

[2] Reception, Staging and Onward Movement
[3] Virtual Reality
[4] Augmented Reality
[5] Unmanned Aerial Vehicle

The risks associated with underestimating the preparation of professional personnel are assessed using the example of required specific skills, and key factors for minimizing them are identified. Insufficient personnel preparedness is considered a significant problem, and the proposed solution is the systematic application of established rules and their verification in the practical deployment of systems. The study focuses on the risks arising from the human factor, which is a significant source of uncertainty [20].

The risks associated with applying "traditional" procedures in an automated process environment are analyzed using the example of military units. It has been found that automation often leads to an underestimation of the professional capabilities of personnel, which can pose a serious operational risk, especially in the event of an automated system failure. The analysis shows that manual calculation of corrections using the proposed analytical approach can mitigate this risk, as it enables rapid and accurate fire control even in degraded conditions. This increases the resilience of units and reduces the likelihood of fire support mission failure [21].

A different perspective on the issue of uncertainty is provided by the proposal to use a Bayesian inference framework, which emphasizes the gradual collection of data over time and the continuous updating of predefined, distributed probabilities. This approach allows models to gradually "learn" from newly available data and thus refine their predictions. A significant advantage of the Bayesian approach is its transparency, as each model decision can be easily explained based on the observation of new data, which strengthens confidence in its reliability [22].

The following text focuses on the application of fuzzy set mathematics in an environment threatened by the loss of defended objects as a result of enemy air attacks. The key point is the use of fuzzy sets to describe states of uncertainty and their combination with the evaluation of the priority of individual defended objects and rational options for their protection [23]. Similarly, another study presents a computer expert system for risk management in the field of air defence, designed to assess the threat of an air strike in real time. The system uses fuzzy methods and is based on expert knowledge of tactics to determine the level of threat to a protected object based on the relationships between the elements of an air attack and potential targets. Verification by experts confirmed the accuracy of the system, which increases the ability to identify and manage risks in a specific military area promptly [24].

While the Bayesian approach works with probabilities and gradual learning, fuzzy logic focuses on processing vague and ill-defined values. Another study focuses on this principle, proposing a multi-level hierarchical model capable of converting informal expert judgments, often expressed in linguistic values such as "low," "medium," or "high," into numerical values suitable for calculations. The proposed framework also allows for the definition of specific scenarios with extreme impacts, such as so-called catastrophic variants, which are often overlooked or underestimated in conventional models [25]. Another study presents a kernel density estimation method for circular data, which it considers key for analyzing phenomena of a periodic nature that may influence decision-making in risk-related areas (e.g., the direction of fire spread, wind, or migration routes). A new bandwidth selection procedure based on cross-validation using the von Mises density kernel is proposed. The method has been verified on both simulated and real data and provides more robust estimates than existing approaches, thereby reducing the risk of erroneous conclusions in modelling [26].

Further work sees effective risk elimination in the simulation of risk states and proposes methods aimed at increasing the accuracy of estimating the size of the band of their occurrence. Commonly used procedures for selecting bandwidth are analyzed, and new approaches inspired by the linear case are proposed, including solutions with variable bandwidth. These proposals were tested on simulations involving multimodal, peaked, and asymmetric distributions and subsequently verified on real data on animal movement and wind direction. The results confirm the potential of the new methods for more reliable modelling, which is key for high-risk applications [27].

The importance of fuzzy logic is growing, especially in the context of large data sets, where traditional methods have limited effectiveness. As another study shows, the developed system can automatically analyze hundreds of thousands of data profiles in real time without the need for manual intervention, thanks to the use of fuzzy logic. The goal of these modern approaches is to maximize the ability of models to adapt to new conditions while maintaining the transparency of the processes leading to the results. While the Bayesian approach is suitable for situations where data is collected gradually over time, fuzzy logic is instrumental where information is uncertain, ambiguous, or incomplete [28].

In industrial practice, a combination of FMEA[6] and MOORA[7] methods have proven effective, combining expert analysis with precise calculations and enabling transparent risk assessment. The FMEA method is used to identify potential failures and assess their impact, while the MOORA method converts input data into numerical form and then ranks it according to significance. This approach reduces the influence of subjective assessment and ensures reliable and repeatable results. The framework also includes the establishment of a so-called RPN[8] reference threshold, which in this case determines the risk acceptance limit, facilitating decision-making and planning of measures to eliminate or mitigate it [29, 30]. However, as another study points out, the mere existence of a risk management system is not sufficient. The proposed measures are feasible. The level of risk that people are willing to accept in a given context and the available means to eliminate it play a decisive role. The study demonstrates the adjustment of weights in risk assessment depending on the specific situation and the current level of risk acceptability [31].

The financial dimension of risk management is a key aspect of decision-making in defence planning and crisis management. Several studies focus on linking costs with the effectiveness of measures, both at the level of individual organizations and at the level of regions and international structures.

In this case, risk analyses are used to determine rational defence costs, combining risk assessment with the costs of eliminating risks in conditions where the assessed entity exhibits risk aversion. This manifests itself as a loss of utility in the event of the loss of an asset or part thereof. The proposed solution, therefore, aims to eliminate the loss of an asset or part thereof by minimizing the loss of utility from it, and this

6 Failure Modes and Effects Analysis

7 Multi-Objective Optimization on the basis of Ratio Analysis

8 Risk Priority Number

approach is considered rational [32]. The risks associated with the decision-making process on the structure of air defence measures are analyzed with a focus on the threat of inefficient use of resources and failure to perform operational tasks. The analysis shows that determining the marginal utility of GBAD[9] elements using game theory makes it possible to optimize the ratio between operational efficiency and economic efficiency. This approach contributes to reducing the risk of misallocation of resources while increasing the resilience and readiness of the entire system [33]. The following study deals with the combination of risks and the costs of their elimination, including the loss of utility from an asset. Still, it approaches the issue through a reverse task. It presents a mathematical model of risk aversion, the aim of which is to determine the level of risk that the evaluator is aware of, depending on the amount of funds they are willing to invest in its elimination [34].

Based on the literature review, the professional literature covers a wide range of approaches to risk analysis in environments characterized by high dynamics, uncertainty, and limited resources. The identified studies agree on the need to use methods that are accurate, flexible, and easy to interpret, with the common goal of ensuring the ability to respond quickly to changing conditions. These include both advanced mathematical and statistical models, such as fuzzy logic, Bayesian approaches, or kernel estimates, as well as practically oriented simulation tools and decision-making frameworks that are used in planning, training, and operations management.

The research further shows that an essential element of modern methods is the ability to combine technical, organizational, and economic aspects of risk management. This approach makes it possible to assess not only the probability and severity of threats, but also the effectiveness of the resources spent on eliminating them or reducing their impact. The combination of analytical models with economic indicators and operational simulations thus creates a comprehensive framework that can be adapted to the specific conditions of both military and civilian environments. The result is a set of tools and methodologies that support informed decision-making, reduce uncertainty, and increase the resilience of systems to threats in both the short and long term.

Despite this progress, many of the existing approaches still face several limitations when applied to military environments characterized by rapidly changing conditions. Conventional risk models often rely on fixed parameter values, discrete risk categories, or static weighting schemes that do not adequately reflect changes in threat levels between peacetime and crisis. In addition, their outputs are typically expressed as single-point estimates that mask the uncertainty and variability inherent in expert assessments. These constraints reduce the transparency and robustness of the decision-making process, particularly in borderline cases where small changes in input parameters can lead to qualitatively different conclusions. These shortcomings motivate the use of fuzzy set theory combined with multi-criteria decision-making methods to provide a more flexible and adaptive framework for risk assessment in defence applications.

[9] Ground-Based Air Defence

3 Method Description

The diagram below presents a conceptual model of risk anatomy in the context of information security (Fig. 1). It visually formalises the interrelationships between key entities, namely asset owners, assets, risks, vulnerabilities, threats, threat agents, and countermeasures. The model describes a causal chain in which vulnerabilities and threats condition the emergence of risks, while the activities of threat agents further influence their intensity and nature. The implementation of adequate countermeasures disrupts this chain, thereby reducing the likelihood or impact of undesirable events. At the same time, the model captures the dynamics of assets, which can be either enhanced or degraded depending on the action of the above factors [35].

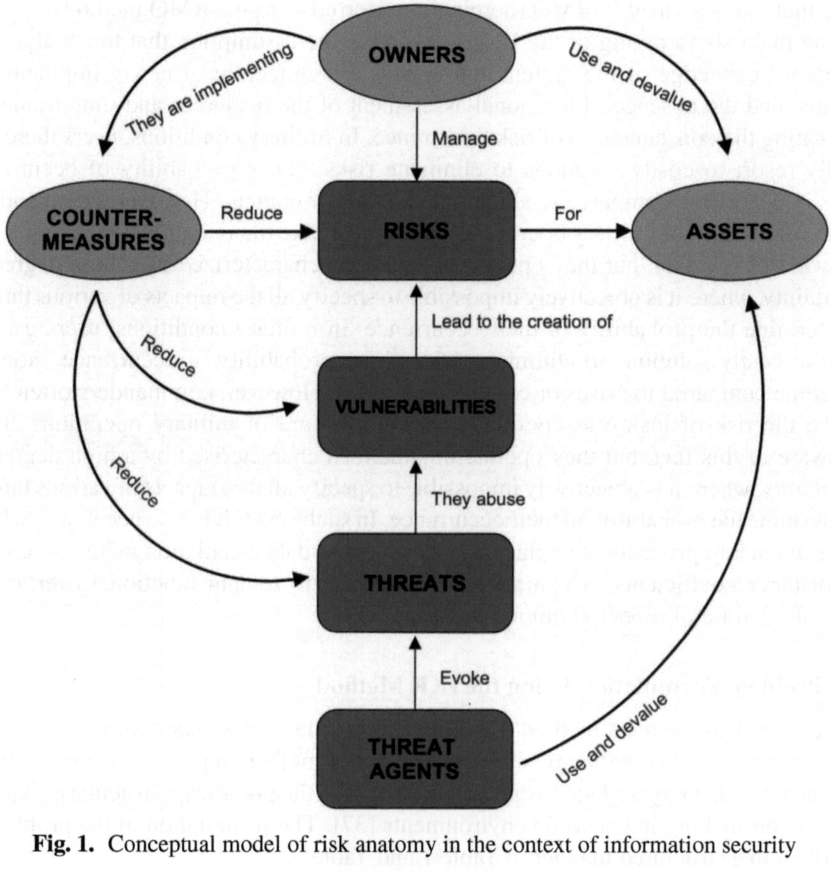

Fig. 1. Conceptual model of risk anatomy in the context of information security

In the Czech Armed Forces (hereinafter referred to as CAF), there is currently a valid order from the Minister of Defense, that sets out the risk management procedure within the Ministry of Defense. This order formulates a procedure that results in the ranking of individual risks based on the criticality of assets and threats. The individual steps of the method address the specification of assets, the assessment of the criticality of assets depending on their reparability and availability, the specification of threats, the evaluation of the criticality of threats about assets, and the calculation and determination of the criticality of risk. The basic analysis procedure consists of assessing the reparability and availability of assets and the criticality of threats on a scale ranging from 1 to 4. Based on the sum of the partial assessments, each asset and each threat is then classified into the appropriate risk category. The overall degree of risk criticality depends on the criticality value of the asset and the degree of threat criticality. Four levels of risk criticality are defined: acceptable without intervention, conditionally acceptable, recommending supervision and prevention, unacceptable without implementation of measures, and completely inappropriate, requiring immediate and systemic solution. Here, the fuzzy risk assessment method (hereinafter referred to as fKR) presented and proposed in this article, combined with the application of the MOORA method, eliminates the shortcomings of the method described in RMO (hereinafter referred to as the RMO method).

The main shortcoming of the RMO method is the assumption that the analyst has extensive knowledge of the system and technical architecture of newly implemented systems, and the absence of a rational assessment of the resources and time frame for eliminating the consequences of risk occurrence. In military conditions, users therefore usually resort to costly solutions to eliminate risks whose probability of occurrence varies in peacetime compared to situations of crisis or combat. However, commanders, by the very nature of military operations, often must take the risk of losing assets. They are aware of this fact, but they operate in situations characterized by a high degree of uncertainty, where it is objectively impossible to specify all the impacts of various threats or determine the probability of their occurrence. In military conditions, users usually resort to costly solutions to eliminate risks whose probability of occurrence varies in peacetime compared to crises or combat operations. However, commanders often have to take the risk of losing assets due to the very nature of military operations. They are aware of this fact, but they operate in situations characterised by a high degree of uncertainty, where it is objectively impossible to specify all the impacts of various threats or determine the probability of their occurrence. In such cases, it is also necessary to have practical backup procedures in place, such as manual data calculation using directional and distance coefficients, which allows fire support to remain functional even in the event of a failure of modern computing systems [36].

3.1 Problem Formulation Using the fKR Method

The fuzzy risk assessment method uses compensated decisions to determine the criticality of an asset and, in combination with the MOORA method, represents a multi-criteria approach to risk analysis. Due to the use of fuzzy sets, the process is particularly suitable for decision-making in uncertain environments [37]. The formulation of the problem is described in a structured manner in Table 1 and Table 2.

Let us have:

- m assets A_i, where $i \in \langle 1; m \rangle$;
- m evaluations KR_i (/) for each of the assets A_i, where $KR_i \in \langle 0; 1 \rangle$, the value KR_i expresses the evaluator's degree of conviction about the criticality of the risk for A_i, depending on the criticality of the asset and the criticality of the threats that endanger the asset, A_i;

- m RC_i (kCZK[10]), where RC_i expresses an expert estimate or, if sufficient information is available, the determination of the Recovery Costs necessary to repair or restore the system or achieve at least an acceptably functional state;
- m RT_i (hours), where RT_i expresses an expert estimate or, if sufficient information is available, the time necessary to repair or restore the system to its original state or to achieve at least an acceptably functional state.

Then, for each asset A_i, the following can be determined:

- F_i (/), which expresses the overall risk assessment of asset A_i;
- KR_i^N (/) – the degree of risk criticality after normalization;
- RC_i^N – expert estimate or, if sufficient information is available, actual Recovery Costs after normalization;
- RT_i^N (/) – expert estimate or, if sufficient information is available, actual Time to Restore Normal Conditions after normalization.
- Ranking KR, which expresses the order according to KR priority;
- Ranking RC, which expresses the order according to the amount of Recovery Costs;
- Ranking RT, which expresses the order according to Time to Restore Normal Conditions;
- Priority ranking, which expresses the order reflecting the compromise between KR, RC, and RT, thus considering the number of resources and time required to restore the system.

Table 1. Formulation of the fKR method before input normalization Source: own processing

Asset	KR	RC	RT
	(/)	(kCZK)	(h)
A_1	KR_1	RC_1	RT_1
A_2	KR_2	RC_2	RT_2
A_i	KR_i	RC_i	RT_i
A_m	KR_m	RC_m	RT_m

Table 2. Formulation of the fKR method after normalization of inputs Source: own processing

Asset	KR^N	RC^N	RT^N	F	Ranking KR	Ranking RC	Ranking RT	Priority ranking
	(/)	(/)	(/)	(/)				
A_1	${KR_1}^N$	${RC_1}^N$	${RT_1}^N$	F_1	$\langle 1; m \rangle$	$\langle 1; m \rangle$	$\langle 1; m \rangle$	$\langle 1; m \rangle$
A_2	${KR_2}^N$	${RC_2}^N$	${RT_2}^N$	F_2	$\langle 1; m \rangle$	$\langle 1; m \rangle$	$\langle 1; m \rangle$	$\langle 1; m \rangle$
A_i	${KR_i}^N$	${RC_i}^N$	${RT_i}^N$	F_i	$\langle 1; m \rangle$	$\langle 1; m \rangle$	$\langle 1; m \rangle$	$\langle 1; m \rangle$
A_m	${KR_m}^N$	${RC_m}^N$	${RT_m}^N$	F_m	$\langle 1; m \rangle$	$\langle 1; m \rangle$	$\langle 1; m \rangle$	$\langle 1; m \rangle$

[10] 1 kCZK = 1 000, – CZK

3.2 Procedure and Relationships for Computation

First, key assets and corresponding potential threats that may affect their availability, integrity, or functionality are systematically identified. In the conditions of the Czech Armed Forces, the assessment is based on the ČSN[11] ISO[12] 31000:2018 standard.

The analysis published here uses a weighted fuzzy approach with values from the discrete set {0; 0.2; 0.4; 0.6; 0.8; 1} to evaluate all levels of variables, which ensures standardization and subsequent data processing [37].

The calculation of the asset criticality index (KA_i) and the risk criticality index (KR_i) uses a compensation coefficient $\gamma \in \langle 0;1 \rangle$, which determines whether the evaluator prefers a pessimistic or optimistic approach to risk assessment. The relationship considers the evaluator's attitude to risk and willingness to accept uncertainty [38]. A demonstration example is given in the following chapter.

The degree of risk criticality is determined according to the following relationship:

$$KR_i = \gamma \times \max\{KA_i; KH_i\} + (1 - \gamma) \times \min\{KA_i; KH_i\}, \quad (1)$$

where the individual symbols mean:

- KR_i (/) – risk criticality level, $KR_i > 0,5$ means that the risk criticality level is rather high, and it is usually necessary to plan measures to eliminate or reduce it; if $KR_i \leq 0,5$, it means that the risk criticality level is rather low, and in the best case, it is not necessary to plan measures to eliminate or reduce it;
- KA_i (/) – asset criticality level;
- KH_i (/) – threat criticality level;
- γ (/) – compensation coefficient, $\gamma \in \langle 0;1 \rangle$, for the purpose of the demonstration example, the values $\gamma = 0.8$ for pessimistic assessment and $\gamma = 0.2$ for optimistic assessment are selected.

The asset criticality level (KA_i) is a function of the fuzzy assessment of the repairability-replaceability and sensitivity-availability of the asset and is calculated according to the following formula:

$$KA_i = \gamma \times \max\{N_i; D_i\} + (1 - \gamma) \times \min\{N_i; D_i\} \quad (2)$$

where the individual symbols mean:

- KA_i (/) – asset criticality level;
- N_i (/) – fuzzy assessment of asset repairability and replaceability with a value from the discrete set {0; 0.2; 0.4; 0.6; 0.8; 1} with the meaning of extreme values:
- 0 – the asset can be replaced immediately, without significant time and financial demands, a user can perform the replacement without special qualifications, or the asset is available as a spare part;
- 0.2, 0.4 – the asset can be repaired or replaced;
- 0.6, 0.8 – the asset cannot be repaired or replaced;

[11] ČSN – Czech Technical Standart

[12] ISO – International Organization for Standardization

- 1 – the asset cannot be replaced immediately, the time and financial demands of repairing the asset are considerable, replacement can only be carried out by a user with exceptional qualifications, loss of the asset means that a backup solution must be implemented in another way, without using the original solution, the fulfillment of the combat task is practically impossible, and a backup solution must be prepared in advance, including organizational measures;
- D_i (/) – fuzzy assessment of asset availability and sensitivity using values from the discrete set {0; 0.2; 0.4; 0.6; 0.8; 1} with the following meanings for the extreme values:

  - 0 – the asset is available;
  - 0.2, 0.4 – the asset is rather available;
  - 0.6, 0.8 – the asset is relatively unavailable;
  - 1 – the asset is completely unavailable;

- γ (/) – compensation coefficient, $\gamma \in \langle 0;1 \rangle$, for the purposes of the demonstration example, the values $\gamma = 0.8$ for pessimistic assessment and $\gamma = 0.2$ for optimistic assessment are selected.

The threat criticality level (KH_i) is expressed by a fuzzy assessment that takes into account the impact of the threat and the intention of its perpetrator to act against the system. Determining this level requires knowledge, assessment of the current situation, and the ability to make at least an approximate prediction of future developments. The article presented here is based on a questionnaire survey, the results of which are based on the opinions of fifty-five experts from the armed forces and the defense industry.

The potential effects of electronic warfare and cyber-attacks, the implementation of system viruses, espionage, unauthorized access to the system, unqualified access to the system by operators, a lack of spare parts, and intentional misuse of the system are considered to be fundamental. The specific KH_i values for individual A_i assets are listed in the following chapter.

The criteria listed in Table 1 are:

- KR – maximization, the higher the more serious and requiring attention;
- RC – minimization, the lower the better for ensuring full system functionality;
- RT – minimization, the lower the better for organizational repair arrangements.

Given that each criterion has a different dimension and, in absolute terms, reaches completely different values, it is necessary to normalize them to a unit vector.

After normalizing the inputs, the resulting value F_i is determined according to the following relationship:

$$F_i = KR_i^N - RC_i^N - RT_i^N \tag{3}$$

Practical experience shows that when working with complex data sets, commonly available software tools such as MS Excel can be used to solve multi-facility location optimisation tasks and quickly generate resource allocation variants for subsequent evaluation [39].

3.3 Demonstration of the Use of the fKR Method

The demonstration of use is described step by step. It summarizes the partial conclusions of the research conducted on risk analysis procedures in connection with the introduction of a new command and control (C2) node for use by armed forces units. To ensure that its potential is fully exploited, the decision-making process must be supported by a functional and integrated C2I system that enables a fast, accurate, and reliable flow of information across all levels of command [40].

Step 1 – Determining Assets and Asset Criticality
Given the sensitivity of the issue, the overview of assets in Table 3 is generalized and presented in a scope that supports the receipt, processing, and display of messages and reports, the receipt and processing of orders and commands, the distribution of information, and the filtering of information with varying degrees of confidentiality.

The assessment of asset criticality uses two complementary scales, each of which is discretized in the interval $\langle 0;1 \rangle$. **Repairability/replaceability** expresses the difficulty of restoring the function of an asset: a value of 0 indicates a quick and inexpensive repair, 0.2 indicates increased effort, 0.4 indicates a complex restoration with a diversion of capacities, 0.6 an almost impossible replacement, 0.8 extreme costs, and 1 a situation where restoration is neither technically nor economically feasible.

Sensitivity/availability describes the security regime and accessibility: 0 represents a freely accessible element, 0.2 partial service restrictions, 0.4 significant restrictions, 0.6 access only under special conditions, 0.8 strict secrecy status, and 1 critical unavailability. The combination of both values creates an integrated vulnerability profile, which is further used to calculate the overall criticality and prioritize protective measures; the methodology converts expert judgment into a transparent numerical metric suitable for quantitative comparison.

Table 3. Overview of assets and asset criticality levels Source: own processing

ID Asset	Asset	Repairability/ replaceability	Sensitivity/ availability	Asset criticality level
		N (/)	D (/)	KA (/)
A_1	Server station classified	1.00	1.00	1.00
A_2	Operator terminal classified	1.00	0.80	0.96
A_3	Security filter	0.80	0.80	0.80
A_4	Server station unclassified	0.60	0.40	0.56
A_5	Operator terminal unclassified	0.40	0.60	0.56
A_6	Operator terminal unclassified	0.40	0.60	0.56

(*continued*)

Table 3. (*continued*)

ID Asset	Asset	Repairability/ replaceability	Sensitivity/ availability	Asset criticality level
		N (/)	D (/)	KA (/)
A_7	Operator terminal unclassified	0.40	0.60	0.56
A_8	Radio station classified	0.80	0.80	0.80
A_9	Radio station unclassified	0.20	0.60	0.52
A_{10}	Radio station unclassified	0.20	0.60	0.52

For example, for asset A_2, the following applies:

$$KA_2 = 0.8 \times \max\{1.0; 0.8\} + (1 - 0.8) \times \min\{1.0; 0.8\} = 0.96$$

$$= \gamma \times \max\{N_2; D_2\} + (1 - \gamma) \times \min\{N_2; D_2\} \quad (4)$$

The KA_2 value = 0.96 expresses the evaluator's (analyst's) degree of conviction about the high criticality of the asset. $KA_2 > 0.5$ so, it can be assumed with a high degree of certainty that measures – tactics to protect the asset – need to be specified and implemented. In the situation demonstrated, a similar partial conclusion is accepted for all assets.

Determining the Criticality Level of a Threat

For each asset, specific threats that may affect it are identified. Each threat is assessed using two components:

- Level of determination/intent of the threat (Z), which indicates whether the threat is random or targeted.
- Level of threat intensity (V), which expresses the strength of the impact.

Both values range from 0 to 1.

The overall Threat criticality level (KH) is obtained as the product of these two components:

$$KH = Z \times V \quad (5)$$

From among multiple threats related to a single asset, the most serious one is selected, i.e., the one with the highest KH value. This highest value is referred to as the threat criticality level [41].

Table 4. Threat criticality rating Source: own processing

ID Asset	Level of determination/ intent of the threat	Level of threat intensity	Threat criticality level
	Z (/)	V (/)	KH (/)
A_1	0.8	0.8	0.80
A_2	1.0	0.6	0.92
A_3	0.8	1.0	0.96
A_4	0.8	0.2	0.68
A_5	1.0	0.2	0.84
A_6	0.8	0.4	0.72
A_7	0.8	0.4	0.72
A_8	1.0	0.8	0.96
A_9	0.4	0.4	0.40
A_{10}	0.4	0.4	0.40

Step 2 – Determining the Degree of Risk Criticality

The degree of risk criticality KR is determined based on the degree of asset criticality KA and the degree of threat criticality KH. In the proposed method, individual assessments are expressed as fuzzy numbers, and the KR value is calculated using a so-called compensated decision. A demonstration calculation is provided in Table 4. The values shown in Table 5 are partial results of research into risk analysis methods carried out in connection with the acquisition process for new C2 nodes.

Table 5. Risk criticality level Source: own processing

ID Asset	Criticality level asset	Threat severity level	Degree of risk criticality
	KA (/)	KH (/)	KR (/)
A_1	1.00	0.80	0.960
A_2	0.96	0.92	0.952
A_3	0.80	0.96	0.928
A_4	0.56	0.68	0.656
A_5	0.56	0.84	0.784
A_6	0.56	0.72	0.688
A_7	0.56	0.72	0.688
A_8	0.80	0.96	0.928
A_9	0.52	0.40	0.496
A_{10}	0.52	0.40	0.496

For example, for asset A_2, the following applies:

$$\begin{aligned} KR_2 &= \gamma \times \max\{KA_2; KH_2\} + (1-\gamma) \times \min\{KA_2; KH_2\} \\ &= 0.8 \times \max\{0.96; 0.92\} + (1-0.8) \times \min\{0.96; 0.92\} = 0.952 \end{aligned} \tag{6}$$

The KR_2 value = 0.952 expresses the assessor's (analyst's) opinion of a high degree of risk criticality. $KR_2 > 0.5$ so, it can be assumed with a high degree of certainty that measures – tactics to eliminate or reduce the impact of the risk – need to be specified and implemented. In the situation demonstrated, the same partial conclusion is accepted for all assets except assets A_9 and A_{10}.

Step 3 – Determining the Final Risk Priority Value

Table 6 provides an integrated overview of the ten monitored assets, where the KR column expresses their calculated risk criticality. At the same time, RC and RT indicate the financial and time requirements for bringing them into operational condition. The combination of these three indicators forms the data basis for a multi-criteria algorithm that determines the order of intervention.

Table 6. Inputs for calculating the resulting risk priority values Source: own processing

Asset	KR (/)	RC (kCZK)	RT (h)
A_1	0.976	2200	5
A_2	0.944	1100	3
A_3	0.832	1900	0.5
A_4	0.656	1300	5
A_5	0.789	700	2
A_6	0.656	700	2
A_7	0.656	700	2
A_8	0.832	1700	4
A_9	0.488	1400	3
A_{10}	0.488	1400	2

Table 7 shows the normalized values of the three input criteria, risk criticality (KR^N), recovery costs (RC^N), and recovery time (RT^N) converted to a scale of 0 to 1. The MOORA method further processes this data into an F, where KR^N acts as a maximization criterion and RC^N with RT^N as a minimization or cost criterion. A positive value of the indicator indicates that adequate resources are available to eliminate risks and that their allocation is effective, as the marginal benefit of the invested funds, measured by the achieved reduction in threat, exceeds the costs incurred; On the other hand, a negative value indicates the opposite ratio, where either resources are lacking or their use would not be effective because the costs of mitigating the risk outweigh the expected benefits.

The ranking in individual criteria (columns Ranking KR, RC, RT) documents the relative position of assets in terms of metrics. In contrast, the Priority ranking column represents the aggregate ranking resulting from the F index. The resulting rankings show that assets A5, A2, and A6/A7 achieve the most advantageous combination of high criticality and low financial and time requirements. At the same time, the riskiest A1 falls in priority due to extremely high costs and long recovery times.

Table 7. Standardized inputs and resulting values of risk analysis Source: own processing

Asset	KR^N	RC^N	RT^N	F	Ranking KR	Ranking RC	Ranking RT	Priority ranking
	(/)	(/)	(/)	(/)				
A_1	1.000	1.000	1.000	-1.000	1	1	1	7
A_2	0.983	0.267	0.556	0.161	2	6	4	2
A_3	0.931	0.800	0.000	0.131	3	2	6	4
A_4	0.345	0.400	1.000	-1.055	5	5	1	8
A_5	0.621	0.000	0.333	0.287	4	7	5	1
A_6	0.414	0.000	0.333	0.080	5	7	5	3
A_7	0.414	0.000	0.333	0.080	5	7	5	3
A_8	0.931	0.667	0.778	-0.513	3	3	2	5
A_9	0.000	0.467	0.556	-1.022	6	4	3	9
A_{10}	0.000	0.467	0.333	-0.800	6	4	5	6

4 Results and Discussion

The discussion of the results consists of a gradual analysis in Table 7. The result of the original RMO procedure is the risk criticality index KR_i, but nominally with different evaluation intervals. Table 7 shows the normalized values of the calculated fuzzy evaluations. In both procedures, the risk criticality level is determined on its own, regardless of the costs and time required to eliminate the impacts of the risk occurrence. Using this procedure, it is necessary to decide on specific tactics for assets A1 to A8. The degree of risk criticality reaches the highest values for assets A1, A2, A3, A5, and A8, as shown in the KR Ranking. From the perspective of the costs of eliminating the consequences of risks, a completely different order emerges in the top positions, see RC Ranking, namely assets A1, A3, A8, A9, and A10. From the perspective of the time needed to eliminate the consequences of risks, a completely different ranking emerges in the top positions, see Ranking RT, namely assets A1, A2, A4, A8, and A9. The priority ranking, based on the Fi value, identifies assets A2, A3, A5, A6, and A7 as assets for which the degree of risk criticality in standardized terms exceeds the costs and time required to eliminate the consequences of their loss. The fKR method, which combines the fuzzy approach with the MOORA value approach, thus provides an entirely different view of the degree of risk. The ranking is not determined by the degree of risk, but also by the ability to eliminate these risks rationally and effectively within the limits of financial and time resources. The assessment of assets A1 and A8, which show high priority in all respects, is interesting. These are assets with a high degree of risk criticality and high financial and time costs for their elimination. Future research will focus on the suitability of the systemic and technical architecture of node C2, which exposes users to a complex situation. In the current state of the technical solution, this situation does not allow the user to implement effective risk management strategies. The presentation of the innovative fKR method thus shows that it can be used during the preparation of the system architecture to limit or prevent the occurrence of assets with similarly highly rated KR, RC, and RT properties.

If the prioritisation were based solely on the KR values, the assets with the highest criticality such as A1 and A8 would consistently appear at the top of the ranking. However, once recovery costs and restoration times are incorporated, the combined fKR and MOORA procedure shows that other assets, particularly A5, A2, A6 and A7, become more suitable candidates for immediate intervention. This highlights the added value of the proposed method: rather than replacing the traditional risk index, it refines it by embedding it into a multi-criteria decision-making framework that reflects real operational constraints related to time and resource availability.

5 Conclusion

The article focuses on the application of a combined risk analysis method in a specific environment where decisions must be made under conditions of uncertainty and limited data availability. The procedure's structure is based on the valid RMO; however, this approach is innovatively extended by applying fuzzy set theory and the MOORA method. The method employs a combination of maximum and minimum risk values and an expertly selected compensation coefficient γ, enabling adaptive risk assessment on a continuum from a pessimistic ($\gamma = 0.8$) to an optimistic ($\gamma = 0.2$) approach [42].

The choice of the coefficient depends on the degree of uncertainty, resource availability, and the acceptable level of residual risk. While an optimistic approach is appropriate when a higher tolerance for failure is satisfactory, a pessimistic approach is used for systems with critical failure impacts. However, the successful implementation of these approaches also depends on their integration into the current doctrinal framework of the armed forces, which must be continuously developed and harmonised with alliance standards [43].

The motivation for using the fKR method is the need to reliably capture uncertainty arising from limited information and dynamically changing conditions. This uncertainty is particularly evident when introducing new technologies, where practical experience is often lacking, yet timely risk assessment remains essential. The method's flexibility allows analysis to be adapted to current operational circumstances without requiring strict standardisation of input data. The outcome of the study is not a single fixed numerical risk value but rather a degree of confidence that reflects the nature of available information and supports qualified decision-making in conditions of high uncertainty and insecurity.

The successful application of the proposed method also depends on the preparedness and adaptability of commanders, which, in the context of the modern battlefield, require systematic reflection in their training and education [44].

Acknowledgments. This research was supported by the project SV23-FVL-K107-PEK at the Faculty of Military Leadership, University of Defence in Brno.

Disclosure of Interests. The authors declare no competing interests.

References

1. Odehnal, J., Neubauer, J., Olejnicek, A., Boulaouad, J., Brizgalova, L.: Empirical analysis of military expenditures in NATO nations. Economies. **9**(3), 107. ISSN 2227-7099 (2021). https://doi.org/10.3390/economies9030107
2. Oulehlova, A., Kudlak, A., Urban, R., Hoke, E.: Competitiveness of the regions in the Czech Republic from the perspective of disaster risk financing. J. Competitiveness. **13**(4), 115–131. ISSN 1804-171X.: (2021). https://doi.org/10.7441/joc.2021.04.07
3. Pamucar, D., Bozanic, D., B, Đorovic.: Fuzzy Logic in Decision Making Process in the Armed Forces of Serbia. LAP Lambert Academic Publishing, Saarbrücken (2011). ISBN 978-3-8465-0602-5.\
4. Sustr, M., Vajda, M., Blaha, M., Ivan, J., Korec, D.: Artillery officer education and the interoperability challenge in Joint fires: a Czech–Slovak comparison. Cogent Educ. **12**(1) ISSN 2331-186X (2025). https://doi.org/10.1080/2331186x.2025.2533308
5. Blaha, M.: Communication as a basic for future artillery fire support control system. In: The European Conference of Communications (ECCOM'10), pp. 140–142. WSEAS Press, Tenerife (2010) ISBN 978-960-474-250-9.
6. Ministerstvo Obrany, Č.R.: Rozkaz ministra obrany č. 20: Řízení rizik v resortu Ministerstva obrany ve znění RMO č. In: 14/2018, ve znění RMO č. 27/2019 a ve znění RMO č. 50/2020 Věstníku, Praha (2015)
7. Voznakova, A., Marin, Z., Santaballa, J.A., Canle, M.: A simple risk Assesment method for continental waters, based on screening contaminants of emerging concern. Adv. Sustain. Syst. **8**(9) ISSN 2366-7486 (2024). https://doi.org/10.1002/adsu.202300651
8. Dobrzanski, Z.: Antropogeniczne źródła rtęci w Morzu Bałtyckim. Realne zagrożenie dla bezpieczeństwa i programy działań. Online. PRZEMYSŁ CHEMICZNY. **1**(8), 54–64 (2024) ISSN 0033-2496. https://doi.org/10.15199/62.2024.8.4
9. Korec, D., Blaha, M., Barta, J., Varecha, J.: Innovative approaches to the use of artillery in wildfire suppression. Fire. **8**, 232 (2025). https://doi.org/10.3390/fire8060232
10. Jan, I., Viktor, V., Ladislav, P., Jan, D., Tomáš, H.: Evaluation approaches for an aggregated meteorological model for artillery operations. In: Prob Ceedings of the 22nd International Conference on Informatics in Control, Automation and Robotics. Marbella, Španělsko: {Neuvedeno}, vol. 1, pp. 208–218 (2025) ISSN 2184-2809. ISBN 978-989-758-770-2
11. Chi, S., Han, S., Kim, D.Y., Shin, Y.: Accident risk identification and its impact analyses for strategic construction safety management. J. Civ. Eng. Manag. **21**(4), 524–538 (2015)
12. Shi, H., Li, W., Meng, W.: A new approach to construction project risk assesment based on rough set and information entropy, 187–190 (2008). https://doi.org/10.1109/iciii.2008.85
13. Wang, X., Tao, W., Xin, Z., Wang, Y.: Research on strategic risk identification method of equipment system development based on system dynamics. J. Syst. Eng. Electr. **34**(5), 1225–1234 (2023) ISSN 1004-4132. https://doi.org/10.23919/jsee.2023.000124
14. Makarova, I., Yakupova, G., Buyvol, P., Abashev, A., Mukhametdinov, E.: Risk management methodology for transport infrastructure security. Infrastructures. **7**(6), 81–81. ISSN 2412-3811. (2022). https://doi.org/10.3390/infrastructures7060081
15. Drozd, J., Prochazka, J.: Constructive Simmulation: an effective tool for an assessment of the operational effectiveness within the Cability planning process. Vojenské Rozhledy. **31**(2), 54–70. ISSN 1210-3292. (2022). https://doi.org/10.3849/2336-2995.31.2022.02.054-070

16. Foltin P, Vlkovsky M, Mazal J, Husak J, Brunclik M, 2018. Discrete event simulation in future military logistics applications and aspects. In: Mazal J (ed.), Modelling and Simulation for Autonomous Systems. Online. Cham: Springer International Publishing. p. 410–421. Lecture Notes in Computer Science. ISBN 978-3-319-76071-1.
17. Pekar, O., Novak, J., Varecha, J., Sotnar, J., Drabek, J.: Bridging theory and practice in military education through advanced technologies. In: European Conference on Games Based Learning. 7 October 2024, vol. 18, pp. 1056–1060 (2024). https://doi.org/10.34190/ecgbl.18.1.2648
18. Havlik, T., Sustr, M., Ivan, J., Pekar, O., Musinka, M.: Evaluation of the effectiveness of a firing battery in self-defense and protection in the area of firing positions using constructive simulation. J. Defense Model. Simul. **0**(0) (2024). https://doi.org/10.1177/15485129241291579
19. Svehlik, M., Sustr, M., Potuzak, L., Varecha, J., Drabek, J.: Creating of minefield breaches with artillery. In: Proceedings of the 20th International Conference on Informatics in Control, Automation and Robotics, pp. 266–272. ISBN 978-989-758-670-5. SCITEPRESS–Science and Technology Publications, Rome, Italy (2023). https://doi.org/10.5220/0012208500003543
20. Blaha, M., Potuzak, L., Sustr, M., Ivan, J., Havlik, T.: Simplification options for more efficient using of Angular and Linear measuring Rules for Fire Control. Int. J. Educ. Inform. Technol. **15**(15), 28–34. ISSN 2074-1316. (2021). https://doi.org/10.46300/9109.2021.15.4
21. Sustr, M., Ivan, J., Blaha, M., Potuzak, L.: A manual method of artillery fires correction calculation. Mil. Oper. Res. **27**(3), 77–94. ISSN 1082-5983. IF 0,700 (2022). https://doi.org/10.5711/1082598327377
22. Savic, M., Đorđevic, P., Nikolic, Đ., Mihajlovic, I., Zivkovic, Z.: Bayesian inference for risk assessment of the position of study program within the integrated university: a case study of engineering management at technical faculty in Bor. Serbian J. Manag. **9**(2), 231–240. ISSN 1452-4864 (2014). https://doi.org/10.5937/sjm9-6391
23. Majek, V., Slouf, V.: Operations with fuzzy numbers in the task divided targets. In: International Conference on Military Technologies 2015, ICMT 2015, p. 641–645. ISBN 978-80-7231-976-3. University of Defence, Brno (2015). https://doi.org/10.1109/MILTECHS.2015.7153670
24. Cimr, D., Tomaskova, H., Cimler, R., Kuhnova, J., Slouf, V.: A system to evaluate an air-strike threat level using fuzzy methods. In: Thanh, N.N., Pimenidis, E., Khan, Z., Trawiński, B. (eds.) Computational Collective Intelligence. Online Lecture Notes in Computer Science, pp. 322–331. Springer International Publishing, Cham (2018) ISBN 978-3-319-98445-2
25. Shamborovskyi, G., Nehoda, Y., Demidova, N., Tarashchenko, V., Breus, S.: Modeling study on risk identification in the process of anti-crisis Enterprise management. J. Risk Financ. Manag. **14**(2), 67–67. ISSN 1911-8066. (2021). https://doi.org/10.3390/jrfm14020067
26. Hasilová, K., Horová, I., Vališ, D., Zámecˇník, S.: A comprehensive exploration of complete cross-validation for circular data. Stat. Trans. New Ser. **25**(3), 1–12 (2024). https://doi.org/10.59170/stattrans-2024-024
27. Zámečník, S., Horová, I., Katina, S., Hasilová, K.: An adaptive method for bandwidth selection in circular kernel density estimation. Comput. Stat. **39**(4), 1709–1728 (2024). https://doi.org/10.1007/s00180-023-01401-0
28. Siami, M., Naderpour, M., Ramezani, F., Lu, J.: Risk Assessment through big data: an autonomous fuzzy decision support system. Online. IEEE Trans. Intell. Transp. Syst. **25**(8), 9016–9027. ISSN 1524-9050. (2024). https://doi.org/10.1109/tits.2024.3392959
29. Yina, R., Ab Rahmana, M.N., Arifinb, K., Abdullahb, M.H.S.B.: Risk identification model for lean manufacturing improvement. J. Kejuruteraan. **35**(4), 945–953 (2023) ISSN 0128-0198. https://doi.org/10.17576/jkukm-2023-35(4)-17

30. Hujer, V., Kratky, M., Farlik, J.: Utilization of modeling and simulation in the design of air defense. In: Mazal, J., Fagiolini, A., Vasik, P. (eds.) Modelling and Simulation for Autonomous Systems, pp. 291–298. ISSN 0302-9743. ISBN 978-3-030-43890-6. Springer Nature, 2020, LNCS 11995, Cham, Switzerland (2019). https://doi.org/10.1007/978-3-030-43890-6_23
31. Selvakumar, J.J., Suganya, G., Arthi, T.S., Pachiyappan, S.: Does risk management components influence on project success? Evidence from IT sector. J. Proj. Manag. **9**(3), 269–276. ISSN 2371-8366. (2024). https://doi.org/10.5267/j.jpm.2024.4.001
32. Slouf, V., Blaha, M., Mullner, V., Brizgalova, L., Pekar, O.: An alternative model for determining the rational amount of funds allocated to defence of the czech republic in conditions of expected risk. Obrana a strategie. (1), 149–172. ISSN 1214-6463. IF 0,300 (2023). https://doi.org/10.3849/1802-7199.23.2023.01.149-172
33. Hujer, V., Slouf, V., Farlik, J.: Utility as a key criterion of a decision-making on structure of the ground based air Defence. In: Mazal, J., Fagiolini, A., Vasik, P., Turi, M., Bruzzone, A., Pickl, S., Neumann, V., Stodola, P. (eds.) Modelling and Simulation for Autonomous Systems. Online Lecture Notes in Computer Science, pp. 249–260. Springer International Publishing, Cham (2022) ISBN 978-3-030-98259-1
34. Pekar, O., et al.: Redefining Defence expenditures in B9 countries: a risk-based model for rational allocation under foreign threat scenarios. Obrana Strat. **25**(1), 71–112 (2025). https://doi.org/10.3849/1802-7199.25.2025.1.71-112
35. Cermak, M.: Řízení informačních rizik v praxi. V Tribunu EU vydání druhé. Knihovnicka.cz. Tribun EU, Brno (2023) ISBN 978-80-263-1794-4.
36. Drabek, J., Sustr, M., Potuzak, L., Ivan, J., Liska, R.: Contingency and emergency manual procedures for calculation firing data using direction and distance coefficients. Eng. Rep. **7**(6) ISSN 2577-8196 (2025). https://doi.org/10.1002/eng2.70252
37. REPKA, R.: Metody rozhodování a jejich aplikace v řízení rizik. Vysoké učení technické v Brně, Brno (2018)
38. Ryczynski, J., Banasik, A., Gajowniczek, K.: Application of fuzzy logic to tactical risk assessment in military supply chains under conditions of uncertainty. Energies. **14**(15), 4679. Available at: (2021). https://doi.org/10.3390/en14154679
39. Nemec, P., Stodola, P., Pecina, M., Neubauer, J., Blaha, M.: Optimization of the weighted multi-facility location problem using MS excel. Algorithms. **14**(7), 191. ISSN 1999-4893. (2021). https://doi.org/10.3390/a14070191
40. Blaha, M., Brabcova, K.: Decision-making by effective C2I system. In: 7th International Conference on Information Warfare & Security, pp. 44–50. ISSN 2048-9870. Academic Publishing Limited, Seattle (2012). isbn:978-1-908272-29-4
41. Slouf, V.: Rozhodování velitelů dělostřeleckých jednotek v podmínkách rizika. Vydání: první. Studijní text. Univerzita obrany, Brno (2024) ISBN 978-80-7582-491-2.
42. Novák, J., Potužák, L., Blaha, M., Šlouf, V., Drábek, J.: The impact of the deteriorated political and security situation on the financial stability of arms companies operating in an oligopolistic market environment. In: Challanges to National Defence in Contemporary Geopolitical Situation, p. 500–511. ISSN 1470-2436. General Jonas Žemaitis Military Academy of Lithuania, 2024, Vilnius (2024). https://doi.org/10.3849/cndcgs.2024.500
43. Zizka, P., Saibert, R.: Development of the Czech armed forces doctrinal framework. Vojenské Rozhledy. **33**(1), 3–20. ISSN 1210-3292. (2024). https://doi.org/10.3849/2336-2995.33.2024.01.003-020
44. Zahradníček, P., Botík, M., Rak, L., Hrdinka, J.: Modern battlefield and necessary reflection in military Leader's education and training. Vojenské Rozhledy. **32**(4), 110–122. ISSN 1210-3292. (2023). https://doi.org/10.3849/2336-2995.32.2023.04.110-122

Learning Tactical Tank Behaviour: From Reward Hacking to Robust Alignment

Martin Krieg[1,2](✉) and Helmut Hlavacs[2]

[1] Theresan Military Academy, Burgplatz 1, 2700 Wiener Neustadt, Austria
[2] University of Vienna, Waehringerstraße 29, 1090 Vienna, Austria
m.krieg@miles.ac.at, helmut.hlavacs@univie.ac.at

Abstract. We investigate reward-design strategies for training a reinforcement learning (RL) agent to control a turreted ground platform that must aim at and engage a moving target in a 3D simulator built with the *Godot* game engine and the *godot-rl-agents* plugin. In our experiments, classical angular shaping consistently led to *reward hacking*: the agent orbits near alignment to collect shaping rewards without meeting the terminal condition. Removing shaping in favour of a terminal-state-only reward prevents this exploitation but results in little to no learning progress. To address both issues, we propose a distance-invariant, potential-based reward formulation using *projected minimum distance* (PMD) with dynamic thresholds, optionally augmented by waypoint milestones. We show that PMD-based rewards both with and without waypoints achieve near-deterministic success, short time-to-target, and stable convergence; ablation studies confirm that each component is individually effective. Beyond this specific aiming behaviour, our results demonstrate that *Godot* provides a practical, open platform for military-relevant RL prototyping.

1 Introduction

Recent conflicts, such as the war in Ukraine, illustrate an intense engineering competition to advance autonomous capabilities in weapon systems and platforms. This is particularly evident in small unmanned platforms that must operate under degraded communications and rapid decision cycles. Reinforcement learning (RL) is well suited to such sequential control problems. It learns control policies from interaction with a virtual environment and offers three practical advantages: it can discover control strategies that are difficult to specify manually, produce compact closed-loop behaviours from limited observations, and directly optimize task-level metrics (e.g., time-to-target). Many computer games have long incorporated military scenarios, making them familiar testbeds for modelling combat-relevant decision tasks. This tradition, together with their accessible tooling, helps explain why game engines are suitable for developing military-relevant RL environments. A further advantage is that these platforms enable fully digital modelling of complex weapon systems and tactical situations at the required level of detail, allowing rapid iteration without the cost and risk of

J. Novotný et al. (Eds.): MESAS 2025, LNCS 16627, pp. 137–148, 2027.
https://doi.org/10.1007/978-3-032-33182-3_8

physical trials. Games and simulators have also served as benchmarks and development platforms for RL, from DQN on Atari [12] to superhuman systems in Go and Chess [21–23], multi-agent esports [15,24], and learned-model planning [19]. Open, configurable engines such as Unity ML-Agents [9], ViZDoom [10], and increasingly Godot RL Agents [3] make it possible to build task-specific RL environments with military relevance at low cost.

These developments in modern warfare and the progress in artificial intelligence motivate this work. We investigate how alternative reward structures in RL influence the aiming sub-task of a turreted, tank-like platform under fixed observations and a static hull, focusing on rapid and accurate target alignment as a fundamental capability for higher-level autonomous systems. It does not address end-to-end gunnery, multi-target selection, or effects assessment. Our results suggest that careful, task-aligned reward design is central to achieving it. In the following, we detail our approach and evaluate alternative reward designs in a series of controlled experiments. The remainder of this paper is organized as follows: Sect. 2 reviews related work, Sect. 3 describes the methodology and research questions, Sect. 4 presents experiments and results, Sect. 5 discusses the findings, and Sect. 6 concludes the paper.

2 Related Work

Our study builds on established RL methods, many of which have been advanced and tested in game-based simulations. Breakthroughs include deep value-based control on Atari [12], policy-gradient methods such as PPO [20], planning with learned models [19], and grand-challenge achievements in games such as Go, Chess, Shogi, and StarCraft [21–24]. Multi-agent self-play has revealed emergent strategies and tool use [2], establishing training patterns such as league systems and large-scale simulation, and highlighting how reward design interacts with exploration and stability. These algorithmic foundations underpin our use of PPO in a controlled 3D simulation to study reward shaping effects on tactical aiming. Game engines as RL platforms vary in fidelity, openness, and configurability. Unity ML-Agents [9] and ViZDoom [10] have catalyzed vision-based control and multi-agent research. More recently, Godot RL Agents [3] has emerged as an open, scriptable alternative with Gym-style interfaces and support for popular RL libraries. In our work, Godot's open-source nature and direct control over environment logic make it well suited for prototyping a defence-relevant aiming behaviour while keeping reward and observation code fully transparent, a property that is crucial for analysing alignment. Reward hacking and broader objective misspecification have been highlighted as central safety risks in reinforcement learning and other optimization-based systems. Amodei et al. [1] discuss "avoiding reward hacking" as a concrete safety problem and outline practical failure modes when proxy objectives are optimized. Complementary work analyzes *reward tampering*, where agents obtain high reward by manipulating the reward-generating process rather than solving the intended task [5]. In our setting, angle-based shaping exhibits a mild form of this phenomenon: the agent increases return by exploiting dense shaping signals without satisfying the terminal success condition. The PMD-based formulation reduces this mismatch by tying intermediate rewards more tightly to the geometric success criterion.

While these advances have been driven largely by research in games and generic control tasks, the same methods and tools are increasingly being explored in military and defence contexts. RL for military and defence applications spans air combat and command-and-control (C2) to naval simulations and decision support. Examples include air-combat manoeuvring and hierarchical RL [11,16], intelligent air-defence C2 [6,25], naval USV simulations with exploration bonuses [18], C2 training in commercial-grade simulators [4], and broader arguments for games and simulators as AI testbeds for C2 [8]. Large language models have also been explored for course-of-action generation [7].

3 Experimental Setup and Methodology

In this section, we describe the experimental setup, research questions, and methodological choices underlying our study. Building on the trends and challenges identified in Sect. 1, we focus our investigation on a core sub-task of turreted ground platforms: rapid and robust target alignment under fixed-hull conditions. The overarching goal is to examine how different reward formulations influence the learning dynamics and resulting behaviours of a RL agent tasked with this aiming problem. We implement an aiming task in a 3D environment in *Godot 4.4.1* with the *godot-rl-agents* [3] plugin. The hull (player) remains fixed and the agent controls turret yaw and cannon pitch, isolating the aiming component from other mobility or stability effects. Enemies spawn uniformly in an annulus with radii $[30, 40]$ engine units, ensuring varied but bounded engagement distances. An episode ends in success when the enemy is held in aim for $H{=}2$ steps, or in failure when the time limit $T_{\max}$ is reached. No explicit firing trigger was required since the goal was to achieve stable aiming. All experiments use an action repeat of 8, meaning each RL step corresponds to eight physics ticks in Godot. In the baseline experiments (Exp01–06) the maximum episode length was set to 10 000–20 000 ticks, after which a timeout occurred. In the PMD experiments (Exp07/07a/07b) this limit was harmonised with the RL step count, resulting in a maximum of 8 000 ticks (1 000 RL steps). In the baseline experiments we ultimately spawn six enemies simultaneously to increase the chance that at least one target spawns at a favourable angular position, as enemies must maintain a minimum separation distance on the ring. Only one enemy can be engaged at a time, but the additional spawns reduce the likelihood of starting with an unfavourable geometry. In the PMD family we spawn a single enemy, removing this advantage and making target position fully dependent on the randomised spawn. Based on this setup, our study is guided by the following research questions and associated hypotheses:

RQ1: How does angle-based shaping affect agent behaviour?

H1: Angle-based shaping is hypothesised to be effective for the aiming task.

RQ2: How do terminal-state-only rewards affect learning?

H2: Terminal-state-only rewards are hypothesised to be less effective due to the sparsity of the reward signal.

RQ3: How does a PMD-based, distance-invariant reward affect learning?

H3: PMD-based rewards are hypothesised to be effective, as similar distance metrics have shown positive results in other RL settings.

RQ4: How does adding waypoints to a PMD-based reward affect learning?

H4: Including waypoints improves learning by providing a deterministic path to the solution and reducing opportunities for reward exploitation.

To address these questions, we first specify the observation and action spaces that the policy operates on, before introducing the reward families under comparison and the overall experimental design. For Exp01–06 we use a compact observation vector consisting of a binary aim flag (enemy in aim or not), the normalised angular error, and the normalised remaining time. In the PMD experiments (Exp07/07a/07b) we expand the observation space and encode the enemy direction as a unit vector in the local turret frame, add a binary front-flag indicating whether the enemy lies within the frontal arc, and the normalised remaining time. The action space is continuous, $\mathbf{a} = (a_{\text{yaw}}, a_{\text{pitch}}) \in [-1, 1]^2$, and maps to angular velocities with a clip applied to the elevation component. This allows smooth control of both yaw and pitch, while constraining elevation changes to avoid unrealistic aiming movements

With the observation and action spaces defined, we now turn to the reward formulations under comparison.

Angle-based shaping (Exp01–05): Angular error shaping plus an aim bonus; variants differ in tracking tolerance, time decay, and timeout penalties.

Final-only (Exp06): Tiered terminal reward on success (by time bands), timeout penalty on failure.

PMD with dynamic thresholds (Exp07/07a/07b). Let $\hat{\mathbf{d}}$ be the unit barrel direction and $\mathbf{v} = \mathbf{p}_{\text{enemy}} - \mathbf{p}_{\text{muzzle}}$. The projected minimum distance is defined as

$$\text{PMD} = \|\mathbf{v} \times \hat{\mathbf{d}}\|.$$

It is normalised via a reference angle $\theta_{\text{ref}} = 50°$:

$$\phi = 1 - \min\left(\frac{\text{PMD}}{\|\mathbf{v}\| \tan\theta_{\text{ref}}}, 1\right) \in [0, 1].$$

In shaping variants, we instantiate a potential function $\Phi(s) := \phi(s)$ according to the formulation by Ng et al. [14], and add the potential-based shaping term

$$F(s, a, s') = \gamma\,\Phi(s') - \Phi(s),$$

which preserves optimal policies under standard assumptions on the MDP and discount factor.

Dynamic angular thresholds make tolerances distance-invariant:

$$\varepsilon_{\text{term}} = \|\mathbf{v}\| \tan\theta_{\text{eps}}, \quad \varepsilon_{\text{wp}} = \|\mathbf{v}\| \tan\theta_{\text{wp}},$$

with $\theta_{\text{eps}} = 6.0°$ and $\theta_{\text{wp}} = 3°$. This formulation ensures that alignment tolerances scale naturally with target distance, preventing bias toward either close or far targets.

To evaluate these reward designs, we train Proximal Policy Optimization (PPO) [20] using Stable-Baselines3 [17] for 10^6 timesteps per run, with a fixed random seed (42) to ensure reproducibility. Training uses eight parallel environment instances and an action repeat of 8, meaning that each policy step corresponds to eight physics ticks in Godot. During training, we record scalar performance metrics to TensorBoard, including `rollout/success_rate`, `ep_len_mean`, and `ep_rew_mean`. For the PMD family of experiments, we additionally log per-episode CSV files containing episode length, return, success flag, and time-to-success (TTS), produced by an in-engine metric logger. This richer logging allows for detailed post-hoc analysis beyond the aggregated statistics available in TensorBoard. These metrics address different aspects of our research questions: reliability (success rate, timeout fraction), efficiency and stability (TTS, episode length), and learning speed (steps-to-0.95). Mean episode return is included for completeness but is only directly comparable within a reward family due to differing reward scales, and Exp01 uses a different reward structure from the other baselines. These settings provide a consistent basis for comparing the effectiveness of the reward designs in the following experiments.

4 Experiments and Results

In this section, we present the results of our experiments, structured according to the research questions introduced in Sect. 3. We first analyse the angle-based and final-only baselines before turning to the PMD-based reward structures and their ablations. Episode length values are reported in RL steps (see Sect. 3). The following Table 1 summarises the configuration of all experiments discussed in this section.

We begin the analysis with the baseline configurations (Exp01–06), which use either angle-based shaping or terminal-only rewards, to address RQ1 and RQ2. Across all six baseline configurations, the success rate remains essentially at zero over the entire 10^6 training steps. Figure 1 shows that no configuration leads to a phase of sustained improvement or a distinct upward trend. This flat behaviour indicates that neither the angle-based shaping nor the terminal-only reward signal was sufficient to drive learning towards consistent target alignment. In the context of our hypotheses, this outcome contradicts H1 and only weakly supports H2: reward hacking is avoided in the terminal-only case, but there is still no evidence of policy improvement.

In Fig. 2 it becomes evident that the mean episode length stays close to the maximum possible value for all baselines, with no downward trend over the course of training. This strongly suggests that episodes typically terminate

Table 1. Experiment configurations.

ID	Targets	Angle shaping	PMD shaping	Waypoints	Final reward	Timeout pen.
Exp01	6	Yes	No	No	High (e.g., 100–500)	None
Exp02	6	Yes (tighter)	No	No	High	Moderate
Exp03	6	Yes	No	No	Very high	High
Exp04	6	Yes	No	No	Very high	High
Exp05	6	Yes (decay/speed)	No	No	Very high	High
Exp06	6	No	No	No	Tiered final only	Moderate
Exp07	1	No	Yes	Yes	Moderate	Moderate
Exp07a	1	No	Yes	No	Moderate	Moderate
Exp07b	1	No	No	Yes	Moderate	Moderate

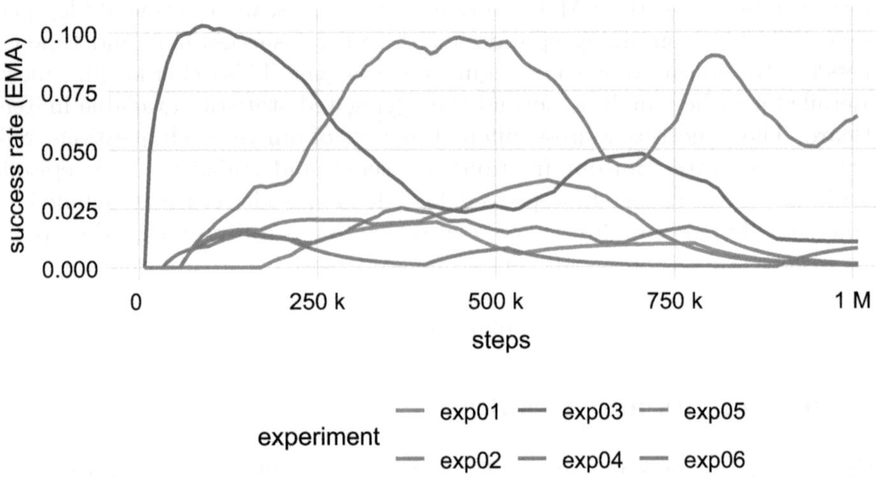

Fig. 1. Baselines (Exp01–06): smoothed rollout success (EMA) over training.

due to the time limit rather than the agent successfully aligning to the target. The absence of length reduction confirms the lack of learning progress already indicated by the success curves.

In shaping-heavy settings, the mean episode return as shown in Fig. 3 increases steadily despite the near-zero success rate. This indicates that the agent learns to collect intermediate shaping rewards without completing the task – a classic case of reward hacking. In other baselines with lower shaping budgets, returns remain lower and more stable, but the lack of task success persists. Since reward scales differ, direct numerical comparison between settings is not meaningful, but the patterns reinforce that shaping can lead to misaligned behaviours when it is not tightly coupled to the terminal objective.

Overall, the baseline results show that angle-based shaping rewards lead to unproductive behaviours and that terminal-only rewards, while preventing

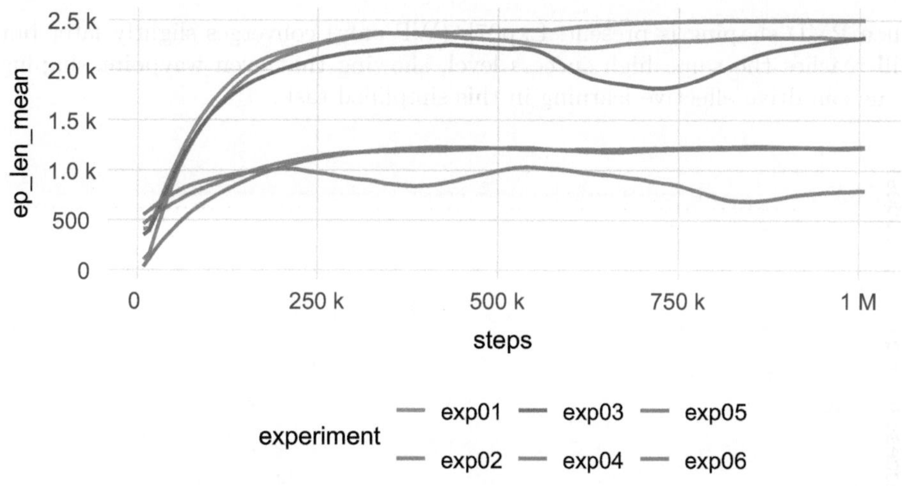

Fig. 2. Baselines (Exp01–06): mean episode length (EMA) over training.

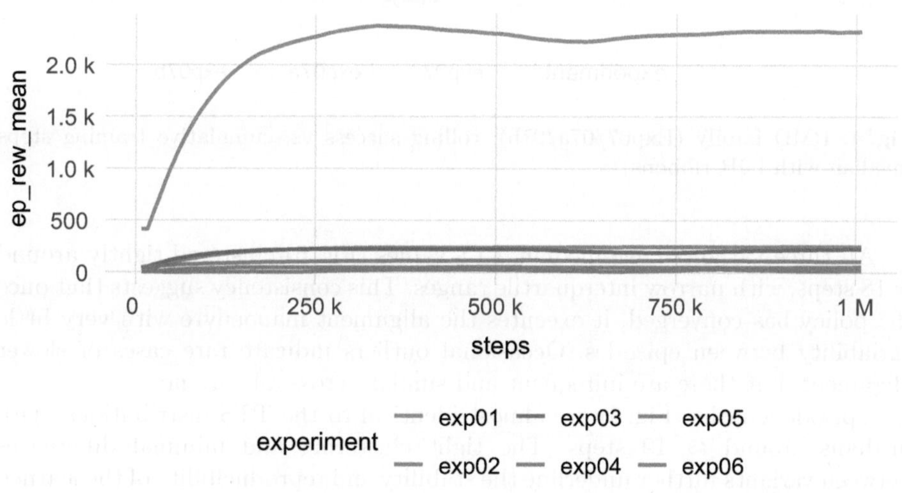

Fig. 3. Baselines (Exp01–06): mean episode return (EMA) over training.

reward hacking, fail to provide sufficient guidance for learning within the available training budget.

Since the baselines failed to achieve consistent target alignment, we next examine the PMD-based experiments, which were designed to address RQ3 and RQ4. Figure 4 shows rolling success over cumulative training steps for the three PMD variants. All PMD variants exhibit rapid learning, with success rates surpassing 95% within the first ≈ 20k training steps and maintaining stability thereafter. The curves for Exp07 (PMD+WP) and Exp07a (PMD-only) are almost indistinguishable, suggesting that the waypoint component adds little benefit when PMD shaping is present. Exp07b (WP-only) converges slightly later but still reaches the same high success level, showing that even waypoint shaping alone can drive effective learning in this simplified task.

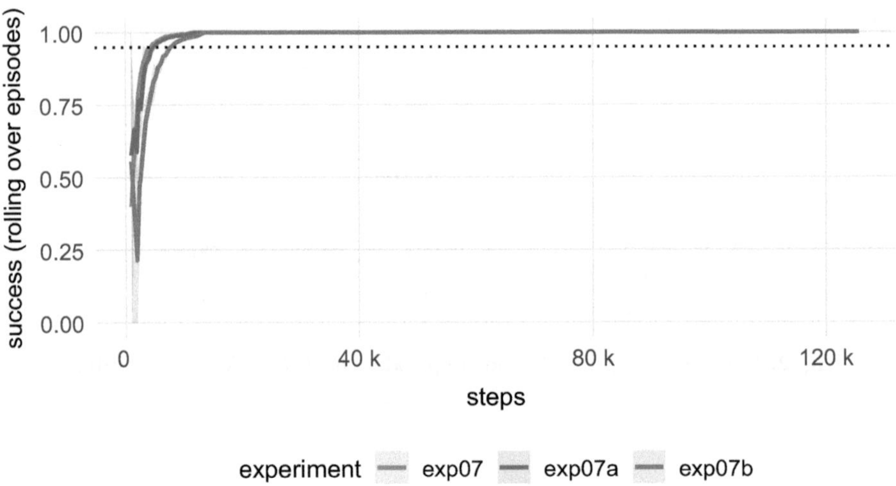

Fig. 4. PMD family (Exp07/07a/07b): rolling success vs. cumulative training steps (median with IQR ribbons).

All three variants have median TTS values (Fig. 5) clustered tightly around ≈ 18 steps, with narrow interquartile ranges. This consistency suggests that once the policy has converged, it executes the alignment manoeuvre with very little variability between episodes. Occasional outliers indicate rare cases of slower alignment, but these are infrequent and similar across all variants.

Episode lengths (Fig. 6) are almost identical to the TTS distributions, with medians around ≈ 19 steps. The tight clustering and minimal differences between variants further underline the stability and reproducibility of the learned behaviours.

Taken together, the PMD results demonstrate that distance-invariant shaping, with or without waypoints, leads to rapid, stable, and efficient learning in this aiming task.

5 Discussion

Our experiments reveal clear differences in how the tested reward structures influence learning outcomes. Angle-based shaping produced persistent exploitation of intermediate rewards without achieving the terminal objective, contradicting H1. This illustrates a classic failure mode in reward design: the agent maximises return by exploiting shaping signals rather than solving the intended task. Terminal-only rewards avoided this issue, as anticipated, but failed to

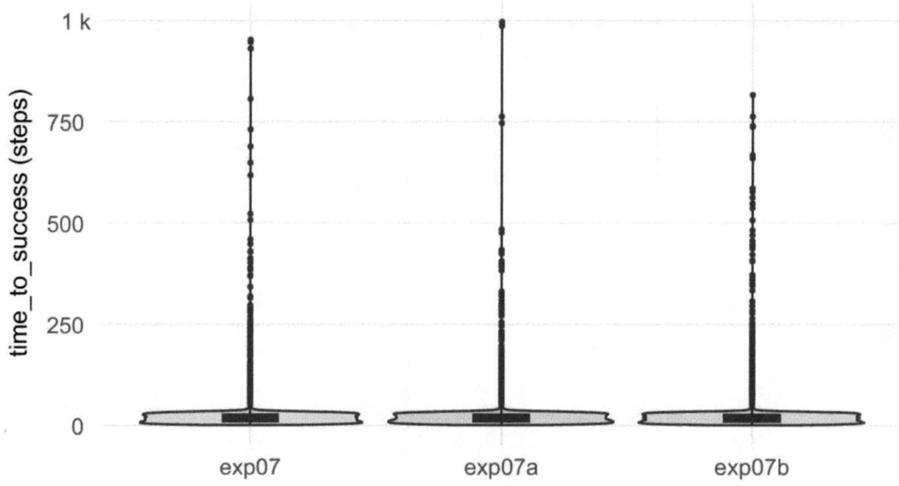

Fig. 5. PMD family: time-to-success distributions per experiment.

achieve high success rates within the given training budget, providing only weak support for H2. The sparse feedback proved insufficient for guiding effective policy learning in this setting.

Robustness. All reported training runs use a fixed random seed (42) to support deterministic reproducibility. This choice does not establish robustness across seeds, initialization noise, or stochastic training effects, and a multi-seed evaluation is required before drawing stronger conclusions about stability in more variable settings.

In contrast, PMD-based shaping led to fast, stable convergence and short time-to-target, even from scratch. The waypoint ablation confirmed that well-aligned intermediate rewards can be introduced without harming convergence, supporting H3 and H4. Taken together, these findings show that distance-invariant shaping, with or without waypoint milestones, is both effective and robust in this aiming context.

Beyond the specific task, these results underline a broader principle: shaping rewards must be geometrically consistent with the success condition to be both effective and resistant to exploitation. The PMD formulation achieves this by normalising tolerances with respect to target distance, ensuring equivalent treatment of close and distant targets in angular terms. In safety-critical domains such as defence, such alignment between reward and task geometry is essential, as poorly designed rewards risk encouraging unsafe or tactically useless behaviour.

The study used a deliberately simplified setup to isolate the aiming behaviour. While this design clarifies the effects of reward formulation, it also limits direct transferability to operational contexts. Real-world aiming tasks involve moving platforms, cluttered environments, multiple simultaneous threats, and noisy or partial observations. They may also require integration

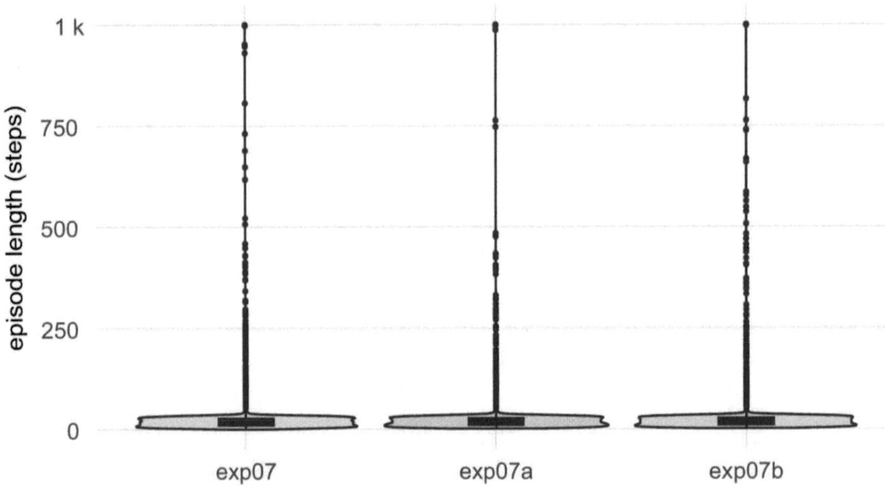

Fig. 6. PMD family: episode length distributions per experiment.

with higher-level tactical decisions such as target prioritisation, evasive manoeuvres, and ammunition management. These additional complexities can interact with reward design in non-trivial ways, potentially reintroducing failure modes absent in the simplified case.

Future work will therefore focus on progressively reintroducing complexity: incorporating hull motion and relative movement between shooter and target, adding terrain features and occlusions, modelling sensor uncertainty, and exploring multi-agent scenarios in both cooperative and adversarial forms. We also plan to investigate alternative RL algorithms, curriculum learning, and hybrid reward structures to further improve learning efficiency and robustness. For example, curriculum learning can sequence increasingly difficult aiming conditions (e.g., tighter tolerances, moving hull, occlusions) to reduce exploration burden, while hybrid rewards can combine sparse terminal objectives with carefully constrained shaping to limit exploitation [13].

6 Conclusion

This study examined alternative reward designs for a reinforcement learning agent tasked with rapid and robust target alignment under fixed-hull conditions in a simulated turreted platform. The experiments demonstrated that reward design is decisive for achieving effective and reliable behaviour. Angle-based shaping (H1) was ineffective due to reward exploitation, terminal-only rewards (H2) avoided exploitation but failed to support learning within the available budget, while PMD-based shaping with or without waypoints (H3, H4) achieved fast, stable convergence and short time-to-target.

These findings confirm that small changes in reward formulation can produce large differences in performance, stability, and susceptibility to reward hacking.

In military and other safety-critical applications, aligning reward structures with the geometry of the success condition and the operational goal is essential for ensuring predictable and tactically sound behaviour. By combining transparent, scriptable simulation environments such as Godot with Godot RL Plugin with careful reward design, it is possible to prototype and test behaviours that show robustness in controlled scenarios. However, their performance under more complex or operational conditions warrants systematic evaluation in the future.

Disclosure of Interests. The authors declare no competing interests.

References

1. Amodei, D., Olah, C., Steinhardt, J., Christiano, P., Schulman, J., Mané, D.: Concrete problems in AI safety. arXiv preprint arXiv:1606.06565 (2016)
2. Baker, B., et al.: Emergent tool use from multi-agent autocurricula (2019). https://arxiv.org/pdf/1909.07528
3. Beeching, E., Dibangoye, J., Simonin, O., Wolf, C.: Godot reinforcement learning agents. arXiv preprintarXiv:2112.03636 (2021)
4. Dimitriu, A., Michaletzky, T.V., Remeli, V., Tihanyi, V.R.: A reinforcement learning approach to military simulations in command: modern operations. IEEE Access **12**, 77501–77513 (2024). https://doi.org/10.1109/ACCESS.2024.3406148
5. Everitt, T., Hutter, M., Kumar, R., Krakovna, V.: Reward tampering problems and solutions in reinforcement learning: a causal influence diagram perspective. arXiv preprintarXiv:1908.04734 (2021)
6. Fu, Q., Fan, C.L., Song, Y., Guo, X.K.: Alpha c2-an intelligent air defense commander independent of human decision-making. IEEE Access **8**, 87504–87516 (2020). https://doi.org/10.1109/ACCESS.2020.2993459
7. Goecks, V.G., Waytowich, N.: Coa-gpt: generative pre-trained transformers for accelerated course of action development in military operations (2024). https://doi.org/10.48550/arXiv.2402.01786
8. Goecks, V.G., et al.: On games and simulators as a platform for development of artificial intelligence for command and control. J. Defense Model. Simul. Appl. Methodol. Technol. **20**(4), 495–508 (2023). https://doi.org/10.1177/15485129221083278
9. Juliani, A., et al.: Unity: a general platform for intelligent agents (2018). http://arxiv.org/pdf/1809.02627
10. Kempka, M., Wydmuch, M., Runc, G., Toczek, J., Jaśkowski, W.: Vizdoom: a doom-based ai research platform for visual reinforcement learning. In: Proceedings of IEEE Conference of Computational Intelligence in Games (2016). https://arxiv.org/pdf/1605.02097
11. Mei, J., Li, G., Huang, H.: Deep reinforcement-learning-based air-combat-maneuver generation framework. Mathematics **12**(19), 3020 (2024). https://doi.org/10.3390/math12193020
12. Mnih, V., et al.: Human-level control through deep reinforcement learning. Nature **518**(7540), 529–533 (2015). https://doi.org/10.1038/nature14236
13. Narvekar, S., Sinapov, J., Leonetti, M., Stone, P.: Curriculum learning for reinforcement learning domains: a framework and survey. J. Mach. Learn. Res. (2020)

14. Ng, A.Y., Harada, D., Russell, S.J.: Policy invariance under reward transformations: theory and application to reward shaping. In: Proceedings of the Sixteenth International Conference on Machine Learning (ICML 1999), pp. 278–287. Morgan Kaufmann, Bled, Slovenia (1999)
15. OpenAI, Berner, C., et al.: Dota 2 with large scale deep reinforcement learning (2019), http://arxiv.org/pdf/1912.06680
16. Pope, A.P., et al.: Hierarchical reinforcement learning for air-to-air combat (2021). http://arxiv.org/pdf/2105.00990
17. Raffin, A., Hill, A., Gleave, A., Kanervisto, A., Ernestus, M., Dormann, N.: Stable-baselines3: reliable reinforcement learning implementations. J. Mach. Learn. Res. **22**(268), 1–8 (2021). http://jmlr.org/papers/v22/20-1364.html
18. Rao, J., et al.: A modified random network distillation algorithm and its application in usvs naval battle simulation. Ocean Eng. **261**, 112147 (2022). https://doi.org/10.1016/j.oceaneng.2022.112147
19. Schrittwieser, J., et al.: Mastering atari, go, chess and shogi by planning with a learned model. Nature **588**(7839), 604–609 (2020). https://doi.org/10.1038/s41586-020-03051-4
20. Schulman, J., Wolski, F., Dhariwal, P., Radford, A., Klimov, O.: Proximal policy optimization algorithms (2017). https://doi.org/10.48550/arXiv.1707.06347
21. Silver, D., et al.: Mastering the game of go with deep neural networks and tree search. Nature **529**(7587), 484–489 (2016). https://doi.org/10.1038/nature16961
22. Silver, D., et al.: A general reinforcement learning algorithm that masters chess, shogi, and go through self-play. Science (New York, N.Y.) **362**(6419), 1140–1144 (2018). https://doi.org/10.1126/science.aar6404
23. Silver, D., et al.: Mastering the game of go without human knowledge. Nature **550**(7676), 354–359 (2017). https://doi.org/10.1038/nature24270
24. Vinyals, O., et al.: Grandmaster level in starcraft ii using multi-agent reinforcement learning. Nature **575**(7782), 350–354 (2019). https://doi.org/10.1038/s41586-019-1724-z
25. Zhao, M., et al.: Intelligent decision–making system of air defense resource allocation via hierarchical reinforcement learning. Int. J. Intell. Syst. **2024**(1) (2024). https://doi.org/10.1155/2024/7777050, https://www.researchgate.net/publication/381226520_Intelligent_Decision-Making_System_of_Air_Defense_Resource_Allocation_via_Hierarchical_Reinforcement_Learning

Advanced Thermal Management of Onboard AI, Power Electronics and Battery Systems in Unmanned Ground Vehicles via Scenario-Based Co-simulation Using Simulink and GT-SUITE

Esra Hicret Uzer(✉) and Tomáš Haniš

Faculty of Electrical Engineering, Czech Technical University in Prague, Prague, Czech Republic
uzeresra@fel.cvut.cz, tomas.hanis@cvut.cz

Abstract. In unmanned ground vehicles (UGVs), artificial intelligence (AI) compute units generate variable thermal loads that are closely tied to scenario and environmental variables. To ensure optimal performance and reliability, and energy efficiency, it becomes vital to prepare for thermal loads and precondition critical subsystems. This study proposes a scenario-based thermal co-simulation using control-oriented platforms, like MATLAB and Simulink, paired with hi-fidelity modeling tools, like GT-SUITE to analyze the thermal impact of dynamic AI in UGVs. Prediction of AI system loads are estimated based on predefined scenarios and decision complication. These scenarios are correlated to compute workload, which is mapped to transient heat. The co-simulation framework entitles dynamic interaction between Simulink-based controllers and GT-SUITE's high fidelity thermal models, enabling the evaluation of control objectives. Results demonstrate that the scenario prediction significantly outperforms non-predictive control in the manner of efficient cooling with less power consumption. By anticipating workload-dependent heat generation and adjusting coolant and refrigerant mass flow rates beforehand, MPC reduces peak GPU and battery temperatures, improves thermal safety margins, and prevents overheating during transient high-load conditions. The co-simulation environment proved essential in capturing these effects by providing high-fidelity transient thermal dynamics within a computationally efficient control framework.

The study highlights the benefits of predictive control for thermal safety and energy efficiency in future systems. Directions for future work include adaptive corrections to account for residual modeling errors and evaluating trade-offs between cooling energy consumption and thermal safety under realistic driving scenarios.

Keywords: artificial intelligence computing units · unmanned ground vehicles thermal management · multi-domain analysis

J. Novotný et al. (Eds.): MESAS 2025, LNCS 16627, pp. 149–165, 2027.
https://doi.org/10.1007/978-3-032-33182-3_9

1 Introduction

Over the past decade, high-performance computing (HPC) units for heavy and dense computations—such as GPUs, CPUs, TPUs, and dedicated AI accelerators—have evolved significantly in terms of computational efficiency, architecture design and optimization, and parallelism. Modern high performance computing processors can execute trillions of operations per second, including increasingly complex neural network models and enabling almost instantaneous decision-making [1]. For Unmanned Ground Vehicles (UGVs), this progress in compute capability allows successful perception pipelines, faster context understanding, and more sophisticated autonomous behaviors in complex environments [2].

However, this performance evolution has come with a proportional increase in thermal density. As transistor sizes get smaller and architectures become more condense, heat is generated in smaller physical cache, making hotspots more critical and more difficult to cool down with traditional ways. The thrust for the higher clock rates, larger memory bandwidth, and wider parallel operations further increases both steady-state and transient thermal loads [3]. Consequently, thermal management has shifted from being a secondary consideration for engineers to a primary design constraint for maintaining reliability, extending hardware lifespan, and preventing mission-disrupting throttling [4].

As a matter of fact, this challenge is not limited to AI processors only. In electric and autonomous platforms—including electric vehicles (EVs), autonomous delivery robots, Unmanned Aerial Vehicles (UAVs) and UGVs—thermal management is noticeably crucial for other onboard components, such as battery packs, inverters, and power distribution units. The combined thermal loads from all heat generating and storing components form a tightly coupled a thermal ecosystem. Any thermal instability can lead to degraded performance, premature component aging, or even safety risks. As mission complexity increases, ensuring unified and predictive thermal control across these systems becomes essential to sustain high performance under dynamically changing conditions [4–6].

Given these challenges, there is a clear need for tools that can accurately capture the complex, scenario-dependent thermal behavior of UGV onboard systems, while also enabling the design and testing of advanced control strategies before deployment. Addressing this gap, this paper proposes a scenario-based co-simulation framework that integrates:

Control-oriented platforms (MATLAB/Simulink) for developing advanced control strategies, and

High-fidelity thermal modeling tools (GT-SUITE) for detailed thermal and physical subsystem simulation.

There are several methods which are effective at preventing thermal damage, but they are sacrificing the performance especially during heavy parallel computing. They work under the assumption that reducing heat output takes priority over maintaining peak computational capability [10]. In routine workloads, this trade-off may be acceptable. However, in critical mission phases—such as navigating through defiant zones, detecting hostile targets alongside civilians via real-time image classification, performing simultaneous high-resolution mapping, and processing multi-source disaster-zone data—any performance degradation can compromise mission success. In these situations, heavy tasks must run simultaneously and at full performance, and traditional reactive methods are not enough anymore.

To overcome these limitations, there is an increasing need for advanced and scenario-based thermal management for the thermal systems in UGVs. By forecasting upcoming computational demands and their associated heat generation, the thermal management system can proactively precondition cooling subsystems, ensuring performance is sustained even during peak workloads. This approach not only prevents throttling but also enables energy-efficient operation, allowing for strategic thermal control that aligns with mission priorities.

In the proposed method, predefined mission scenarios—involving the utilization of heavy kernels, or real-time data processing and decision-making processes—are mapped to corresponding computational workloads. These workloads are then translated into transient heat generation profiles within GT-SUITE. The co-simulation framework Functional Mockup Interface (FMI) allows continuous interaction between the control algorithms in Simulink and the high-fidelity multi-domain system in GT-SUITE, enabling the evaluation and refinement of advanced predictive cooling strategies.

In the following sections, Sect. 2 provides a review of related work about thermal management strategies for AI accelerators and the essentials of co-simulation interfaces and alternative approaches of multi-domain co-simulation tools. Section 3 describes the methodology, detailing the physics and mathematical modeling and control of the thermal systems. The results of the proposed modeling and simulation framework are presented in Sect. 4, followed by a discussion of the findings in Sect. 5. Finally, Sect. 6 and 7 concludes the study and highlights the implications of the work, along with potential directions for future research.

2 Related Work

2.1 HPC Thermal Management

Effective thermal management in autonomous vehicles (AVs) such as unmanned ground vehicles (UGVs) is increasingly recognized as a mission-critical enabler for reliable, high-performance autonomous operation. Recent research has explored both hardware- and software-level strategies to address the growing thermal challenges posed by modern onboard AI computing systems and power electronics [3–6]. There are several power management techniques to overcome these challenges in both hardware and software levels such as in circuit level, architectural, and scheduling methods [14].

For certain UGV applications, particularly in defense and reconnaissance missions, thermal uniformity across the vehicle's overall surface and with the ambient background becomes a critical requirement. Uneven heat distribution can create distinct hotspots that are easily detectable by infrared (IR) and thermal imaging systems, revealing the vehicle's location or operational state. By maintaining a uniform thermal profile—through coordinated cooling of AI processors, power electronics, battery and propulsion components—UGVs can minimize their thermal signature, enhancing stealth capabilities and reducing the risk of detection in hostile environments [17].

To perform mission-critical tasks such as multi-sensor fusion, real-time object detection and classification, simultaneous localization and mapping (SLAM), and autonomous path planning, UGVs are equipped with advanced high performance computing systems (HPCs). These workloads are computationally intensive and inherently dynamic, with their complexity fluctuating based on mission context, environmental conditions, and real-time sensor inputs. The direct consequence of these fluctuating workloads is variable thermal load on the onboard electronics, often changing in seconds as mission requirements shift.

In conventional embedded computing systems, thermal management relies on reactive techniques. Common approaches are:

Dynamic Voltage and Frequency Scaling (DVFS) — lowering processor voltage and clock frequency to reduce power consumption and heat generation [7, 8].

Task Scheduling and Load Balancing — postponing or redistributing computational tasks to spread out the thermal load [9–11, 13].

Thermal Throttling — aggressively limiting computational performance when temperature thresholds are approached to prevent overheating [10].

Designing efficient thermal control for HPC components commonly relies on co-simulation to couple physical models with control environments. Fast, compact thermal models such as Hot-Spot provide RC-network based transient temperature estimates and are widely used as surrogate models in control/scheduling loops because they balance accuracy and computational speed [15]. For liquid cooling architectures, multi-scale thermal management systems illustrate chip/ package-level thermal dynamics and complex heterogeneous heat dissipation models [16]. Complementary research on thermal-aware scheduling, including DVFS runtime management allows simultaneous assessment of workload management and actuator control such as Model-in-Loop approach which is significantly important for dynamic changes of GPU workloads where transient hotspots occur [18].

Recent advancements emphasize the importance of future-aware, advance predictive thermal control methods for high-performance computing systems. These strategies aim to anticipate workload-induced heat generation, rather than entirely reacting to temperature threshold values.

In the context of data centers, which are heavily running GPUs and requiring efficiency cooling performance to predict server temperatures and maintain thermal-aware workload distribution and future demands are combined with Model Predictive Control (MPC) to optimize the workload allocation and energy utilization, with the demand predictions, the controller can find near-optimal solutions for transient thermal models with dynamic power demands [12, 19].

2.2 Multi-domain Analysis

For the analysis and design of control systems, the starting point is often a block diagram representation of the plant. While this process is relatively straightforward for simple, single-domain systems, translating more complex physical models into block diagrams can be challenging. Over the past four decades, research in modeling and simulation has produced increasingly mature tools that allow these conversions to be performed automatically, even for large and multi-domain systems.

Such systems frequently combine several interacting domains. Electrical subsystems involve power drawn by actuators and sensors or the charging and discharging behavior of batteries. Mechanical subsystems capture vehicle motion or detailed structural dynamics through finite element methods. Fluid subsystems include heating and cooling loops or airflow processes, while thermal subsystems represent heat generation and its dissipation through conduction and convection. Despite their diversity, each of these domains can be represented in terms of input–output relationships, enabling their integration within block diagram models [20].

To support this integration, a wide range of co-simulation frameworks has been developed. Depending on the used application, these frameworks can be control-oriented, physics-oriented, or distributed. Examples include High-Level Architecture (HLA), MOSAIK, and Ptolemy II [22, 23], which are suited for multi-physics systems as well as control applications. A widely adopted standard interface in this context is the Functional Mock-up Interface (FMI), which allows subsystem models to be packaged as Functional Mock-up Units (FMUs). These FMUs can be exchanged between different simulation environments, enabling the use of high-fidelity, multi-domain models in combination with advanced control platforms [24].

In the control community, one of the most widely adopted solutions is the use of the S-Function interface in Simulink (MathWorks). High-fidelity plant models developed in other environments can be exported as FMUs and integrated into Simulink through this mechanism. The interface provides a standardized, low-level input–output framework for exchanging models between tools. This approach combines the strengths of physics-based simulators with control design platforms, allowing realistic co-simulation of multi-domain systems. By linking detailed plant models with control algorithms, engineers can construct digital twin environments that capture physical complexity while supporting the development and validation of advanced control strategies (Fig. 1).

3 Methodology

3.1 Thermal Load Prediction

Thermal loading in the AI accelerator can be estimated from its dynamic and leakage power characteristics. Scenario generation is based on frame rates, utilization ratios, voltage, and temperature values. On the computational side, heat arises primarily from two sources: dynamic power, which depends on switching activity and scales with capacitance, supply voltage, and operating frequency; and leakage power, which increases with both voltage and temperature.

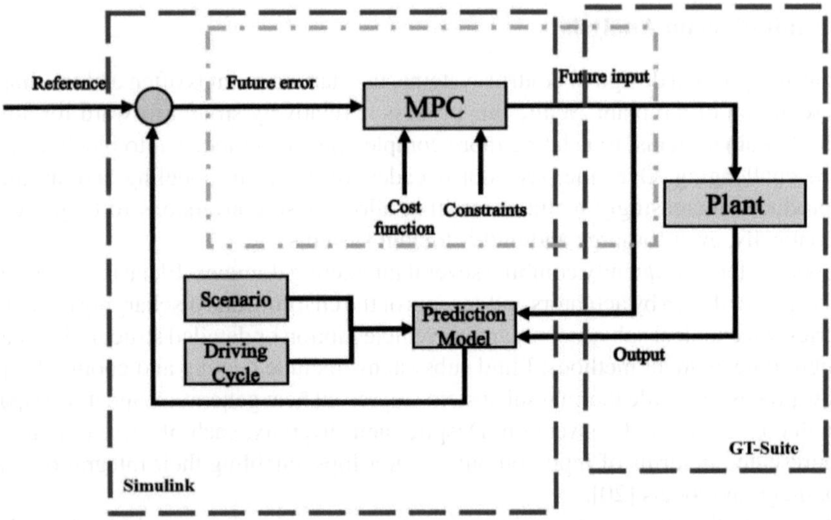

Fig. 1. Block diagram of the distribution between Simulink and GT-Suite

The workload of the GPU—determined by factors such as the number of active sensors, frame rates, neural network size, and planning frequency—directly influences utilization. In response, power management mechanisms adjust the GPU's voltage and frequency through dynamic voltage and frequency scaling (DVFS). Prior studies indicate that actual power consumption also depends on application-level behavior, particularly memory access patterns. Therefore, an accurate power model must incorporate both core and memory operating states.

Practically, a power and temperature estimator can be identified from benchmark data representing various computational densities (e.g., image processing, route generation, target detection, communication). The components of power calculation are then mapped to equivalent heat inputs for the electro-thermal or thermo-electric model. This time-varying heat source is injected into a compact thermal RC network that represents the chip, package, and heatsink structure. Such modeling provides a well-validated yet lumped transient temperature prediction.

To derive a prediction model suitable for advanced control, the temperature dynamics of the electronics and other physical subsystems are formulated in state-space form, with scenario-based heat sources from the battery and GPU serving as inputs. Linearization around multiple operating points or along representative operating trajectories yields Jacobians that relate system states and inputs (e.g., GPU utilization, voltage, frequency, coolant flow rate, refrigerant flow rate, vehicle speed) to time-varying temperature rates (Fig. 2).

In cases with strong nonlinearities—especially under DVFS operation and conditions of high leakage power—the Jacobians may need data-driven corrections while preserving the physical structure of the model. The use of such linearized models enables the development of credible predictors for control design and preconditioning strategies.

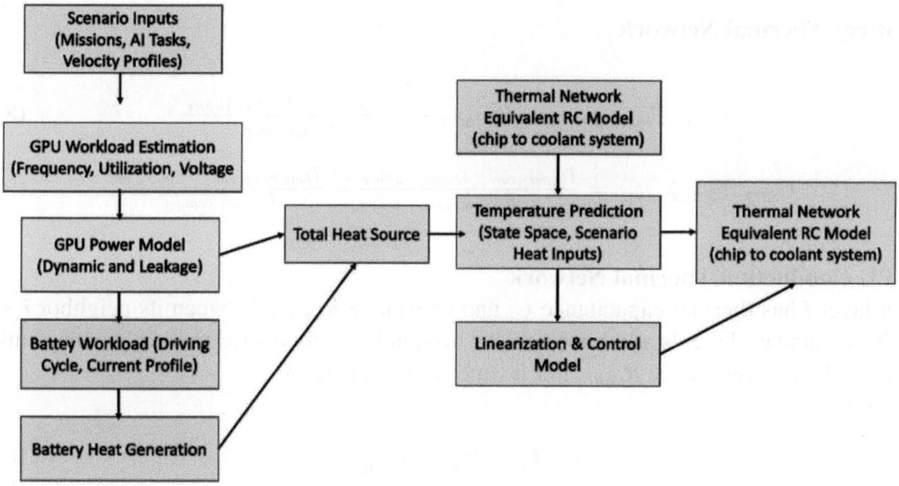

Fig. 2. Flow chart of thermal load prediction

3.2 System Model

Instantaneous Power of GPU

$$P(t) = C_{eff}\ V(t)^2 f(t)\ Util(t) + P_{leak}\big(T_{chip}(t), V(t)\big) \tag{1}$$

$$P_{leak}\big(T_{chip}(t), V(t)\big) = \alpha\ V(t)\ e^{\beta T_{chip}(t)} + \gamma \tag{2}$$

Battery Power

$$Q_{batt}(I_{batt}, T) = I_{batt}^2 R_{int}\ (T, SOC) + I_{batt} \mathrm{T}\Delta V_{OC}(SOC, T) \tag{3}$$

Thermal Dynamics

$$C_{chip}\ \dot{T}_{chip}(t) = P_{GPU}(t) - \frac{T_{chip}(t) - T_{coolant}(t)}{R_{chip,coolant}} \tag{4}$$

$$C_{coolant}\ \dot{T}_{coolant}(t) = \frac{T_{chip}(t) - T_{coolant}(t)}{R_{chip,coolant}} - \frac{T_{coolant}(t) - T_{evap}(t)}{R_{coolant,evap}} \tag{5}$$

$$C_{plate}\ \dot{T}_{plate}(t) = P(t) - \frac{T_{plate}(t) - T_{amb}(t)}{R_{plate,amb}} \tag{6}$$

$$C_{battery}\ \dot{T}_{battery}(t) = Q_{battery}\big(I_{battery}, T_{battery}\big) + \frac{T_{battery}(t) - T_{evap}(t)}{R_{battery,evap}} \tag{7}$$

Battery Thermal Network

$$C_{core}\,\dot{T}_{battery,core} = Q_{battery} - \frac{T_{battery,core} - T_{battery,surface}}{R_{core,surface}} \tag{8}$$

$$C_{surf}\,\dot{T}_{battery,surf} = \frac{T_{battery,core} - T_{battery,surface}}{R_{core,surface}} - \frac{T_{battery,surface} - T_{coolant,in}}{R_{battery,coolant}} \tag{9}$$

GPU Conduction Thermal Network

Let layer i has thermal capacitance C_i and resistance $R_{i,\,i+1}$ between its neighbor $i+1$. Top boundary layer is adiabatic, and the bottom layer connected to the plate/ heatsink via conductive resistance R_{plate}. For layers $i = 1 \ldots n$ (Fig. 3):

For $i = 1$:

$$C_1\,\dot{T}_1 = P_{GPU} - \frac{T_1 - T_2}{R_{1,2}} \tag{10}$$

Between $i = 2 \ldots n-1$:

$$C_i\,\dot{T}_i = \frac{T_{i-1} - T_i}{R_{i-1,\ i}} - \frac{T_i - T_{i+1}}{R_{i,\ i+1}} \tag{11}$$

For $i = n$:

$$C_n\,\dot{T}_n = \frac{T_{n-1} - T_n}{R_{n-1,n}} - \frac{T_n - T_{plate}}{R_{plate}} \tag{12}$$

Between the cold plate and coolant there is convective resistance

$$\mathrm{R_{convective}} = \frac{1}{h_c A_c} \tag{13}$$

h_c convective heat transfer coefficient is a function of $\dot{m}_{coolant}$:

$$h_c = \frac{Nu\,k}{D},\ Nu = a + bRe^m + \mathrm{Pr}^{0.3},\ \mathrm{Re} = \frac{4}{\pi\,\mu\,\dot{m}_{coolant}} \tag{14}$$

$$\begin{aligned} C_{cool,in}\,\dot{T}_{cool,in} = \dot{m}_{cool} c_{plate,cool}\left(T_{cool,out} - T_{cool,in}\right) + \frac{T_{plate} - T_{cool,in}}{R_{convective}} \\ + \frac{T_{bat,surf} - T_{cool,in}}{R_{batt,cool}} - Q_{loss,coolant} \end{aligned} \tag{15}$$

$$\begin{aligned} C_{cool,out}\,\dot{T}_{cool,out} = \dot{m}_{cool} c_{plate,cool}\left(T_{cool,in} - T_{cool,out}\right) + \frac{T_{plate} - T_{cool,in}}{R_{convective}} \\ + \frac{T_{bat,surf} - T_{cool,in}}{R_{batt,cool}} - Q_{HX}\# \end{aligned} \tag{16}$$

Given that the safe operating temperature range of the battery is lower than that of the GPU, the coolant is routed first through the battery pack in order to absorb and dissipate the battery heat. Then, the coolant flows through the GPU cold plate to remove the GPU heat load. It can be also dealt with separate coolant loops for each subsystem.

To simplify evaporation process, Lumped Volume Thermal Model is used for evaporator heat exchange process under the parallel flow and single-phase refrigerant assumption,

$$\frac{1}{UA} = \frac{1}{h_{coolant} A_{coolant}} + \frac{t_{wall}}{k_{wall} A_{wall}} + \frac{1}{h_{refrig} A_{refrig}} \tag{17}$$

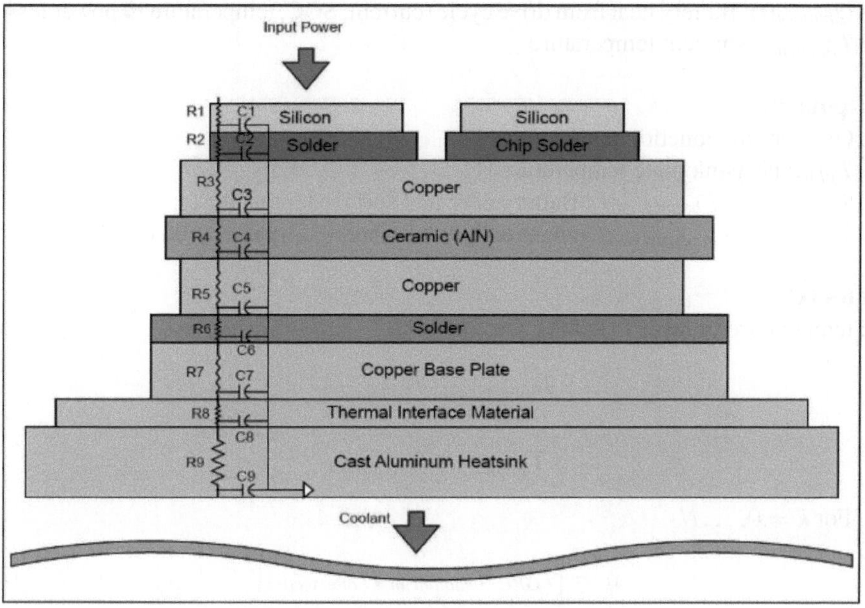

Fig. 3. Block representation of the chip stack RC model

where UA is overall conductance of heat exchanger [W/K]

$$NTU = \frac{UA}{C_c} \tag{18}$$

$$\epsilon = 1 - e^{-NTU} \tag{19}$$

$$Q_{HX} = \epsilon \, C_c\left(T_{cool,in} - T_{refrig,in}\right) \tag{20}$$

$$P_{pump,k} = P_{pump}\left(\dot{m}_{cool,k}\right), P_{compressor,k} = P_{comp}\left(\dot{m}_{refrig}\right) \tag{21}$$

3.3 Control Strategy

To have a proper preconditioning and better usage of scenario generating, we decided to apply MPC for the system with slack variables. System parameters and cost function is as following.

Inputs (u):

$\dot{m}_{coolant}$: Coolant mass flow rate [kg/s]

$\dot{m}_{refrig}$: Refrigerant mass flow rate [kg/s]

Disturbances (d)

$Q_{GPU}(t)$: GPU heat from mapped scenario (frequency, voltage, utilization, temperature ➔ dynamic and leakage power)

$Q_{battery}(t)$: Battery heat from drive cycle (current, SOC, temperature ➔power losses)
$T_{ambient}$: Ambient temperature

Outputs (y)
T_j: GPU on- die junction temperature
T_{plate}: heatsink plate temperature
$T_{battery,\ core}$, $T_{battery,\ surf}$: Battery core and surface temperatures
$T_{coolant,\ in}$, $T_{coolant,\ out}$: Coolant temperature before and after cold plate

States (x)
T_i: temperature of layer I (I, TIM, Cu, AlN, Al)

$$T_{battery,core}, T_{battery,surf}$$

$$T_{coolant,in}, T_{coolant,out}$$

For $k = 0, \ldots N$

$$x_k = \left[T_{GPU}\ T_{coolant,in}\ T_{battery,core}\right]^T \tag{22}$$

$$u_k = \left[\dot{m}_{cool,k}\ \dot{m}_{refrig,k}\right]^T \tag{23}$$

$$d_k = \left(Q_{GPU}\ Q_{bat,k}\ I_{bat,k}\ T_{amb,k}\right) \tag{24}$$

$$x_{k+1} = F(x_k, u_k, d_k) \tag{25}$$

Power and mass flow rate through coolant and refrigerant loops are mapped to the consumed power during the operation.

$$P_{pump,k} = P_{pump}\left(\dot{m}_{cool,k}\right), P_{compressor,k} = P_{comp}\left(\dot{m}_{refrig}\right) \tag{26}$$

$$\dot{m}_{cool,k} \leq \dot{m}_{cool,\max}, \dot{m}_{refrig,k} \leq \dot{m}_{refrig,\max} \tag{27}$$

Constraints for the GPU and battery temperature with slack variables:

$$T_{GPU} \leq T_{GPU,ref} + s_{T1,k}, s_{T1,k} \geq 0, \tag{28}$$

$$T_{battery,core} \leq T_{batt,core,ref} + s_{Tb,k}, s_{Tb,k} \geq 0, \forall \mathrm{k} = 1 \ldots \mathrm{N} \tag{29}$$

Reference temperature vector for the states:

$$x_k = \left[T_{GPU,ref}\ T_{coolant,ref}\ T_{battery,ref}\right]^T \tag{30}$$

Cost function and final version of the optimization process is as following:Stage cost:

$$l(x_k u_k s_k) = \left(x_k - x_{k,ref}\right)^T Q\left(x_k - x_{k,ref}\right) + u_k^T R u_k + w_1\, s_{T1,k}^2 + w_2 s_{Tb,k}^2 \tag{31}$$

Terminal cost (The final cost for the end of prediction horizon):

$$V_f(x_N) = \left(x_N - x_{N,ref}\right)^T P\left(x_N - x_{N,ref}\right) \tag{32}$$

$$\min_{\{x(\cdot),u(\cdot),s(\cdot)\}} \sum\nolimits_{i_y \in \Gamma_y} \left[l(x_k u_k s_k) + V_f(x_N)\right] \tag{33}$$

Subject to:

$$x_{k+1} = F(x_k, u_k, d_k) \tag{34}$$

$$T_{GPU} \le T_{GPU,ref} + s_{T1,k}, s_{T1,k} \ge 0, \tag{35}$$

$$T_{battery,core} \le T_{batt,core,ref} + s_{Tb,k}, s_{Tb,k} \ge 0, \forall \mathrm{k} = 1 \ldots \mathrm{N} \tag{36}$$

$$\dot{m}_{cool,k} \le \dot{m}_{cool,\max}, \dot{m}_{refrig,k} \le \dot{m}_{refrig,\max} \tag{37}$$

4 Co-simulation Framework

In most cases, co-simulation systems function as a middle layer between control software and detailed physical models. The interfaces between subsystems are defined through different variable types. Conventional input and output ports capture the signal connections used in block diagrams. Potential and flow variables define physical interactions, such as voltage and current in electrical systems or pressure and flow in fluid systems. Stream variables are used to model bidirectional fluid exchanges and intensive properties, such as specific enthalpy or mass fraction.

When the governing equations of each subsystem are assembled into a complete model, the result is typically a set of differential-algebraic equations (DAEs). Multi-domain simulation tools adopt various strategies for solving these systems. Some of them directly apply numerical methods, often using implicit integration techniques. Others transform the equations into an equivalent set of ordinary differential equations (ODEs) and then apply explicit or implicit solvers. To achieve computational efficiency when handling models with very large equation sets, graph-theoretic approaches and sparse matrix techniques are commonly employed [20].

The **Functional Mock-up Unit (FMU)** standard provides a way to package such subsystem models—including their equations, parameters, and interfaces—into a portable representation. In this context, FMU serves as the bridge between GT-SUITE's high-fidelity plant model and Simulink's control design environment. The controller in Simulink interacts with the plant FMU through well-defined inputs and outputs, enabling real-time co-simulation without the need to replicate the full physical equations inside Simulink.

Also, the FMU-based co-simulation makes the high-fidelity thermal dynamics from GT-SUITE are consistently communicated to the Simulink controller sure, by enabling the controller to operate with both computational efficiency and physical accuracy.

5 Results

The co-simulation parameters are determined by Simulink, and Worldwide Harmonized Light Vehicles Test Cycle (WLTC) and 30 C° ambient temperature are chosen for the battery and a combination of idle, light and heavy intensity cases are selected for the GPU heat generation. The material specifications to calculate RC model of the GPU stack are given in Table 1. The reference temperatures for the battery are 40 °C and for the GPU is 81 °C. Sampling time is 0.1 s for both systems and final temperature profile is captured at the end of simulation (Figs. 4, 5, 6 and 7).

5.1 Finite Element Results

Fig. 4. Temperature distribution over the heatsink. Upper image non- predictive (on-off temperature controller) controller (which can reach up to 414 K at the hottest point), lower image predictive controller

Fig. 5. Temperature distribution over the silicon chip where heat is generated. Upper results are from the non-predictive (on-off temperature controller) controller (which can reach up to 393 K), lower results are of the predictive controller

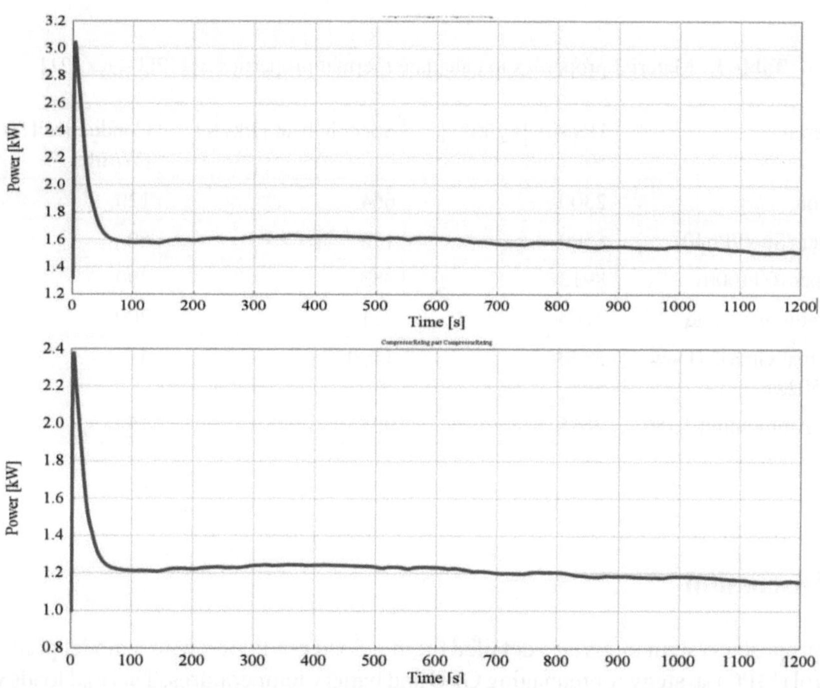

Fig. 6. Total power consumption. Upper results are from the non-predictive (on-off temperature controller) controller, lower results are of the predictive controller

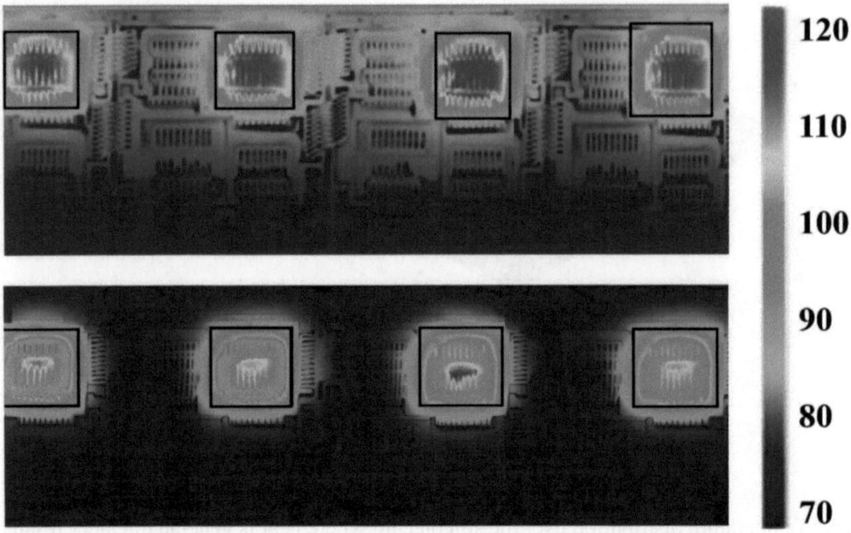

Fig. 7. Temperature distribution of the parallel computing HPC system showing both chipset modules within the same temperature range (70–120 °C). The color map illustrates localized hot spots and uniformity across processors under identical thermal scaling

Table 1. Material properties to calculate thermal properties of GPU stack [21]

Material	Density [kg/m^3]	Specific heat [J/kgK]	Conductive HTC [W/mK]
Silicon	2300	664	120
Solder (Sn60/Pb40)	8500	176	60
Copper (C11000)	8913	383	390
Aluminum Nitride	3200	711	200
Thermal Grease (Dow TC-5022)	3230	1100	4
Cast Aluminum (A356)	2685	935	159

6 Discussion

The proposed system integrates detailed thermal load prediction with a model predictive control (MPC) strategy for managing GPU and battery temperatures. Thermal loads were estimated from a benchmarking process that included different intensity computations (e.g., heavy and light calculations) and a driving cycle to implement battery temperature dependency. The co-simulation environment, which utilizes GT-SUITE as the plant model and Simulink as the controller environment via the Functional Mock-up Interface

(FMU), ensures the controller receives physically consistent thermal responses without replicating high-order physics in the control domain.

The results indicate that the scenario-based modeling approach can successfully predict the overall temperature rise of the GPU and battery under different workloads, ambient conditions, and cooling scenarios, preventing overheating. However, significant temperature differences were observed between the predictive and non-predictive temperature control strategies. Specifically, the MPC was able to anticipate upcoming thermal loads based on scenario predictions and adjust coolant and refrigerant mass flow rates proactively. In contrast, the non-predictive controller, which is a simple on-off temperature controller, responded only after temperature deviations occurred. This led to superior thermal safety margins in the predictive case, particularly during workload transients, and a reduction in peak GPU and battery temperatures.

The co-simulation framework was critical in highlighting these differences. Since GT-SUITE provides transient thermal responses, the temperature prediction in Simulink was tested against conditions close to physical reality. The FMU interface allowed for the smooth integration of these high-fidelity dynamics into the control loop, making it possible to directly compare the predictive versus non-predictive approaches in a realistic plant setting.

7 Conclusion

Predictive control demonstrated clear advantages in managing thermal control of HPC components and battery safety margins, especially under high-intensity computational workloads. While HPCs are treated as power electronics, the importance of more sophisticated control is underscored. Co-simulation ensured the credibility of the comparison by coupling the optimization-based controller with a detailed thermal plant model. This highlights the importance of using FMU-based frameworks for evaluating advanced controllers in complex multi-domain systems.

In summary, the co-simulation study shows that while both strategies can ensure some amount of cooling; by utilizing the correlation between scenarios and temperature rise, predictive control significantly improves thermal performance by preempting critical temperature rises. The FMU-based integration of GT-SUITE and Simulink proved essential for evaluating such advanced control strategies under realistic operating conditions.

Future work should extend the MPC formulation with adaptive models or data-driven corrections with different driving cycles for the battery, complex missions for the HPC units and variety of the environmental conditions to account for residual modeling errors to make highly accurate predictions, as well as assess the trade-offs between cooling energy consumption and thermal safety in real mission scenarios.

Disclosure of Interests. The authors declare no competing interests. This research was supported by the Grant Agency of the Czech Technical University in Prague, grant No. SGS25/145/OHK3/3 T/13.

References

1. Jouppi, N.P., et al.: In-datacenter performance analysis of a tensor processing unit. In: Proceedings of the 44th ACM/IEEE International Symposium on Computer Architecture (ISCA '17), pp. 1–12. ACM/IEEE, New York (2017)
2. Stepanas, K., Willians, J., Hernander, E., Ruetz, F., Hines, T.: OHM: gpu based occupancy map generation. arXiv:2206.06079v1 [cs.CV] 26 Apr 2022 (2022)
3. Stan, M.R., Skadron, K., Barcella, M., Huang, W., et al.: HotSpot: a dynamic compact thermal model at the microarchitectural level. Microelectron. J. **34**(12), 1153–1165 (2003)
4. Kong, J., Chung, S. W.: Recent Thermal Management Techniques for Microprocessors. ACM Comput. Surv. **44**(3), 13 (2012)
5. Sheikh, H.F., Ahmad, I., Wang, Z., Ranka, S.: An overview and classification of thermal-aware task scheduling techniques for multi-core processing systems. Sustain. Comput. Inform. Syst. **2**(3), 151–169 (2012)
6. Asim, M., et al.: Advancements in thermal management solutions for electric vehicle high-power electronics: innovations, cooling methods, and future perspectives. J. Energy Storage. **111**, 115344 (2025)
7. Yang, J., Zhou, X., Chrobak, M., Zhang, Y., Jin, L.: Dynamic thermal management through task scheduling. In: Proceedings of the 2008 International Symposium on Performance Analysis of Systems and Software (ISPASS 2008), pp. 191–201. IEEE, San Francisco (2008)
8. Ajmal, M.S., Iqbal, Z., Khan, F.Z., Bilal, M., Mehmood, R.M.: Cost-based energy efficient scheduling technique for dynamic voltage and frequency scaling system in cloud computing. Sustain. Energy Techn. and Assess. **45**, 101210 (2021)
9. Hung, W.-L., Xie, Y., Vijaykrishnan, N., Kandemir, M., Irwin, M.J.: Thermal-Aware Task Allocation and Scheduling for Embedded Systems. In: Proceedings of the 2005 Design, Automation and Test in Europe Conference and Exhibition (DATE 2005), vol. 1, pp. 898–899. IEEE, Munich (2005)
10. Maity, S., Majumder, A., Roy, R., Hota, A., Dey, S.: Harnessing Machine Learning in Dynamic Thermal Management in Embedded CPU–GPU Platforms. ACM Trans. Des. Autom. Electron. Syst. **30**(2), 19 (2025)
11. Yu, C.H., Lung, C.L., Ho, Y.L., Hsu, R.S., Kwai, D.M., Chang, S.C.: Thermal-aware on-line scheduler for 3-D many-core processor throughput optimization. IEEE Trans. Comput. Aided Des. Integr. Circ. Syst. **33**(5), 763–773 (2014)
12. Amarnath, A., et al.: HetSched: quality-of-mission aware scheduling for autonomous vehicle SoCs. In: Proceedings of the 2022 IEEE International Symposium on Performance Analysis of Systems and Software (ISPASS), pp. 79–90. IEEE, Singapore (2022)
13. Yun, B., Shin, K.G., Wang, S.: Proactive thermal-aware multicore scheduling using job migration and power-gating. In: Proceedings of the 2012 IEEE 15th Real Time and Embedded Technology and Applications Symposium (RTAS), pp. 85–94. IEEE, Beijing (2009)
14. Ajmal, M.S., Iqbal, Z., Khan F.Z., Bilal, M., Mehmood, R.M.: cost-based energy efficient scheduling techniques for dynamic voltage and frequency scaling system in cloud computing. Sustain Energy Technol Assess **45**, 101210 (2021)
15. Huang, W., Ghosh, S., Velusamy, S., Sankaranarayanan, K., Skadron, K., Stan, M.R.: HotSpot: a compact thermal modeling methodology for early-stage VLSI design. IEEE Trans. VLSI Syst. **14**(5) (2006)
16. Hunang, W., Humenay, E., Skadron, K., Stan, M.R.: The need for a full-chip and package thermal model for thermally optimized IC designs. In: ISLPED '05. Proceedings of the 2005 International Symposium on Low Power Electronics and Design (2005)
17. Rosique, F., Lorente, P.N., Fernandez, C., Padilla, A.: A systematic review of perception system and simulators for autonomous vehicles research. Sensors. **19**(3), 648 (2019)

18. Rodriguez, J. P., Yomsi, P.M., An efficient proactive thermal-aware scheduler for DVFS-enabled single-Core processors. In: Association for Computing Machinery, 29th International Conference on Real-Time Networks and Systems (RTNS), ACM, France (2021)
19. Rostami, S., Down, D. G., Karakostas, G.: Thermal-aware workload distribution for data centers with demand variations. arXiv:2308.12559v1 [eess.SY] (2023)
20. Baillieul, J., Samad, T.: Encyclopedia of Systems and Control, 1st edn. Springer, London (2015)
21. Remsburg, R.: Direct integration of IGBT power modules to liquid cooling arrays. In: Electric Vehicle Symposium Conference (2007)
22. Negreiros, A.L.V., Brito, A.V: Allowing Large-Scale Systems Evaluation with Ptolemy through Distributed Simulation. Brazilian Symposium on Computing Systems Engineering (SBESC) (2013)
23. Steinbick, C. et al.: Smart grid co-simulation with MOSAIK and HLA: a comparison study. arXiv:1811.06877v1 [cs.OH] 15 Nov 2018 (2017)
24. Hatledal, L.I., Styve, A., Howland, G., Zhang, H.: A language and platform independent co-simulation framework based on the functional mock-up Interface. IEEE Access. **7**, 109328–109339 (2019)

Color-Enhanced FPFH-Based ICP for Robust Point Cloud Registration in Support of Autonomous Tactical Behavior

Jana Procházková(✉)

Brno University of Technology, Brno 616 69, Czech Republic
prochazkova.j@fme.vutbr.cz

Abstract. The objective of our research was to investigate the efficacy of point cloud registration in natural environments. Standard algorithms are typically employed in urban settings or in situations where vehicles are traversing traffic roads. However, when the environment has a limited number of well-resolved areas, the performance of these algorithms tends to decline significantly.

This article explores the use of the Iterative Closest Point (ICP) algorithm with the color-enhanced Fast Point Feature Histogram (FPFH) descriptor in the context of autonomous driving. Autonomous vehicles designed for rescue missions or research operations in hard-to-reach areas, such as dense forests, mountainous regions, or disaster-stricken zones, require robust perception systems to navigate effectively. In such cases, reliable scene interpretation is critical for Autonomous Tactical Behavior, where real-time decision-making and autonomous path adjustment are essential for mission success.

The augmentation of the descriptor with colour information enhances the precision with which the algorithm composes the scene, thereby facilitating more optimal vehicle path planning for navigating the landscape. In addition, we have tested a variety of color spaces to ensure that the influence of different lighting conditions on the color information does not affect the result. The LAB space was identified as the most suitable. Furthermore, a series of experiments were conducted on both real and artificial datasets to illustrate the advantages of the proposed approach.

Keywords: Iterative Closest Point · Feature Point Histogram · Color Spaces · Autonomous Driving

1 Introduction and Literature Overview

1.1 Context and Motivation

Modern technology advancements are centered on autonomous driving, which aims to transform the transportation sector by improving ease, safety, and efficiency. Real-time perception and comprehension of the environment is a crucial feature of autonomous driving systems, or the objective is to create an accurate three-dimensional representation of the environment.

J. Novotný et al. (Eds.): MESAS 2025, LNCS 16627, pp. 166–180, 2027.
https://doi.org/10.1007/978-3-032-33182-3_10

This involves the precise and robust matching of 3D point clouds, which is essential for tasks such as object detection or localization. Advanced methods like point cloud registration and Simultaneous Localization and Mapping (SLAM) are used to overcome these challenges.

Simultaneous Localization and Mapping technologies allow the system to automatically create a map of an unknown environment while simultaneously maintaining an awareness of the system's location within that environment. This dual capability is of high importance for autonomous navigation, particularly in complex or dynamic environments. Autonomous vehicles may move and make decisions in real time by using SLAM, which combines sensor data to produce detailed maps. It integrates data from a variety of sensors, including LiDAR, cameras, and IMUs (Inertial Measurement Units), to provide a comprehensive understanding of the vehicle's surroundings and its position (see more e.g. in [1–3]).

However, despite its numerous advantages, SLAM presents several challenges and limitations when applied to specific terrain reconstruction. SLAM algorithms are computationally intensive, requiring high processing power and memory resources. This complexity arises from the need to perform continuous real-time data processing, including feature extraction, data association, and map updating. For example, authors in [4] examine three state-of-the-art visual SLAM frameworks to evaluate how each one addresses critical systems-level challenges: specifically, timeliness, concurrency, and context awareness under real-time operational constraints. Their findings show that while global-map-based SLAM systems often deliver the highest accuracy, they struggle in resource-constrained, highly concurrent environments.

The accuracy of SLAM is substantially influenced by the quality and calibration of the sensors employed. In terrain reconstruction, standard sensors include LiDAR, cameras, and IMUs. Any discrepancies in sensor calibration, such as misalignment or drift, can result in significant errors in the generated maps.

SLAM algorithms are sensitive to environmental influences that can slow down their performance. For example, homogeneous or feature-poor environments, such as open fields or woods, need more distinct landmarks for effective SLAM operation, resulting in localization and mapping inaccuracies. Furthermore, dynamic environments with moving objects or changing conditions (e.g., weather, vegetation growth) can introduce complexities in maintaining an accurate and consistent map.

In this context, the Fast Point Feature Histograms (FPFH) descriptor stands out as a powerful tool for capturing geometric features of point clouds. FPFH has been widely recognized for its efficiency and robustness in describing local surface characteristics. In this paper, we propose to extend the FPFH descriptor with color information. The combination of a neighborhood description with the addition of color will result in a more accurate description of the point's neighborhood, especially in very hard terrain conditions. To ascertain which color space is least dependent on illumination, several color spaces (RGB, HSV, XYZ, LAB) were selected for testing. This is because in the natural environment, a change in illumination intensity leads to a significant change in color values. Moreover, the combination of geometric and color features helps to distinguish between similarly shaped objects that differ in appearance, thereby improving matching accuracy.

In the second phase, FPFH descriptor with color information is used with the standard ICP algorithm. We performed multiple tests with both artificial and real data, and at the end of the thesis, we show a comparison of the use of different color models with reconstruction accuracy. By leveraging the advanced capabilities of ICP and the enriched FPFH descriptor, autonomous vehicles can achieve higher levels of situation awareness in natural and difficult terrains. This not only enhances their operational effectiveness in Autonomous Tactical Behavior or research missions but also contributes to the broader goal of enabling autonomous systems to operate reliably in diverse environments.

1.2 Literature Overview

The registration of point clouds is a well-documented challenge in the field of computer vision. Several algorithms and techniques have been developed to obtain a correct transformation. The most basic distinction is whether there is a rigid or non-rigid transformation between the two scenes. In the present study, we will limit our consideration to rigid variant. The primary objective, therefore, is to identify the rotation matrix and translation vector that describe the motion between two point clouds. The initial and most frequently utilized algorithm is ICP—Iterative Closest Point (first published in [5]). The principle of the Iterative Closest Point (ICP) algorithm is to iteratively refine the alignment of two point clouds by minimizing the distance between corresponding points until convergence.

A comprehensive overview of the various methods for extending the ICP algorithm, including different distance computations, point descriptors, and artificial intelligence algorithms, can be found in [6]. ICP is a well-established algorithm, yet it continues to be refined and enhanced in recent research. The article [7] presents the most efficient means of explaining uncertainty estimates produced by point cloud registration algorithms, with a particular focus on variants of ICP. Employing methodologies derived from explainable AI, the authors undertake a comprehensive analysis of the factors influencing ICP outcomes, encompassing variables such as noise, occlusion, and ambiguous geometry. The paper [8] presents a new calculation using a combination of point-to-line and point-to-plane constraints. This allows the system to assess whether reliable registration in a given area of the scene is even possible. The method is designed for use in unstructured environments (e.g., caves, forests, disaster-stricken areas) and achieves higher robustness and accuracy.

The use of descriptors with the registration was adapted from image analysis. Their principle is simple, to express a mathematical description of a given point's surroundings to make it as identifiable as possible in a second point cloud.

Descriptors can be based on the description of the surroundings using curvature or other geometric properties. In our work, we used the FPFH descriptor (first introduced in [9]), which is based on the geometric connection of points in the surroundings (description in Sec. 2.1). Its utilization in ICP algorithms is well documented [10, 11], however, its association with color information represents a novel extension.

Integrating color information into the Fast Point Feature Histogram (FPFH) descriptor significantly enhances its discriminative capability for point cloud alignment tasks. While FPFH captures local geometric structures based on curvature and surface relationships, it may have difficulty in environments with geometric redundancy or ambiguity.

By incorporating color features - typically from perceptually uniform color spaces such as HSV, LAB, RGB, XYZ (described in Sec. 2.2) - the descriptor becomes more robust in distinguishing between visually similar but structurally identical regions. This fusion improves correspondence matching, reduces the number of false positives, and accelerates convergence in subsequent alignment process. Furthermore, the use of color information enables more stable registration under challenging lighting conditions, making the method particularly suitable for natural environments.

2 Methodology

The following section will describe the theoretical background of the proposed algorithm. The following Sect. 2.1 describes the theoretical foundations of the FPFH descriptor, followed by color spaces (Sec. 2.2) and the extension of the descriptor with color information in Sect. 2.3. The last Sect. 2.4, then describes the data sets.

2.1 Point Feature Histogram Background

The use of descriptors is a common practice when describing 2D images or point clouds for the purpose of representing spatial data. The fundamental characteristic of these descriptors is to provide a representation of feature points based on the intrinsic characteristics of the points themselves or their neighboring points. The FPFH descriptor was firstly described in [9].

Let p_q be a point in Euclidean space and the set $\mathcal{P}_q^k = \{p_1^k, p_2^k \ldots p_n^k\}$ are neighbors' points given by inequality:

$$|\, p_i^k - p_q \,| \leq d \tag{1}$$

where d is maximal distance and $|.|$ is given norm. The neighborhood can be defined by maximal number k of points p_i^k. Then, vector function F describes the local geometry given by set $\mathcal{P}_q^k$ around point p_q as:

$$F\left(p_q, \mathcal{P}_q^k\right) = \{x_1, x_2, x_3 \ldots x_m\}, \tag{2}$$

where x_i, $i \in \{1 \ldots m\}$ is i-th dimension of point feature vector. Point Feature Histogram is defined for point and its neighbor's points given by Eq. (1). For each pair of points, the descriptor is to describe the parameters (see Fig. 1 for geometry view):

$$\alpha = \arccos(v \cdot n_t),$$

$$\phi = \arccos\left(n_s \cdot \frac{p_t - p_s}{|\, p_t - p_s \,|}\right),$$

$$\theta = \arctan\left(\frac{w \cdot n_t}{n_s \cdot n_t}\right),$$

$$d = |p_t - p_s|$$

for $\forall p_s, p_t \in \mathcal{P}_{\mathrm{II}}^k$, where n_s, n_t are corresponding normals, $v = n_s \times \frac{p_t - p_s}{|p_t - p_s|}$ and $w = n_s \times v$. The relation between a pair of points in the neighborhood of $\mathcal{P}_q^k$ is characterized by the quartet $(\alpha, \phi, \theta, d) = (f_1, f_2, f_3, f_4)$. These quartets then yield a histogram characterizing the geometry of the neighborhood of the points. The index of the histogram for given quartet is given by following equation (in case of generalized index function):

$$idx = \sum_{i=1}^{n} step_i(f_i) \cdot \frac{1}{div_1} \prod_{j=1}^{i} div_j \tag{3}$$

where div_j is number of subintervals for given features f_i and $step_i$ is a generalized step function with arbitrary interval splits $s_j \in [f_{min}, f_{max}], j \in 1, 2, \ldots, div_i - 1$. Value of $step_i$ is given by this evaluation:

$$step_i(f) = \begin{cases} 0, & f_i < s_1 \\ & \vdots \\ 1, & s_1 < f_i < s_2, \\ div_i - 1, & f_i \geq s_{div_i - 1} \end{cases} \tag{4}$$

In the original work of Rusu [9], the description of the neighborhood of a point consists of four values. However, acceleration of computation time, the distance is not used because this value is not relevant due to sensing distortion and is subject to large changes due to the distance of the point from the sensor. So that only these three values α, ϕ, θ are used and they are called Simplified Point Feature Histogram.

For each value, we determine the number of bins in the histogram (due to Eq. (3, 4) and then we will construct this histogram for all pairs of points. Unlike the basic PFH, the FPFH does not use all possible pairs of points in the spherical neighborhood of a point, but it works with histograms of connected points. Thus, this algorithm evaluates with respect to the properties of the bound points, and it speeds up the computation.

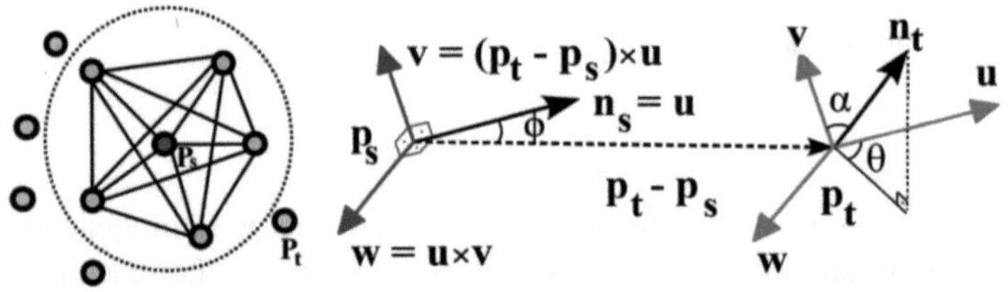

Fig. 1. Computation of FPFH descriptor - geometric visualization

In practice, it would be computationally expensive to calculate the FPFH histogram for each point. It is therefore necessary to find the points that are most representative of a given cloud. In this case, it is not advisable to use the change of curvature with differently scaled data, because due to noise the behavior of the normals is not stable (their deviations can be very large at the noise points) and this will lead to a false selection. The authors in [12] propose a method based on the analysis of the so-called μ– histogram that is suitable for this case.

2.2 Color Spaces

The light is described by its Spectral Power Distribution (SPD); however, human eyes are not cannot perceive the SPD. This section outlines alternative approaches to representing color, that attempt to model the human eye and its trichromatic perception. These approaches are based on the observation, that any color can be recreated using an additive mix of three primary colors, thus representing color with a triplet of values of intensities of the primary colors. The system of primaries used to represent a color is called the color model or the color space. The following subsections describe some of the most used color spaces, using [13–15] as the primary source.

RGB Space. The most widely adopted representation of color is using the Red, Green, and Blue (RGB) primaries. Colors are represented by a triplet of intensities of the primary colors, creating the desired color through an additive mixture. A common misconception is that RGB is a color space, while in fact, it is a family of color spaces, where a concrete choice of the RGB primaries determines the specific color space. This is the reason why the RGB approach is called device dependent - each camera sensor and display have their own set of primaries. The Commission Internationale de l'éclairage (CIE) in 1931 devised the CIE RGB color space. Monochromatic reference stimuli R, G, and B were selected as primaries, with respective wavelengths [16]:

$$\begin{aligned} \lambda_R &= 700.0 \sim \text{nm} \\ \lambda_G &= 546.1 \sim \text{nm} \\ \lambda_B &= 435.8 \sim \text{nm} \end{aligned} \tag{5}$$

In their study, Wright and Guild instructed observers to perform color matching of a series of lights with defined wavelengths by adjusting the intensities of the primary colors R, G, B. The averaged responses obtained from these experiments were subsequently used to derive the color matching functions $\overline{r}(\lambda)$, $\overline{g}(\lambda)$, $\overline{b}(\lambda)$ for the standard observer [17]. The resulting functions are illustrated in Fig. 2.

A monochromatic light $\mathrm{E}_{\lambda_\mathrm{i}}$ with the wavelength λ_i is perceptually identical to the additive mixture using the color matching functions.

$$\mathrm{E}_{\lambda_\mathrm{i}} \approx \overline{\mathrm{r}}(\lambda_\mathrm{i})\mathrm{R} + \overline{\mathrm{g}}(\lambda_\mathrm{i})\mathrm{G} + \overline{\mathrm{b}}(\lambda_\mathrm{i})\mathrm{B} \tag{6}$$

This provides an additive representation for any light stimulus Q. A light stimulus Q is a sum of monochromatic lights E_{λ_i} weighted by a factor Q_{λ_i} Then

$$Q(\lambda_i)E_{\lambda_i} \approx \overline{r}(\lambda_i)Q(\lambda_i)R + \overline{g}(\lambda_i)Q(\lambda_i)G + \overline{b}(\lambda_i)Q(\lambda_i)B \tag{7}$$

Using Grassman's linearity laws,[1] the light stimulus Q has the same color as the additive mixture:

$$Q \approx RR + GG + BB, \tag{8}$$

where

$$R = \int_{380}^{740} \overline{r}(\lambda)\, Q(\lambda)\, \mathrm{d}\lambda,\; G = \int_{380}^{740} \overline{g}(\lambda)\, Q(\lambda)\, \mathrm{d}\lambda,\; B = \int_{380}^{740} \overline{b}(\lambda)\, Q(\lambda)\, \mathrm{d}\lambda.$$

[1] https://doi.org/10.1002/andp.18531650505

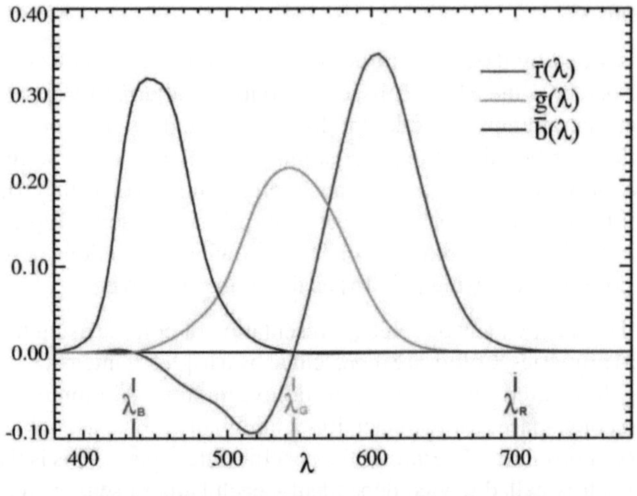

Fig. 2. CIE 1931 RGB color matching functions

Color Space XYZ. The CIE XYZ color space, introduced by the International Commission on Illumination (CIE) in 1931, represents a fundamental model for describing human color perception. It was specifically designed to overcome the limitations of the earlier CIE RGB color space, most notably the issue of negative component values, which significantly restricted its practical applicability.

CIE XYZ was derived from CIE RGB with three set requirements. The first is for the color matching functions $\overline{x}(\lambda), \overline{y}(\lambda), \overline{z}(\lambda)$, see Fig. 3, to be a linear combination of $\overline{r}(\lambda), \overline{g}(\lambda), \overline{b}(\lambda)$, such that $\overline{x}(\lambda), \overline{y}(\lambda), \overline{z}(\lambda)$ are non-negative.

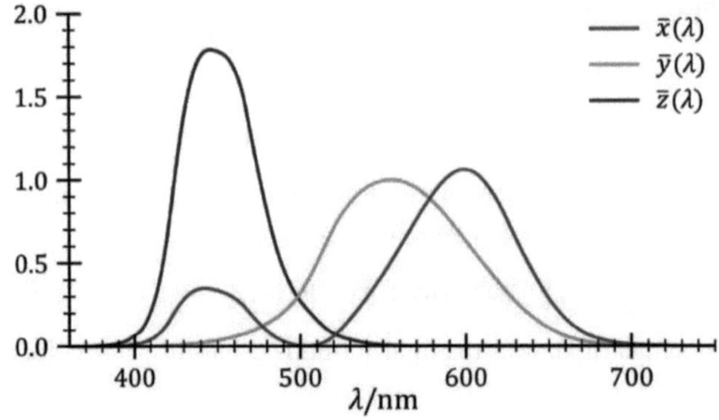

Fig. 3. CIE 1931 XYZ color matching functions [18]

When CIE XYZ was developed the computational ability was a limiting factor and dealing with non-negative numbers allowed to simplify the calculation [16]. The second requirement was that the $\overline{y}(\lambda)$ be identical to the standard luminosity function so that the Y primary would correspond to the luminance of the color. The final requirement was to normalize the color matching functions so that the tristimulus values $X = Y = Z$ are equal for white light. The tristimulus (X, Y, Z) for light stimulus Q is obtained as:

$$X = \int_{380}^{740} \overline{x}(\lambda)\, Q(\lambda)\, \mathrm{d}\lambda,\ Y = \int_{380}^{740} \overline{y}(\lambda)\, Q(\lambda)\, \mathrm{d}\lambda,\ \ Z = \int_{380}^{740} \mathrm{z}(\lambda)\, Q(\lambda)\, \mathrm{d}\lambda.$$

The primaries of CIE XYZ are sometimes called virtual primaries, as they do not correspond to a real color. The conversion between CIE RGB and CIE XYZ is possible via a simple linear transform:

$$(X\ \ Y\ \ Z)^T = \begin{pmatrix} 0.49 & 0.31 & 0.20 \\ 0.17697 & 0.81240 & 0.01063 \\ 0 & 0.01 & 0.99 \end{pmatrix} \begin{pmatrix} R \\ G \\ B \end{pmatrix} \tag{9}$$

Color space HSV (Hue, Saturation, Value). RGB representation and the CIE XYZ color space are highly effective for storing and transmitting color information, as displaying a color simply involves converting it into the device's specific color space by multiplying the color vector by the device's transformation matrix. However, without visual output, it is challenging to assess the characteristics of a color based solely on its tristimulus values. Neither the RGB nor the CIE XYZ representations correspond directly to the way humans intuitively perceive.

In practical applications, such as color editing software, users commonly adjust attributes like brightness, increase or decrease the color's intensity, or shift its hue. To enable more intuitive color manipulation, RGB values can be transformed into the HSV color space, which encodes colors in terms of hue, saturation, and value. Similar to RGB, HSV is device-dependent, as it represents a transformation of device-specific RGB tristimulus values into an alternative framework.

When defining the HSV components, first a set of helper variables are defined, the maximum M, minimum m and the chroma C (Fig. 4).

$$M = \max(R, G, B), m = \min(R, G\ B), C = M - m \tag{10}$$

Value V describes the intensity of color on a scale of 0 to 1. Value of 0 means the color is pure black, while value 1 can be either pure white or colorful, depending on the saturation value, it means that $V = M$. Saturation S describes the intensity of the color in interval 0 to 1. The value is given by:

$$S = \begin{cases} C/V, & \text{everywhere except } V = 0 \\ 0, & V = 0 \end{cases} \tag{11}$$

Color Space LAB. An essential property of point feature representations is their ability to differentiate between points. When using color as such a representation, it must be also possible to quantify differences between colors. HSV is advantageous over RGB for this purpose, as it facilitates intuitive comparisons of lightness, saturation, and hue. However, HSV lacks perceptual uniformity, meaning that equal distances in this space do not correspond to equal perceived color differences. A perceptually uniform color space ensures that distances between points correspond proportionally to perceived

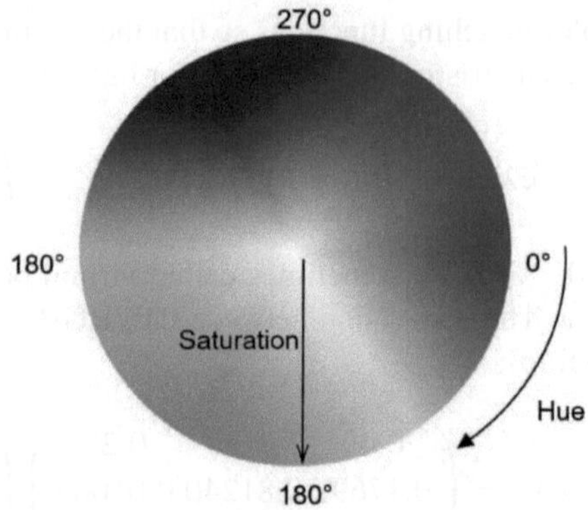

Fig. 4. Color model HSV – slice for Value = 1

differences between their associated colors [4]. To address this, CIE introduced the CIE LAB color space in 1976, explicitly designed for perceptual uniformity. CIE LAB is three-dimensional: $L\star$ represents lightness (0–100), while $a\star$ and $b\star$ encode chromaticity, both ranging from -1 to 1. Fig. 5 shows the LAB space. More specific formulation of conversion in LAB space can be found in [19].

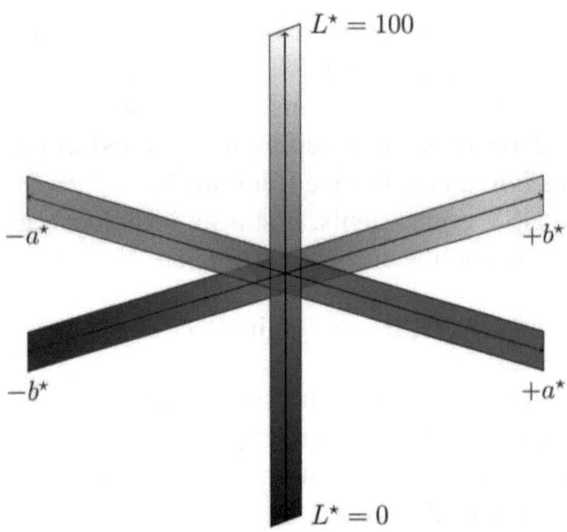

Fig. 5. Axis of CIE LAB color space.

2.3 The Extension of the FPFH Descriptor with Color Information

A key advantage of employing a perceptually uniform color space, such as CIE LAB, is that perceptual differences between colors can be directly quantified using the Euclidean metric. To enhance point discrimination within a point cloud, not only spatial proximity but also color similarity is considered. During point set registration, points from the source and target clouds may be spatially close; however, if their colors differ significantly or their lightness values diverge, this suggests they originate from distinct surface regions. Incorporating color information in CIE LAB is straightforward: the tristimulus values are simply appended as additional dimensions to the Cartesian coordinates, enabling distance computation without altering the underlying metric.

$$d(p, q, \alpha) = \left| \left(p_x, p_y, p_z, \alpha p_{L*}, \alpha p_{a*}, \alpha p_{b*}\right)^T - \left(q_x, q_y, q_z, \alpha q_{L*}, \alpha q_{a*}, \alpha q_{b*}\right)^T \right| \quad (12)$$

where α is a scalar used to weigh the color information against the coordinates. We can use color with already exiting point registration methods without the need to modify the implementation. Note, that although CIE LAB was designed to be perceptually uniform, it didn't achieve the set out goal perfectly. Since its introduction in 1976 more color spaces were introduced [20], offering better perceptional uniformity, however, for purposes of point set registration CIE LAB is sufficient.

2.4 Dataset Description

To test the proposed descriptor, it was necessary to obtain data from the natural environment that also contained color information. The utilization of Cyclomedia services[2], in conjunction with Street Smart software, facilitated the acquisition of diverse sets of data within natural environments. This data was stored in a zenodo repository (link is at the end of the article). The area of point cloud covers 50x50 meters of terrain with color information stored in format uint16. These data are described in Table 1 as ptCloud A – ptCloud D and in Fig. 6, 7 is visualization of these scenes.

Because the processing of real data is both time-consuming and computationally demanding, the initial tests were performed on several smaller models (Model1-Model4 in Table 1) to obtain preliminary results and evaluate the most appropriate color model.

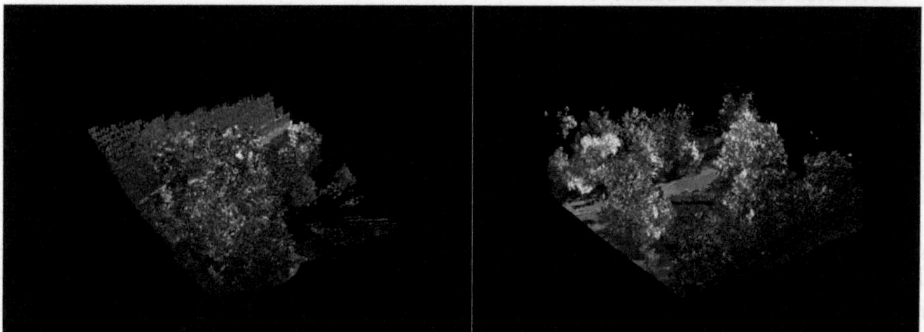

Fig. 6. Testing point clouds A, B of natural environment

[2] https://www.cyclomedia.com/uk

Fig. 7. Different lighting conditions in real data environment

Table 1. Description of datasets

Name	Number of points	Size (m)	Precision
ptCloud A	6 737 523	50x50	0.06 m
ptCloud B	7 502 250	50x50	0.06 m
ptCloud C	9 160 257	50x50	0.06 m
ptCloud D	17 845 904	50x50	0.06 m
Model1 (Squirrel)	8 353	–	0.14-0.2 cm
Model2 (Duck)	25 109	–	0.14-0.2 cm
Model3(Rabbit)	13 944	–	0.14-0.2 cm
Model4(Mario)	41 702	–	0.14-0.2 cm

3 Results and Discussion

3.1 Overview of Testing Process

In the first phase of testing, we applied all combinations of color spaces with the FPFH descriptor to simple models created by the Kinect system[3] (Model 1 - Model 4). The program was written in Python using standard libraries (NumPy, SciPy, Skimage, Sklearn). The only inputs required are a point cloud, the number of neighborhood points for calculating the FPFH descriptor, and the threshold for terminating the ICP algorithm. A simple variant of the algorithm for these data is proposed in the work [21]. After this first testing, we choose suitable combinations for application on complex point clouds of real environment.

The algorithm consists of three parts. First, the point cloud can be downsampled (this is highly recommended to speed up the calculation on real data). Then, the FPFH descriptor is calculated and color information from the data file containing the point cloud is attached. The last step is to apply the ICP algorithm (standard iteration process described in original work [5]), which searches for the rotation matrix and translation

[3] University of Bologna, laboratory DEIS vision.deis.unibo.it/SHOT

vector that correspond to the transformation of the given point cloud. This geometric transformation is usually written in projective space as:

$$\mathrm{T} = \begin{pmatrix} \boldsymbol{R} & \boldsymbol{t} \\ \boldsymbol{0} & \boldsymbol{1} \end{pmatrix} \quad (13)$$

As illustrated in Table 2, first test on artificial models show that the number of iterations is observed to decrease in instances involving the combination of ICP and descriptor FPFH with color space representation HSV. Also, the color space LAB without FPFH and combination ICP, FPFH and RGB give promising results.

Table 2. Comparison of application ICP with different color spaces applied on Model 1 (rotation 30°)

Algorithm	Iterations	Dist. mean	Dist. variation
ICP	40	2.4160e-15	2.7334e-33
ICP + FPFH	16	2.4832e-15	4.4776e-33
ICP + RGB	10	2.4637e-15	2.2721e-33
ICP + HSV	8	2.3831e-15	3.5547e-33
ICP + LAB	9	2.4456e-15	1.5085e-33
ICP + FPFH+RGB	8	2.7547e-15	4.4718e-33
ICP + FPFH+HSV	7	2.4145e-15	3.6235e-33
ICP + FPFH+LAB	8	2.4445e-15	2.2009e-33

Following the initial testing phase, the proposed algorithms were applied to the ptCloud A-D point cloud data, which already contains millions of points.

To test the FPFH descriptor, we calculated it for all these points; the calculation time for this number is approximately 25 min. Such a long calculation makes the method unsuitable for immediate calculation in the field and is more suitable for post-processing of the acquired data. Therefore, it is necessary to use descriptors only on selected points. The simplest solution is to perform regular subsampling. If the areas are indistinct and vary in structure, it would be more appropriate to choose the more complex Intrinsic Shape Signatures Keypoints [22] method. However, it is necessary to realize that this again requires computing time for the characteristic covariance matrix of the neighborhood and the calculation of eigenvalues. In terms of time consumption, it is therefore more appropriate to select points by regular subsampling.

Testing on real data (ptCloud A-D) was performed with various settings for the number of surrounding points used to calculate FPFH (5–30 neighborhood points) and with various values for the rotation angle (0–30°) and displacement vector. Given the ICP algorithm, the displacement can be ignored because in the first phase of the ICP algorithm, the point clouds are aligned to the center of gravity, so calculating the displacement is a very simple task, and no combination of methods resulted in degraded results. The calculation was performed on a MacBook Air M1 with 8GB of memory.

3.2 Results and Conclusion

The results demonstrated that augmenting the ICP algorithm with the FPFH descriptor incorporating color information significantly reduces computational complexity when applied to real-world data. For instance, in the case of rotating point cloud C, the standalone ICP algorithm required 170 iterations, whereas the FPFH-enhanced version with color information converged in only 5 iterations (using 10 neighboring points for the FPFH computation). Comparable improvements were observed for the remaining point clouds. Detailed values for distance mean and distance variance are summarized in Table 3.

Table 3. Comparison of application ICP with different color spaces applied on ptCloud C (rotation 15°, neighboring points 10)

Algorithm	Iterations	Comp. time (s)	Dist. mean	Dist. var.
ICP	170	96	1.4256e-10	9.3488e-13
ICP + FPFH	5	0.625	1.0819e-9	9.1778e-20
ICP + RGB	170	134	1.1425e-6	8.3434e-13
ICP + FPFH+RGB	5	0.670	1.7547e-9	9.4912e-19
ICP + FPFH+HSV	4	0.701	1.4822e-10	8.6338e-20
ICP + FPFH+LAB	5	0.681	1.4845e-10	8.3109e-20

The results of other point clouds demonstrate a high degree of similarity and correspond closely to the presented data for ptCloud C. Since this is real data, the addition of noise to the data was not a factor in the study, as it is already naturally present.

Several significant conclusions can be drawn from the results. In the context of post-processing data, the computational complexity of a given method is of negligible significance. To facilitate real-time computation, it is necessary to select suitable points for calculating the FPFH descriptor. It should be noted that the computational complexity of this process increases with both the number of selected points and the number of points in the neighborhood. In terms of practical implementation, the findings of our research indicate that the most effective solution is to reduce the point cloud size by approximately 10%, and to select 8-10% of the most significant points for the calculation of the FPFH descriptor. In the case of the ptCloud C point cloud, 90,000 points were used to achieve excellent accuracy.

The selection of the color model is an additional significant outcome of our work. It has been determined that the RGB color processor does not reflect color changes due to lighting. Therefore, it is advisable to use the HSV or LAB color processor, which, when used in combination with the FPFH descriptor, provide excellent accuracy and are not sensitive to lighting conditions. A further advantage of the LAB space is the property mentioned in Sect. 2.2 on color spaces - that it is a uniform color space, which ensures that the distance between two points corresponds proportionally to the difference between their associated colors. Integrating multi-channel color information into the FPFH descriptor enhances object recognition accuracy, which is crucial for Autonomous Tactical Behavior in real-world scenarios.

Data Availability. The datasets and source code supporting the findings of this study are available at https://doi.org/10.5281/zenodo.16779949

Acknowledgement. This publication was supported by the project "Innovative Technologies for Smart Low Emission Mobilities", funded as project No.CZ.02.01.01/00/23_020/0008528 by Programme Johannes Amos Comenius, call Intersectoral cooperation.

Disclosure of Interests. The authors have no competing interests to declare. The authors declare no competing interests. This research was supported by by Programme Johannes Amos Comenius. The authors used ChatGPT (OpenAI) for English language editing and stylistic improvement of the manuscript. All scientific content was created and validated by the authors.

References

1. Alsadik, B., Karam, S.: The simultaneous localization and mapping (SLAM)-an overview. J. Appl. Sci. Technol. Trends. **2**(04), 120–131 (2021)
2. Khairuddin, A.R., Talib, M.S., Haron, H.: Review on simultaneous localization and mapping (SLAM). In: ICCSCE 2015, pp. 85–90. IEEE, Penang, Malaysia (2015)
3. Taheri, H., Xia, Z.C.: SLAM: definition and evolution. Eng. Appl. Artif. Intell. **97**, 1–25 (2021)
4. Murali, V., Chandramouli, B., Gavrilovska, A., Krishnamurthy, A., Phanishayee, A., Sharma, D.: A comprehensive study of systems challenges in visual simultaneous localization and mapping systems. Proc. ACM Measurement Anal. Comput. Syst. **5**(1), 1–34 (2021)
5. Besl, P.J., McKay, N.D.: A method for registration of 3-D shapes. IEEE Trans. Pattern Anal. Mach. Intell. **14**(2), 239–256 (1992)
6. Li, L., Wang, R., Zhang, X.: A tutorial review on point cloud registrations: principle, classification, comparison, and technology challenges. IEEE Access. **11**, 35392–35413 (2023)
7. Qin, Z., Li, D., Fang, C., Yang, L.: Towards explaining uncertainty estimates in point cloud registration. arXiv preprint (2024). https://arxiv.org/abs/2412.20612
8. Yue, H., Yu, J., Su, H., Ma, W., Ren, H., Li, Y.: LP-ICP: general localizability-aware point cloud registration for robust localization in extreme unstructured environments. arXiv preprint (2025). https://arxiv.org/abs/2501.02580
9. Rusu, R.B., Blodow, N., Beetz, M.: Fast point feature histograms (FPFH) for 3-D registration. In: Proceedings of the IEEE International Conference on Robotics and Automation (ICRA 2009), vol. 5, pp. 3212–3217, Kobe, Japan (2009)
10. Sun, R., et al.: Optimization of the 3D point cloud registration algorithm based on FPFH features. Appl. Sci. **13**(5), 3096 (2023)
11. Xiang, J., Fan, W., Liu, P., Wang, M.: Point cloud alignment method based on improved ISS-ICP algorithm. In: IEEE Conference Proceedings, ICICSP, vol. 2022, pp. 249–253 (2022)
12. Rusu, R.B., Marton, Z.C., Blodow, N., Beetz, M.: Persistent point feature histograms for 3-D point clouds. In: Proceedings of the 10th International Conference on Intelligent Autonomous Systems (IAS-10), pp. 119–128 (2008)
13. Kasson, J.M., Plouffe, W.: An analysis of selected computer interchange color spaces. ACM Trans. Graph. **11**(4), 373–405 (1992)
14. Dubois, E.: The Structure and Properties of Color Spaces and the Representation of Color Images. Video, and Multimedia Processing. Morgan & Claypool Publishers, Burlington, Synthesis Lectures on Image (2009)
15. Foley, J.D., van Dam, A., Feiner, S.K., Hughes, J.F.: Computer Graphics: Principles and Practice, 2nd edn. Addison-Wesley, Reading, Mass (1990)

16. Ohta, N., Robertson, A.R.: Colorimetry. Wiley, Chichester (2005)
17. Fairman, H.S., Brill, M.H., Hemmendinger, H.: How the CIE 1931 Color-Matching Functions Were Derived from Wright–Guild Data. Color. Res. Appl. **22**(1), 11–23 (1997)
18. Wikimedia Commons. https://commons.wikimedia.org/wiki/File:CIE_1931_XYZ_Color_Matching_Functions.svg. Accessed 07 Aug 2025
19. Bertalmío, M.: Vision Models for High Dynamic Range and Wide Colour Gamut Imaging. Academic, Cambridge, MA (2020)
20. Xue, Y.: Uniform Color Spaces Based on CIECAM02 and IPT Color Difference Equations. Dissertation. Rochester Institute of Technology, Rochester, NY (2008)
21. Markovsky, A.: Colour Extension of Image Fast Point Feature Histogram, Diploma Thesis. (2024).
22. Zhong, Y.: Intrinsic shape signatures: a shape descriptor for 3-D object recognition. In: Proceedings of the 12th International Conference on Computer Vision Workshops (ICCV Workshops), pp. 689–696 (2009)

Sub-agent Level BPMN Programming for Military Autonomous Platforms

Levent Hakkı Şenyürek[1(✉)] and Erkin Çilden[2]

[1] STM Defense Technologies Engineering and Trade Inc., Çankaya, Ankara, Turkey
lhakki.senyurek@stm.com.tr,levent.senyurek@gmail.com
[2] ASELSAN, Gölbaşı, Ankara, Turkey
erkincilden@aselsan.com
https://www.stm.com.tr/en , https://www.aselsan.com.tr/en

Abstract. For programming the behavior of complex agents such as military platforms which contain a bunch of sensors and actuators, adapting a multi-agent programming approach would increase effectiveness by providing a complete and user-friendly control over the platform, either real or virtual. Especially in an emerging era of nontechnical user programmable products, this approach is increasingly gaining attention. BPMN provides a powerful means to define collaborative missions and processes, and is currently incorporated in agent programming for multi-robot applications. In the traditional sense, the common definition of an agent includes sensors, actuators, and a decision logic providing interaction with the environment. However, when complexity of platforms increases, with increasing number and complexity of organic sensors, actuators and command and control systems, encapsulating each platform as an agent may decrease its elasticity.

This paper proposes an approach to incorporate BPMN for military autonomous platform visual programming. This approach allows the platform or its model to be programmed in a user-friendly and expressive way for both end-users and model designers. This is achieved by representing the platforms' sub-systems with discrete agents, enabling multi-agent collaborative programming at the sub-platform level. In this context, we aim to extend the widely known use of BPMN in multi-robot programming to complex military autonomous platform task planning. We first make a comparative analysis of the related state-of-the-art and the proposed approach. Then, we present the potential advantages of our approach through autonomous platform task planning for selected maritime operation scenarios.

Keywords: Visual Scripting · Mission Planning · Business Process Model and Notation · Agent Programming · Multi-Agent Systems · Autonomous Platforms

1 Introduction

The motivation behind the approach described in this paper is to program complex agents and make them easily programmable for both their designers and

J. Novotný et al. (Eds.): MESAS 2025, LNCS 16627, pp. 181–193, 2027.
https://doi.org/10.1007/978-3-032-33182-3_11

end-users, such as drone or simulator operators. Generally, a military doctrine is hard-coded by the programmer into the behavior models of simulator- or real-world agents. However, when it is required to allow the user reprogram the entities -like when testing a new and classified tactic or finetuning a consumer robot behavior- the simulation framework or entity control software should provide enough flexibility in a user-friendly manner, since end-users are generally non-programmers (Defining action-tuning inputs to behaviors for instance, the required speed input for a simple cruise behavior increases programmability/flexibility/genericity but in such a way that only a limited space of possible platform behaviors can be explored.).

In the related literature, there are competing approaches for programming agents via user-friendly methods. Most of the recent work underlines the visual methods that make use of action, function, and condition blocks together with connecting lines to form conditional plans as agent programs. Even this approach splits into different sub-approaches with slightly different notations for describing/representing agent behavior, such as behavior trees or activity diagrams.

Nowadays, for describing agent actions, in other words, visual agent programming, one of the most promising methods is Business Process Model and Notation (BPMN). BPMN visual programming (VP) is especially fruitful for creating a synchronized and concurrent plan for multi-agent systems (MAS), and specifically for multi-agent based simulation (MABS), since it provides tools to describe separate, concurrent, and synchronized action flows for collaborating agents, such as units in a task force. Moreover, familiarity with BPMN to non-programmers makes it a strong alternative for user-friendliness.

On the other hand, BPMN is not used for single-agent programming so far. This is something not unexpected, since collaborative behavior is traditionally imagined as a teamwork of multiple agents and platforms (like tanks, people, UAVs, or robots) which are usually handled as atomic mission elements. But a single platform might itself be and usually is a complex multi-system architecture. Since systems like sensors and actuators are not traditionally considered as separate agents, and are sub-agents by definition, traditional MAS approaches are usually discarded when dealing with such single-agent-multiple-sub-system constructs.

Our approach focuses on sub-agents (systems) for programming and creating programmable, single complex agents that achieve full action genericity without sacrificing user-friendliness. We used BPMN at the system (sub-agent) level, which provides the required user-friendliness and full programmability aspects for agents. We successfully incorporated the proposed method for closed-loop simulation agents, which are essentially autonomous, but it might also be used for programming real agents like autonomous vehicles.

In this paper, after a quick review of the relevant literature, we will present our approach in more detail and conclude with the demonstration of an example platform task plan.

2 Literature Overview

MABS has emerged as a foundational simulation paradigm for representing and understanding interacting complex phenomena, including military systems-of-systems [11]. The representation of the entities, either systems or subsystems, usually requires a certain level of autonomy, aligned with the fidelity and the interaction context required by the intended use.

A challenge that emerges from this body of research is the programmability of autonomous behaviors of models, not only by model designers, but also by subject matter experts and end-users. This capability is thought to enhance the utility of the underlying simulation framework for doctrine development, mission planning, analysis of alternatives, and so on. This challenge motivates the transfer and enhancement of existing approaches as practical behavior design tools, via high-level specification of complex autonomous behaviors, while preserving the computational and cognitive capacities.

A few representative methods had already been used for this purpose, including behavior trees, subsumption architecture, and sequential behavior compositions [5,10,12].

2.1 Behavior Trees (BT)

VP for autonomous agents (or bots/models in the following context) in the form of BTs is a popular approach, especially for game development and robotics. Moreover, model programming ability through BTs are also embedded to simulation frameworks such as AFSIM [3]. BTs are by definition hybrid structures integrating behaviors with decision trees to create conditional behavior plans consisting of two categories of execution nodes, namely the actions and the conditions, which are the basic building blocks of most visual programming tools. Here, procedural state transition logic is organized in a hierarchical tree structure (with the atomic behaviors as leaves). BTs have effectively replaced finite state machines (FSMs) as the prime method of implementing autonomous behavior [8,9,12].

But this technique is primarily intended for model developers rather than end-users, and it requires a new mindset with a relatively long learning curve for non-programmers. Thus, creating a new low-level behavior as a synchronized usage of the bots'/models' systems is mostly not directly available to the end-users. Moreover, there are other drawbacks: after the completion of any action, a depth-first search of the entire tree is executed to find the correct successor according to the plan. Although there are some techniques to limit these repetitions, using them makes the plan structure more complex. Similarly, action interruption is not a built-in functionality in BTs, although it is very common in real-world processes. Again, introducing interruptibility to BT actions is possible, but the process is cumbersome. Another limitation is that the BT structure forces the user to sequential agent programming instead of parallel programming although bots/models can execute different behaviors concurrently in real life through their multiple embedded systems (i.e. sensors and actuators) [4,8,12,14,15].

2.2 Subsumption Architecture

BTs describe repeated but sequential and mostly short action plans. On the other hand, chronologically older subsumption architecture allows concurrent functioning behavior mechanisms. Subsumption approach is a product of behavior-based design, where different, distinct behaviors of an entity can be fired and executed concurrently, using priorities or requirement merging methods when necessary for source sharing (competing and interacting behaviors create a collective output). This architecture can also be used for creating sequential action plans by allowing a predecessor action to trigger a successor one after its conclusion, but this enforces a concurrent structure to behave sequentially and increases program complexity.

Subsumption architecture is mostly used in robotic systems. The interval programming-based Mission Oriented Operating Suite (MOOS-IvP) developed by MIT [2], for example, provides autonomy for platforms, particularly in the marine context, and is based on a subsumption-type architecture. Each behavior has a condition for firing and an action code, which are both created by the programmer (not an end-user) through conventional (non-visual) coding and scripting. As mentioned before, a large mission plan can only be constructed through sequential triggering of different behaviors, which is not a trivial task. For behavior synchronization (creating sequential plans is a subset of behavior synchronization), condition-action tables are constructed. In Stage, for example (a simulation framework developed by Presagis), behaviors of platform models are programmable through condition-action tables. When organized hierarchically with suppression mechanisms, such rule-based structures can approximate a subsumption-style behavior architecture.

2.3 Sequential Behavior Compositions

BTs and subsumption architecture are both memoryless or short-memory behavior models, such as FSMs. This means that they let the entities they control behave as there is no past and no future. Entities with such kind of decision making and behavior models are simply reactive. Sequential structures such as a plan or a policy, on the other hand, without having a distinct memory model, provide an implicit focus on time, or rather on timeline, which naturally provides a kind of context-based reasoning, as we mentioned in [14], since different parts of the plan can be considered as different contexts. Explicit temporal structuring and context partitioning are first-class citizens in BPMN, whereas they are implicit or emergent in reactive architectures. This also paves the way towards a more deliberative approach, not necessarily sacrificing reactivity. Here, we mention structures or notations like flowcharts, activity diagrams, and business process modeling notation (BPMN). UML activity diagrams can describe only high-level abstract models rather than an analytical model guiding developers for implementation, let alone interpreters, because of drawbacks as limited notations, which decreases their understandability. These problems have been solved in BPMN language, which can precisely describe the logical flow of the activities within a process.

In [14] we proposed that using BPMN might be a practical way for planning/programming the behavior for simulated military agents, especially in complex and long-duration collaborative scenarios. That study focused on higher-level task plans rather than programming single lower-level tasks.

There are already examples for the exploitation of such sequential mechanisms for robot programming at any levels. Choregraph, for example, is a visual tool, the agent programming approach of which is based on organizing robot behaviors as several concurrent sequences [14]. Here, concurrent sequences are not necessarily distinct plans for distinct entities; they rather build a joint plan for different autonomous agents, focusing on the job done instead of the actuator entities.

On the other hand, [7] describes another sequential (and concurrent) action model for robot parts (Gripper, Arm, Planner, etc.) strictly synchronized through shared time -it is set from the beginning, which part acts and stops acting in which order and which time.

Swimlane activity diagrams and especially BPMN introduces the concept of lanes into sequential approaches where plan activities are distributed according to some real or conceptual classifications -each corresponding to different lanes [7]. ROS2 Robot Operation System, described in [7], is an extension to ROS for multi-robot programming and may therefore be integrated to BPMN tools more easily, while ROS is developed for single robot programming where multi-entity (multiple sensors and actuators) collaborative action design is accomplished through more conventional and low level/hard coded methods (distributed publish-subscribe mechanisms for communication and action scripting/coding). Distribution of activities according to the actuators that execute them is a preferred classification increasing clarity about roles taking part in a plan and simplifies plan construction. At the end, a joint plan consisting of different synchronized plans for different collaborating entities is formed, and synchronization is not only accomplished through shared time but rather through shared events or semaphores, of which time and time events are just a subclass. Such an approach is not a common practice in reactive behavior design.

In mission engineering, where sequential method is a standard for action design, capturing how the mission activities are related to actors, systems and organizations is considered as one of the key elements [1].

3 Sub-agent Level BPMN Programming

3.1 Overview

In real life, super-actions of super-entities consist of sub-actions of their sub-entities as Aristotle stated before Christ in the Philosophy of Nature [13]. As a result, for describing an action of an agent, considering the ontological/structural hierarchy of its sub-agents might be much more expressive.

In [14] we labeled this approach as intuitive since when writing a simulation scenario, it was obvious that we should create distinct plans for each team agent to build a collective task plan. But when it comes to the detailed programming of each lower-level task or action inside an entity's plan, we used traditional BTs without considering sub-agent structure. This was partly because there was no example in the related literature where BPMN approach penetrates into sub-agent level. BPMN is mostly used for creating collaborative plans for distributed agents (like human teams or multi-robot systems) instead of programming a task for a single robot or platform [6].

When the platform itself is a complex structure, such as a military ship or an unmanned underwater vehicle, consisting of several sensors, actuators and decision logic, we can and possibly should expand our multi-agent or multi-entity approach to analyze or decompose single agent actions as well, for being able to program and reprogram the agent behavior in a more efficient, user-friendly, comprehensive, enabling, and standardized way. The so-called primitive or atomic tasks or actions of such a complex agent is usually not primitive or atomic at all (even the simplest cruise mission of a platform is in fact a complex and usually long-duration process -with a time-line- consisting of several sub-actions of a bunch of actuators). But BPMN, being one of the most understandable and expressive ways for multi-entity programming, is originally used to describe business processes where actors themselves are single agents [6,7]. Thus, an extension of the BPMN to the sub-agent world is needed. As we mentioned before, there are attempts for visual agent/robot programming considering sub-agent level but these lack the multi-entity programming opportunities BPMN can provide.

Another advantage of using BPMN even in sub-agent level is that we can create a recursive hierarchy from down (sub-agent level) to top (agent, multi-agent/group, and scenario) level. In other words, each level can be constructed with a standardized plot: Each agent action would be programmed as a synchronized, collaborative/joint plan of its sub-agents, without excluding the lowest-layer agent actions.

3.2 Conceptual Description of the Proposed Task Design Process

Our approach can be summarized as a disciplined usage of BPMN for the description of platform tasks as sub-agent joint plans consisting of sub-agent primitive/atomic functions. So, the first step is determining the sub-agents (or systems) that should take part in the task description. Here, there are not strict rules but main idea is just discarding those systems that have no role in or no contribution to the task effort. In addition, periodical activities like the tactical picture compilation which run in parallel to any kind of action plan, should also be left aside while focusing on the task-specific activities. Using the ontological platform structure for guidance to determine sub-agents makes the methodology free of abstraction, and no abstraction effort is required. As a result, no unbalanced abstraction problem will be encountered, which is a problem for many VPE-based frameworks as described in [5].

Next step is determining the primitive/atomic behaviors of the selected sub-agents/systems. If enough system granularity is reached in the previous step, determining those behaviors is also a trivial task. For example, if an electrical motor is selected as a sub-agent, the primitive actions of that might be determined as (1) turning in both directions (in different speeds), (2) changing torque (to different levels), (3) staying idle, etc.

The last step is to design the collective task effort in BPMN in a disciplined manner as a set of concurrent, synchronized behavior/action plans for the selected sub-agents. BPMN has enough functionality to express any kind of complex multi-entity behavior. But it should be treated carefully for creating an executable, complete plan (instead of an abstract plan which cannot be directly translated from the model into the code) down in the sub-agent level. Firstly, we try to create one lane for each actuator where no transition line should reach from one actuator's plan to another. Synchronization should only be done through shared parameters or events instead. This is for forcing the user to write complete plans for each actuator, which is necessary for executability. As a result of this preference, we do not use the parallel gateway of BPMN since no concurrent action in our one-lane-one-actuator plans is possible. But as we stated above, we are not sacrificing concurrency, instead promoting and completely making use of it through executing concurrent sub-agent plans. In this approach, parallel gateways are simply not necessary.

Another symbol which is not used here is the end or exit event symbol. All the lanes should be finished with idle actions instead of exit symbols. This is important for not letting the systems uncontrolled even when the job is done, since these might be the last plans dictated to the platform systems. It is better, for example, to shut down the engines before simply going out. (Exiting the task can be done from a higher-level task plan instead, when necessary.) Lastly, we should emphasize that each plan should start by considering any possible initial conditions, which are usually limited in number. This can somewhat complicate the plan, but we cannot see any other way to create a fully and securely executable action plan in any design format.

4 An Example Task Programming

4.1 Dipping Sonar Search Task of Rotary Wing Platforms

For a complex military closed-loop simulation project where a lot of ready-to-use tasks are to be implemented as part of platform models and where the operators required the ability to design and test their own platform tasks, we used the above-described approach effectively and got a high customer satisfaction. In addition to expected advantages like a high communication efficiency among modelers and customers/users -due to the use of BPMN as a common notation for both programmers and military operation designers- we also faced unexpected positive results like that the user-friendliness of the approach and the standardization of task structure also increased the efficiency of the action modelers and the learning curve of new team members gradually decreased. Considering the difficult-to-satisfy requirements for implementing tens of different, complex tasks for several military platforms, this efficiency increase was critical.

In this study, one of these military tasks of a marine rotary wing platform is chosen for its simplicity and expressiveness to demonstrate the above-mentioned advantages of our proposed approach.

The task chosen is a submarine search task in the scope of anti-submarine warfare (ASW) where dipping sonars are used for localizing hidden submarines - especially in layered waters where ship mounted sonars cannot detect platforms under water layers.

4.2 Determining the Sub-agents Which Take Part in The Task Execution

Our approach for programming the behavior plan of the platform, according to the doctrine or a new tactical design, begins with determining the sensors and the actuators that will take part in the corresponding task. Here, obviously, the dipped sonars (either active or passive) are systems that should be considered as vital companions. Also, the winch which is used to dip and pull back the sonar structure should be considered as a separate actuator since dipping/releasing the sensor is a totally separate action which shouldn't be mixed with the primary sensing activity of the sonars. Another important actuator is, of course, the propeller of the platform, which is responsible for the displacement. A total movement suite of a rotary wing consists of several propellers and other equipment for orienting the platform to gain movement in all directions in 3D. This whole suite can be considered as a single actuator (the mover) since their combined duty is simply orienting and moving the platform. Since our focus was closed-loop simulation, this preference seemed to be a better choice, but while dealing with real platforms, each of these parts of the mover suite may also be considered as distinct units.

Note that, the ontological/modular structure of the platform is copied for determining the sub-agents here, which makes our duty rather simpler. In the scope of such a search task, other sensors and actuators like radars, data-link, countermeasure and command and control systems should also be used for sharing tactical picture with a base and responding to an emergency but we omitted these functions and corresponding systems for decreasing complexity and increasing clarity to focus on the main point of our study.

4.3 Determining the Primitive Actions as Building Blocks of Task Description

As a second step after starting with the determination of the actuators, we determine the atomic/primitive actions of these chosen systems. For sensors, "activating", "deactivating", "parameter set", and "idle" are 4 actions we have chosen as atomic/primitive. (When the sensor is in idle mode, it detects/tracks targets or does nothing according to whether it is activated or deactivated.) For the winch, obviously, "dipping/releasing" and "pulling" (with different speeds when important), together with "idle" can be considered as the 3 action primitives.

The mover, on the other hand, as a combined actuator suite, has more primitives than the previous ones. In that case determining the primitive actions is not trivial, and there are no strict rules for action selection. The designer should decide which selected atomics could be used to describe all the subsystem behaviors in an optimum way (the minimum number of atomic actions should be determined for describing the maximum number of behaviors with minimal complexity and minimal action overlapping). One possible action package might consist of the following primitive actions: "Idle", "starting/stopping the engine", "changing height", "changing speed", "flying with constant speed in heading direction", "turning to right or left", "flying towards some coordinate in constant height", "flying in line with a constant bearing" and "hovering". Here, since there are actually more actuators than one in the mover suite, determining primitives becomes more challenging. There are several different primitive action group choices which all can lead to the same results in different ways. For example, here we can combine speed change with flying-with-constant speed action by programming the speed change action in a way that, after reaching the desired speed, it can force the platform to continue flying at that speed. Using that combined action for speed change and flying with constant speed have nearly no difference from triggering first the speed change action and then the constant-speed-flying action. Similarly, flying towards a coordinate might obviously be considered as the combination of turning, flying, and speed change.

4.4 Describing the Task in BPMN as A Sub-Agent Joint Action Plan

After determining the sub-agents and action primitives we can proceed to BPMN behavior design. Figure 1 shows the task plan constructed for a simple, one-coordinate, and single-depth dipping sonar search task with bpmn.io -a web-based BPMN tool created by Camunda Community. Note that the task/plan diagram consists of different lanes corresponding to different systems. Each lane is a BPMN flow diagram consisting of primitive actuator actions. The three lanes are synchronized with events/conditions that are usually created by one of the plans and used in other ones to trigger action transitions.

Task plan (or program) described in the figure, states that while pulling the sonar -if released- the rotary wing platform (the mover thereof) should change its height to cruising height -if not yet reached the search coordinate- and should fly towards that search coordinate. After reaching its destination it should change its height to the search height this time, send a signal that the conditions are ready for sonar analysis, and wait until the analysis is finished with the sonar pulled back. Rest of the movers' plan is changing height -if the platform is not yet at the base coordinate- flying towards the base, changing height again for landing, stopping the engine, and going into the idle state.

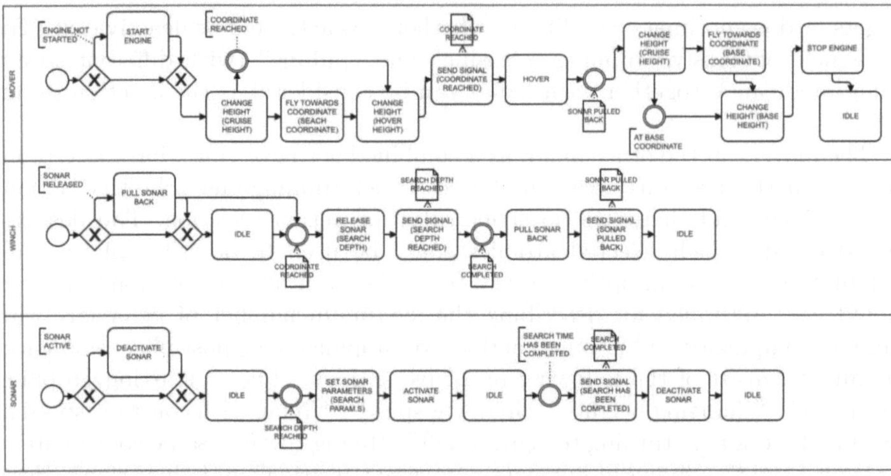

Fig. 1. An example BPMN-based sub-agent action plan describing a rotary wing platform's one-coordinate, single-depth dipping sonar search task.

Meanwhile, the winch pulls the sonar back -if released and until the search coordinate is reached- since the platform shouldn't move with a released sonar and waits in the idle state until the movers' "coordinate reached" signal arrives. If the destination is reached, the sonar is dipped to the search depth and is triggered for activation. The winch then waits until the sonar analysis is completed for pulling the sonar back, sending "sonar pulled back" information and going into the idle state.

The sonar, at the beginning of the task, is deactivated if active, and goes into the idle state until reaching the search depth. Then the search parameters are set and the sonar starts analysis by being activated in its idle state. When analysis is completed, other systems are informed, and the sonar is deactivated before going into its idle state.

Note that the sonar both makes an analysis or does nothing in its idle state according to whether it is activated or not, since, according to the separation of concerns principle, we are not putting periodical, concurrent, and long-lasting functions like tactical picture compilation into our task plans. These can better be modelled as FSMs or BTs running permanently in parallel with the task or plan flow.

Complementary Plans. In the real world such a task plan should not be executed alone. It should work in parallel with other same- or higher-level task plans. For example, in this plan it is not stated what to do when a submarine is spotted, an anti-air missile is approaching or when the fuel reaches a low threshold level. Adding all these alarming conditions in this level would make the plan seem unnecessarily complicated since from all the atomic actions transitions should be drawn indicating alarm conditions, which is unnecessary since these transitions can be done from a higher-level that can be considered as another one lane plan for the whole platform this time where we can dictate the platform firstly do its search job (the high level task described in detail above) and when alarms are activated, it should behave accordingly by executing an engagement, an anti-missile defense or a return to base task (other high level tasks which are out of the scope of this paper) after abandoning the dipping sonar search plan.

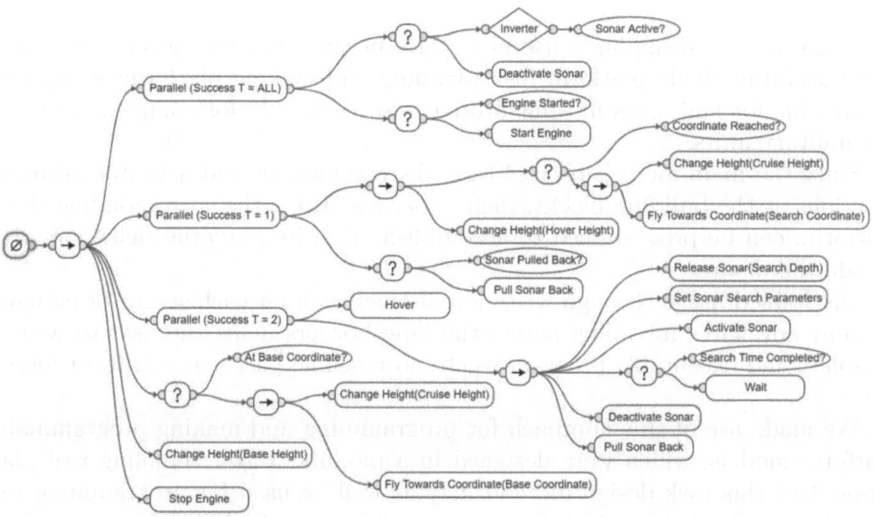

Fig. 2. Rotary wing platforms' one-coordinate, single-depth dipping sonar search task described in BT format.

5 Designing the Dipping Sonar Search Task in a BT Editor for Comparison

Figure 2 shows the design of the same task in behavior tree format drawn using the Behavior3 Editor (https://www.behaviortrees.com/). Here, ellipses stand for conditions and other leaves of the tree are the sub-agent atomic behaviors or actions. "?" operator is a selector which is usually known as Fallback operator in BT literature. This operator might be used for checking a condition before firing an action. If the condition is not fulfilled, the corresponding action is bypassed. "→" operator is generally known as the Sequence operator. This is used for sequentially firing a list of actions when some condition is fulfilled, if any. "Parallel" operator, on the other hand, is succeeded/passed according to the condition stated in the corresponding operator box (Success T = 1,2,..., ALL etc.). This indicates whether the operator can be succeeded/passed when one or all of the sub-branches are succeeded/passed.

In addition to that the BT approach obviously requires more experience for design, comprehension and communication. It also has a branch factor problem, as seen in the figure: As the number of sub-agents increases, for each episode of the task plan, an extra branch should be introduced. This makes the complexity grow geometrically with increasing sub-agent number. Adding one more system into a BPMN design only requires the introduction of one extra lane.

6 Conclusion and Future Work

Our approach -a disciplined use of BPMN in the sub-agent level- has proved to be useful in single platform task planning and making platforms easily programmable for end-users in a facilitative way, especially for complex platforms like military units.

Since the main focus is on real (not abstract) sensor and actuator primitive functions as the building blocks, their super-agent, i.e. the corresponding single platform, can be programmed to accomplish all of its potential behaviors, in a standardized way.

Disciplined usage through writing a distinct plan for each sensor or actuator without any wires intruding across the lane borders helps the user to write a complete and executable program where no machine part gets adrift, or forgotten.

We made use of this approach for programming and making programmable platform models, which were designed in a modular way resembling real platforms. But this task design method may as well be used for programming real autonomous platforms, which is among our future work plans.

Another planned future work is using this approach in a hierarchical manner to program and make programmable multi-platform groups, robotic systems, or even swarms. Although practical deployment may require addressing additional problems concerning real-time constraints, uncertainty, and fault handling, we believe that fundamental architectural modifications will not be necessary.

Next, we can make use of traditional AI tools for fine-tuning task plan parameters (action inputs, transition function parameters etc.) through simulation. This can be followed by autonomous planning to enable agents and agent groups to create their own plans -in the described notation- which can lead to a real/full autonomy. (Note that, since planning is a process of creating action sequences, BPMN is naturally a better approach for planners as well, compared with BTs, FSMs, and subsumption architecture).

Acknowledgments. The authors acknowledge the support of their respective institutions and declare no financial relationship with the owners of the third-party software trademarks referenced in this article.

Compliance with ethical standards

Disclosure of Interests. The authors declare no competing interests. The views expressed in this paper are those of the authors and do not necessarily reflect the official position of their affiliated institutions.

References

1. Department of Defense Mission Engineering Guide. Technical Report, Office of the Under Secretary of Defense for Research and Engineering (2023). https://ac.cto.mil/wp-content/uploads/2023/11/MEG_2_Oct2023.pdf
2. Benjamin, M.R.: MOOS-IvP autonomy tools users manual. User Manual MIT-CSAIL-TR-2010-039, MIT Computer Science and Artificial Intelligence Lab (CSAIL) (2010). https://dspace.mit.edu/handle/1721.1/57509
3. Clive, P.D., Johnson, J.A., Moss, M.J., Zeh, J.M., Birkmire, B.M., Hodson, D.D.: Advanced framework for simulation, integration and modeling (AFSIM) (Case Number: 88ABW-2015-2258). In: Proceedings of the international conference on scientific computing (CSC), p. 73. (2015). http://worldcomp-proceedings.com/proc/p2015/CSC7058.pdf
4. Colledanchise, M., Ögren, P.: Behavior Trees in Robotics and AI: An Introduction (2018). https://doi.org/10.1201/9780429489105
5. Coronado, E., Mastrogiovanni, F., Indurkhya, B., Venture, G.: Visual programming environments for end-user development of intelligent and social robots, a systematic review. J. Comput. Lang. **58**, 100970 (2020). https://doi.org/10.1016/j.cola.2020.100970
6. Corradini, F., Pettinari, S., Re, B., Rossi, L., Tiezzi, F.: A BPMN-driven framework for multi-robot system development. Robot. Auton. Syst. **160**, 104322 (2023). https://doi.org/10.1016/j.robot.2022.104322
7. Ingrand, F., Ghallab, M.: Deliberation for autonomous robots: a survey. Artif. Intell. **247**, 10–44 (2017). https://doi.org/10.1016/j.artint.2014.11.003
8. Iovino, M., Scukins, E., Styrud, J., Ögren, P., Smith, C.: A survey of behavior trees in robotics and AI. Robot. Auton. Syst. **154**, 104096 (2022). https://doi.org/10.1016/j.robot.2022.104096
9. Kedalo, A., Zykov, A., Aslam, H., Mazzara, M.: Comparing behaviour tree and hierarchical task network planning methods for their impact on player experience. In: 2023 IEEE Symposium Series on Computational Intelligence (SSCI), pp. 135–139. IEEE, Mexico City (2023). https://doi.org/10.1109/SSCI52147.2023.10371841
10. Michel, F., Ferber, J., Laur, P.-A., Aleman, F.: Situational programming: agent behavior visual programming for MABS novices. In: Bosse, T., Geller, A., Jonker, C.M. (eds.) MABS 2010. LNCS (LNAI), vol. 6532, pp. 1–15. Springer, Heidelberg (2011). https://doi.org/10.1007/978-3-642-18345-4_1
11. North, M.J., et al.: Complex adaptive systems modeling with Repast Simphony. Complex Adapt. Syst. Model. **1**(1), 3 (2013). https://doi.org/10.1186/2194-3206-1-3
12. Özkahraman, Ö., Ögren, P.: Combining control barrier functions and behavior trees for multi-agent underwater coverage missions. In: 2020 59th IEEE Conference on Decision and Control (CDC), pp. 5275–5282 (2020). https://doi.org/10.1109/CDC42340.2020.9304151
13. Ross, D.: Aristotle. Taylor & Francis (1995)
14. Şenyürek, L.H., et al.: Visual mission scripting for multi-agent-based simulation of autonomous platforms. In: Mazal, J., et al. (eds.) Modelling and Simulation for Autonomous Systems, pp. 68–81. Springer, Cham (2026). https://doi.org/10.1007/978-3-031-99732-7_5
15. Sewell, B.: Blueprints Visual Scripting for Unreal Engine: Build Professional 3D Games with Unreal Engine 4's Visual Scripting System, 1st edn. Packt Publishing (2015)

Computer-Generated Forces Team Behavior within Air Combat Simulations: A Tactic Template Approach for Modeling Team Tactics and Trajectory Planning

Fabian Reinisch(✉), Michael Strohal, and Peter Stütz

Institute of Flight Systems, Universität der Bundeswehr Munich, Werner-Heisenberg-Weg 39, 85577 Neubiberg, Germany
{fabian.reinisch,michael.strohal,peter.stuetz}@unibw.de

Abstract. Due to the increasing complexity of modern air combat engagements, simulators for pilot training must not only replicate the physical properties of adversarial forces, but also provide them with a situationally adaptive, tactically intelligent behavior. Addressing this demand, our work aims to model computer-generated forces (CGF) behavior for use in pilot training simulations as well as tactics validation and enable coordinated CGF behavior based on adaptive team tactics incorporating explicit tactical knowledge. This paper is focused on the final phase within our overarching CGF behavior agent function and generates a behavior plan driven by inputs from the previous situation analysis and risk assessment phases. Central to the representation of the behavior plan is the use of *tactic templates* - which are a modular representation of tactical maneuver sequences incorporating knowledge derived from Subject Matter Experts (SME). These templates are used to encode typical air combat tactics, and specify how the participating CGF should be coordinated during engagements. They also enable the CGF to respond to pre-defined triggers due to increased risk by performing certain actions, deviating from their maneuver sequences. In the second half, we present a planning methodology to generate trajectories, allowing each CGF to intercept their assigned target within the chosen tactic, while incorporating incoming risks from the adversary side. The proposed solution supports dynamic replanning, allowing the CGF to perform a replanning when situational risk assessments indicate that the current plan is no longer viable. To validate our research, we implement and test our approach within an experimental system simulating air combat beyond-visual-range (BVR) training missions. The simulation results, showing tactics execution as well as trajectory planning, are discussed in this paper.

Keywords: Computer Generated Forces · Behavior Modeling · Decision-Making · Planning · Air Combat · Pilot Training · Tactics · Trajectory Planning

J. Novotný et al. (Eds.): MESAS 2025, LNCS 16627, pp. 194–210, 2027.
https://doi.org/10.1007/978-3-032-33182-3_12

1 Introduction

The modeling and simulation domain increasingly requires higher accuracy levels of the adversary computer-generated forces (CGF) / red forces, especially in the context of training simulations and tactical evaluation. Achieving this requires more than accurately replicating the physical characteristics of the simulated entities, it also demands behavior that is both situationally adaptive and tactically intelligent. Especially in beyond-visual-range (BVR) engagements, where the two sides striving for air superiority influence each other directly with their maneuvering, ensuring coordinated CGF which are able to adapt to a constantly changing scenario is essential. Meeting these requirements ensures that pilot candidates remain continuously challenged, thereby yielding an efficient training outcome [1].

To create CGF capable of behaving with such situationally adaptive as well as tactically intelligent team behavior, their behavior models must be capable of analyzing the current situation, assess potential risks and opportunities, and finally select and execute tactical plans in real-time. This requires CGF to coordinate their actions, plan their maneuvers and trajectories, and react dynamically to situation changes or adversary risks while they are working together.

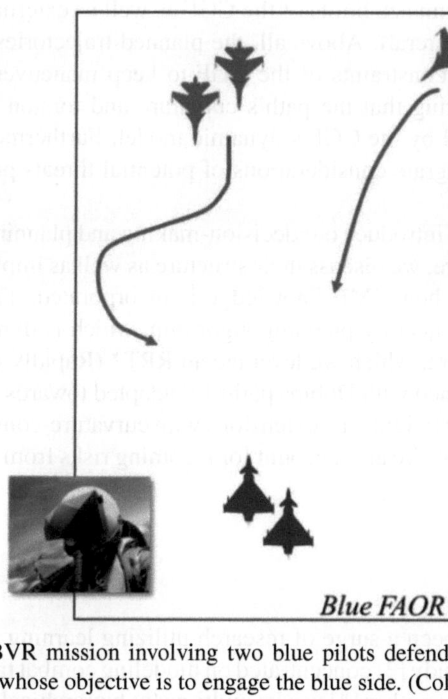

Fig. 1. A sample BVR mission involving two blue pilots defending their FAOR against four incoming red CGF, whose objective is to engage the blue side. (Color figure online)

Our research focuses on BVR air-to-air scenarios where up to four blue aircraft, piloted by humans in VR simulators, defend their Fighter Area of Responsibility (FAOR) against up to eight incoming red threats (see Fig. 1). While the pilots aim to protect their assigned airspace, the CGF red forces pursue offensive objectives, working cooperatively to reach air superiority. To reach their objectives, the engaging CGF must synchronize with each other, select their respective targets and fly chosen tactics to intercept the blue side.

Generating such tactically-intelligent behavior suitable for pilot training requires more than scripted CGF control, it demands a structured concept that governs how the CGF tactics are executed in a coherent manner. To address this demand, we introduce a behavior planning concept based on tactic templates, which are a modular representation of tactical maneuver sequences derived from Subject Matter Expert (SME) knowledge. These templates represent established air combat tactics and specify how the CGF should act in groups when facing different adversary configurations. Our approach applies these tactic templates to model the behavior of CGF groups during the engagement. While the templates define intended roles, maneuver sequences, and coordination patterns, their execution in air combat scenarios requires adaptive trajectory planning for target interception during, and synchronizing the CGF after an engagement cycle. As adversary behavior is not fixed and the geometry between the aircraft evolves over time, feasible flight trajectories need to be computed for each CGF, so it can fulfil its assigned role within the chosen tactic.

Trajectory planning in this context poses significant challenges, as it must account for both the physical performance limits of the CGF as well as external influences such as approaching adversary aircraft. Above all, the planned trajectories must be flyable, adhering to the kinematic constraints of the CGF to keep maneuvers within feasible limits. This includes ensuring that the path's curvature and torsion never exceed the maximum values permitted by the CGF's dynamic model. Furthermore, the trajectory planning process must integrate considerations of potential threats posed by opposing entities.

In this paper, we briefly introduce our decision-making and planning concept, focusing on *tactic templates*. Here, we discuss their structure as well as implementation using Behavior Trees (BTs) and how SME knowledge is incorporated. The second part of the paper focuses on the trajectory planning algorithm, which is dynamically invoked by the *tactic templates*. Here, which we leverage an RRT* (Rapidly exploring random tree-Star) algorithm combined with Dubins paths [2] adapted towards our requirements, replacing the conventional straight-line extensions with curvature-constrained paths that align with aircraft dynamics. We also account for incoming risks from adversary entities during path exploration.

2 Related Work

In recent years, there has been a surge of research utilizing learning techniques for air combat simulations. One study [3] concentrated on modeling combat tactics with a learning classifier system, while another [4] used a multi-agent hierarchical policy gradient in order to discover and generate air combat tactics via self-play. More recently, researchers have been actively applying reinforcement learning (RL) techniques to generate air combat maneuvering [5, 6]. Although RL-based simulations have shown promising results, their practical implementation will require extensive verification, since interpreting the maneuvering principles and situational judgment learned by RL-based systems may present challenges for human operators and limit the comprehension of the learned decisions. Additionally, using RL-based approaches also impose challenges to incorporate subject-matter-expert (SME) knowledge into the decision-making of the models. However, in this domain, including SME knowledge and having explainable behavior plays a central role. This requirement was reinforced during our meetings with pilots: It is an indispensable prerequisite for them in order to be willing to accept generated behavior. In [7], air combat behavior is modeled as a Markov process combined with Bayesian Inference, which enables better integration of SME knowledge. However, this research, similar to the majority in the field, mostly concentrates on modeling air combat behavior within a 1-vs-1 scenario [4, 6, 8, 9]. As a result, tactical coordination between the entities is often overlooked or not fully incorporated into these studies. Since a while, BTs have been used in computer games and the simulation industry due of their modularity and scalability [10]. However, manually crafting BTs for a large number of entities and training scenarios needs repetitive work and results in rigid behavior and therefore predictable learning experience [1, 11, 12].

Addressing trajectory planning, advancements in research have produced a range of methods. Trajectory planning can be divided into three main stages: path planning, guidance logic, and motion control. Path planning methods are typically grouped into four categories: graph-based algorithms, potential field techniques, sampling-based planners, and learning-driven approaches. Graph-based algorithms like Dijkstra's and A* construct paths based on discrete representations of the space. Dijkstra's algorithm seeks the shortest path using an exhaustive search, but its computational load makes it often impractical in unless combined with faster methods. A*, by incorporating heuristic cost estimates, directs the search toward the goal more efficiently [13]. However, A* works best on discrete graphs or grids and becomes computationally expensive with increasing resolution. Virtual potential field methods construct an artificial force field over the environment, where attracting forces can pull the entity toward the goal and repulsive forces push it away from obstacles. This results in smoother trajectories and supports dynamic collision avoidance by continuously adjusting the path in response to nearby adversary entities [14]. Custom potential field formulations allow for more precise control over avoidance behavior, but also make the method computationally heavier. Finally, the Rapidly-Exploring Random Tree (RRT) algorithm belongs to the class of sampling-based planners. It incrementally builds a tree by randomly sampling the state space and extending branches toward unexplored regions, enabling efficient coverage of larger search-spaces [15]. RRT is well-suited for applications in dynamic environments due to its speed and scalability. However, the resulting paths are typically suboptimal for our requirements and require post-processing to incorporate dynamic constraints of the CGF models, adding more computational time. Reinforcement learning has also recently been applied to path planning in simulations, offering an alternative to traditional methods by enabling agents to learn suitable actions through interaction with the environment. For instance, Q-learning has been used to develop planning strategies for autonomous platforms and showed improved adaptability compared to conventional algorithms [16]. Deep reinforcement learning variants, such as the Deep Deterministic Policy Gradient (DDPG) algorithm, have also been employed to handle continuous action spaces relevant to vehicle dynamics [17]. While these methods allow agents to generate paths that adapt to dynamic environments, though they often require extensive training data and tuning to ensure reliability. This is especially challenging with respect to the requirement of explainability in air combat training applications.

3 Overall Concept and Agent Structure

In our approach to model CGF behavior with the goal of achieving both situational adaptivity and tactical intelligence, we build an expert-system designed around a centralized agent function [18]. Based on human behavior, we conceived a functional chain composed of three main stages: *situation analysis*, *risk/opportunity assessment*, and *decision-making and planning*. The planning stage (see Fig. 2) operates across three hierarchical levels:

1. *Team Level*: Grouping own entities according to adversary formations, assigning both

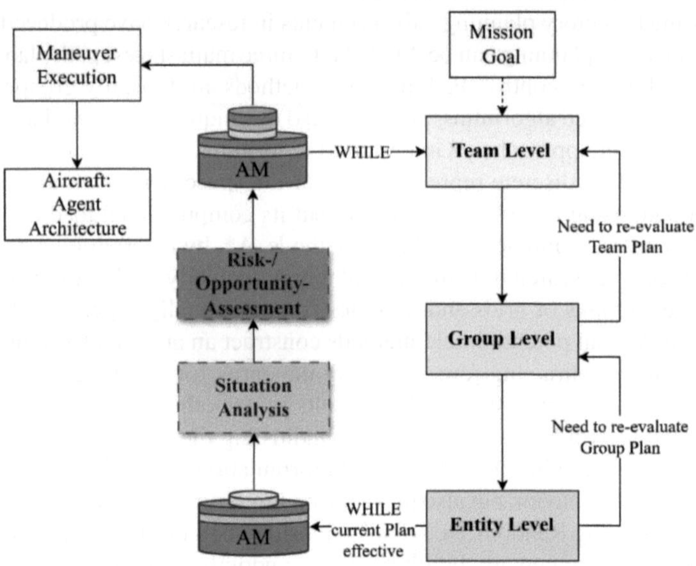

Fig. 2. Decision-Making and Planning: This process begins at the Team Level, where own entities are grouped, and tactics are assigned. The selected tactics are then executed and evaluated at the Group Level, where derived subtasks are assigned to participating entities while ensuring correct tactics execution. At the Entity Level, suitable trajectories are generated based on the current task, and appropriate maneuvers are selected and sent to the simulated CGF dynamic models. The current tactical plan is continuously evaluated through the Risk-/Opportunity-Assessment stage. If the chosen tactics become infeasible or the risks unacceptable, a signal is sent to the upper level to re-evaluate the plan.

targets and tactical templates to the resulting groups.

2. *Group Level*: Executing the assigned tactics and continuously evaluating their effectiveness for the specific group context.

3. *Entity Level*: Generating executable trajectories, selecting suitable maneuvers, and dispatching them to the simulated entities.

As of now, our target assignment and tactic selection are primarily modeled based on SME-derived rules. Accordingly, the focus in this work is on the representation and modeling of tactics through *tactical templates* and the generation of corresponding trajectories.

To evaluate the situational adaptivity and tactical decision-making capabilities of the CGF red force behaviors, we implemented an experimental apparatus. It enables two CGF teams to engage in simulated air combat scenarios, with simulations running faster than real time, enabling tactical evaluations (CGF vs. CGF). Additionally, it supports mixed trials in which a CGF team competes against a team of subject matter experts (SME) operating within VR-based simulators, thereby also serving as a training environment.

4 Tactic Templates

4.1 Introduction

In BVR air combat training, pilots are taught to execute predefined tactics based on available mission and threat information. Each tactic provides high-level maneuver sequences for entities cooperating towards a common objective through coordinated behavior. The Team Lead assigns both tactics and targets to his teammates, which are then executed in accordance with established air combat pilot knowledge rules. This is also reflected in our requirements, due to which we chose a modular approach where the different pilot tactics are modeled using so-called *Tactic Templates*. Each *Tactic Template* contains structured information about the possible number of participating own entities, engageable targets as well as tactical maneuver sequences, coordination points between entities, and permissible deviations (like evading an incoming Missile), directly allowing us to include SME knowledge. Storing Tactics in such a way also enables the SME to both understand as well as modify the tactical rules. Additional elements, such as risk levels or pilot experience levels, can be incorporated into the decision-making using this approach as well (see Fig. 3).

An example of a Tactic is the "Loose Deuce" [19] (see Fig. 4), which involves two aircraft engaging their assigned targets. Here, initially, both entities fly in opposite directions, with one facing towards (hot), and one facing away(cold) from the target. After the hot aircraft fired a missile and starts turning cold, the counterpart takes its role and advances towards the target. Therefore, the adversary side was never left untargeted. This Tactic requires synchronization between the entities, facilitating the need to model these synchronization points as well as the involved tactical maneuvers using rule-based systems.

4.2 Implementation

Behavior Trees (BTs) [20] are tree-based data structures in which each node represents a condition check or an action performed by an entity. They are commonly used for implementing AI for non-player-characters (NPCs) in computer games. More sophisticated

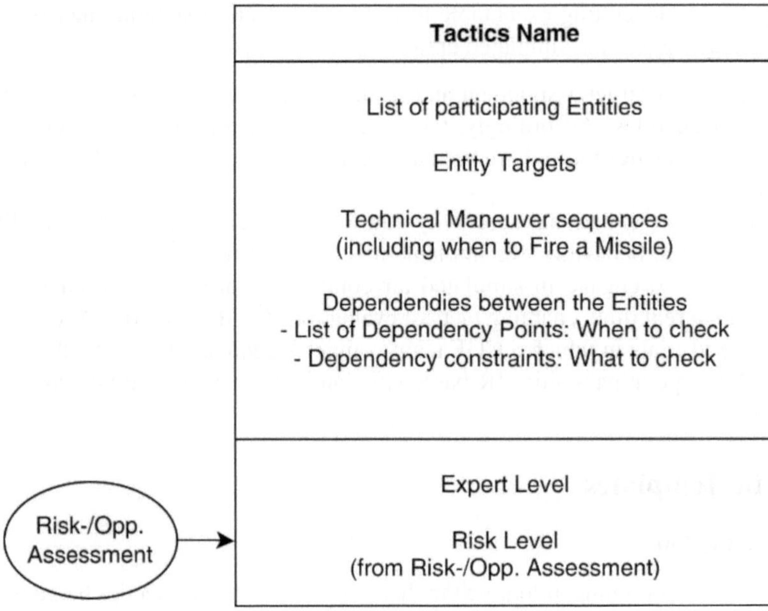

Fig. 3. Schematic representation of a tactic knowledge base. For each modeled tactic, a *tactic template* is implemented, containing information such as own entities, assigned targets, tactical maneuver sequences and coordination points between entities

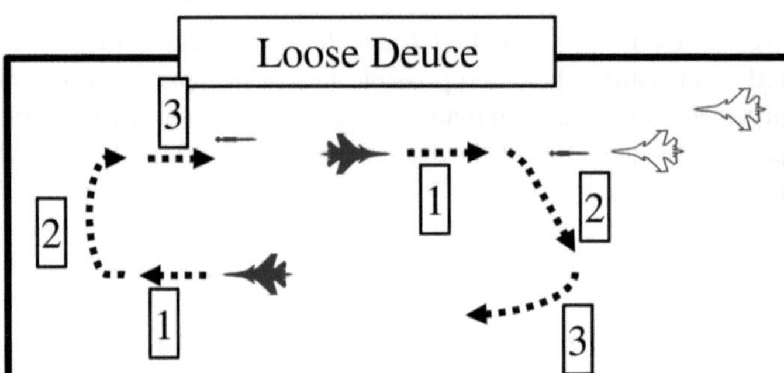

Fig. 4. Sequence of the *Loose Deuce* tactic: While one aircraft engages the targets, the other initially remains cold, after which both aircraft turn simultaneously, so their roles are switched.

behaviors are constructed by organizing simple control flow and action nodes into a tree structure, which is traversed in a depth-first manner to determine which actions should be executed. Behavior trees offer flexibility through their hierarchical design, allowing smaller trees that represent basic behaviors to be reused as subtrees within larger trees that govern more complex, high-level behavior.

In contrast to most designs which use a single BT to model either the entire team behavior or only use individual BTs for each entity [12], our approach is a trade-off between these two. We implemented a single overarching BT, which is used only for entities with fixed, defined roles, such as support units like AWACS[1] that only follow simple, rule-based patterns (e.g., continuous circle flight). The behavior of the entities executing tactics in groups is instead modeled with the help of modular BTs, each representing a different *tactic template*. These tactic template BTs define the high-level coordination logic and maneuver sequences for all CGF working together in a particular tactic and allow us to directly incorporate SME knowledge. Therefore, these entities not governed by the overarching BT are dynamically assigned to tactics and targets if a replanning is required. Once assigned, their behavior is driven by the tactic's BT, which is executing rules to either directly generate and send maneuvers to the CGF, execute coordination rules between participating entities or call other methods for different tasks. The advantage of the latter one especially shows when the CGF need to execute tasks such as synchronizing themselves [2], estimating the adversary Weapon Engagement Zone (WEZ) or when intercepting targets. Modeling the latter task will be the focus of the following chapter.

Figure 5 shows an example of a part of such a BT template. This template is responsible for executing a defensive maneuver in case an incoming missile is detected.

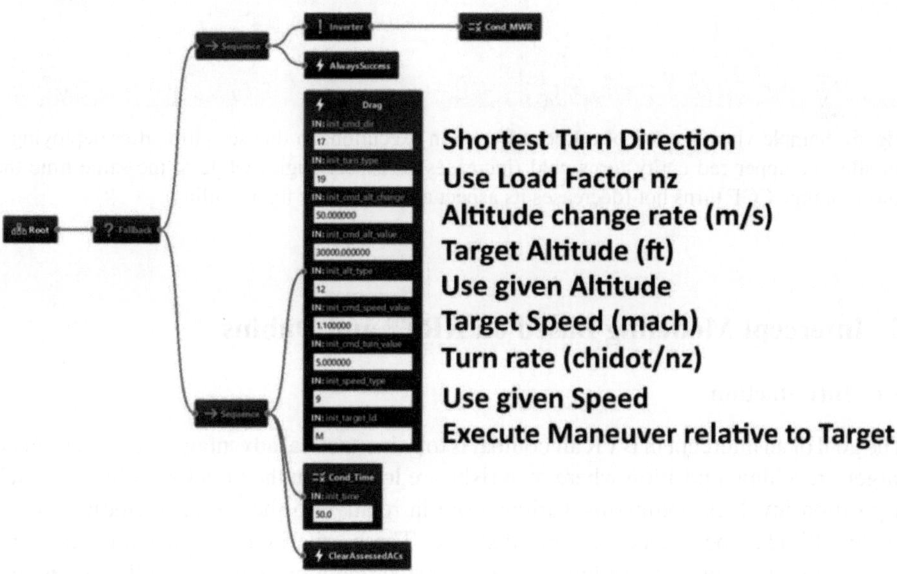

Fig. 5. Sample visualization of a Behavior Tree Snippet used for incorporating rule-based knowledge into our experimental apparatus: This tree is used to model defensive maneuvering: When an incoming Missile is detected, a drag [21] (flying away from the adversary) is executed and the stored assessed aircraft are reset.

Figure 6 depicts a sample scenario with two red CGF. The red side is executing a *Loose Deuce*: After deploying a missile, the upper red entity turns cold (increases its

[1] An Airborne Warning and Control System (AWACS) is a long-range radar-equipped aircraft designed to provide early threat detection by monitoring airspace.

aspect angle) while at the same time the lower, orange CGF turns hot (decreases its aspect angle). Visualization is performed using Tacview [22].

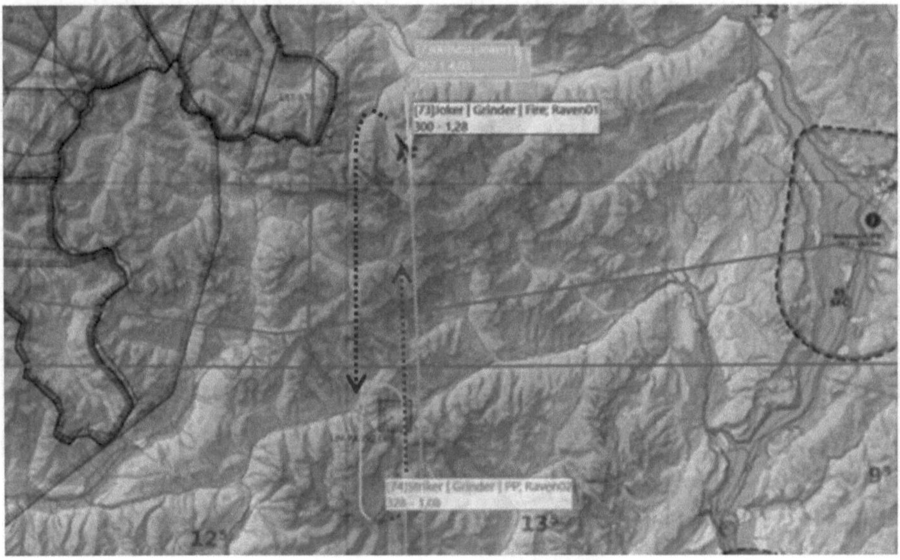

Fig. 6. Sample visualization of a Loose Deuce in execution: In this scenario, after deploying a missile, the upper red entity turns cold (increases its aspect angle) while at the same time the lower, orange CGF turns hot (decreases its aspect angle). (Color figure online).

5 Intercept Modeling Based on RRT* and Dubins

5.1 Introduction

The goal of an intercept in BVR air combat is to gain a tactical advantage over the assigned target - reaching a position where own risks are lower than the target's. Achieving such a position involves optimizing various criteria relative to the target, including aspect angle, altitude, speed (energy), and distance. These criteria are further influenced by the maximum allowable risk level, the recognized intent or maneuver of the target, and the target's Weapon Engagement Zone (WEZ). Planning and successfully executing a trajectory suitable for this task becomes especially challenging after the engagement has been commencing for longer, resulting in often chaotic situations.

In the following (see Fig. 7), a sample offensive scenario is considered, in which a red CGF plans a trajectory toward an assigned target in order to reach a tactically advantageous position and deploy a missile.

We formulate the task as a trajectory planning problem, therefore solving it should yield a suitable trajectory to intercept the target. We implement a three-stage solution based on the RRT* algorithm, which employs Dubins paths during the exploration phase. This enables the incorporation of curvature constraints in the flight trajectories, consistent

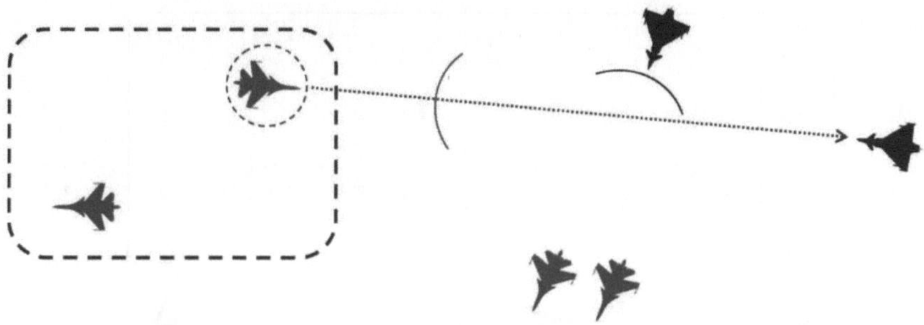

Fig. 7. Possible offensive scenario: The red marked CGF needs to engage the blue entity on the right side. The half-circles mark the boundaries of the respective WEZ. (Color figure online).

with limitations imposed by the allowable load factors of the CGF dynamic models. Trajectory smoothing is required due to the dynamic constraints of the CGF motion models, as well as the enforcement of the maximum permissible tactical engagement range with respect to the target. In addition, constraints for the avoidance of specific regions can be incorporated, including both static obstacles and weapon engagement zones (WEZ) of other entities. Finally, the generated trajectories are transformed into executable tactical maneuver commands.

5.2 Algorithm Selections

The RRT algorithm is a widely used sampling-based method for path planning. It incrementally builds a path tree by randomly selecting points in the environment and connecting them to the nearest node in the tree. This makes this algorithm also suitable for exploring feasible paths in cluttered or dynamic scenarios. However, while RRT quickly finds a feasible path, it does not guarantee path optimality.

To improve on this, the RRT* (RRT Star) algorithm extends RRT by incorporating a path optimization step. As the tree grows, RRT* rewires connections to minimize the overall path cost, resulting in shorter paths compared to RRT. Due to these advantages with no drawbacks, we continued with the RRT* algorithm for our purposes.

Dubins paths are paths that are proven to be the fastest ones from one point to another given a maximum allowed curvature and initial and terminal headings (orientation). A resulting path can consist of either three circular arcs connected tangentially, (example: "LRL") or two circular arcs with a straight-line segment tangentially positioned between them (example: "LSR"), where "L" and "R" denotes a left or right turn arc and "S" represents a straight-line flight segment. We refer to these differences in paths as path types. For example, in Fig. 8, the Entity follows an "LSR" path type.

Considering the dynamic constraints and maneuverability limitations of combat aircraft, and therefore our CGF models, we analyzed an improved Dubins-RRT path planning algorithm adapted for our scenario requirements. Unlike the standard RRT, which extends its search tree using straight-line segments, our approach replaces these with Dubins paths, curves that respect the aircraft's minimum turning radius constraints.

We compared three algorithmic combinations to identify the most suitable for our research:

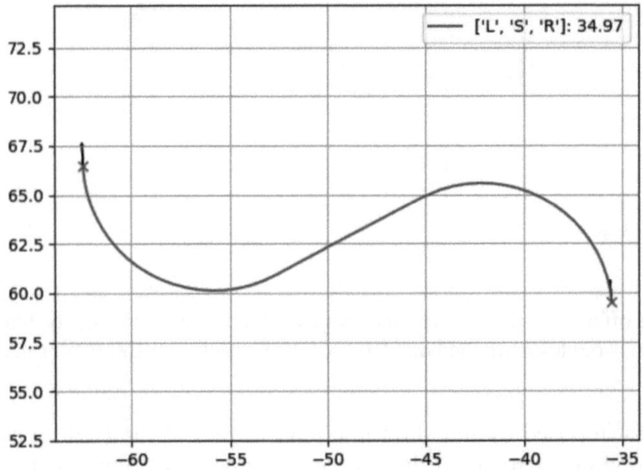

Fig. 8. Sample Dubins Path: The path consists of a Left turn, then a straight-line segment, and finally a right turn.

- RRT*: without Dubins paths
- RRT-Dubins: Standard RRT with curvature-constrained paths
- RRT*-Dubins: Improved RRT* with curvature-constrained paths

The evaluation scenario consisted of fixed start and goal configurations, along with multiple obstacles (represented by grey circles) along the path. Table 1 lists the parameters used for this comparison.

Table 1. RRT / Dubins test case parameters

Parameter	Chosen Value
Start State	Position: (0, 0), Heading: 90 Deg
Terminal State	Position: (10, 10), Heading: 90 Deg
Algorithm Search Area	17 × 17
Goal Sample Rate	10
Max. Distance per Expansion	50
Curvature	1.0
Max. Iterations	100

The first tested algorithm was the RRT*, which found a path within 0.2865 s, however here additional post-processing is required for it to be useable (see Fig. 9). Further, the RRT variant with Dubins paths found a solution as well (0.2344 s), however due to the curvature constraints the discovered path was much longer and still has improvement potential (see Fig. 10). Finally, when using the algorithm combining RRT* and Dubins Paths, the resulting path (0.255 s) was significantly shorter than the previous RRT Dubins result (see Fig. 11). Finally, another variation involves running the algorithm until a predefined maximum number of iterations is reached. Applying this approach to the RRT*-Dubins algorithm and allowing it to run for 100 iterations results in noticeably improved paths, shorter and therefore more suitable for our purposes (see Fig. 12). While this algorithm took more runtime, the resulting timeframe (0.6533 s) is still acceptable for our application.

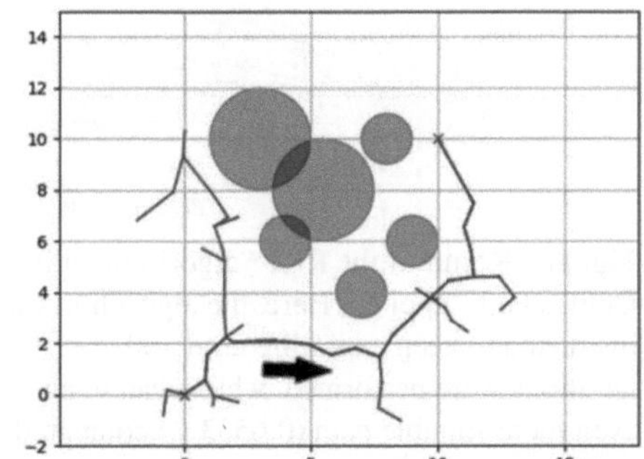

Fig. 9. Result of the regular RRT* algorithm without any Dubins Paths applied. A potential path within an acceptable timeframe (0.2865 s.) was found, but it still requires post-processing to smooth out the sharp turns.

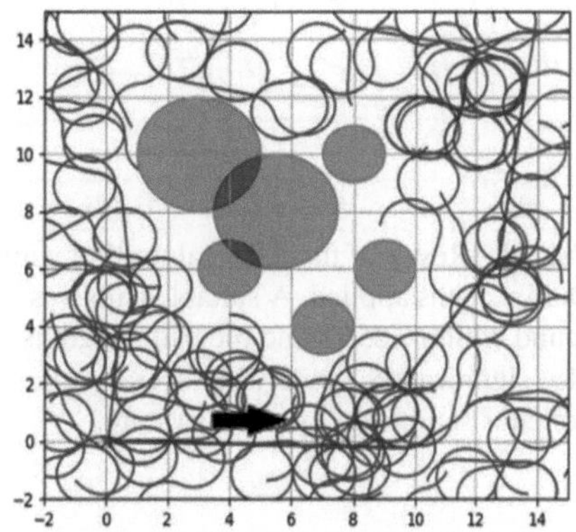

Fig. 10. Result of the RRT algorithm with Dubins Paths applied during the exploration phase. A suitable path within an acceptable timeframe (0.2344 s.) was found, but it is significantly suboptimal.

Most path planning algorithms like Dubins paths and RRT expect a start and terminal state consisting of position and angle (yaw) values. For us this corresponds to the positions and headings of the intercepting CGF. Since our overarching concept includes a preceding situation analysis process capable of recognizing flown maneuvers and selected targets (intentions) of adversary entities, we can use this information to estimate the adversaries' flight trajectories. For simplification, we currently assume that the recognized maneuvers and intentions are accurately identified and do not account for uncertainties in the given information.

To integrate this incoming information the path generation algorithm, we derive a custom implementation of the RRT*-Dubins algorithm which is able to accept a goal area instead of a position as well as a target angle threshold. Based on the own speed, allowed risk and the targets' speed and intention we compute an estimated goal area in which the CGF would be able to engage the target. Feeding this area information instead of an exact position not only speeds up the path planning algorithm runtime, since it's more likely to find a path ending up in the goal if it's an area, but it also allows us to factor in uncertainties in the future.

During the exploration phase, an additional adaptation of the method replaces the static obstacle check with a dynamic adversary prediction (see Fig. 13). While the entity to be planned (red) generates its trajectory, the other two entities (grey ovals) are extrapolated and incorporated into the trajectory planning. For adversaries maneuvering relative

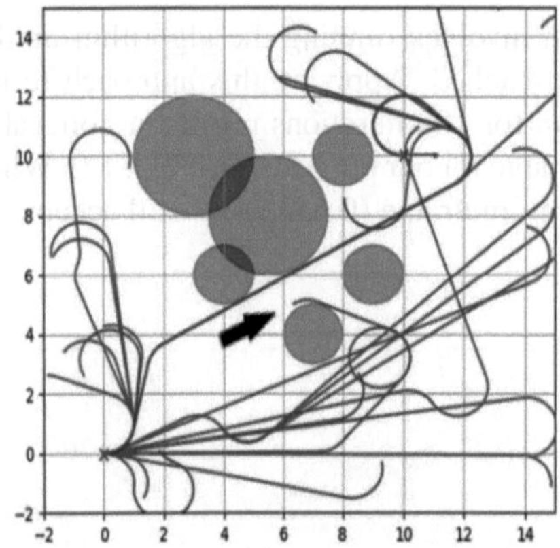

Fig. 11. Result of the RRT* algorithm with Dubins Paths applied. A suitable path was found within 0.255 s and the path length is also significantly shorter, however, it still contains significant excess curvature.

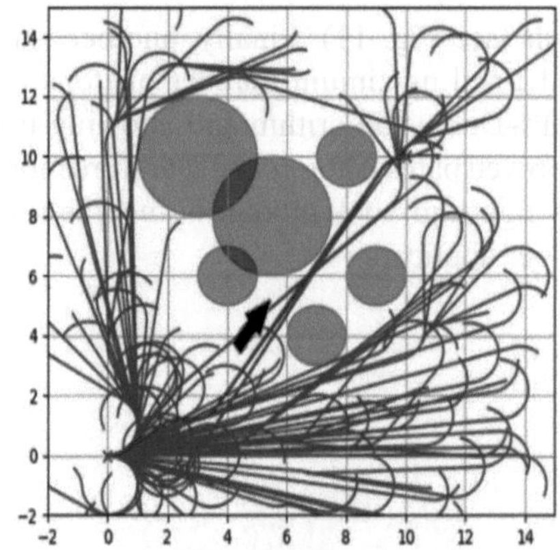

Fig. 12. Result of the RRT* algorithm with Dubins Paths applied. Here, the algorithm was instructed to keep exploring until 100 iterations were performed, which lead to an even more suitable path (0.6533 s.) compared to Fig. 11.

to other targets, trajectories are extrapolated based on observed maneuvers, for entities without identifiable intent, extrapolation is performed using their current motion states. For adversaries targeting the planning CGF, their predicted pursuit is simulated at each planning step. Through this extrapolation of opponents during the RRT*-Dubins exploration phase, the evolution of the scenario geometry for a candidate path can be assessed, determining whether the path can be further expanded. The shape and extent of the obstacles are defined by an approximated weapon engagement zone (WEZ) of the adversary and the maximum permissible risk level of the own platform.

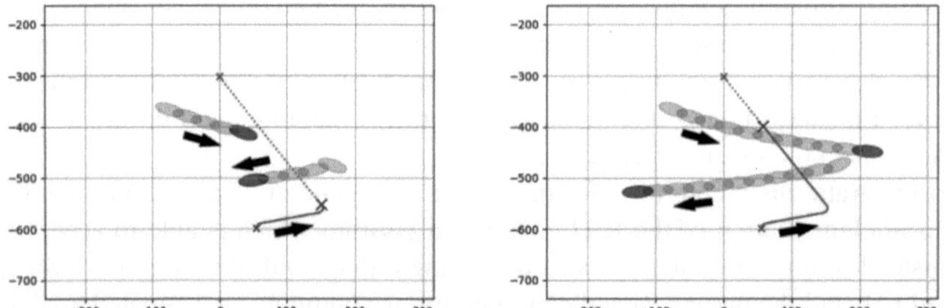

Fig. 13. Visualization of the dynamic extrapolation of trajectories during execution.

5.3 Results

The validation of the suitability of the proposed approach for modeling offensive trajectories was conducted using CGF vs. CGF scenarios. In these scenarios, a red CGF was instructed to intercept an incoming blue CGF, while simultaneously avoiding other blue entities. The remaining blue CGF execute a predefined intent, pursuing other red CGF. Based on the previously selected algorithm, the RRT*-Dubins algorithm is employed for these tests. Additionally, a two-dimensional NED plane is defined, with axes scaled in kilometers (used for the following figures).

In the test scenario (see. Fig. 14), the red CGF labeled "Planned Entity," which is positioned at the bottom of the image, is tasked with intercepting the incoming blue CGF approaching from above. An additional blue CGF pursues another red CGF in parallel and therefore acts as a moving obstacle. Red points indicate the starting positions of the CGF. Here, the RRT* algorithm with Dubins paths is applied, initially modeling obstacles as static during path generation. The left image illustrates the various paths explored during the execution of the algorithm. The right image depicts the resulting trajectory, which completely avoids the flight path of the passing blue CGF. The planned red entity (bottom) follows a trajectory that initially turns left before steering right toward the target.

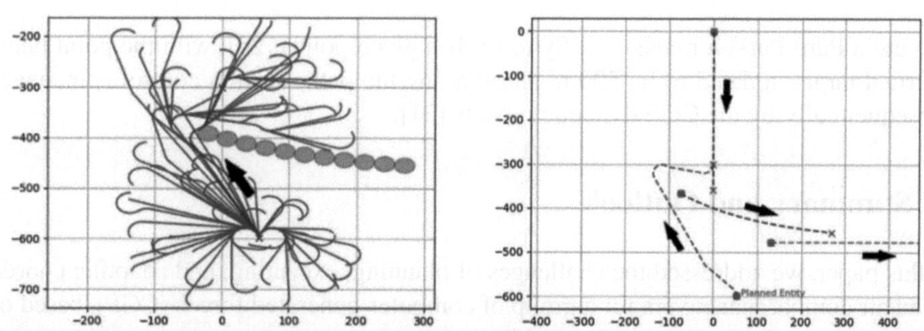

Fig. 14. Scenario with two total blue CGF, the RRT* algorithm with Dubins Paths was applied. Here, the algorithm was instructed to statically avoid obstacles while generating the path. The left picture shows the different paths that were explored during the algorithm execution. At the right side, the resulting path of this scenario is visualized. (Color figure online).

Figure 15 highlights the advantages of dynamic obstacle avoidance (for the underlying mechanism, see Fig. 13). The red CGF at the bottom center ("Planned Entity") is tasked with intercepting the incoming blue CGF from above. On the left, the complete trajectories of the blue CGF are treated as static obstacles, resulting in an interception path that entirely avoids the full blue flight path. On the right, the same scenario is depicted using dynamic obstacle avoidance. Here, the time component of the moving blue CGF is incorporated during trajectory generation. This allows the interception trajectory to interact with the motion of the blue CGF and intersect it at specific points.

It should be noted that while the method produces a valid solution in most cases, approximately 10% of the trials fail to yield a feasible path due to unfavorable random exploration. This limitation could be mitigated by increasing the default maximum number of iterations (currently 100), enlarging the goal region, or reducing obstacle sizes, representing potential directions for future improvements. Finally, in order to ensure smooth trajectory traversal, we use a virtual target approach and instruct the CGF to

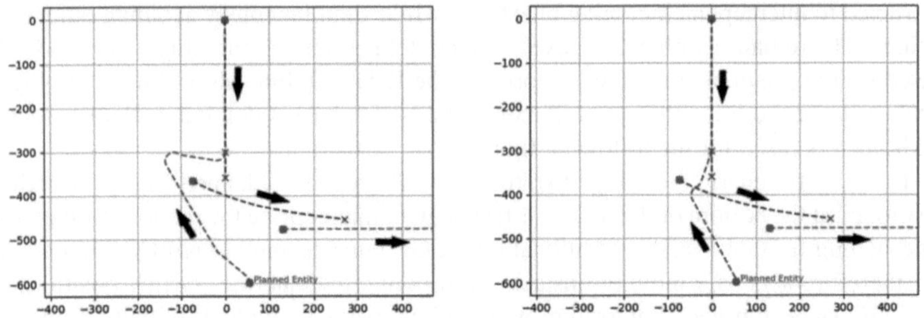

Fig. 15. Left: The red CGF at the bottom right is tasked with intercepting the incoming blue CGF at the top. The full flight paths of the blue CGF are treated as static obstacles, resulting in an intercept trajectory that completely avoids all blue flight paths. Right: The same scenario, but with the time component of the blue CGF taken into account, allowing the intercepting path to account for the dynamic movement of the blue aircraft over time and therefore intersect it at certain points. (Color figure online).

execute a Pure Pursuit maneuver (fly towards a given point) [23], with the point being a virtual target updated to lie 500 m ahead along the path. Motion control is managed subsequentially by the CGF dynamic models [21].

6 Summary and Outlook

In this paper, we addressed the challenges of planning, executing, and adapting coordinated air combat maneuvers for a group of computer-generated forces (CGF), based on adversary behavior and engagement objectives.

This work outlines a behavior planning framework in which CGF are assigned to tactical templates modeled using BTs, representing tactical maneuver sequences containing SME knowledge and corresponding coordination between the involved CGF to achieve their assigned objectives. Our implementation using BTs outlined the capability to incorporate SME knowledge into the CGF behavior ruleset and therefore showed suitability of this approach for pilot air combat training application.

We then integrated a trajectory-planning component capable of generating dynamically feasible flight paths for intercepting the adversary, while respecting aircraft maneuvering constraints. To this end, we compared different path planning algorithms and discussed their performance in generating suitable trajectories. Here, we decided on an improved RRT*-Dubins algorithm, which replaces the straight-line extensions of standard RRT* with Dubins paths. Finally, we presented an implementation of this hybrid algorithm and showed that we were able to generate flight trajectories suitable to intercept other incoming entities.

Future planned work consists of refining the trajectory generation process further, as well as incorporating uncertainties and changing adversary intents.

Disclosure of Interests. The authors declare no competing interests.

References

1. Toubman, A.: Calculated Moves: Generating Air Combat Behaviour (2020)
2. Reinisch, F., Strohal, M., Stütz, P.: Computer-generated forces team behavior within air combat simulations: coordinated path planning with constraints. In: AIAA SCITECH 2025 Forum
3. Smith, R.E., Dike, B.A., Mehra, R.K., Ravichandran, B., El-Fallah, A.: Classifier systems in combat: two-sided learning of maneuvers for advanced fighter aircraft. Comput. Methods Appl. Mech. Eng. (2000). https://doi.org/10.1016/S0045-7825(99)00395-3
4. Sun, Z., et al.: Multi-agent hierarchical policy gradient for air combat tactics emergence via self-play. CRANK. Eng. Appl. Artif. Intell. (2021). https://doi.org/10.1016/j.engappai.2020.104112
5. Dongyuan, H., Yang, R., Zuo, J., Zhang, Z., Jun, W., Wang, Y.: Application of deep reinforcement learning in maneuver planning of beyond-visual-range air combat. IEEE Access (2021). https://doi.org/10.1109/ACCESS.2021.3060426
6. Wang, X., et al.: Deep reinforcement learning-based air combat maneuver decision-making: literature review, implementation tutorial and future direction. Artif. Intell. Rev. (2024). https://doi.org/10.1007/S10462-023-10620-2
7. Changqiang, H., Kangsheng, D., Hanqiao, H., Shangqin, T., Zhuoran, Z.: Autonomous air combat maneuver decision using Bayesian inference and moving horizon optimization. J. Syst. Eng. Electron. (2018). https://doi.org/10.21629/JSEE.2018.01.09
8. Wang, Z., Wang, L., Ai, J., Dong, Y.: High-Fidelity decision-making and simulation for cooperative autonomous air combat considering the effect of flight controller. IEEE Access (2022). https://doi.org/10.1109/ACCESS.2022.3227386
9. Sun, T.-Y., Tsai, S.-J., Huo, C.-L.: Intelligent maneuvering decision system for computer generated forces using predictive fuzzy inference system. J. Comput. (2008). https://doi.org/10.4304/JCP.3.11.58-66
10. Steve Rabin: AI Game Programming Wisdom (2014)
11. Zhang, Q., Yin, Q., Xu, K.: Towards an integrated learning framework for behavior modeling of adaptive CGFs. In: 9th International Symposium on Computational Intelligence and Design, ISCID 2016, vol. 2, pp. 7–12. IEEE, Hangzhou, China, December 10–11, 2016 (2016). https://doi.org/10.1109/ISCID.2016.2011
12. Yao, J., Huang, Q., Wang, W.: BT optimization: adaptive human behavior modeling for air combat simulation. In: 19th IEEE/ACM International Symposium on Distributed Simulation and Real Time Applications, DS-RT 2015, pp. 100–103. IEEE Computer Society, Chengdu, China, October 14–16, 2015 (2015). https://doi.org/10.1109/DS-RT.2015.12
13. He, Z., Liu, C., Chu, X., Negenborn, R.R., Qing, W.: Dynamic anti-collision A-star algorithm for multi-ship encounter situations. Appl. Ocean Res. (2022). https://doi.org/10.1016/j.apor.2021.102995
14. Liu, W., et al.: COLREGS-based collision avoidance algorithm for unmanned surface vehicles using modified artificial potential fields. Physical Commun. (2023). https://doi.org/10.1016/j.phycom.2022.101980
15. Lee, M., Noh, G., Park, J., Lee, D.: Real-time directed rapidly exploring random tree path planning for air collision avoidance. J. Aerosp. Inf. Syst. (2022). https://doi.org/10.2514/1.I011016
16. Xiaofei, Y., Yilun, S., Wei, L., Hui, Y., Weibo, Z., Zhengrong, X.: Global path planning algorithm based on double DQN for multi-tasks amphibious unmanned surface vehicle. Ocean Eng. (2022). https://doi.org/10.1016/j.oceaneng.2022.112809
17. Guo, S., Zhang, X., Zheng, Y., Yiquan, D.: An autonomous path planning model for unmanned ships based on deep reinforcement learning. Sensors (2020). https://doi.org/10.3390/S20020426

18. Fabian Reinisch, Philippe Ruther, Luca Winkler, Michael Strohal, Peter Stütz (ed.): Computer-Generated Forces Team Behavior within Air Combat Simulations: Concept and Agent Structure (2024)
19. Leone, D.: Loose deuce Vs fluid four: during the Vietnam War the fighting tactics used by US Naval Aviators were better than those of the USAF pilots – here's why. https://theaviationgeekclub.com/loose-deuce-vs-fluid-four-during-the-vietnam-war-the-fighting-tactics-used-by-us-naval-aviators-were-better-than-those-of-the-usaf-pilots-heres-why/
20. Davide Faconti, E.: BehaviorTree.CPP - Nodes (2018)
21. Reinisch, F., Strohal, M., Stütz, P.: Behaviour modelling of computer-generated-forces in beyond-visual-range air combat. In: Wagner, G., Werner, F., De Rango, F. (eds.) Proceedings of the 12th International Conference on Simulation and Modeling Methodologies, Technologies and Applications, SIMULTECH 2022, pp. 327–335. SCITEPRESS, Lisbon, Portugal, July 14–16, 2022 (2022). https://doi.org/10.5220/0011306600003274
22. Raia Software Inc.: Tacview
23. ALSSA: Multi-service tactics, techniques, and procedures for multi-service brevity codes (2023). https://rdl.train.army.mil/catalog-ws/view/100.ATSC/5773E259-8F90-4694-97AD-81EFE6B73E63-1414757496033/atp1-02x1.pdf

Multi-platform Task Allocation in Airborne Reconnaissance Missions: A Genetic Algorithm Approach Based on Target Features

Sebastian Bening(✉) and Peter Stütz

Institute of Flight Systems, University of the Bundeswehr Munich, Werner-Heisenberg-Weg 39, 85579 Neubiberg, Germany
{sebastian.bening,peter.stuetz}@unibw.de

Abstract. This paper presents a planning and scheduling approach for ISR (Intelligence, Surveillance, and Reconnaissance) missions involving heterogenous platforms and sensors. A genetic algorithm is used to assign and schedule tasks based on expected target features, sensor performance, and mission constraints. The algorithm supports both, pre-mission planning and dynamic in-mission adaption. To ensure feasibility of the generated schedules, a hybrid combination of the Rapidly Exploring Random Tree* and the Dubins path planning algorithm is integrated, enabling the calculation of platform-specific flight trajectories. We provide a systematic evaluation of the proposed hybrid path planner across a range of simulated environments with varying complexity. The implementation of the genetic algorithm is based on the DEAP framework and evaluates chromosomes using multi-objective fitness criteria, including mission duration, cost, risk, and measurement quality. The system provides a scalable and adaptable solution for mission planning in dynamic and constrained environments.

Keywords: Multi-Agent-Systems · Task Allocation · Unmanned Aerial Vehicles · Multi-Domain-Operations

1 Introduction

The quality of reconnaissance and surveillance data forms a critical foundation for a wide range of military operations. In the civilian domain - such as in search and rescue missions - high-quality reconnaissance data can significantly increase the chances of locating and saving missing persons.

To enhance both the rate and quality of data collection, it is increasingly common to deploy a combination of multiple airborne sensor platforms equipped with diverse sensor types. While this approach offers significant potential, it also introduces considerable complexity due to heterogeneous sensor capabilities, platform constraints, and the need for coordinated execution. Manual planning of such missions is therefore often inefficient and suboptimal.

J. Novotný et al. (Eds.): MESAS 2025, LNCS 16627, pp. 211–237, 2027.
https://doi.org/10.1007/978-3-032-33182-3_13

Automation enables the exploitation of synergies between different systems through cooperative approaches. It also allows for more efficient utilization of available resources and can lead to improved data quality. Various approaches are being explored in the area of task allocation for groups of Unmanned Aerial Vehicles (UAVs). In [15], a survey was conducted to review centralized and decentralized task allocation approaches for UAVs networks. The authors conclude that effective systems must be capable of adapting to both the objectives of the assignment and the constraints imposed by the environment.

In [8], a heuristic grouping ant colony optimization algorithm is applied for reconnaissance task allocation for heterogeneous targets. The authors demonstrate the algorithm's ability to handle multiple target types. However, targets are divided among the available UAVs and processed independently, rather than being addressed cooperatively.

Similarly, the authors of [17] propose a genetic algorithm for cooperative reconnaissance that considers the required target resolution. Though, their approach does not take into account environmentally constrained sensor performance or the use of cooperative measurements to achieve the required target resolution. In [7], the authors employ a reinforcement learning approach to generate the initial population for a genetic algorithm, which subsequently refines the solutions through optimization.

To support the planning and monitoring of Intelligence, Surveillance and Reconnaissance (ISR) missions involving multiple airborne sensor platforms, we propose a customized genetic algorithm for task allocation and scheduling. Tasks derived from a mission order are evaluated based on expected target features and anticipated sensor performance under environmental conditions, forming the basis for their assignment. Comparable to our work, the authors of [19] consider path planning and task allocation as an inseparable problem. They propose a genetic algorithm for planning multi-UAV, multi-target attack missions. The authors of [15] also emphasize that task allocation and path planning are strongly interconnected. To address this dependency, we integrate a hybrid Rapidly Exploring Random Tree (RRT)* path planning algorithm with our genetic algorithm-based task allocation approach. Our genetic algorithm's structure allows for dynamic re-evaluation and schedule modification when new information becomes available during mission execution or when additional tasks are assigned to the system.

The remainder of the paper is organized as follows, Sect. 2 presents the problem formulation and outlines the underlying assumptions. Section 3 introduces the system design and details the genetic algorithm. In Sect. 4, we describe a prototype implementation and discuss initial simulation results. Finally, Sect. 5 concludes the paper and outlines directions for future work aimed at improving the algorithm.

2 Problem Definition

We aim to design a generalized planning system capable of planning, monitoring, and evaluating ISR missions for a heterogenous group of airborne platforms.

We assume the availability of a set of sensor-equipped airborne platforms and relevant environmental data. The objective is to generate feasible mission plans that adhere to operational constraints. A feasible mission plan must be executable with the assigned resources; flight plans must be implementable within platform constraints, and reconnaissance tasks must be performed within the specified time windows. If these conditions are not met, the plan is considered invalid and excluded from further evaluation.

To support a variety of ISR mission types, each mission order is first decomposed into a set of tasks required to fulfill the overall mission objective (e.g., detecting, identifying, or locating specific object types; mapping an area). Based on an analysis of typical ISR missions, we identified various combinations of sensor types and measurement methods applicable to the execution of these tasks.

These sensor types are deployed on a diverse range of airborne platforms, both manned and unmanned. In general, the platforms differ in performance characteristics, operational value, and risk of loss. Platform-specific capabilities influence flight path design, safety margins, and mission timelines.

Moreover, the performance of the sensors and the achievable quality of measurement methods are strongly influenced by environmental conditions (e.g. weather) and the relative geometry between the sensor and the point or area of interest. Consequently, the selection of appropriate measurement positions significantly impacts overall mission effectiveness.

Considering the interdependent factors - task type, measurement method, sensor-carrying platform, sensor type, measurement position, and temporal scheduling - we obtain a high-dimensional solution space. The resulting NP-hard optimization problem aims to produce valid, cost-effective, and high-quality mission plans under multiple operational constraints. The objective of the optimization is to minimize execution duration, path length, operational cost, and operational risk, while maximizing sensor performance and, consequently, information gain. The final mission plan defines which platform-sensor-combinations are assigned to fulfill specific tasks and specifies the schedule items that must be integrated into the respective platform and sensor timelines for execution. The obtained solution must be consistent with the tasks already assigned to the platforms and sensors.

To enable proper task scheduling, it is necessary to compute flight paths that comply with platform specific constraints and avoid obstacles, no-fly zones, and areas posing a risk to platform safety. Proper flight paths are essential for estimating travel time and ensuring that platforms can reach their assigned measurement positions within the required time constraints. To address the path planning requirements, we apply a hybrid RRT*-Dubins approach. The method first uses an RRT* search to identify a viable path to the target position, and then transforms it into a feasible Dubins path that complies with the platform's motion constraints. The objective is to generate flight paths that comply with the minimum turn-radius constraint of a fixed-wing platform while navigating through an area containing no-fly zones between two points with predefined headings.

To explore this solution space effectively, we present a genetic algorithm that searches for suitable task assignments and generates corresponding schedule items for both platforms and sensors. Constraints are enforced through tailored mutation and crossover operations, which prevent the generation of invalid solutions such as unassigned tasks or duplicate task assignments.

3 System Architecture and Genetic Algorithm Design

The genetic algorithm operates on a structured representation of the planning problem, composed of a task pool and relevant contextual data.

Each mission order provided to the system is first translated into a task pool, which defines a set of possible execution options for individual tasks. When combined appropriately, these tasks fulfill the overall mission objectives.

In addition to the task pool, the genetic algorithm requires information about the operational environment, including weather conditions, terrain data, and identified risk zones within the operating area. It also considers the current schedules of platforms and sensors to avoid conflicts with ongoing tasks and to support dynamic replanning when needed.

An overview of the inputs and outputs of the genetic algorithm is shown in Fig. 1.

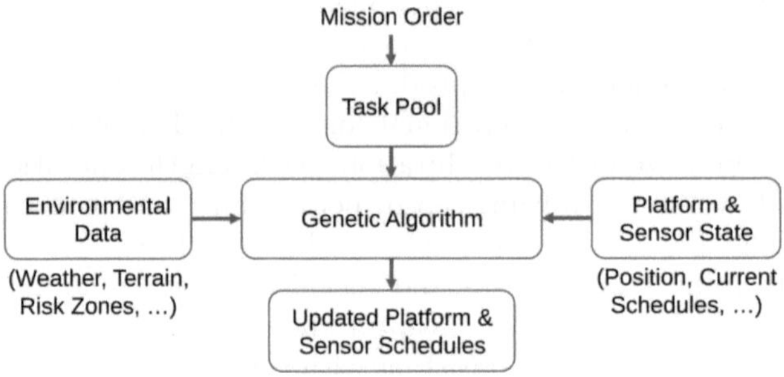

Fig. 1. The figure shows the main inputs and outputs of our genetic algorithm as it is used by our system.

To better illustrate the application of the genetic algorithm for ISR mission planning, the following Subsect. 3.1 provides a brief overview of the process used to interpret and translate mission orders provided by operators. For further details, the foundational system design is presented in [1], and a more comprehensive description of the overall process is provided in [2].

To connect individual schedule items and ensure the feasibility of the resulting mission plan, it is essential to determine the flight paths between scheduled positions. This enables the calculation of transit distances and durations which are required to sequence tasks into executable platform schedules. Given the critical role of path planning in the overall system, we briefly describe our approach in the dedicated Subsect. 3.2.

The remaining Subsect. 3.3 presents the genetic algorithm in detail.

3.1 Task Pool Generation

In a pre-processing step, the mission order is analyzed to identify individual tasks. The considered tasks include the detection, identification, and localization of objects, as well as the mapping of defined areas. We account for various object types, ranging from humans and different types of vehicles to buildings and infrastructure installations.

We analyzed task-object-type combinations commonly encountered in standard ISR missions and mapped them to various measurement methods capable of fulfilling those tasks. In the analysis, we identified target features (e.g., shape, color, temperature, material, velocity) required to fulfill various tasks (e.g., detection, identification, localization), as well as the sensors capable of collecting these features with sufficient quality to satisfy the task requirements. The measurement methods include single measurements of target feature and combination of multiple measurements (e.g.,triangulation). The use of multiple measurements may involve simultaneous or sequential execution.

We formalized this mapping in what we refer to as *cooperation blueprints*, which define the relationship between tasks, targets and applicable measurement methods. The applicability of measurement methods is based on features specific to the target types. During the pre-processing step, these blueprints are accessed to associate each identified task with a set of feasible solution options that can fulfill the mission requirements.

The possible solutions for each tasks are then filtered based on the sensors currently available. To enable parallel task execution by multiple platforms and sensors, the mission area is divided into cells, and the mission tasks are applied to every cell. The remaining task-sensor combinations are evaluated using sensor performance models. These performance models asses the expected effectiveness of each sensor in measuring target features under anticipated environmental conditions and identify suitable measurement positions where the required data can be acquired with sufficient quality to fulfill the task objectives. This process enables the system to assess the operational context autonomously and estimate the expected mission outcome and is shown in Fig. 2.

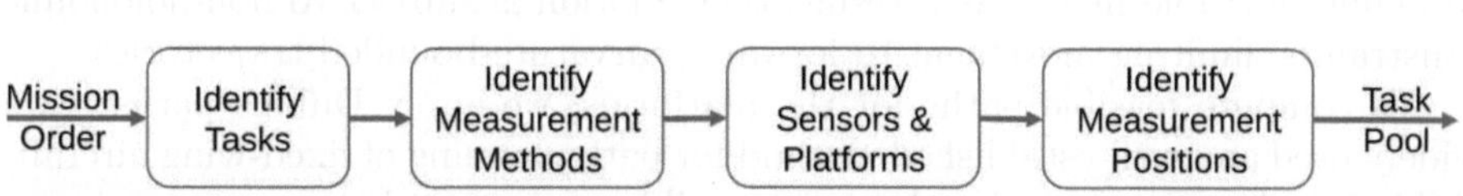

Fig. 2. The figure illustrates the pre-processing workflow. The figure shows how a mission order is interpreted and transformed into a structured task pool, which is then used as input for the genetic algorithm.

At the end of this process, the system generates a list of possible solutions for each task in every cell. Each solution candidate includes the following information:

- Cell identifier
- Task identifier and associated object type
- Selected measurement method
- Assigned sensor and platform combination
- Measurement position with estimated performance score

This pool of items serves as the input for the genetic algorithm. Based on these solution candidates, new schedule items for sensors and platforms are generated.

Platform and sensor schedule items are closely interconnected. The platform's task is to transport the sensor to the designated measurement position in time. Each sensor schedule item specifies not only the time at which the measurement should be performed, but also the exact location at which the task is to be executed. As a result, every sensor schedule item is inherently linked to a corresponding platform schedule item.

To enable scheduling of the items, it is necessary to estimate the expected travel duration between consecutive schedule items. In the current simplified version, the flight path is estimated assuming constant platform speed. In a more advanced version, which we intend to realize in the future, more realistic flight profiles can be incorporated - including variations in velocity, as well as holdings patterns and maneuvering behaviors. The method used to determine the flight path is described in detail in the following subsection.

3.2 Path Planning

Automated task assignment, scheduling, and evaluation require the generation of feasible flight paths for the involved platforms. These paths are essential to ensure that platforms can traverse between assigned measurement positions, compute the corresponding transfer times, assess risk levels along the route, and generate executable trajectories for mission execution.

Since we primarily consider fixed-wing platforms such as tactical UAVs, High-Altitude Long-Endurance (HALE) platforms or manned jets, the planned flight paths must be continuous and free of abrupt direction changes or reversals. These platforms have a minimum turning radius and require a minimum forward speed to maintain stable flight. As a result, their motion is subject to non-holonomic constraints, limiting movement to forward, curvature-bounded trajectories.

To compute feasible paths for the platforms, we apply Dubins paths [4], a widely used and well-established method for path planning of fixed-wing aircraft. Dubins paths represent the shortest possible trajectory between two poses - defined by position and heading - for a vehicle that moves forward at a constant speed and is constrained by a minimum turning radius. Each path consists of a sequence of straight segments, right turns, and left turns.

In addition to platform-specific performance constraints, operation constraints such as restricted airspace and safety margins around target areas must be considered during the path generation. These constraints can be abstracted as three-dimensional barriers or obstacles that may not be entered or crossed. As a result, standard path planning and obstacle avoidance techniques can be applied.

One such method is the RRT algorithm [13]. It is a sampling-based path planning algorithm designed to efficiently explore high-dimensional constrained spaces. RRT incrementally builds a tree by randomly sampling the state space and extending the tree towards these samples. For our obstacle-aware path planning we use RRT* [11], a variant introduced to address the lack of optimality in original RRT. RRT* introduces a rewiring step that enables asymptotical convergence towards the optimal solution as the number of samples increases.

Inspired by the approaches presented in [20] and [12], we investigated the use of a modified RRT* algorithm that, instead of connecting samples with straight-line segments, directly generates Dubins paths.

A discussion of our implementation of a modified RRT* with Dubins path integrations is provided in Subsect. 4.1. It is worth noting, that this modification significantly increases both the number of iterations required to find a solution and the overall computation time. Since scheduling requires path calculations for a large number of candidate solutions, computational efficiency is of utmost importance.

To address this, we employ a hybrid multi-step approach. Initially, we attempt to generate a Dubins path directly between the start and end points of the trajectory. If this path is not collision-free, we apply the RRT* algorithm to find a feasible path through the environment. A Dubins path is then constructed based on the result of the RRT* algorithm. Further details of this implementation are provided in Subsect. 4.1.

3.3 Genetic Algorithm Based on Target Features

In this subsection we present our genetic algorithm designed for multi-platform task allocation and scheduling in airborne reconnaissance missions. The algorithm is tailored to match expected target features with sensor capabilities and optimizes mission execution with respect to total mission time, platform cost, platform risk and reconnaissance quality.

General. Genetic algorithms are a class of metaheuristic optimization techniques inspired by the process of natural selection [9,14,18]. They begin with a randomly initialized population of valid candidate solutions and apply evolutionary operators as selection, crossover, and mutation to iteratively evolve better solutions. Each candidate solution is represented by a set of properties, often referred to as chromosome, which can be modified throughout the process. During each iteration, known as generation, the fitness of each individual in the population is evaluated. The most promising candidates are then selected and recombined to produce the next generation.

Genetic algorithms are particularly well suited for exploring large and complex search spaces [9]. They are effective for multi-objective optimization, as they support the evolution of trade-offs between conflicting goals [3]. By operating on a population of candidate solutions, genetic algorithms enable simultaneous evaluation of multiple candidates, making them inherently compatible with parallel computing and scalable to larger problems [5]. Furthermore, their population-based and stochastic nature makes them less susceptible to get trapped in local optima.

On the downside, evaluating a large number of candidate solutions over many generations can be computationally expensive, particularly when the fitness evaluation is complex. Moreover, due to their heuristic nature, genetic algorithms do not guarantee convergence to a globally optimal solution.

Chromosome Design. In a genetic algorithm, a *chromosome* represents a complete solution to the problem being addressed. Each individual in the population corresponds to a chromosome, and these individuals compete based on their fitness. As part of the evolutionary process, the fitness value of each chromosome has to be evaluated to guide the selection and reproduction. A chromosome is composed of smaller components called *genes*, where each gene represents a part of the overall solution or a decision variable.

In our case, there is one gene for every platform considered in the planning process. Each gene represents the schedule of the corresponding platform, including the schedule items allocated to it. The overall chromosome consists of theses genes and thus represents the complete mission plan across all platforms involved in mission execution. Each chromosome corresponds to a valid solution for the assigned tasks.

The system supports dynamic replanning during mission execution by maintaining platform schedules that integrate both previously assigned tasks and new tasks introduced during the current planning cycle.

Task Assignment Pool. The basis for all chromosomes is the current state of the platform schedules. Chromosomes differ in the additional schedule items that are introduced to fulfill the new tasks. Based on the tasks identified in the task generation process described in Subsect. 3.1, the pool of task assignments is created. This pool contains all solutions for the tasks derived from the mission order. These solutions, referred to as task assignments, are organized according to the tasks they address and the specific cells within the mission area to which they are associated.

This structure allows the genetic algorithm to select appropriate solutions for each task and to generate corresponding schedule items for both sensors and platforms. By enabling the selection of a single solution per task and cell the structure ensures that no task is assigned more than once.

Population Generation. To create the initial population, a random set of chromosomes is generated. For each chromosome, the gene corresponding to each platform is initialized based on its current schedule. In addition, the pool of possible task assignments is used to randomly select a single solution per task per mission area cell. Based on these selected solutions, new schedule items are created and assigned to the involved platforms and sensors.

In the simplified version, the new items are appended to the end of each platform's existing schedule. In a more advanced version, these schedule items may be inserted at arbitrary positions within the schedules. This would require adjusting the timing of subsequent schedule items and verifying that all relevant constraints are still satisfied.

To generate future population generations, the fitness of each individual in the current generation is evaluated. Based on this evaluation, individuals are selected for crossover, and mutation is applied to the resulting offspring. These steps are repeated until a complete new population has been created.

Fitness Evaluation. The fitness evaluation in the genetic algorithm is performed to assess the quality of the individuals, hence the quality of candidate solutions. Based on the resulting fitness value, individuals are selected for crossover and mutation operations. The goal of this approach is to guide the evolutionary search towards high-quality solutions.

We apply a multi-objective optimization approach and evaluate each individual using five fitness criteria: *mission duration*, *latest finish time*, *costs*, *risk level*, and *measurement quality*.

The *mission duration* is defined as the time between the earliest expected start time and the latest finish time among all schedule items generated from the task assignment pool. Specifically, the start time is determined by the earliest scheduled execution of a task related to the current mission. Since minimizing overall mission time is desirable, this value is treated as an objective to be minimized.

The *latest finish time* objective is used to discourage delaying the execution of a new mission until all currently running missions are completed, particularly in cases where earlier execution could reduce the total duration of the new mission. It is determined by the finish time of the latest schedule item associated with newly assigned task, assuming the plan is executed as expected and without delays. During optimization, this value is treated as a minimization objective.

The *cost* of a chromosome is defined as the sum of the operating cost of all platforms involved in executing mission-related tasks. For each platform represented by a gene, the duration of the mission-related schedule items is computed and multiplied by the platform's specific operating cost per time unit. High-value assets such as HALE platforms or manned platforms are associated with higher operating cost compared to low-value tactical UAVs. The total cost for the chromosome is obtained by summing the individual costs across all genes. This objective is also minimized in the optimization process.

The *risk* value is also calculated separately for each gene and then aggregated to obtain the total risk for the entire chromosome. Platform-specific risks vary depending on the mission and environment. To account for this, the mission area is divided into zones with predefined risk levels, forming a mission-specific risk map. The risk levels may be influenced by various factors, depending on the mission objectives. For example, in covert operations, the risk of detection and thus potential mission failure, increases with proximity to the target. In contrast, for other missions, platform survivability may be affected by the presence of know or suspected hostile air defense systems.

To incorporate risks into the planning process, the flight path of each platform is analyzed to determine how much time is spent in mission specific zones of different risk levels. A risk value is then computed for each platform based on its exposure to these zones. The genetic algorithm minimizes the total risk value across all platforms as part of the optimization process.

The final objective is the *measurement quality*, which the genetic algorithm aims to maximize. During the selection of feasible measurement positions, sensor performance models are used to identify the expected performance value of each sensor at various measurement locations, considering operational constraints and environmental conditions. As long the estimated performance exceeds a predefined threshold, a measurement position is considered acceptable for fulfilling the associated task. However, even among acceptable options, differences in expected measurement quality remain and are taken into account in the evaluation.

Based on the five defined objectives, a five-dimensional fitness tuple is computed for each chromosome.

Selection. To select suitable parents for the next generation based on the fitness tuple, various selection methods can be applied. Common approaches include roulette wheel selection, tournament selection, and rank selection. In all methods, the fitness of each individual in the population is first evaluated, after which a fixed number of individuals are selected for the crossover and mutation operations.

In *roulette wheel selection*, each individual is assigned a selection probability proportional to its fitness. Individuals are then randomly selected based on these probabilities. This methods can be sensitive to outliers, particularly when the population contains individuals with significantly higher fitness values than others, which may skew the selection process.

In *tournament selection*, a random subset of a fixed size is selected from the population. The best-performing individuals within this subset are then chosen for the evolution process. This method has proven to be robust and effective across a wide range of applications.

In *rank selection*, individuals are sorted based on fitness, and selection probabilities are assigned according to their rank rather than raw fitness values. This approach mitigates issues related to fitness scaling and offers a balanced trade-off between exploration and exploitation.

In our genetic algorithm, we chose to apply tournament selection. It is simple and efficient to implement, allows for tunable selection pressure through the tournament size parameter, and is robust to fitness scaling. Furthermore, the inherent randomness of the methods helps preserve population diversity and reduces the risk of premature convergence.

Crossover Function. The *crossover* is used to combine parts of two parent chromosomes to produce one or more offspring. Analogous to biological reproduction, its purpose is to exploit advantageous traits from both parents and recombine them into new candidate solutions.

In our genetic algorithm, the crossover function begins by merging the two list of assigned task solutions from the parent chromosomes to a single combined list. From this, two child chromosomes are generated. For each task-cell combination in the combined list, the crossover operator randomly selects the assignment from one of the two parents. Once a complete set of assignments has been selected, new schedules are generated for each gene in the child chromosome. The resulting offspring are then passed to the mutation step for further variation.

Mutation Function. Mutation introduces random alteration to a gene or a small number of genes within a chromosome to promote diversity and prevent premature convergence. With a predefined mutation probability, an individual may undergo mutation after the crossover operation has been completed.

In our genetic algorithm, we define a set of five mutation functions, each modifying a single element within the selected task assignments. Following a mutation, the platform and sensor schedules of the chromosome are repaired and updated to maintain completeness and feasibility.

If a chromosome is selected for mutation, one of the following mutation function is applied at random:

- **Heading**: Modifies the heading at with which a platform arrives at the measurement position
- **Measurement Position**: Replaces the assigned measurement position for a task
- **Sensor**: Changes the assigned sensor, and if necessary, the associated platform
- **Measurement Method**: Changes the measurement method used to fulfill a task. This may trigger reassignment of sensors and platforms.
- **Reorder**: Moves an item to another position in a platform's schedule.

After mutation, the resulting individuals are added to the next generation until the desired population size is reached. Once the new population is complete, the evolutionary process continues by discarding the previous generation and repeating the cycle with the new population until a termination condition is satisfied.

4 Implementation and Discussion

In this section we provide an overview of our implementation and present the first simulation results for both the path planning component and the genetic algorithm. The simulation environment, pre-processing component, path-planning component, and the initial version of the previously described genetic algorithm for task allocation and scheduling in airborne reconnaissance missions were implemented in Python version 3.10.12 [16].

4.1 Implementation of the Path Planning

For the path planning component, we implemented and evaluated three different algorithms across multiple sets of randomly generated environments.

Algorithms: The first method is a basic RRT* algorithm. While it cannot generate paths that are directly feasible for the platforms, it provides a fast first estimate of path lengths. Additionally, it serves as a baseline for comparison with the two other methods.

The second method is a modified RRT* that replaces straight-line connections with Dubins curves to respect the platform's non-holonomic constraints. When a new node is created, a Dubins path is generated between the nearest node and the sampled point. This path is then followed incrementally and truncated when the predefined RRT step size is reached. If the sampled point is reached before exceeding the step size, it is directly added as the new node in the tree. For clarification, the procedure is illustrated in Fig. 3.

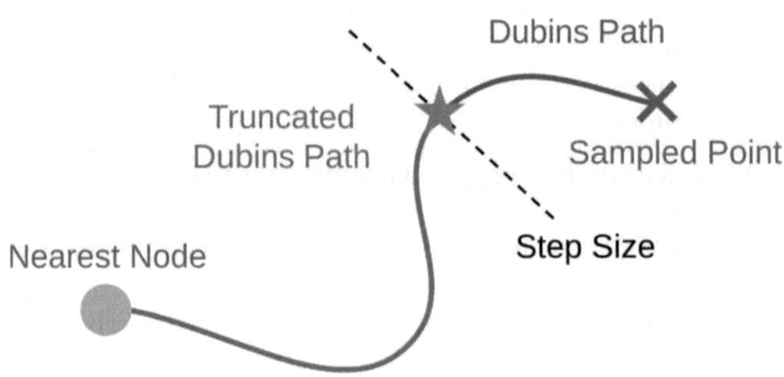

Fig. 3. Illustration of the procedure used to generate truncated Dubins segments during the tree expansion phase of the RRT*-Dubins algorithm. The Dubins path is truncated at the maximum step size, which is indicated by the dashed line.

The third variant is a hybrid solution. It first attempts to directly generate a Dubins path between the start and goal position. If this fails, a standard RRT* algorithm is executed to find a feasible path. Once a path is found, the algorithm attempts to connect the nodes along this path using Dubins curves. To reduce the number of segments and smooth the path, it tries to skip as many intermediate nodes as possible by directly connecting the current node to a later one. If a Dubins path cannot be generated for a segment, a local RRT*-Dubins search is performed in a smaller region to bridge the gap. This allows the algorithm to retain the benefits of Dubins-constrained planning while keeping the additional computational cost minimal. The full procedure is summarized in pseudocode in Fig. 4.

```
1. Try Dubins path from start to goal.
2. If successful, return this path.
3. Else:
    a. Run RRT* to find a path.
    b. Traverse the RRT* path:
        - Attempt Dubins connection to furthest possible node.
        - If not feasible:
            - Run local RRT*-Dubins for that segment.
4. Return the constructed path.
```

Fig. 4. Pseudo code for our Hybrid RRT*-Dubins path planning algorithm.

All three algorithms were implemented in their two-dimensional variants. The two-dimensional setting allows for easier visualization, which is beneficial for debugging and analysis. Moreover, the three-dimensional versions can be readily adapted from the two-dimensional implementations, and similar relative performance among the algorithms can be expected in three-dimensional space. While the computational complexity will increase with higher dimensionality, the core behavior of each algorithm remains consistent. In the initial version of our simulation, platforms are assumed to operate in separate altitude layers to ensure collision avoidance. Therefore, a two-dimensional path planning approach is sufficient for our current evaluation.

Test Setup: To compare the algorithms, we evaluated all of them in identical environments with the same start and goal positions. We selected a test area of 10.000 m × 10.000 m which is representative of typical mission scales for tactical UAVs. If the algorithms perform well in such a constrained area, they can be expected to scale to larger environments as well. In larger areas, the influence of Dubins path constraints diminishes as path curvature becomes less critical relative to the overall trajectory length.

Although typical mission areas are expected to contain only a small number of restricted zones or obstacles, we also tested environments with higher obstacle densities to evaluate the limits of the algorithms. For each environment configuration, we generated 50 randomized instances using the NumPy [10] random number generator, with a unique seed assigned to each run to ensure reproducibility. The tested environment variations are as follows:

- 5 obstacles with sizes ranging from 500 m to 1000 m
- 15 obstacles with sizes ranging from 500 m to 1000 m
- 5 obstacles with sizes ranging from 1500 m to 2000 m

Table 1. Parameters used for the three path planning algorithms during the comparison

Parameter	Value
Start position	(1000, 9000)
Goal position	(7500, 1000)
Area size	10000×10000
RRT* step size	200
Neighborhood radius	400
Max. number of iterations	2000
Turning radius	100
Dubins step size	100

In all cases, the specified size range refers to the maximum distance from the center of an obstacle to one if its corners. The obstacles are generated as polygons with a random number of vertices between four and eight. In total, we conducted 150 simulation runs for each algorithm.

For all three algorithms, the same set of parameters was used, as summarized in Table 1.

Figure 5 shows one example simulation environment along with the resulting solutions for each of the three algorithms. The red polygons represent obstacles or no-fly zones within the area. the green tree-like structures indicate the search trees generated by the algorithms, the blue lines represent the final paths found. In the plot corresponding to the hybrid variant, the red path shows the solution initially found by the RRT* component, while the blue path shows the final Dubins-smoothed trajectory derived from it.

As illustrated, the RRT* enables all variants to effectively guide the search process towards the goal location. In case of the RRT*-Dubins algorithm, the additional heading constraint results in a denser search tree before a feasible path to the goal is identified.

The analysis of the performance metrics supports the observations made from the visualization of the search trees. Figure 6 presents the results in the environment with five small obstacles. In the top-left subplot, a box plot illustrates the computation time required for 50 runs of each algorithm.

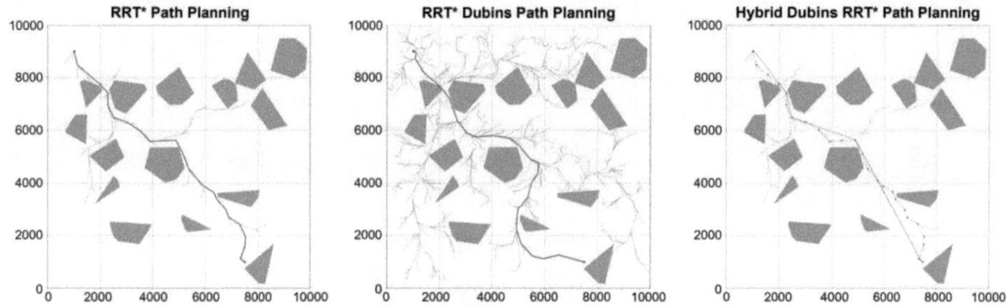

Fig. 5. The figure illustrates the results of the three path planning algorithms - RRT* (left), RRT*-Dubins (center), and the proposed hybrid method (right) - in an environment containing 15 obstacles (shown as red polygons). The exploration tree is visualized in green, and the selected final path is shown in blue. For the hybrid variant, the best path from the underlying RRT* is also displayed in red for comparison. (Color figure online)

As shown, the classic RRT* demonstrates consistently fast performance, with most runs falling within a narrow range, aside from two outliers. The hybrid algorithm exhibits greater variability in computation time, but still remains below 0.5 s in most cases. In contrast, the RRT*-Dubins variant is significantly slower, with median times approaching one second and some outliers reaching up to approximately two seconds.

This trend continues when examining the number of iterations, as shown in the center plot of Fig. 6. The RRT*-Dubins variant consistently requires more iterations compared to the classic RRT*, which is expected, due to the added complexity considering heading constraints during expansion. The hybrid algorithm, on the other hand, requires fewer iterations on average. This can be attributed to its ability to generate a direct Dubins path at the beginning of the planning process, allowing it to bypass the need for extensive tree expansion in some cases.

The rightmost plot in Fig. 6 presents the analysis of the path lengths produced by each algorithm. Here, we observe a strong similarity between the classic RRT* variant and the RRT*-Dubins variant. However, the Dubins variant tends to produce slightly longer paths, which can be attributed to the additional heading constraints that often result in less direct trajectories. In contrast, the hybrid variant consistently generates shorter paths, indicating that its smoothing mechanism effectively reduces unnecessary detours and produces more efficient connections between the start and goal positions.

The plot in the lower half of the figure shows that, in this sparse environment, all three variants successfully find a solution in all runs within the maximum limit of 2000 iterations. In the sparse environment, it is rather unlikely that a Dubins curve with the minimum turning radius cannot be fitted between obstacles. This situation changes in the denser environments.

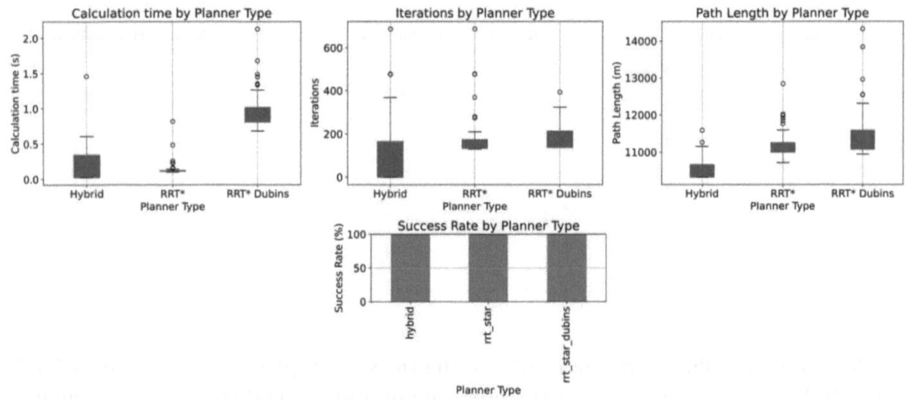

Fig. 6. The figure presents a comparison of the results from 50 simulation runs for each of the three path planning algorithms in random environments containing five small obstacles. The box plots provide statistical summaries of key performance metrics. In each box plot, the horizontal line within the box represents the median. The box spans the interquartile range (IQR), covering the values between the 25th and 75th percentiles. The whiskers extend to the most extreme data points within 1.5 times the IQR from the lower and upper quartiles. Outliers beyond this range are displayed as individual circles. The top left subplot shows the calculation time required by each planner. The top center displays the number of iterations needed to find a solution. The top right shows the path length of solutions. Finally, the bottom subplot presents the success rate of each planner across the 50 evaluated environments.

Since larger no-fly zones are also expected in reconnaissance and surveillance scenarios, we conducted a similar set of experiments using larger obstacles. The results of these simulation runs are presented in Fig. 7.

The trends observed seen in the environment with smaller obstacles are confirmed in this setup as well. Due to the additional heading constraint, the RRT*-Dubins variant performs slightly worse than the basic RRT*, as increased complexity of path computation between nodes significantly increases the calculation time.

Furthermore, because the larger obstacles reduce the available free space and create narrower passages, a small number of runs fails to find a solution within the 2000-iteration limit. It is more difficult for randomly curve segments to find a feasible path through densely populated obstacle areas. This is why the hybrid version achieves a higher success rate than the RRT*-Dubins variant. The hybrid version benefits from the path generated by the RRT* and subsequently smooths or curves the trajectory to satisfy the Dubins motion constraints. Hence, the RRT*-Dubins variant exhibits the highest failure rate, as it is more constrained by its curvature limitations (Fig. 7).

In the final simulation set, we investigated a more densely populated environment, resulting in narrower passages between obstacles Fig. 8. The trends observed in the previous simulations are confirmed in this scenario. The hybrid

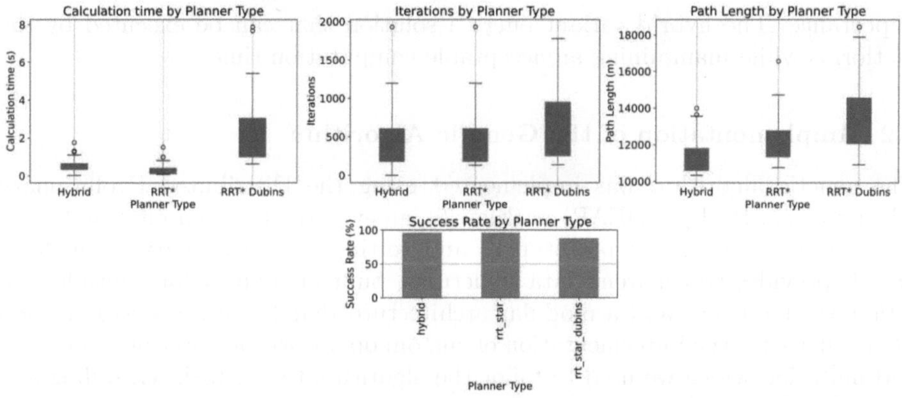

Fig. 7. Similar to Fig. 6, this figure compares the performance of the three path planning algorithms in 50 environments with five large obstacles.

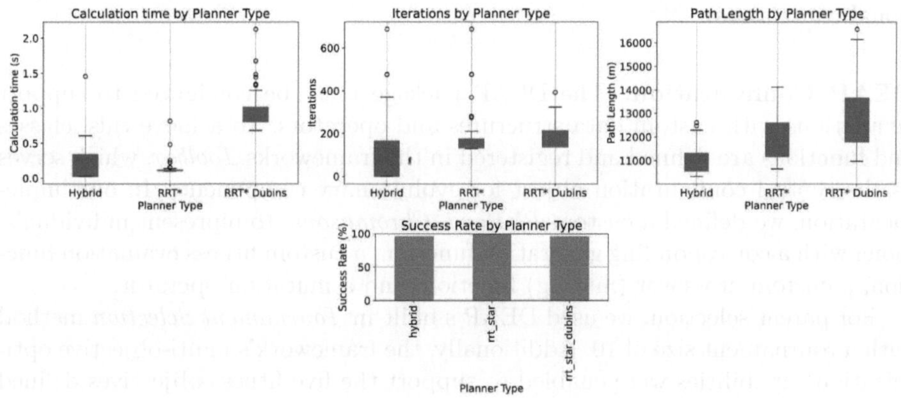

Fig. 8. As prior in Fig. 6 and Fig. 7, this figures compares the performance of the three path planning algorithms in 50 environments with 15 small obstacles.

variant consistently produces shorter paths on average, while maintaining acceptable computation time. In this regard, it significantly outperforms the RRT*-Dubins variant.

However, due to the increased complexity of the environment, the hybrid approach occasionally fails to find a valid path. Given that such densely populated environments are expected to be rare in practice, this limitation is considered acceptable.

During task allocation and scheduling, it can be expected that a large number of flight paths must be computed. For each candidate solution under consideration, a path must be calculated to estimate the flight duration and to generate a feasible execution schedule. As a result, short computation times are of utmost importance. The hybrid variant offers a solution that can be executed by the platforms while maintaining an acceptable computation time.

4.2 Implementation of the Genetic Algorithm

The genetic algorithm was implemented using the Distributed Evolutionary Algorithms in Python (DEAP) package [6], an evolutionary computation framework designed for rapid prototyping and testing of evolutionary algorithms. DEAP provides transparent data structures, built-in support for multiple evolutionary strategies, and a modular architecture that facilitates customization [6]. It allows for the implementation of custom operators for selection, crossover, and mutation which we used to tailor the algorithm to our task scheduling and path planning problem.

As input, the genetic algorithm component receives the list of tasks to be assigned in the current planning cycle, the list of available platforms and their associated sensors, access to the planning component, and any relevant operational constraints.

DEAP Configuration. The DEAP package must be configured to support simulations with custom data structures and operators. To achieve this, classes and functions are defined and registered in the frameworks *Toolbox*, which serves as the central configuration object for evolutionary components. In our implementation, we defined a custom *Platform Chromosome* to represent individuals, along with a corresponding generation function, a custom fitness evaluation function, a custom crossover (mating) function, and a mutation operator.

For parent selection, we used DEAP's built-in *Tournament Selection* method with a tournament size of 10. Additionally, the framework's multi-objective optimization capabilities were enabled to support the five fitness objectives defined in Sect. 3.3.

To run the genetic algorithm, the *population size*, the *number of generations* and the *mutation rate* must be specified. DEAP also provides a built-in statistics tool that can be used to collect and track evolutionary statistics throughout the simulation process.

Platform Chromosome. We defined a custom *Platform Chromosome* class that contains a list of *Platform Gene* objects, a list of tasks assigned to the chromosome, and a fitness value. The list of assigned tasks is initially used for the gene generation, to construct platform specific schedules. In this process, tasks are randomly selected from the list, and schedule items are created for the corresponding platforms and sensors. These items are then appended to the corresponding schedule.

The generation of the schedule items includes the calculation of a flight path from the previous schedule item using the path planning component, the estimation of the flight duration, and based on this the expected start and end times. Each platform gene also store the original schedules its associated platforms and sensors, to track changes and enable proper updates during crossover and mutation operations.

In addition, each platform gene stores the total path length of the platform's schedule, the total flight duration, the accumulated risk along the route, and the summed measurement quality of all sensor schedule items. These values are later used during the fitness evaluation phase to assess the quality of the overall chromosome.

In the current implementation, the new schedule items generated during the planning cycle are appended to the end of each platform's existing schedule. This approach provides a straightforward way to integrate new tasks without disrupting the existing mission plan. In a more advanced version, we intend to randomly insert new schedule items into the existing schedule, which would require a more sophisticated repair mechanism. Such a mechanism must ensure that the modified schedule still satisfies all mission objectives and operational constraints. Additionally, a task prioritization scheme could be introduced to determine wether newly introduced tasks are allowed to override or influence existing assignments.

In addition to the newly generated schedule items stored within each platform gene, the raw list of assigned tasks is also retained in the platform chromosome. This list is used during the crossover and mutation operations in later stages of the evolutionary process.

Fitness Evaluation. For the fitness evaluation, each gene is evaluated individually, and the results are aggregated to compute the overall fitness of the chromosome.

For the *duration* and *latest finish time* fitness objectives, the total flight duration is calculated by determining the start time of the first newly added schedule item and the finish time of the last one. The *operating cost* is computed by summing the durations of all newly added schedule items and multiplying them by the platform's specific cost rate.

To evaluate the *risk* objective, a risk map of the environment is required. The flight path is segmented based on the risk zones it traverses, and the length of each segment is weighted accordingly. However, since the risk map is not yet implemented in the current simulation environment, this objective is currently set to zero.

The *measurement quality* is determined based on the quality values of the measurement positions, as defined by the sensor performance models. Because these values are not yet standardized across all sensor types, a generalized model is still under development. As a result, this fitness objective is also currently set to zero.

In summary, the initial implementation of the fitness evaluation considers only the duration, end time, and operating cost objectives.

Based on the evaluated fitness values of the chromosomes, parent selection for the crossover operation is performed using the integrated tournament selection method provided by the DEAP package.

Crossover. The crossover, also referred to as mating operation in the DEAP package, takes two parent chromosomes as input and produces two offspring chromosomes. In our custom crossover function, the task assignment lists from both parents are combined, and for each cell-task combination, a solutions is randomly selected from one of the two parents. If a cell-task combination is assigned only in one parent, that assignment is directly inherited by the offspring chromosome. A safeguard mechanism ensures that only one solution per task and mission area cell is chosen, thereby preventing duplicate task assignments.

Once a complete set of task assignments has been selected, new platform genes are generated, including the updated schedules based on the selected tasks and associated platform-sensor assignments.

The result is two valid offspring chromosomes, each representing a unique combination of tasks inherited from the parents, which are then passed on to the mutation stage.

Mutation. The mutation stage is applied with a predefined probability, determined by the mutation rate parameter. If triggered, one of the five mutation functions introduced in Sect. 3.3 is selected at random with equal probability. Mutations are applied exclusively to tasks introduced during the current planning cycle, leaving previously scheduled tasks untouched. Each of the five mutation functions requires a corresponding repair mechanism to ensure that the resulting chromosome remains valid after the modification. If a selected mutation results in an invalid schedule, it is discarded, and the original chromosome remains unchanged.

In the *heading* mutation, the heading of a randomly selected platform schedule item is modified by a random angle. Following this change, a new path must be generated from the previous schedule item to the mutated schedule item. If a subsequent schedule item exists, the path from the mutated item to the next item must also be recalculated. If either of the newly generated paths differs significantly in length, compared to the original, the timing of the modified item and all subsequent schedule items must be updated accordingly.

The mutation of a *measurement position* follows a similar procedure. First, alternative task solutions with different valid measurement positions for the same cell-task-sensor combination must be identified. Once an alternative is selected, the measurement position of the corresponding schedule item is updated. As a result, the flight path and timing of the schedule item and potential subsequent items must be recalculated to maintain schedule consistency.

In the *sensor* mutation, the assigned sensor along with its associated measurement position is changed. As a result, two schedules must to be modified. First, the measurement item is removed from the original sensor's schedule The flight path to the next item in the platform's schedule and the timing of all subsequent schedule items are then adjusted accordingly. Next, the task is inserted into the schedule of the new sensor and its corresponding platform. In the current implementation, this insertion is limited to appending the item at the end of the schedule. In future versions, it is intended to support insertion between existing schedule items, which will require more advanced consistency checks. This mutation is only applied if both modified schedules remain valid after the change.

The mutation of the *measurement method* is similar to the sensor mutation. In this case, an alternative task solution with a different measurement method is selected for a random schedule item. This may also involve assigning the task to a different platform-sensor combination, depending on the selected method. As with the sensor mutation, all affected schedules have to be reconstructed and verified for validity following the change.

In the final mutation function, the *reorder* mutation, a schedule item from a platform gene is moved to the end of its schedule. This operation also requires recalculating the platform's flight path and updating the timing of all affected schedule items. In future implementations, we intend to allow random insertion of the item at any position within the same schedule, rather than restricting it to the end.

Discussion. To verify the functionality of the algorithm, we applied it to the task allocation and scheduling of a mission to detect vehicles in an area of 10000 m × 10000 m. The mission processing component decomposes the mission area into 16 cells of 2500 m × 2500 m, with the center of each cell designated as a measurement point.

Three tactical UAVs are available for the mission. Each of the UAVs is equipped with an electro-optical sensor. Two are deployed from the southwest corner of the area, and one from the northeast corner. The scenario is illustrated in Fig. 9.

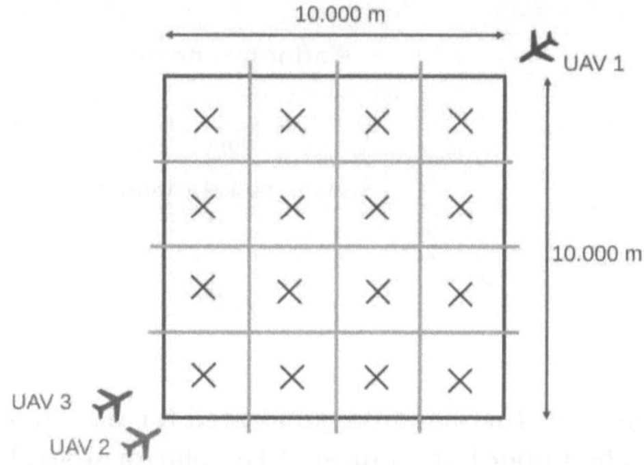

Fig. 9. The figure illustrates the scenario in which the genetic algorithm is applied to schedule platform tasks. Each cell center represents a location that must be measured.

The pre-processing component used the mission order, along with the data of the available platforms and sensors, to generate a task pool based on cooperation blueprints and sensor performance models. This task pool provides the candidate solutions for the genetic algorithm. The configuration of the genetic algorithm is as follows:

- Population size: 100
- Tournament size: 3
- Number of generations: 30
- Mutation rate: 0.1

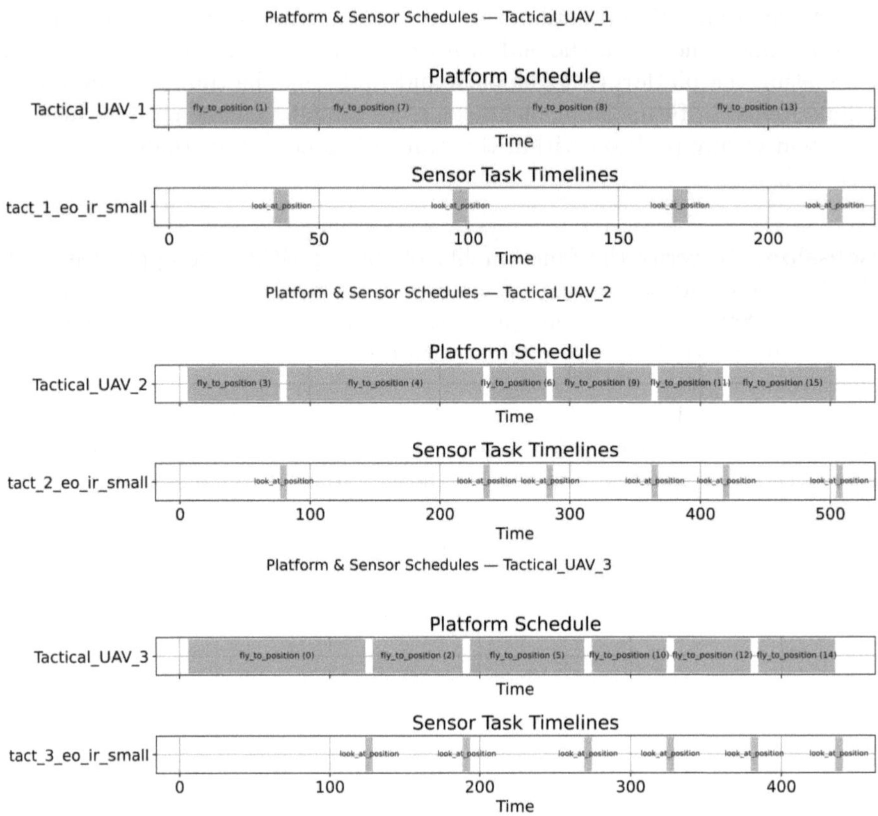

Fig. 10. The figure illustrates the schedules generated for the three tactical UAVs using the genetic algorithm. The upper bars represent the platform-level, while the lower bars depict the corresponding sensor-level schedules.

The resulting schedules from the simulation for the three UAVs are shown in Fig. 10. In the upper half of each plot, the platform schedule is shown, illustrating the tasks involving flight to the designated measurement positions. In the lower half the sensor schedule displays the corresponding measurement tasks directed at the specified target locations.

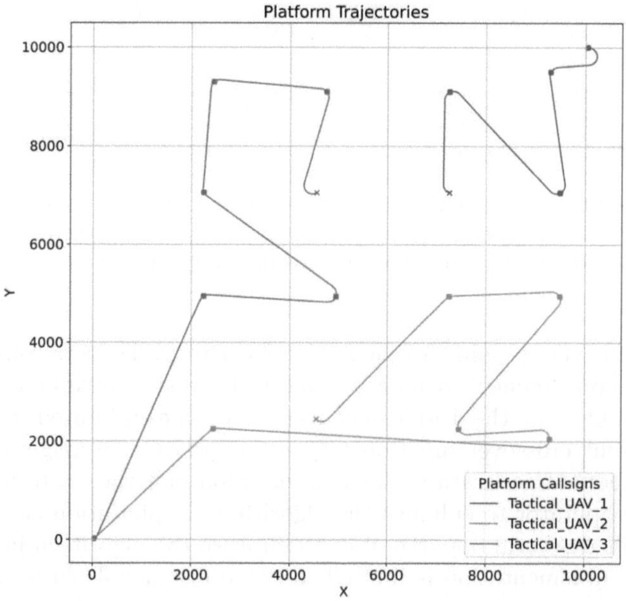

Fig. 11. The figure shows the trajectories of the three tactical UAVs, corresponding to the generated platform and sensor schedules.

The plots indicate that the algorithm assigned four tasks to the UAV deployed in the northeast corner, and six tasks each to the two UAVs launched from the southwest corner. It can also be observed, that the schedule for UAV 2 takes the longest, with a duration of just over 500 s, whereas UAV 1 completes its assigned tasks in approximately 230 s. Furthermore, it can be observed that all schedule items are properly sequenced, with no overlaps between the tasks.

Figure 11 shows that each platform was assigned a flyable Dubins path connecting its designated measurement positions. It can also be observed that the paths are not yet optimal, and there is potential to shorten the trajectories between the measurement positions. The results of the preliminary evaluation of the algorithm suggest that further parameter tuning and refinement of the processes are necessary to improve overall performance.

Running 30 generations of the genetic algorithm with a population of 100 individuals required approximately 94 s. While the current implementation is suitable for pre-mission planning, its computational demands limit its applicability for real-time or online replanning scenarios.

We also analyzed the performance of the genetic algorithm over successive generations as illustrated in Fig. 12.

We deliberately focused on the cost and duration objectives, as the risk and performance objectives are set to zero. The plots in Fig. 12 show the minimum,

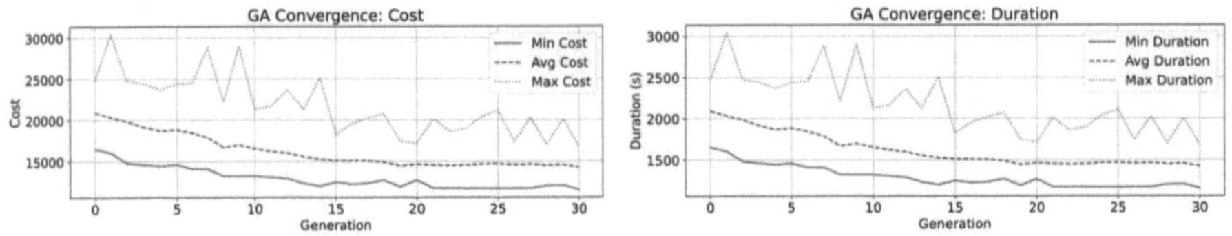

Fig. 12. The left side of the figure illustrates the convergence of the cost objective over the generations of the genetic algorithm. The right side shows the convergence of the mission duration objective throughout the evolutionary process.

maximum, and average values of each objective across all generations. The results indicate slow convergence, with occasional peaks in the maximum values caused by mutations. Overall, the degree of convergence appears limited, which suggests that the current crossover function may not effectively propagate high-quality traits to subsequent generations. This observation motivates a future revision of the crossover operator to enhance the algorithm's exploitation capability.

We identified several opportunities to improve the algorithm in future work. The current implementation is limited to two-dimensional platform movement. Allowing altitude changes and incorporating three-dimensional sensor performance models, with spatially distributed measurement positions, would significantly increase the number of available solutions per task. This in turn would likely require a larger number of generations for convergence and lead to increased simulation times.

Therefore, various approaches can be applied to reduce the computational effort. In the current implementation, a separate task per target type is generated for each cell and passed to the genetic algorithm via the task assignment pool. However, this leads to redundancy, since a sensor capable of detecting a person using a specific method will typically also be able to detect a vehicle using the same method. Thus solving the task with the highest quality requirement can often satisfy multiple task with lower quality constraints. Reducing such duplication would allow computational resources to be used more efficiently and could significantly decrease the overall simulation time.

A similar reduction in computational effort can be achieved by defining tasks for smaller subsets of the area and then performing localized scan patterns. This approach reduces the number of cells considered by the genetic algorithm. To support this, schedule items must be allocated additional time for task execution and must include not only the transfer path to the task location but also a dedicated trajectory for the scanning operation itself.

The mutation stage in particular, requires a complex implementation and involves a series of operations on platform schedules. These operations may increase the overall computation time, and it remains uncertain whether their impact on solution quality justifies the additional effort.

Another potential improvement to the implementation is the adaption of the algorithm for better parallelization. This is particularly relevant if such planning algorithms are to be deployed in cloud environments or computing clusters in the future, where parallel processing can significantly enhance performance. However, this aspect lies outside the scope of our research.

As part of future work, a more detailed evaluation will require the setup of a simulation environment with simulated platforms, sensors and targets. The simulated system will use the genetic algorithm to generate new schedule items in response to sensor detections, triggering follow-up tasks such as target identification and tracking. Running simulations in such an environment will increase the realism and significance of the evaluation results.

5 Conclusion

This work addressed the challenge of scheduling, planning, and monitoring ISR missions for a heterogenous group of airborne platforms and sensors, based on target specific features.

We presented a genetic algorithm that generates feasible schedules for both platforms and sensors to fulfill an overall mission objective. The algorithm is designed for use in pre-mission planning. where it generates an initial schedule, and in online operation during mission execution, where it can adapt the schedule in response to new information and dynamically arising tasks.

The algorithm relies on path planning to generate feasible flight paths for the platforms and to schedule sensor operations accordingly. To this end, we introduced a hybrid RRT*-Dubins algorithm that combines the advantages of the classic RRT* approach with the Dubins path constraints ot produce executable trajectories. We presented an implementation of this hybrid planner and discussed simulation results in comparison with the classic RRT* and the RRT*-Dubins variant.

In addition, we presented a prototype implementation of the genetic algorithm, discussed initial results, and outlined future steps to enhance its capabilities. Planned improvements include extending the planning framework to three dimensions, integrating a risk zone calculator for the environment, and evaluating the algorithm with simulated platforms, sensors, and targets.

Acknowledgments. This work was financially supported by Airbus Defence & Space.

Disclosure of Interests. The authors declare no competing interests. The views expressed in this paper are those of the authors and do not necessarily reflect the official position of their affiliated institutions.

References

1. Bening, S., Albert, A.E., Stütz, P.: Cooperative airborne sensor platforms for enhanced reconnaissance: a concept for managing task-based cooperation. In: AIAA SCITECH 2024 Forum. American Institute of Aeronautics and Astronautics. https://doi.org/10.2514/6.2024-2798, https://arc.aiaa.org/doi/abs/10.2514/6.2024-2798

2. Bening, S., Stütz, P.: A generalized feature-based approach to dynamic planning for airborne reconnaissance missions. In: 2025 AIAA DATC/IEEE 44th Digital Avionics Systems Conference (DASC), pp. 1–10 (2025).https://doi.org/10.1109/DASC66011.2025.11257374
3. Deb, K.: Multiobjective Optimization Using Evolutionary Algorithms. Wiley, New York (2001)
4. Dubins, L.E.: On curves of minimal length with a constraint on average curvature, and with prescribed initial and terminal positions and tangents. Am. J. Math. **79**(3), 497–516 (1957). https://doi.org/10.2307/2372560, https://www.jstor.org/stable/2372560
5. Eiben, A., Smith, J.: Introduction To Evolutionary Computing, vol. 45 (2003). https://doi.org/10.1007/978-3-662-05094-1
6. Fortin, F.A., De Rainville, F.M., Gardner, M.A., Parizeau, M., Gagné, C.: DEAP: evolutionary algorithms made easy. J. Mach. Learn. Res. **13**, 2171–2175 (2012)
7. Gao, S., Zuo, L., Bao, S.X.: UAV reconnaissance task allocation with reinforcement learning and genetic algorithm. In: 2022 International Conference on Automation, Robotics and Computer Engineering (ICARCE), pp. 1–3 (2022). https://doi.org/10.1109/ICARCE55724.2022.10046603, https://ieeexplore.ieee.org/abstract/document/10046603
8. Gao, S., Wu, J., Ai, J.: Multi-UAV reconnaissance task allocation for heterogeneous targets using grouping ant colony optimization algorithm. Soft. Comput. **25**(10), 7155–7167 (2021). https://doi.org/10.1007/s00500-021-05675-8
9. Goldberg, D.E.: Genetic Algorithms in Search, Optimization and Machine Learning. 1st edn. Addison-Wesley Longman Publishing Co., Inc, USA (1989)
10. Harris, C.R., et al.: Array programming with NumPy. Nature **585**(7825), 357–362 (2020). https://doi.org/10.1038/s41586-020-2649-2
11. Karaman, S., Frazzoli, E.: Sampling-based algorithms for optimal motion planning. Int. J. Robot. Res. **30**(7), 846–894 (2011). https://doi.org/10.1177/0278364911406761
12. Khanal, A.: RRT and RRT* Using Vehicle Dynamics (2022).https://doi.org/10.48550/arXiv.2206.10533, http://arxiv.org/abs/2206.10533, arXiv:2206.10533 [cs]
13. LaValle, S.: Rapidly-exploring random trees: a new tool for path planning. The annual research report (1998). https://www.semanticscholar.org/paper/Rapidly-exploring-random-trees-%3A-a-new-tool-for-LaValle/d967d9550f831a8b3f5cb00f8835a4c866da60ad
14. Mitchell, M.: An Introduction to Genetic Algorithms. The MIT Press (1996). https://doi.org/10.7551/mitpress/3927.001.0001
15. Poudel, S., Moh, S.: Task assignment algorithms for unmanned aerial vehicle networks: a comprehensive survey. Veh. Commun. **35**, 100469 (2022). https://doi.org/10.1016/j.vehcom.2022.100469. https://www.sciencedirect.com/science/article/pii/S221420962200016X
16. Python Software Foundation: Python language reference, version 3.10 (2023). https://docs.python.org/3.10/reference/index.html
17. Tian, J., Shen, L., Zheng, Y.: Genetic algorithm based approach for multi-UAV cooperative reconnaissance mission planning problem. In: Esposito, F., Raś, Z.W., Malerba, D., Semeraro, G. (eds.) ISMIS 2006. LNCS (LNAI), vol. 4203, pp. 101–110. Springer, Heidelberg (2006). https://doi.org/10.1007/11875604_13
18. Whitley, D.: A genetic algorithm tutorial. Stat. Comput. **4**(2), 65–85 (1994). https://doi.org/10.1007/BF00175354

19. Yan, F., Chu, J., Hu, J., Zhu, X.: Cooperative task allocation with simultaneous arrival and resource constraint for multi-UAV using a genetic algorithm. Expert Syst. Appl. **245**, 123023 (2024). https://doi.org/10.1016/j.eswa.2023.123023. https://www.sciencedirect.com/science/article/pii/S095741742303525X
20. Yang, Y., Leeghim, H., Kim, D.: Dubins path-oriented rapidly exploring random Tree* for three-dimensional path planning of unmanned aerial vehicles. Electronics **11**(15), 2338 (2022). https://doi.org/10.3390/electronics11152338. https://www.mdpi.com/2079-9292/11/15/2338

The Effects of Terrain Surface and Vegetation on Autonomous Navigation of Ground Robotic Systems

Jan Nohel(✉), Pavel Zahradníček, Dana Křišťálová, Jan Zezula, Zdeněk Flasar, and Luděk Rak

University of Defence, 662 10 Brno, Czech Republic
{jan.nohel,pavel.zahradnicek,dana.kristalova,jan.zezula, zdenek.flasar,ludek.rak}@unob.cz

Abstract. The utilization of robotic systems has become an integral part of military operations. While aerial and naval robotic systems are commonly used for reconnaissance or enemy destruction, ground systems face numerous challenges that hinder their effective deployment. The main issue is terrain traversability, particularly in terms of the presence of micro-relief terrain features and vegetation. While digital information systems and tactical-geographical data on the area, terrain relief, weather, and enemy can be used for planning ground robotic system tasks, the actual conditions for traversability in unknown terrain can be highly variable. Current terrain traversability can be identified using laser radar, although this has its limitations in terms of range and the accuracy of obstacle identification. This article examines three case studies to characterize the advantages and disadvantages of using autonomous navigation for ground robotic systems using laser radar, and proposes potential improvements.

Keywords: UGS · traversability · LIDAR · manoeuvre · navigation

1 Introduction

The use of unmanned aerial systems (UAS) has already become a standard component of military operations. UAS are used as reconnaissance assets to provide commanders with situational awareness on the battlefield, as carriers of weapon systems, loitering munitions, and as so-called "kamikaze drones". This use is primarily due to the current technological advancement of UAS and the airspace being an operational environment free of unexpected obstacles. In the case of unmanned ground systems (UGS), however, the situation is entirely different. Many commanders see UGS as a potential replacement for infantry and military combat vehicles. UGS can move using wheeled, tracked, or legged platforms with high terrain traversability. They can be equipped with high-performance radio stations, computing units, and optoelectronic, infrared, or night vision sensors. UGS navigation can be conducted either remotely by an operator using the outputs of the vehicle's observation sensors and radio communication, or autonomously using a

J. Novotný et al. (Eds.): MESAS 2025, LNCS 16627, pp. 238–252, 2027.
https://doi.org/10.1007/978-3-032-33182-3_14

laser radar (LIDAR) for scanning the surroundings. Experiments are now underway with the integration of weapon stations on UGS, including automatic machine guns, large-calibre cannons, grenade launchers, anti-tank guided missiles, mine dispensers, and kamikaze drones. So-called "combat UGS" are used by the Israel Defense Forces (IDF) for border fence security along the Gaza Strip [1]. The combat deployment of the Russian UGS URAN-9 in the Syrian conflict on the side of the Republican Army faced significant challenges. In contrast, the deployment in this conflict of the Russian engineering UGS URAN-6 and combat UGS Platforma-M and ARGO was more or less successful, operating in coordination with and under the cover of infantry units [2–6].

In the conflict in Ukraine, the deployment of combat UGS can be considered largely unsuccessful, primarily due to the high level of weapon system technology used by both sides [7]. This is primarily due to electromagnetic interference, which significantly restricts the effective deployment of remotely controlled or autonomous systems. The limited situational awareness of operators (who are relying solely on the vehicle's onboard sensors) complicates dynamic manoeuvring in the terrain, which is essential for taking cover from enemy fire and securing advantageous firing positions. UGS are being destroyed by direct enemy fire, artillery support, or strikes from first-person view (FPV) UAS carrying, for example, an RPG-7 warhead [8]. Moreover, if the connection between the operator and the system is lost, the system is highly likely to be destroyed, isolated, or captured by the enemy.

The only option for the return of combat UGS to friendly forces in the event of a loss of satellite navigation signal and communication with the operator is an inertial navigation system for determining its position and autonomous vehicle navigation using LIDAR. However, during this autonomous movement through the terrain, "local" UGS navigation can be highly problematic, primarily due to the unexpected presence of various obstacles along the route and the limited range of LIDAR. To identify the limitations of autonomous movement, three case studies were conducted, focusing on the "local" LIDAR-based navigation of the UGS Taros Furbo on different terrain surfaces with variable vegetation.

2 Literature Review

The issue of the conflict in Ukraine, in terms of the current use of modern technologies and their impact on unit operations at the tactical level of the command and control process, as well as the necessity of enhancing NATO unit mobility, is addressed in [9, 10]. Laser terrain scanning, methods of utilizing LIDAR functions, the impact of terrain surface data accuracy on the navigation of off-road vehicles when capturing the structure and parameters of terrain vegetation, and the quality of data acquisition on vegetation traversability by off-road vehicles are characterized in [11–14]. The ability of UGS sensors to assess terrain traversability is further linked to models quantifying their level of autonomy, which are described in [15]. Here, the level of UGS autonomy is expressed on a scale from fully non-autonomous to fully autonomous, represented by a single numerical parameter describing the UGS's performance capabilities. The mobility level of UGS for military applications across different reaction times, operational modes, and degrees of autonomy is characterized in [16].

The planning of autonomous UGS movement based on tactical terrain analysis is addressed in [17]. This work presents a new approach to acquiring tactical geospatial information from terrain data, and demonstrates its potential application in the military decision-making process for deploying autonomous UGS. Using a terrain model as a foundation, terrain characteristics such as elevation, vegetation density, and soil composition are combined to calculate visibility, traversability, and the cover properties of the terrain. Based on these calculations, optimal observation post locations for a given area and movement routes to these points are determined. Autonomous UGS navigation in urban environments is described in [18]. The movement of UGS in built-up areas that are not significantly disrupted or destroyed by combat operations is less affected by terrain traversability and more dependent on the ability of onboard sensors to scan the vehicle's surroundings and identify obstacles.

One method of autonomous UGS navigation, described in [19], engages with a high level of obstacle detection, distance estimation, and obstacle avoidance using an optical camera combined with the fusion of LIDAR sensor outputs. It explores the potential use of 3D point clouds obtained from LIDAR depth sensors for detailed object shape recognition. This approach helps eliminate the issue of object occlusion, which often occurs when recognizing objects using an optical camera alone. Precise mapping of unknown areas with a 360° range in real time can then be applied, for example, in logistics operations with small payloads, as discussed in [20].

In an effort to minimize UGS navigation issues in the terrain, [21] describes the potential cooperation of UGS with UAS, with the latter conducting terrain mapping within a wide field of view to create digital surface models (DSM). DSM effectively encode geometric information about the terrain that is crucial for assessing its traversability, which can be utilized in UGS information and control systems for route planning. However, this cooperation can be disrupted or entirely suppressed by electronic warfare measures, which can identify the positions of the ground control station (GCS) and UAS, interfere with their communication and satellite navigation signal reception, or even take control of them, as described in [22–24]. A similar method could also be applied in the case of GCS for UGS.

3 Global and Local Navigation of UGS

UGS navigation must be addressed from both the perspective of "local" navigation – traversing traversable terrain between obstacles, and "global" navigation – moving from the starting point to the final destination based on time, distance, and security requirements. The "global" movement routes of the UGS Taros Furbo can be calculated using the functionality of the Manoeuvre Control System CZ (MCS CZ) Tactical Decision Support System (TDSS), as described in [25, 26]. MCS CZ employs the Optimal Manoeuvre Route Model, detailed in [27], for the deterministic calculation of the tactically and spatially coordinated swarm manoeuvres of UGS. The spatial course of manoeuvre routes is calculated by a model based on the mathematical raster layer of operational influences on space, known as the Combined Cost Surface (CCS). This layer incorporates the majority of critical battlefield situational factors. These factors include the mathematical raster layer of surface and vegetation terrain characteristics, CS_1, represented as a digital terrain model. It specifies the average time required to traverse different types of terrain surfaces and vegetation. CS_1 includes all paved and unpaved roads, forests, pastures, fields, urban areas, and water bodies. The influence of slope gradient on the time required to traverse specific terrain surfaces or vegetation is represented by the terrain relief layer, expressed through a digital terrain model labeled as VF_2. The effects of weather conditions on overall terrain traversability are captured in the HF_3 layer, which utilizes weather forecasts. Based on the currently identified enemy positions, their visibility range, and the effective range of their weapons, the HF_4 layer defines the impact of enemy activity on space traversability. The influence of HF_4 on the safe traversal of the operational space can be mitigated by the HF_5 layer, which incorporates the presence of friendly forces, their visibility range, and their effective weapon range into the traversability calculations. The described operational situation factors affect space traversability in terms of both speed and security [26].

Due to the unpredictable occurrence of unexpected natural changes in complex terrain (such as vegetation fires, landslides, or floods) and combat-related alterations (such as destroyed building blocks, newly laid minefields, or chemical contamination), the CCS calculation can incorporate an additional raster layer, $CS_{1.2}$, which specifies NO GO and SLOW GO areas. NO GO areas are not safely traversable and are excluded from manoeuvre calculations. SLOW GO areas impose mobility constraints, increasing traversal time. A slowdown coefficient can be applied, representing a multiplier for the extended time required to cross areas defined by CS_1, which are affected by unforeseen natural events or combat-related terrain disruptions. The presence, extent, and impact of these constraints must be identified through reconnaissance assets and intelligence analysis, and subsequently entered manually into the Tactical Decision Support System (TDSS) [26].

The mathematical algorithms and criterion-based settings of each raster layer quantify their influence on the overall traversability of the operational space. The final CCS is derived from a mathematical algorithmic combination of the continuous impact of all raster layers on terrain traversability, as expressed in Eq. 1. Based on this equation and utilizing a combination of Floyd–Warshall and Dijkstra's algorithms [28–30], the model calculates the fastest and safest manoeuvre route [26].

$$CCS = \frac{CS_1 \cdot CS_{1.2}}{VF_2 \cdot HF_3 \cdot \min(1, HF_4 \cdot HF_5)} \tag{1}$$

The Optimal Manoeuvre Route Model mathematically distinguishes three primary movement types – foot, wheeled, and tracked – due to their differing capabilities in terrain traversability, slope climbing ability, and manoeuvreability on inclines, as well as their response to the effects of rainfall and snowfall. Specific types of military vehicle and foot soldiers can be defined in MCS CZ based on their average speeds on different surface and vegetation types in CS1. However, for accurate calculations, these values must be experimentally validated in the field. The speed values in the model can also be adjusted based on factors such as soldiers' physical condition, driver experience, load weight, a vehicle's technical condition, and tactical movement requirements [26].

The "global" movement route calculated by MCS CZ TDSS is exported into a text file containing a set of coordinate waypoints that the vehicle must traverse to reach its destination. This text file can then be uploaded into the computing unit of the UGS Taros Furbo, which executes the predefined route in the field.

The "local" navigation of the UGS in the terrain is managed by LIDAR, which scans the vehicle's surroundings. Based on LIDAR outputs, the UGS computing unit generates a raster-based traversability map, see Fig. 2, which accounts for the mobility parameters of the vehicle's chassis. For identified obstacles, the computing unit creates alternative routes within the LIDAR's spatial range to bypass them. Once the obstacles are cleared, the UGS resumes movement along the "global" route toward its destination.

LIDAR is an active system, meaning it generates its own energy – light – to measure distances to objects on the ground. In LIDAR, light is emitted in the form of a rapidly pulsing laser. The light energy reflects off surfaces such as the ground, vegetation, tree branches, buildings, and other objects, returning to the LIDAR sensor, where the time of return is recorded. The precise spatial positioning of the reflected points is determined by LIDAR using GPS [31]. By utilizing these points, the UGS computing unit constructs a traversability map of the surrounding environment.

4 The Case Studies

To test the autonomous movement capabilities of UGS in the terrain and compare the calculations of "global" and "local" navigation, three case studies were conducted, each differing primarily in terms of surface characteristics and vegetation.

Case Study 1 focuses on the use of MCS CZ TDSS for the manoeuvre route planning of a group of three UGS Taros Furbo, which, in this study, are positioned in a built-up area on the right side of Fig. 1. The commander-operator received a mission to conduct reconnaissance in the area northwest of their current position, moving through the farmstead in the upper left of Fig. 1 and continuing northwest along the forest edge. The MCS CZ TDSS was used for route planning. Aerial reconnaissance assets identified an enemy terrain vehicle at the forest edge, approximately 150 m south of the farmstead. The vehicle reconnaissance speed for unpaved roads, fields, and pastures was set to 7 km.h^{-1}. For other terrain types, the speed was reduced to exclude them from tactical calculations. The spatial and temporal characteristics of the reconnaissance routes, along with their execution in the field, are presented in Table 1.

Table 1 Characteristics of UGS Taros Furbo manoeuvres during reconnaissance

UGS position	C-UGS manoeuvre	Direct distance (metres)	Manoeuvre distance (metres)	Calculated manoeuvre time (minutes)	Actual time in terrain (minutes)
centre	Frontal attack	887	1,045	7:40	7:44
north	Frontal attack	869	1,073	7:32	7:38
south	Frontal attack	907	1,034	7:56	7:57

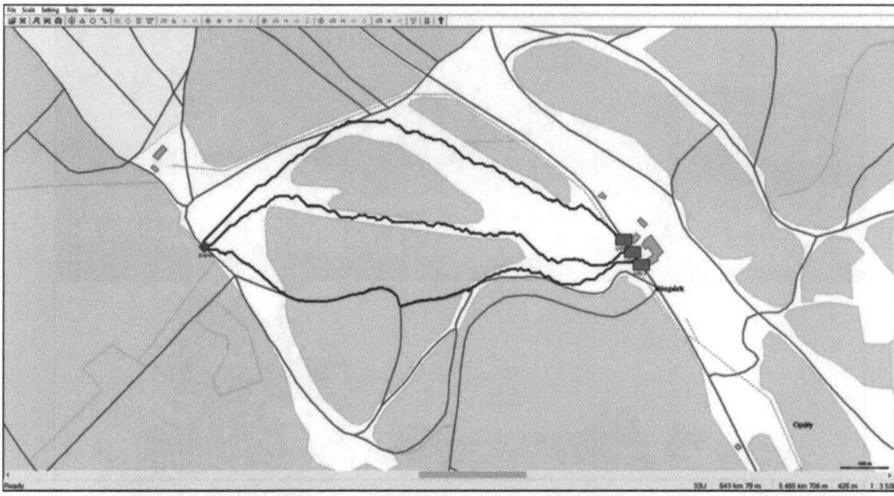

Fig. 1 Survey routes of the UGS Taros Furbo [source: own, TDSS]

The so-called "global" manoeuvre route calculated by MCS CZ TDSS was uploaded into the UGS computing unit, which, in cooperation with the vehicle's GPS receiver and control unit, manages the vehicle's chassis operation. In the upper right of Fig. 2, an example of the scanning of the traversability of the surrounding area by the UGS LIDAR is shown. In the same Figure, at the bottom, the processing of LIDAR outputs into a "local" traversability map by the UGS computing unit is illustrated, where the green coloured squares represent traversable areas in a raster format. Using the traversable space, the UGS control unit transmits commands to the drive and control mechanisms of individual wheels to navigate between obstacles in the surrounding terrain toward the destination. However, the enemy vehicle was not found in the reported area!

In **Case Study 2**, after failing to locate the enemy vehicle, the commander-operator decided to continue reconnaissance along the edge of the forest toward the northwest. Approximately 200 m northwest of the farm building, in the meadow area with self-seeded trees, see Fig. 3, the UGS was attacked by fire from the targeted enemy vehicle. Offensive manoeuvres – frontal attack, envelopment, turning movement, and fire attack – enable commanders to shape the planned approach of their units toward the enemy through their distinct spatial execution. This allows them to select the most suitable course of action considering the terrain and time constraints. The frontal attack in MCS CZ TDSS is implemented through the Optimal Manoeuvre Route Model and represents the fastest approach route to the target. The envelopment is defined as an approach to the target from a lateral direction and, in MCS CZ, is delineated by an invisible circular impassable area between the UGS and the enemy vehicle. During the execution of the turning movement, the UGS approaches the enemy from the opposite side of its initial position, while the MCS CZ is delineated by an invisible impassable area in the shape of a heart, with the target enemy positioned at the centre between its two upper arcs.

Fig. 2 Local navigation of UGS Taros Furbo [32]

The commander-operator of the UGS, using MCS CZ, calculated the offensive manoeuvre routes against the enemy, with their distance and time characteristics presented in Table 2. The reaction speeds to enemy attacks were uniformly set to 10 km.h^{-1}. The routes of the frontal attack, envelopment, and turning movement are shown in Fig. 4. The enemy vehicle would have been destroyed by fire from the weapon stations on the UGS Taros Furbo, however, this is beyond the scope of this article.

The attacked UGS Taros Furbo could engage the enemy vehicle with fire almost immediately. The offensive manoeuvre routes calculated by MCS CZ provided the group with tactical breadth, enabling engagement with the enemy from multiple directions.

Case Study 3 focuses on the issue of traversability of forested terrain by military vehicles. From the perspective of so-called "global" navigation, this is not a complex process, provided that the spacing between trees and shrubs in the forested terrain allows

Fig. 3 Movement of UGS Taros Furbo along the manoeuvre route in the terrain

Table 2 Characteristics of UGS Taros Furbo manoeuvres during attack

UGS position	C-UGS manoeuvre	Direct distance (metres)	Manoeuvre distance (metres)	Calculated manoeuvre time (minutes)	Actual time in terrain (minutes)
centre	Frontal attack	189	189	0:50	0:57
north	Flanking manoeuvre	188	295	1:31	1:44
south	Bypass	202	429	2:18	2:32

the vehicles to pass through. The spacing between trees and shrubs must therefore at least allow for the safe and smooth passage of the vehicle, as well as the vehicle's minimum turning radius for manoeuvring between trees and shrubs. It was experimentally measured that the forest must be mature and maintained, with obstacle spacing of at least twice the vehicle's width in the transverse direction and one and a half times the vehicle's length in the driving direction for the UGS Taros Furbo, see Fig. 5. However, data on obstacle spacing can only be obtained through ground reconnaissance of the specific operational area. For the calculation of the manoeuvre route, it is then only necessary to measure the average speed of the vehicle through forested vegetation in flat terrain.

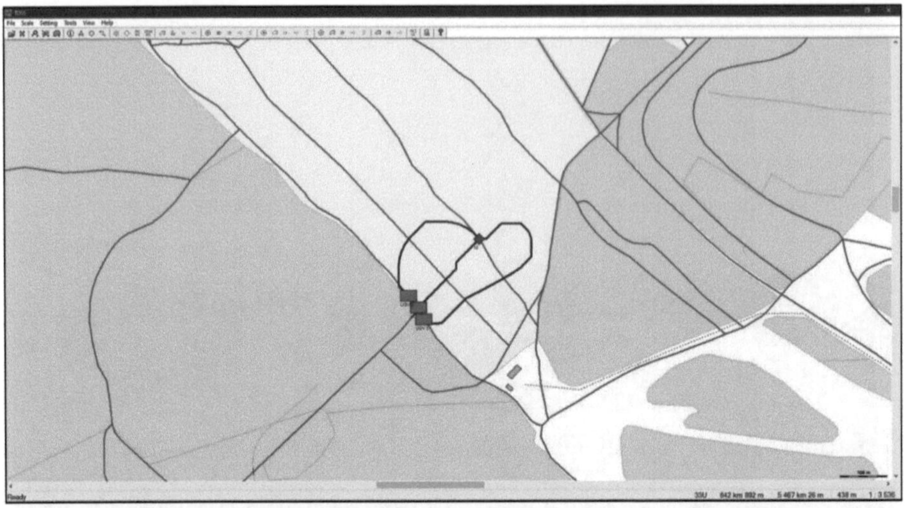

Fig. 4 Offensive manoeuvre routes of UGS Taros Furbo in TDSS

Fig. 5 Passable forested terrain along the manoeuvre route of UGS Taros Furbo

However, "local" navigation is much more complex, as the UGS Taros Furbo must execute it along the calculated "global" route while accounting for the current presence of obstacles. For this purpose, it utilizes two LIDARs – one at the front and another mounted on a superstructure in the middle of the vehicle bed – which continuously scan the vehicle's immediate surroundings. The computing unit of the UGS Taros Furbo then searches for a traversable path between obstacles in the direction of the "global" manoeuvre route calculated by MCS CZ. The task of the UGS was to traverse a section of the forest in a northeasterly direction and identify enemy activity in the open area beyond its edge. The "global" manoeuvre route, calculated by MCS CZ, is shown in Fig. 6.

The direct distance between the manoeuvre initiation point and the edge of the forest is 211 m. The movement speed for this forested area, as well as for other types of terrain – excluding water surfaces and built-up areas – was set to 3 $km.h^{-1}$. The length of the route calculated by MCS CZ in the terrain is 216 m, with a required time of 3:33 min to traverse it. However, the actual time required to traverse the forest was more than twice as long, due to the constant search for passable corridors between trees along the calculated manoeuvre route.

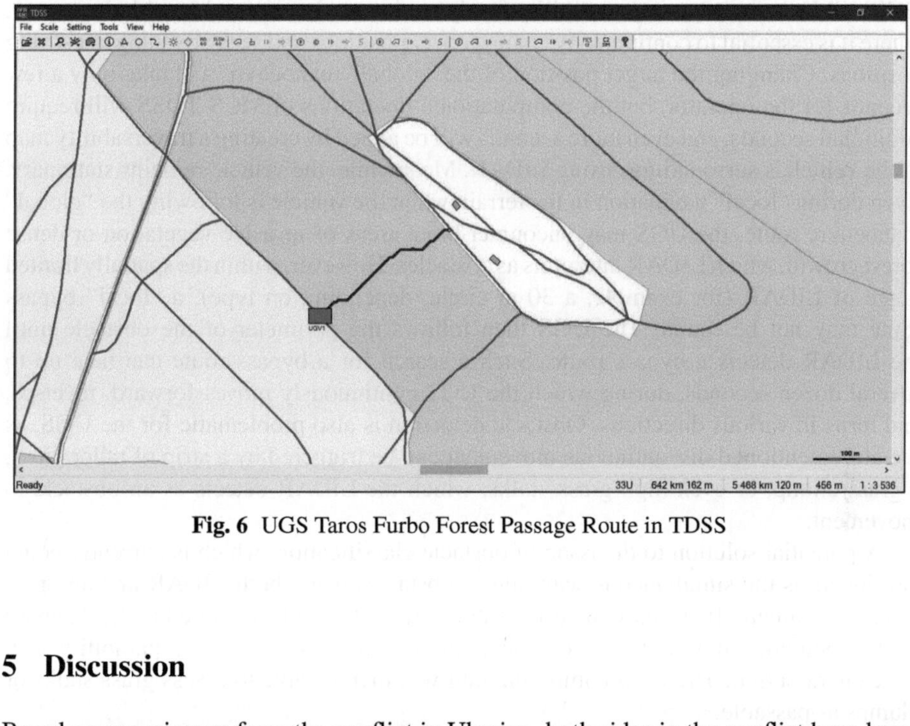

Fig. 6 UGS Taros Furbo Forest Passage Route in TDSS

5 Discussion

Based on experiences from the conflict in Ukraine, both sides in the conflict have been actively striving to utilize UGS to support combat operations. However, their control is mostly carried out using satellite navigation, image outputs from onboard electro-optical sensors, radio communication, and remote vehicle operation by an operator. This form of control is simple, with a range of several hundred metres, depending on the power of the radio stations and the complexity of the terrain. In the case of using radio signal relay via a UAS, another vehicle, or the radio station of another unit, the range can be extended up to several kilometres. The biggest challenge in the radio control of UGS is electromagnetic interference to communication with the operator and the reception of satellite navigation signals. In this case, robotic systems execute the tasks they have been programmed to execute. UAS will typically descend to the ground. The UGS will only come to a stop if they do not have an inertial navigation system that can be used for returning along the same route to the starting area. This could be a viable solution in flat terrain without tall vegetation. Problems with satellite navigation or the use of an inertial navigation unit arise primarily when precise "local" navigation is required, for example, between terrain obstacles and tall trees, as is also discussed in [33–35].

A potential solution could be autonomous UGS control, largely independent of operator interventions. MCS CZ TDSS calculates the "global" manoeuvre route to the target based on the current battlefield situation, while the UGS computing unit, together with GPS or an inertial navigation unit and outputs from the LIDAR, guides the vehicle through the terrain to the target. Although this does not guarantee the completion of the assigned task, it at least provides a realistic chance for the recovery of the UGS.

However, even with the use of the aforementioned autonomous navigation elements, UGS still lack the necessary capability for dynamic reaction in combat with the enemy, where it is essential to continuously change cover positions and seek advantageous firing positions. Changing the target position of the "global" manoeuvre will take only a few seconds for the operator, but the computational operations of MCS TDSS will require additional seconds, and even more seconds will be added by creating a traversability map of the vehicle's surroundings using LIDAR. Meanwhile, the vehicle remains stationary. Even during "local" navigation in the terrain when the vehicle is following the "global" manoeuvre route, the UGS may encounter large areas of invasive vegetation or dense forest growth, which LIDAR interprets as obstacles. However, within the spatially limited range of LIDAR (for example, a 30-m circle, depending on type), a "local" bypass route may not be found. The UGS then follows the perimeter of the obstacle until the LIDAR detects a bypass route. Such a search for a bypass route can take up to several dozen seconds, during which the UGS continuously moves forward, reverses, and turns in various directions. Obstacle detection is also problematic for the UGS, as the aforementioned discontinuous movement can be triggered by a strip of taller grass, a grass clump, or even high grass stalks, which the LIDAR detects as an obstacle to movement.

A potential solution to the issue of obstacle classification, which is currently being developed, is the simultaneous scanning of obstacles using both LIDAR and an opto-electronic camera. In the case of "traversable" grass, it must be recorded in the database of the computing unit under various daylight conditions to ensure comparability with the camera output. The UGS computing unit will then be able to assess grass stalks or clumps as passable.

6 Conclusion

The results of the conducted case studies indicate that MCS CZ models are applicable both in the planning of offensive manoeuvre routes and in reconnaissance operations. From the perspective of validation verification, the applicability of the shortest path search algorithm in the creation of the UGS manoeuvre route has been confirmed. The calculated results, however, will always only be as accurate as the current and precise tactical-geographical digital data of the operational area on which MCS CZ TDSS bases its evaluation of overall terrain traversability. The verification of the calculated manoeuvres of the UGS Taros Furbo during their actual execution in the field identified temporal inaccuracies, primarily caused by the challenging implementation of "local" navigation in areas with a high density of obstacles. Another issue limiting the effective combat use of UGS is their inability to dynamically manoeuvre across the battlefield toward enemy positions. The optimization of taking cover behind obstacles in response to enemy activity, along with the search for advantageous firing positions for the enemy's destruction – while simultaneously ensuring protection against radio communication interference – represents a significant challenge and a necessary prerequisite for the further realistic development of combat UGS.

In the case of flat terrain without dense vegetation, it is possible to consider the use of individual types of offensive manoeuvres and their combinations with UGS featuring enhanced ballistic protection to achieve maximum surprise and destructive effect. The activities of multiple manoeuvre and fire elements can be coordinated simultaneously by a single operator-commander, based on knowledge of the sequence and duration of individual precomputed manoeuvres. This may include, for example, reconnaissance of the area and the operation of autonomous weapon systems for fire support, see [36]. The deployment of combat UGS can also be considered for monitoring gaps in the formation beyond the direct line of sight of one's own units in already surveyed areas, in the second echelon of one's own forces, or in the rear area, among other scenarios.

However, a larger deployment of combat UGS for executing high-risk and time-intensive tasks can also be expected in future military operations, see [37]. To ensure the successful use of these systems, it will be necessary to always upload current and accurate geographical data into decision-support information systems for manoeuvre planning. The accuracy of MCS CZ TDSS calculations would be significantly improved by laser scanning the entire operational area using a UAS immediately before the commencement of the military operation. On this basis, a current digital terrain model would then be created and the digital area model updated. The manoeuvre routes calculated using updated digital models would then reflect the current terrain traversability conditions of the operational area. Another necessity will be continuous secure communication between the operator-commander and all UGS units in the group on the battlefield, as well as their long-term sustainability in the operation. Given the insights from the conflict in Ukraine, it is also necessary to take into account the changing operational environment. An unconventional or irregular conflict influenced by asymmetric threats, such as those that have taken place in Afghanistan or Mali, allowed for the effective and nearly unrestricted use of modern technologies. In the case of a conflict between two regular armies equipped with advanced technologies, complications in the use of radio communication can be expected on the battlefield due to intense jamming by electronic warfare systems. Thus, continuous use of radio communication and satellite navigation signals cannot be reliably assumed.

From the perspective of the strategic outlook for the deployment of UGS in military operations and their implementation into doctrinal use in the formation of friendly units, the persistent technological limitations of their operation are a key factor. While operator-controlled UGS can perform support tasks on the front line, the use of USG with higher autonomous control can currently only be considered in secure rear areas, for example for supply purposes. Combat contact with the enemy is difficult to deal with even for controlled UGS, and if the vehicle is not covered by infantry or quickly withdrawn to a safe area, it will most likely be destroyed. However, autonomous vehicles are currently unable to respond to the enemy's variable actions at all, let alone conduct any offensive action and search for targets.

References

1. Saballa, J.: Israel Deploys Semi-Autonomous Machine Gun Robot to Gaza Border. The Defense Post (2021). https://thedefensepost.com/2021/07/01/israel-machine-gun-robot-gaza-border/
2. Roblin, S.: What Happened when Russia Tested its Uran-9 Robot Tank in Syria? The National Interest. Center for the National Interest, Washington, DC, USA (2021) https://nationalinterest.org/blog/reboot/what-happened-when-russia-tested-its-uran-9-robot-tank-syria-182143
3. Uran-6 Mine-Clearing Robot. Army Technology. Verdict Media Limited, London, United Kingdom (2016). https://www.army-technology.com/projects/uranium-6-mine-clearing-robot/?cf-view
4. Türke, A.I.: Russian Robot Technology in Syria. CERPESC. Europa Varie-tas Institute, Switzerland (2016). https://europavarietas.org/csdp_new/index.php/2016/02/15/russian-robot-technology-in-syria/
5. Thomas, T.: Russian Lessons Learned in Syria: an Assessment, pp. 1–27. MITRE Corporation, McLean, Virginie, USA (2020) Case Number #19-3483
6. Uppal, R.: Russia Deployed Family of Killer Robots, for Combat and Demining in Syria and for Counter Terrorism Operations. IDST International defense, Security & Technology, San Jose, USA (2019) https://idstch.com/military/army/russia-developing-family-of-killer-robots-conduct-war-games/
7. Roblin, S.: War of the Robots: The Battle for Avdiivka. In: Inside Un-manned Systems (2024). https://insideunmannedsystems.com/war-of-the-robots-the-battle-for-avdiivka/
8. RPG-FPV – Rocket Launcher Drones in Ukraine. The Armourer's Bench (2024). https://armourersbench.com/2024/09/21/rpg-fpv-rocket-launcher-drones-in-ukraine/
9. Zahradníček, P., Botík, M.: Technologies in the Ukrainian Conflict: reflection and perspectives from viewpoint of combat Unit's utilization. In: Bekesiene, S. (ed.) Challenges to National Defence in Contemporary Geopolitical Situation, pp. 351–356. ISSN 2669-2023. General Jonas Zemaitis Military Academy of Lithuania (2024). https://doi.org/10.3849/cndcgs.2024.351
10. Kompan, J., Hrnčiar, M.: Challenges for enhanced military mobility on the eastern flank of NATO. In: Lecture Notes in Intelligent Transportation and Infrastructure, Part F2296, pp. 239–248 (2024). https://doi.org/10.1007/978-3-031-52652-7_24
11. Wang, X., Pan, H., Guo, K., Yang, X., Luo, S.: The evolution of LiDAR and its application in high precision measurement. IOP Conf. Ser. Earth Environ. Sci. 502, 012008. (2020). doi:https://doi.org/10.1088/1755-1315/502/1/012008. Beijing, China
12. Rybansky, M., Rada, J., Dohnal, F.: The impact of the accuracy of terrain surface data on the navigation of off-road vehicles. ISPRS Int. J. Geo Inf., 10(3), 106 (2021). doi:https://doi.org/10.3390/ijgi10030106. ISSN 2220-9964

13. Rybansky, M., Brenova, M., Cermak, J., Van Genderen, J., Sivertun, A.: Vegetation structure determination using LIDAR data and the forest growth parameters. In: 8th IGRSM International Conference and Exhibition on Geospatial and Remote Sensing, IGRSM 2016. Kuala Lumpur, Malaysia: IOP publishing LTD (2016). doi:https://doi.org/10.1088/1755-1315/37/1/012031. Dirac House, Temple Back, Bristol BS1 6BE, England, ISSN 1755–1307.
14. Rada, J., Rybansky, M., Dohnal, F.: Influence of quality of remote sensing data on vegetation Passability by terrain vehicles. ISPRS Int. J. Geo Inf., 9(11), 684 (2020). doi:https://doi.org/10.3390/ijgi9110684. ISSN 2220-9964
15. Durst, P., Gray, W., Trentini, M.: A non-contextual model for evaluating the autonomy level of intelligent unmanned ground vehicles. In: 2024 NDIA Michigan Chapter Ground Vehicle Systems Engineering and Technology Symposium, Michigan USA (2024). https://doi.org/10.4271/2024-01-3267
16. Cole, M., Crean, C., Gorsich, D., Jayakumar, P., Jain, A., Ersal, T.: Evaluating mobility performance of unmanned ground vehicles. In: 2024 NDIA Michigan Chapter Ground Vehicle Systems Engineering and Technology Symposium, Michigan USA (2024). https://doi.org/10.4271/2024-01-3730
17. Maaiveld, T., Domela, D., de Reus, N., Schadd, M., Kuijper, F.: Where to go and how to get there: tactical terrain analysis for military unmanned ground-vehicle mission planning. In: Conference: MESAS 2023 (2024). https://doi.org/10.1007/978-3-031-71397-2_7
18. Durst, P., Goodin, C., Song, P., Du, T.: Route planning for autonomous unmanned ground vehicle operations in urban environments. In: 2024 NDIA Michigan Chapter Ground Vehicle Systems Engineering and Technology Symposium (2024). https://doi.org/10.4271/2024-01-3435
19. Yusefi, A., Durdu, A., Toy, I.: Camera/LiDAR sensor fusion-based autonomous navigation. In: 2024 23rd International Symposium Infoteh-Jahorina (INFOTEH), pp. 1–6, East Sarajevo, Bosnia and Herzegovina (2024). https://doi.org/10.1109/INFOTEH60418.2024.10495974
20. Gadekar, A., Fulsundar, S., Deshmukh, P., Aher, J., Kataria, K., et al.: Rakshak: a modular unmanned ground vehicle for surveillance and logistics operations. Cogn. Robot. (3), 23–33 (2023). https://doi.org/10.1016/j.cogr.2023.02.001. ISSN 2667-2413
21. Brand, H., Li, B.: Semantic digital surface map towards collaborative off-road vehicle autonomy. In: 2024 NDIA Michigan Chapter Ground Vehicle Systems Engineering and Technology Symposium, Michigan USA (2024). https://doi.org/10.4271/2024-01-3877
22. Časar, J., Starý, V., Hanuš, V.: Evaluation methodology for counter unmanned aerial system detectors. In: 2023 9th International Conference on Military Technologies, ICMT 2023 - Proceedings, p. 9. Institute of Electrical and Electronics Engineers Inc., Brno (2023). https://doi.org/10.1109/ICMT58149.2023.10171326. ISBN 979-8-3503-2568-3.
23. Kratky, M., Minarik, V., Sustr, M., Ivan, J.: Electronic warfare methods combatting UAVs. Adv. Sci. Technol. Eng. Syst. J. **5**(6), 447–454 (2020). https://doi.org/10.25046/aj050653
24. Plátěnka, V., Vršecká, M., Novotný, J.: Analysis of UAV control signals. In: Barath J., Dedera L., Ockay M. 2021 Communication and Information Technologies Conference Proceedings, KIT 2021 - 11th International Scientific Conference. Liptovský Mikuláš, Slovakia: Institute of Electrical and Electronics Engineers Inc., pp. 52–56 (2021). doi:https://doi.org/10.1109/KIT52904.2021.9583746. ISBN 978–1–6654-2881-1
25. Nohel, J., Flasar, Z.: Manoeuvre Control System CZ. In: Modelling and Simulation for Autonomous Systems MESAS 2019. Switzerland, Cham: Springer International Publishing AG, 11995, pp. 379–388. (2020). doi:https://doi.org/10.1007/978-3-030-43890-6_31. ISSN 0302–9743. ISBN 978–3–030-43890-6
26. Nohel, J., Stodola, P., Zezula, J., Zahradníček, P., Flasar, Z.: Area reconnaissance modelling of modular reconnaissance robotic systems. J. Defense Model. Simul. Appl. Methodol. Technol. (2023). doi:https://doi.org/10.1177/15485129231210302. ISSN 1548-5129. IF 0,800

27. Nohel, J.: Possibilities of raster mathematical algorithmic models utilization as an information support of military decision making process. In: Modelling and Simulation for Autonomous Systems MESAS 2018. Cham, Switzerland: Springer International Publishing AG, pp. 553–565 (2019). doi:10.1007/978-3-030-14984-0_41/. ISSN 0302–9743. ISBN 978–3–030-14984-0
28. Pradhan, A., Kumar, M.G.: Finding all-pairs shortest path for a largescale transportation network using parallel Floyd-Warshall and parallel Dijkstra algorithms. J. Comput. Civ. Eng. **27**(3), 263–273 (2013). https://doi.org/10.1061/(ASCE)CP.1943-5487.0000220
29. Stodola, P., Mazal, J.: Planning algorithm and its modifications for tactical decision support systems. Int. J. Math. Comput. Simul., 6(1), pp. 99–106 (2012). http://www.naun.org/jour-nals/mcs/17- 474.pdf. . ISSN 1998–0159
30. Risald, R., Mirino, A.E., Suyoto, S.: Best Routes Selection Using Dijkstra and Floyd-Warshall Algorithm, pp. 155–158, Indonesia, Surabaya (2017). https://doi.org/10.1109/ICTS.2017.8265662
31. Wasser, A. L.: The Basics of LiDAR - Light Detection and Ranging - Remote Sensing. [online]. 7.2.2025, The U.S. National Science Foundation's National Ecological Observatory Network. (2024). https://www.neonscience.org/resources/learning-hub/tutorials/lidar-basics.
32. The source is LIDAR data processed by the UGV Taros Furbo computing unit, in co-operation with Ing. Jan Bayer from FEL CTU and Ing. Roman Adámek from BUT.
33. Křišťálová, D. et al.: Modelling and simulation of microrelief impact on ground path Extension. In: et al. (eds) Modelling and Simulation for Autonomous Systems (MESAS 2021). Cham: Springer International publishing AG, 13207, pp. 93–112. ISSN 0302–9743 (2022). doi:https://doi.org/10.1007/978-3-030-98260-7_6. ISBN 978-3-030-98259-1
34. Čapek, J., Hubáček, M., Křišťálová, D., Mertová, E.: Effect of tree location accuracy on vegetation passability analysis. In: 2023 International Conference on Military Technologies (ICMT). Brno: Institute of Electrical and Electronics Engineers Inc. (2023). doi:https://doi.org/10.1109/ICMT58149.2023.10171323. ISBN 979–8–3503-2569-0
35. Křišťálová, D., Čapek, J., Adámek, R., Nohel, J.: Practical applicability of tree spacing Passability analysis on vehicle path planning. In: Modelling and Simulation for Autonomous Systems (MESAS 2023). Cham: Springer Cham, pp. 68–91 (2024). doi:https://doi.org/10.1007/978-3-031-71397-2_6. ISSN 0302–9743. ISBN 978–3–031-71397-2, 14615
36. Ivan, J., Potužák, L., Šotnar, J.: Artillery reconnaissance to ensure the operation of autonomous weapon systems and basic requirements for reconnaissance units. Vojenské rozhledy, 4, pp. 63–77 (2019). doi:https://doi.org/10.3849/2336-2995.28.2019.04.063-077. ISSN 1210–3292
37. Mazal, J., et al.: Tactical behavior optimization for a UGV teams. In: Bruzzone A.G. (ed) Proceedings of the International Defense and Homeland Security Simulation Workshop, DHSS. Genoa, Italy: Cal-Tek srl, pp. 14 (2024). doi:https://doi.org/10.46354/i3m.2024.dhss.009. ISSN 2724–0363. ISBN 9791281988057

Modelling and Simulation of Scatterable Minefield Effectiveness Compared to UAV-Based Low-Discrepancy Quasi-Random Distribution

Michal Bilina(✉), Kamila Hasilová, Lenka Balusová, and Radek Procházka

University of Defence, Kounicova 65, 66210 Brno, Czech Republic
{michal.bilina,kamila.hasilova,lenka.balusova,
radek.prochazka2}@unob.cz

Abstract. This paper compares two distinct approaches to minefield establishment and evaluates their operational effectiveness using numerical modelling and simulation analysis. The first method examines the standard scatterable technique, which employs a mine launcher—commonly used by engineering and mechanized units. While this approach enables rapid field coverage, it typically results in less spatial uniformity. The second method utilizes Unmanned Aerial Vehicles (UAVs) to establish minefields based on low-discrepancy quasi-random sequences, such as Halton or Hammersley sequences. These mathematical distributions support more accurate and evenly spaced mine placement, thereby increasing the tactical effectiveness of the minefield. To analyse both approaches, a custom simulation platform was developed in MATLAB, enabling the testing of various establishment scenarios, including interactions with moving targets such as armoured vehicles. Key performance indicators include spatial coverage, hit probability, redundancy (overlap), and pattern predictability. The simulation results indicate that UAV-based establishments using quasi-random algorithms achieve higher coverage efficiency, lower predictability, and greater tactical value. This approach also provides enhanced precision and flexibility, which is particularly advantageous in modern combat operations that demand adaptability and resource optimization. In conclusion, integrating autonomous systems with algorithm-driven establishment strategies presents a promising and scalable alternative to traditional minefield methods, significantly improving the effectiveness of combat engineering support in both current and future operational environments.

Keywords: Combat effectiveness · Spatial uniformity · UAV minelaying

1 Introduction

In the Czech Army, the establishment of minefields is a specialized task assigned to engineer units. Within NATO forces, however, this role can also be performed by non-engineer units, such as artillery or mechanized units. Minefields are generally categorized as either scatterable or standard-pattern [1], each requiring specific deployment systems [2].

J. Novotný et al. (Eds.): MESAS 2025, LNCS 16627, pp. 253–268, 2027.
https://doi.org/10.1007/978-3-032-33182-3_15

Scatterable minefields are characterized by the random distribution of mines. They are typically established using artillery munitions, mine launchers, air- or ground-based scatter systems, cluster munitions, or dispensers [3]. Examples include the Volcano system, GATOR, Baobab-K, MV-3, ISDM Zemledeliye, and others. These systems share a key advantage: they operate remotely, so no personnel need to enter the minefield area [2].

While scatterable systems offer tactical benefits for both offense and defence, they also have drawbacks—particularly high munition consumption. Since mines are dispersed randomly, coverage is uneven, often resulting in clusters and gaps [2]. To increase effectiveness, more munitions are used, but due to the law of diminishing returns, additional mines eventually fail to significantly enhance battlefield effect. The effectiveness of such minefields follows an exponential curve.

Experience from the ongoing war in Ukraine has shown that traditional minelaying methods—such as artillery or ground-based systems—have limitations, especially in terms of accuracy and high ammunition consumption [4]. In response, both sides have increasingly used UAVs for precise, individual mines placement. This approach reduces risk to personnel and allows for flexible, repeatable minelaying in dynamic environments [5]. To fully leverage UAV capabilities, new layout patterns and algorithms must be developed, efficient, evenly distributed, and unpredictable to the enemy [6]. Quasi-random sequences offer a promising solution, enabling high effectiveness with fewer mines and better control over mine distribution [7].

Within the Czech Armed Forces, scatterable minefields are established using the MV-3 mine launcher. The MV-3 (Fig. 1) is a short-range remote minelaying system mounted on a medium truck. It can also be dismounted and used in a stationary role [3]. It deploys mines at ranges from 500 m up to 3000 m, in 500-m increments, which is a suitable distance for establishing an anti-tank barrier [8]. The launcher consists of three rocket tubes, which can be fanned out to an 8° spread, adjusted based on desired range. It fires KS/PT-Mi rockets (*Container-type anti-tank rockets*), each carrying four full-width PT Mi-D1 anti-tank mines.

Fig. 1. MV-3 Mine Launcher [9]

2 Minefield Model

To assess the combat effectiveness of minefields established using the MV-3 mine launcher in comparison with those created by UAVs following quasi-random low-discrepancy distributions, a valid and representative model of a scatterable minefield is required.

Since conducting live-fire field experiments is logistically demanding, this study is based on previously performed but unpublished internal experiments, carried out for the needs of military units and research institutions. While theoretical models describing the general shape of MV-3 minefields exist within the Czech Armed Forces, they have not been previously validated or fitted to empirical data.

To estimate the parameters of a typical MV-3 minefield, two original records of minelaying tests were used. These records were created during capability evaluations of the MV-3 mine launcher. Although dated, they remain valid and accurate. The records were made on A2-sized millimetre paper, marking the positions and quantities of all detected mines. The data were digitized and prepared for simulation. It is assumed that the mine distribution follows a normal distribution (Fig. 2).

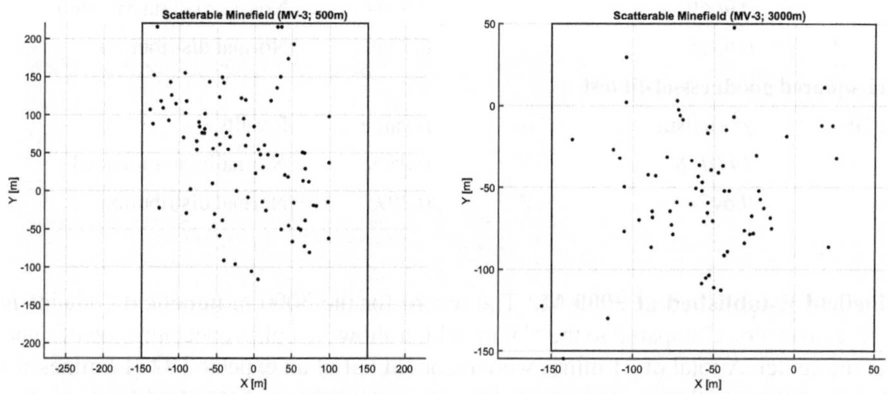

Real minefield established at 500 meters   Real minefield established at 3000 meters

Fig. 2. Mine distribution scheme in the recorded minefields

Minefield Established at 500 M. The original record contains some anomalies—possibly caused by a lack of space on the recording sheet. Some mines appear unnaturally aligned in a row, though no detailed annotations were available to clarify this. The mines were distributed around the intended aim point. The effective length and depth of the minefield were estimated at 300 m and 450 m, respectively, and this area was retained for simulation purposes to ensure comparable conditions.

The recorded number of mines was 91, while the expected number was 96 (12 mines per salvo, 8 salvos). Simulations assume the full 96 mines.

Distribution parameters are listed in Table 1, with results of one-dimensional statistical tests in Table 2.

Table 1. Minefield distribution parameters; 500 m

Mean value:	$\mu = \begin{bmatrix} -16.62 \\ 49.06 \end{bmatrix}$
Covariance matrix:	$\Sigma = \begin{bmatrix} 4351.7 & -1824.6 \\ -1824.6 & 6123.1 \end{bmatrix}$
Standard deviations:	$\sigma_x \approx 65.97; \sigma_y \approx 78.25$
Correlation coefficient:	$\rho = \frac{-1824.6}{65.97 \bullet 78.25} \approx -0.3534$

Table 2. Results of one-dimensional tests 500 m

Shapiro–Wilk test				
Variable	Test statistic *W*		*p*-value	Result
X	*0.9669*		*0.0204*	Non-normal distribution
Y	*0.9845*		*0.3569*	Normal distribution
Chi-squared goodness-of-fit test				
Variable	χ^2 statistic	df	*p*-value	Results
X	*14.0168*	*7*	*0.0509*	Normality not rejected
Y	*9.6471*	*7*	*0.2095*	Normal distribution

Minefield Established at 3000 M. The record for the 3000 m minefield contains no significant errors. Compared to the 500 m field, it shows a higher concentration of mines near the center. A total of 71 mines were recorded out of an expected 72 (12 mines × 6 salvos), suggesting that one mine may have been missed or unaccounted for.

The minefield was slightly offset to the left and downward from the intended aim point due to weather conditions. Its dimensions were set at 200 × 200 m, although a few mines fell outside this area. For simulation purposes, 72 mines are assumed. See distribution parameters in Table 3. Results of one-dimensional statistical tests are provided in Table 4.

For variable *X*, the results of the two normality tests were contradictory. The Shapiro–Wilk test ($p = 0.2483$) did not reject normality, while the χ^2 goodness-of-fit test ($p = 0.0046$) indicated a deviation from the normal distribution. Given the sensitivity of the Shapiro–Wilk test for small to medium sample sizes, the assumption of normality for *X* may still be considered reasonable, although caution is advised.

Table 3. Minefield distribution parameters; 3000 m

Mean Value:	$\mu = \begin{bmatrix} -58.26 \\ -53.93 \end{bmatrix}$
Covariance matrix:	$\Sigma = \begin{bmatrix} 1513.99 & 360.85 \\ 360.85 & 1518.95 \end{bmatrix}$
Standard deviations:	$\sigma_x \approx 38.91; \sigma_y \approx 38.97$
Correlation coefficient:	$\rho = \frac{360.85}{38.91 \bullet 38.97} \approx 0.238$

Table 4. Results of one-dimensional tests; 3000 m

Shapiro–Wilk test				
Variable	Test statistic *W*		*p*-value	Result
X	*0.9794*		*0.2483*	Normal distribution
Y	*0.9922*		*0.8849*	Normal distribution
Chi-squared goodness-of-fit test				
Variable	χ^2 statistic	df	*p*-value	Result
X	*16.9651*	*5*	*0.0046*	Non-normal distribution
Y	*3.4412*	*5*	*0.6323*	Normal distribution

2.1 Validation of the Model in MATLAB

The model operates using estimated parameters derived from the real minefields. These parameters — summarized in Tables 1 and 3 — define the statistical characteristics of the spatial distribution and serve as the input for the simulation.

Both tables include the mean values, covariance matrix, standard deviations, and correlation coefficient, which together describe the overall shape, spread, and orientation of the mine distribution.

- The **mean vector** defines the central position of the distribution, representing the expected location around which mines are concentrated.
- The **covariance matrix** expresses both the degree of spread in each direction and the relationship between the x and y coordinates.
- The **standard deviations** quantify how widely the mines are dispersed along each axis.
- The **correlation coefficient** indicates whether the distribution is rotated or aligned with the coordinate axes.

Based on these parameters, the model generates a synthetic distribution of mines that statistically reproduces the spatial characteristics observed in the real minefields.

To further refine the simulation, the model also considers the physical deployment process. In practice, the actual distribution depends on the crew's operational behavior during minelaying. One important factor is the angular traverse (i.e., horizontal offset) of the outer rocket tubes, which directly influences the overall spread and orientation of the resulting minefield [10].

At 500 m, a total traverse of 8° is typically set, ranging from −4° to +4°, which results in three distinct aim points—one for each rocket tube [10]. Since the rockets disintegrate in mid-air, it is not possible to determine the exact point at which they release their mines. Official documentation provides no detailed specification for this.

Therefore, based on empirical observations, the model assumes that each rocket breaks apart within a 10-m radius of its aim point. With every salvo, new random disintegration points are generated within this area. When multiple salvos are fired, the simulation usually reveals three concentrated mine clusters—each corresponding to one of the rocket tubes. This element of randomness is not directly definable by formula and has been approximated based on repeated simulation results.

In contrast, at a range of 3000 m, the launcher typically operates without any traverse—all three tubes are aligned in parallel. Nevertheless, some sources note that angular adjustment is still technically possible, and the decision to apply it lies with the operator or commander [11]. To ensure a comprehensive validation of the simulation data, both configurations—with and without traverse—will be tested for each distance (500 m and 3000 m).

The models are mostly accurate according to the methodology. The minefield established at 500 m with traverse has a length of approximately 150 m. Without traverse, it should be around 20 m. However, this layout reflects only a single salvo, whereas the Fig. 3 shows 8 and 6 salvos, respectively. This significantly increases the number of mines and thus enlarges the impact area.

The 3000-m minefield with traverse reaches nearly 600 m in length, which matches expectations. Without traverse, its length is approximately 150 m. Since the mine distribution changes with each simulation run, the total field length cannot be precisely defined.

2.2 Modelling and Simulation of Tank Passage through a Minefield

To verify and validate the proposed models, experiments are conducted in MATLAB, where a tank moves through a minefield and combat effectiveness is evaluated—expressed as the probability of triggering a mine.

Simulation Setup: A tank with a width of 3.7 m is randomly placed along the X-axis, and its centerline defines its trajectory. It moves along the Y-axis through the minefield, which is confined to a defined area. The tank's centerline may lie at the edge of the minefield, meaning part of the hull can move outside the minefield. If a mine center falls within the blue-shaded area representing the tank's path, it is considered triggered, and the tank is eliminated [2].

Activated mines are shown in red, inactive ones in black. The experiment ends when the tank crosses the top boundary, and only the first mine hit is counted. Each scenario corresponds to a vehicle passing through the minefield. It is simulated 10.000 times

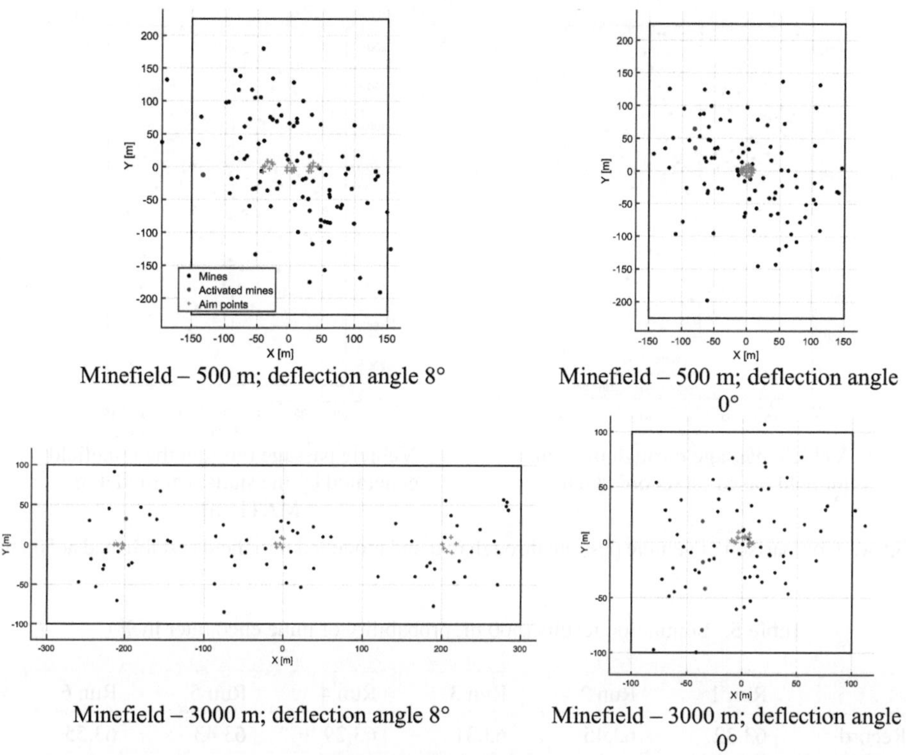

Fig. 3. Visualization of minefields with and without deflection angle (green – aim points; black – non-activated mines; red – mines activated by tank traverse)

and repeated across six identical runs to ensure statistical robustness. The average hit probability, standard deviation, and min/max values are then calculated.

Simulation of a Minefield Established at 500 M. The real mine distribution was compared to the simulated model (Fig. 4). The average combat effectiveness based on the recorded minefield was 63.39%. Due to the fixed layout, the standard deviation between runs was very low (0.006–0.007%).

The simulated model achieved an average effectiveness of 64.69%, differing by only 1.3%, which is considered acceptable. The model is therefore deemed valid and suitable for further simulations. The maximum traverse was used in the model, as it would also be applied in a real layout scenario.

Simulation results are summarized in Table 5.

Simulation of a Minefield Established at 3000 M. When simulating the combat effectiveness of the recorded 3000 m minefield, an average hit probability of 57.62% was reached (Fig. 5). The standard deviation was again very low due to the fixed mine distribution.

The simulated model for the 3000 m minefield achieved an average probability of 60.86%. The difference of 3.24% is higher than in the 500 m case, but still acceptable. The model shows a larger standard deviation, since the mine distribution changes in every

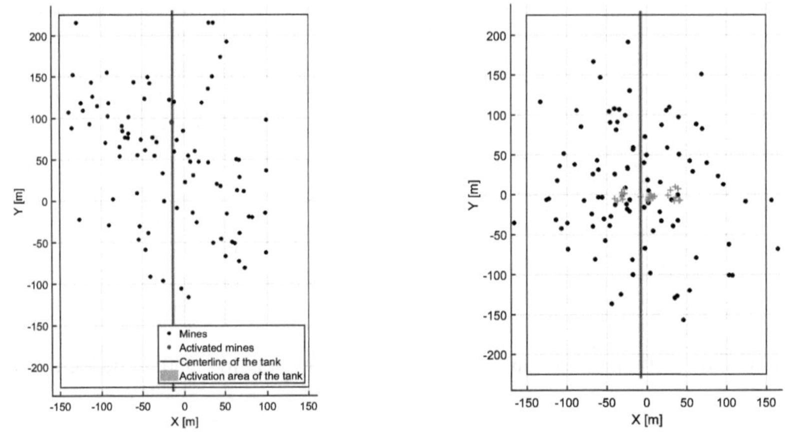

Vehicle passage through the real minefield based on recorded data.

Vehicle passage through the minefield generated by the statistical model in MATLAB.

Fig. 4. Comparison of vehicle passage through real and modelled minefields established at 500 m

Table 5. Simulation results (500 m; probability of mine encounter in %)

	Run 1	Run 2	Run 3	Run 4	Run 5	Run 6
Record	63.32	63.45	63.31	63.29	63.43	63.55
Model	64.20	62.83	65.36	64.10	66.48	65.17

simulation. The gap between the minimum and maximum probability reached nearly 8%, which is expected in scatterable minelaying, where randomness plays a significant role. The model uses an 8° traverse, based on real-world deployment parameters. Thus, the model is considered valid and suitable for further simulations.

Simulation results are presented in Table 6.

2.3 Quasi-Random Sequences

Quasi-random sequences are point sets that may appear random, but are generated based on well-defined, deterministic rules. Each coordinate (i.e., the position of a mine) can be precisely calculated using a deterministic algorithm, which ensures repeatability and simulation accuracy [12]. These methods fall under deterministic point generation techniques [13].

Among the most widely used quasi-random sequences are the Halton, Hammersley, and Sobol sequences, though others like Lloyd's algorithm or optimized variants also exist [14]. Each sequence follows its own logic, resulting in different spatial distributions and computational costs [15]. The common metric for evaluating these methods is discrepancy—a mathematical measure of how uniformly the points fill a given space [16]. Lower discrepancy values indicate a more even distribution and less clustering or gaps

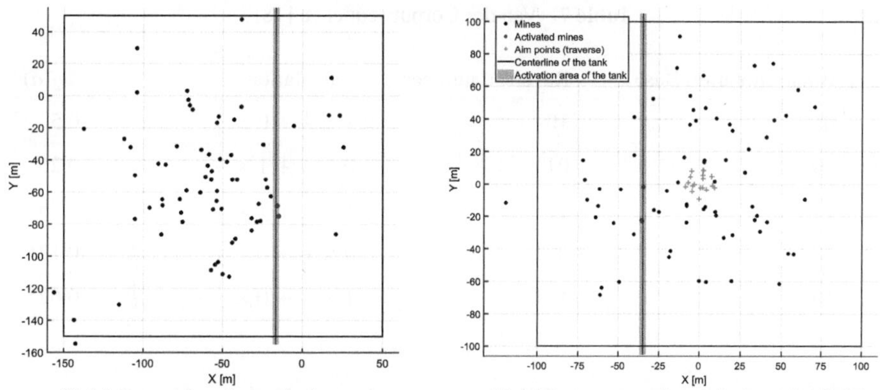

Vehicle passage through the real minefield based on recorded data.

Vehicle passage through the minefield generated by the statistical model in MATLAB.

Fig. 5. Comparison of vehicle passage through real and modelled minefields established at 3000 m

Table 6. Simulation results (3000 m; probability of mine encounter in %)

	Run 1	Run 2	Run 3	Run 4	Run 5	Run 6
Record	57.42	57.70	57.67	57.61	57.56	57.73
Model	61.68	57.13	63.73	63.96	56.25	62.41

[17]. This paper focuses on the Hammersley and Halton sequences, which are used for simulating mine distributions. Figure 6 compares their performance against traditional grid-based layouts and purely random dispersal.

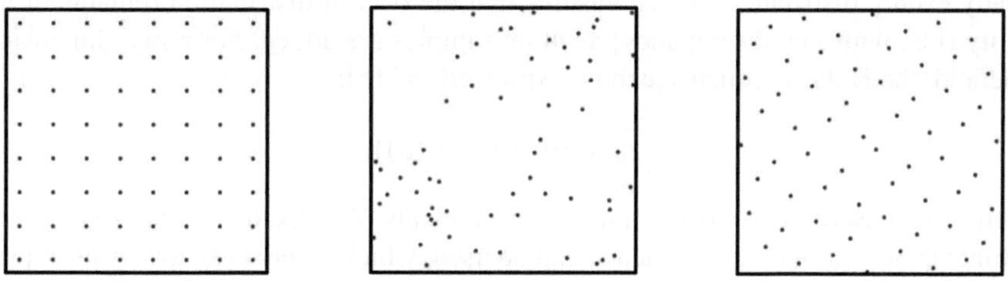

Regular grid　Random distribution　Quasi-random sequence

Fig. 6. Point distribution over an area [15]

The modelling follows the same parameters as those used for minefields established by the MV-3 mine launcher. Both scenarios—at 500 m and 3000 m—are tested. A shared foundation of both point sequences is the Van der Corput sequence (Table 7), a one-dimensional sequence defined using radical inverse functions in base 2, $\Phi_2(a)$.

Table 7. Van der Corput sequence [18]

a	Binary notation Base 2	Reversed number	Calculation	$\Phi_2(a)$
1	01	10	$1 \times \frac{1}{2} + 0 \times \frac{1}{4}$	0.5
2	10	01	$0 \times \frac{1}{2} + 1 \times \frac{1}{4}$	0.25
3	11	11	$1 \times \frac{1}{2} + 1 \times \frac{1}{4}$	0.75
4	100	001	$0 \times \frac{1}{2} + 0 \times \frac{1}{4} + 1 \times \frac{1}{8}$	0.125
5	101	101	$1 \times \frac{1}{2} + 0 \times \frac{1}{4} + 1 \times \frac{1}{8}$	0.625

The Halton sequence uses the Van der Corput sequence in bases 2 and 3 to determine coordinates: base 2 for the x-coordinate and base 3 for the y-coordinate. Base 2 converts digits into binary numeral system, while base 3 converts them into ternary one [18].

The Hammersley sequence uses the Van der Corput sequence only in base 2 to generate the y-coordinates. For the x-coordinates, it simply divides the index of each mine by the total number of elements (mines), meaning the total number of mines in the field must be known in advance [16].

Halton Sequence. The Halton sequence is a vector extension of the Van der Corput sequence into multiple dimensions. To generate points in an n-dimensional Halton sequence, different bases are used for each dimension, with each base serving as the foundation for radical inversion. All bases must be pairwise coprime, making the use of the first n prime numbers $(p_1, p_2, \ldots, p_n)$ a natural choice: [19]

$$\chi_a = \left(\Phi_{p_1}(a), \Phi_{p_2}(a), \Phi_{p_3}(a), \ldots, \Phi_{p_n}(a)\right) \tag{1}$$

One of the main advantages of the Halton sequence is that it can be used even when the total number of required points is not known in advance. The first few points are already evenly distributed, which ensures that the overall distribution remains of high quality (i.e., with low discrepancy) as more samples are added. For a two-dimensional minefield, the Halton sequence can be expressed as [18]:

$$\chi_a = (\Phi_2(a), \Phi_3(a)). \tag{2}$$

Hammersley Sequence. If the number of elements N is fixed (i.e., the total number of mines), the Hammersley sequence can be used, which offers even lower discrepancy compared to other quasi-random sequences. For the index $a \in \{0, 1, \ldots, N-1\}$, where N is the total number of elements (e.g., mines), the Hammersley sequence is defined as follows [19]:

$$\chi_a = \left(\frac{a}{N}, \Phi_{b_1}(a), \Phi_{b_2}(a), \ldots, \Phi_{b_n}(a)\right) \tag{3}$$

where: $\frac{a}{N}$ is the first coordinate from a uniform distribution; $\Phi_{b_i}(a)$ is the radical inverse of the number a in base b_i.

The coordinates are thus a combination of the deterministically evenly spaced value $\frac{a}{N}$ and the radical inverse $\Phi_{b_i}(a)$, which ensures quasi-random distribution in the remaining dimensions. For application in a minefield, which is two-dimensional, the formula must be adapted to a form suitable for two dimensions [16]:

$$\chi_a = \left(\frac{a}{N}, \Phi_2(a)\right). \quad (4)$$

2.4 Modeling and Simulation of Minefields Using Quasi-Random Sequences

Mines are generated using quasi-random sequences, but the dimensions of minefields created by the MV-3 mine launcher are retained to ensure identical input conditions. The simulations are conducted in the same manner.

Simulation of a Minefield Generated Using the Halton Sequence. Minefields are modelled in the same way as those created with the MV-3 mine launcher, either 300 × 450 m or 200 × 200 m (Fig. 7) following established procedures. The 500-m minefield uses a fan angle of 8°, while the 3000-m one assumes 0°. The number of mines corresponds to actual MV-3 deployment: 96 and 72, respectively. Depth is not critical here, as the Y-position of a mine is irrelevant with perpendicular entry. This would only matter if the vehicle entry angle were included, which it is not. The 500-m model achieved an average combat effectiveness of 88.91%, and the 3000-m model reached 99.39%.

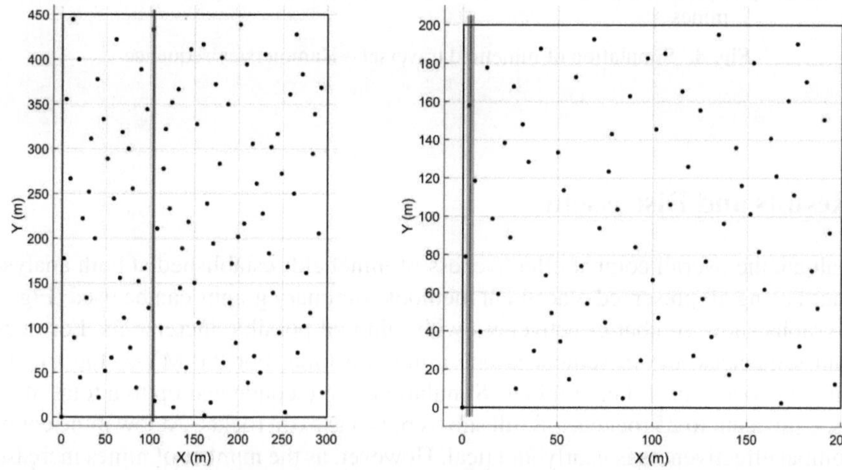

Halton sequence; 500 m – 96 mines Halton sequence; 3000 m – 72 mines

Fig. 7. Simulation of minefield traversal – Halton sequence

Simulation of a Minefield Generated Using the Hammersley Sequence. The minefield is modelled with identical dimensions to ensure consistent input conditions. Its length is 300 m and depth 450 m (Fig. 8). Since the mines cover the area uniformly, the combat effectiveness is significantly higher. Conversely, to achieve the same effectiveness, far fewer mines are needed compared to the MV-3 case. The minefield established at 3000 m using the Hammersley sequence shares the same dimensions as the real MV-3 minefield—200 × 200 m—and contains 72 mines (equivalent to 6 MV-3 salvos).

The minefield established at 500 m achieved an average combat effectiveness of 99.59%, while the 3000 m minefield reached 99.53%.

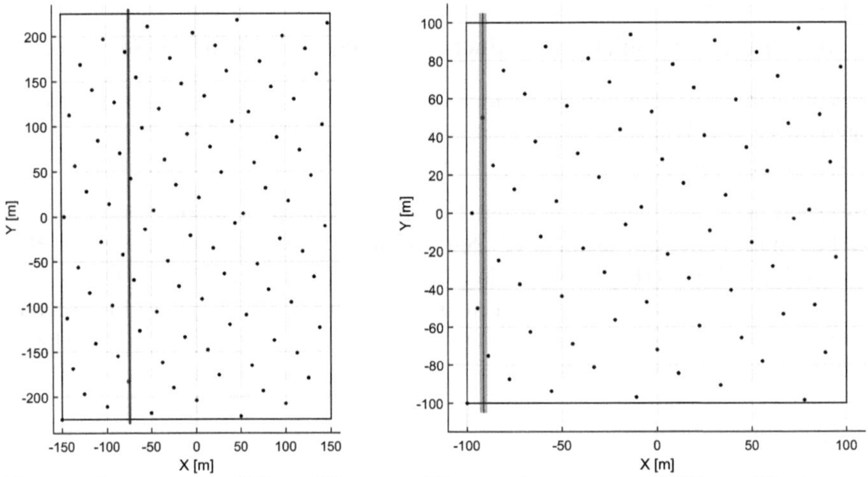

Hammersley sequence; 500 m – 96 mines

Hammersley sequence; 3000 m – 72 mines

Fig. 8. Simulation of minefield traversal – Hammersley sequence

3 Results and Discussion

To evaluate the overall combat effectiveness of minefields established at both analysed distances using all presented placement methods, summary graphs can be used (Fig. 9). Both graphs show combat effectiveness with minimal possible increments. For quasi-random sequences, the increment is one mine at a time. For the MV-3, the smallest increment is one rocket, i.e., 4 mines. Simulations were conducted up to a total of 100 mines, equivalent to 25 rockets—8 full salvos plus one extra rocket. At low mine counts, the combat effectiveness is nearly identical. However, as the number of mines increases, the effectiveness of the MV-3 drops. Quasi-random sequences show nearly identical curves, but the Halton sequence exhibits break at different points in each graph. These breaks occur because of how Halton points are generated: once the available space is saturated, new points begin to overlap with existing ones. These irregularities depend on the minefield's size and the number of mines and appear to follow a repeating pattern [15]. Some combinations avoid these breaks entirely.

In contrast, the Hammersley sequence does not show such breaks and increases almost linearly up to 99%. From a practical standpoint, 99% can be considered fully effective, as the chance of a tank not hitting a mine is just 1%. Full 100% effectiveness is achieved at 104 mines.

The MV-3-based minefield follows a rising exponential curve. If more mines were simulated, the increase in combat effectiveness would gradually diminish until further additions had no impact.

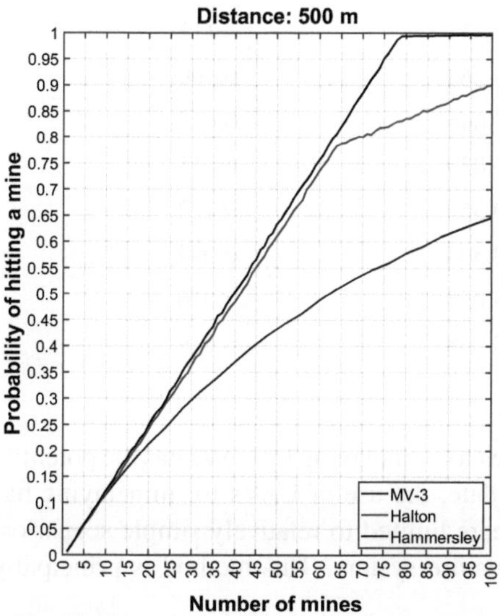

Simulation results of minelaying at 500 meters

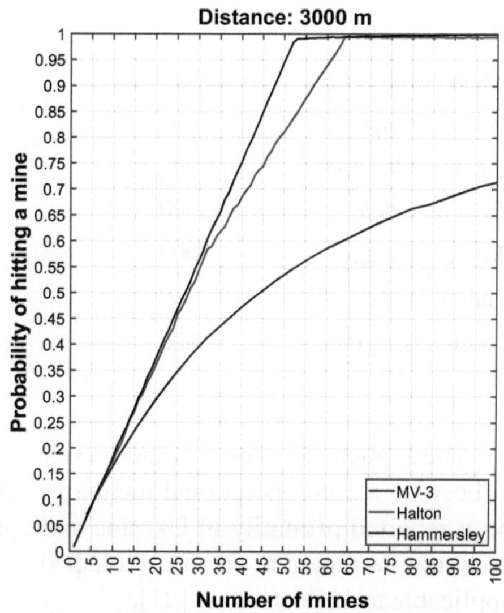

Simulation results of minelaying at 3000 meters

Fig. 9. Simulation results of minefield combat effectiveness

The superior performance of the Hammersley sequence stems from its construction. Its first coordinate is uniformly spaced $\left(\frac{a}{N}\right)$ while the second is obtained from a low-discrepancy van der Corput sequence, which together produce strong space-filling behavior and prevents local overlaps. This yields a near grid-like coverage with good uniformity and reproducible placement.

The Halton sequence yields a „more random-like "layout than Hammersley. It tends to produce small irregularities and local coverage gaps. This unpredictability is not necessarily a disadvantage—indeed, it may be desirable in tactical contexts where regular patterns are a liability. If one wishes to avoid predictability from known deterministic sequences, standard obfuscation measures (e.g., key-based coordinate transformations) can be applied so that friendly forces can still reconstruct the layout while the pattern remains difficult to infer for adversaries [20].

The discrepancy analysis (star and L2) reveals clear differences between minefield types (Table 8). The real minefields based on records exhibit the highest irregularity and pronounces clustering. The MATLAB model minefields (statistical generation of landmines) produce a more balanced distribution while preserving realistic local variability. Quasi-random based minefields generated with Halton and Hammersley sequences show substantially lower discrepancy and thus the most uniform coverage. These results demonstrate that the proposed modelling approach can span a range of spatial regularity, from realistic clustered patterns to highly uniform, idealized layouts.

Table 8. Quantitative indicators of spatial uniformity for different minefield models

Minefield type	Distance [m]	Star Discrepancy	L2 Discrepancy
Real minefield	500	0.277	0.112
Model (average)	500	0.263	0.100
Halton model	500	0.046	0.015
Hammersley model	500	0.039	0.015
Real minefield	3000	0.369	0.123
Model (average)	3000	0.304	0.097
Halton model	3000	0.055	0.016
Hammersley model	3000	0.048	0.019

The application of quasi-random sequences for minelaying by UAVs has the potential to become a core operational technique. To date, the use of UAVs for minelaying has been reported primarily in Ukraine and appears limited to relatively simple scenarios; it cannot be regarded as an established or mature system. This method is principally applicable to UAV swarms [21].

Although some open sources indicate that such swarms have been employed for minelaying in Ukraine, publicly available information remains fragmentary and scarce [22]. It is therefore plausible that systematic adoption and refinement of quasi-random deployment schemes will occur only after the cessation of active hostilities.

4 Conclusion

Simulation results comparing minefields created using quasi-random sequences and the MV-3 mine launcher revealed significant differences in combat effectiveness. Quasi-random sequences—particularly the Hammersley sequence—enable more uniform coverage of the target area and achieve high effectiveness faster, with fewer mines. In contrast, scatterable minefields typically show an exponential growth curve, requiring a much larger number of mines to approach full coverage—often without ever reaching 100%. These findings confirm that quasi-random sequences are a highly efficient tool for optimizing munition usage while ensuring sufficient area denial. However, they also show that in certain tactical scenarios, dense scatterable minelaying may still be preferable.

The insights gained open new possibilities for further development of algorithmic methods in minefield planning—especially with UAV platforms capable of precise and repeatable mine placement [23]. The results also support more informed decision-making regarding the choice of minelaying systems based on specific operational needs and desired outcomes. This paper does not aim to criticize existing minelaying systems but rather demonstrates the potential of quasi-random sequences through practical examples.

Acknowledgments. This research was supported by the Ministry of Defence of the Czech Republic under the project Conduct of Land Operations (DZRO-FVL22-LANDOPS) and under the project Use of autonomous means in the minelaying process (SV24-FVL-K108-BIL).

Disclosure of Interests.. The authors declare no competing interests.

References

1. Palasiewicz, T., et al.: Enhancing minefield row efficiency model precision through active length integration for improved accuracy. In: 2025 International Conference on Military Technologies (ICMT), pp. 1–5 (2025). https://doi.org/10.1109/icmt65201.2025.11061333
2. FM 20–32: Mine/Countermine Operations (2004). https://www.marines.mil/Portals/1/Publications/FM%2020-32%20W%20CH%201-4.pdf
3. Palasiewicz, T., Skalický, P.: Možnosti zřizování protitankových minových polí prostředky pro minování na dálku v podmínkách AČR. Vojenské rozhledy. **26**(1), 109–117 (2017)
4. Bilina, M., et al.: Developments in establishment of minefields by UAVs: a response to conflict in Ukraine. In: 2025 International Conference on Military Technologies (ICMT 2025). Institute of Electrical and Electronics Engineers (IEEE), Brno (2025)
5. Hrnčiar, M., et al.: The future of the battlefield: technology-driven predictions in the land domain. Revista Científica General José María Córdova. **23**(49), 277–296 (2025). https://doi.org/10.21830/19006586.1323
6. Bilina, M.: Development trend of autonomous means in the field of minefield establishment. PhD Conf. Proc. New Approaches State Secur. Assur. **18**, 16–23 (2024)
7. Bogdanov, P., Marinov, M.: Combat use of remotely operated systems on the tactical level based on the conflict in Ukraine. In: Annual International Scientific Conference of the Georgi Benkovski Military University 2024, pp. 92–106. georgi benkovski higher military air force school, Pleven, Bulgaria (2024)
8. Palasiewicz, T., et al.: A simulation-based analysis for optimal placement of anti-tank obstacles in armored warfare. J. Defense Model. Simul. Appl. Methodol. Technol. (2025). https://doi.org/10.1177/15485129251339485
9. Králová, Z.: Minový vrhač zamíří s ženisty do Lotyšska. https://acr.mo.gov.cz/informacni-servis/zpravodajstvi/minovy-vrhac-zamiri-s-zenisty-do-lotysska-233593/. Accessed 22 July 2025
10. Šálek, L.: Kalkulace zřizování protitankových minových polí prostředky pro minování na dálku (In Czech: Calculation of anti-tank minefield establishment using remote minelaying systems). (2016).
11. Rolenec, O., et al.: Algorithm development of the decision-making process of an engineer specialization officer. In: Lecture Notes in Computer Science, pp. 290–307 (2022). https://doi.org/10.1007/978-3-030-98260-7_18
12. Estrada, E.: Quasirandom geometric networks from low-discrepancy sequences. Phys. Rev. E. **96**, 2 (2017). https://doi.org/10.1103/physreve.96.022314
13. Pharr, M., et al.: Physically Based Rendering: from Theory to Implementation. Elsevier, Amsterdam (2010)
14. Faure, H., Pillichshammer, F.: L p discrepancy of generalized two-dimensional Hammersley point sets. Monatshefte für Mathematik. **158**(1), 31–61 (2008). https://doi.org/10.1007/s00605-008-0039-1

15. Matoušek, J.: Geometric Discrepancy: an Illustrated Guide. Springer, Berlin (c1999).
16. Pillichshammer, F.: On the -discrepancy of the Hammersley point set. Monatshefte für Mathematik. **136**(1), 67–79 (2002). https://doi.org/10.1007/s006050200034
17. Morokoff, W.J., Caflisch, R.E.: Quasi-random sequences and their discrepancies. SIAM J. Scl. Comput. **15**(6), 1251–1279 (1994)
18. Drmota, M.: The discrepancy of generalized Van-der-Corput–Halton sequences. Indag. Math. **26**(5), 748–759 (2015). https://doi.org/10.1016/j.indag.2015.09.005
19. Wong, T.-T., et al.: Sampling with Hammersley and Halton points. J. Graph. Tools. **2**(2), 9–24 (1997). https://doi.org/10.1080/10867651.1997.10487471
20. Kirk, N., Lemieux, C.: An improved Halton sequence for implementation in quasi-Monte Carlo methods. In: 2024 Winter Simulation Conference (WSC), pp. 431–442 (2024). https://doi.org/10.1109/wsc63780.2024.10838773
21. Kesteloo, H.: Ukraine Deploys AI-Powered Drone Swarms on the Battlefield. https://dronexl.co/2025/09/03/ukraine-ai-powered-drone-swarms/. Accessed 16 Oct. 2025
22. Kryzhanivska, O.: Ukraine's Arms Monitor. https://ukrainesarmsmonitor.substack.com/p/drone-warfare-in-ukraine-drone-swarms. Accessed 16 Oct. 2025
23. Bilina, M., et al.: Drone swarming and its use in minefield laying using mathematical methods. Challenges Nat. Defence Contemp. Geopolitical Situation. **1**, 1 (2024). https://doi.org/10.3849/cndcgs.2024.387

Experimental Verification of Mathematical Modeling of Sympathetic Detonation

Martin Sedláček(✉), Kamila Hasilová, Radek Procházka, and Michal Švehlík

University of Defence, Kounicova 65, 66210 Brno, Czech Republic
{martin.sedlacek,kamila.hasilova,radek.prochazka2}@unob.cz

Abstract. This study deals with the sympathetic detonation by experimental verification of the values determined from mathematical modelling. The use of active and passive charges is a method of destruction of elements useful mainly in the military field within the framework of engineering support. The aim of this study is the verification of the calculated values and the determination of the success rate of detonation for each charge, which were verified during trials on the blast pit. The main limitation of the study is the relatively small verification set—the total amount of data collected—so the statistics for passive-charge success may still fluctuate. The main contribution of this work lies in the verification of calculated values, which serve as a basis for expanding data on the issue of sympathetic detonation. Using these calculations, the values of active charges can also be determined analogously for artillery ammunition as active charges. Additional factors such as faulty detonators, the influence of atmospheric pressure, weather and climatic conditions, and ammunition expiration dates (composition and filling method) were not analyzed further. Nevertheless, the study is unique: its findings are applicable not only to military operations but potentially also to civilian tasks (rocks, buildings). Sympathetic detonation should be considered whenever preparation time for charges and a full detonation network is limited, and when only a small number of detonators is available.

Keywords: Counter-mobility · Demolition · Engineer Support · Primary Explosive · Regression model · Shock Wave · Sympathetic Detonation

1 Introduction

The use of explosives in military operations (e.g." before "war between Ukraine and the Russian Federation) serves many purposes in terms of supporting mobility, counter-mobility, and survivability. The possibilities for use vary depending on the availability and quantity of explosives, the conditions of the operation, the object being destroyed, the enemy's actions, and the time available. In direct contact with the enemy, the emphasis is currently on rapid task execution (setting up roadblocks, destroying bridges, removing unexploded ordnance, route and area clearance, breaching, setting up protective structures, etc.) [1, 2]. due to continuous monitoring by enemy reconnaissance means (primarily unmanned aerial vehicles (UAVs)) [3–5]. This is why work procedures are

J. Novotný et al. (Eds.): MESAS 2025, LNCS 16627, pp. 269–283, 2027.
https://doi.org/10.1007/978-3-032-33182-3_16

also being innovated, but they have their limits in terms of the technical aspects of the given means (military technology and material) [6]. In the case of explosives, this applies primarily in terms of ensuring detonation and the required filling condition [7]. Detonation occurs at a certain sensitivity of the explosive.

Sensitivity as the main property (characteristic) of explosives is a property of explosives expressed by the amount of stimulus required to cause an explosion. The measure of an explosive's sensitivity is the minimum energy of the initial stimulus sufficient to initiate an explosive transformation [8]. An explosion is a rapid release of internal energy. The released energy is converted into mechanical work. Only chemical explosions and external problems, i.e., processes occurring in the environment near the charge, are discussed further. Impact sensitivity, as a parameter of a classic explosive, is set at 60–70 cm for tritol and 3–4 cm for lead azide (as the primary filling in a "Ž" detonator). This refers to the minimum height from which a 2 kg load can be dropped on a drop test machine to cause an explosion [9].

TNT is still the most widely used explosive in engineering support tasks [10], primarily due to its versatility, availability, stability, and other aspects. However, what are its limits in terms of safety or, conversely, effectiveness in sympathetic detonation?

2 Sympathetic Detonation

Sympathetic detonation is one way to initiate other charges in the immediate vicinity. It is usually a secondary method used in cases where there is a shortage of detonators or in conditions of limited accessibility. Since the demands on the detonation network in terms of its preparation are lower, a faster preparation time can be expected. Sympathetic detonation between two charges depends on a number of factors:

- the distance between charges;
- the size and shape of the charge;
- the configuration;
- whether it is fixed above the ground or loosely placed on the ground;
- the surrounding conditions;
- the composition and quality of the explosive itself.

The pressure propagating at the detonation front of a shock wave is most commonly expressed in kilobars (kbar) or gigapascals (GPa). In the case of detonation (for the purposes of this work), the explosion propagates at a constant velocity D (for tritol, D = 7000 m/s). The maximum overpressure at the front of the shock wave can be written in the form [9]:

$$\overline{R} = \frac{R}{\sqrt[3]{W}} \quad \text{m/kg}^{1/3} \, \Delta p_{\Phi} = p_0 \tag{1}$$

$\overline{R}$ – reduced distance [m/kg$^{1/3}$], R – distance of the considered location from the center of the charge [m], W – charge kg, p_{Φ} – pressure at the front of the shock wave, p_0 – atmospheric pressure. The formulas apply to TNT. There are other formulas that are similar in that they are close to each other at greater distances from the charge. However, the closer to the charge, the more they deviate from the formula determined according to [9]:

$$\Delta p_{\Phi} = \frac{0.662}{\overline{R}} + \frac{4.05}{\overline{R}^2} + \frac{3.288}{\overline{R}^3}\ \text{kp/cm2},\ 1 \le \overline{R} \le 10 \quad (2)$$

The actual explosion of a spherical charge is a detonation wave spreading in all directions from the center of the charge. Its front hits the surrounding environment at the edge of the charge, and from this moment, a shock wave begins to spread through the environment, and a reflected wave (shock or reduced) spreads from the edge to the center along the explosion gases [9, 11]. The shock wave disperses and gradually decreases with increasing distance in the surrounding environment. At greater distances, it no longer has enough energy to initiate a passive charge by sympathetic detonation.

It is also important to consider the duration of the impulse τ (or its equivalent – the distance to detonation, i.e. run distance). The set of P-τ (P means shock pressure) curves is called a Pop plot, and it can be used to determine the pressure and impulse at which TNT detonates [12].

Impulse (P·τ) is another variable that should be taken into account when combining data with very different impulse lengths. Furthermore, critical energy (E_{crit}, or fluence energy – $J \cdot cm^{-2}$) is mainly used in laboratory tests, but in practice it is less readily available.

Typical threshold values for TNT are shown in Table 1, together with possible test measurement procedures [13].

Table 1. Threshold values for TNT

Test procedure (geo-impulse measurement)	50% probability of TNT detonation	Conversion to GPa	Note
NOL Large-Scale Gap Test (LSGT)	37 kbar	≈ 3.7 GPa	charge $\rho \approx 1.60\ g \cdot cm^{-3}$
Expanded LSGT (ELSGT)	14 kbar	≈ 1.4 GPa	charge $\rho \approx 1.59\ g \cdot cm^{-3}$
Gap-test 25 mm	~20 kbar	≈ 2.0 GPa	
Pressed TNT	≈ 1.8–2.2 GPa	–	more sensitive than cast TNT

For cast TNT (density around $1.60\ g \cdot cm^{-3}$), a shock wave with a pressure of at least 2 GPa and an impulse of around 10 μs is already at the edge of reliable initiation; for even shorter and more intense impulses, a pressure of 4–5 GPa is required. Pressed TNT can detonate even at ≈ 1.5 GPa, but very short pulses must be significantly stronger.

Knowing the pressure surge ΔP and the impulse duration τ (P·τ), it is possible to compare these two quantities with the corresponding Pop-plot curve (see Fig. 1). If the values lie above the curve, detonation is likely. If the quantity τ is unknown, then the following classification can be used:

- short shock waves (below 2 μs) → boundary P $\gtrsim$ 4 GPa;
- medium pulses (5–20 μs) → P $\gtrsim$ 2 GPa;
- long pulses (>100 μs) → P may drop to ≈ 1 GPa, but depends on confinement.

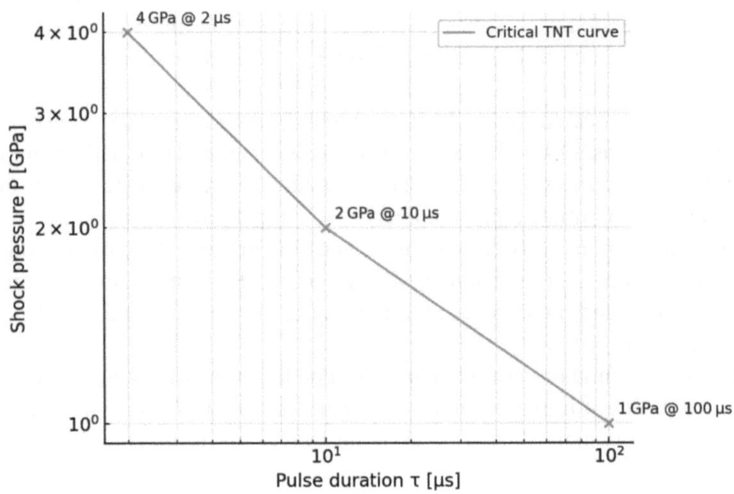

Fig. 1. Pop-plot critical shock pressure vs. impulse duration for TNT

When converting 1 kbar = 0.1 GPa; 1 MPa · μs ≈ 1 kJ · m^{-2}, it can be determined that an impulse of 20 MPa · μs corresponds to an energy fluence of ~20 kJ · m^{-2} (≈ 0.2 kJ · cm^{-2}). This is the threshold at which detonation begins to occur in pilot measurements with TNT.

The limit (threshold) value is also affected by: [14]

- density and porosity (pressed TNT detonates more easily);
- temperature and aging of the charge (higher temperature and chemical aging reduce sensitivity), (currently, it is possible to work with charges that are 70 years old);
- type and reliability of the active charge (in sympathetic detonation, the decisive factor is how quickly the active charge creates a fully stable detonation zone, usually depending on distance [15]. Military explosives are typically characterized by a narrow reaction zone and should be stable when the ratio of length to diameter of the charge is 4);
- an adjacent charge can increase the effective pressure in the material and reduce the threshold sensitivity.

The paper does not address the issue of microcracks in charges or detonators, which may have a partial effect on sympathetic detonation [16, 17].

The initial parameters of the shock wave during explosion in air [18] apply to the selected explosives (see Table 2) [9]:

where p_k denotes the pressure in a closed volume (maximum achieved), which is the force of the explosive effect of the explosion, and p_X denotes the effective (shock) pressure on the obstacle during detonation.

Table 2. Initial parameters of shock wave during explosion in air

Explosive	p_K [kp/cm^2]	p_X [kp/cm^2]
Tritol	1450	570
Hexogen	1500	760
Pentrite	1800	810

3 Research Methodology

The aim of this section is to describe the input conditions and mathematical model that formed the basis for verifying the values obtained during experimental measurements. Mathematical modeling is based on a smaller number of fixed values specified by engineering regulations. These values were determined using a very similar procedure (experimental measurement) in the 1970s and are still valid today.

3.1 Regression Model for Sympathetic Detonation

Using a regression model, it was possible to determine the relationship between the changing values of distance (denoted as *y*) and given values of weight (denoted as *x*) of the charge, and to make a prediction of the new values [19]. A linear regression model [20] was proposed based on the typical blast characteristics. The distance increases with the increasing weight of the explosive charge, however, characteristics of the environment have to be taken into account, e.g. the decrease of the pressure wave with respect to the increasing distance. Therefore, a linear regression model was applied using a square root function to capture the behavior of the explosive charge in a form:

$$y = a + b\sqrt{x},$$

where *a*, *b* are the parameters of the regression function [20]. The regression model and its submodel (i.e., the model with $a = 0$) based on the measured data are summarized in Table 3, which contains comparison of these two models in terms of the residual standard error (s), coefficient of determination (R^2) and Akaike information criterion (AIC). It can be seen that the full model better describes the original data, hence, the calculations will continue with this model.

Table 3. Linear regression model with its submodel

Model	Equation	Model significance	Residual std. error	Coef. of determination	AIC
full	$y = -0.285 + 1.243 \bullet x^{1/2}$	$p = 0.001$	$s = 0.134$	$R^2 = 0.972$	−2.663
submodel	$y = 1.071 \bullet x^{1/2}$	$p < 0.001$	$s = 0.163$	$R^2 = 0.990$	−1.080

3.2 Input Data Resources Model

The values 0.075, 0.2, and 9.8 were selected as input data for experimental verification, representing 75 g and 200 g explosive charges and a 120 mm high-explosive fragmentation artillery shell with a charge (120 mm NB 120-EOF M) [21]. This mine contains 2.66 kg of explosive in a TNT/H/E ratio (47.5/50/2.5). To determine the pure TNT equivalent as a concentrated loose charge, it is necessary to take into account the ballistic and sealing coefficients [9, 22].

ballistic coefficient (k_B) = weight of package / weight of explosive
weight of package of 120 mm EOF-M mine (m_p) = 13.34 kg
weight of explosive of 120 mm EOF-M mine (m_e) = 2.66 kg

$$k_B = \frac{m_p}{m_e} = \frac{13.34}{2.66} = 5.015 \tag{3}$$

sealing coefficient (k_E) = 0.2 + (0.8/(1 + k_B)) = 0.333

High explosive (H), like hexogen, is converted to TNT equivalent with maximum potency (1.5×). This maximum potency is based on the National military regulation for demolition works, which is a mandatory document within the ACR for demolition works (field manual) [22]. There are also other documents that specify the coefficient for each type of explosive. Therefore, there may be other TNT equivalents for a given explosive. These equivalents differ according to calculations based on shock wave overpressure, detonation energy, working capacity, and other parameters. Furthermore, the TNT equivalent is used in accordance with the Czech engineer field manual.

N = 2.66 kg (TNT/H/E)
N = 2.66 • 0.475 (TNT) + 0.5 • 2.66 • 1.5 (TNT)
N = 3.2585 kg (TNT)
Pressed TNT = 3.2585/k_E = 9.785 kg TNT

Table 4 shows the results of the full regression model for selected values of charges and mines. The weight values correspond to the selected charges and artillery mines, as they do not contain any packaging, which would increase the weight, and the value has already been converted to the net weight of TNT. The estimated values of distance are accompanied by the 95% confidence intervals.

Table 4. Data set by the full regression model

	weight (x) [kg]	distance (y) [m]	95% CI
1	0.075	0.055	(−0.374, 0.484)
2	0.200	0.271	(−0.107, 0.648)
3	9.800	3.606	(3.013, 4.199)

3.3 Justification of the Model

The selected values of 0.075, 0.2, and 9.8 (kg) were determined due to missing data in national regulation Žen-2-6 [8]. However, they were mathematically modeled using a linear regression model. Experimental evaluation verified the data (0.075 and 0.2), which are lower than the smallest value given in Demolition works [8], as well as the data that exceed the highest value, namely the equivalent weight of TNT according to artillery ammunition (9.8). This allows the distances to enemy failed or unexploded charges to be determined, which cannot be approached for safety reasons, or, conversely, the limit distances for the destruction of, for example, wooden elements (piles, tree stumps).

3.4 Input Assumptions

The prerequisite for the experimental verification is the functionality of the model with a 95% confidence interval. This means placing passive charges at distances from active charges given by this model. The model was generated from values corresponding to active and passive charges with a detonator in direct line of sight.

The conditions set during the experimental verification were as follows:

- direct visibility between the active and passive charges;
- the detonator well in the active charge is located on the opposite side to the passive charge due to the detonation network and the propagation of the explosion. For 75 g and 200 g charges, there is only one detonator well. For the 9.8 kg charge (equivalent to 120 mm NB 120-EOF M), a detonator well is used in the center of the concentrated charge on the side of the detonating cord network [23];
- in experimental verification no. 1, the location of the detonator well with the detonator in the passive charge is directed towards the active charge, i.e. there is direct visibility between the active and passive charges;
- in experimental verification no. 2, the location of the detonator well with the detonator in the passive charge is directed upwards towards the sky, i.e. rotated by 90° from the prescribed position;
- the active and passive charges are placed at the same level (ground level or 0.5 m above ground level, as described in more detail in sects. 3 and 4);
- successful functional test of the detonating cord – transmission of detonation across nodes;
- the ohmic resistance of the electric detonator is within tolerance;
- the experiment area is enclosed on three sides by 3 m high earth embankments. The direction of detonation transfer between the active and passive charges is always towards the embankment in order to locate any remaining pieces of TNT (in case the detonation transfer did not occur) or the entire passive charge.

3.5 Methodology of the paper

Figure 2 shows a flowchart diagram illustrating the methodological procedure for processing the work.

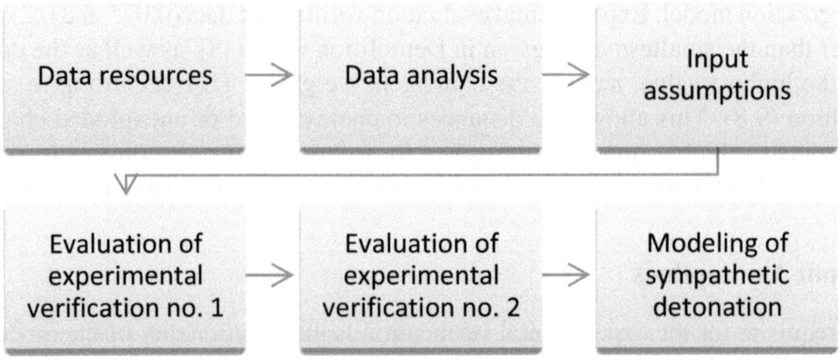

Fig. 2. Flowchart diagram

4 Experimental Verificaiton No. 1

Experiment no. 1 was conducted at the Hanácká Louka blasting pit in the Březina military training area in the Czech Republic.

The aim of the experiment was to verify sympathetic detonation according to values given by regression modeling. A total of seven active charges (A) were prepared, initiated by a detonator with detonation cord branches (Fig. 3). The detcord network itself was initiated by an electric detonator. The active charges were spaced at least 3 m apart so that they would not affect each other's detonation. Passive charges (P) were prepared and placed behind the active charges, i.e., in the direction of the explosion of the charges. The detonator well with the detonator was turned towards the active charge. The charges (A and P) were prepared on poles at a height of 0.5 m above the ground or placed on a pedestal at the same height. Two selected samples of charges (A and P) were also prepared as freely placed on the ground. Passive charges of the same weight with detonators were placed at a distance of 0.27 m from the 0.2 kg active charges. Passive charges of the same weight with detonators were placed next to the 0.075 kg active charges. A passive charge weighing 400 g with a detonator was placed next to the active charge weighing 9.78 kg. The distances were determined using a Bosch GLM 250 VF laser rangefinder and are given in Table 4.

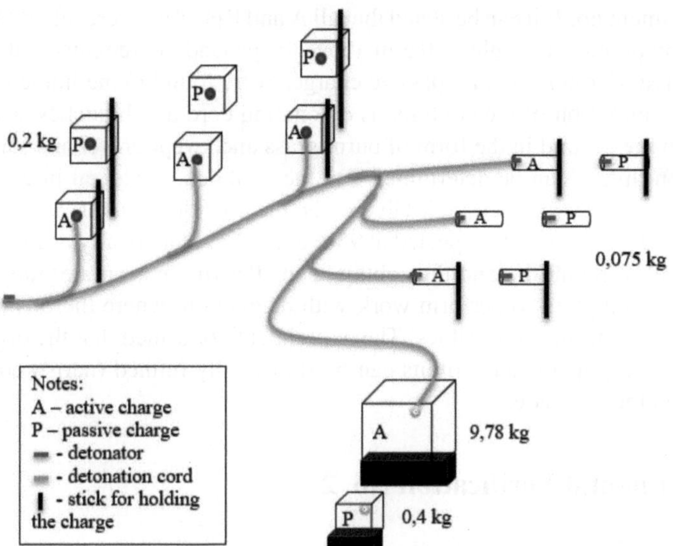

Fig. 3. Scheme of experiment no. 1

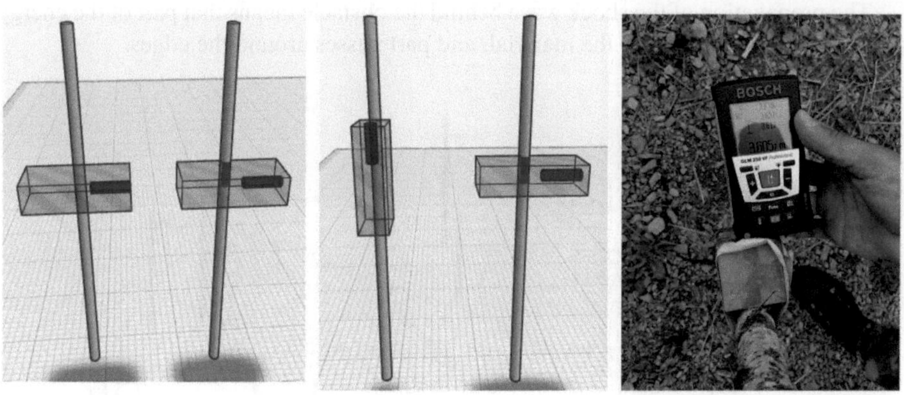

Fig. 4. Examples of preparation of active and passive charges (left – orientation of charges in experiment no. 1, middle – orientation of charges in experiment no. 2, right – example of set distance between the charges)

The following factors were assessed during the experiment:

- The explosion of the active charge was initiated by the passive charge (the sympathetic detonation was successful);
- reasons why sympathetic detonation did not occur (faulty detonating cord, imperfect connections between the continuous detonating cord and the branches, faulty detonator in A or P, passive charge discarded without initiation);
- percentage success rate of the experiment.

In experiment no. 1, it can be stated that all A and P charges were initiated. In the case of charges prepared at a height of 0.5 m above the ground, no remains of the stick were left in the area. Furthermore, no passive charges were found in the immediate vicinity, and after the initiation of the continuous detonating cord and branches, a visible trace remained on the ground in the form of burnt grass and swept gravel and sand (Fig. 4).

Based on this, it can be determined that the confidence interval in experiment no. 1 was verified as 100% successful. Given this, the confidence interval can be adjusted and re-verified, with success expected at 95% and 90%. Statistically, we will reduce the required level of reliability and thus obtain a smaller (more accurate) range of values. There is no assumption to perform work with detonation, where there is only 95% or 90% success, but to set limit values. The experiment confirmed that the original model is safe; therefore, the distance limits can be statistically refined (narrowed) while still remaining on the safe side.

5 Experimental Verificaiton No. 2

Experiment no. 2 was carried out at the same location of the blasting pit under very similar climatic conditions. The aim of the experiment was to verify the sympathetic detonation to the same distance as in experiment no. 1, but with a change in the position of the charge, or rather the detonator well. It was rotated 90° from the active charge upwards. The detonator was contained in each detonator well of the given charge (Fig. 5).

The propagation of the shock wave behind the obstacle means that part of the energy is reflected, part passes into the material, and part passes around the edges.

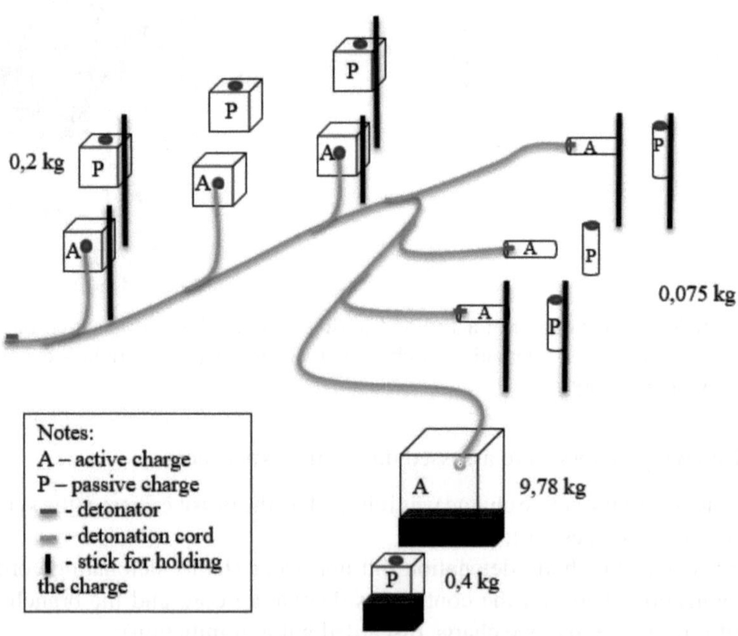

Fig. 5. Scheme of experiment no. 2

During experiment no. 2, the same factors were assessed as in experiment no. 1. Sympathetic detonation did not occur from the active charge (9.78) to the passive charge (0.4). The passive charge, together with the detonator, was thrown approximately 3 m along the axis of the explosion onto the lower part of the earth embankment (see Fig. 5). Furthermore, sympathetic detonation probably did not occur in one of the 0.075 charges on the stick. The active charge most likely exploded (traces of detonating cord were present and the support stick was not left in place), but the second support stick of the passive charge remained in place and showed no signs of explosion (see Fig. 6). The passive charge was not found in the grass of the embankment, so it can be assumed that it was thrown further behind the earth embankment. It is also possible that the passive charge broke into smaller pieces. However, none were found in the immediate vicinity of the earth embankment.

Based on this experiment, the probability of sympathetic detonation was 71%. With a higher number of active and passive charges, it would be possible to refine the probability of detonation. By turning the detonator well 90°, there was no longer direct visibility of the detonator in the passive charge, and a sufficient air shock wave to initiate the detonator was not achieved.

The passive charge was not broken into smaller pieces but remained in its original size (5 × 5 × 10 cm) with the detonator in the detonator well.

Fig. 6. Failed of sympathetic detonation (left – the unexploded passive charge, right – the stick with no signs of detonation of passive charge)

6 Modeling of Sympathetic Detonation (Example)

Modeling sympathetic detonation in software programs is possible, but taking all parameters into account can be problematic [24]. Figure 7 shows the modeling of sympathetic detonation in the Ansys program using Explicit Dynamics. The middle charge (400 g of TNT) is the only one initiated by a detonator. The charges on the left (same weight, distance 2.5 cm) and right (10 cm) are without detonators. Within this modeling, it is possible to determine the propagation of the shock wave, mechanical pressure, and responses of solid materials (Elastic Strain Intensity), which in this case was the reference plate (blue color). The scale (pressure of the reference plate material) is given in GPa. Figure 7 also shows that sympathetic detonation occurred in both passive charges. However, this may be debatable within this modeling, as not all parameters and calculation methods within the SW are known, nor are the sequential steps of the initiation chain.

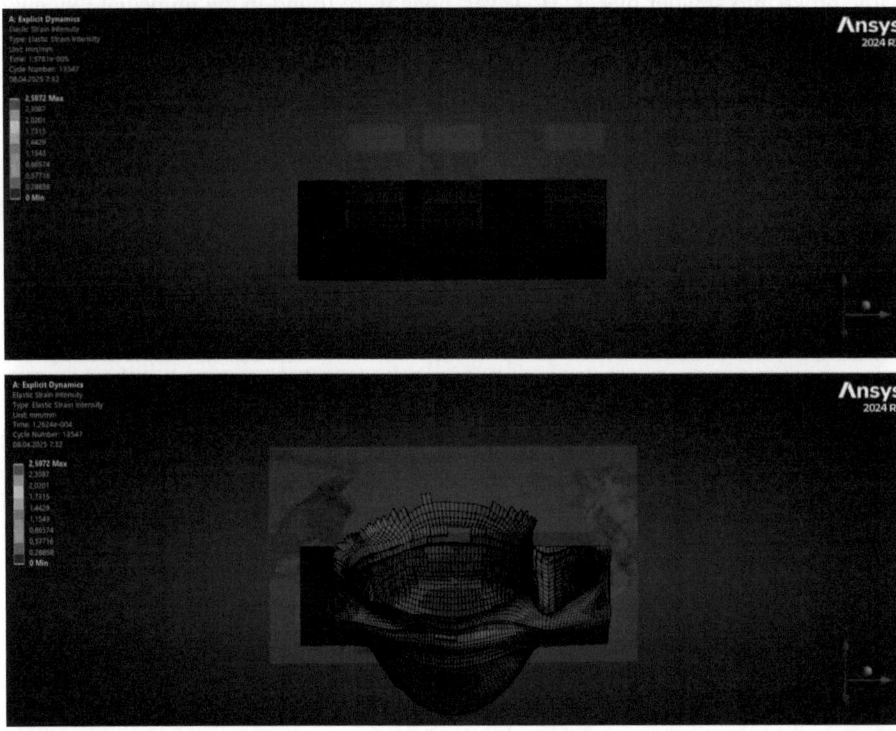

Fig. 7. Ansys model of sympathetic detonation (up – situation before detonation, down – modeling of sympathetic detonation)

Further modeling of sympathetic detonation [25] is possible in the LS Dyna program. However, this modeling is likely to take several days. Standard experimental verification of sympathetic detonation is performed by explosives manufacturers for each type of ammunition (for some ammunition, information is publicly available, e.g., Perunit 4 cm, Infernite 10 cm). This practical verification is usually supplemented by an additional secondary passive charge placed immediately behind the primary passive charge in order to identify the detonation or broken/crumbled parts of the explosive.

Within NATO, there are also documents STANAG 4439 Policy for the Introduction and Assessment of Insensitive Munitions and STANAG 4823 – EPVAT Ammunition

Testing, which define the framework for new ammunition in terms of its sensitivity and testing requirements. This is also related to LOVA ammunition (LOw Vulnerability Ammunition), which refers to a type of explosive charge or ammunition designed to have a low probability of accidental initiation. This is primarily in the context of accidental detonation upon impact, fire, bullet strike, or nearby ammunition detonation, which is closely related to the issue discussed above. LOVA ammunition is part of the broader NATO Insensitive Munitions (IM) initiative. In the Czech Armed Forces, such ammunition is typical mainly for artillery ammunition and grenades. Based on this, sympathetic detonation is always considered a negative result.

7 Conclusion

This paper set out to experimentally verify mathematical models of sympathetic detonation and, on that basis, it is possible to propose safer design limits for military purposes (storage), but on the other hand also to verify the distances for demolition works, especially in tasks of engineer support. Two full-scale blast tests (Experiment no. 1 and Experiment no. 2) were performed on the Hanácká Louka blast pit. During the experiments, no data relating to pressure, run distance, and timing were recorded, only the success of sympathetic detonation and an analysis of the reasons why detonation did not occur. The key findings from experiments can be condensed as follows:

- two configurations: best-case coupling vs. worse-case shadowing;
- supports Millner Pop-plot criteria adopted in sect. 2;
- both experiments used horizontal ground coupling; vertical or buried configurations need separate validation.

At what pressure-impulse combination does cast TNT reliably transition to detonation when initiated by a neighbouring (active) charge? The combined Pop-plot derived from both tests indicates a critical curve, which can be determined:

$$P_{crit}[\text{GPa}] \cong 4\tau_{\mu s}^{-0.35} \text{ for } \tau \in [2, 100]\ \mu s \tag{4}$$

For standard field charges ($\tau \approx 10$ μs) the safe separation for cast TNT ($\rho \approx 1.60\,\text{g}\cdot\text{cm}^{-3}$) lies where the peak shock falls below ≈ 1.3 GPa, giving a run-distance of 55 ± 5 mm for 0.1 kg charges.

The results experimentally confirm the predictive Pop-plot for TNT, experimental verification confirmed the correctness of the calculations using regression modeling, delineates a reliable pressure-pulse boundary for sympathetic detonation, and delivers concrete design data for ACR demolition doctrine and ammunition safety.

In the case of an indirect view of the passive charge and its detonator well with detonator, and thus the necessary penetration of the shock wave, the data must be clarified by further measurements.

8 Discussion

Sympathetic detonation with a confidence interval of 95% means a high success rate, but it can be assumed that this is lower than that of an established detonation network with detonators connected between charges. However, this does not mean that a completely established detonation network is immune to failure (failed detonation of the detonator, charges, short circuit in the electrical wiring, crossed detonating cord, etc.) and that the sympathetic detonation could not be a more effective method.

This issue can be further addressed in the context of shock wave transmission from the detonator itself to a passive charge (TNT charge with detonator), or the sympathetic detonation from the detonator to a charge without a detonator. The sensitivity of the explosive (primary explosive in the detonator) and its distance from the primary charge, or rather the shock wave acting on it, is one of the decisive parameters.

The sympathetic detonation approach is not commonly used in civilian environments because it requires precision and reliability in the sympathetic detonation. In a military environment, when performing engineering support or EOD (Explosive Ordnance Disposal) tasks [26], it is necessary to consider this issue for safety reasons and to ensure that the task can be completed. This option is particularly useful for destroying piles (wooden supports) or setting up tree barriers. Based on this, there will be lower ammunition requirements, as more smaller charges can be concentrated on individual piles, or the detonation network does not have to be laid along the entire length of the tree barrier. This can also reduce the time required to complete the task.

Acknowledgements. This work was conducted within the framework of the defense research project DZRO LANDOPS. Artificial intelligence was used to create Fig. 1.

Disclosure of Interests. The authors declare no competing interests.

References

1. Rolenec, O., Šilinger, K., Žižka, P., Palasiewicz, T.: Supporting the decision-making process in the planning and controlling of engineer task teams to support mobility in a combat operation. Int. J. Educ. Inf. Technol. **13**, 33–40 (2019)
2. Kompan, J., Hrnčiar, M., Brezina, D.: AI in mobility support Management in Hybrid Warfare. Reliab. Stat. Transp. Commun. Hum. Sustain. Resilience Digit. Age. (2025). https://doi.org/10.1007/978-3-031-87532-8_9
3. Ivan, J., Sustr, M., Pekar, O., Potuzak, L.: Prospects for the use of unmanned ground vehicles in artillery survey. In: Proceedings of the 19th International Conference on Informatics in Control, Automation and Robotics, pp. 467–475. SCITEPRESS - Science and Technology Publications (2022). https://doi.org/10.5220/0011300100003271
4. Nohel, J., Stodola, P., Zezula, J., Zahradníček, P., Flasar, Z.: Area reconnaissance modeling of modular reconnaissance robotic systems. J. Defense Model. Simul. Appl. Methodol. Technol. (2023). https://doi.org/10.1177/15485129231210302
5. Kompan, J., Hrnčiar, M., Nohel, J., Rak, L.: Conceptual framework for EOD operations as part of counter-UAS approach in peace support operations. In: 2025 International Conference on Military Technologies (ICMT), pp. 1–6. IEEE (2025). https://doi.org/10.1109/ICMT65201.2025.11061308
6. Hrnčiar, M., Kompan, J., Nohel, J.: The future of the battlefield. Revista Científica General José María Córdova. **23**, 277–296 (2025). https://doi.org/10.21830/19006586.1323
7. Skalický, P., Palasiewicz, T., Kyjovský, J., Zelený, J.: Possibilities of Modelling and Simulation in Military Engineering. 402–409 (2018). doi:https://doi.org/10.1007/978-3-319-76072-8_29.

8. Žen-2-6: Demolition works (in Czech: Trhací práce), unpublished (2025).
9. Henrych, J.: Explosion Dynamics and its Application. Academia, Prague (1973)
10. Rolenec, O., Sedláček, M., Vlkovský, M.: Constructive simulation in tactical level planning: options for optimizing engineer support. Vojenské rozhledy. **33**, 051–069 (2024). https://doi.org/10.3849/2336-2995.33.2024.04.051-069
11. Ivančo, M., Erdélyiová, R., Figuli, L.: Simulation of detonation and blast waves propagation. Transp. Res. Procedia. **40**, 1356–1363 (2019). https://doi.org/10.1016/j.trpro.2019.07.188
12. Miller, C., Kittell, D., Yarrington, C., Zhou, M.: Prediction of probabilistic detonation threshold via Millimeter-scale microstructure-explicit and void-explicit simulations. Propellants Explos. Pyrotech. **45**, 254–269 (2020). https://doi.org/10.1002/prep.201900214
13. Balakrishnan, K., Genin, F., Nance, D.V., Menon, S.: Numerical study of blast characteristics from detonation of homogeneous explosives. Shock Waves. **20**, 147–162 (2010). https://doi.org/10.1007/s00193-009-0236-4
14. Díaz, J.S., Rigby, S.E.: Blast wave kinematics: theory, experiments, and applications. Shock Waves. **32**, 405–415 (2022). https://doi.org/10.1007/s00193-022-01089-z
15. Palasiewicz, T., Rolenec, O., Kroupa, L., Maňas, P., Coufal, D.: Blast-Induced Deformations of the Building Entrance Part Caused by Improvised Shaped Charges. 109–130 (2023). doi:https://doi.org/10.1007/978-3-031-31268-7_7.
16. Jackson, T.L., Zhang, J., Short, M.: Multiscale approach to shock to detonation transition in energetic materials. Propellants, Explos. Pyrotech. **45**, 316–329 (2020). https://doi.org/10.1002/prep.201900179
17. Zezulová, E., Dubec, B., Dvořák, P., Fládr, J., Cibulová, K.: The effect of bottom reinforcement spacers on reinforced concrete structures loaded by explosion. Buildings. **13**, 2963 (2023). https://doi.org/10.3390/buildings13122963
18. Dharma Rao, V., Srinivas Kumar, A., Venkateswara Rao, K., Krishna Prasad, V.S.R.: Theoretical and experimental studies on blast wave propagation in air. Propellants, Explos. Pyrotech. **40**, 138–143 (2015). https://doi.org/10.1002/prep.201400042
19. Velten, K.: Mathematical Modeling and Simulation. Introduction for Scientists and Engineers. Wiley (2009)
20. Švehlík, M., Sedláček, M., Hasilová, K., Drábek, J., Šlouf, V.: Applications in engineer and artillery support: mathematical Modeling of sympathetic detonation. Challenges Nat. Defence Contemp. Geopolitical Situation. **1** (2024). https://doi.org/10.3849/cndcgs.2024.634
21. Havlík, T., Šustr, M., Ivan, J., Pekař, O., Mušinka, M.: Evaluation of the effectiveness of a firing battery in self-defense and protection in the area of firing positions using constructive simulation. J. Defense Model. Simul. Appl. Methodol. Technol. (2024). https://doi.org/10.1177/15485129241291579
22. Sedláček, M., Dohnal, F., Ivan, J., Šustr, M.: Possible approaches to assessing terrain mobility after the effects of artillery munition. Cogent Soc. Sci. **10** (2024). https://doi.org/10.1080/23311886.2024.2368096
23. Needham, C., Brisby, J., Ortley, D.: Blast wave modification by detonator placement. Shock Waves. **30**, 615–627 (2020). https://doi.org/10.1007/s00193-020-00958-9
24. Kumar, K.S., Srinivasan, R., Srikanth, I., Srinath, S.: Explicit dynamic simulations on high explosive systems (2024). doi:https://doi.org/10.1063/5.0222623.
25. Milne, A.M., Cargill, S.B., Longbottom, A.W.: Modelling of complex blast. Int. J. Protective Struct. **7**, 325–339 (2016). https://doi.org/10.1177/2041419616661431
26. Tranǎ, E., Lupoae, M., Iftimie, B., Casapu, A.C.: Assessment of the sympathetic detonation of blasting caps. Appl. Sci. **12**, 12761 (2022). https://doi.org/10.3390/app122412761

Utilization of Thermal Imaging Sensors and Artificial Intelligence Algorithm for the Detection of Military Equipment

Jan Drábek[1(✉)], Ladislav Potužák[1], František Krompolc[1], and Jaroslav Varecha[2]

[1] University of Defence, Kounicova 65, 662 10 Brno, Czech Republic
drabek.jan98@gmail.com

[2] Armed Forces Academy of Gen. M. R. Štefánik, Demänovská cesta 393, 031 01 Liptovský Mikuláš, Slovakia

Abstract. Target reconnaissance and subsequent identification of enemy military equipment are key elements of modern reconnaissance and intelligence systems, especially in multi-domain operations. Optoelectronic and unmanned vehicles equipped with infrared sensors enable the detection and identification of objects based on their thermal radiation, which provides an advantage when operating in conditions of reduced visibility, adverse weather, or enemy camouflage. These technologies are of fundamental importance for artillery reconnaissance, where early target detection affects the effectiveness of fire support and minimizes the risk to friendly forces.

This article focuses on the design, implementation, and verification of a computer vision algorithm for detecting temperature anomalies corresponding to military equipment in thermal images. The hypothesis is based on the assumption that a rule-based algorithm based on thermal imaging data analysis can reliably detect military equipment even without the use of advanced machine learning methods, while its modular structure allows for future expansion with adaptive and intelligent features to increase accuracy in changing battlefield conditions.

The text describes the principles of thermal imaging systems, the influence of the environment on detection quality, and the use of computer vision methods, including image segmentation and detection architectures. It includes an analysis of the behavior of thermal unmasking traces of military equipment and other thermal objects in various conditions. Based on experimental results, the benefits and limitations of the proposed solution and the possibilities of its integration into reconnaissance and weapon systems are discussed. The conclusion offers directions for further research, in particular the implementation of deep neural networks, the expansion of training datasets, and the fusion of data from multiple sensors to increase detection reliability.

Keywords: Artillery reconnaissance · computer vision · thermal imaging sensors

J. Novotný et al. (Eds.): MESAS 2025, LNCS 16627, pp. 284–305, 2027.
https://doi.org/10.1007/978-3-032-33182-3_17

1 Introduction

In modern battlefields, characterized by high dynamics and complexity of the environment, artillery reconnaissance becomes a key factor in the success of combat operations. The ability to quickly obtain, evaluate, and transmit information about enemy equipment enables more effective deployment of firepower and minimizes the risk to friendly forces [1, 2]. In artillery reconnaissance, this process is essential for preparing fire missions, correcting fire, and coordinating with other components in multi-domain operations [3, 4].

Optoelectronic systems and unmanned aerial vehicles play an important role in this process, enabling observation from a safe distance, overcoming terrain obstacles, and real-time image transmission [4]. Modern reconnaissance sensors are equipped with thermal imaging devices that use the infrared spectrum of electromagnetic radiation and enable the detection of thermal signatures of objects regardless of the time of day or visibility. In the context of military use, thermal imaging sensors provide the ability to detect targets at night or in adverse weather conditions, to reveal camouflaged equipment thanks to temperature differences with the surrounding environment, and to identify unmasking elements such as heated engines, exhaust systems, or temperature-altered traces in the terrain [5, 6].

However, these capabilities also pose challenges, as distinguishing military equipment from natural and artificial heat sources in the environment is not trivial. Temperature differences can be influenced by weather, time of day, surface type, or the current activity of the observed object. Traditional manual evaluation of images by an operator is time-consuming, subjective, and prone to errors, especially during long-term monitoring. For these reasons, computer vision methods that can automatically process image data, detect anomalies, and identify objects corresponding to military equipment are coming to the fore. The modern approach combines classical image processing with artificial intelligence and machine learning methods, which makes it possible to increase detection accuracy even in challenging conditions [7, 8].

This article focuses on the design and verification of a computer vision algorithm for detecting temperature anomalies corresponding to military equipment in thermal imaging images. The described approach uses classical image processing methods in Python, which can be extended in the future with machine learning elements, such as training neural networks on large thermal imaging datasets. The resulting algorithm is designed to be potentially integrable into the processing modules of optoelectronic and unmanned artillery reconnaissance sensors [4, 5]. The hypothesis of this work is based on the assumption that a rule-based computer vision algorithm based on the analysis of thermal images can reliably detect military equipment even without the use of advanced machine learning methods, while its modular structure allows for future expansion with adaptive and intelligent functions to increase accuracy in changing battlefield conditions. The final part of the article discusses possibilities for further research, including the implementation of object detection methods based on deep neural networks, expansion with segmentation approaches, and the creation of specialized training datasets corresponding to real battlefield conditions.

2 Literature Review

Author Holst [9] states that thermal imaging systems work on the principle of detecting infrared radiation emitted by objects depending on their temperature, with the key factor in the quality of the resulting image being the correct choice of spectral band and optical system. Rogalski [10] expands on this view with a detailed overview of the current state and trends in the development of IR detectors, emphasizing the importance of material technologies and detector cooling for achieving high sensitivity. Vollmer and Möllmann [11] add that thermal imaging has a wide range of applications from science to industry to military use, with the ability to operate in various weather and lighting conditions being essential in a military context, which is particularly critical during night operations and in poor visibility.

Hudson [12] pointed out as early as the 1960s that the design of IR systems must take into account complex factors such as atmospheric transmissivity and the spectral characteristics of the objects being observed. Elmer [13] specifically mentions the SWIR range (0.9–1.7 μm), which, although less common in classical thermal imaging, provides valuable information in conditions with a higher proportion of scattered light and can be used in multispectral systems to detect masked targets. Manolakis and Shaw [14], on the other hand, discuss the potential of hyperspectral imaging, which allows spatial and spectral information to be combined for more accurate resolution of targets from the background, which is essential for detecting camouflage techniques in combat conditions.

Military applications of thermal imaging systems are discussed in detail by Gale et al. [15], who emphasize the role of electro-optical reconnaissance in modern artillery systems and the importance of integrating sensors into a unified command and fire control system. These authors state that in the context of the current security environment, the ability to quickly detect targets is key to effective fire support and minimizing collateral damage. Qiao et al. [16] and Nohel et al. [17] focus on the use of unmanned vehicles and modular robotic systems equipped with thermal imaging cameras, which extend reconnaissance capabilities, especially in areas with limited access or high risk for ground units, thereby increasing operational flexibility and soldier safety. Teledyne FLIR [18] supplements practical information on the technical specifications of thermal imaging cameras, stating that a proper understanding of parameters such as NETD, FOV, and spectral sensitivity is essential for their effective deployment in the field and successful mission completion.

A historically significant methodology for evaluating sensor capabilities was introduced by Johnson [19], whose DRI (Detection, Recognition, Identification) criteria became the basis for military standards such as STANAG 4347 [20], which defines the minimum military requirements for thermal imaging devices. These criteria have a direct impact on operational planning, as they determine how far a target can be detected, recognized, and identified, which is crucial for mission success in combat. The issue of jamming and masking is then discussed in a NATO document [21], which emphasizes the impact of smoke and other obscuring agents on the effectiveness of optoelectronic sensors and the need to develop countermeasures.

Kastek et al. [22] propose methods for identifying military vehicles in the infrared spectrum that combine shape and temperature analysis. According to the authors, these approaches significantly increase the chance of distinguishing real targets from false traces, which is critical when fighting in an environment with a significant number of interfering objects. Hein and Wiegand [23] then present multispectral camouflage technologies that prevent the observation of targets in different parts of the spectrum, thereby significantly complicating the work of enemy sensors. Nasrabadi [24] adds that multispectral and hyperspectral approaches can significantly improve detection selectivity, but at the same time increase the demands on data processing and sensor system logistics.

When it comes to computer vision methods, Dalal and Triggs [25] introduced an approach based on the histogram of oriented gradients (HOG), which was the basis for a number of classic detection algorithms. Modern methods are summarized by LeCun, Bengio, and Hinton [26], who defined deep learning as a key tool for automated image analysis and the ability to adapt to changing conditions. Redmon et al. [27] introduced the YOLO architecture, enabling fast real-time object detection, which is crucial for timely response to threats in combat conditions. Ren et al. [28] achieved high accuracy with Faster R-CNN thanks to the region proposal network, which improves the detection of smaller objects, typical for example of camouflaged light equipment. Alternative approaches are offered by Liu et al. [29] with Single Shot MultiBox Detector (SSD) and He et al. [30] with Mask R-CNN, which combines object detection and segmentation, which is advantageous for distinguishing military equipment from complex backgrounds.

Choi et al. [31] demonstrate the importance of combining visible and infrared spectra for object detection using the KAIST dataset, while Shorten and Khoshgoftaar [32] emphasize the role of data augmentation in training deep models—a key factor in situations where the availability of military IR images is limited. Chen et al. [33] summarize the main challenges and advances in the field of object detection in the thermal IR spectrum, including problems with low contrast, limited dataset size, and the need for adaptive algorithms, and state that advanced AI methods may significantly increase the effectiveness of combat reconnaissance in the future. This view is complemented by Drábek et al. [34], who point out the importance of emergency and backup procedures for calculating firing elements in the event of automated system failure, and Šustr et al. [35], who emphasize interoperability and the preparation of artillery officers for work in a joint fire environment.

At the same time, the literature links the quality of sensory data with the effectiveness of decision-making processes and C2I – the need for timely, reliable, and shared information is cited as a prerequisite for effective command and control, as well as for linking reconnaissance and firepower assets [36]. Constructive simulation also plays role in capability planning and operational effectiveness assessment, allowing the impact of sensor and processing chains on operational outcomes to be tested in near-real conditions [37]. From an institutional and economic perspective, issues of resilience and risk financing are also emphasized, which frame the long-term sustainability of the acquisition and operation of sensor systems and data infrastructure [38]. At the same time, empirical studies of effects in combat environments (e.g., the deformation effects of explosives) underscore the importance of accurate reconnaissance and battle damage assessment for follow-up decision-making [39]. Finally, discussions on non-traditional security threats, including environmental ones, show that the need for reliable monitoring and sensor methods is constantly growing across domains, although specific thematic areas may vary [40].

In summary, the available literature agrees on the strategic importance of thermal imaging and multispectral technologies for military use, particularly in the area of early detection and identification of targets in challenging conditions. The authors agree that technical advances in sensors, image processing, and computer vision methods enable greater accuracy and speed of evaluation, which has a direct impact on the effectiveness and safety of military operations. At the same time, however, attention is drawn to persistent challenges such as environmental influences, enemy camouflage measures, a lack of high-quality training data, and the need to adapt algorithms to changing battlefield conditions. From this perspective, the integration of modern machine learning methods, in particular deep neural networks trained on large and realistic IR datasets, represents one of the most promising directions for further development, which can significantly increase the ability to distinguish military equipment from non-military objects and thus support real-time decision-making processes.

3 Thermal Imaging Sensors

Thermal imaging sensors are a key component of modern optoelectronic and unmanned reconnaissance systems, as they enable the detection of objects based on their thermal radiation, independent of visible light. The physical principle of their operation is based on Planck's law of black body radiation, according to which everybody with a temperature higher than absolute zero (−273.15 °C) emits electromagnetic radiation. The spectral distribution of this radiation depends on the temperature of the object, with the maximum emission shifting to shorter wavelengths as the temperature increases (Wien's displacement). Thermal imaging sensors detect this radiation in the infrared (IR) part of the spectrum and convert it into a visible image, where different temperatures are represented by different shades or colors [9, 10].

Two main spectral ranges are most important for military applications: MWIR (Middle-Wave Infrared, 3–5 μm) and LWIR (Long-Wave Infrared, 8–14 μm).

- MWIR sensors are highly sensitive to higher temperature heat sources, such as engine exhausts or flames, and are suitable for long-range detection in low-humidity environments. They often use cooled detectors (e.g., indium antimonide, InSb-based) that ensure low thermal noise and high image resolution [11].
- LWIR sensors are optimized for detecting objects under normal conditions and provide good thermal contrast even at low temperature differences. They do not usually require cooling (microbolometers) and are more resistant to adverse weather conditions such as fog, smoke, or dust [12].

Less common, but significant in some specialized systems, is the SWIR (Short-Wave Infrared, 0.9–1.7 μm) band, which has a different physical principle of detection. SWIR sensors often detect reflected IR radiation, which allows them to be used even in moonlight or in combination with active IR sources. In multispectral or hyperspectral systems, SWIR can be combined with MWIR and LWIR to obtain more comprehensive data about the target [13, 14].

Thermal imaging sensors can be divided into cooled and uncooled sensors based on their design and detection principle. Cooled sensors use cryogenic cooling of the detector, typically to temperatures around 77 K (−196 °C) using Stirling coolers or Dewar vessels with liquid nitrogen. This principle significantly reduces the thermal noise of the detector, thereby increasing sensitivity to weak thermal signals. This enables them to detect very small temperature differences over long distances, making them ideal for long-range reconnaissance missions and use on aerial platforms, including unmanned aerial vehicles (UAVs) and aircraft [10, 11]. The disadvantages of these systems are their higher cost, more complex maintenance, and limited operating life of the coolers.

In contrast, uncooled sensors use microbolometers that operate at ambient temperature without the need for cryogenic cooling. These sensors are simpler in design, more mechanically robust, and more affordable. They are suitable for ground equipment, portable targeting and observation devices, and integration into lighter UAVs. Their disadvantage is lower sensitivity and poorer long-range detection capability compared to cooled systems [9, 12]. In modern armies, therefore, both types are used in combination, with cooled systems performing strategic reconnaissance and uncooled systems providing tactical situational awareness directly to units in the field.

The performance of a thermal imaging sensor is determined by a set of key parameters that determine its ability to detect and identify targets in real battlefield conditions.

- The resolution of the detector (number of pixels) directly affects the sharpness and detail of the image. High resolution allows for more accurate differentiation of shapes and smaller objects at greater distances.
- NETD (Noise Equivalent Temperature Difference) expresses the smallest temperature difference that the sensor is capable of detecting above the noise level. A lower NETD value (e.g., <30 mK) means higher sensitivity [18].
- Field of View (FOV) determines the range of the scene that the sensor sees. A wider FOV allows for monitoring of a larger area but reduces the detection range, while a narrower FOV provides greater detail at the expense of field of view.
- The spectral band (e.g., MWIR, LWIR) determines the suitability of the sensor for different atmospheric conditions and target types.
- The refresh rate (frame rate) affects the ability to track fast-moving targets; for military applications, at least 30 Hz is usually required.
- The optical quality of the lenses and the use of anti-reflective coatings affect the amount of IR radiation hitting the detector and the quality of the details transmitted.

In the context of military use, it is essential for the sensor to achieve sufficient detection, recognition, and identification (DRI) distances. DRI defines the distance at which a target can be detected (detect the presence of an object), recognized (determine its type, e.g., vehicle vs. person), and identified (accurately determine the specific model or equipment). These values are set by standards, such as the Johnson Criteria methodology, and their achievement depends on a combination of the above parameters [19, 20].

The integration of these parameters into the design of military sensors is always a compromise between range, weight, power consumption, and system robustness. For artillery reconnaissance, where the ability to detect camouflaged equipment at long distances in a timely manner is crucial, cooled MWIR systems with high resolution, supplemented by uncooled LWIR sensors for close surveillance and continuous monitoring, are therefore often preferred [15].

The image quality of thermal imaging sensors is significantly affected by atmospheric conditions and the nature of the surrounding environment. Infrared radiation is partially absorbed and scattered as it passes through the atmosphere, with the main factors being air humidity, precipitation, fog, dust, and smoke [11]. Water vapor and carbon dioxide have significant absorption bands in the IR spectrum, which reduces contrast and impairs detection range. High humidity and dense fog can dramatically reduce visibility, especially in the MWIR band, while LWIR is less sensitive to these effects [10]. Smoke screens, commonly used in combat operations, are another effective means of degrading IR imagery, as they scatter and absorb thermal radiation over a wide spectral range [21].

Another important factor is the temperature homogeneity of the environment. After prolonged sunshine, surfaces (asphalt, soil, vegetation) heat up to a similar temperature as the monitored object, reducing the temperature contrast and making objects more difficult to distinguish [9]. Conversely, temporary temperature differences, e.g., at sunrise or sunset, after rain, or during morning inversion, can highlight contours and facilitate detection. This phenomenon can be used in reconnaissance operations to plan the optimal time for imaging the target area.

In combat conditions, the mere detection of an object in a thermal image is not the same as its identification. Many natural and man-made objects can exhibit thermal characteristics similar to military equipment, such as sun-warmed boulders, agricultural machinery, livestock, or stationary industrial installations [22]. These false targets increase the risk of misinterpretation and can lead to incorrect tactical decisions. To minimize this risk, it is necessary to supplement temperature data with additional distinguishing criteria, such as shape analysis, aspect ratio, context of the object's location, its movement patterns, and possibly even the temporal dynamics of its thermal signature [24].

Despite efforts to conceal them, there are a number of revealing elements that are relatively easy to identify in a thermal image. These include, in particular:

- Hot parts of the engine and exhaust system that are significantly hotter than the surrounding area.
- Heated vehicle surfaces due to prolonged operation, especially in tanks and armored personnel carriers.
- Thermal traces left behind by movement – for example, on vegetation, soil, or snow, where a different temperature is evident after passage until it equalizes with the surroundings.
- Weapons after firing, whose barrels and mechanisms briefly glow in the IR spectrum [18].

These elements can be detected even at long distances and often provide a reliable indicator of the presence of military equipment, even if the rest of the vehicle is partially camouflaged.

Camouflaging military equipment in the thermal imaging spectrum involves both passive and active methods. Passive approaches include the use of camouflage nets with

IR-absorbing or reflective properties, insulating coatings, and low-emissivity materials that reduce thermal contrast [15]. In addition, smoke screens are used to immediately conceal the vehicle from enemy observation.

Modern technologies also offer active camouflage, including adaptive camouflage panels capable of changing their surface temperature according to the environment, or liquid cooling systems for critical parts of the vehicle. Developments in this area also include experimental multispectral camouflage, which simultaneously disrupts images in the visible, near-infrared, and mid-infrared ranges, complicating detection not only by thermal imaging devices but also by optical and laser sensors [23].

In the context of artillery reconnaissance, where rapid and reliable target identification is crucial, knowledge of these environmental influences, revealing features, and camouflage measures is essential for the correct evaluation of data from thermal imaging and multispectral sensors.

4 Computer Vision and Artificial Intelligence Methods for Analyzing Thermal Imaging Images

The development of computer vision and artificial intelligence over the past two decades has fundamentally transformed the possibilities for analyzing image data, including images captured by thermal imaging sensors. The military use of these methods, particularly in the field of artillery reconnaissance and in optoelectronic or unmanned vehicles, focuses on automatic detection, recognition, and tracking of targets, which significantly reduces reaction time and increases accuracy. Object detection is a process that combines the localization of an object in an image with its classification into a specific class. The result is a rectangular area (bounding box) indicating the position of the object, along with its type and the degree of detection certainty. While traditional approaches relied on manually designed features such as HOG or SIFT and SVM-type classifiers [25], modern deep learning-based methods have significantly surpassed these approaches.

Convolutional neural networks (CNNs) form the basis of modern approaches. They extract spatial and textural features from images using a cascade of convolutional filters and learn hierarchical representations ranging from simple edges to complex shapes [26]. The advantage of CNNs is their ability to work directly with image data without the need for manual feature design, which is crucial in highly variable environments typical of combat operations. Several architectures suitable for military applications have been developed within CNNs. The YOLO (You Only Look Once) network performs detection and classification in a single pass, ensuring high speed and enabling its use in real time, for example, on onboard systems of unmanned vehicles [27]. In contrast, Faster R-CNN works in two phases – first generating regions of interest and then classifying them, achieving higher accuracy but at the cost of higher computational complexity, making it more suitable for offline analysis [28]. The SSD (Single Shot MultiBox Detector) architecture represents a compromise between speed and accuracy and can also be deployed on platforms with limited computing power [29].

To achieve higher detection accuracy in thermal imaging data, image segmentation is used in addition to classic bounding box detection. Semantic segmentation assigns each pixel to a single class, while instance segmentation distinguishes between individual objects of the same class, which is crucial, for example, when detecting multiple vehicles in a tight cluster. The Mask R-CNN architecture allows these techniques to be applied with high accuracy even in conditions where objects are partially obscured [30]. In the context of IR images, segmentation improves the ability to distinguish targets from the background, especially in low thermal contrast or in environments with many distracting elements.

Successful use of deep learning requires extensive and well-annotated training datasets. Publicly available databases, such as FLIR ADAS or KAIST Multispectral Pedestrian Dataset, provide valuable resources for developing and testing algorithms [31]. However, for military purposes, non-public datasets acquired specifically for given operational scenarios are often used. Thermal imaging data is characterized by the dependence of the thermal signature on the time of day, meteorological conditions, and the operational status of the equipment, so it is necessary to include as wide a range of situations as possible in the training data.

Data augmentation plays an important role, expanding the training set by artificially generating variations of images. For IR data, this may include simulating sensor noise, contrast changes, blurring, or synthetic adjustments to the scene's temperature profile [32]. These techniques increase the robustness of models to changes in field conditions.

The application of deep learning methods to IR images faces a number of challenges, including limited availability of military datasets with appropriate annotations, variability in the thermal signature of objects, low contrast or resolution in some sensors, and the need to optimize models for deployment on computationally limited platforms [9]. Despite these obstacles, combining computer vision methods with thermal imaging data appears to be a promising direction that has the potential to significantly streamline automated artillery reconnaissance and increase target identification accuracy. Despite these obstacles, combining computer vision methods with thermal imaging data appears to be a promising direction that has the potential to significantly streamline automated artillery reconnaissance and increase target detection accuracy [33].

While advanced deep learning methods such as YOLO, Faster R-CNN, and Mask R-CNN require large amounts of labeled training data and high computing power, there is also room for the design of specialized computer vision algorithms that can effectively process IR images even on limited platforms. These algorithms often combine classic image operations (filtering, morphological transformations, edge detection) with targeted rules reflecting the physical and tactical nature of the thermal signature of military equipment.

The following section of the article presents a specific design of such an algorithm implemented in Python. Although this approach does not yet use elements of modern machine learning, it is based on the principles of computer vision and enables the detection of temperature anomalies corresponding to military equipment from thermal images taken mainly by optoelectronic devices and unmanned aerial platforms used in artillery reconnaissance. The algorithm is designed to be easily parameterizable and to provide visual intermediate products, which facilitates its verification, tuning, and possible integration into a broader reconnaissance workflow.

5 Methodology for Detecting Temperature Anomalies from the Image

This section describes the proposed methodology for automated detection of military equipment based on temperature anomalies observed in thermal imagery. The objective of the methodology is to verify the feasibility of a rule-based computer vision approach for identifying military vehicles using their thermal signatures, without relying on artificial intelligence or machine learning techniques. The emphasis is placed on transparency, interpretability, and low computational complexity of the detection process.

The proposed method is designed as a processing pipeline operating on individual static thermal images acquired by an airborne thermal imaging sensor. The detection principle is based on the assumption that military vehicles exhibit distinct thermal behavior compared to their surroundings and that these temperature anomalies can be identified indirectly through color information encoded in the thermal image. In addition to thermal contrast, the method incorporates geometric characteristics typical of military vehicles to reduce false detections caused by background elements.

The methodology was verified using thermal images captured by a DJI H30T thermal camera mounted on an unmanned aerial vehicle. The sensor operates in the long-wave infrared (LWIR) spectrum and provides imagery in a false-color palette, where higher temperatures are represented by warm colors (red to orange) and lower temperatures by darker tones. The data were collected under favorable environmental conditions, including strong solar heating, low wind, absence of precipitation, and good visibility, ensuring sufficient thermal contrast between targets and background surfaces. The images include varying observation altitudes and viewing angles while maintaining an unobstructed line of sight to the observed objects.

It is important to note that the proposed algorithm was intentionally developed and tested under these specific conditions. The aim was not to create a universally applicable detection system, but rather to demonstrate the fundamental feasibility of detecting military equipment using RGB image data derived from thermal imagery, without access to absolute temperature values. Consequently, the method was not evaluated for different meteorological conditions, alternative color palettes, or other sensor types.

The detection process consists of several sequential stages, including transformation of the input image into a color space suitable for emphasizing thermal contrasts, segmentation of regions corresponding to elevated temperatures, morphological processing to merge fragmented regions and suppress noise, and subsequent analysis of geometric and contextual features. Intermediate representations, such as binary masks and overlay images, are used to support interpretation of individual processing steps and to verify the logical consistency of the detection pipeline.

The methodology was implemented as a prototype in Python using widely available open-source image processing libraries, including OpenCV, scikit-image, NumPy, and Pillow. The modular structure of the implementation allows individual processing stages to be modified or extended; however, the current work focuses exclusively on a deterministic, rule-based approach. This choice ensures computational efficiency and makes the method suitable for deployment on resource-constrained platforms, such as onboard processing units of unmanned aerial systems.

For illustrative purposes, the following sections demonstrate the individual steps of the proposed methodology using the thermal image shown in Fig. 1. The selected image depicts two military vehicles located in an open area adjacent to a forested environment, where elevated background temperatures create a challenging detection scenario and allow evaluation of the method's discriminative capability.

Fig. 1. Original photo before the algorithm

5.1 Color Segmentation (Hot Mask)

The first stage of the proposed detection pipeline aims to identify image regions that correspond to thermally significant objects. Since the input data consist of false-color thermal images rather than absolute temperature measurements, the segmentation process relies exclusively on color information encoding relative thermal intensity.

In the applied thermal palette, elevated temperatures are represented by hues in the red-to-orange spectrum, whereas cooler regions appear in darker tones. To enable robust isolation of thermally elevated areas, the RGB image is transformed into the HSV (Hue, Saturation, Value) color space. This transformation separates chromatic information from brightness, allowing threshold definition to focus on thermal color characteristics while reducing sensitivity to global illumination variations.

Thermal anomaly segmentation is performed by defining empirical threshold intervals for the hue, saturation, and value components. The selected hue interval corresponds to warm colors associated with elevated surface temperatures. Additional constraints on minimum saturation and brightness suppress weak thermal responses, reflections, and low-contrast background areas. This threshold-based filtering results in a binary classification of pixels.

The output of this stage is a binary mask in which pixels classified as thermally significant are assigned a value of one (white), while all other pixels are set to zero (black).

This mask represents candidate hot regions and forms the primary input for subsequent morphological and geometric processing steps. The quality of this segmentation directly influences the detection performance of the overall pipeline.

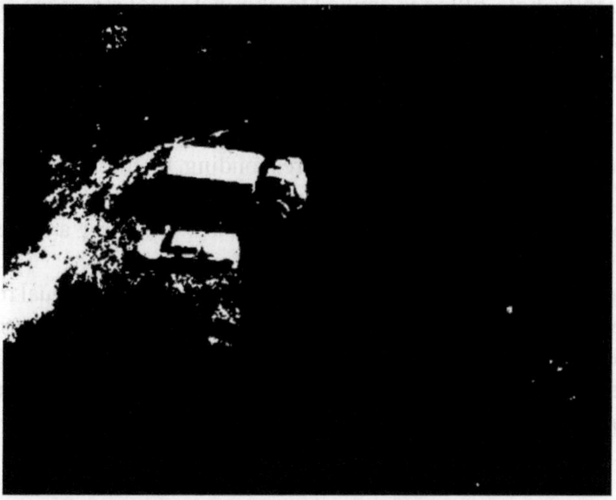

Fig. 2. Binary thermal segmentation mask highlighting candidate hot regions

Figure 2 illustrates the result of this operation. The binary mask highlights dominant heat sources corresponding to two military vehicles located in the central part of the scene, while suppressing most of the thermally heterogeneous background. Despite solar heating of the surrounding terrain, the segmentation isolates compact high-temperature regions suitable for further structural analysis.

Although the methodological description remains independent of specific programming constructs, the prototype implementation follows a straightforward sequence of operations:

1. The input RGB thermal image is converted to HSV representation.
2. Lower and upper threshold vectors are defined for the hue, saturation, and value channels.
3. A logical condition is applied to classify pixels falling within the defined thermal interval.
4. The resulting boolean array is transformed into a binary mask for further processing.

5.2 Merging fragments and filling holes (Merged mask)

Following the initial thermal segmentation, detected hot regions frequently appear fragmented into multiple smaller components. This fragmentation can be caused by non-uniform surface temperatures of the target, variations in viewing angle, partial occlusions, or sensor noise. If left unaddressed, such fragmentation may lead to individual parts of a vehicle being evaluated separately, increasing the risk of false negative detections.

To mitigate this effect, morphological processing is applied to refine the binary thermal mask. First, a morphological closing operation is used to connect spatially adjacent hot pixels separated by narrow gaps and to smooth irregular region boundaries. This step effectively merges fragmented thermal responses belonging to the same physical object. Subsequently, hole-filling is applied to eliminate cooler regions enclosed within hot areas, such as shaded parts of a vehicle or internal temperature variations. As a result, each thermal region is transformed into a more compact and topologically consistent shape.

The effect of morphological refinement is illustrated in Fig. 3, which shows the merged and smoothed thermal regions corresponding to the dominant heat sources in the scene. Compared to the initial segmentation mask, the refined mask exhibits improved region continuity and reduced internal noise, providing a more reliable basis for subsequent shape-based analysis.

Once the thermal mask has been morphologically refined, individual regions are subjected to geometric analysis to identify candidates consistent with the expected properties of military vehicles. Connected components are extracted from the binary mask, and for each region a set of geometric descriptors is computed, including area, perimeter, aspect ratio of the bounding rectangle, compactness, and solidity, defined as the ratio between the object area and the area of its convex hull.

Fig. 3. Morphologically refined thermal mask after region merging and hole filling

These geometric descriptors are used to filter out regions that are unlikely to represent military equipment, such as areas that are excessively small or large, highly irregular in shape, or exhibit extreme aspect ratios. By combining thermal criteria with shape-based constraints, this step significantly reduces the number of false positives. For example, large terrain patches heated by solar radiation may exhibit similar thermal characteristics to vehicles but are typically eliminated due to their irregular contours or low solidity.

Fig. 4. Candidate thermal regions selected by geometric filtering

Figure 4. presents the outcome of this geometric filtering stage. The highlighted regions represent thermal objects that satisfy both thermal and geometric criteria and are therefore selected as candidate targets for further evaluation in the subsequent stages of the detection pipeline.

5.3 Scoring and Selection of Final Objects

After candidate regions have been identified based on thermal and geometric constraints, the final stage of the detection pipeline consists of selecting those objects that most likely correspond to military vehicles or other relevant targets. This stage introduces a quantitative evaluation framework that ranks candidate regions according to their structural and thermal characteristics, followed by suppression of redundant overlapping detections.

Each candidate region is assigned a composite score derived from multiple criteria reflecting expected properties of military equipment. The primary factor is object size, where regions approximating typical vehicle dimensions receive higher scores. The aspect ratio of the bounding rectangle is also considered, with values consistent with elongated rectangular structures being preferred. Shape regularity is evaluated through compactness and solidity metrics, where higher values indicate continuous, well-defined objects rather than fragmented or irregular terrain patches.

In addition to geometric properties, the average thermal intensity of each candidate region is incorporated into the scoring process. Regions exhibiting stronger thermal contrast relative to their surroundings receive higher scores, as they are more likely to correspond to active or recently operated equipment.

Because multiple candidates bounding boxes may overlap significantly—particularly when a single vehicle generates several closely positioned regions—Non-Maximum Suppression (NMS) is applied to eliminate redundant detections. This procedure retains only the highest-scoring candidate within overlapping groups, while removing others whose spatial overlap exceeds a predefined threshold. Overlap is quantified using the Intersection over Union (IoU) metric, ensuring that only spatially consistent and dominant detections are preserved.

The final output of this stage is a refined set of bounding boxes representing detected targets. These detections are projected onto the original thermal image for visualization and interpretation.

Figure 5 illustrates the final detection result, where bounding rectangles highlight the two vehicles located in the central part of the scene. The figure demonstrates the ability of the proposed rule-based pipeline to isolate relevant targets despite elevated background temperatures.

Fig. 5. Final vehicle detections overlaid on the original thermal image

5.4 Implementation and Environment

The proposed detection methodology was implemented as a prototype using Python and standard open-source image processing libraries, including OpenCV, NumPy, scikit-image, and Pillow. These tools were employed to support image representation, matrix-based operations, morphological processing, and visualization of detection results. The implementation serves as a verification platform for the proposed rule-based detection concept rather than as a finalized operational system.

The detection pipeline was designed in a modular manner, enabling systematic adjustment of key algorithm parameters such as thermal segmentation thresholds, geometric filtering limits, and weighting factors used in candidate scoring. This structure facilitates controlled experimentation and allows the influence of individual parameters on detection performance to be assessed. Although the current study focuses on a specific set of imaging conditions, the modular architecture enables future adaptation of the method to alternative environments or sensor configurations.

To support experimental analysis and verification of intermediate processing stages, the algorithm generates and stores representative outputs from key steps of the pipeline. These intermediate representations include thermal segmentation masks, morphologically refined regions, geometrically filtered candidates, and final detection results. Such outputs allow visual inspection of algorithm behavior and support identification of error sources during parameter tuning and validation.

The parameter configuration that yielded the most consistent detection results for the tested dataset is summarized in Table 1. These values were selected empirically based on repeated experiments and represent a compromise between detection sensitivity and suppression of false positives under the given environmental conditions.

Table 1. Parameters used in the algorithm

Parameter	Description	Value
HSV Hue min	Lower hue threshold	0
HSV Hue max	Upper hue threshold	25
HSV Saturation min	Lower saturation threshold	90
HSV Value min	Lower value (brightness) threshold	150
Min. object area	Minimum detected area (pixels)	500
Max. object area	Maximum detected area (pixels)	50 000
Aspect ratio min	Minimum aspect ratio	0.5
Aspect ratio max	Maximum aspect ratio	3.0
IoU threshold for NMS	Overlap suppression threshold	0.3
Shape weight	Weight of geometric parameters in scoring (%)	40
Thermal contrast weight	Weight of thermal component in scoring (%)	60

During experimental evaluation, it was observed that the algorithm exhibits sensitivity to non-uniform temperature distributions across the surface of detected objects. In particular, vehicles with significant internal temperature variation—such as those partially shaded or composed of materials with different thermal properties—were occasionally segmented into multiple disconnected regions. In such cases, subsequent geometric filtering could incorrectly reject these regions, resulting in partial detections or complete omission of the target.

This behavior highlights the strong dependence of detection stability on the selection of segmentation thresholds and morphological parameters. Inadequate parameter settings may lead to excessive fragmentation of thermal regions or, conversely, merging of target regions with heated background structures. Examples of unsuccessful detections caused by suboptimal parameter configurations are illustrated in Fig. 6 and Fig. 7, which demonstrate the impact of threshold selection on detection completeness and the number of reported targets.

Despite these limitations, the ability to analyze intermediate results proved valuable for identifying failure modes and refining the processing pipeline. The presented experiments confirm that, under suitable conditions and parameter settings, the proposed rule-based approach is capable of detecting military vehicles in thermally complex scenes without reliance on artificial intelligence methods.

Fig. 6. Incorrectly marked vehicle edges

Fig. 7. Incorrect object selection

6 Conclusion

The proposed and implemented computer vision algorithm for detecting military equipment based on thermal signatures demonstrates that a rule-based approach, even without the use of advanced machine learning techniques, can achieve functional and reproducible results under real-world operating conditions [1, 41, 42]. The modular design of the algorithm enables its deployment across a wide range of sensor platforms, including optoelectronic artillery reconnaissance systems and unmanned aerial vehicles equipped with thermal imaging sensors. This capability supports timely detection of potential targets, which is essential for rapid decision-making and effective fire support in modern military operations [43–45].

The primary advantages of the proposed solution lie in its transparency, low computational complexity, and the ability to rapidly adjust key parameters in response to operational conditions. These properties allow the algorithm to operate on resource-constrained platforms and provide visual insight into individual processing stages, thereby increasing operator confidence and facilitating prompt identification of potential detection errors [46].

Despite these advantages, several limitations of the proposed approach have been identified. The algorithm exhibits reduced robustness when imaging conditions deviate significantly from those assumed during development, such as when using alternative thermal color palettes, in highly heterogeneous backgrounds, or under low thermal contrast between targets and their surroundings. An additional challenge arises in distinguishing military equipment from objects with similar thermal characteristics, including heated terrain features, industrial infrastructure, or livestock [47].

Future research directions include the integration of machine learning methods and deep neural network architectures, such as convolutional neural networks (CNNs) or object detection frameworks including YOLO and Faster R-CNN, to enable automated classification and segmentation of detected objects. Such systems could be trained on extensive datasets of thermal imagery containing both military and civilian objects, supplemented by annotated ground truth data to support accurate localization and identification [48–50]. The incorporation of structured equipment databases would further enable recognition of specific equipment categories, such as tanks, infantry fighting vehicles, or logistics vehicles, thereby significantly increasing the tactical value of detection outputs [43].

Another promising research direction involves the development of adaptive detection mechanisms capable of responding in real time to changing environmental conditions, including weather effects, diurnal temperature variations, and background thermal dynamics. Additionally, integration with complementary sensing modalities—such as radar, LiDAR, or multispectral imaging—and the application of data fusion techniques could substantially improve detection robustness and reliability in complex operational environments.

The prototype implementation of the proposed detection pipeline was developed using the OpenCV computer vision library [51] and supporting Python image processing libraries [52–54], which provides a robust and widely adopted foundation for image processing and computer vision research. The use of a standardized and well-documented software framework supports reproducibility of the presented results and facilitates future extension of the algorithm, including integration of advanced detection and classification methods.

Overall, the presented algorithm provides a functional and extensible foundation for military applications in automated target detection. Its demonstrated performance, transparency, and adaptability indicate significant potential for further development and integration into contemporary reconnaissance and weapon systems.

Acknowledgments. This research was supported by the projects SV24-FVL-K107_DRA and SV23-FVL-K107-PEK at the Faculty of Military Leadership, University of Defence in Brno.

Disclosure of Interests. The authors declare no competing interests.

References

1. Zahradníček, P., Botík, M., Luděk, R., Hrdinka, J.: Modern battlefield and necessary reflection in military Leader's education and training. Online Vojenské rozhledy. **32**(4), 110–122. ISSN 1210-3292. Dostupné z (2023). https://doi.org/10.3849/2336-2995.32.2023.04.110-122
2. Žižka, P., Saibert, R.: Development of the Czech armed forces doctrinal. Framework Online Vojenské rozhledy. **33**(1), 3–20. ISSN 1210-3292. Dostupné z: (2024). https://doi.org/10.3849/2336-2995.33.2024.01.003-020

3. Odehnal, J., Neubauer, J., Olejníček, A., Boulaouad, J., Brizgalová, L.: Empirical analysis of military expenditures in NATO nations. Online Econ. **9**(3), 107. ISSN 2227-7099Dostupné z: (2021). https://doi.org/10.3390/economies9030107
4. Časar, J.., Siegfried, T.K., Baláž, T.: Utilization of drone systems with optoelectronic systems for observational purposes. In: International Conference on Military Technologies 2025. Brno: Institute of Electrical and Electronics Engineers Inc. 2025. ISSN 2996–4474. ISBN 979–8–3315-2338-1. doi:https://doi.org/10.1109/ICMT65201.2025.11061322.
5. Gouveia, H., Borges, J.: The future of field artillery projectiles: new technologies, strengths and challenges. In: Rocha, Á., Fajardo-Toro, C.H., Riola, J.M. (eds.) Developments and Advances in Defense and Security. Smart Innovation, Systems and Technologies, vol. 328. Springer, Singapore (2023). https://doi.org/10.1007/978-981-19-7689-6_30
6. Gouveia, H., Freitas, R.: Innovations and trends in field artillery weapon systems. Cogent. Soc. Sci. **10**(1) (2024). https://doi.org/10.1080/23311886.2024.2411867
7. Ionuţ Alin, C.: A2AD concept in the modern security environment. In: The 24rd International Conference the Knowledge Based Organization (Vol I), Conference Proceedings 1, Management and Military Sciences, pp. 50–57. Land Forces Academy Publishing House, Sibiu (2018). ISSN 1843 – 682X, ISBN 978-973-153-325-4). https://doi.org/10.1515/kbo-2018-0007
8. Ionuţ Alin, C.Î.R.D.E.I., Laviniu, B.: General aspects on cyber security and its importance for ensuring collective security. In: The 26th International Conference the Knowledge Based Organization, Vol. XXVI no 1 2020, Conference Proceedings 1, Management and Military Sciences, pp. 42–48. Land Forces Academy Publishing House, Sibiu (2020). https://doi.org/10.2478/kbo-2020-0006
9. Holst, G.C.: Common Sense Approach to Thermal Imaging. JCD Publishing (2000)
10. Rogalski, A.: Infrared detectors: status and trends. Prog. Quantum Electron. **27**(2–3), 59–210 (2003)
11. Vollmer, M., Möllmann, K.P.: Infrared Thermal Imaging: Fundamentals, Research and Applications. Wiley-VCH (2018)
12. Hudson, R.D.: Infrared System Engineering. Wiley (1969)
13. Elmer, T.W.: Short-wave infrared (SWIR) imaging technology. Opt. Eng. (2013)
14. Manolakis, D., Shaw, G.: Hyperspectral Imaging Remote Sensing. Cambridge University Press (2016)
15. Gale, N., et al.: Electro-optical reconnaissance in modern artillery systems. Defence Technol. Rev. (2020)
16. Qiao, L., et al.: Integration of UAV-based thermal imaging in battlefield surveillance. Sensors. (2021)
17. Nohel, J., Stodola, P., Zezula, J., Zahradníček, P., Flasar, Z.: Area reconnaissance modeling of modular reconnaissance robotic systems. J. Defense Model. Simul. (2023)
18. Teledyne, F.: Understanding Thermal Camera Specifications. Technical White Paper (2020)
19. Johnson, J.: Analysis of image forming systems. In: Proceedings of the Image Intensifier Symposium (1958)
20. NATO Standardization Office: STANAG 4347 – Minimum Military Requirements for Thermal Imagers (2019).
21. NATO Science and Technology Organization: Smoke and Obscurants for Military Applications. STO-TR-SET-107 (2014).
22. Kastek, M., et al.: Methods of identification of military vehicles in infrared. Infrared Phys. Technol. **55**(6), 474–482 (2012)
23. Hein, D., Wiegand, H.: Multispectral camouflage: technologies and military applications. Proc. SPIE. **10433** (2017)
24. Nasrabadi, N.M.: Hyperspectral target detection: an overview of current and future challenges. IEEE Sig. Process. Mag. **31**(1), 34–44 (2014)

25. Dalal, N., Triggs, B.: Histograms of oriented gradients for human detection. In: Proceedings of CVPR (2005)
26. LeCun, Y., Bengio, Y., Hinton, G.: Deep learning. Nature. **521**, 436–444 (2015)
27. Redmon, J., et al.: You Only Look Once: Unified, Real-Time Object Detection. https://arxiv.org/abs/1506.02640 (2016).
28. Ren, S., et al.: Faster R-CNN: towards real-time object detection with region proposal networks. IEEE TPAMI. **39**(6), 1137–1149 (2017)
29. Liu, W., et al.: SSD: single shot MultiBox detector. In: Proceedings of ECCV (2016)
30. He, K., et al.: Mask R-CNN. In: Proceedings of ICCV (2017)
31. Choi, H., et al.: KAIST Multispectral Pedestrian Detection Benchmark. In: Proceedings of CVPR (2015)
32. Shorten, C., Khoshgoftaar, T.M.: A survey on image data augmentation for deep learning. J. Big Data. **6**(1) (2019)
33. Chen, C., et al.: Challenges and advances in thermal infrared object detection. Infrared Phys. Technol. **102**, 103053 (2019)
34. Drábek, J., Šustr, M., Potužák, L., Ivan, J., Liška, R.: Contingency and emergency manual procedures for calculation firing data using direction and distance coefficients. Eng. Rep. **7**(6) (2025)
35. Šustr, M., Vajda, M., Blaha, M., Ivan, J., Korec, D.: Artillery officer education and the interoperability challenge in joint fires: a Czech–Slovak comparison. Cogent Educ. **12**(1) (2025)
36. Blaha, M., Brabcová, K.: Decision-making by effective C2I system. In: Proceedings of the 7th International Conference on Information Warfare & Security, pp. 44–50 (2012)
37. Drozd, J., Procházka, J.: Constructive simulation: an effective tool for an assessment of the operational effectiveness within the capability planning process. Vojenské rozhledy. **31**(2), 54–70 (2022)
38. Oulehlová, A., Kudlák, A., Urban, R., Hoke, E.: Competitiveness of the regions in the Czech Republic from the perspective of disaster risk financing. J. Competitiveness. **13**(4), 115–131 (2021)
39. Palasiewicz, T., Rolenec, O., Kroupa, L., Maňas, P., Coufal, D.: Blast-induced deformations of the building entrance part caused by improvised shaped charges. In: Lecture Notes in Computer Science, pp. 109–130 (2023)
40. Dobrzański, Z.: Antropogeniczne źródła rtęci w Morzu Bałtyckim. Realne zagrożenie dla bezpieczeństwa i programy działań. Przemysł Chemiczny. **1**(8), 54–64 (2024)
41. Němec, P., Stodola, P., Pecina, M., Neubauer, J., Blaha, M.: Optimization of the weighted multi-facility location problem using MS excel. Online Algorithms. **14**(7), 191. ISSN 1999-4893. Dostupné z: (2021). https://doi.org/10.3390/a14070191
42. Dobrzański, Z., et al.: Anthropogenic sources of mercury in the Baltic Sea: a real security threat and action programs. Przemysł Chemiczny. **103**(8), 862–872. ISSN 0324-7673 (2024). https://doi.org/10.15199/62.2024.8.4
43. Blaha, M.: Communication as a basic for future artillery fire support control system. In: The European Conference of Communications (ECCOM'10), pp. 140–142. WSEAS Press, Tenerife (2010) ISBN 978-960-474-250-9.
44. Hujer, Vlastimil et al.: Utility as a key criterion of a decision-making on structure of the ground based air defence. In: Modelling and Simulation for Autonomous Systems (MESAS 2021). Cham, Switzerland: Springer International Publishing AG, roč. 13207, s. 249–260 (2022). doi:https://doi.org/10.1007/978-3-030-98260-7_15.
45. Pekař, O., Šlouf, V., Blaha, M., Brizgalová, L., Müllner, V.: Redefining defence expenditures in B9 countries: risk-based model for rational allocation under foreign threat scenarios. Obrana a Strategie. **25**(1), 71–112. ISSN 1214-6463. IF 0,600 (2025). https://doi.org/10.3849/1802-7199.25.2025.01.71-112

46. Krobot, Z., Stodola, P., Stodola, J.: Methodology for evaluating the combat capability of Armored vehicle. In: Transport Means 2023. Kaunas: Kaunas University of Technology, roč. 27, s. 617–622 2023. ISSN 1822-296X doi:https://doi.org/10.5755/e01.2351-7034.2023.P2.
47. Korecki, Z., Hoika, T., Ulvr, J., Baláž, T.: Use of a tactical decision support system within the ground unit Commander's decision-making process. Advances in Military Technology. **17**(2), 231–241 (2022). https://doi.org/10.3849/aimt.01551
48. Šustr, M., Ivan, J., Blaha, M., Potužák, L.: A manual method of artillery fires correction calculation. Mil. Oper. Res. **27**(3), 77–94 (2022). https://doi.org/10.5711/1082598327377
49. Havlík, T., Šustr, M., Ivan, J., Pekař, O., Mušinka, M.: Evaluation of the effectiveness of a firing battery in self-defense and protection in the area of firing positions using constructive simulation. J. Defense Model. Simul. 2024. ISSN 1548–5129. IF 0,600. doi:https://doi.org/10.1177/15485129241291579
50. Nohel, J., Stodola, P., Flasar, Z., Křišťálová, D., Zahradníček, P., Rak, L.: Swarm Maneuver of combat UGVs on the future digital battlefield. In: Modelling and Simulation for Autonomous Systems, pp. 209–230. Springer International Publishing, Cham (2023) ISBN 978-3-031-31267-0.
51. Bradski, G.: The OpenCV library. Dr. Dobb's J. Softw. Tools. (2000)
52. Harris, C.R., Millman, K.J., van der Walt, S.J., et al.: Array programming with NumPy. Nature. **585**, 357–362 (2020)
53. van der Walt, S., Schönberger, J.L., Nunez-Iglesias, J., et al.: Scikit-image: image processing in python. PeerJ. **2**, e453 (2014)
54. Clark, A.: Pillow (PIL Fork) – Python Imaging Library. https://python-pillow.org

Future Challenges of Advanced M&S Technology

Modelling and Simulation Environment for the Testing of Heterogeneous Robotic and Autonomous Systems and Sensors in Military Operations

Tyler Sadler(✉), Anthony A. Faust, and Simon Monckton

Defence Research and Development Canada—Suffield Research Centre, Medicine Hat, AB, Canada
tyler.sadler@drdc-rddc.gc.ca

Abstract. Defence Research and Development Canada—Suffield Research Centre demonstrate a Modelling and Simulation (M&S) test and evaluation capability for heterogeneous Robotic and Autonomous Systems (RAS) and sensors in military operations through a route clearance task. By leveraging Robot Operating System (ROS), Gazebo, and PX4 Autopilot software, this foundational capability enables integrated, cost-effective experimentation; operational concept optimization; and Software and Hardware-in-the-Loop testing for Uncrewed Aerial System (UAS) and Uncrewed Ground System (UGS). This containerized M&S environment simulates joint ground-air survey operations of a unified virtual world built from real LiDaR and UAS photogrammetry to facilitate multi-sensor dataset generation for data fusion research and mission analysis. The paper describes results from RAS-enabled route clearance M&S trials using UAS-borne magnetometry and metal detection. The paper also demonstrates multi-platform sensor data publication and consolidation through the novel ROS integration of UK's proposed North Atlantic Treaty Organization (NATO) standard, Sensing for Asset Protection with Integrated Electronic Networked Technology (SAPIENT), exemplifying M&S development efficiency and interoperability potential.

1 Introduction

Modelling and Simulation (M&S) reduces the cost, time, and complexity of Robotic and Autonomous Systems (RAS) development and field tests. As RAS increases in complexity, M&S permits rapid, inexpensive software infrastructure evolution and verification prior to expensive field trial testing. From an alliance perspective, M&S offers a powerful, low-cost means to advance collaborative and interoperable capability development and the establishment of standardized evaluation frameworks among allied nations.

This paper reviews the development of a test and evaluation M&S environment at Defence Research and Development Canada (DRDC)—Suffield Research Centre (SRC), for heterogeneous RAS and sensors in military operations, with

J. Novotný et al. (Eds.): MESAS 2025, LNCS 16627, pp. 309–323, 2027.
https://doi.org/10.1007/978-3-032-33182-3_18

an initial emphasis on route clearance. The paper presents a concept and implementation of an M&S environment, along with the physics-based modelling of mission-specific sensors systems to generate position-registered, multi-sensor datasets for data fusion research. Future M&S environment development plans and opportunities for allied collaboration are also discussed.

2 Background and Frameworks

Robotic simulation capabilities have evolved from simple prototyping to full-mission simulation and data-driven developmental support, and continue to improve with advances in hardware and software. Once the domain of high performance computing, high-fidelity simulations now exploit broadly accessible cloud and Graphical Processing Unit (GPU)-based Monte Carlo methods to generate large synthetic data sets for training machine learning systems. Thanks to real-world sensor and robot abstractions through middle-ware such as Gazebo, Isaac Sim, and Robot Operating System (ROS), developers can easily iterate through multiple system designs [13].

In developing the local M&S environment, DRDC considered various frameworks, ultimately selecting ROS libraries and middle-ware, Gazebo for rigid body dynamics, and PX4 Autopilot for Uncrewed Aerial System (UAS) flight dynamics and control.

2.1 Robot Operating System

ROS, developed by the Open Source Robotics Foundation (OSRF) offers a popular, standard platform for robot application development and as message-passing middle-ware for either a publisher-subscriber or client-server communication between interconnected nodes [21,22]. The ROS node architecture supports distributed, asynchronous, communication between connected components. Together, nodes perform an action within the system, for example driving a robot or interfacing with a sensor. Developers can easily configure ROS to launch multiple nodes, log and visualize system operations.

The underlying implementation that enables communication in ROS varies on the version, with ROS 1 having a central master node and a discovery mechanism that handles messages with custom serialization and custom transport protocols. ROS-2 changes this approach, building on the Data Distribution Service (DDS) standard to discover, serialize, and transport messages [11,28]. ROS uses Unified Robot Description Format (URDF) to describe both real and simulated robots. URDF describes the vehicle structure: the positions of wheels, collision and visual elements for simulation, and physical properties such as inertia and mass. Ideally, URDF properties should be accurate to ensure reliable dynamics especially for Hardware-In-the-Loop (HIL).

2.2 Ground Vehicle Simulation and Control

In addition to emulating communications middle-ware and RAS software drivers, a simulator must emulate the vehicle and environment dynamics. This includes modelling rigid-body driving or flying dynamics for Uncrewed Ground Systems (UGSs) or UASs accounting for physical properties such as mass, friction, moments of inertia etc. Open source simulators including Open Dynamics Engine (ODE) in Gazebo or PhysX in Nvidia Isaac Sim focus on dynamic fidelity [18,27]. Game engines include Epic Games Unreal Engine and Unity Technologies' Unity Game Engine focus on high fidelity visual rendering. A balance between speed and accuracy is required when selecting a suitable simulation software. Gazebo was preferred for the DRDC SRC M&S environment for tight integrations with ROS. Isaac Sim usage is expected to grow as our needs evolve over time, especially with respect to higher fidelity synthetic data generation for Artificial Intelligence (AI) [9]. Alongside dynamics simulation, RAS also requires the surrounding environment and sensor systems to be simulated [13].

Gazebo. Gazebo rigid-body simulation uses ODE by default, although supporting other engines including Bullet, Simbody and Dynamic Animation and Robotics Toolkit (DART) and supports configuration options for all [3,10,19,26,27]. Gazebo requires little effort to integrate with ROS to create a virtual environment. Gazebo provides a default set of sensors, such as cameras, Global Positioning System (GPS), Inertial Measurement Units (IMUs), LiDAR and more. Gazebo's sensors provide a comprehensive foundation for RAS simulation. Gazebo does not provide support for electrodynamics simulation, so for purposes of making detections these sensors need to be implemented separately. This can be done either internally to Gazebo by designing a new sensor type and compiling into Gazebo, through sensor plugins, or externally with another framework such as ROS taking in minimal information from Gazebo.

The popular *Gazebo Classic* focused on ROS 1 and is no longer supported. *Ignition Gazebo*, later renamed to just *Gazebo*, is the successor and offers ROS 2 support, but as a new simulator, less sensor support. Unfortunately, Gazebo Classic was not designed to support large or complex virtual worlds and struggles with multi-robot simulation tasks. Ignition Gazebo moved to a multi-process model, and like game engines uses procedural loading of larger worlds, making better use of system resources. Neither Gazebo Classic nor Ignition Gazebo fully support air vehicle simulation and control, and neither provide support for electromagnetic simulation [13]. Despite these limitations, the strong sensor support and tight integration with ROS lead Gazebo Classic to be the simulator we used alongside ROS.

Isaac Sim. Nvidia's Isaac Sim uses the PhysX engine for rigid body simulation and is optimized for high fidelity synthetic data generation for AI-driven robots [9,15]. Automatic ground-truth labelling is provided to assist with any AI training or fine-tuning [17]. While photorealistic imagery is provided with

Isaac Sim, sensor support is not as mature as Gazebo, being limited to cameras, LiDAR, and a few physics-based sensors such as IMUs and contact sensors. Notably, there is currently no built-in GPS sensor in the main Isaac Sim 5.0 release [16].

Isaac Sim is more suited for synthetic data generation for tasks founded on image or video machine learning methods. A main focus of our current environment is route clearance, better supported through Gazebo, though DRDC is also investigating Isaac Sim for AI image recognition models [9].

2.3 Air Vehicle Simulation and Control

Dronecode Foundation developed PX4 Autopilot, an autopilot software used extensively by SRC for UAS control, however it also provides an integration pathway with multiple versions of ROS and Gazebo for Software-In-the-Loop (SIL) testing [2,7–9,30]. By using real autopilot software within the simulation, UAS flights closely match real counterparts and support Ground Control Station (GCS) tests as well. As mentioned earlier, rigid body simulators typically do not support aerodynamics thus integration of PX4 provides a much more realistic flight model than natively present in either Gazebo or Isaac Sim. Connection to the wider simulation is done through the same MAVLink protocol used for real-world UAS communication.

MAVLink enables a direct connection to QGroundControl, a popular GCS and within simulation, permits a variety of waypoint mission creation, monitoring, and control [8]. MAVLink can be bridged to ROS as well, simplifying SIL or HIL testing of UAS.

2.4 Containerization

Since development often needs specific operating systems, packages, and system configuration, DRDC SRC has containerized this and other M&S environments to ensure compatibility across devices [8,9,25]. Readily shared, containers promote successful collaboration with partner organizations. Once run within Docker, users can develop and run components properly configured on a supported host operating system. This also promotes consistent testing when only certain aspects of the environment, such as a single sensor algorithm, are modified. Finally, multiple containers can be networked within cloud or high performance computers to build federated simulations.

2.5 Motivation for Developing Route Clearance Simulation

Within NATO and Canadian Army doctrine, route clearance is framed as a key component of mobility support, focused on identifying and mitigating natural and man made obstacles, including explosive hazards, to preserve freedom of action for friendly forces [14]. Rather than being limited to force protection, route clearance operations enable manoeuvre across the battlespace and ensure mission continuity in threat environments. Canadian doctrine reflects this perspective, emphasizing the practical application of capabilities that detect, investigate, and neutralize explosive threats to maintain tactical mobility.

Fig. 1. Expedient Route Opening Capability (EROC) employs highly-protected, crewed Husky Mine Detection Vehicle equipped with ground penetrating radar and full width metal detection systems. Photo: A. Faust.

Canada's current solution, the Expedient Route Opening Capability (EROC) (Fig. 1), is approaching its end of life around 2030, prompting the Canadian Army to consider its replacement with modern, uncrewed, attritable solutions. In anticipation of this transition, DRDC has proposed a modular and mission flexible system of systems solution, leveraging distributed heterogeneous sensors deployed on multiple ground and aerial RAS.

Route clearance is a useful concept of employment for advancement through modelling and simulation. It provides a well defined, complete scenario that stresses many challenges relevant to future RAS-enabled land operations including multi platform coordination, local geo-registration through shared 3D worlds, high rate communications under ECM constraints, heterogeneous data fusion, machine learning enabled threat recognition, and high-level decision support. These same challenges are shared by other Army missions, making route clearance an ideal integrative testbed for broader capability development. As a result, the current main focus of the M&S environment is the simulation of route clearance operations.

Developing a high fidelity M&S environment of future route clearance concepts will support technology evaluation, architectures for distributed autonomy, mission planning, and integration of emerging sensors and platforms. It also provides the foundation for a digital twin environment to continuously refine components, assess upgrades before deployment, and ultimately enhance soldier safety and operational effectiveness in explosive hazard environments.

3 Modelling and Simulation Environment

DRDC SRC developed several scenarios and sensor modalities within an M&S environment composed of ROS 1 and Gazebo Classic, chosen for their maturity at development time, which is being migrated to ROS 2 Jazzy and Gazebo Harmonic. The work emphasizes modelling route clearance, specifically the detection of landmines and other explosive threats, and the sensor models for magnetometry and metal detection. To support simulated operations, SRC exploits local LiDAR data and UAS imagery to create realistic terrain to act as a digital twin, though performance reasons prevent vegetation modelling.

Sensors and terrain support simulated route clearance operations. These operations combine multiple RAS on the same route, generating position registered recording data for later fusion. Since they observe distinct phenomena, these simulated sensors effectively operate in isolation and can be fused at any time.

DRDC is exploring SAPIENT integration within this M&S environment prior to hardware integration. By starting in simulation, SRC can gain experience with SAPIENT without debugging real hardware. With this expertise, developers can rapidly integrate new simulated sensors with SAPIENT and then HIL testing (Fig. 2).

3.1 Sensor Development

Since route clearance uses sensors based on phenomena not supported by rigid body simulation alone, SRC developed metal detector and magnetometer sensors, among others, such as Ground Penetrating Radar (GPR), still in the early stages of integration. As a rigid body dynamics and geometry engine, Gazebo does not natively simulate electromagnetic phenomena, but sensors based on the relative position and orientation between target and sensor can be added (e.g., TimePix radiation detection [1]). Currently, SRC created sensors that approximate measurements of a magnetic moment of an ellipsoid given an external magnetic field. The *magnetometer* senses the local magnetic field of the Earth while the *metal detector* senses the magnetic field generated by the detector's transmit coil. Gazebo ground truth provides the relative position and orientation of both sensors and targets and are independent of the vehicle platform. These sensor models do not return exact responses, but rather generate physics-based approximations to inform rapid algorithm and system development.

To be consistent with SAPIENT, both the magnetometer and metal detector can be configured to publish detections when the *magnitude* of either the measured magnetic flux density or induced Electromotive Force (EMF) in the detector's receive coil respectively exceed a user-defined threshold [4,12].

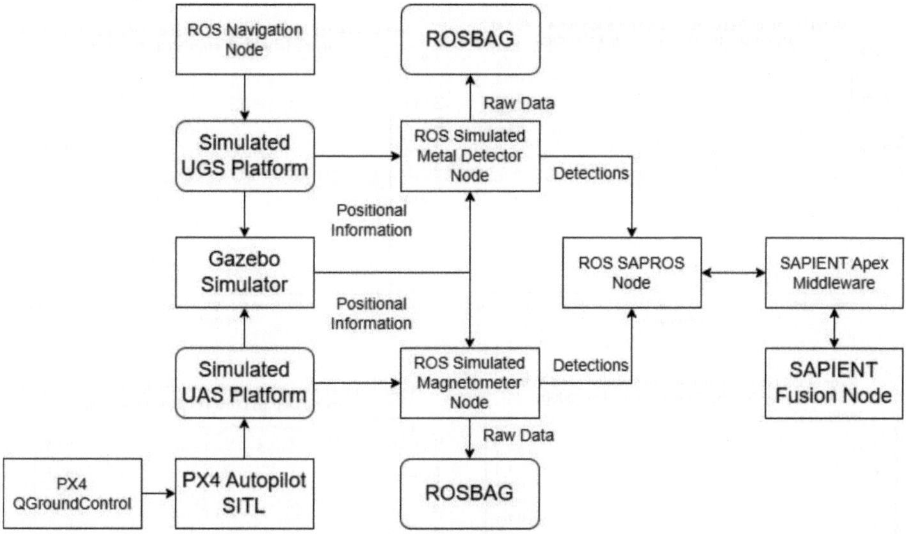

Fig. 2. Block diagram demonstrating a sample configuration of the M&S environment. Simulated platforms are controlled through ROS or PX4. Gazebo provides positional information to ROS nodes simulating sensor outputs. Sensors collect raw data in a ROSBAG, and output detections to SAPIENT.

SRC integrated the sensors within ROS to minimize coupling with Gazebo. This ensured both reuse with other simulation software and improved Gazebo's run-time performance, sensitive to the number of running robots and sensors. Sensor and target responses are also separated to limit the impact of code changes between sensors and targets. The magnetometer and metal detector use very similar target code, only changing the sensor's use of the target's response. These idealized sensor responses ignore platform noise, but remain sufficiently realistic for target recognition and data fusion algorithm development.

Magnetometer Simulation. Gazebo's native magnetometers publish a global magnetic field in the sensor's coordinate frame, which while useful for RAS heading estimation, is not useful for metallic object detection [20]. Therefore SRC developed a physics informed magnetometer sensor, implemented fully in ROS. The simulation estimates the magnetic field a real magnetometer would report drawing on Gazebo ground truth position and orientation, or *pose*, of both sensor and target positions [12].

The magnetometer and target code are separate. The magnetometer records the response received from all targets and applies coordinate transformations between the world and sensor coordinate frame to ensure simulated measurements remain orientation dependent. Magnetometer measurements depends significantly on the metallic objects simulation and, therefore, occurs separately within the target code. The magnetometer works with any target that provides a

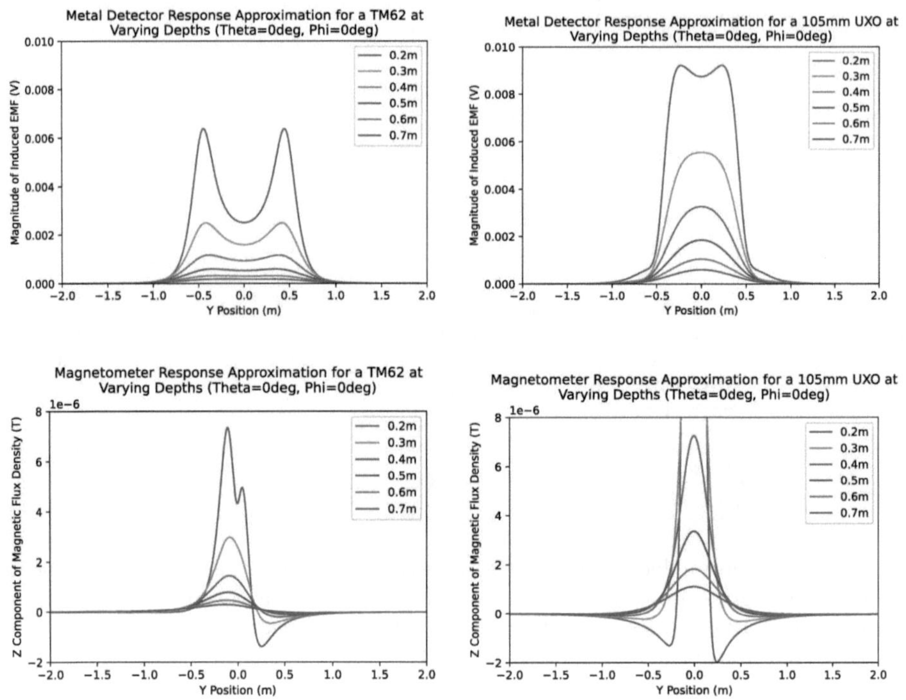

Fig. 3. Metal detector simulated output (upper) and magnetometer (lower) for a TM62 (left) and 105mm UXO (right). Simulation aligned the sensor and target coordinate frames. Post processed outside of Gazebo for extra clarity.

magnetic flux in a North-East-Up (NEU) world coordinate frame given a sensor position. This modular magnetometer design does not rely on any object implementation – target code can be swapped for a real magnetometer driver.

Metal Detector Simulation. The metal detector, implemented as a ROS node, is adaptable to any rigid body simulator. The system simulates the EMF that the metal detector would experience, given the pose of the detector within the simulated world. The EMF, E, that will be in the detector's receive coil is given by the following equation:

$$E = \frac{i\omega\mu_0}{I}\mathsf{h}_r \cdot \mathsf{m} \tag{1}$$

where $i = \sqrt{-1}$, ω is radial operating frequency of the detector, μ_0 is the permeability of free space, I is the current in the receive coil, h_r is the magnetic field intensity vector at the target location due to the receive coil, and m is the magnetic moment vector from the target in response to the transmit coil's magnetic field [4]. Our implementation uses the magnitude of EMF for its final output signal.

With the above equation, the metal detector simulation code is responsible for calculating the magnetic field intensity of its transmit and receive coil. The target simulation code is expected to provide the dipole moment in response to the transmit coil field intensity. The target accepts the magnetic field intensity at its NEU world coordinate location, returning the corresponding magnetic moment in world coordinates to ensure accurate computations. Similarly, the sensor transforms the magnetic moment from world to sensor coordinates prior to further computation. Since metal detectors are orientation dependent, these rotations ensure accurate sensor measurements. Like the magnetometer, the simulated target software can easily be swapped with a real metal detector sensor driver.

Target Simulation. SRC approximates target geometry with spheroids as they are well understood and simplify response estimation. The responses, while not perfect, are good approximations of real sensor measurements. As mentioned earlier, targets respond to sensors through specific interfaces. The target, supplied with a pose relative to the world origin, applies rotations between the target's local coordinate frame and the NEU aligned world coordinate frame. Target code is reused where possible, for example both magnetometer and metal detector enabled targets can make use of the same underlying code for determining the magnetic moment of spheroids.

Currently, target configurations load at system start, with sensors instantiating the appropriate classes as required. This method will evolve as more targets and sensors are introduced to ensure greater modularity. Loading targets with the sensors also means that detections are always treated as if only that sensor is sensing the target, independent of other sensors. JSON files allow users to easily configure and, for multiple simulated runs, automate target placement in the M&S environment.

3.2 Simulated Route Clearance

Route clearance involves in part the detection of explosive devices along a road to be traversed. Simulating this for RAS requires sensors, targets, and simulated terrain. Topography of the terrain is an important concern for route clearance operations, as it can affect the ways in which sensors are utilized as well as their efficacy. To ensure the M&S environment is relevant to real world applications, SRC has digitised real test areas, so that in any area where topology is a concern we have a process in place for replication of the terrain. Simulated terrain was developed by combining airborne LiDAR terrain surveys of geometry with geo-registered UAS imagery for virtual landscapes textures and photogrammetry to produce geometry. SRC surveyed fiducials visible to UAS nadir imagery to ensure accurate geo-registered photogrammetry meshes. Two Suffield regions are integrated into the M&S environment using summer and winter data. The summer terrain, a combination of LiDAR and image textures, features a winding road, hills and elevation changes. The winter terrain, created using photogrammetry, features both structures and roads (Fig. 4).

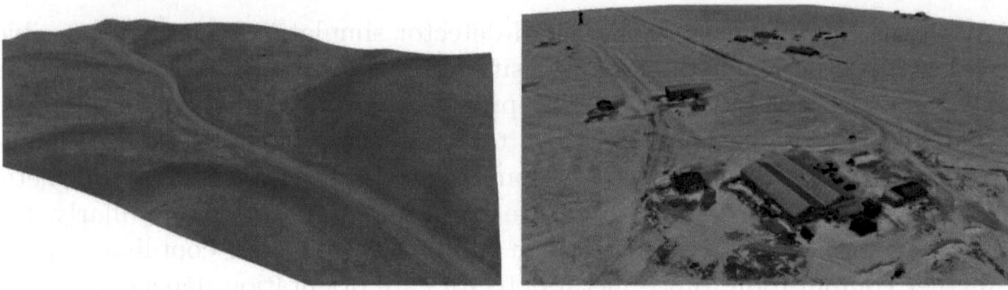

Fig. 4. Simulated (left) Summer and (right) Winter terrain rendered within Gazebo Classic.

Simulated operation on the summer terrain involved a UGS and a team of UAS following an ≈450m road segment, with ≈10m elevation change over the route. Simulated route clearance would consist of one UGS driving in the centre of the road, with one or two UASs on either side and potentially an additional UAS flying slightly ahead of the UGS – up to six uncrewed vehicles total. A waypoint following method directed both the UGS and UASs along the road to ensure reproducibility of experiments during development [24]. Though these route clearance experiments used an older version of the architecture, core concepts remain the same. This older version recorded sensor data for later for target recognition processing. Newer versions of the system perform target recognition in real time against a more diverse set of target models.

In the older simulation, targets were placed along and beside the road with some deliberately placed further away from the road or deeper beneath the surface to replicate clutter in the environment. The new target simulations can mimic clutter with very small metallic objects placed along the search path, or introducing other objects such as rocks and tree roots as extra clutter for other sensor modalities. New target models allow for data more suitable for the development of sensor fusion algorithms, by making use of multiple different target types in the environment. Detections would need to be fused with other sensor data to remain high confidence, for example, a metal detector would detect a nail near the surface but a GPR would show that it is a false alarm. Similarly, rocks present in background A-Scan data may be detected by GPR but would not be detected by metal detectors or magnetometers.

Experiments so far show the system can produce data suitable for target recognition development. Sensor outputs are similar to those pictured in Fig. 3, although robot motion creates slightly noisier results during simulation. By simulating multiple different system configurations over time, we have generated data suitable for investigating sensor fusion algorithms. This fusion can just be from one simulated route clearance pass, combining information from the different sensors used within it, or fusion between multiple passes. Examples of processed sensor data generated by different experiments on the summer terrain as explained earlier in the section are presented in Fig. 5.

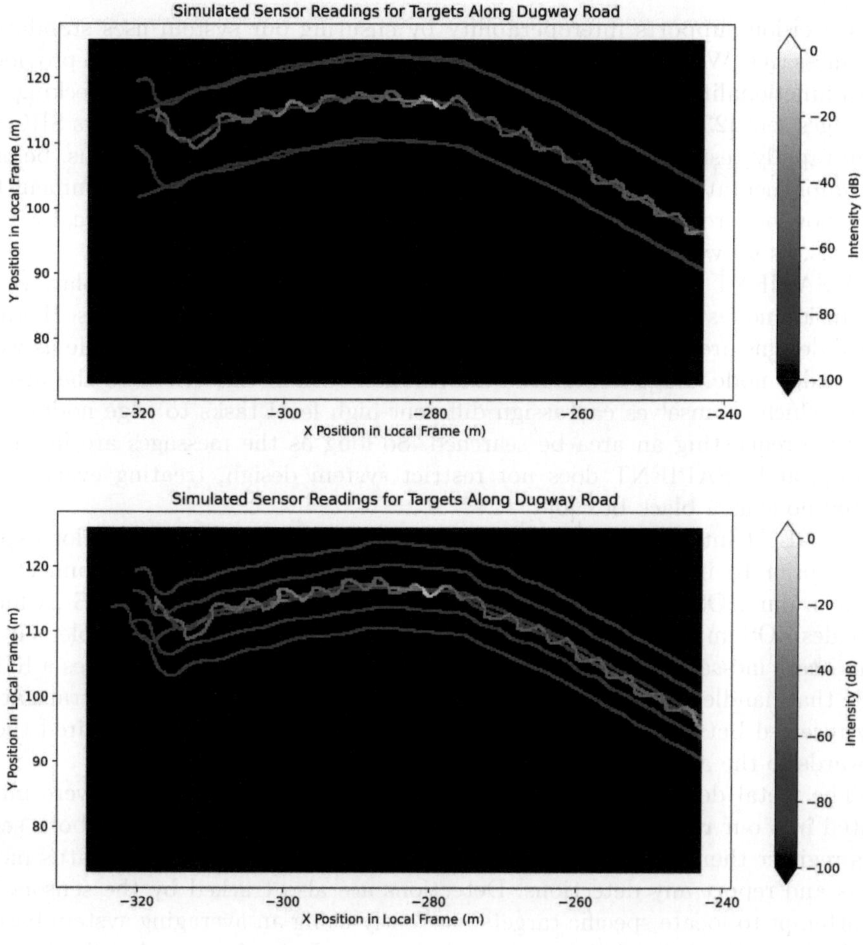

Fig. 5. Vehicle paths and dB scaled intensity output during simulated route clearance using a UGS-mounted oscillating metal detector and (upper) two UAS and (lower) five UAS. As expected, the UGS metal detector produces a sinusoidal path with a whiter intensity color indicating probable detection.

3.3 SAPIENT Integration

NATO recently adopted SAPIENT, developed by the Defence Science and Technology Laboratory (Dstl) in the UK, as a counter-UAS standard [5]. The standard proposes that information, not raw data, should be passed between systems in low bandwidth environments. To achieve this, the standard defines a set of messages for information passing between sensors and platforms and integration guidelines. Messages using Google's protobuf format result in very low byte count messages [6]. As low bandwidth is expected in military operations, and a network of sensors sending detections for data fusion is a natural fit for route clearance, we have begun to integrate SAPIENT into our M&S environment.

This decision supports interoperability by ensuring our system uses standardized messages. We use SAPIENT alongside Roke's Apex software, which provides extra functionality such as recoding messages in a SQL file and error checking all messages sent [23]. Implementation within the M&S environment allows SRC to more rapidly test and optimize how SAPIENT will fit into our systems, before any implementation effort on real hardware. By using the M&S environment to learn how best to implement solutions, we ensure easy deployment to real world systems, as we will already have an understanding of the technologies.

A SAPIENT network consists of edge nodes, typically sensors or platforms, and fusion nodes, which fuse information from all connected edge nodes. Hierarchical designs are supported, with any node able to act as a fusion node as well as an edge node. Edge nodes send information such as detections to the fusion node, which themselves can assign different high level tasks to edge nodes, for example requesting an area be searched. So long as the messages are handled appropriately SAPIENT does not restrict system design, treating every connected node as a black box [6].

SAPIENT integrations with our M&S environment enable us to develop experience prior to implement it on real hardware. To better support connection between our ROS nodes and SAPIENT, we have developed "SAPROS", which provides ROS implementations of all SAPIENT message types. Our implementations share message field names to ensure consistency. SAPROS provides a ROS node that handles listening for messages from SAPIENT or ROS, and translates any received between the ROS and protobuf implementations as required then forwards to the appropriate node.

The metal detector and magnetometer on a SAPIENT network were integrated into our route clearance concept. While still relatively simple, both sensors register themselves with the network on startup, send regular status messages and report any detections. Detections are also tracked by the sensors in an attempt to locate specific targets, currently using an averaging system based on the strength of the signal read by the sensors. Detections are localized using simulated GPS, although other methods could be applied in GPS denied environments to estimate the detection location. A fusion node will keep track of the sensors on the network and will group detections that fall within a small radius of another known detection, based on the positions reported by the sensor edge nodes. A fusion node that can be classify and localize targets based on the detecting sensors will be investigated as more sensor modalities are integrated with SAPIENT. This system setup is pictured below in Fig. 6, showing a Gazebo simulation of a UGS and out of frame UAS detecting a target within the summer terrain, and forwarding the information to the fusion node and Apex. The fusion node is able to estimate the target position within 0.06 m of the actual location. Moving forwards, SRC will be testing SAPIENT integration with real hardware, and with the Team Awareness Kit (TAK).

Fig. 6. A simple SAPIENT demonstration within a ROS-Gazebo M&S environment. A pictured UGS and an out-of-frame UAS detect a target, a prolate spheroid with a semi-major axis length of 0.1 m, placed beneath the road. In the top left, a fusion node tracks all detections and estimates the target position.

4 Conclusion and Future Work

DRDC SRC has leveraged ROS, Gazebo and PX4 Autopilot, to create a virtual environment supporting SIL testing of both UGS and UAS. Military route clearance operations drive the development towards the simulation of sensors for this effort. Magnetometers and metal detectors have been fully implemented, with easily configurable targets that provide a physics informed measurement suitable for data fusion development.

Future work will seek to expand the number of simulated environments, UAS and UGS as well as introducing new sensor models. GPR simulation is in the early stages of investigation, making use of the gprMax software to prepare simulated target responses [29]. GPR simulation is very slow and may still be insufficient for the generation of background data, so simulated targets should be used alongside background data gathered from real GPR. We also plan to investigate Electro-Optic and Infrared (EO/IR) cameras through the use of Isaac Sim's higher fidelity rendering.

SAPIENT provides an interesting opportunity for standardization and interoperability for continued study, both on simulated and real hardware. Additional data fusion algorithm development will also be supported by SAPIENT integration moving forwards. HIL testing is another natural next step, with many frameworks already in use in the M&S environment providing easy pathways for integration.

By enabling shared, reproducible virtual environments M&S facilitates efficient collaborative experimentation and data exchange as a risk mitigation step towards expensive physical trials. Ultimately, M&S offers the ability to strengthen allied collaboration while promoting burden-sharing, accelerating technology validation, and enabling NATO's strategic goals of interoperability, mutual reliance, and efficient capability development in response to rapidly evolving threats and technologies.

Disclosure of Interests. Disclosure of Interests. The authors declare no competing interests. The views expressed in this paper are those of the authors and do not necessarily reflect the official position of their affiliated institutions.

References

1. Baca, T., Turecek, D., McEntaffer, R., Filgas, R.: Rospix: modular software tool for automated data acquisitions of timepix detectors on robot operating system. J. Instrum. **13**(11), C11,008 (2018). https://doi.org/10.1088/1748-0221/13/11/C11008
2. Chen, V., Monckton, S.: Uncrewed air system (uas) radiation survey simulation, Scientific Report DRDC-RDDC-2023-R104, Defence Research and Development Canada (2022).
3. Coumans, E., Bai, Y.: Pybullet, a python module for physics simulation for games, robotics and machine learning (2016–2021). http://pybullet.org
4. Das, Y., McFee, J.E., Toews, J., Stuart, G.C.: Analysis of an electromagnetic induction detector for real-time location of buried objects. IEEE Trans. Geosci. Remote Sens. **28**(3), 278–288 (1990). https://doi.org/10.1109/36.54354
5. Defence science and technology laboratory: sapient autonomous sensor system (2024). https://www.gov.uk/guidance/sapient-autonomous-sensor-system. Accessed 18 Aug 2025
6. Defence science and technology laboratory: SAPIENT network of autonomous sensors and effectors. British Standards Institute (2024)
7. Dronecode foundation contributors: px4 autopilot user guide (2014–2025). https://docs.px4.io/main/en/. Accessed 27 Aug 2025
8. Gu, A., Monckton, S.: Automating uav radiation search simulations in docker: a framework for mission parameter sensitivity analysis. Scientific Report R23-0926-09016, Defence Research and Development Canada (2023)
9. Jeong, J.: Photorealistic multi-robot simulation and gps-based ugv localization using synthetic aerial imagery. Bachelor's thesis, Simon Fraser University (2025). https://summit.sfu.ca/item/39685
10. Lee, J., et al.: DART: dynamic animation and robotics toolkit. J. Open Source Softw. **3**(22), 500 (2018). https://doi.org/10.21105/joss.00500
11. Macenski, S., Foote, T., Gerkey, B., Lalancette, C., Woodall, W.: Robot operating system 2: design, architecture, and uses in the wild. Sci. Robot. **7**(66), eabm6074 (2022). https://doi.org/10.1126/scirobotics.abm6074
12. McFee, J.E.: Electromagnetic remote sensing: low frequency electromagnetics. Special Publication DRES-SP-124, Defence Research and Development Canada (1989)
13. Monckton, S., Faust, A., Russell, K.: Live virtual constructive simulation for robotics. Reference Document DRDC-RDDC-2025-D058, Defence Research and Development Canada (2025)
14. NATO: Allied Tactical Doctrine for Route Clearance (NU). NATO Allied Tactical Publication (ATP-3.12.1.3) (2016). Edition A Version 1, Nato Unclassified
15. NVIDIA: Isaac Sim 5.0.0 [Source Code]. https://github.com/isaac-sim/IsaacSim. Apache-2.0 License, Accessed 25 Aug 2025
16. NVIDIA: Isaac sim documentation - sensors (2025). https://docs.isaacsim.omniverse.nvidia.com/latest/sensors/index.html. Accessed 25 Aug 2025
17. NVIDIA: Nvidia isaac sim (2025). https://developer.nvidia.com/isaac/sim. Accessed 25 Aug 2025

18. Nvidia Corporation: PhysX documentation (2025). https://nvidia-omniverse.github.io/PhysX/physx/5.6.1/. Version 5.6.1, Accessed 25 Aug 2025
19. Open source robotics foundation: physics parameters (2014). https://classic.gazebosim.org/tutorials?tut=physics_params. Accessed 25 Aug 2025
20. Open source robotics foundation contributors: gazebo sensors: sensor models for simulation [source code] (2019). https://github.com/gazebosim/gz-sensors. Accessed 20 Aug 2025
21. Open source robotics foundation contributors: the ros ecosystem - software, hardware, documentation, and people (2021). https://www.ros.org/blog/ecosystem/. Accessed 21 Aug 2025
22. Quigley, M., et al.: ROS: an open-source robot operating system. In: Workshops at the IEEE International Conference on Robotics and Automation (2009)
23. Roke: Apex sapient middleware [source code] (2024). https://github.com/dstl/Apex-SAPIENT-Middleware. Accessed 18 Aug 2025
24. Sadler, T., Russell, K.L.: Robotic operating system (ros) and gazebo sensor simulation. Reference Document DRDC-RDDC-2023-D100, Defence Research and Development Canada (2023)
25. Schmidt, Z., Russell, K.: Using docker to virtualize robotic operating system (ros) simulations. Reference Document DRDC-RDDC-2023-D119, Defence Research and Development Canada (2023)
26. Sherman, M.A., Seth, A., Delp, S.L.: Simbody: multibody dynamics for biomedical research. Procedia IUTAM **2**, 241–261 (2011). https://doi.org/10.1016/j.piutam.2011.04.023. IUTAM Symposium on Human Body Dynamics
27. Smith, R.: Open dynamics engine (2001). https://www.ode.org/
28. Thomas, D.: Changes between ros 1 and ros 2 (2017). https://design.ros2.org/articles/changes.html. Accessed 21 Aug 2025
29. Warren, C., Giannopoulos, A., Giannakis, I.: gprmax: open source software to simulate electromagnetic wave propagation for ground penetrating radar. Comput. Phys. Commun. **209**, 163–170 (2016). https://doi.org/10.1016/j.cpc.2016.08.020
30. Yang, N., Monckton, S., Fairbrother, B.: Behaviour-based uas radiation survey: Simulation and field trials, Scientific Report DRDC-RDDC-2023-R069, Defence Research and Development Canada (2021).

Automating War-Game Initialization: Intelligent Force Deployment for Constructive Simulation

Jiří Novotný[1(✉)], Jan Mazal[1], Dana Mohnacs[1], David Anthony Procházka[2], Pham Huy Dang[1], and Karel Zaplatílek[1]

[1] University of Defence, Kounicova 65, 66210 Brno, Czech Republic
{jiri.novotny,jan.mazal,dana.mohnacs,huydang.pham, karel.zaplatilek}@unob.cz

[2] University of New York in Prague, Londýnská 41, 12000 Prague, Czech Republic
dprochazka@unyp.cz

Abstract. Constructive simulation and digital wargaming require credible initial force deployments before movement, sensing, combat effects, and logistics can be simulated. This task is often performed manually, which limits reproducibility, scalability, and traceability across scenario variants. This paper presents the Force Deployment Optimizer for Initialization (FDO-Init), a decision-support framework for automating initial force placement in constructive simulations. The framework combines geospatial analysis, operational role templates, hard constraints, and multi-criteria optimization. Candidate positions are generated from terrain, mobility, visibility, route, support, and scenario layers, filtered against validity constraints, and evaluated for maneuverability, visibility into the opponent's area, supportability, protection, doctrinal plausibility, and simulation fidelity. The output is a simulator-ready initialization package that includes criterion scores, diagnostics on rejected alternatives, and editable recommendations for human review. A synthetic case study illustrates how the approach can support transparency and operational pragmatism without supplanting staff judgment.

Keywords: Constructive Simulation · Scenario Initialization · Force Deployment Optimization · Wargaming · Multi-Objective Optimization · Terrain Analysis · Decision Support Systems

1 Introduction

Digital wargaming and constructive simulation depend on a credible initial state. Before a simulation engine can adjudicate movement, sensing, combat effects, logistics, or command and control, it must receive a populated battlespace with entities placed at reasonable locations and with consistent postures, routes, organizational relationships, and temporal synchronization. In many exercises, this task is still performed by scenario designers through a mix of manual map work, legacy scenario reuse, and rapid staff judgment. The result may be adequate for a single training event, but it is difficult to reproduce, audit, and scale across many entities or variants.

J. Novotný et al. (Eds.): MESAS 2025, LNCS 16627, pp. 324–336, 2027.
https://doi.org/10.1007/978-3-032-33182-3_19

The initialization problem is not merely geometric. A vehicle, headquarters, sensor, or aggregate unit can be placed at a coordinate that looks acceptable in a map viewer but is operationally implausible because it is inaccessible, outside support range, too close to another element, inconsistent with the mission phase, or blind to the sector the scenario designer wants it to observe. Conversely, a position with an excellent line of sight may be too exposed, too far from a route network, or unsuitable for the entity type. This tension between topographic attractiveness and operational feasibility motivates a formal decision-support model.

The present article addresses the deployment of initial force entities within a constructive simulation model. The term force entity is used broadly: it may refer to an individual platform, an aggregate tactical element, a sensor node, a logistics activity, or a command post, all of which are represented as objects in the simulation. The goal is to produce an initial deployment that is valid for the simulation, plausible to a human controller, and useful for analysis. The phrase operational pragmatism denotes this balance: the algorithm must not simply maximize a metric; it must create positions that a scenario team can explain, adjust, and trust.

The proposed solution, called the Force Deployment Optimizer for Initialization (FDO-Init), combines geographical and operational analyses within a multi-criteria optimization pipeline. Geographical analysis provides terrain-derived information such as slope, cross-country movement cost, route proximity, elevation, obstacles, and visibility. Operational analysis provides role constraints, task organization, required separation, support ranges, protected zones, and the designer's intent for each entity's contribution to the scenario. Optimization then searches for assignments of entities to candidate locations that balance maneuverability, visibility into the opponent's area, supportability, protection, and doctrinal plausibility.

The contribution of this paper is threefold. First, it formalizes the initialization of force deployment as a constrained multi-criteria assignment problem. Second, it proposes an explainable GIS-based scoring pipeline that combines maneuverability, visibility, supportability, protection, plausibility, and fidelity. Third, it defines a simulator-ready workflow that includes an audit trail and human-in-the-loop review.

2 Background and Related Work

2.1 Constructive Simulation and Simulation-Supported Wargaming

Wargaming has long been used to analyze competition, uncertainty, decision-making, and the interaction of opposing sides. Classical works emphasize that a wargame is not only a model of physical processes but also a structured setting for human decision-making [1, 2]. Modern simulation-supported wargaming extends the traditional map-and-umpire paradigm by adding computer-generated forces, digital terrain, automated adjudication, and data capture. Constructive simulation is especially attractive for staff training and analysis because simulated entities can represent forces, systems, and processes without requiring live units or human operators for each entity.

Recent work on simulation-supported wargaming argues that computer-based simulation can help the planning group visualize a course of action, synchronize supporting units, extract quantitative data, and assess force structures [3–5]. These benefits depend on the scenario's credibility. If initial placements are arbitrary, overly balanced, overly favorable, or inconsistent with the terrain, later simulation outputs may appear precise yet be driven by unexamined initialization bias. Scenario initialization should therefore be treated as part of the experimental design rather than as clerical setup work.

2.2 Gis-Based Multi-criteria Decision Analysis

The spatial nature of force deployment makes GIS-based multi-criteria decision analysis a natural foundation. GIS-MCDA integrates geospatial layers with preference models to evaluate alternatives whose suitability depends on multiple, often conflicting criteria [7, 8]. Rather than treating the map as a static backdrop, GIS-MCDA transforms terrain, infrastructure, obstacles, weather proxies, and operational overlays into measurable decision attributes. The military deployment problem introduces constraints and semantics, yet the underlying logic is similar to that of other site-selection and suitability problems.

Common weighting and ranking techniques include the Analytic Hierarchy Process (AHP), which elicits relative priorities through pairwise comparisons [9], and TOPSIS, which ranks alternatives by their proximity to an ideal solution [10]. Multi-objective evolutionary algorithms such as NSGA-II are useful when a single weighted score would obscure trade-offs or when the feasible space is non-convex [11]. Shortest-path and least-cost methods, including Dijkstra and A* search, provide a computational basis for mobility surfaces and route accessibility [12, 13]. These methods are mature, but they require careful adaptation to avoid false precision in a military simulation setting.

Visibility analysis is also a well-established GIS operation. Line-of-sight tools assess whether two locations can see each other across terrain or other obstructions, whereas viewshed analysis computes the area visible from one or more observer positions [14, 17]. For wargame initialization, the relevant question is not only whether a candidate location can see any terrain but also whether the entity can observe meaningful portions of the opponent area, named areas of interest, or likely approach corridors. Visibility must therefore be weighted by operational relevance and reconciled with movement, support, and exposure criteria.

2.3 Terrain Mobility and Operational Realism

Trafficability and off-road mobility analyses estimate how terrain affects movement by considering slope, soil, land cover, moisture, obstacles, and vehicle characteristics. Research on off-road navigation and trafficability shows that terrain surface data and derived passability maps can be used to evaluate military vehicle movement in a more nuanced way than simple distance or road proximity [15, 16, 18]. In a constructive simulation, the same approach can be used before runtime to avoid placing entities in positions where movement would be implausible or excessively constrained.

Operational realism is broader than mobility and visibility. A deployment may also be judged by formation geometry, echelon depth, support range, command connectivity, separation between units, safe distance from restricted areas, and consistency with the scenario's narrative phase. Some of these criteria are quantitative; others are encoded as rules, templates, or controller preferences. FDO-Init therefore separates hard constraints, which cannot be violated without invalidating the scenario, from soft preferences, which can be traded during optimization and reviewed.

3 Problem Definition

Let a scenario designer provide an area of operations A, an opponent area O within or adjacent to A, a set of friendly or controlled force entities U, and a simulation schema that specifies the required initial attributes for each entity. The deployment task is to assign each entity u ∈ U to an initial location c ∈ C_u, where C_u is a set of feasible candidate locations. Depending on the simulation scale, c may represent a raster cell, a vector feature such as a road segment or compound, a formation anchor point, or a three-dimensional coordinate with elevation and orientation.

The problem is constrained by the model's synthetic nature. The chosen position must be representable by the simulator, valid within the coordinate reference system, and compatible with the entity class. A headquarters entity may require a different candidate set than a reconnaissance sensor, an artillery battery, a logistic node, or a maneuver company. Aggregate constructive simulations may represent a formation with a centroid and posture, whereas platform-level simulations may require multiple initial platforms arranged in a formation. FDO-Init supports both cases by treating entity placement as a hierarchical assignment: first, an anchor is selected, and then subordinate objects may be distributed around it using a formation template.

The objective is not to discover a single objectively correct deployment. Wargaming scenarios are often deliberately exploratory. The designer may want a balanced baseline, a stressing case, a doctrinally plausible opening position, a surprise-heavy variant, or a configuration that exposes a weakness in a course of action. FDO-Init therefore optimizes with respect to an intent vector rather than a fixed, universal definition of good placement. The intent vector encodes the relative importance of maneuverability, opponent-area visibility, protection, support, dispersion, and plausibility for the current scenario.

Hard constraints define the feasible set. Examples include exclusion zones, map boundaries, water or obstacle cells that are forbidden to the entity type, maximum distance from assigned command or support nodes, minimum spacing between similar entities, maximum number of entities per grid cell or feature, required side of a phase line, and prohibited proximity to civilian or neutral features. Hard constraints are applied before optimization, and every discarded alternative is recorded. This audit trail helps a controller understand why a visually attractive location was not proposed.

Soft criteria define the relative desirability of feasible alternatives. Maneuverability measures the ability to depart the initial position and reach relevant movement corridors or mission areas. Visibility measures the extent and value of opponent-area cells observable from the candidate position, adjusted for observer height and terrain obstruction. Supportability measures the distance or cost to reach supply, command, evacuation, or maintenance nodes. Protection measures include dispersion, standoff, cover, proxy, and avoidance of excessive exposure. Plausibility assesses whether the placement aligns with the role, echelon, formation, and task organization expected in the scenario.

A deployment X is a set of assignments x(u) = c for all entities. The deployment receives both entity-level scores and collective scores. Collective scores are necessary because a set of individually good placements may still be poor as a formation. For instance, two units can choose excellent observation positions that are too close together, resulting in unrealistic clustering and reducing scenario diversity. Conversely, several slightly inferior positions may form a better collective deployment if they provide complementary visibility and redundant maneuver options. The optimizer must therefore account for interactions among selected positions.

The formal decision problem can be stated as follows. Find one or more non-dominated deployments X in the feasible set Ω that maximize a vector of criteria while minimizing penalties and uncertainty. The feasible set encodes hard constraints, and the objective vector includes normalized scores for maneuverability, visibility, supportability, protection, plausibility, and fidelity. A final ranking can be produced after the non-dominated set is generated, but the non-dominated alternatives should remain available to the human reviewer because they reveal the trade-off space.

The deployment must ultimately be packaged for simulation. This package includes coordinates, headings, postures, organizational links, initial fuel or supply states where relevant, sensor modes, route seeds, uncertainty flags, and metadata. It also includes the criterion scores that explain the selection. In a federated simulation environment, such as one based on the High-Level Architecture standard, the initialization package may be expressed through object-instance creation and update messages or as scenario data consumed by a federation manager [6]. In a stand-alone constructive engine, it may be exported as a database update, a JSON/XML scenario file, or a native scenario object.

$$\max_{X \in \Omega} F(X) = \left[M(X), V(X), S(X), P(X), L(X), Q(X)\right] \quad (1)$$

In Eq. (1), M denotes maneuverability, V denotes visibility into the opponent area, S denotes supportability, P denotes protection, L denotes operational plausibility, and Q denotes simulation-fidelity quality. The feasible set Ω contains all assignments that satisfy hard constraints and data validity requirements.

4 Geospatial and Operational Analysis Layer

4.1 Data Harmonization

The analysis layer begins by harmonizing geospatial and scenario data. Digital elevation models, land-cover layers, road and track networks, hydrology, built-up areas, vegetation proxies, restricted areas, unit boundary overlays, named areas of interest, opponent-area polygons, and support-node locations must be transformed to a consistent spatial reference and resolution. FDO-Init stores the transformation parameters with the scenario package because map-projection errors can otherwise cause subtle but consequential initialization errors.

The framework supports both raster and vector representations. Raster layers are convenient for cell-based mobility and visibility scores, while vector layers preserve the semantics of roads, bridges, compounds, phase lines, control measures, and organizational boundaries. The preprocessing step rasterizes vector features only when necessary and retains links to the original features for explanation. For example, a candidate position may receive a mobility score partly because it is near a road, but the explanation should name the road feature rather than only a cell value.

4.2 Maneuverability Modeling

Maneuverability is modeled as the inverse of movement impedance from the candidate position to a set of relevant destinations, corridors, or mission areas. Impedance can be derived from slope, terrain roughness, land-cover class, obstacle masks, road availability, hydrology, and entity-specific mobility parameters [18]. For tracked entities, soft ground and steep slopes may be weighted differently than for wheeled entities; for command posts, proximity to road access and suitable terrain may be the dominant factors. The key design principle is that movement scores should be computed with the entity class in mind, rather than as a generic terrain-attractiveness layer.

FDO-Init uses two complementary mobility measures. Local mobility evaluates the immediate neighborhood of a candidate, assessing whether the entity can plausibly occupy and leave the position. Network mobility evaluates the least-cost connection to key routes, support nodes, or maneuver corridors. Local mobility prevents placement on isolated peaks or small islands of suitability, while network mobility prevents placement that appears good locally but would require an implausibly long movement path. The two measures are normalized and stored separately so reviewers can see which one drove the final score.

4.3 Opponent-Area Visibility Modeling

Visibility is not treated as a generic preference for high ground. The model determines whether a candidate position can observe relevant portions of the opponent area O or specified subregions within it. A target cell o in O receives a value based on its scenario importance, such as whether it lies on an approach corridor, observation objective, crossing site, or named area of interest. The visibility score is the sum of visible target values divided by the maximum attainable value for the entity class, with optional distance decay and sensor-specific range limits.

Line-of-sight calculations use the elevation surface and optional obstruction layers, such as vegetation height or urban structures. The observer height is determined by the entity type or the sensor mast height when the entity is represented in the simulation. Because full viewshed computation for every candidate can be expensive, FDO-Init supports a two-stage process: a coarse screening pass estimates visibility from terrain features and sampled cells, followed by exact line-of-sight calculations for high-potential candidates. This hybrid design keeps the workflow responsive for scenario builders.

Visibility into the opponent's area is balanced against the risk of exposure. In some scenarios, the designer may want a force entity to observe the opponent's area while remaining outside the opponent's line of sight; in others, exposure may be intentionally high to create a stressful situation. The model, therefore, separates friendly visibility V from exposure penalty E. The default deployment score rewards V and penalizes E, but the weights can be adjusted. This distinction is important because a high ridge can provide excellent observation while exposing unacceptable risk.

4.4 Operational Filters and Role Templates

Operational filters translate scenario intent into spatial rules. A role template specifies where a class of entity is allowed to appear, which other entities it should be near, the spacing it should maintain, and which criteria matter most. A reconnaissance element may emphasize visibility, maneuver corridors, and forward position; a logistics node may emphasize road access, support range, dispersion, and protection; a command post may emphasize communications, accessibility, and separation from obvious threat axes. Templates are editable because scenario designers must adapt them to the exercise's purpose.

The filter stage is deliberately conservative. It removes locations that would be invalid, incoherent, or highly implausible before the optimizer sees them. This choice reduces the risk that a clever algorithm finds a mathematically attractive but operationally nonsensical solution. For example, if a support element must remain behind a control line, positions beyond that line are not assigned low utility; they are excluded. This distinction between low desirability and infeasibility is central to operational pragmatism.

The analysis layer also supports grouping. Many constructive simulations represent hierarchical units. FDO-Init can first position a parent entity or formation anchor, then create subordinate candidate sets relative to that anchor. This two-level process supports coherent formation geometry while still allowing subordinates to be adjusted for local terrain and visibility. A deterministic random seed can introduce small variation across scenario replications without compromising reproducibility (Fig. 1).

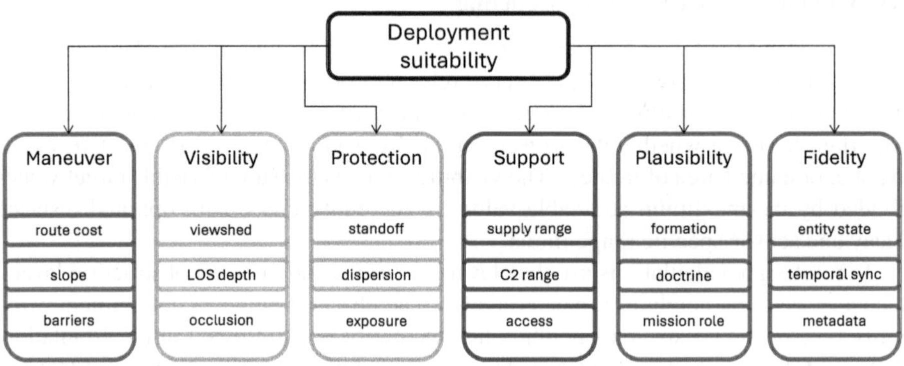

Fig. 1. Decision hierarchy used to translate operational intent into deployment suitability criteria. Criterion weights can be elicited using AHP, calibrated from exercise data, or varied during sensitivity analysis to expose trade-offs.

5 Multi-Criteria Optimization Workflow

The algorithmic workflow is designed for scenario-building time rather than real-time combat control. It must be fast enough for interactive use, though it can run longer than a runtime agent because initialization typically occurs before the exercise starts. The workflow consists of eight stages: ingest scenario inputs, harmonize geospatial layers, generate candidates, compute criteria, apply constraints, optimize assignments, explain alternatives, and export the simulation package.

The workflow is intentionally modular. A simulation organization can replace the viewshed engine, mobility model, ranking method, or export adapter without changing the overall concept. This modularity is essential because constructive simulation engines vary widely in entity resolution and scenario formats. FDO-Init should therefore be implemented as a service or library with clear data contracts, rather than as a monolithic feature embedded in a single simulation client (Fig. 2).

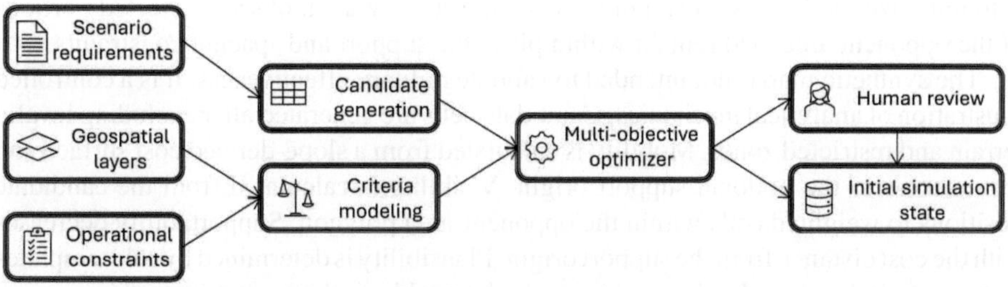

Fig. 2. FDO-Init processing architecture from scenario inputs to simulator-ready state, with the audit log, random seed, criterion weights, and rejected alternatives stored as part of the scenario package

Algorithm 1.Force deployment initialization with multi-criteria optimization.

```
Input: scenario S, entity set U, geospatial layers G, opponent area O,
constraints H, weights W
Output: initial entity deployment X*, diagnostics D, and simulator-ready
initialization package P
•1: preprocess G into aligned rasters and vector overlays; compute no-go
    mask and trafficability mask
•2: for each entity class u in U, generate candidate cells C_u using
    mission boundary, role, and spacing rules
•3: for each c in C_u, compute criteria f_mob, f_vis, f_sup, f_prt,
    f_pls, and uncertainty indicators
•4: discard c if any hard constraint in H is violated; retain reasons
    for discard in D
•5: form objective vectors q(u,c) and either solve the assignment MILP
    or run Pareto search plus local repair
•6: rank non-dominated deployments using stakeholder weights W and
    regret/sensitivity checks
•7: present X* with explanations, alternatives, and editable overrides
    to a human controller
•8: export P as deterministic entity state, seed, spatial reference,
    criterion scores, and provenance metadata
```

6 Illustrative Synthetic Case Study

To demonstrate the workflow without using sensitive or real operational data, consider a synthetic area of operations represented by a 5-by-5 km raster, a notional opponent-area polygon, a route and support-origin proxy, and a digital elevation-like surface. The scenario includes several force entities with different roles: two observation-oriented entities, three maneuver entities, one command element, and one support element. The goal is to initialize the force so it can move from the starting area, observe selected portions of the opponent area, and remain within plausible support and spacing constraints.

The synthetic map is not intended to validate military effectiveness. It is a controlled illustration of analytical mechanics. Candidate cells are generated after excluding invalid terrain and restricted zones. Mobility is calculated from a slope-derived cost surface and from access to the notional support origin. Visibility is calculated from the candidate positions to weighted cells within the opponent-area polygon. Supportability decreases with the cost distance from the support origin. Plausibility is determined by role templates that constrain forward depth, spacing, and relationship to the formation anchor.

To make the demonstration reproducible, the synthetic area was discretized into regular candidate cells. Each cell was assigned normalized terrain and operational attributes in the interval [0,1]. Mobility was derived from the local slope and access to the notional route network. Visibility was computed as the weighted proportion of opponent-area cells observable from the candidate position. Supportability decreased with movement-cost distance from the support origin. Protection was computed from dispersion, standoff from the opponent area, and an exposure penalty. Plausibility was assigned from role templates that encoded expected depth, spacing, and relationship to the formation anchor. Candidates that violated hard constraints, such as restricted terrain, insufficient spacing, or incompatible role zones, were removed before optimization (Figs. 3, 4 and 5).

The three scenarios illustrate different spatial configurations produced by the same workflow. Scenario 1 emphasizes a compact friendly deployment with concentrated observation opportunities. Scenario 2 separates the friendly and opponent candidate sets more clearly and produces longer observation or connectivity links. Scenario 3 shows a wider distribution of opponent-area targets and highlights the importance of balancing visibility with exposure and supportability. These examples demonstrate how FDO-Init can generate alternative initial states while preserving explicit diagnostic information for human review.

The case study is intentionally synthetic and does not validate combat effectiveness. Its purpose is to demonstrate how FDO-Init transforms heterogeneous terrain and scenario inputs into candidate positions, criterion scores, rejected-alternative diagnostics, and a simulator-ready initial state. A full empirical evaluation would require comparison with expert-created baselines, measurement of scenario setup time, reviewer trust, invalid placement rate, and the sensitivity of simulation outcomes to initial deployment variants.

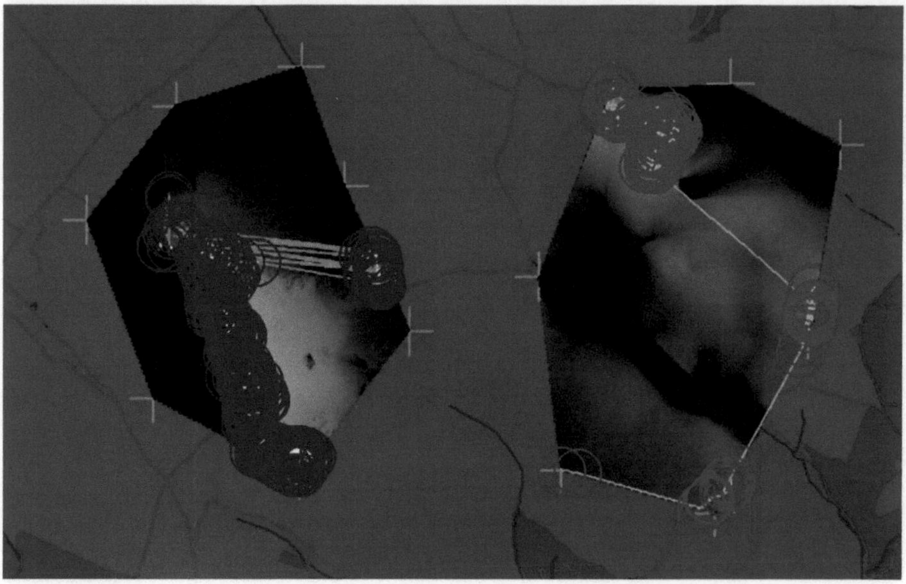

Fig. 3. Scenario 1: suitability candidate position/points with friendly and opponent-area outline. (blue = friendly candidate positions, red = opponent-area candidates/targets, grayscale = terrain/suitability surface, green areas = forest/vegetation)

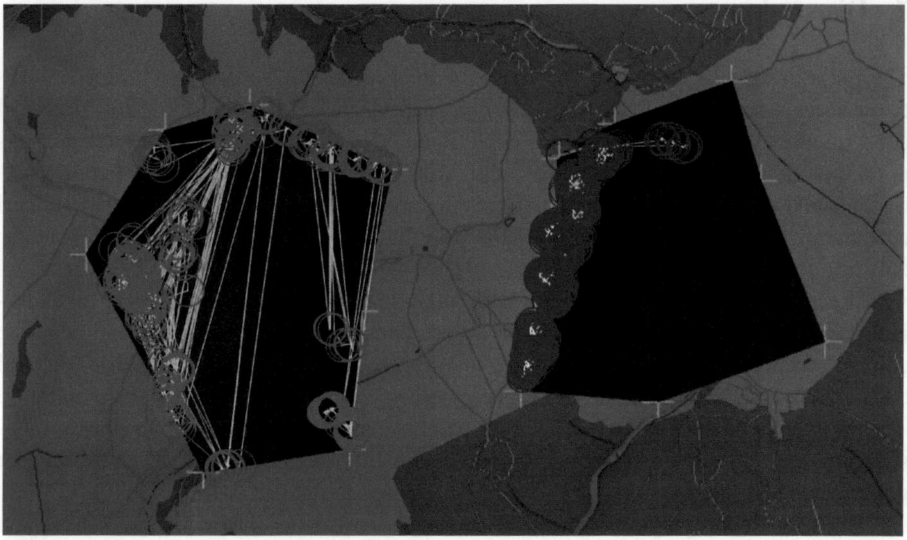

Fig. 4. Scenario 2: suitability candidate position/points with friendly and opponent-area outline. (blue = friendly candidate positions, red = opponent-area candidates/targets, grayscale = terrain/suitability surface, green areas = forest/vegetation)

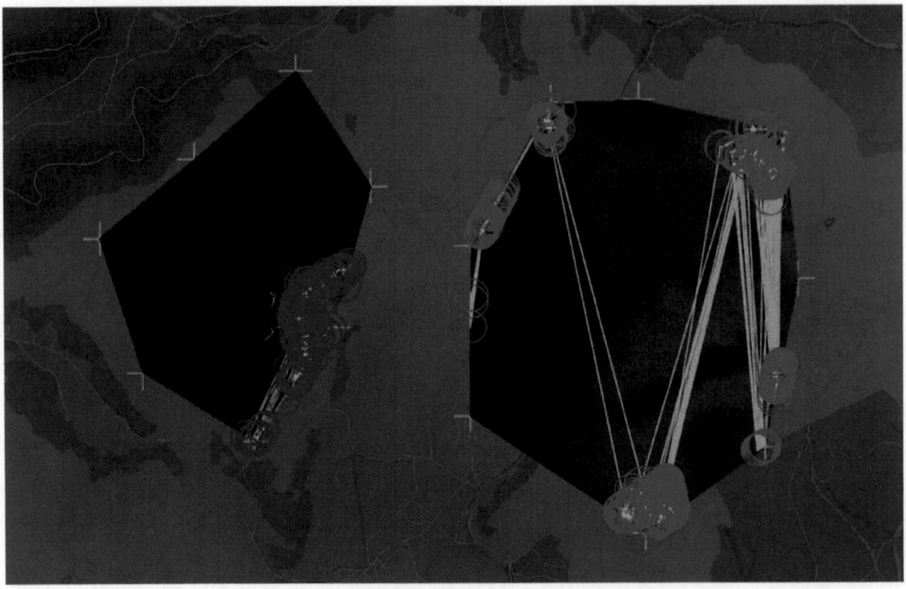

Fig. 5. Scenario 3: suitability candidate position/points with friendly and opponent-area outline. (blue = friendly candidate positions, red = opponent-area candidates/targets, grayscale = terrain/suitability surface, green areas = forest/vegetation)

7 Discussion

The main design decision in FDO-Init is to treat initialization as a constrained multi-criteria decision problem rather than a map-editing task. This reframing has practical consequences. It makes assumptions explicit, enables repeatable scenario variants, supports quantitative sensitivity analysis, and strengthens the connection between geospatial data and simulation state. It also forces the organization to distinguish between hard constraints and soft preferences, a distinction that is often blurred in manual scenario construction.

The approach is compatible with both analytical and training wargames. In analytical studies, reproducibility and sensitivity are paramount. The optimizer can generate controlled initial-state variants, enabling analysts to assess whether conclusions depend on a specific placement. In training exercises, speed and plausibility are paramount. The optimizer can accelerate setup and provide instructors with alternatives that emphasize different learning objectives. The same technical pipeline serves both purposes, but governance and the user interface should be adapted to the use case.

The most challenging research issue is not choosing an optimizer. Many optimization algorithms can search the feasible space. The harder problem is criterion validity: ensuring that the scores reflect what scenario designers actually mean by maneuverability, visibility, supportability, and plausibility. This requires iterative work with subject-matter experts, not just algorithm engineering. It also requires humility about what geospatial data can prove. A high score should be interpreted as a structured recommendation under stated assumptions, not as operational truth.

A second challenge is scale. Large constructive simulations may involve thousands of entities and many scenario variants. Exact optimization may be too slow, and full viewshed calculation may be expensive. The framework addresses this through candidate pruning, cached mobility surfaces, approximate visibility screening, parallel computation, and hierarchical deployment. Future work should investigate surrogate models that predict visibility or mobility scores for candidate generation while preserving auditability and avoiding opaque recommendations.

8 Conclusion

This article presented a scientific, implementation-oriented solution for automating initial force deployment in constructive wargaming simulations. The proposed FDO-Init framework integrates geospatial analysis, operational role templates, hard constraints, multi-criteria scoring, and optimization. Its central idea is that initialization should be treated as a transparent decision-support problem rather than as manual placement or black-box automation.

The solution directly addresses the requirement for operational pragmatism. It optimizes maneuverability and visibility into the opponent's area while considering a broader set of criteria, including supportability, protection, plausibility, simulation fidelity, uncertainty, and human judgment. By presenting a portfolio of alternatives and maintaining an audit trail, this approach enables scenario designers to understand and adjust the deployment rather than merely accepting a computed answer.

Future work should implement the framework in a representative constructive simulation environment, evaluate it with professional scenario designers, and compare setup time, invalid initialization rate, reviewer trust, and outcome stability against manual baselines. Additional research should also examine learning from approved human edits, integrate richer obstruction and weather data, and extend the method to multi-side scenario initialization. The expected benefit is not a perfect automated staff officer but a disciplined, explainable, and reusable initialization capability for digital wargaming.

Acknowledgments. The article uses only notional examples and synthetic figures. No real operational plan, classified dataset, or real-world deployment recommendation is represented.

Disclosure of Interests. The authors have no competing interests to declare.

References

1. Perla, P.P.: The Art of Wargaming: a Guide for Professionals and Hobbyists. Naval Institute Press, Annapolis (1990)
2. Sabin, P.: Simulating War: Studying Conflict through Simulation Games. Bloomsbury Academic, London (2012)
3. Page, E.H.: Modeling and Simulation, Experimentation, and Wargaming: Assessing a Common Landscape. MITRE Corporation, McLean (2016)
4. Bruvoll, S., et al.: Simulation-Supported Wargaming for Analysis of Plans. In: NATO STO-MP-MSG-133, 12 (2015)

5. Evensen, P.-I., Martinussen, S.E., Halsor, M., Bentsen, D.H.: Simulation-supported Wargaming for assessing force structures. Scandinavian J. Mil. Stud. **5**(1), 323–333 (2022). https://doi.org/10.31374/sjms.128
6. IEEE Computer Society: IEEE Std 1516–2025, IEEE Standard for Modeling and Simulation (M&S) High Level Architecture (HLA). IEEE, New York (2025)
7. Malczewski, J.: GIS-based multicriteria decision analysis: a survey of the literature. Int. J. Geogr. Inf. Sci. **20**(7), 703–726 (2006). https://doi.org/10.1080/13658810600661508
8. Malczewski, J., Rinner, C.: Multicriteria Decision Analysis in Geographic Information Science. Springer, Berlin (2015)
9. Saaty, T.L.: The Analytic Hierarchy Process: Planning, Priority Setting. Resource Allocation. McGraw-Hill, New York (1980)
10. Hwang, C.L., Yoon, K.: Multiple Attribute Decision Making: Methods and Applications. Springer, Berlin (1981)
11. Deb, K., Pratap, A., Agarwal, S., Meyarivan, T.: A fast and elitist multiobjective genetic algorithm: NSGA-II. IEEE Trans. Evol. Comput. **6**(2), 182–197 (2002). https://doi.org/10.1109/4235.996017
12. Dijkstra, E.W.: A note on two problems in connexion with graphs. Numer. Math. **1**, 269–271 (1959). https://doi.org/10.1007/BF01386390
13. Hart, P.E., Nilsson, N.J., Raphael, B.: A formal basis for the heuristic determination of minimum cost paths. IEEE Trans. Syst. Sci. Cybern. **4**(2), 100–107 (1968). https://doi.org/10.1109/TSSC.1968.300136
14. Kim, Y.-H., Rana, S., Wise, S.: Exploring multiple viewshed analysis using terrain features and optimisation techniques. Comput. Geosci. **30**(9–10), 1019–1032 (2004). https://doi.org/10.1016/j.cageo.2004.07.008
15. Rada, J., Rybansky, M., Dohnal, F.: The impact of the accuracy of terrain surface data on the navigation of off-road vehicles. ISPRS Int. J. Geo Inf. **10**(3), 106 (2021). https://doi.org/10.3390/ijgi10030106
16. Khan, M.N., Kashif, M., Shah, A.: Off-road Trafficability for military operations using multicriteria decision analysis. Int. J. Adv. Remote Sens. GIS. **10**(1), 3425–3437 (2021). https://doi.org/10.23953/cloud.ijarsg.489
17. Esri: Using Viewshed and Observer Points for visibility analysis. ArcGIS Pro Documentation. Accessed 25 Jun 2026
18. Esri: What is Military Ground Mobility? ArcGIS AllSource Documentation. Accessed 25 Jun 2026

Integrating Digital Twins into Simulation Systems: A UAS Proof of Concept

Jan Hodický[1](✉) and Graham Long[2]

[1] NATO HQ SACT, Norfolk, VA 23455, USA
jan.hodicky@nato.int
[2] Thales UK, Reading, UK

Abstract. This paper presents a proof of concept demonstrating the integration of Digital Twins (DTs) into simulation environments to enhance the fidelity and adaptability of autonomous systems modelling. The study explores the implementation of a DT architecture for an Uncrewed Aerial System (UAS), combining a physical quadcopter with its digital counterpart, which includes a flight dynamics model, AI-based control system, and ground control interface. The DT is constructed and continuously refined using real-world telemetry data, enabling bi-directional, real-time synchronization between physical and digital entities. This persistent linkage allows the DT to reflect dynamic state changes in the physical system, while also supporting optimizations and control feedback.

The approach leverages open standards and composable, modular simulation architectures to replace selected functionalities of the Computer Generated Forces (CGF) system with DT-derived behaviors. The evolving AI flight model, trained using data from the physical asset, was progressively integrated and assessed within the simulation to validate performance gains across training iterations. Comparative analyses showed significant improvement in mission execution, particularly in precision path following and search pattern adherence.

The results underscore the feasibility and advantages of embedding AI-enhanced DTs into constructive simulation environments, offering enhanced realism, system adaptability, and analytical transparency. This work lays foundational insights for the broader application of DTs in simulation-based testing, optimization, and decision support for military applications.

Keywords: Digital Twin · Constructive simulation · High Level Architecture Modelling and Simulation

1 Introduction

NATO is tracking technology that can influence modelling and simulation domain itself. Besides big data and artificial intelligence a digital twin has been identified as a technology that may change the way the current simulation system capabilities can be extended to reach higher resolution in modelling the problem space [1]. In the context of the paper a concept of Digital Twin and simulation system is elaborated to enable understanding of a proof of concept demonstrating the integration of Digital Twins (DTs) into constructive simulation to enhance the fidelity and adaptability of autonomous systems modelling.

J. Novotný et al. (Eds.): MESAS 2025, LNCS 16627, pp. 337–349, 2027.
https://doi.org/10.1007/978-3-032-33182-3_20

1.1 Digital Twin and Basic Replated Concepts

From NASA's pioneering use of digital replicas of spacecraft for real-time simulation, troubleshooting, monitoring, and managing complex mission systems to Dr. Michael Greives's first credited use of the term and application of digital twins to manufacturing [2], digital twins are rapidly evolving in capability and expanding to many diverse fields, products, and services. They have become a foundation of Industry 4.0, revolutionizing decision-making processes, product design, production optimization, and predictive maintenance in manufacturing, and are now finding applications in energy, construction, infrastructure, urban planning, and healthcare. In essence, DTs consist of a digital or virtual representation of a physical asset, system, system of systems or process with a dynamic data connection between the physical and digital counterparts. However, the lack of consensus and common understanding of the precise definition of a digital twin is a common theme across industry and research [3, 4] and various definitions have emerged and been subject to review [5, 6]. Furthermore, the expanding adoption of digital twins across many domains and applications has led to a plethora of use-case specific definitions [3, 4] and served to further increase ambiguity and diverging digital twin definitions.

For this research, the NATO created the working definition on Digital Twins:

"A Digital Twin is a virtual representation of a connected physical asset. The key word 'connected' indicates a synchronous and asynchronous exchange of data and a feedback loop between the model and physical asset."

Despite the extensive variation in Digital Twin definitions across different application, domain and usecase contexts, they share a fundamental common understanding of a digital twin as a digital counterpart of a physical entity. Nevertheless, this concept is blurred by related terms such as Digital Shadows and Digital Models which are often used synonymously with Digital Twin, but which reflect different levels of data integration between physical and digital counterparts.

To overcome these multiple interpretations and concepts and achieve a more common understanding, Kritzinger proposes a classification of Digital Twins into three subcategories, according to their level of data integration [4]. A Digital Model is a digital representation of an existing or planned physical object that does not use any form of automated data exchange between the physical object and the digital object. A change in state of the physical object has no direct effect on the digital object and vice versa. A Digital Shadow provides an automated one-way data flow between the state of an existing physical object and a digital object, and a change in state of the physical object leads to a change of state in the digital object, but not vice versa. Finally, in a Digital Twin, the data flows between an existing physical object and a digital object are fully integrated in both directions. In such a combination, the digital object might also act as controlling instance of the physical object. There might also be other objects, physical or digital, which induce changes of state in the digital object. A change in state of the physical object directly leads to a change in state of the digital object and vice versa. The digital thread, a critical concept in the operation of digital twins, serves as a communication framework within DT systems. It facilitates the seamless flow of data across the entire lifecycle of a product, from design and manufacturing to operation and maintenance. More than just a conduit for data, the digital thread ensures the synchronization between physical and virtual models, maintaining a continuous connection between different stages of a product's lifecycle and various digital twins. This integrated flow of information is not just essential for creating a comprehensive and accurate digital representation of a physical entity, but also for supporting more informed decision-making and efficient operations. In the context of Industrie 4.0, the digital thread plays a crucial role in advancing from a basic digital model to a predictive twin, enabling real-time updates and predictive analytics. By ensuring data continuity, the digital thread enhances the effectiveness and accuracy of digital twin systems, allowing for continuous evolution and maturation of these digital representations.

1.2 Simulation System

References to "simulation system" in this report shall adopt NATO's definition of a simulation system as: "a combination of interacting elements or components organized to provide a representation of a system or of a part of the real world for an intended use. Example of simulation components are hardware, software, models, databases, human operators and procedures." [7]. NATO uses a constructive simulation for collective education and training and analytical purposes. Therefore, in the context of the paper, we limit simulation system to a constructive simulation that is defined by NATO: "A simulation involving simulated control entities, including agents, operating simulated systems. (Human operators make inputs to such simulations, but are not directly involved in determining the outcomes.)" [7]. In certain literature the computer generated forces (CGF) is a synonym for a constructive simulation.

1.3 Problem Statement

Despite the growing maturity of Digital Twin (DT) technology and its proven value in representing physical systems with high-fidelity, bi-directionally connected models, there remains a significant gap in methodologies for integrating DTs into constructive simulation and stimulation environments at scale. Current approaches and practices are often limited to isolated, single-asset implementations, lacking the interoperable aspects assuring composing multiple DTs into a constructive simulation. This limits the exploitation of DT capabilities for dynamic scenario evaluation, real-time optimization, and adaptive control in complex, multi-level simulation contexts.

2 Proof of Concept Design, Methods and Material

2.1 Main Objective

The proof of concept demonstrates the integration of Digital Twins (DTs) into a constructive simulation environments to enhance the fidelity and adaptability of autonomous systems modelling. The study explores the implementation of a DT architecture for an Uncrewed Aerial System (UAS), combining a physical quadcopter with its digital counterpart, which includes a flight dynamics model, AI-based control system, and ground control interface while exploring the limitation of current standards, best practices architectures.

The main objective of this concept was to design and implement a mechanism to demonstrate how open standards, and modular, composable architectures can be used to integrate a DT into a simulation system, and replace a selected functionality of the constructive simulation with the DT.

Modularity is defined as: "A measure of the extent to which a program is composed of modules, such that a change to one module has minimal impact on other modules." [7] and composability is explained as: "A simulation design principle that deals with the inter-relationships of components (a highly composable system provides recombinant components that can be selected and assembled in various combinations to satisfy specific user requirements)". Open standard is generally understood as a technical specification that is publicly available and free to use, modify, and distribute without restrictions.

2.2 Operational Concept

The user operational concept concerns the integration of a DT to replace a simulation component of a modular, open architecture simulation system (Fig. 1) that:

- Enables severable functionality and system components to be developed added, removed, or replaced separately and independently.
- Allows inclusion of new capabilities, components, user applications and technical services with an expected level of resources (e.g. time, procedural steps).
- Adopts open modelling standards.
- Is extensible with compatible and pluggable content, functionality, and models.
- Enables the coupling of applications and services via standardized APIs and interfaces.

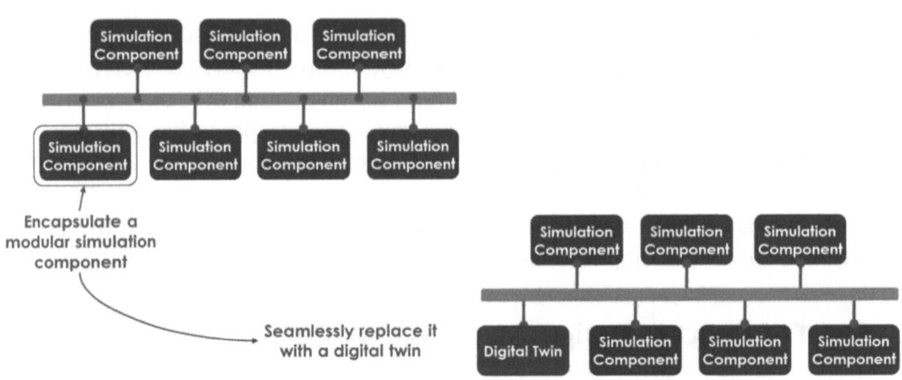

Fig. 1. Simulation component replacement with a Digital Twin

2.3 Main Architecture

The solution is based on the Thales Air and Space Operational Environment Digital Twin (AOEDT), which combines a synthetic environment, simulation components, digital models, shadows and DTs to provide offline and online, high fidelity decision aiding, optimization and control capabilities. The two primary objectives of the proof of concept design and architecture are to enable the encapsulation of simulation components, including DTs, and to support and provide the capability to orchestrate and compose the system with the required combination of components, including the potential to integrate DTs into the system in place of or in addition to existing components.

Encapsulating simulation components as loosely coupled, modular, composable assets using open modelling, API and interface standards has been fulfilled through the implementation of a distributed simulation (DS) [8] architecture (Fig. 2) that orchestrates the AOEDT simulation components around a High Level Architecture (HLA) framework [9], integrated in a federated, interoperable simulation environment.

The capability to configure and adapt the simulation environment with the addition and removal of simulation component and DT assets is provided by discovering, orchestrating and deploying the simulation system and its components through the implementation of a Modelling & Simulation as a Service (MSaaS) [10] environment managed by the Thales NUADA MSaaS tool.

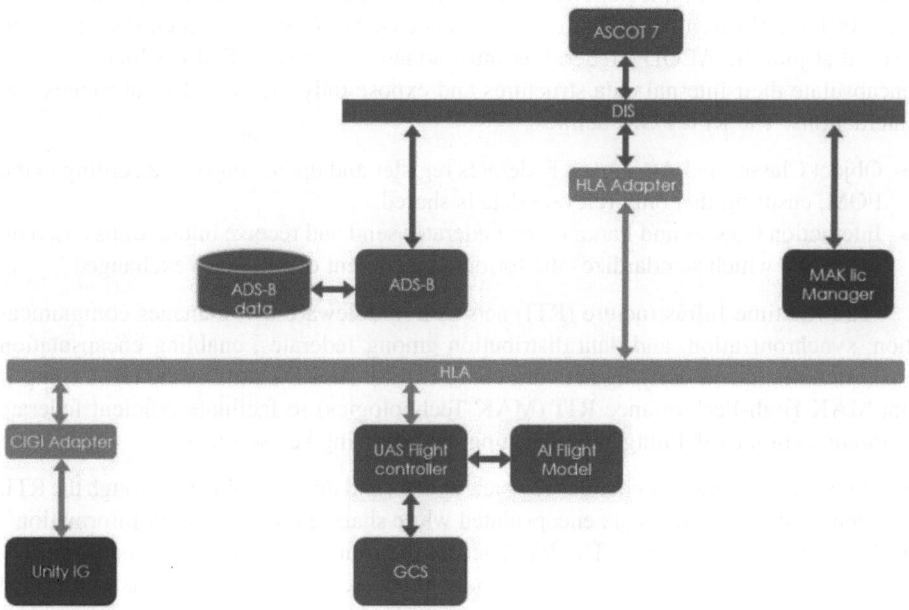

Fig. 2. System architecture

The AOEDT system (Fig. 2) is designed and implemented as a standards based, distributed simulation architecture designed to provide an open, versatile, adaptable system that provides a framework and capability to compose solutions from appropriate synthetic environment and simulation components, digital models, shadows and DTs. This approach enables the flexible composition of the AOEDT system from existing Thales simulation assets and DTs, as well as the provision and integration of DT related services, such as data and analytics services.

The baseline AOEDT system is configured with the following simulation federates:

- Unity IG - 3D real-time visualization of the virtual environment (terrain, entities etc.)
- Test UAS Digital Twin - Ground Control Station and AI driven performance model (AI Flight Dynamics)
- ASCOT7 - Computer-Generated Entity (CGE) platform for the simulated environment covering operations in land, air, maritime, cyber and space domains
- ADS-B (Automatic Dependent Surveillance–Broadcast) data - aviation surveillance broadcasts of position and other related data.

The baseline configuration was used as the starting point to demonstrate the encapsulation of components and system adaptation by adding DT components, associated data analytics services, and removal of simulation components, such as a CFG federate.

The AOEDT HLA federation employs HLA Evolved (IEEE 1516–2010), and adopts an industry standard implementations of HLA rules, interface specification, object models, management and optimization of federate communication and interoperability.

The Federation Object Model (FOM) defines the common data and interactions that federates use to communicate. The AOEDT system employs the industry standard SISO-STD-001.1-2015 Real-time Platform Reference (RPR) FOM. All federates, including DTs, that join the AEODT federation must adhere to the RPR FOM, which serves to encapsulate their internal data structures and expose only the necessary attributes and interactions. The RPR FOM defines:

- Object Classes and Attributes: Federates register and update objects according to the FOM, ensuring that only relevant data is shared.
- Interaction Classes and Parameters: Federates send and receive interactions based on the FOM, which standardizes the format and content of messages exchanged

The Runtime Infrastructure (RTI) acts as a middleware that manages communication, synchronization, and data distribution among federates, enabling encapsulation by abstracting the underlying network complexities. AOEDT utilises the HLA compliant MAK High-Performance RTI (MAK Technologies) to facilitate efficient federate communication by defining and managing the following key services:

- Object Management: Federates register, update, and discover objects through the RTI, keeping their internal state encapsulated while sharing only necessary information
- Interaction Management: The RTI handles the routing of interactions between federates, ensuring that each federate only processes interactions it has subscribed to.
- Data Distribution Management (DDM): DDM allows federates to publish and subscribe to data based on regions of interest, further encapsulating data exchange by ensuring that federates only receive relevant information.

Adapters and mediators facilitate communication and integration between federates, acting as intermediaries to manage and optimize federate interaction and perform specific tasks to ensure seamless data exchange, synchronization and compatibility between heterogeneous federate systems. Within the AOEDT system, ASCOT7 and the ADS-B data components use the DIS IEEE 1278 standard and are integrated into the simulation with an HLA adapter that bridges between HLA and DIS using the RPR FOM. A

CIGI adapter is used to bridge between HLA and the CIGI (Common Image Generator Interface) interface to the Unity Image Generator component.

2.4 Material - Digital Twin

The UAS DT consists of a physical asset, a small quadcopter drone (Fig. 3), and its digital counterpart (Fig. 4) comprised of a flight dynamics model, drone flight controller that provides route and waypoint management, and ground control station.

Fig. 3. UAS physical quadcopter drone

2.5 Method - UAS Flight Model Training

The UAS Digital Twin (Fig. 5) models the flight dynamics of the physical UAS from actual flight data captured from the physical quadcopter drone which is then used to train an Artificial Intelligence (AI) flight dynamics and drone battery model.

In the scenario proposed to support the proof of concept development, the DT flight model is at an early stage of development and evolutions of the AI flight model were integrated into the simulation system and its capability and maturity were evaluated as it progressed through the AI training process, with an expectation that the model performance would improve as model training progressed (Fig. 6).

Several drone flights were completed to capture suitable flight data that would form the training data set for the AI flight dynamics model. These flights included both free flight and prescribed flight patterns to ensure a sufficient range and variety of data was captured across the flight envelope to support effective AI model training. The prescribed flight pattern was also used as one of the comparative benchmarks to evaluate the flight performance of the physical and digital UAS counterparts.

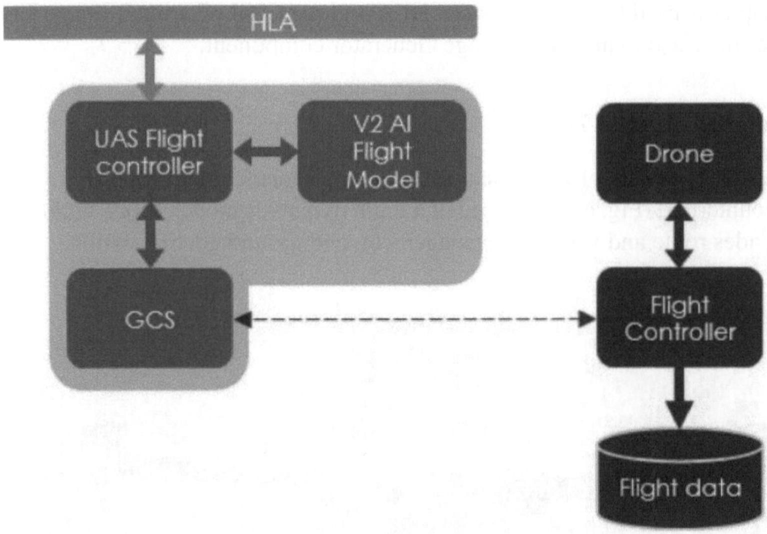

Fig. 4. UAS Digital Twin – digital counterpart

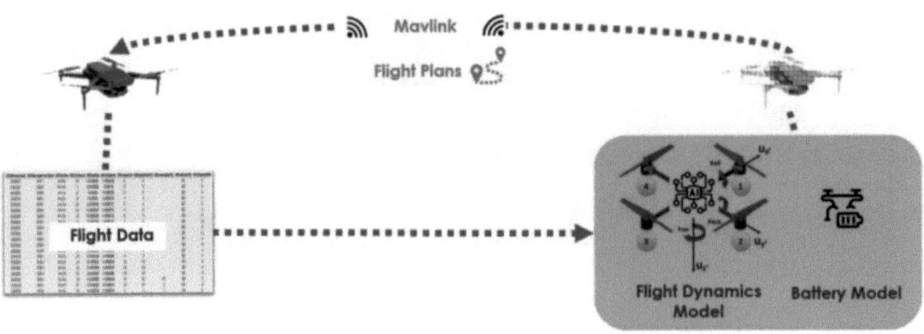

Fig. 5. Digital twin flight model

The flight data was pre-processed to clean and organize the data, by removing noise, synchronizing timestamps and extracting relevant features including accelerations, angular rates and control responses.

A neural network model for predicting flight dynamics and reinforcement learning model for control optimization were then iteratively trained on the flight data to learn the relationship between control inputs and quadcopter responses, minimizing prediction errors. Approximately 50 iterations of the AI models were run to achieve a plausible level of UAS flight performance. Model iterations were validated and tested by evaluating performance using RMSE and other metrics on key flight parameters, like angular velocities, and by analyzing AI flight model predictions compared to ground-truth flight data, and the execution and adherence to flight plan profiles relative to the performance of the real UAS.

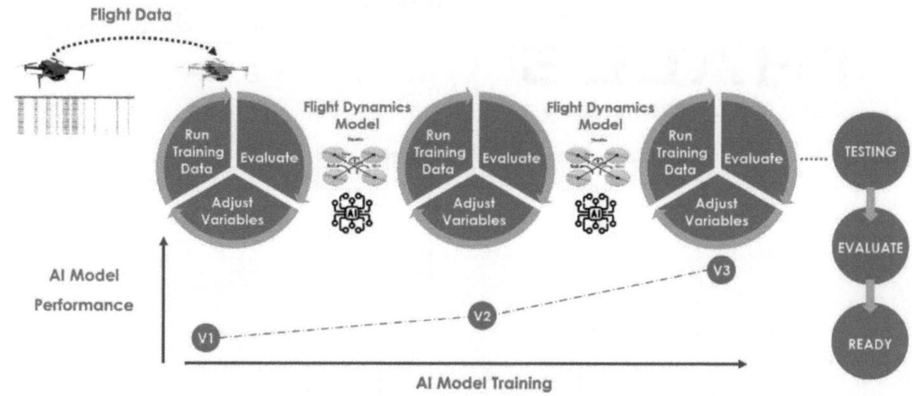

Fig. 6. AI flight model training process

The objective within the limited scenario and scope of the proof of concept was to achieve a plausible level of flight performance and conduct a level of appropriate validation to verify this. In practice, the flight models will be developed and matured to the level of fidelity required by each target use case and application of the final DT, which will dictate the appropriate level of verification and validation applied to the flight model.

3 Results

In the scenario proposed to support the proof of concept development, the DT flight model is at an early stage of development and evolutions of the AI flight model were integrated into the simulation system and its capability and maturity were evaluated as it progressed through the AI training process, with an expectation that the model performance would improve as model training progressed.

3.1 Real Uas Versus Ai Flight Model Analysis

The first step performed analysis of the AI flight model performance compared to the real UAS, to verify it accurately represents real UAS flight performance. A spatial analysis (Fig. 7) of the relative performance of the twin and real UAS was used to illustrate the comparison of their flight path plots on a map and confirm that the AI flight model achieved a plausible level of flight performance that accurately replicated the flight of the real UAS.

3.2 Ai Flight Model Versus CGF Flight Analysis

In the demonstration scenario, the user requires a higher fidelity model of the UAS than can be provided by a CGF UAS, and the DT UAS is integrated into the simulation system to provide an accurate, realistic representation of UAS performance. A spatial analysis

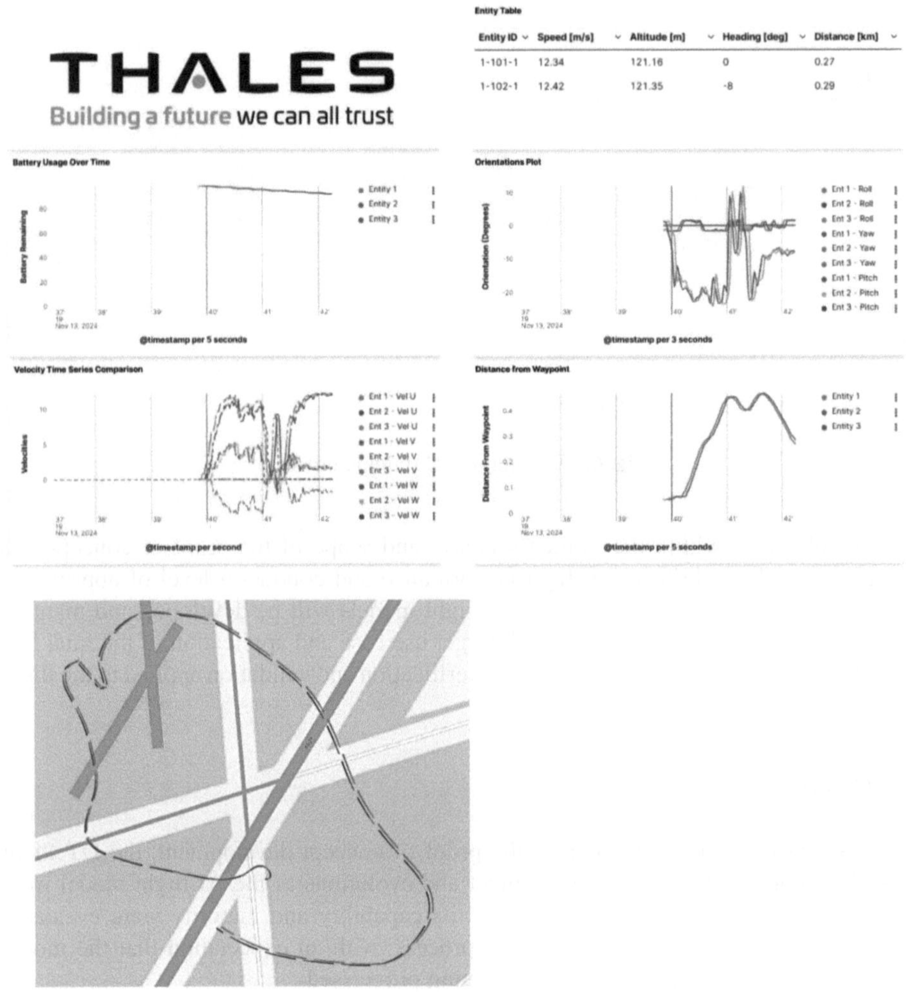

Fig. 7. Real UAS flight vs. AI flight model

(Fig. 8) of the relative performance of the twin and CGF UAS was used to illustrate and evaluate the AI flight models capability to provide a realistic flight performance when executing a search pattern (illustrated with the solid red line) compared to a CGF. This analysis highlighted that the CGF (the blue dashed line) follows an artificially smooth flight path compared to the AI flight model (green dashed line).

3.3 AI Flight Model V1 Versus CGF Flight Model V2

The demonstration scenario also reflects the development phase of the DT and the iteration of the AI flight model that results from the progression of the AI training process. A comparison of iterations of the AI flight model as it progresses through training (Fig. 9) was undertaken to verify that flight performance and the capability to

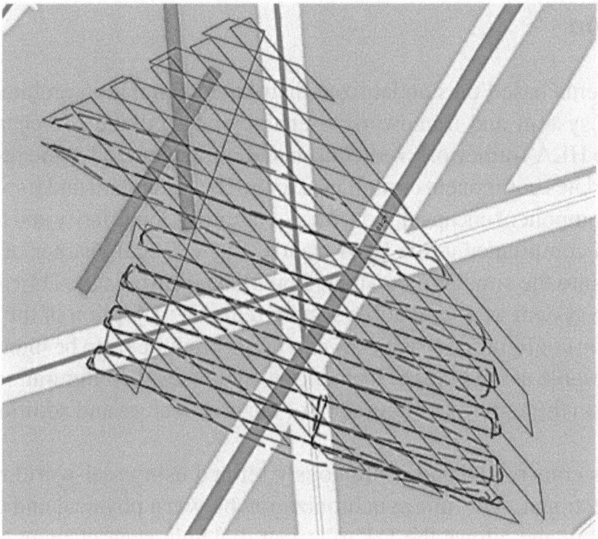

Fig. 8. CGF UAS flight vs. AI flight model

accurately fly a search pattern improves between the earlier model on the left and later model on the right.

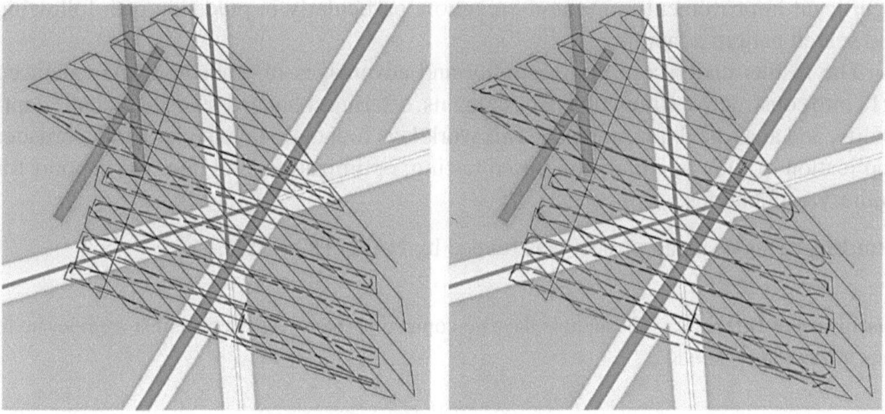

Fig. 9. AI flight model V1 versus V2

This process also illustrates the analysis capability that will be required in many deployed DTs that will utilize the dynamic data connection with their physical counterpart to evolve the digital model over time to reflect the latest state of the physical entity.

4 Conclusion

Simulation systems based on standardized distributed simulation architectures provide a structured ecosystem and framework to enable and facilitate DT encapsulation and integration. The HLA framework was chosen and implemented for the proof of concept solution. It mandates component compliance to the HLA standard and implementation of HLA imposes component encapsulation, interoperability, modularity and loose coupling.

Digital twin compliance to the HLA standard is a critical enabler of encapsulation and integration into the simulation system. Compliance ensures the DT can perform and interact with the system as a compatible system federate. Adoption of the HLA standard provides a system configuration "pattern" enabling components to be interoperable, integrated & composable using MSaaS. It enables well managed configuration and seamless system adaptation through re-configuration of the architecture and addition and removal of federates.

The DT was constructed and continuously refined using real-world telemetry data, enabling bi-directional, real-time synchronization between physical and digital entities. This persistent linkage allows the DT to reflect dynamic state changes in the physical system, while also supporting optimizations and control feedback.

The approach leverages open standards and composable, modular simulation architectures to replace selected functionalities of the Computer Generated Forces (CGF) system with DT-derived behaviors. The evolving AI flight model, trained using data from the physical asset, was progressively integrated and assessed within the simulation to validate performance gains across training iterations. Comparative analyses showed significant improvement in mission execution, particularly in precision path following and search pattern adherence.

The results underscore the feasibility and advantages of embedding AI-enhanced DTs into constructive simulation environments, offering enhanced realism, system adaptability, and analytical transparency. This work lays foundational insights for the broader application of DTs in simulation-based testing, optimization, and decision support for military applications.

Funding This research project was funded by NATO HQ SACT.

Disclosure of Interests. The authors have no competing interests to declare that are relevant to the content of this article

References

1. The future of Modelling and Simulation: Open Publications. ISSN 2957–7160. 8. (2023)
2. Michael, G.: Origins of the Digital Twin Concept (2016). https://doi.org/10.13140/RG.2.2.26367.61609.
3. Van der Valk, H., Haße, H., Molle Fr, Otto B.: Archetypes of Digital Twins (2021). https://doi.org/10.1007/s12599-021-00727-7
4. Kritzinger, W., Karner, M., Traar, G., Henjes, J., Sihn, W.: Digital Twin in manufacturing: A categorical literature review and classification (2018). https://doi.org/10.1016/j.ifacol.2018.08.474

5. Tao, F., Zhang, H., Liu, A., Nee, A.: Digital twin in industry: state-of-the-art. IEEE Trans. Industr. Inform. **15**(4) (2019)
6. Mihai, S., et al.: Digital Twins: A Survey on Enabling Technologies, Challenges, Trends and Future Prospects (2022). https://api.semanticscholar.org/CorpusID:252486716
7. NATO Term: https://nso.nato.int/natoterm/Web.mvc
8. Misra, J.: Distributed discrete-event simulation. ACM Comput. Surv. **18**(1), 39–65 (1986)
9. Hodický, J.: HLA as an experimental backbone for autonomous system integration into operational field. In: Hodický, J. (ed.) Modelling and Simulation for Autonomous Systems: First International Workshop, MESAS 2014, Rome, Italy, May 5–6, 2014, Revised Selected Papers (Lecture Notes in Computer Science, Vol. 8906, Pp. 121–126). Springer (2014)
10. Shahin, M., Babar, M.A., Chauhan, M.A.: Architectural design space for modelling and simulation as a service: a review. J. Syst. Softw. **170**, 110752 (2020). https://doi.org/10.1016/j.jss.2020.110752

Supporting MRSI Calculations for Legacy Mortar Systems: Structured Software Tool for Operational Use and Future Development

Tomáš Havlík[1(✉)], Jan Nohel[1], Miroslav Mušinka[2], and Janusz Materac[3]

[1] University of Defence, Brno Kounicova 65, 66210, Czech Republic
tomas.havlik@unob.cz

[2] Armed Forces Academy, Demänová 393, 03101 Liptovský Mikuláš, Slovakia

[3] Military University of Land Forces, Piotra Czajkowskiego 109, 51-147 Wrocław, Poland

Abstract. This paper presents a support tool developed to assist mortar fire controllers in calculating parameters for achieving Multiple Rounds Simultaneous Impact (MRSI) with conventional, manually operated mortar systems. The tool is implemented as a structured software library in C#, enabling consistent computation of firing combinations based on digitized firing tables and simplified ballistic models. It is designed for use with legacy systems that lack automated fire control capabilities and rely on manual input.

Developed independently as a research initiative, the tool was created with the intention of potential integration into systems such as PVNPG-14 m. Its main objective is to complement and streamline current manual procedures, especially where standardized methods for MRSI are not available. By assisting in the selection of appropriate munition and timing combinations, the tool increases calculation speed and supports operational decision-making in the field.

Although the current version does not use artificial intelligence, the software's internal structure allows for further expansion. The paper concludes with a conceptual proposal for the future development of enhanced versions, including the potential application of AI and machine learning techniques to support adaptive fire planning, automation of routine calculations, or scenario-based evaluations in indirect fire support.

The presented solution contributes to practical fire control capabilities and may serve as a foundation for broader application in field operations, with the possibility of future use in training and doctrine development as the system evolves.

Keywords: Artillery · Mortar · MRSI · Software

1 Introduction

Multiple Rounds Simultaneous Impact (MRSI) represents an advanced artillery firing technique in which multiple projectiles are fired along different trajectories to achieve simultaneous impact on the target (see Fig. 1), thereby increasing target neutralization effectiveness and limiting the adversary's opportunity to implement countermeasures.

J. Novotný et al. (Eds.): MESAS 2025, LNCS 16627, pp. 350–368, 2027.
https://doi.org/10.1007/978-3-032-33182-3_21

The principles and practical applicability of MRSI have been examined in the context of conventional artillery employment, demonstrating both its tactical benefits and its sensitivity to firing data accuracy and timing precision [1].

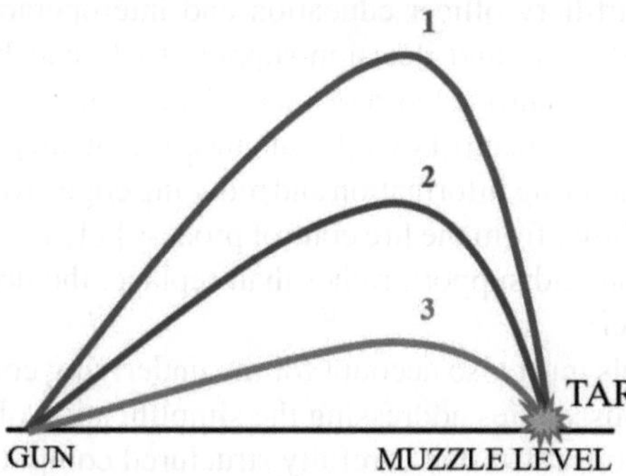

Fig. 1. Conceptual illustration of the Multiple Rounds Simultaneous Impact (MRSI) principle. Different projectile trajectories, achieved by varying elevation angles and firing times, result in a simultaneous impact on the target despite differing times of flight

In contemporary self-propelled artillery systems, MRSI capability is typically achieved through a high degree of automation, integrated ballistic computers, and sophisticated fire control architectures that enable rapid trajectory selection and precise synchronization of firing times [2]. Such systems rely on advanced mathematical models for the determination of firing units, providing high computational accuracy while minimizing human intervention in the fire control process [3]. However, these solutions are primarily associated with modern platforms and are not directly transferable to older or manually operated systems.

Despite ongoing modernization efforts, many armed forces (including members of NATO and the Visegrád Group) continue to operate a mixed inventory of modern artillery platforms alongside legacy towed howitzers and mortar systems. In these legacy systems, the adoption of automated fire control has often been partial, resulting in hybrid operational environments where modern computational tools coexist with manual gunnery procedures [4]. This disparity creates an operational gap between modern and legacy systems, affecting efficiency, interoperability, and tactical flexibility within joint and multinational operations [5, 6].

Operational constraints further influence the practical employment of mortar units, particularly in expeditionary or high-mobility scenarios. Factors such as ammunition transport, securing, and handling during movement can significantly affect deployment speed and firing readiness, thereby impacting the feasibility of time-sensitive fire missions [7]. These constraints reinforce the need for fire control solutions that improve responsiveness without imposing additional logistical or technical burdens on the unit.

While automation in modern platforms simplifies the computation of firing solutions, operators of manual or semi-digital systems must rely on traditional procedures involving printed firing tables, step-by-step calculations, and sequential corrections based on meteorological and topographic data [8]. Manual correction methods and contingency procedures remain essential in such environments, particularly when automated fire control support is unavailable or degraded [9]. The time and cognitive demands associated with these procedures directly limit the feasibility of advanced techniques such as MRSI when applied to legacy systems.

Recent research into artillery officer education and interoperability highlights the importance of training solutions and decision-support tools capable of bridging the technological divide between automated and manual fire control environments [10]. Decision-support systems have been shown to enhance the quality and consistency of command decisions by structuring information and reducing cognitive workload, without removing human responsibility from the fire control process [11, 12]. From this perspective, computational tools should support, rather than replace, the decision-making role of the crew and commander.

The design of such tools must also account for the underlying computational principles of fire control. Previous studies addressing the simplification of angular and linear measuring rules have demonstrated that carefully structured computational support can significantly improve the efficiency and reliability of firing data determination, even in systems not originally designed for automation [13, 14]. In parallel, optimization-based approaches to firing data computation, including algorithmic methods, have shown potential for improving accuracy and robustness under complex ballistic conditions [15].

Interoperability and communication considerations further shape the development of artillery fire control solutions. Experience from the design of automated and semi-automated artillery fire support systems underscores the importance of open architectures, modular software design, and compatibility with existing doctrinal and technical frameworks [16]. Such an approach enables incremental capability enhancement and facilitates integration within joint and multinational fire support environments.

Against this background, the application of MRSI to legacy mortar systems emerges as a problem well suited to targeted computational support. Although MRSI has traditionally been associated with modern self-propelled artillery, its execution fundamentally depends on accurate time-of-flight estimation, precise sequencing of firing times, and a clear understanding of ballistic constraints. These requirements can be addressed through lightweight, modular software tools that build upon existing manual gunnery procedures while extending them with computational support. In this context, the present study introduces a software-based tool designed to enable MRSI firing with legacy mortar systems, aiming to improve operational feasibility, reduce crew workload, and support interoperability across multinational artillery units.

2 Problem Context and Objectives

While modern artillery platforms equipped with advanced fire control systems perform MRSI calculations automatically [3], such capabilities remain unavailable to many mortar units, particularly in reserve formations or in countries maintaining large inventories of legacy towed or man-portable weapons. In these cases, fire direction relies on manual computation based on firing tables, a process that is both time-consuming and prone to human error under operational pressure [8].

The absence of standardized MRSI procedures for mortars results in highly variable performance, with outcomes heavily dependent on the skill, experience, and coordination of individual crew members [10]. Additional factors, such as mechanical constraints of the weapon (e.g., the speed and precision of elevation adjustment) and variations in ammunition performance, further limit the achievable simultaneity of impacts [17].

Previous research into manual fire control methods and contingency calculation procedures [8, 9, 13] shows that computational efficiency can be significantly improved through optimized algorithms and simplified firing data derivation, even without automated systems. Techniques such as improved genetic algorithms [15] and constructive simulation-based training [18] have proven effective in accelerating solution times while maintaining acceptable accuracy.

The primary objective of this research is to develop a low-complexity, platform-independent software tool capable of:

- Calculating feasible MRSI firing solutions for various mortar calibers.
- Minimizing computation time and hardware requirements.
- Providing outputs through a standardized interface for potential integration into existing or future systems.
- Serving as training and operational aid for manual MRSI execution.

The software is implemented as a C# Dynamic Link Library (DLL) for portability and modularity, enabling integration with command-and-control systems or simulation platforms. While the current version focuses on Czech 120 mm and 81 mm mortar systems, its architecture was developed in cooperation with Slovak and Polish partners to ensure adaptability to additional mortar types and ammunition sets. This multinational approach lays the groundwork for enhanced interoperability within the Visegrád Group and potentially with other allied forces.

3 Software Design, Architecture and Implementation

In response to the operational challenges outlined in Chapter 2, the developed solution aims to provide a versatile and low-complexity software tool capable of generating Multiple Round Simultaneous Impact (MRSI) firing solutions for legacy mortar systems. The implementation takes the form of a modular Dynamic Link Library (DLL) written in C#, chosen for its object-oriented structure, efficiency in managing complex data types, and compatibility with Windows-based environments commonly used in both operational and training contexts [19]. This modular approach to defence software architecture reflects established practices in systems engineering and decision-support modelling within the military domain [20].

The DLL architecture enables seamless integration into a variety of host applications, from stand-alone calculation tools to full-scale fire control systems (FCS), while maintaining minimal hardware requirements for deployment on portable field devices and simulation servers. This approach follows current defence software development practices, where modularity and reusability reduce costs and accelerate deployment cycles [19].

3.1 Architecture Overview

The software is structured into four independent modules, ensuring that updates or expansions in one component do not require modifications to the others. This modularity simplifies maintenance, supports gradual capability growth, and allows adaptation to new weapon systems with minimal changes to the computational core.

Topographic Computation Module. Processes positional data for both mortar and target to calculate topographic range, deflection, and elevation difference. These calculations form the foundation for determining feasible firing solutions. While based on established manual artillery computation methods, the module employs automated algorithms to increase speed and reduce human error [9]. Its design supports multiple coordinate systems and allows for future integration of terrain correction using digital elevation models. Environmental assessments of artillery impact zones may provide valuable reference data for terrain evaluation during firing data preparation [21].

Firing Tables Module. Manages access to digitized firing tables for various mortar types and ammunition. Printed tables were converted into standardized CSV files, enabling rapid data retrieval. Accurate digital replication of firing tables is essential for reliability, particularly when ammunition lots differ in ballistic characteristics [4]. Each propellant charge is stored with parameters such as range, quadrant elevation, time of flight, and angle of fall.

Weapons Module. Contains weapon-specific constraints, including elevation limits, available ammunition types, charge configurations, and mechanical limits such as maximum elevation speed. This ensures computed solutions remain safe and operationally feasible [3]. The stored parameters can be updated without altering the computational logic, enabling rapid adaptation to new mortar systems or multinational environments.

Input/Output Module. Standardizes the exchange of data between the library and host applications, handling inputs such as coordinates, weapon type, and ammunition selection, and producing outputs in a structured format. This facilitates integration into simulation platforms, tactical decision-support systems [22], or existing FCS. Communication architecture considerations for artillery fire support systems have been explored in earlier works [23], which informed the interface design for potential integration. Practical use of tactical decision support systems within ground unit command processes demonstrates the potential value of such integration [24].

3.2 Implementation Details

The library automates the entire MRSI planning process—from initial topographic calculations, through firing table lookups, to determining timing intervals for simultaneous impacts. In operational practice, such computations are often performed manually at the Fire Direction Centre (FDC), requiring multiple calculation steps, environmental corrections, and look-ups for each charge, a process that is time-consuming and prone to errors under combat stress. Automating these steps significantly reduces crew workload and increases precision [9].

Performance optimization was a priority. The implemented algorithms deliver results within one second, even when processing multiple ammunition types and complex firing scenarios. Statistical evaluation has confirmed that generated solutions remain within acceptable error margins when compared to manual calculations and live-fire calibration trials [25]. Advanced statistical validation methods, including approaches adapted for non-linear and circular data, can further improve accuracy assessment in future iterations [26]. Low resource requirements allow the software to run on ruggedized laptops, embedded systems, or older computing platforms still used in some military contexts.

3.3 Data Preparation and Security Considerations

During the research phase, a proof-of-concept version was implemented in Microsoft Excel using macros and embedded formulas to validate algorithm performance and firing table integration. Similar validation techniques using spreadsheet-based prototyping have been successfully applied in other optimization and computational modelling projects [27]. These prototyping approaches are common in military software development to ensure algorithm validity before full implementation [25].

The current version does not incorporate encryption or access control but is intended for deployment within secure military networks. Future iterations are planned to include encrypted firing tables, access-restricted interfaces, and adaptive computation features inspired by reinforcement learning principles [28] to dynamically adjust firing solutions based on observed impact patterns.

3.4 Advantages of the Modular Approach

The modular design ensures flexibility, maintainability, and scalability. Each module can be independently replaced or extended—allowing updates to firing tables, integration of new weapon profiles, or inclusion of advanced ballistic models [15]. The standardized interface ensures compatibility with diverse host applications, while the low hardware demands make the system equally suitable for operational deployment and training simulations [29].

By combining rapid computation, adaptability to multiple weapon systems, and straightforward integration into existing fire control workflows, the developed software provides a sustainable foundation for extending MRSI capabilities to legacy mortar systems, supporting both current operational needs and future doctrinal developments.

The developed software tool is structured into several core functional components, including an input handling module for parameter validation, a ballistic computation core for time-of-flight determination, an MRSI engine responsible for firing sequence timing, a data management component for handling digitized firing tables, and an output interface presenting computed firing solutions to the operator.

4 MRSI Algorithm

The developed algorithm utilizes as input the geographic data of the weapon and target (coordinates E, N, A), the selected weapon system (see Fig. 2), and the available ammunition. The output consists of all feasible combinations of ammunition types and the calculated firing intervals between rounds necessary to achieve a simultaneous impact effect on the target.

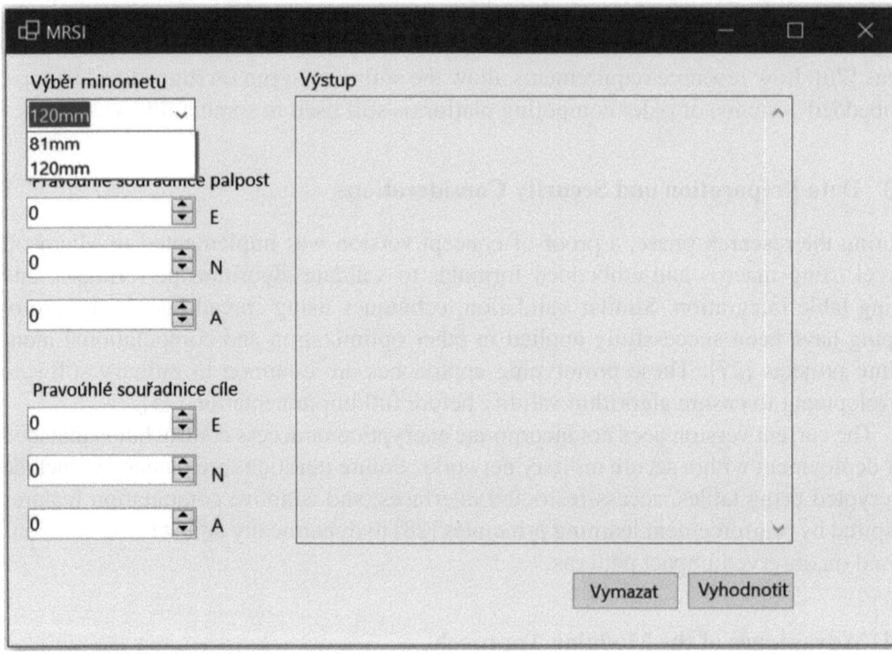

Fig. 2. MRSI Demonstration Software 1.1—mortar selection and input interface of the developed software tool. The figure shows the environment used to define the mortar type and to enter the coordinates of the mortar position and the target, forming the initial input for subsequent ballistic calculations

In the first phase, the algorithm determines the target's topographic range. Based on the selected weapon system, the program filters out ammunition types that cannot engage the target (e.g., targets located outside the minimum or maximum range for a given munition). The resulting set of potential ammunition is further compared against the unit's actual inventory, as mortar crews may not have access to the full spectrum of munitions (e.g., absence of extended-range rounds or limited propellant charges, such as only charges 1–4 for 120 mm HE rounds). The output of this stage is a set of ammunition types that are both technically and logistically feasible for the given weapon system and target.

In the second phase, the program retrieves the necessary firing parameters from the firing tables for each selected munition type, determining the projectile's time of flight to the target. Ammunition types are then sorted in ascending order by time of flight, and the program iterates through all possible combinations, calculating differences in flight times.

The first computational step of the MRSI algorithm begins by comparing the munition with the shortest time of flight to all munitions with longer times of flight. If the time-of-flight difference exceeds a predefined threshold—representing the crew's capability to adjust and fire within that interval, the pair is added to the result list, designated MRSI2 (two-round MRSI combinations). This process repeats for the second munition in the sequence, comparing it to all munitions to its right, and so on, until the last munition has been processed (Figs. 3 and 4).

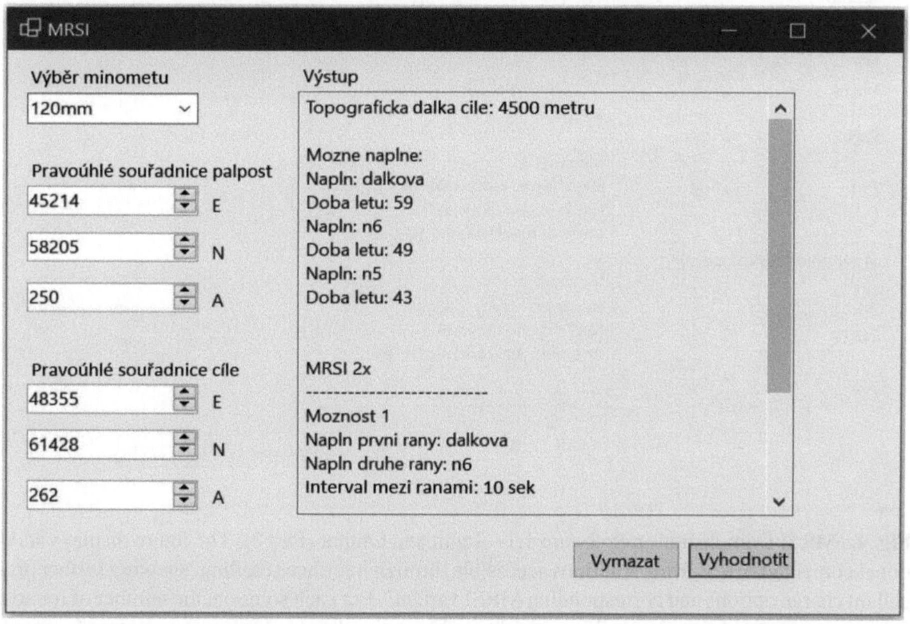

Fig. 3. MRSI Demonstration Software 1.1—Input and Output (Part 1). The left side of the interface shows the input parameters, including mortar type selection, mortar position coordinates, and target coordinates. The right side presents the computed output, illustrating the topographical target distance, available propellant charge options, and feasible MRSI firing solutions, including the number of rounds, firing order, and corresponding firing time intervals. The figure represents the actual operational interface of the software; original variable names and labels are preserved to reflect real-world usage, and their meaning is explained in the accompanying text

Formally, the initialization step creates a sequence **M** of feasible munitions, sorted in ascending order by time of flight. Let **n** denote the total number of munitions in sequence **M**. Each element (munition type) is indexed from 1 to **n**. For each element **i**, the algorithm compares its time of flight with all elements **i + 1, i + 2, …, n**. If the difference exceeds the crew capability threshold, the pair is added to MRSI2. This loop continues until **i = n**.

The MRSI2 list is then used to compute MRSI3 (three-round MRSI combinations) by applying a similar procedure, but now the search space is reduced to the combinations from MRSI2. The process iteratively identifies an additional munition whose time of flight satisfies the firing interval constraints, producing MRSI3. The algorithm can be extended to handle MRSI solutions with four or more rounds, thus allowing the library to compute MRSI combinations of arbitrary size.

The code is implemented in the C# programming language with a strong emphasis on object-oriented principles. It contains the following primary classes: CTable, CMortar, CCoordinates, CMRSI, and CInterface.

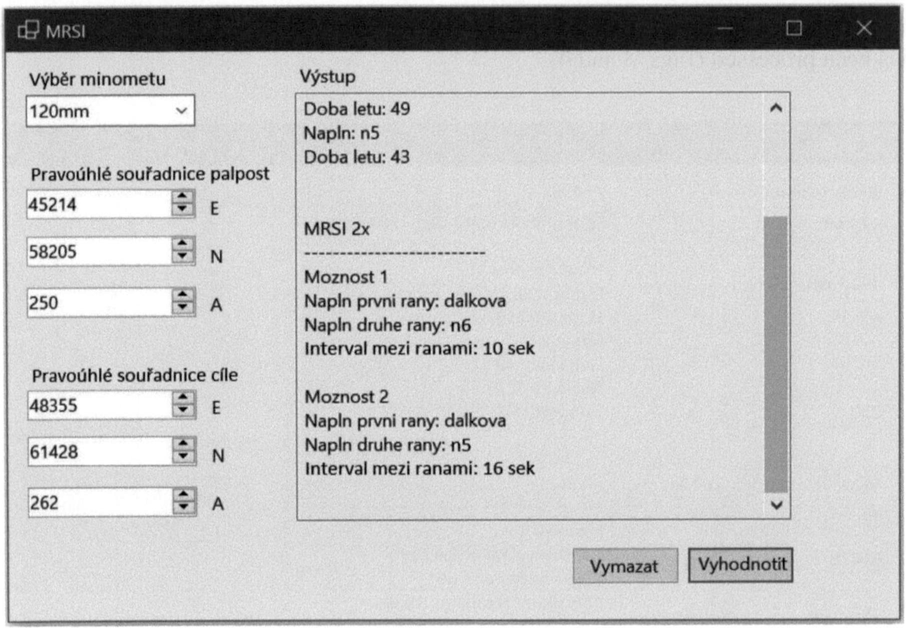

Fig. 4. MRSI Demonstration Software 1.1—Input and Output (Part 2). The figure displays additional computed MRSI firing solutions accessible through interface scrolling, showing further propellant charge options and corresponding MRSI variants. For each solution, the number of rounds, firing sequence, and time intervals required to achieve simultaneous target impact are presented. The values shown are representative and serve for demonstration and validation purposes

- **CTable** handles loading and processing mortar firing tables. Each instance corresponds to a single table, which was manually digitized from hardcopy into MS Excel, refined, and converted into CSV format. Seven tables are defined per mortar, each corresponding to a propellant charge (e.g., for the 81 mm mortar: n0–n6; for the 120 mm mortar: n1–nD). Typical columns include range, quadrant elevation, maximum trajectory height, time of flight, and angle of fall. Public methods, such as FindDistance, allow retrieval of the appropriate row for a given range.
- **CMortar** represents a generic mortar model, with enumerations defining weapon types and propellant charges. The constructor loads the corresponding CSV tables for each charge into an array of **CTable** instances. The method *FindPossibleCharges* returns a list of all charges capable of engaging a target at a given range.
- **CCoordinates** defines a structure to store geographical coordinates (E, N, A) and provides methods for calculating distances and elevation differences between points.
- **CMRSI** implements the MRSI combination search algorithm, offering public methods CalculateMRSI2 and CalculateMRSI3, which return lists of valid MRSI combinations.
- **CInterface** serves as the link between the computational library and user interfaces.

Two user interfaces (UIs) were developed to demonstrate the library's capabilities:

- **Console UI**—implemented via CInterface, handling user input/output and basic visualization in the console.
- **Graphical UI**—developed in Windows Forms, with functionality similar to the console UI but designed for Windows-based systems. Here, the main method's logic is distributed across multiple event-driven methods triggered by Windows messages.

The algorithm's efficiency is achieved by comparing each munition only to subsequent elements in the sequence, significantly reducing the number of operations. As a result, computational time decreases with each iteration, making the method suitable for real-time applications and simulations involving multiple parallel scenario branches.

4.1 Mathematical Formulation of the MRSI Algorithm

Let:

- **C**—be the set of feasible ammunition/charge options for the selected mortar (after weapon/stock filtering),
- **r**—the topographic range (and implicitly other firing conditions),
- **τ(c)**—the time of flight (TOF) for option $c \in C$ obtained from firing tables for range r,
- **Δmin**—the minimum separable inter-shot interval determined by crew capability / FCS latency,
- **Δmax**—(optional) an upper bound reflecting rate-of-fire / heating constraints,
- **ε**—the simultaneity tolerance on impact time (e.g., a few tenths of a second).

Define the TOF-sorted sequence:

$$\tau = (\tau_1, \tau_2, \ldots, \tau_n), \text{ with } \tau_1 \le \tau_2 \le \ldots \le \tau_n, \tag{1}$$

corresponding to the ordered munitions:

$$M = (C_1, \ \ldots, \ C_n). \tag{2}$$

Two-Round Feasibility A pair (i, j) with:

$$1 \le i < j \le n, \tag{3}$$

is MRSI-feasible if:

$$\Delta_{min} \le \tau_j - \tau_i \le \Delta_{max} \text{ (upper bound optional)}. \tag{4}$$

The firing schedule that yields (near-)simultaneous impact is then:

$$t_{fire}(j) = t_0, \tag{5}$$

$$t_{fire}(i) = t_0 + \left(\tau_j - \tau_i\right), \tag{6}$$

so that

$$\mid \left(t_{fire}(j) + \tau_j\right) - \left(t_{fire}(i) + \tau_i\right) \mid \le \varepsilon. \tag{7}$$

K-Round Feasibility (K ≥ 3) A k-tuple

$$(i_1 < i_2 < \cdots < i_k) \tag{8}$$

is MRSI-feasible if adjacent TOF gaps satisfy:

$$\Delta_{min} \le \tau_{i(m+1)} - \tau_{i(m)} \le \Delta_{max} \tag{9}$$

for all

$$m = 1, \ldots, k - 1, \tag{10}$$

and the schedule:

$$t_{fire}\ (i_1) = t_0 + \left(\tau_{i(k)} - \tau_{i(1)}\right), \tag{11}$$

$$t_{fire}\ (i_2) = t_0 + \left(\tau_{i(k)} - \tau_{i(2)}\ \right), \ldots, \tag{12}$$

$$t_{fire}\ (i_k) = t_0, \tag{13}$$

produces impacts within ε. Longer-TOF shots fire earlier; shortest-TOF fires last.

Pair construction is $O(n^2)$ but strictly upper-triangular comparisons (only $i < j$) halve work. Extending to triples and higher uses the precomputed pair set to prune the search, reducing work relative to naive $O(n^3)$, $O(n^4)$, … enumeration.

To ensure practical applicability of the proposed MRSI formulation in operational and training environments, the mathematical model was implemented as a modular software tool. The following section therefore focuses on the system architecture and implementation aspects that enable real-time computation and integration with existing fire control workflows.

5 Practical Evaluation and Prototype Development

Based on the described system architecture, the developed tool was evaluated with respect to computational performance, correctness of firing data, and usability under realistic operational conditions. The evaluation of the developed MRSI computation tool was conducted in two phases, focusing first on verifying algorithmic correctness under operational conditions, and later on extending capabilities to further reduce crew workload and preparation time.

5.1 Version 1.1—Field Testing

The first prototype (version 1.1) was tested in live-fire exercises using 120 mm and 81 mm mortars under conditions representative of real operational deployment. The software generated firing data consisting of propellant charge selection and calculated time intervals between rounds, which were passed to the Fire Direction Centre (FDC) for translation into standard firing commands [1]. This ensured minimal disruption to existing workflows and reduced the need for additional crew training during the trial phase.

The live-fire trials confirmed that MRSI engagements are technically feasible with manually operated mortars; however, precise simultaneity of impacts proved difficult to achieve. Contributing factors included crew timing deviations, variability in ammunition performance, and mechanical limitations of mortar elevation adjustment rates [17]. These findings are consistent with previous research on the operational constraints of manual indirect fire systems [10].

An additional observation was that crew endurance and physical readiness had a measurable effect on timing accuracy during high-tempo fire missions. Recent studies link physical work capacity with operational performance, suggesting that realistic physical training regimes should be incorporated into preparation for MRSI missions [30]. Despite these challenges, the software significantly reduced the cognitive load associated with manual timing calculations, allowing crews to focus on weapon handling. Comparable automation initiatives in artillery modernization have demonstrated similar benefits in improving reaction time and reducing error rates [19].

5.2 Version 2.0—Extended Capability

Building on the lessons of version 1.0, the second prototype (version 2.0) was designed to further streamline the MRSI process by providing complete firing data directly to the commander. In addition to charge selection and firing intervals, version 2.0 outputs aiming elements (sight elevation and deflection), effectively removing the intermediate computation step by the FDC [11]. This modification shortens mission preparation time and aligns with trends in integrating decision-support tools directly into field artillery units.

The current version exists as an Excel-based calculation tool (Fig. 5), selected for its rapid prototyping capability and ease of distribution during the testing phase [18]. After inputting necessary data, users can obtain MRSI firing solutions by triggering a dedicated command macro (Fig. 6). This format allows rapid adjustment of algorithms and firing tables during multinational trials prior to full software deployment.

International collaboration has been a key component in the development of version 2.0. Technical documentation, firing tables, and operational procedures have been exchanged between partners in the Czech Republic, Poland, and Slovakia to ensure cross-platform compatibility. A coordinated test campaign is planned to evaluate performance under different national doctrines, training levels, and mortar systems [31]. If proven effective, the solution may be standardized within the Visegrád Group (V4), with potential extension to other regional partners such as Hungary, enhancing interoperability in indirect fire capabilities [32].

Planned upgrades include the integration of terrain mobility data into firing solution planning, enabling commanders to account for weapon system positioning constraints and ammunition supply routes when coordinating MRSI missions [33]. Such capability would also support the integration of the tool into constructive simulation environments, enabling realistic scenario-based crew training under operational constraints [29].

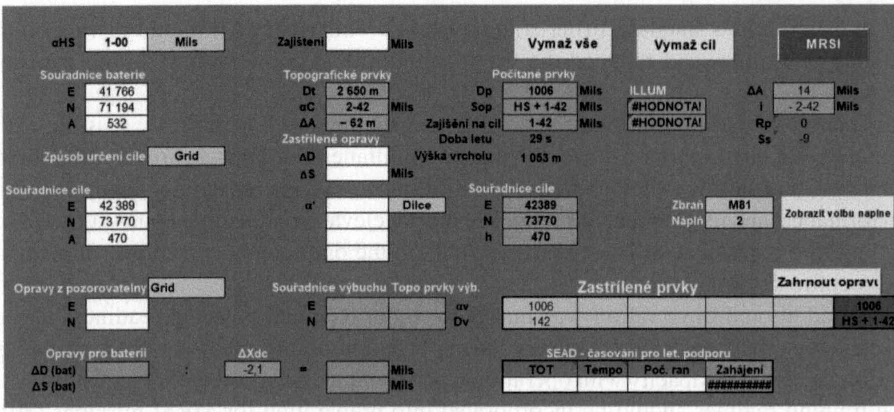

Fig. 5. MRSI Demonstration Software 2.0—MS Excel Interface—Input-oriented environment of the developed software tool demonstrating the definition of firing parameters prior to MRSI evaluation. In addition to basic target distance and bearing, the interface computes auxiliary values such as target elevation difference and related supporting parameters. The figure illustrates the general ballistic computation environment without displaying MRSI firing sequence results

Fig. 6. MRSI Demonstration Software 2.0—MS Excel MRSI table presenting information relevant for the fire unit, including available MRSI options, firing order, and timing constraints. The figure illustrates how the computed results are transformed into actionable data supporting practical execution by the mortar crew

6 Discussion

The results demonstrate that the proposed approach is technically feasible for enabling Multiple Rounds Simultaneous Impact (MRSI) calculations on legacy mortar systems. Although MRSI techniques are commonly associated with modern self-propelled artillery, the conducted research confirms that they can be successfully adapted for manually operated mortars when supported by dedicated computational tools. The developed software framework reduces the manual calculation burden on fire direction centers (FDCs), allowing crews to focus primarily on weapon handling and execution of firing procedures [8]. This approach reflects broader artillery modernization trends, where partial automation is employed as an intermediate step toward fully integrated fire control systems [13].

6.1 Technical and Operational Challenges

One of the primary challenges identified during testing was balancing computational precision with practical execution. While the algorithms generate accurate firing solutions, actual battlefield performance is influenced by the crew's ability to adjust elevation and deflection rapidly, load ammunition consistently, and coordinate timing precisely. Similar constraints have been documented in research on manual artillery fire correction and meteorological adjustments, underlining the continuing need for rigorous crew training and doctrinal refinement [4, 9].

6.2 Adaptability and Interoperability

The integration of multinational firing data during the development phase demonstrated the flexibility of the software's architecture. Differences in firing tables, weapon configurations, and procedural norms required an adaptable computational framework capable of accommodating diverse inputs without compromising accuracy [3, 15]. This design philosophy aligns with successful practices from other joint defense projects, where early standardization of data formats and procedures supports interoperability and reduces integration costs.

6.3 Environmental and Contextual Considerations

Operational planning for MRSI must also consider environmental and terrain-related factors. Studies on the environmental impact of artillery activities highlight the importance of incorporating environmental assessment into mission planning [34, 35]. Future iterations of the software could include modules that account for terrain degradation, accessibility after impact, and environmental protection constraints, ensuring tactical effectiveness while adhering to environmental regulations.

6.4 Integration with Decision-Support Systems

A promising development path is the integration of the MRSI computation tool with Tactical Decision Support Systems (TDSS), enabling real-time coordination that considers enemy positions, friendly force locations, and terrain mobility constraints [18,

22]. This would create a more comprehensive and responsive fire control environment, suitable for both high-intensity engagements and joint multinational operations.

6.5 Logistics and Resource Efficiency

From a capability planning perspective, the low hardware requirements and modular structure of the software make it a cost-effective modernization option for forces operating under budget constraints. Research on defense resource allocation indicates that tools like this should be evaluated not only for their tactical performance but also for their cost-effectiveness compared to alternative modernization paths [31, 32].

6.6 Regional Defense Cooperation

The collaboration between Czech, Slovak, and Polish partners during testing of version 2.0 reflects the increasing emphasis on regional defense integration. If validated, adoption within the Visegrád Group (V4) could lead to the creation of a standardized methodology for MRSI computation, improving collective indirect fire capabilities [5]. Such standardization would also reinforce interoperability with potential future partners, including Hungary.

6.7 Implications for Military Education

The evolving character of modern battlefields requires artillery leaders to maintain adaptability and proficiency in emerging technologies, including semi-automated MRSI computation systems. This requirement is consistent with broader trends in military education, where curricula are being restructured to incorporate advanced fire control concepts and decision-support tools [36].

7 Conclusion and Future Research

This paper presented the development of a structured software tool supporting MRSI calculations for legacy mortar systems. By digitizing firing tables and embedding calculation algorithms into a modular C# library, the tool provides rapid determination of feasible munition combinations and firing intervals, reducing reliance on manual computation.

This study has demonstrated that Multiple Round Simultaneous Impact (MRSI) techniques (traditionally associated with modern self-propelled artillery) can be adapted for legacy, manually operated mortar systems through the use of a lightweight, modular computational tool. The developed prototype translates complex ballistic calculations into actionable firing data, significantly reducing the cognitive and procedural workload on mortar crews and enabling faster mission preparation. While the tool cannot replace the need for thorough crew training, it increases the likelihood of achieving near-simultaneous impacts under realistic operational conditions.

The principal limitations remain linked to the mechanical characteristics of the weapon systems and the proficiency of their operators. Even with precise computational outputs, live-fire execution is subject to human reaction times, variations in ammunition performance, and environmental factors. These findings are consistent with broader research indicating that technology can mitigate (but not fully eliminate) human and mechanical constraints in weapon system performance [19].

Future development will prioritize the migration of the current Excel-based prototype into a fully integrated, standalone application capable of real-time data exchange with fire control systems and adaptable to multiple weapon platforms. Another key objective will be the incorporation of advanced trajectory optimization methods, such as the Gauss pseudospectral approach [37], to improve the precision of firing sequence calculations, particularly in scenarios involving mixed-calibre or mixed-weapon systems. In the longer term, selected optimization or artificial intelligence–based methods could be explored to support adaptive firing sequence selection and reduce operator workload, while preserving the transparency and controllability required for operational fire control systems.

A further area of focus will be the establishment of a robust methodology for the statistical evaluation of live-fire test data, drawing on established models for simulation study analysis [25]. Such an approach will enable an objective assessment of accuracy, repeatability, and operational reliability across varied conditions and national systems. In parallel, the project will continue its international collaboration with Czech, Slovak, and Polish armed forces to validate the tool's adaptability and performance. If these trials confirm its operational value, the tool could be adopted more widely within the Visegrád Group and by NATO partners, enhancing regional interoperability in indirect fire support.

By pursuing these directions, the research aims to expand the operational utility of MRSI for legacy mortar systems, contributing both to national capability enhancement and to multinational standardization efforts in indirect fire doctrine.

Acknowledgments. This study was funded by **LANDOPS (*DZRO-FVL22-LANDOPS*)** Conduct of land operations.

Disclosure of Interests. The authors declare no competing interests.

References

1. Šustr, M., Potužák, L., Blaha, M., Ivan, J.: Multiple round simultaneous impact fires and possibilities of its application in Czech Army. Vojenské rozhledy—Czech Mil. Rev. **29**(4), 84–93 (2020)
2. Majstrenko, O.V., Makeev, V.I., Prokopenko, V.V., Andreiev, I.M., Kamentsev, S.Y., Onofriychuk, A.Y.: An improved mathematical model of the method of fully preparing the determination of firing units for hitting the information and calculation component of the automated fire control system of combat vehicles of reactive artillery. Radio Electron. Comput. Sci. Control. **4**, 195–209 (2024). https://doi.org/10.15588/1607-3274-2024-4-19
3. Lahti, J., Sailaranta, T., Harju, M., Virtanen, K.: Control of exterior ballistic properties of spin-stabilized bullet by optimizing internal mass distribution. Def. Technol. **15**, 38–50 (2019). https://doi.org/10.1016/j.dt.2018.10.003

4. Ivan, J., Šustr, M., Blaha, M., Havlík, T.: Evaluation of possible approaches to meteorological techniques of artillery manual gunnery after the adoption of automated fire control system. Vojenské rozhledy—Czech Mil. Rev. **30**(3), 75–92 (2021). https://doi.org/10.3849/2336-2995.30.2021.03.075-092
5. Žižka, P., Saibert, R.: Development of the Czech armed forces doctrinal framework. Vojenské rozhledy—Czech Mil. Rev. **33**(1), 3–20 (2024). https://doi.org/10.3849/2336-2995.33.2024.01.003-020
6. Gouveia, H., Freitas, R.: Innovations and trends in field artillery weapon systems. Cogent Soc. Sci. **10**(1), 2411867 (2024). https://doi.org/10.1080/23311886.2024.2411867
7. Neubauer, J., Vlkovský, M., Michálek, J.: Statistical modeling of cargo securing on selected military trucks and road surfaces. J. Defense Model. Simul.—Appl., Methodol., Technol. **21**(3) Special Issue SI) (2024). https://doi.org/10.1177/15485129241227012
8. Drábek, J., Šustr, M., Potužák, L., Ivan, J., Liška, R.: Contingency and emergency manual procedures for calculation firing data using direction and distance coefficients. Eng. Rep. **7**(6) ISSN 2577-8196 (2025). https://doi.org/10.1002/eng2.70252
9. Šustr, M., Ivan, J., Blaha, M., Potužák, L.: A manual method of artillery fires correction calculation. Mil. Oper. Res. **27**(3), 77–94 (2022). https://doi.org/10.5711/1082598327377
10. Šustr, M., Vajda, M., Blaha, M., Ivan, J., Korec, D.: Artillery officer education and the interoperability challenge in joint fires: a Czech-Slovak comparison. Cogent Educ. **12**(1), 2533308 (2025). https://doi.org/10.1080/2331186X.2025.2533308
11. Stodola, P., Mazal, J.: Tactical decision support system to aid commanders in their decision-making. In: Hodicky, J. (ed.) Modelling and Simulation for Autonomous Systems, MESAS 2016 Lecture Notes in Computer Science, vol. 9991, pp. 396–406. Springer, Cham (2016). https://doi.org/10.1007/978-3-319-47605-6_32
12. Blaha, M., Brabcová, K.: Decision-making by effective C2I system. In: 7th International Conference on Information Warfare & Security, pp. 44–50. Academic Publishing Limited, Seattle (2012) ISBN 978-1-908272-29-4. ISSN 2048-9870.
13. Blaha, M., Potužák, L., Šustr, M., Ivan, J., Havlík, T.: Simplification options for more efficient using of angular and linear measuring rules for fire control. Int. J. Educ. Inf. Technol. **15**, 28–34 (2021). https://doi.org/10.46300/9109.2021.15.4
14. Blaha, M., Šilinger, K., Potužák, L.: Linear and angular issues in perspective artillery fire control system. MATEC Web Conf. **210**, 02055 (2018). https://doi.org/10.1051/matecconf/201821002055
15. Du, L., Lv, W., Kong, L., Guan, C.: A study on artillery firing data solving method based on improved genetic algorithm. IEEE Access **12**, 158471–158477 (2024). https://doi.org/10.1109/ACCESS.2024.3487247
16. Blaha, M., Brabcová, K.: Communication environment in the perspective automated artillery fire support control system. In: Proceedings of the 10th WSEAS International Conference on Applied Informatics and Communications (AIC 2010), pp. 236–239. WSEAS Press, Taipei (2010). ISBN 978–960–474-216-5. ISSN 1792-4634
17. Sedláček, M., Dohnal, F., Ivan, J., Šustr, M.: Possible approaches to assessing terrain mobility after the effects of artillery munition. Cogent Soc. Sci. **10**(1), 2368096 (2024). https://doi.org/10.1080/23311886.2024.2368096
18. Rolenec, O., Sedláček, M., Vlkovský, M.: Constructive simulation in tactical level planning: options for optimizing engineer support. Vojenské rozhledy—Czech Mil. Rev. **33**(4), 051–069 (2024). https://doi.org/10.3849/2336-2995.33.2024.04.051-069
19. Drozd, J., Procházka, J.: Weapon system acquisition process utilizing design simulation as decision support. Vojenské rozhledy—Czech Mil. Rev. **33**(4), 37–50 (2024). https://doi.org/10.3849/2336-2995.33.2024.04.037-050

20. Hujer, V., Slouf, V., Farlik, J.: Utility as a key criterion of a decision-making on structure of the ground based air Defence. In: Mazal, J., Fagiolini, A., Vasik, P., Turi, M., Bruzzone, A., Pickl, S., Neumann, V., Stodola, P. (eds.) Modelling and Simulation for Autonomous Systems (MESAS 2021) Lecture Notes in Computer Science, vol. 13207, pp. 249–260. Springer, Cham (2022). https://doi.org/10.1007/978-3-030-98260-7_15
21. Ivan, J., Šustr, M., Gregor, J., Potužák, L., Varecha, J.: Advancing soil sampling techniques for environmental assessment of artillery impact zones. J. Ecol. Eng. **26**(5), 1–14 (2025). https://doi.org/10.12911/22998993/196688
22. Stodola, P., Nohel, J., Mazal, J.: Model of optimal maneuver used in tactical decision support system. In: 2016 21st International Conference on Methods and Models in Automation and Robotics (MMAR), Miedzyzdrojepp, 1240–1245. IEEE (2016). https://doi.org/10.1109/MMAR.2016.7575287
23. Blaha, M.: Communication as a basic for future artillery fire support control system. In: The European Conference of Communications (ECCOM'10), pp. 140–142. WSEAS Press, Tenerife (2010) ISBN 978-960-474-250-9.
24. Korecki, Z., Hoika, T., Ulvr, J., Baláž, T.: Use of a tactical decision support system within the ground unit Commander's decision-making process. Adv. Mil. Technol. **17**(2), 231–241 (2022). https://doi.org/10.3849/aimt.01551
25. Neubauer, J., Mazal, J.: Statistical evaluation of simulation study data. In: Bruzzone, A., Pickl, S., Mazal, J., Fagiolini, A., Vasik, P., Pacillo, F., Stodola, P. (eds.) Modelling and Simulation for Autonomous Systems, MESAS 2023, Lecture Notes in Computer Science, vol. 14615, pp. 364–370. Springer, Cham (2025). https://doi.org/10.1007/978-3-031-71397-2_23
26. Hasilová, K., Horová, I., Vališ, D., Zámecník, S.: A comprehensive exploration of complete cross-validation for circular data. Stat. Transition New Series **25**(3), 1–12 (2024). https://doi.org/10.59170/stattrans-2024-024
27. Nemec, P., Stodola, P., Pecina, M., Neubauer, J., Blaha, M.: Optimization of the weighted multi-facility location problem using MS excel. Algorithms **14**(7), 191 (2021). https://doi.org/10.3390/a14070191
28. Alipio, M., Bures, M.: Deep reinforcement learning perspectives on improving reliable transmissions in IoT networks: problem formulation, parameter choices, challenges, and future directions. Internet Things **23**, 100846 (2023). https://doi.org/10.1016/j.iot.2023.100846
29. Mazal, J., Zezula, J., Procházka, J., Procházka, D.: The use of modeling and simulation in the development process optimization of the armed forces of the Czech Republic. Vojenské rozhledy—Czech Mil. Rev. **31**(4), 140–158 (2022). https://doi.org/10.3849/2336-2995.31.2022.04.140-158
30. Drozd, J., Neubauer, J., Sekanina, J., Sedlačík, M.: Bridging the gap: aligning physical work capacity testing with actual endurance performance in military settings. Front. Psychol. **16**, 1536197 (2025). https://doi.org/10.3389/fpsyg.2025.1536197
31. Pekař, O., Šlouf, V., Blaha, M., Brizgalová, L., Müllner, V.: Redefining Defence expenditures in B9 countries: risk-based model for rational allocation under foreign threat scenarios. Obrana Strategie—Defence Strategy **25**(1), 71–112 (2025). https://doi.org/10.3849/1802-7199.25.2025.1.71-112
32. Šlouf, V., Blaha, M., Pekař, O., Brizgalová, L., Müllner, V.: An alternative model for determining the rational amount of funds allocated to Defence of the Czech Republic in conditions of expected risk. Obrana Strategie—Defence Strategy. **23**(1), 149–172 (2023). https://doi.org/10.3849/1802-7199.23.2023.01.149-172
33. Křišťálová, D., et al.: Ground visibility analyses, algorithms and performance. In: Mazal, J., Fagiolini, A., Vasik, P., Turi, M., Bruzzone, A., Pickl, S., Neumann, V., Stodola, P. (eds.) Modelling and Simulation for Autonomous Systems (MESAS 2021) Lecture Notes in Computer Science, vol. 13207, pp. 61–73. Springer, Cham (2022). https://doi.org/10.1007/978-3-030-98260-7_4

34. Dobrzański, Z., et al.: Anthropogenic sources of mercury in the Baltic Sea. A real security threat and action programs. Przemysł Chemiczny. **103**(8) (2024). https://doi.org/10.15199/62.2024.8.4
35. Hanáková, N., Manas, P., Rolenec, O., Palasiewicz, T.: National Defense and environmental protection: on the Czech armed forces′ approach to the development of environmental legislation in the Czech, EU and NATO context. Vojenské rozhledy—Czech Mil. Rev. **31**(4), 172–202 (2022). https://doi.org/10.3849/2336-2995.31.2022.04.172-202
36. Zahradníček, P., Botík, M., Rak, L., Hrdinka, J.: Modern battlefield and necessary reflection in military Leader's education and training. Vojenské rozhledy – Czech Mil. Rev. **32**(4), 110–122 (2023). https://doi.org/10.3849/2336-2995.32.2023.04.110-122
37. Liu, C., Zhang, C., Wang, J.: Multi-stage trajectory optimization for time-on-target of tactical rockets using gauss Pseudospectral method. In: Chen, X., Zhao, Q.C. (eds.) Proceedings of the 37th Chinese Control Conference (CCC 2018), pp. 2119–2124. IEEE, Wuhan (2018)

Author Index

J. Novotný et al. (Eds.): MESAS 2025, LNCS 16627, pp. 369–370, 2027.
https://doi.org/10.1007/978-3-032-33182-3

MIX
Papier aus verantwortungsvollen Quellen
Paper from responsible sources
FSC® C105338

If you have any concerns about our products,
you can contact us on
ProductSafety@springernature.com

In case Publisher is established outside the EU,
the EU authorized representative is:
Springer Nature Customer Service Center GmbH
Europaplatz 3, 69115 Heidelberg, Germany

Printed by Libri Plureos GmbH
in Hamburg, Germany